The Dynamics of Criminological Research

The Dynamics of Criminological Research

Jennifer L. Schulenberg

OXFORD
UNIVERSITY PRESS

OXFORD
UNIVERSITY PRESS

Oxford University Press is a department of the University of Oxford.
It furthers the University's objective of excellence in research, scholarship,
and education by publishing worldwide. Oxford is a registered trade mark of
Oxford University Press in the UK and in certain other countries.

Published in Canada by
Oxford University Press
8 Sampson Mews, Suite 204,
Don Mills, Ontario M3C 0H5 Canada

www.oupcanada.com

Library and Archives Canada Cataloguing in Publication
Schulenberg, Jennifer L., author
The dynamics of criminological research / Jennifer L. Schulenberg.

Includes bibliographical references and index.
ISBN 978-0-19-543902-1 (paperback)

1. Criminology—Research—Methodology. 2. Criminal
justice, Administration of—Research—Methodology. I. Title.

HV6024.5.S38 2015   364.072   C2015-903454-X

Cover image: © iStock/francisblack

Oxford University Press is committed to our environment.
This book is printed on Forest Stewardship Council® certified paper
and comes from responsible sources.

MIX
Paper from
responsible sources
FSC® C103567

Printed and bound in Canada

5 6 7 - 23 22 21

In memory of Jolanda Lina Schulenberg (1942–1992)

Contents

Chapter 7 • Ethnographic Field Research   197

Chapter 8 • Unobtrusive Methods and Secondary Data   227

Chapter 12 • Mixed Methods: An Integrated Approach   367

Appendix A • The Research Proposal and "Writing It Up"   398

Appendix B • Reading and Interpreting Published Research   405

Appendix C • Random Number Table   410

Preface

I confess that I was an undergraduate student who dreaded the required research methods course, more out of fear than content. Other than hearing that the course was not for the faint of heart, I really didn't know what research methods entailed. The fall term arrived, and I sat in this class much like a deer caught in the headlights. The professor might as well have been speaking a different language. At this point, doing a graduate degree was not in my plans. Thus, I not only struggled with the material but also truly questioned its usefulness. How on earth does any of this material matter in the real world?

Fast forward several years, and I now sit on the other side of the desk, teaching the course that you look forward to, grudgingly accept, or positively dread. While serving as the associate chair for legal studies, I advised students on their degree plans. If I had a dollar for every time I saw that look of fear at the mention of taking a research methods course, I could buy a lot of pizza for my students at the end of the term.

While conceptualizing what this book would look like, I was acutely aware of my classroom experiences and feedback from undergraduate and graduate students. Each year, I find myself adopting a different book for my course because relevant content is lacking or the examples do not resonate with my students. Despite many research methods books being available on the market, a focus on criminological examples is missing. Moreover, we do not have a Canadian textbook for courses in criminology, criminal justice, and legal studies.

I wrote this book so that students can not only understand the material but also see how it lives and breathes in everyday life. As such, research methods is presented in a way that helps to remove any fear, dread, and confusion that may confront them. The text is also written with instructors in mind; it provides comprehensive coverage on traditional and emerging methods in the discipline and fosters teaching this course with a focus on applying concepts rather than strictly disseminating knowledge. Accomplishing these objectives involves going beyond the nuts and bolts of methodological practice and reaching a place where you can see how the material fits together more consistently with the reality of conducting crime and justice research.

Research is a messy process conducted in the real world under imperfect conditions. Producing knowledge isn't as straightforward as following a recipe to get through the research process. Yet research methods need not be daunting, foreign, or overwhelming. It does involve a new way of thinking about the world around us, but the skills gained in this course will help you understand the research process, creation of knowledge, appropriateness of using one method over another, and factors to consider when assessing the conclusions.

Have you ever read a journal article and skipped the methods section? Do you know how the latest crime statistics you read about in the newspaper are created? What are the strengths and weaknesses of the official statistics that produced the crime rate? How do you know you can trust the conclusions? You can answer these questions once you gain an appreciation of the research process.

Purpose and Goals

Research methods are the techniques used to produce knowledge. Methodology is the study of methods and the research approach employing these methods. Similarly, methodology includes analyzing the philosophy and debates surrounding mixed methods. Understanding the methodological logic is as important as the method itself when it comes to conducting and, more important, evaluating research.

Thus, the purpose of this book is to develop your methodological skills and your ability to critically evaluate what you read so that the conclusions can be contextualized by how they were developed. The corresponding goal for the book is to provide the information required to prepare students to conduct research but, more important, become informed consumers of research findings. To accomplish this goal, the underlying philosophy guiding the text's structure and content is simple: the research question drives the method. All methodological decisions come back to whether the method will allow you to address the research question and achieve the research objective.

The book's writing style is accessible and user-friendly to demystify the research process without sacrificing depth or scope of coverage. No assumptions are made about student knowledge. Concepts are presented, followed by both research and everyday life examples that illustrate these methods in action. The examples—many of which are from Canadian research—become more complex as the book progresses, further encouraging comprehension. Analysis chapters emphasize interpreting the data, equipping students with research evaluation skills.

In respect to substantive content, this book is distinguishable from others in three ways. First, it produces a balanced approach by placing much greater attention on qualitative methods. Research methods textbooks often have a stronger emphasis on quantitative methods. Here, the content is consistent with the philosophy that the research question drives the method. Different questions require quantitative, qualitative, or more than one type of data. This book offers students the opportunity to be comfortable and knowledgeable with all approaches.

Second, the disciplines of criminology and criminal justice are constantly evolving, and the area of research methodology is no exception. To better reflect the contemporary debates and methods used when conducting crime and justice research, this text covers two areas that are usually excluded or receive only brief coverage. Evaluation research is becoming increasingly important in the current environment of fiscal constraint and the need to demonstrate evidence-based practice. A separate chapter is devoted to mixed methods research, as its use in addressing our questions about the causes and responses to crime is also increasing. Many concepts from previous chapters are reintroduced while discussing this paradigm.

The third distinctive feature is the integrative approach to discussing ethical and political considerations. It's common for research methods books to devote a separate chapter to ethics. Chapter 2 of this text provides a general overview of the topic, but ethical principles and political considerations are discussed in conjunction with the approaches, methods, and techniques covered in each chapter. In this way the importance, role, and complexity of ethics is highlighted in specific methodological contexts throughout the research process.

Organization

The book's presentation of material is designed to take you on a journey that emphasizes cumulative learning. Concepts introduced in earlier chapters, particularly data analysis and mixed methods, are discussed later in the book to show the interconnectedness of the material. Too often, research methods are seen as distinct units without little connection to each other.

Content Overview

The book's 5 sections and 12 chapters are organized based on substantive logic and student feedback. Topics move from the theoretical to the mechanics of data collection and analysis to the integrative approach of mixed methods. A brief description of each part and chapter follows.

Part I introduces students to the logic of scientific inquiry, research design, and ethics. Chapter 1 offers students a theoretical introduction to research methods. The difference between scientific and everyday types of knowledge, along with ideology versus theory, leads to assumptions about knowledge in different worldviews. These abstract concepts are applied to everyday examples, such as the difference between inductive and deductive profiling and arguments about why most published research is false. Chapter 2 delves into the scientific method and what it looks like for both quantitative and qualitative research. The Wallace Wheel is used to illustrate the research process. The chapter also introduces ethical and political considerations by discussing codes of ethics, minimal risk, voluntary participation, and conflicts of interest. Material is applied to contemporary topics such as the Canadian racial profiling controversy and scientific misconduct by professors.

Part II covers the components of qualitative and quantitative research designs. Chapter 3 focuses on a difficult but important aspect of the research process: measurement. On a theoretical level, researchers use deductive or inductive logic to conceptualize and operationalize key ideas in research questions. The chapter covers challenging aspects of measurement, such as the language of causality and the identification of dependent, independent, and control variables. It also discusses assessing the quality of measurement (i.e. reliability, validity, trustworthiness) and applies the material to the ways we measure violent behaviour, fear, and crime in Canada. An everyday life example applies the concepts of reliability and validity to crime lab evidence.

Chapter 4 devotes equal attention to probability and nonprobability sampling techniques. Topics include the lingo, probability theory at the more abstract level, and types of sampling techniques, sample quality, and sample size at the practical level. Techniques are related to student samples, incarceration experiences, and the ways the media can mislead the public.

Chapter 5 focuses on experimental designs, a topic that often eludes and overwhelms students. To make sense of experimental designs, the chapter begins with appropriate topics, the purpose, and experimental settings. It also looks at the lingo, dependent and independent variables, and the ways research subjects are assigned to groups. The true experiment is introduced as the point of reference, followed by pre- and quasi-experimental designs. The chapter concludes with threats to internal and external validity, strengths, weaknesses, and ethics. An extended discussion on examples, such as whether being homeless affects criminal behaviour, helps bring these designs into perspective with the real world.

Part II presents the most commonly used methods for collecting data in criminology and criminal justice research. The chapters emphasize understanding the logic, components, and topics that are appropriate to each methodology. Chapter 6 enters the more familiar territory of surveys and interviews. The chapter reviews the when and why, types, structure, question logistics, and challenges of surveys. Interview types, questions, and processes are discussed, including a section on focus groups. Examples include navigating a job interview, uncovering the hidden secrets associated with police misconduct, and using surveys in mixed methods designs.

Chapter 7 contextualizes the basics of field research in a historical context. Material focuses on field roles, gaining and maintaining access, entering the field, field notes, group relations, leaving the field, and ethics. In addition to these usual topics, the chapter covers contemporary approaches, including systematic social observation, netnography, and ethnomethodology. Examples of research in criminal subcultures and challenges associated with collecting data while on police patrol contextualize the material.

Chapter 8 introduces material on unobtrusive measures, such as historical analyses of documents and pictures, content, and secondary data analysis. Attention is directed to measuring crime and agency records from criminal justice organizations. The chapter provides content on frequently neglected methods, including physical trace, crime mapping, legal research, meta-analysis, digital media, and online data. Examples of research on graffiti and use of the Uniform Crime Reporting Survey illustrate these techniques.

Part IV covers techniques used to analyze quantitative and qualitative data. Equal attention is devoted to each approach, in a manner that develops the ability to interpret data and findings. Interpreting quantitative data typically evokes legitimate fear in students. Therefore, Chapter 9 makes every effort to present statistics in ways that allow students to interpret their meaning. The chapter focuses on descriptive statistics (describing and summarizing data with measures of central tendency and dispersion), bivariate (cross-tabulations), statistical significance, and regression. A section devoted to the elaboration paradigm examines how multivariate statistics can help us understand the complexity of life and investigate causal relationships.

Chapter 10 revisits the Wallace Wheel to introduce analytic induction and the link between theory and method (e.g. ideal types, analytic comparisons) and presents the details of qualitative data analysis, including strategies such as fracturing the data, coding, sensitizing concepts, and identifying relationships in grounded theory and thematic analyses. In addition, the often excluded strategies of discourse analysis, qualitative content analysis, narrative analysis, and semiotics are discussed. Criteria to evaluate qualitative research, authenticity, and ethical considerations conclude the chapter.

Part V recognizes that, in criminology and criminal justice, evaluation research and mixed methods are emerging as valuable approaches to investigating complex phenomena and research problems. Chapter 11 highlights the distinctions between cross-sectional, longitudinal, basic, and applied research. The chapter revisits the Wallace Wheel and brings the relationship between theory and practice to the forefront, with an overview of the research steps and types of evaluation research. The politics and ethics of negotiating the relationship with stakeholders are included, as well as examples such as the effectiveness of the D.A.R.E. (Drug Awareness Resistance Education) program.

Chapter 12 defines mixed methods, its historical development, the paradigm wars, philosophical assumptions and introduces the more common mixed methods designs. The chapter also covers the matter of the research question driving the method, the rationale for using mixed methods (e.g. development, triangulation), the purpose (e.g. explanatory), and characteristics of all designs (e.g. sequence, priority). To demonstrate the required methodological gymnastics, everyday examples include adopting this approach to investigate social media and research examples regarding the prevalence of different methodologies in published crime and justice research.

Four appendices discuss topics that will help you as you continue your studies in criminology and criminal justice. This part of the text includes information on writing a research proposal and reading and interpreting published research, provides a random number table, and lists secondary data sources that are used in criminology and criminal justice research.

Pedagogical Features

This text uses several pedagogical features to assist with cumulative learning and the application of the material. Each chapter opens with a quotation intended to provoke critical thinking and point to contemporary debates. Learning objectives outline the skills and knowledge that students should achieve by the end of the chapter. Pedagogical boxes appear throughout the chapters, providing more in-depth research and everyday examples, making the material accessible, and assisting in applying research methods in different contexts.

- "Key Thinker" boxes present the life and work of an influential thinker in the substantive area of that particular chapter. For instance, students learn about Malcolm Klein's views on defining a criminologist (Chapter 3), Joan McCord's work on the Cambridge-Somerville Youth Study (Chapter 5), Robert Merton's contribution to survey methodology (Chapter 6), Howard Becker's ethnographic work (Chapter 7), and Mark Progrebin's experiences as a field researcher (Chapter 10).
- "Methods in Action" boxes highlight the implementation of key concepts and strategies in a real-life context, such as being a psychic to illustrate the different types of knowledge in comparison to scientific approaches (Chapter 1), reporting public opinion polls (Chapter 6), or using tips for "statsy" success when interpreting quantitative research (Chapter 9).
- "Research Highlights" take a variety of criminology and criminal justice topics to highlight methods covered in the chapter. Examples include combining sampling techniques to investigate perceptions on justice (Chapter 4), accessing and relating to active offenders (Chapter 7), and measuring hot spots of criminal activity using different types of unobtrusive data (Chapter 8).
- "Vignette: Breaking It Down" uses the one substantive topic of police work. This continuous vignette acts as an application example for the content of each chapter. Examples are looking at sampling in quantitative, qualitative, and mixed methods research on police discretion (Chapter 4) and interpreting crime statistics to inform police policy and patrol strategies (Chapter 9).

Each chapter ends with a list of important points, which summarizes the key ideas and serves as a review. A list of key terms includes the terms defined in the chapter's margins (and included in a glossary at the end of the book). Students can do the review questions and exercises to synthesize information, prepare for examinations, and apply the skills learned in the chapter. A selection of online exercises and websites of interest tap into the wealth of information available online and allow students to engage with the content by using the methods and techniques. Finally, an annotated list of additional resources provides articles and books that are not limited to academic research. These titles can serve as a resource for students who would like to gain more in-depth knowledge on the subject or who intend to use chapter material for a course assignment, such as a research proposal.

Acknowledgements

This book reflects a collaboration between my students and me, as both student and teacher are on a continuous learning curve. Teaching research methods at the undergraduate and graduate levels has taught me so much about student comprehension, aspirations, frustration, bewilderment, and excitement to conduct research. The excitement is contagious. My students may not realize the impact of their questions, challenges, fears, and satisfaction regarding their coursework and research projects. However, all that and more have shaped the development and writing of this book. To see the look in a person's face when he or she understands an abstract or complex concept is incredibly rewarding. I have endeavoured to pay respect to my students by passing on the lessons learned from them. Thus, I dedicate this book to all the students I have had the honour to work with and those who, in the future, will make me a better methodologist and teacher.

I would be remiss not to extend immense gratitude to the team at Oxford University Press. Many thanks go to Nancy O'Reilly, who believed in my dream of bringing research methods to life with a book that focuses specifically on criminology and criminal justice in Canada. I have been blessed to work with Sarah Carmichael, Amy Gordon, and Mark Thompson, whose experience and expertise as developmental editors had a profound influence on the version of the finished book. I am especially grateful to Mark for reading chapter drafts, making editorial suggestions, remaining positive, and showing concern for me as a person while I wrote this book and battled many serious health problems. An integral part of the Oxford team is the work of the copy editor—in this case, Janna Green, who patiently cleaned up my prose, including all my commas. There is also the conscientious work of the reviewers, whose thoughtful feedback challenged me to see the material from a different perspective and organize the material in a manner that more accurately reflects research methods in practice. I join Oxford in thanking Jon Frauley (University of Ottawa), Alicia Horton (Simon Fraser University), Miriam Levitt (University of Ottawa), Gavin Slade (University of Toronto), and Eric Tompkins (College of New Caledonia), as well as the two reviewers who chose to remain anonymous.

I would also like to extend thanks to my colleagues in the Department of Sociology and Legal Studies, who helped to keep me focused on what is important. Just as it takes a village to raise a child, making sense of research methods is not an individual endeavour. I am also indebted to the University of Waterloo, whose emphasis on research productivity and teaching excellence made it possible to take on a project of this magnitude.

Finally, embarking on this journey required a sense of humour that transcended the parameters of my expectations. My most heartfelt thanks to my son, not only for his love and support but also for not outwardly laughing at me when papers flew across the floor, or when I thought aloud, had a pencil in my hair, and lived a generally cloistered life as I wrote each chapter. I can't forget Max, my orange 18-pound tabby, who felt it necessary to lie on the exact manuscript page that I needed at any given moment. Equal kudos go to the other feline in the household, Sparkie, who is fascinated with any liquid in a glass and computer keyboards. He made sure that I took breaks for cuddles and repeatedly reminded me where to find the delete and backspace keys. There is never a dull moment—life is filled with learning, and I'm loving every minute of it. Thank you to all.

Part I
An Introduction to Scientific Inquiry

Chapter 1

What Is Scientific Inquiry?

"Almost everything that distinguishes the modern world from earlier centuries is attributable to science."
Bertrand Russell, *A History of Western Philosophy,* 2nd ed. (1946/2004, p. 484)

Learning Objectives

- To differentiate between sources of knowledge, an ideology, and a theory.
- To identify if a theory is falsifiable and adheres to the principles of parsimony and serendipity.
- To associate epistemological and ontological assumptions with nomothetic and idiographic explanations and the positivist, interpretivist, and pragmatist worldviews.

- To understand the relationship between deductive and inductive reasoning.
- To recognize how middle-range theories bridge the gap between empirical evidence and abstract theories.
- To define and provide examples of basic, applied, exploratory, descriptive, and explanatory research.

Introduction

Odds are that taking a research methods course isn't on your top-ten list of fun things to do. You may be asking yourself, "Why do I need to study research methods when I have no desire to go to graduate school? Why is this course mandatory?" As you work through the chapters in this book, you will find answers to these questions. You will be exposed to many facets of how research in criminology and criminal justice impacts society, how science is a way of thinking, and how we seek and validate knowledge that affects our daily lives.

Everyday knowledge is typically based on information that is available or, as a result of familiarity, based on prior experience. Scientific knowledge is much more specific, as attention is focused on the accuracy and legitimacy of knowledge. If something

Research Highlights

Why Most Published Research Findings are False

In "Why Most Published Research Findings Are False," Ioannidis (2005) claims that there is less than a 50 per cent chance that the results from any random research study are true. Why has this finding caused such disagreement about the legitimacy and accuracy of scientific knowledge? One of the principles of the scientific method is replication, in which other researchers repeat a study to see whether they get similar results. If they do, they add legitimacy to the original findings. If not, the different findings question the accuracy of the knowledge.

It is not uncommon to see subsequent research refute previous findings. For instance, deterrence theorists argue that a secure custody sentence shows offenders the consequences of their criminal behaviour (specific deterrence). At the same time, institutionalization of some offenders shows others what can happen (general deterrence), providing further support for the use of secure custody to control criminal behaviour. As a result, debates developed as to whether community-based sanctions are less, equally, or more effective than incarceration at deterring future offending.

In their "Beyond Probation" study, Murray and Cox, Jr (1979) found that, for chronic young offenders, institutionalization is more effective at reducing the number of future offences than are community-based sanctions (e.g. probation, group homes, vocational training). Schneider (1990) replicated this study in terms of the young offenders, community-based sanctions, research methods, and data analysis. However, Schneider found that the decrease in the number of offences is the same whether youths receive community-based or secure custody sentences. Based on these two studies, is Murray and Cox, Jr's conclusion legitimate and accurate? Unfortunately, answering this question would be premature because there isn't a single research study that can "prove" with absolute certainty the effectiveness of secure custody.

Ioannidis (2005) argues that over half the results from any random research study are false for several reasons, including small sample sizes, poor study design, and selective reporting. Furthermore, there is a tendency to treat statistically significant results as substantively significant (i.e. relevant in the real world). Statistical significance will be covered in Chapter 9—for now, think of it as the degree of confidence that the result did not occur by chance. Scientific convention states that a finding is statistically significant if the odds of it occurring by chance are only 1 in 20. Statistical significance doesn't automatically suggest importance in the real world.

Ioannidis (2005, p. 700) states: "A major problem is that it is impossible to know with 100 per cent certainty what the truth is in any research question." Thus, we should accept that most research findings will be refuted, that some will be validated (upon replication), and that the replication process is more significant than any particular research finding. When you read conclusions, it may be better to view the findings as something to think about and not as facts to be considered categorically as knowledge. This approach, of course, would include the conclusions from Ionnadis, despite his failure to acknowledge it!

is to be considered a fact or knowledge in the scientific community, it must be supported by research findings that use appropriate research methods and analytical techniques. Evaluations of knowledge typically use assessments—such as multiple-choice questions or class participation—that measure the ability to retain and synthesize this knowledge. Thus, the capacity to assess whether knowledge is legitimate and accurate is extremely important.

Let's say a police officer asks a murder suspect where he or she was the night of the crime. Clearly, the officer is asking the right question, but his or her ability to evaluate the response is just as important. Not all information or data are created equal and, in many cases, the data collection method affects validity or the ability to represent reality accurately. Just as we must contextualize responses to questions in ordinary life, we must question the research methods used to generate the data and interpretations. An understanding of research methods makes us aware of what an analysis does and does not say. We should use both to assess claims to knowledge.

This chapter will help orient you to the assumptions and worldviews that shape how research questions are developed, how research methods are chosen, and why the findings are interpreted in a certain way to generate knowledge. As you learn the **scientific method** of creating knowledge about human behaviour and the intersection between research and criminal public policy, you will develop and refine your skills to understand, interpret, and question the research results that often influence social institutions' opinions and responses to crime.

scientific method a model of inquiry used to systematically create knowledge based on a set of principles and procedures.

Ability to Question Information

Whether we realize it or not, we consume research throughout our lives, regardless of our occupation. We can't escape it. Consider TV ads that state nine out of ten dentists prefer a particular toothbrush. Much like there is a focus in elementary and secondary schools on media literacy, it is equally important to develop critical thinking and methodological skills that put you in a better position to recognize whether evidence is true or imperative. Scientific inquiry requires critical thinking as it systematically examines claims to knowledge before reaching any conclusions.

Society, particularly in the workplace, places a great deal of emphasis on critical thinking skills. We are all conditioned from birth not to question authority figures, be they our parents, teachers, books, or the media. Critical thinking is "the ability to think for oneself and reliably and responsibly make those decisions that affect one's life" (Schafersman, 1991). We are taught what to think but not necessarily how. Science is a method of thinking, and critical thinking is the use of reason and evidence to evaluate knowledge claims. In this way, scientific reasoning and critical thinking go hand in hand.

An argument can be made that every chapter in this book contributes to developing your critical thinking skills. Understanding research methods and the logic of the scientific method will dramatically enhance your potential for success, personally and professionally. If you hone the ability to think critically, you can ask the right questions, identify and find the required information, analyze data, and assess conclusions. Understanding research methods can also help you deal with the universal problem of information overload. These methods give you practical skills to find and evaluate the information you actually need to be an informed consumer and decision-maker. For example, suppose you are a lawyer defending a person who is charged with producing obscene material. How do you define *obscene*? Typically, the first approach would involve seeking applicable case law. Since the Criminal Code's definitions apply to "a reasonable person," another way to answer this question could be to conduct a survey to see if impartial individuals deem the material obscene.

Types of Knowledge

We are always engaged in an interpretive process through our interactions with people, places, and things that create or modify our knowledge. "Everyday life presents itself as a reality [that is] interpreted by men and subjectively meaningful to them as a coherent world" (Berger & Luckmann, 1967, p. 19). In other words, how we interpret and classify information as knowledge is shaped by the degree that it is meaningful to us. Taken-for-granted knowledge is situated knowledge; it is grounded in one's personal experiences, interpretations, and assessments of the knowledge source.

Analyzing our world makes us susceptible to misinformed opinions, distorted assumptions, skewed interpretations, and rigid ideological beliefs. That said, our common-sense understanding of the world isn't always wrong and scientific knowledge isn't always right. Neither knowledge source is perfect, but the latter is systematic and empirical, making it more likely to be credible and accurate. Taken-for-granted knowledge is pre-scientific but nonetheless still serves an integral function in daily life. For instance, one can safely assume that you would put your hand on a hot stove only once! Non-scientific sources of knowledge include appeals to authority, tradition, common sense, legends, myths, and personal experience.

Authority

An expert or authority could be your professor, textbook author, parents, politicians, scientists, or even the media. Authority figures make a claim to knowledge that becomes true by virtue of their experience, expertise, or credentials. The person's status influences our judgment on the truth of the knowledge. Knowledge by authority means that something must be true if an expert says it is. For example, the media and many parents tell children that Santa Claus will bring them presents on Christmas Eve. Without evidence to the contrary and the skills required to question this statement, children tend to believe what these authority figures tell them.

Authoritative knowledge is a double-edged sword. On the one hand, it can provide a starting point to seek further knowledge. In many ways, we grant experts unquestionable authority to create knowledge. However, even well-respected scientists can be wrong, which is one reason that ideas are repeatedly tested under different conditions. We may also overestimate an expert's qualifications or the data used to support his or her assertions. It is common for authority figures to state opinions and conclusions in areas outside their expertise. Given the above, a critical question to ask is, "How do we know the process they use to reach their conclusions?" There are many ways to gain knowledge, and the ability to assess its usefulness and truthfulness is an important skill to use, even with information provided by experts.

Tradition

Knowledge based on tradition is grounded in the past; something is true because it has always been believed or been done a certain way. For centuries, people believed that the world was flat. Tradition said so, and Galileo suffered the consequences for claiming that the earth was actually round. From a different perspective, moral questions can be informed by faith and tradition. But even in this circumstance, the answers may differ because the belief or tradition does not apply to everyone (e.g. atheist, agnostic, Christian). As is the case with authority, not all traditional knowledge is false. Tradition involves accessing a body of cumulative knowledge amassed over time, which can serve as a springboard to develop and learn new knowledge scientifically.

A facet of tradition is provincialism, the tendency to ignore or disparage knowledge and viewpoints from cultures other than one's own. Our cultural perspective impacts our acceptance or rejection of facts and theories regardless of the evidence presented (Kahane, 1988). This practice can manifest by accepting rigid ideological beliefs or adopting popular or politically correct views.

For instance, pro-death penalty activists are adamant about the deterrent effect that capital punishment provides. Views against the death penalty are equally strong. Both sides rely on tradition-based knowledge and can refer to research that supports their position. Taking a different approach, Land, Teske, Jr, and Zheng (2009) analyzed the death penalty's deterrence effect in a manner that resolved some of the methodological weaknesses in previous research. Although the authors discovered a small short-term reduction in homicides in the first and fourth months following an execution, they also found evidence of displacement from one month to another, suggesting that any deterrence effect was reduced to almost nothing within 12 months.

Common Sense

Common-sense knowledge—knowledge based on ordinary reasoning commonly accepted by others in society—arguably plays a critical role in our lives. Intuition is a powerful source of knowledge, but it does not meet the scientific standards required to have confidence in the claim's veracity. We use intuition when we hope that something is true or when we make decisions based on a "gut feeling." If a person plays the slot machines at a casino, his or her intuition may justify pulling the lever just one more time. The logic associated with the intuition may be "The law of averages states I am due to win money" or "I have a gut feeling that this will be the one." Research into gambling finds that slot machines are mathematically programmed to provide small payoffs frequently enough to feed into common-sense knowledge and intuition (Cosgrove & Klassen, 2009).

The second variant of common-sense knowledge is idiomatic expressions. Consider the expression "opposites attract." We often refer to this saying when we talk about two seemingly different individuals who are in what appears to be a successful personal relationship. Yet this idiom does not constitute a claim to knowledge consistent with scientific reasoning.

Knowledge based on common sense can be valuable as we negotiate and understand the world. It can make us question our understanding further by seeking additional corroborating evidence. However, to support this type of knowledge, the evidence must derive from scientific investigations and not from other sources of alternative knowledge.

Legends and Myths

Legends are stories that relate to a particular group of people and are popularly accepted as historical and true. Myths are unproven or false collective beliefs used as evidence to justify a story, idea, or concept. The media is one of the primary sources of knowledge based on legends and myths. Crime and responses to criminal behaviour are presented in a manner that reflects the objective of any corporation: to make money. The question remains whether these portrayals are accurate in terms of the event and claims to knowledge.

Research on portrayals of crime, societal responses, and offenders often finds significant disparities between the event's context and facts and the media's message. The coverage of Hurricane Katrina evacuees being relocated to Houston, Texas, in 2005 provides an example. Although research using crime mapping techniques found no increase in property or violent crime six months after the event, self-report surveys found that media reports of the relocation created a fear of unmanageable growth in crime, to the extent that the Houston Police Department increased its presence in areas near evacuees (Lawton & Schulenberg, 2007). Warren (2009) conducted a content analysis of print and television media coverage 6 months before and 12 months after Hurricane Katrina. The findings suggested that the Texas media depicted the New Orleans evacuees negatively by using small and biased snippets and repeating coverage from the first three days after the hurricane. Consequently, Houston residents developed an unfounded distrust of the evacuees.

In 2005 and 2006, media coverage of the hurricane constituted a myth for some and a legend for others. An example is Neal Boortz's response to a caller to his nationally syndicated radio show:

Why is it that the people who are being affected by the floods in Iowa and the upper Midwest . . . seem to be so much more capable of taking care of themselves and handling this disaster than were the people of Katrina in New Orleans? I think the answer's pretty clear, is that up there in that part of the country, you find a great deal of self-sufficiency. Down there in New Orleans, it was basically a parasite class totally dependent on government for their existence (Media Matters for America, 2010).

As this example shows, what we believe to be true is socially constructed. In everyday life, we typically do not discover knowledge but construct it through an active process. Similarly, employing scientific reasoning and method is a conscious activity. We assemble these interpretations within the context of shared understandings, language, and practices within our society. The media portrayal of Hurricane Katrina evacuees created a moral panic by constructing a myth of dangerousness and various justifications for distrusting the evacuees. Moral panics occur when a group of people "become defined as a threat to societal values and interests" (Cohen, 1973, p. 9). Societal reactions are then based on a false knowledge about that particular group of people, which is perceived as representing a danger to society. Research finds that media and political interests are often intertwined and that the media portrayals of events are a large contributor to the creation of moral panics (Herman & Chomsky, 1988).

Consider what is now referred to as the "CSI effect," stemming from the popular television series *CSI: Crime Scene Investigation* and its spinoffs (*CSI: Miami* and *CSI: New York*). This concept captures such shows' exaggerated portrayal of forensic science labs as producing findings very quickly and always get the criminal. As a result, trial juries have made greater demands for forensic evidence in order to eliminate reasonable doubt. Unfortunately, the myth, glamour, and authority misrepresent the criminal investigation process. On *CSI*, investigators appear to receive DNA results within hours. But not all police services have a crime lab. The Royal Canadian Mounted Police (RCMP) has forensic laboratories in Halifax, Ottawa, Regina, Edmonton, and Vancouver. In Quebec, the police wait over a year for DNA results in cases deemed non-urgent—which accounts for 99 per cent of all cases (Dupuis, 2009, p. 10). Once again, there is a disconnect between alternative sources of knowledge and scientific knowledge.

Personal Experience

Our personal experiences shape who we are and who we become. However, they can distort reality and our ability to reason impartially about the relationship between our experiences and those of others. There are four ways that our personal experience can lead us astray: overgeneralization, selective observation, premature closure, and the halo effect.

Overgeneralization occurs when we make statements and draw conclusions that go beyond what the available data or information can support. Based on the evidence so far, we make a faulty assumption and apply it to other situations or other people. Unfortunately, we are not good mirrors and interpreters of ourselves. For instance, eyewitness testimony is not the most reliable method because we miss the obvious, have trouble recalling detailed information, and can be influenced unconsciously by emotions and information after the fact. Moreover, different people perceive the same situation differently.

A further complication is that our personal experiences may not be typical or comprehensive. Our experiences are also based on a particular standpoint. Imagine that your professor holds up a book in class. You are sitting in the centre of the classroom and thus can see the book's cover. A student sitting at the end of a row may see the thickness of the book.

Methods in Action

Psychic for a Day

Personal experience, tradition, faith, and (often) hope have a powerful hold on our emotions and reasoning ability, particularly during stressful times in our lives. We discussed how some claims to knowledge may not be legitimate and accurate under some circumstances. In 2003, the PBS show *Eye on Nye* aired a segment on psychics with Michael Shermer, founding publisher of *Skeptic* and executive director of the Skeptics Society. Shermer (2003) was asked to see how successful a psychic he could be with only little knowledge of psychic techniques. Despite the fact that he was to do cold readings (i.e. without any prior knowledge about the five randomly selected subjects), he did not prepare until the day before the show.

Using a book on the subject, Shermer learned the importance of a pre-reading setting, which involves behavioural modifications such as a soft voice and non-confrontational body language. In the preamble, the reader should tell subjects that he or she senses things weighing on their hearts and will use his or her special gift of intuition to help them find their way through their current life challenges. The reading is supposed to start general and focus on the present, then the past, and finally peek at the future. Shermer (2003, pp. 48–49) developed this opening statement:

> You can be a very considerate person, very quick to provide for others, but there are times, if you are honest, when you recognize a selfish streak in yourself. I would say that on the whole you can be rather quiet . . . but when the circumstances are right, you can be quite the life of the party if the mood strikes you. Sometimes you are too honest about your feelings and you reveal too much of yourself. You are good at thinking things through and you like to see proof before you change your mind about anything . . . You are wise in the ways of the world, a wisdom gained through hard experience rather than book learning.

The professor will see the back cover and feel how heavy the book is. Each of these observations is true but, in isolation, portrays only one perspective of knowledge about that book.

Selective observation occurs when we notice only those things that support and reinforce our current thinking and views on a subject. Here, knowledge is built by reaffirming preconceived notions about the world and the reasons for behaviour and events. In other words, we see things that support our opinions and ignore or minimize any evidence that conflicts with this understanding.

We fall into the trap of premature closure when we reach a conclusion before we have sufficient evidence to do so. Think of it as knowing the answers and not needing to look at, listen to, or question any additional information. Premature closure is often associated with mishaps in logic, such as missing evidence, insufficient evidence, and unjustified conclusions. The adequacy of the evidence should be assessed prior to using it in support of a conclusion. Insufficient evidence combines overgeneralization and premature closure. For example, when someone is released on parole and reoffends shortly thereafter, the conclusion is that our correctional system is too lenient; however, this statement is based on one incident and does not include sufficient supporting evidence. Conclusions based on insufficient evidence manifest when researchers generalize their findings to topics, people, or places that the data do

All five subjects nodded their heads vigorously in agreement.

During the tarot card reading, Shermer couldn't remember what the ten-card configuration stood for, so he winged it. With palm readings, experts state that you should direct comments toward the colour and texture of the skin, hair on the back of the palm, the shape of the hands, and any differences between the left and right hand. This practice lends an air of scientific observation to the reading as it represents empirical evidence that subjects can see. Consequently, they do not typically question the interpretations. For the astrological reading, Shermer downloaded a chart for a man born on 9 May 1961; the female subject was born on 3 September 1982.

Think about this reasoning and types of knowledge while you read the following statement:

> I discovered that her father had died when she was 27, so I deduced that it must have been a sudden death (correct) and that she did not have the opportunity to make her peace with him (also correct). Finally, I accurately deduced that she was sad because she would have liked to share her many life experiences over the past two decades with her father (Shermer, 2003, p. 55).

We have a bit of authority, halo effect, and selective observation at work here in the various claims to knowledge.

What can we conclude from this exercise? Shermer states that there is little evidence to support a psychic claim to knowledge. One idea is that the sources of knowledge and reasoning used to interpret and derive conclusions make people susceptible to believing in psychics. All five subjects believed Shermer's interpretations and thought that he was a psychic.

not corroborate. An explanation may seem reasonable and logical but is unjustified because it lacks the evidence required to support it (see the Methods in Action box on page 8).

The **halo effect** creates knowledge through the overgeneralization of authority figures. The perception of one personality trait is seen as outstanding and extends to all qualities of that person. If we succumb to the halo effect, we designate the source as highly prestigious and fail to scrutinize any of the knowledge claims. There are many examples in society, including scientists, dynamic leaders, and others we admire. Think about your personal relationships. You believe your girlfriend, boyfriend, spouse, or friend because you admire other qualities about him

or her. The admiration, or pedestal such people are placed on, leads to an uncritical examination of their words and actions. This effect causes us to lose our neutrality and objectivity about what we believe to be true and to draw conclusions on prior reputations.

halo effect a predisposition to admire all actions and words of a person, based on the perception of a distinguished quality demonstrated in the past.

Scientific Knowledge

As previously explained, the scientific method is the way we gain understanding and test other forms of knowledge. This book is about using the scientific method to create knowledge. At this juncture, several characteristics are integral to understanding how scientific knowledge differs from those we have already discussed:

- **Prediction and explanation:** Based on **theory,** predictions are made to explain the social world.
- **Systematic observation and empiricism:** Using the five senses as predicted by theory, data on events and behaviours are collected.
- **Scientific reasoning:** Using rationality and logic, a theory or model is created based on the findings (knowledge).
- **Transparency:** The research process is documented so that another person could conduct the study again.
- **Provisional:** The results are analyzed by other researchers for limitations and alternative explanations.

Keep in mind that the scientific method can produce knowledge, but the evidence supporting these conclusions can be misinterpreted. It is always important to question everything you read, much as you would with knowledge created by authority, tradition, or common sense.

theory a set of statements or a model based on empirical evidence and reasoning that helps to explain and predict social phenomena.

Theoretical Foundations

Every criminological theory contains assumptions about human nature and causality, describes the criminological phenomena to be understood, and explains the behaviour or facet of the criminal justice system. Theories discuss the causes or reasons for crime but can also speak to central aspects of actors and responses by the criminal justice system. Crime and justice research is both theoretical and empirical. It's theoretical as it is primarily concerned with creating and testing theories or ideas about how the world works in relation to crime. It is empirical because it systematically measures and observes the social world and our perceptions of it. To this end, all research endeavours have underlying theoretical foundations that influence the development of research questions and largely determine the research methods adopted to address these questions. These foundations include assumptions about knowledge, aspects of theory, and types of theoretical perspectives or worldviews.

The Difference between Ideology and Theory

We have looked at the various types of knowledge that are, for the most part, used in everyday life. Quite often, conclusions based on authority, tradition, common sense, legends, myths, and personal experiences can form the basis of ideologies. However, scientific research can also make claims to knowledge and miss evidence, provide insufficient evidence, or present unjustified conclusions. If both ideology and theory can have problems with their claims to knowledge, it is important to understand the distinction between the two terms prior to contemplating theoretical assumptions and the scientific method.

Ideology

Ideological explanations are presented with absolute certainty, purport to have all the answers, are fixed and closed, avoid tests of the ideas, dismiss contradictory evidence, are typically linked to specific moral beliefs, provide partial explanations, are inconsistent, and advocate for a specific position. They are quasi-theoretical explanations that lack several elements of scientific theories that increase the legitimacy of a knowledge claim.

Even within a particular ideology, you can find differences in logic, reasoning, and assumptions. Ideologies cannot be "proven" wrong and therefore are not amenable to modification on the basis of new, contradictory evidence. Upon examination, the conclusions are based on selective observation but also rely largely on personal experiences or overgeneralization and premature closure. A main point to remember is that "all ideologies are just words, abstractions used for particular political, social, economic purposes" (Zimbardo & Wang, 2010, point 15). This description contrasts with theories, which are conditional in the sense that the conclusions are understood to be incomplete and uncertain, to welcome modification based on new or contradictory evidence, to be divorced from appeals to morality, to represent neutrality, to seek logical consistency, and do not align with social positions.

Theory

Theories organize observations of the world and allow researchers to predict what will happen in the future under certain conditions. With scientific knowledge, even ideas repeatedly tested and supported by research are not unequivocally true. There are no guarantees that future research will continue to support the ideas, interpretations, and explanations. Theories have characteristics that tend to promote the advance of scientific knowledge, including sufficient description, precision in specifying ideas, interpretability, internal consistency (i.e. no contradictory propositions), and clear and specific predictions. Theories are also falsifiable, parsimonious, and serendipitous; they contain breadth on the subject and are amenable to applications or testing in the real world. Let's take a look at a few of these qualities, which are integral to distinguishing theory from ideology.

Falsifiability

A theory is falsifiable when research questions are structured so that the data collected can invalidate or modify a theoretical assertion. Unlike quasi-theories, such as ideologies, scientific theories use empirical research methods in the development of theoretical statements. As Popper (1963, p. 36) succinctly states, "a theory which is not refutable by any conceivable event is non-scientific" as it is not testable or falsifiable. Thus, the status of a theory rests with its falsifiability.

Falsifiability represents a characteristic of the scientific community known as skepticism. This term simply means that researchers and theorists are open to challenges and that findings are seen as provisional. In this way, the theoretical statements derived from research are scrutinized to ensure that the research methods and ideas within the theory are congruent with scientific standards, such as falsifiability. Thomas Kuhn (1970/1996, p. 146) summarizes skepticism in his highly influential book, *The Structure of Scientific Revolutions*: "No theory ever solves all of the puzzles with which it is confronted at a given time; nor are the solutions already achieved often perfect. On the contrary, it is just the incompleteness and imperfection of the existing data-theory fit that, at any given time, define many of the puzzles that characterize normal science."

When a researcher submits an article to a scholarly journal, it is sent out to (usually) three anonymous reviewers. This peer review process represents organized skepticism as the reviewers evaluate the links between previous literature, theory, research questions, research methods, analytical techniques, data interpretation, and conclusions. With some academic journals, the acceptance rate of articles can be 5 per cent or less, and the reviewer reports can be scathing. It is much more likely for an article to be rejected or to receive a "revise and resubmit," which requires that the author address the reviewers' comments in order for the article to be reconsidered for publication.

There are several warning signs that indicate a closer link between ideology and a concern regarding the veracity of the claims to knowledge:

1. The theoretical statements and research findings are initially released to the media. The integrity of research depends on exposing ideas and findings to vetting by the scientific community. An attempt to bypass the peer review process suggests that the research might not measure up to the theoretical and methodological standards of the scientific community.

2. The researcher claims that a powerful entity in industry or government is trying to suppress the

research findings. There have been cases, particularly in respect to medical research sponsored by pharmaceutical companies, where such a claim has been made. One must carefully evaluate this assertion, as it is another justification for bypassing the peer review process.

3. The researcher states that the findings are difficult to detect, such as clear photographs of flying saucers. The results are only as good as the analyst and the analytical technique used to test the theoretical statements and research questions.

4. The evidence presented to support the findings is largely anecdotal. Anecdotal evidence often has associated emotional connotations that perpetuate legends or myths and fall into the sphere of ideologies. This type of evidence can keep superstitions or old wives' tales alive. For example, your mother may have told you to bundle up or you'll catch a cold. Yet scientific research finds that colds are viruses and not associated with exposure to the cold.

5. The researcher claims that the theoretical explanation is credible and accurate because it has always existed. This is traditional knowledge.

6. The researcher has worked in isolation on the project, which is why he or she is the only one who was able to make this discovery. True breakthroughs do not occur in a vacuum but involve a cumulative process in which many researchers who test theoretical explanations in different contexts with different people (recall replication). (Park, 2003)

Of course, these signs are only indicators, as the research and theoretical statements may still be legitimate; however, as Park points out, it is more often a reason to seriously question the findings and resulting theoretical propositions.

To illustrate these points, consider the court's use of "expert" testimony. Remember, not all scientific research is created equal based on the research methods used, the interpretation of the data, and the scientific community's assessment of the claim to knowledge.

Daubert v. Merrell Dow Pharmaceuticals, Inc. (1993), argued in the US Supreme Court, brought this issue to the forefront by creating the Daubert standard for admission of expert testimony as evidence. This standard established five criteria for assessing the truth of a claim to scientific knowledge. First, the evidence must be subjected to empirical testing in the real world so that the theory or technique is demonstrated to be falsifiable, refutable, and testable. The use of fingerprints has withstood this challenge, but the use of a polygraph has had inconclusive results and, in Canada, is not admissible as evidence in court. Second, consistent with the first point raised by Park, the proposed testimony must be subjected to peer review and publication in a scientific journal or book. Third, we must have an indication of the potential error rate or likelihood that the prediction could be wrong. Fourth, standards and controls for the application of the theory and research findings must be developed and consistently applied. As new forensic science techniques are developed, they are often controversial because their instruments do not fulfill this criterion or cannot specify the likelihood of a false positive. Finally, the testimonial evidence must indicate the degree to which the theory or technique is accepted by the scientific community.

Following the Daubert standard, the Supreme Court of Canada's *R v. Mohan* (1994) decision further clarified the admissibility of expert testimony. The testimony must be relevant, required to marshal facts, eligible (i.e. not be hearsay), and provided by a person with the appropriate credentials. Closely related is both countries' requirement that testimony be the result of reliable principles and research methods, which are then reliably applied to the facts of the case.

Parsimony

There are multiple theories to explain events and behaviours. For instance, in our quest to understand why some youth break the law and others do not, we have theories that are based on the neighbourhood (social disorganization theory), a disjuncture between societal goals and the means to achieve them (Merton's modes of adaptation, differential opportunity theory), psychological explanations (conduct disorder), biological explanations (nature versus nurture), social learning (differential association, operant conditioning), societal reaction (labelling theory), social inequality (feminist and conflict theories), life course (Moffit's typology of adolescent-limited and life course persisters), and many others. Which one is the most accurate explanation for juvenile delinquency? Can this question be answered?

In science, a parsimonious theory simplifies reality and combines essential elements to promote our understanding of a social phenomenon. Parsimony represents an economical theory with a few principles that explain many events but do not oversimplify reality. Integrated theories combine two or more theories to create a more holistic explanation (such as Sampson and Laub's [2003] age-graded theory of crime). Parsimony is one way to achieve some consistency in the operationalization of these concepts. Therefore, a parsimonious theory is also testable and falsifiable.

Serendipity

In ordinary life, serendipity often refers to good fortune, or luck. In scientific theory formulation, serendipity involves an open mind to chance observations that are typically unassociated with the research questions under investigation but lead, nonetheless, to new knowledge. Another way of looking at serendipity is to imagine a "eureka" moment, when a researcher realizes the potential impact, clarification, and understanding about crime based on this unexpected finding.

Merton (1968) makes a valuable distinction between serendipity and serendipity patterns. Serendipity is a finding that was not originally part of the theory being investigated. A serendipity pattern is a surprising and irregular system that is potentially important. In research on factors affecting police discretion with youth, a serendipitous finding

could be a relationship between the degree of parental involvement and the type of crime committed. A serendipity pattern could simply be a trend across people, places, and events regarding parental involvement and the type of crime. Serendipity played a part in Alexander Fleming's discovery of penicillin, as Fleming was conducting experiments for a completely different reason.

Theories make predictions based on the evidence available, relationships between ideas, and factors found to have a certain effect on our topic of interest, providing a gateway to future research. A powerful theory helps to organize the current body of knowledge on a subject and inform practices in the criminal justice system. (Table 1.1 presents the attributes of theoretical research and identifies the chapters in this book that will discuss these topics in further detail.) There are times when the label of a scientific theory is actually applied to an ideology. However, Wolfgang (1980, p. 50) reinforces the distinction between theory and ideology: "When there is research and carefully developed theory supported by research, then information is available, ignorance is denied its power to permit any kind of decision, and the principle of best evidence is invoked."

Assumptions about Knowledge

Research differs based on the epistemological and ontological assumptions that underlie the theoretical approach and research design. All theoretical perspectives operate with a conception of reality, truth, and knowledge. **Epistemology** is a philosophical concept that describes how we know that a claim to knowledge is legitimate. Epistemological assumptions are the criteria embedded in any research design that determine how we are to know what we know. **Ontology** establishes what is deemed to be true. Hence, epistemology reflects the process and ontology

epistemology a philosophical concept regarding the nature and criteria of legitimate knowledge based on how we know what we know.

ontology a philosophical concept about establishing truth.

Table 1.1 Components of theoretical research

Theoretical component and attributes	Relevant chapter(s)
I Theoretical scope	Chapter 1
1. Universally applicable	
2. Culturally specific	
3. Historically specific	
4. A social group	
5. Certain individuals	
6. A phenomenon	
II Units of analysis	Chapter 4
1. Individual	
2. Society	
3. Culture	
4. Institution	
5. Group	
6. Organization	
7. Social role	
8. Interaction	
9. Process	
10. Phenomena	
11. Method	
III Hypotheses stated linguistically and symbolically	Chapter 3
IV Assumptions	Chapter 1
V Logic of inquiry	Chapters 1 and 2
1. Theoretical propositions not emphatically derived but logically derived according to a theoretical structure	
2. Theoretical propositions not emphatically derived or logically derived (e.g. based on author's opinion)	
3. Theoretical propositions partially empirically derived	
4. Theoretical propositions based on empirical evidence	
VI Empirical support offered from	Chapters 2 and 6–8
1. Author's own experience (e.g. clinical, law enforcement, teaching)	
2. Official data (e.g. police records, Statistics Canada)	
3. Nonofficial data (e.g. surveys, field observations, interviews)	
4. Other published sources (e.g. theoretical works)	
VII Definitions and concepts	Chapter 4
VIII Dependent and independent variables	Chapter 2
IX Type of conclusions and interpretations	Chapters 9–11
1. Theoretical	
2. Methodological	
3. Policy-oriented	
X Internal consistency	Appendix B
1. Interpretations logically follow from assumptions and definitions	
2. Interpretations logically follow from empirical evidence	
XI Testability	Chapter 1 and
1. Demonstrated (tested)	Appendix A
2. Suggested	
3. Problem not referred to	

Table 1.1 *Continued*	

XII Contribution to conceptualization
  1. Construction of theory
  2. Construction of methodology
  3. Construction of the concept
	All chapters

XIII Extent to which the theory can be generalized
  1. Universally applicable
  2. A culture
  3. Historically specific
  4. A society
  5. A social group
  6. Certain individuals
  7. A specific issue
	Chapters 1 and 4–5
	and Appendix B

Source: Adapted from Wolfgang (1980, pp. 35–36).

reflects the conclusions. Quantitative and qualitative research operate with a different set of assumptions about the definition of reality (ontology), the acknowledgement of reality or how we know what we know (epistemology), and the ways that reality is understood (methodology) (Lincoln & Guba, 1985).

Types of Explanations

Nomothetic research seeks to develop laws or rules about the general case or norm (*nomos* in Greek) to explain observable phenomena. Arguably, a substantial amount of crime and justice research is nomothetic and uses numerical data. This type of research is probabilistic as the goal is to determine the possibility that an event, situation, condition, or behaviour will occur, how often, and under what circumstances. For example, a nomothetic perspective would investigate recidivism by examining what factors account for variations in the probability of someone breaking the law again (or being arrested, convicted, or incarcerated).

At the other end of the spectrum, **idiographic research** studies the individual to understand the properties that differentiate him or her from others. It is a complete, in-depth understanding of the self (*idios* in Greek), characteristics, and

events. According to Wilhelm Windelband, idiographic explanations are socio-historically situated behaviours and events (Lamiell, 1998). They are in contrast to nomothetic interpretations, which focus on studying individual events to create general laws as guides to a broader understanding of the social phenomenon.

For example, seeking psychological counselling reflects a more idiographic approach. However, psychology research that looks at the coping mechanisms used by those with post-traumatic stress disorder (PTSD) represents more of a nomothetic inquiry. The ontological assumption of nomothetic inquiry is that there is one truth that we can get close to but not necessarily pinpoint because of our research methods and the nature of social science data. The epistemological assumption is objectivist in the sense that knowledge constitutes the laws and regularities as determined and supported by empirical observational data. The idiographic perspective takes a different approach with the ontological assumption that there is more than one truth,

nomothetic research research that focuses on establishing universal principles or laws about social reality.

idiographic research research that focuses on understanding behaviours and events within a socio-historic situated approach.

as multiple realities exist based on the socio-historical context of the event, situation, or behaviour. The epistemological assumption is subjectivist; we know what we know based on the language and perceptions of those in the situation. There is more than one reality, owing to a process of interpretation whereby social actors negotiate meaning and understanding through social interaction.

Direction of Theorizing

Deductive reasoning, which moves from the general to the specific, relies on the principle of empiricism (empirical evidence). To be considered knowledge, the observations must be detected and tested empirically by our five senses (i.e. sight, smell, taste, hearing, and touch). Thus, this approach to research starts with a theory, develops a research hypothesis, collects observational data, and interprets the data so that the findings support, modify, or refute a theoretical statement.

> **deductive reasoning** an approach to research that moves from the general to specific by taking an existing idea or theory and applying it to a situation to test whether it is true.

> **inductive reasoning** an approach to research that moves from the specific to the general by using observations to formulate an idea or theory.

Research using **inductive reasoning** moves from observing specific facts to detecting a pattern

in the observational data and to a tentative hypothesis about these regularities, which leads to the development of a theory. Accordingly, it is more open-ended and exploratory than deductive reasoning. Inductive reasoning is most often associated with qualitative research as it investigates how social actors make sense of their world through everyday processes.

Even with seemingly incompatible differences, most research uses both deductive and inductive reasoning processes. Approaches to research are not as dichotomous, or black and white, as this demarcation between deductive/inductive and quantitative/qualitative implies.

Let's say you are pulled over by the police. The officer asks if you are aware that you were exceeding the speed limit. Employing deductive reasoning, you might develop the following argument:

1. Everyone appears to travel 10 to 20 kilometres over the speed limit on this highway (theoretical statement).
2. Travelling 10 to 20 kilometres over the speed limit is acceptable, as measured by not receiving a speeding ticket (hypothesis).
3. Empirical evidence is based on your personal driving experience and the observations of other drivers and passengers (observation).
4. The empirical evidence supports this theoretical statement (confirmation).

The officer, armed with his or her radar gun, could be working with inductive reasoning. A possible argument would go as follows:

1. The officer observes a car travelling at a rate exceeding the posted speed limit, as measured by visual observation and the reading from the radar gun (observation).
2. The officer finds other vehicles travelling at speeds that also appear to exceed the limit (pattern).

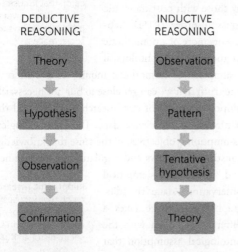

Figure 1.1 Deductive and inductive reasoning

Methods in Action

Inductive and Deductive Criminal Profiling

John Douglas from the FBI Behavioural Science Unit at Quantico is arguably one of the most famous criminal profilers. During the late 1970s, Douglas and his colleague Robert Ressler interviewed 36 serial killers to investigate the patterns between the offender's life and personality and the nature of his or her crimes and evidence at the crime scenes (Turvey, 1999). Their typology of organized and disorganized killers reflects inductive reasoning.

Inductive criminal profiling develops a description of the offender based on findings and patterns from other crime scenes, the profiler's abilities, and publicly available data to guide law enforcement investigations. Inductive reasoning often results in a conclusion, which is interpreted as likely but not certain. With inductive criminal profiling, the conclusion goes beyond the information contained in its premises (Turvey, 1999).

In contrast, deductive criminal profiling relies solely on information connected to that particular crime scene and victim. For instance, if a cigarette butt left at the scene is found to be unavailable locally, the deductive profiler might posit that the killer is wealthy enough to afford imported cigarettes. Unlike an inductive profile, this conclusion isn't compared to other crime scenes with similar evidence.

Although depicted in the media as accurate, inductive profiling may not be that different from tips the police receive from psychics. The British Home Office examined 184 solved crimes to ascertain how often the FBI's profile of organized and disorganized killers accurately described the person who was ultimately arrested (Gladwell, 2007). The study found that profiles worked in 2.7 per cent of these cases.

Other problems are linked to the research methods employed in inductive profiling. For instance, Douglas and Ressler cannot demonstrate that the 36 murderers interviewed represent characteristics of the larger population of killers. These killers were chosen based on convenience. Much research looking to verify the accuracy of inductive profiling finds that it falls short because these types of crimes do not fall neatly into either an organized or disorganized crime scene, nor do these crime scene characteristics typically match a certain type of offender accurately (Gladwell, 2007). Turvey (1999) explains that this discrepancy is caused by different offenders exhibiting the same behaviours for completely different reasons.

With deductive profiling, conclusions are based on forensic crime scene reconstruction and not evidence based on similar offenders, offences, or crime scenes. The criminal profile uses deductive reasoning to construct an offender profile from one crime scene. The offender's behaviours in committing the crime are analyzed, as are the characteristics of the crime scene and the victim(s). This technique, referred to as behaviour evidence analysis, depends on the profiler's ability to use deductive reasoning to recognize patterns and regularities in the behaviour of a single offender. The accuracy of deductive criminal profiling is much higher than that of inductive profiles (Gladwell, 2007).

3. The officer reasons that, if the original vehicle is pulled over for exceeding the speed limit, other drivers will understand that the action as unacceptable (tentative hypothesis).

4. During the traffic stop, other vehicles slowed down. Thus, exceeding the speed limit by 10 to 20 kilometres an hour is not seen as acceptable by others on this highway if they see a car pulled over (theory).

Levels of Social Reality

Both individual (micro) and structural (meso and macro) levels of theorizing are important to understand the causes of, and responses to, criminal behaviour. **Micro-level** explanations of social reality depict social processes within small-scale settings and events that involve a few individuals or small groups. For instance, explaining the relationship between the victim and the offender or decision-making by jury members represents micro-level analysis.

The **meso-level** explanation of social reality investigates social processes at a stage between micro- and macro-level theories. For instance, Shaw and McKay's (1942) explanation for the ecological distribution of juvenile delinquency in Chicago was the result of community-level social disorganization. Meso-level theories and research look at social movements, differences between and within communities and organizations, or variations between types of crime. These social processes are typically examined over longer periods of time, such as a few months or several years.

The **macro-level** explanation of social reality investigates how larger aggregates, such as social institutions in society, operate and interact with other institutions and groups of people. Macro-level social processes represent the big picture, large-scale settings, societal processes, patterns, and structures across time. For example,

micro-level a theory and research focus on explaining processes that occur over short periods of time, involve a small-scale setting, or include only a few people in a social interaction or encounter.

meso-level a theory and research focus on explaining phenomena that link micro- and macro-level social processes at an intermediate level (e.g. organizations, time periods of several months or years).

macro-level a theory and research focus on explaining phenomena that occur in large-scale settings, exist across significant periods of time, or involve the relations and impact of social institutions in society.

positivism a worldview that asserts that scientific knowledge, which describes and explains observable phenomena, is the only true knowledge.

macro-level theories address groups such as the family, education, social class, ethnicity, or government and investigate topics such as trends in crime by social class over a twenty-year period.

Theoretical Worldviews

To appreciate the relationship between theoretical foundations and research methods, we begin with the connection between theory and science. Scientific statements describe how and why social phenomena operate the way they do. In contrast, normative statements tell us whether certain acts or conditions are morally acceptable. The former reflect the theoretical foundations used in crime and justice research. The latter reflect statements used in various non-scientific types of knowledge.

In scientific thinking, all theoretical foundations depend on observations, procedures, and methods used to create legitimate and accurate knowledge. Weight is not placed on the knowledge producer per se. In short, science can be defined as "a way of generating and testing the truth of statements about events in the world of human experience" (Wallace, 1971, p. 11). Therefore, science is a way of thinking. Each theoretical worldview acts as a frame of reference, shaping the inquiry and organizing our observations and reasoning processes when interpreting the data. The relationship between these theoretical foundations, paradigms, or worldviews and research is best highlighted by the contrasts found among positivism/post-positivism, interpretivism/constructionism, pragmatism, and middle-range theories.

Positivism and Post-Positivism

Introduced by Auguste Comte, **positivism** is a theoretical worldview that adopts the natural science model to describe and explain the social world. Positivists argue that legitimate knowledge is obtainable only by studying empirical data. The goal of knowledge claims is to describe social phenomena that can be directly observed and measured. Science is the best way to get at the truth so that we can predict and control processes and events in social life.

Positivism represents a **deterministic** approach as social reality operates by the laws of cause and effect. It is also reductionist; scientific inquiry and theories reduce ideas into small and more discrete concepts that are testable. Through the scientific method, we can detect patterns, regularities, causes, and consequences on the basis that events do not occur at random. These patterns and regularities occur independently and externally to the individual. The epistemological and ontological basis of knowledge is that an objective reality can be discovered with the proper research methods and analytical techniques. This objective truth or reality is patterned, ordered, and is often investigated with quantitative research methods.

The primary distinction between positivism and post-positivism is that the latter recognizes that our data, methods, and interpretations are not perfect, which means that we can get close to this objective, singular truth but not with absolute certainty. For both, the indicator of an adequate explanation is the ability to predict an outcome. Thus, much post-positivistic research seeks to identify the key causes in the variation of a behaviour, process, or event (e.g. the factors that affect illegal drug use). Knowledge is separate from the knower and knowledge producer, as post-positivistic research embraces objectivity and value-free scientific inquiry. An objective researcher is unbiased. In the same way, the research methods adopted have no effect on the social reality being observed. Specifically, objective claims to knowledge are created independently of the researcher's beliefs and desires and are supported with reasons based on empirical evidence.

Post-positivists point out that evidence is not perfect; hence, we cannot prove a theoretical statement right or wrong. We can simply investigate whether empirical evidence supports the theoretical statement. Although assigning quantitative research as positivistic is quite problematic, this demarcation

can help to appreciate the differences in the approaches to scientific research. Post-positivistic research "assumes there is a reality composed of atomistic, discrete, observable events in which antecedent variables operate in a law-like fashion to produce events" (Schulenberg, 2007a, p. 100). Here are the key tenants of the positivistic worldview:

> **determinism** a view that sees all behaviours and events as determined, or caused by, prior events, conditions, and laws.

1. The purpose for conducting research is to create a scientific explanation that provides evidence for universal causal laws about criminal behaviour. If we know a cause, we can predict and prevent its occurrence.
2. The assumption about social reality is that it exists, is real, and is waiting for scientific discovery. As reality is patterned and ordered, we can generate universal laws of behaviour.
3. Individuals respond to external forces in the same way they do to physical forces. Consequently, we can see external forces by observing the behaviour of individuals.
4. Human behaviour and its causes are external to the individual and not entirely up to his or her decision-making (deterministic approach).
5. Knowledge claims based on scientific methods are more legitimate and accurate than claims to knowledge based on common sense or other appeals to knowledge.
6. Replication ensures that knowledge is logically consistent with observed facts.
7. Empirical evidence is falsifiable and therefore cannot be proven with absolute certainty. Findings are approached with healthy skepticism.
8. Scientific research is to be objective and value-free (devoid of opinions and bias) during the data collection and interpretation process.

This worldview is not without its critics. For instance, the natural science model is more of an ideal than a reality when conducting research in the social sciences. Additionally, some aspects of the model are not feasible as they are unethical when conducting research on human behaviour. One exemplar of this criticism is the Milgram experiment conducted in 1962. Milgram (1963) was interested in understanding how regular German people could permit the Holocaust to occur. His research interest was to understand human behaviour and the social conditions under which it operates. His experiment on blind obedience to authority was conducted in a laboratory. Research participants were "teachers" and a research assistant served as the "student." The teacher asked the student questions and administered powerful electric shocks with every wrong answer. The assistant expressed increasing pain and discomfort as the intensity of the shock increased. The participants could not see the assistant and did not know that the shocks were simulated. Although two-thirds of the "shocks" were at dangerous levels, the participants were pressured to continue even if they wished to stop.

Although these types of experimental conditions are consistent with the natural science model, many argue that Milgram's experiment is highly unethical because of the extreme emotional stress, the participants' inability to withdraw from the study, and the deception regarding the true research questions under investigation. For more on Milgram's study, see Chapter 2.

Another criticism of (post-) positivism is that it is impossible for any research endeavour to be completely objective or value-free. Some critics charge that post-positivistic research can help to support the existing social order. For example, studies on crime rate reduction may assist in maintaining the status quo for society's wealthy and powerful by focusing on street versus white-collar crimes. Finally, positivism cannot recognize that different people may experience and perceive the same events differently, which is classified as a subjective experience and is incompatible with the principles of positivism.

Interpretivism and Social Constructionism

Max Weber (1921/1978)'s contribution to scientific theory is the importance placed on people's perception of their own behaviour and other people's reactions to this behaviour. These ideas influenced theorists who were instrumental in articulating symbolic interactionism, ethnomethodology, labelling theory, and phenomenology. Weber's concept of verstehen is synonymous with the **interpretivist** worldview as it reflects an empathetic understanding of intention and a context of human behaviour. Interpretivists seek to understand how we make sense of our lives, how we define situations in the ways that we do, and how we define ourselves when we interact with others. We can understand human behaviour only by entering the subjects' setting or situation to see their definition of the situation, what they take into consideration when deciding to act, and how they interpret the words, behaviour, and events around them. Meaning is validated based on **intersubjectivity**, in which a phenomenon is commonly understood in the same way. The principle of verstehen implies that accurate knowledge "is attained when, through sympathetic participation, we can adequately grasp the emotional context in which the action took place" (Weber, 1921/1978, p. 5). Accordingly, interpretive research typically uses qualitative methods, such as participant observation and in-depth interviews.

Social reality is considered to be subjective rather than objective. Interpretivists see it as socially constructed and interpreted through social interaction, whereas positivists focus on a social reality that is external to the individual and acts

interpretivist a worldview that sees meaning as socially constructed, action as intentional, and the goal of research as understanding how people create and maintain meaning about the world around them.

intersubjectivity a term that describes a situation with a meaning or definition held by more than one person and that is constructed through interactions with others.

to constrain his or her behaviour. From a methodological standpoint, interpretivists argue that individuals react to the research methods adopted in a research study. For example, if you suspect you are being watched, there is a good possibility that you will adjust your behaviour. In the same way, the manner in which researchers collect their data can fundamentally alter the social reality they witness or have access to.

The research goal is not to explain but to create an understanding. Everything in life is viewed as a process, and the research needs to identify generic social processes that reflect how people make sense of their worlds. As the famous dictum states: "If people define situations as real, then they are real in their consequences" (Thomas & Thomas, 1928, pp. 571–572). Meanings are a social and historical construction and must be subjected to and negotiated within a social and historical context. Interpretivists argue that life does not occur in a vacuum and that it is problematic for research to rely solely on the philosophy that external forces explain human behaviour.

Interpretivist and constructivist research is based on the assumption that there is more than one reality, due to a process of continuous interpretation whereby individuals negotiate meaning and understanding. However, this idea is too simplistic for research in crime and justice. **Constructionist** research emphasizes the social actor's definition of the situation and how he or she recognizes, produces, and reproduces behaviour. Thus, the explicit focus is on the interpretation process. Contextualism works from the assumption of human nature that behaviour is specified and understandable only in the context in which it occurs—the precise focus is on the context around a behaviour, situation, or event. These variations all operate from the same notion, that we create our view of the world based on our perceptions of it. The main principles of the interpretivist worldview are as follows:

1. The research purpose is to create an in-depth understanding of how people construct meaning and experience everyday experiences.

2. Social reality is assumed to be a social construction built on individuals' perceptions within social interactions.

3. Individuals are engaged in an ongoing process of socially constructing meanings used to interpret and understand the world. Social reality may be patterned or exhibit regularities, but such features are caused by social norms created through social interactions, not laws of nature.

4. Human behaviour is a consequence of free will (conscious decision-making) because we create subjective meanings of situations and adjust our actions accordingly.

5. Common-sense knowledge influences human behaviour; therefore, knowledge can be contradictory. Interpretivists, constructionists, and constructivists do not see law-like regularities as an invalid way to understand the social world but approach the subject by focusing on generic social processes in the construction of common-sense knowledge.

6. Claims to knowledge are true if they make sense based on intersubjectivity. A fact is true if it provides empirical evidence of the social actor's point of view and allows us to enter the world of the individuals under investigation.

> **constructivism** a theoretical worldview that emphasizes how people interpret the social world around them.

7. Scientific evidence cannot be interpretable if it is removed from the context in which it occurs and from the meanings that individuals assign to the behaviours, situations, and events.

8. Instead of strict adherence to objectivity and value neutrality, the interpretive tradition advocates reflection (reflexivity) and analysis of values as part of the research process. Failing to do so represents an inability to develop an empathetic understanding.

Pragmatism

Qualitative and quantitative methods and their underlying theoretical assumptions are philosophically consistent with the use of certain research methods. But we must not fall into the trap of assuming that all researchers who operate under the interpretivist paradigm use qualitative research methods or that all post-positivists who conduct research with the natural science model use quantitative research methods. Mixed methods research is centred on the worldview of **pragmatism**.

pragmatism the position that knowledge is a tool for organizing experience and for merging theory and practice; scientific inquiry cannot avoid the multiple theoretical foundations, perspectives, and philosophical assumptions if it is to fully understand social phenomena.

With pragmatism, action—not just any type of experience—is the source and test of knowledge. Scientific knowledge is a tool for organizing experience and merging theory and practice together. If we are to have a holistic understanding of the social world, we can't avoid the multiple theoretical foundations, perspectives, or philosophical assumptions. Post-positivistic and interpretivist worldviews both have strengths and weaknesses; in isolation, neither has all the answers.

Pragmatists focus on what works and solutions to problems. The guiding principle is not the purity of the worldview but how well the research questions are addressed. At the same time, research is to be contextual and socially, historically, and politically situated. "Pragmatists consider the research question to be more important than either the method they use or the worldview that is supposed to underlie the method. Most good researchers prefer addressing their research questions with any methodological tool available" (Tashakkori & Teddlie, 1998, p. 21).

Pragmatism is both a philosophical and a methodological approach. Research is not about antecedent conditions but actions, situations, and consequences. It isn't permanently aligned with any philosophy or definition of reality because truth is what works at that particular point in time. The focus is on what leads to an intended outcome and the process and context in which it occurs.

With a pragmatist worldview, mixed methods research allows for a larger spectrum of divergent views on a subject, which can lead us to question the theories that were used to inform the research questions (deductive) while also generating theory (inductive). For instance, if you are investigating police discretion from a pragmatist worldview, you are seeking an understanding of not only what officers appear to do but also of what they say they do and why. Invariably, there will be differences, which are welcome research outcomes because pragmatist research has the potential to test, verify, and generate theory within the same research study. The research question drives the method by demanding different data collection and analytical techniques. Pragmatism features the following ideas:

1. The research purpose is to identify what works, solve problems, and address the research questions using philosophical and methodologically appropriate methods.
2. Social reality is not a unified object but is context bound.
3. Individuals act within social, historical, and political contexts.
4. Human behaviour is influenced by both external forces and the freedom of choice.
5. The approach is problem-centred, not a question of defining reality and laws or choosing between common sense and scientific claims to knowledge.
6. Knowledge and truth are what work at a particular point in time.
7. Empirical evidence is based on actions, situations, and consequences.
8. The degrees of objectivity and subjectivity, as well as the criteria to assess claims to knowledge, depend on the theoretical assumptions and worldview associated with a particular research question.

There is no one correct way to approach research in criminology and criminal justice. Although there are distinct differences between positivism, interpretivism, and pragmatism (see Table 1.2), they all share several commonalities. Systematic empirical approaches are used to understand the social world. The basis of inquiry is theoretically driven research questions. Finally, none of these theoretical worldviews claim that knowledge is certain. Our knowledge base is dynamic and evolving, not static and fixed.

Middle-Range Theory

In much the same way that positivism and interpretivism seem to be at opposite ends of the spectrum, so too are criminological theories that offer explanations for the causes of and responses to criminal behaviour. Merton (1968) criticized the approaches to research used to generate theoretical explanations. He argues that current theories have two critical faults: they are too empirically based in the sense that data collection occurs without any theoretically based research questions, and they are becoming abstract because they attempt to explain all aspects of social life. Researchers seem almost obsessed with creating a unified explanation for behaviour, one that becomes so broad and general that the theoretical statements cannot be tested and thus do not meet the criteria of falsifiability. Merton says that the future of social sciences rests in producing, collecting, and applying empirical evidence to generate new research questions continuously.

Merton proposed **middle-range theories** as a solution to the current atheoretical or abstract higher-level theory to explain human behaviour. To theorize is to start with specific aspects of a social phenomenon (e.g. individual motivation to continue committing crime) instead of abstract concepts and institutions in society, such as the reasons why the lower class commit more crime than other classes do. For research to advance our knowledge base, it must "develop special theories from which to derive hypotheses that can be empirically investigated and by evolving a progressively more general conceptual scheme that is adequate to consolidate groups of special theories" (Merton, 1968, p. 51). What does all this mean? Let's examine the middle-range theory in relation to what we have covered so far.

Middle-range theory consists of a limited set of theoretical assumptions that are used to develop research questions to be confirmed by empirical evidence. These theories are not separate entities in and of themselves; they belong to a network of theories that explain the causes and responses to criminal behaviour. They were also extremely abstract prior

> **middle-range theory** a theoretical approach (or set of theoretical statements) that create a bridge between empirical evidence and abstract theories.

Table 1.2 Three theoretical worldviews in crime and justice research

Post-Positivism	Interpretivism/ Constructionism	Pragmatism
Determinism	Understanding	Consequences of actions
Reductionism	Multiple participant meanings	Problem-centred
Empirical observation and measurement	Social and historical construction	Pluralistic measurement and research methods
Theory verification	Theory generation	Real world practice-oriented; theory verification and generation
Quantitative	Qualitative	Mixed methods

Source: Adapted from Creswell (2014, p. 6).

to being reconceptualized and tested as a middle-range theory. Middle-range theories cut across the micro-, meso-, and macro-levels of social reality and explicitly acknowledge that there are missing facts and shortcomings to the explanation provided for human behaviour.

The goal with middle-range theories is to create explanations that are just abstract enough that we can generalize about human behaviour but are still sufficiently grounded in the real world that we can empirically verify the statements in a variety of contexts and situations. This objective is accomplished by focusing on measurable sections of social life rather than all variants of that social phenomenon (e.g. specific types of crime versus all types of crime in all places at all times). Merton's middle-range theory has had a profound impact on testing and explaining ideas about the causes and responses to crime. It constitutes a set of techniques to analyze the world in order to create theoretical explanations that are still connected to the real world, communicate knowledge to academics and policy-makers across disciplines, and provide a springboard for new ideas and future research.

> **basic research** research that attempts to advance knowledge and theoretical understanding of a particular social phenomenon; the intent of the research and the results are not explicitly meant to address a concern or to solve a problem.

Types of Research in Criminology and Criminal Justice

Regardless of its purpose or type, research is a systematic inquiry on a subject to discover or revise facts, theories, or applications. Zora Neale Hurston (1942, p. 143) describes research as a "formalized curiosity. It is poking and prying with a purpose." The main types of research conducted in criminology and criminal justice are basic and applied. You conduct basic research if you want to understand a social situation and applied if you want to address a problem or concern. However, the distinction between the two types isn't clear-cut, "as much basic research may later have unanticipated social applications" (Wolfgang, 1980, p. 50), especially when using multiple types of data.

Basic Research

The goal of **basic research** is to advance knowledge and theoretical understanding of a particular social phenomenon. In practice, this approach means that the research is conducted with no immediate practical application in mind. The primary purpose is not to create knowledge that can address a crime-related problem or decisions in the criminal justice system. Basic research seeks to answer a question for the sake of answering a question as it exists, and findings are often seen as an end in themselves.

Basic research designs are a set of instructions and procedures for data collection, analysis, and interpretation, but the choice of research method is driven by the type of data required to answer the research questions. For instance, Comack and Brickey (2007) investigated how violent female offenders define and create their identity in respect to the various meanings and connotations associated with violence. Using a feminist theoretical framework, the authors required data that allowed the women to unpack their identities in their own words. Hence, the most appropriate research method for addressing the research questions was conducting face-to-face interviews.

In contrast, Winterdyk and Thompson (2008) found that research demonstrates the increasing rate of identity theft but that we still don't know much about the public awareness of this crime. Thus, their research questions investigated the "self-reported perception and awareness about the nature, extent, risk, and effects of identity theft and a variety of fraudulent behaviours" by statistically analyzing survey data (Winterdyk & Thompson, 2008, p. 153). In this way, they addressed the questions of how much knowledge and the types of victimization effects that are associated with identity theft. Research questions in basic research are defined and derived from theoretical statements about how the world works, which act as a framework for the study.

Most basic research is conducted in a university environment. This setting allows for the production of disinterested knowledge, which helps us understand the world but doesn't necessarily have a direct practical implication. Do not interpret the lack of a direct focus on practical applications as indicative of how vital basic research is in criminology and criminal justice. Basic research produces foundational knowledge, including theories that explain criminal behaviour and criminal justice responses, trends over time, the impact of social structures (such as the neighbourhood), or the factors affecting the likelihood of reoffending.

How can we use the findings from basic research? Let's look at an example. Research finds that a larger percentage of chronic young offenders have a history of child abuse and maltreatment than what exists in the overall youth population. Yet this difference by no means implies that all victims of child abuse will go on to break the law. Basic research findings develop a theory of the relationship between child abuse and chronic youth offending and the additional factors that contribute, in varying degrees, to some child abuse victims breaking the law. It typically does not look for effective ways to respond to chronic offenders who were physically, sexually, or emotionally abused. These responses could be intervention strategies to reduce future reoffending or programs to prevent child abuse victims from starting a criminal career. However, the theoretical and empirical implications of basic research findings often suggest effective responses. These suggestions are then tested in the real world by conducting applied research.

An important reason to conduct basic research is that it can change how we think about and approach crime-related issues. Major breakthroughs in our knowledge about criminal behaviour and the criminal justice system's responses come from the findings of basic research. For instance, Chambliss (1973)

argues that, within the context of economic inequality, a youth's visibility is a significant factor in the likelihood of being labelled in some way. Based on such findings, labelling theory suggests that criminal behaviour is perpetuated by the criminal justice system because successfully applied labels become part of a person's self-identity, leading to future actions that are in accordance with that label. This idea implies that diversion programs and less formal processing through the criminal justice system are effective responses.

The extent that basic research impacts our views on responding to criminal behaviour is profound. For instance, Canada's *Youth Criminal Justice Act* (*YCJA*) emphasizes diverting youth out of the youth criminal justice system through extrajudicial measures—even those who have committed an offence in the past. We can't reasonably respond to youth crime without some knowledge of what causes some individuals to break the law, commit certain types of crimes, specialize in property or violent offences, co-offend, or continue to commit crimes into adulthood.

Increasingly, research funding agencies support research with some type of identifiable use or practical utility in the real world. In many ways, this stance is in direct opposition to basic research's main characteristic, producing disinterested knowledge. For example, the Social Science and Humanities Research Council (SSHRC) is the primary funding agency for research in criminology and criminal justice. Its goal is to "support and foster excellence in social sciences and humanities research intended to deepen, widen, and increase our collective understanding of individuals and societies as well as to inform the search for solutions to societal challenges" (Social Sciences and Humanities Research Council, 2014). The Insight Grant Program encourages researchers to examine "what we think, how we live, and how we interact with each other and the world around us" (Ibid.). Some argue that, "for scientific knowledge to be trustworthy, it needs to be dissociated from material interests" (Ziman, 2002, p. 397). Yet much research requires financial support to be feasible. Applied research shares this problem, but there are additional dimensions to consider in relation to the creation of disinterested knowledge.

Applied Research

Basic research results need to be combined with the results from other studies to have policy implications. With **applied research**, decision-making in the criminal justice system and related organizations is based on knowledge created by research findings. The goal of applied research is to inform and develop evidence-based practice, which it does in three ways.

> **applied research** research that aims to address an identified concern or to solve a specific problem.

First, applied research applies results to a specific problem in the real world. For instance, basic research finds that crime occurs at a much higher rate in certain neighbourhoods in a city, known as hot spots (Sherman, Gartin, & Buerger, 1989). Applied research assesses whether saturation patrol is an effective solution to this problem or has only a displacement effect by moving the crime to areas without such patrol (Sherman & Weisburd, 1995; Smith et al., 1992; Smith, 2001; Weisburd & Green, 1995; Weisburd & Braga, 2006). As a result, we now know some of the negative consequences of responding to crime through saturation patrol, including a short-term impact, an adverse effect on police–community relations caused by the use of highly aggressive enforcement tactics, a potential for the abuse of police authority, the large financial expense, an increased workload for the criminal justice system (leading to more lenient sentences), and various opportunity costs, such as diverting resources from other areas and problems (Scott, 2003).

Second, applied research can assess the outcomes and effectiveness of prevention programs and intervention strategies or the impact of policies and legislative change. For instance, the *YCJA* structures police discretion by making clear that substituting extrajudicial measures (e.g. no action, informal warning, formal caution, diversion program) for laying a charge is appropriate for most young offenders. Research finds that, after implementation of the *YCJA*, the number of youth charged decreased by 23 per cent from 2002 to 2005: 69 per cent of apprehended youth were charged in 1990, 56.4 per cent in 2002, 44.6 per cent in 2003, and 43.5 per cent in 2005 (Carrington & Schulenberg, 2008, pp. 355–356). This percentage decrease for youth referred to court is much greater for minor offences than for serious youth crime, which is consistent with the principles set forth in the *YCJA*.

Finally, applied research builds on the findings of basic research and influences policy decision-making. Further research is then conducted on the unexpected applications in the real world. The potential explanation for unexpected findings could be political and ethical concerns. Research sponsors can influence the questions asked, the data made available for analysis, the research methods adopted, and the presentation of results. Sponsors may want to suppress research findings that reflect negatively on the program. For instance, a social skills and employment training program may need to demonstrate effectiveness to have its funding renewed. Limitations imposed by sponsors include restricting the type of data available, the timeline for performing the research, the questions to be asked, and the type of analysis to be conducted (Leiber & Mawhorr, 1995).

When looking at the relationship between basic and applied research, the theoretical findings can take on a life of their own because theories are interpreted and measured in different ways by different people. For instance, Martinson (1974) evaluated 231 studies on prison rehabilitation programs, finding that they are largely ineffective. This "nothing works" doctrine became the most politically influential criminological citation for 40 years. For there to be no misunderstandings of the basic research findings, Martinson (p. 25) concludes: "With few and isolated exceptions, the rehabilitative efforts that have been reported so far have had no appreciable effect on recidivism."

Martinson (1974, p. 49) goes on to say that current "strategies . . . cannot overcome, or even appreciably reduce, the powerful tendencies of offenders to continue in criminal behavior." This argument spurred applied research that compared the effectiveness of secure custody and community-based rehabilitation programs. The outcome was the opposite of what Martinson (1979) envisioned with his nothing works mantra. Society, particularly in the United States, started to incarcerate even more offenders for even more types of offences. Correctional authorities were also reluctant to invest resources in any rehabilitative efforts.

Martinson's doctrine demonstrates the relationship between, and the need for, basic and applied research. It also shows the diversity of research in the field of criminology and criminal justice and the importance of both types of research in expanding our understanding of the causes and responses to crime.

Some crime and justice research has more than one purpose. It is important to bear in mind that the research purpose affects what methodological strategies are included in the overall research design. For instance, if you want to understand how someone becomes a prostitute, you would not design an explanatory study that statistically analyzes crime data for individuals charged with solicitation. Instead, you would likely interview prostitutes, thereby making your research design exploratory or descriptive.

Exploratory Research

Exploratory research findings develop insights into a problem when we know very little about the subject or when the relationship and scope are not clearly defined. Exploratory research allows researchers to familiarize themselves with the problem and formulate more precise research questions for future research. The results can also help us assess the feasibility of conducting further research and to develop an appropriate research design. Research questions are not always set in stone;

therefore, the findings may not fully address them. The results give us some indication of what, when, where, how, and why something occurs but no reliable information on how much or how often. Exploratory research is often qualitative but will also use existing data or surveys.

One example of exploratory research brings together several concepts that we have covered (including disinterested knowledge, political interests, and applied research) and introduces ethical concerns involved in scientific research. Before the negative effects of smoking cigarettes received much attention, the Beaumont Organization (1981) interviewed young adults to explore how and why they started smoking, their health fears regarding smoking, and the importance of smoking imagery. The study's report, "The Benefits of Cigarettes: Exploratory Research," provided cigarette companies with step-by-step instructions on how to exploit these fears (without the subjects' knowledge) by creating ads that reduce them, consequently contributing to the development and marketing of "light" cigarettes. The study also violated two ethical principles of scientific research: to disclose the research purpose and to avoid causing or minimizing any harm to research participants.

Descriptive Research

If one were to randomly peruse several articles published in leading scholarly journals, it would be difficult not to conclude that a large proportion of crime and justice research is descriptive in nature. **Descriptive research** details situations or events using all types of data collection methods, with the exception of experiments. Quantitative surveys and qualitative interviews—examples of this type of research—are often used to answer research questions about current or past social phenomena. The results from

exploratory research research that is directed at little-understood subjects or developing ideas and that refines research questions for future research.

descriptive research research that creates a picture or profile with words or numbers to answer who, when, where, or how.

descriptive research can be used to implement changes in the criminal justice system, related policies, or legislation. For instance, descriptive research on the cycle of domestic violence led to the implementation of mandatory arrest policies.

Explanatory Research

Sometimes a study is both exploratory and explanatory or descriptive and explanatory. **Explanatory research** builds on the findings from exploratory and descriptive research by identifying a cause–effect relationship behind a particular event. In other words, it tries to explain why a pattern exists or an event occurs. Once a researcher establishes a relationship between two ideas, such as prior record and recidivism,

explanatory research research conducted to explain why something occurs and to test and refine theory.

explanatory research will try to specify how prior record (the cause) affects recidivism (the effect). It is well established that prior record is one of the best predictors of recidivism. However, explanatory research is still conducted to specify how this relationship changes based on other factors, such as successfully completing a treatment program.

If there isn't a lot of literature or theory to guide the development of research questions, exploratory or descriptive research is conducted first to detect any recurrent patterns or relationships. Then these patterns are used to create the more focused research questions required in explanatory research. Whether it's exploratory, descriptive, or explanatory research, quantitative and qualitative methods are used to address the research questions.

Summary of Important Points

Introduction

- An understanding of research methods and science as a way of thinking are important in being an informed consumer of research on crime and justice issues and in everyday life.
- Learning research methods will make you a better decision-maker and increase your marketability in terms of an ability to understand evidence-based practices, to question, to support arguments with data, and to communicate complex information.

Types of Knowledge

- Non-scientific knowledge makes us vulnerable to errors in reasoning and logic, misinformed opinions, distorted assumptions, skewed interpretations, and rigid ideological beliefs.

- Non-scientific sources of knowledge which can be valuable in daily life and create an awareness of the need for corroborating evidence, include appeals to authority, tradition, common sense, legends, myths, personal experience, and the halo effect. Yet knowledge claims based on scientific reasoning are more likely to produce legitimate and accurate knowledge that can be verified empirically.

Ideology versus Theory

- Typically, ideologies are associated with moral beliefs, dismiss contradictory evidence and absolute certainty, and advocate for a specific position.
- Theories organize observations of the world to predict what will happen in the future under certain conditions.
- Unlike ideologies, theories are falsifiable, parsimonious, and serendipitous.

Theoretical Foundations

- Social research is theoretical, as it creates and tests ideas about how the world works, and empirical, as it measures and observes the social world and our perceptions of it.
- Quantitative and qualitative research operate with different assumptions about the definition of reality (ontology), the acknowledgement of reality or how we know what we know (epistemology), and the ways in which reality is understood (methodology).
- Nomothetic research seeks to develop laws or rules about the general case, whereas idiographic research is an in-depth understanding of socio-historically situated behaviours and events.
- Deductive reasoning moves from general theory, testable hypotheses, and observation to specific confirmation of proposed theoretical statements.
- Inductive reasoning moves from specific observations to patterns, tentative hypotheses, and general theoretical statements.
- Most research in criminology and criminal justice uses both deductive and inductive reasoning.
- Both individual (micro) and structural (meso and macro) levels of theorizing are central to understand the causes of, and responses to, criminal behaviour.

- Research adopting a post-positivistic worldview describes and explains observable social phenomena in terms of law-like patterns and regularities. It is nomothetic and usually quantitative.
- Research adopting an interpretivist worldview investigates how we make sense of our lives and define situations as we interact with others. It is idiographic and usually qualitative.
- A pragmatist worldview is not committed to one set of philosophical assumptions or methodology but typically adopts a mixed methods approach. The focus is on what the research question demands, intended consequences, and the context in which these processes occur.
- Middle-range theories create a bridge between empirical evidence and abstract theories to generalize about human behaviour and empirically verify theoretical statements in the real world.

Types of Research

- Research is a systematic inquiry on a subject to discover or revise facts, theories, or applications.
- Research can be basic or applied, but a study often contains elements of both types. Research can explore, describe, or explain behaviours, situations, and events.

Key Terms

applied research 26
basic research 24
constructivism 21
deductive reasoning 16
descriptive research 27
determinism 19
epistemology 13
explanatory research 28

exploratory research 27
halo effect 9
idiographic research 15
inductive reasoning 16
interpretivist 20
intersubjectivity 20
macro-level 18
meso-level 18

micro-level 18
middle-range theory 23
nomothetic research 15
ontology 13
positivism 18
pragmatism 22
scientific method 4
theory 10

Review Questions and Exercises

1. Choose an article on any criminological or criminal justice topic from a local and a national newspaper. Identify whether conclusions are based on scientific or non-scientific knowledge, whether the stories reflect deductive or inductive reasoning, and the degree of objectivity in the reporting of the events.
2. Pick any crime- or criminal justice–related issue, identify the current sources of knowledge you have on this topic (e.g. personal experience), and develop three research questions that would be appropriate for an exploratory, descriptive, and explanatory study (one question for each type).
3. Create three theoretical statements explaining the overrepresentation of Aboriginal peoples in Canadian correctional institutions. Make the first statement cover the micro-level of social reality, the second the meso-level, and the third the macro-level.
4. How would you investigate sentencing decisions in post-positivistic research? What about research with an interpretivist or pragmatist worldview?

Online Exercises and Websites of Interest

Max Weber's View of Objectivity in Social Science

www.criticism.com/md/weber1.html
This site provides a good overview of Weber's approach and philosophical assumptions and the process of conducting research.

Original Milgram Experiment (1962)

www.youtube.com/watch?v=fCVlI-_4GZQ
This video features Stanley Milgram describing his research interests and motivation and includes footage of the experiment.

The Pat Brown Criminal Profiling Agency

www.patbrownprofiling.com/
Based on the information from this website, does Pat Brown use inductive or deductive criminal profiling techniques? Give evidence to support your answer.

Web Center for Social Research Methods

http://socialresearchmethods.net
A knowledge base on applied social research methods, this site has information on topics covered throughout this book.

Additional Resources

Halliday, S., & Schmidt, P. (2009). *Conducting Law and Society Research: Reflections on Methods and Practices.* **Cambridge Studies in Law and Society. New York: Cambridge University Press.**

The authors offer a peak into the challenges, uncertainties, and "messiness" of conducting research by interviewing 21 prolific and influential scholars about their reflections and advice on the scientific study of law and society.

Kuhn, T. (1970/1996). *The Structure of Scientific revolutions* **(3rd ed.). Chicago: University of Chicago Press.**

Considered one of the most influential books in the field, this text forms part of the debate on the relationship between worldviews and research methods. Kuhn argues that science doesn't create knowledge in a linear fashion.

Merton, R.K. (1968). *Social Theory and Social Structure.* **New York: The Free Press.**

This book is a landmark in sociology and criminology. Pay particular attention to Chapter 1, on the relationship between theory and research; and Chapter 2, which outlines Merton's concept of middle-range theories.

How Are Research Projects Structured?

"At the root of science and scientific research is the urge, the compulsion, to understand the nature of things."
David Ruelle, *The Mathematician's Brain* (2007, p. 57)

Learning Objectives

- To describe the iterative process between theory and methods.

- To describe the hypothetico-deductive method and how the scientific method is associated with quantitative, qualitative, and mixed methods research designs.

- To understand the relationship between informational components, methodological controls, and ethical considerations in the scientific research process.

- To differentiate between cross-sectional and longitudinal research designs.

- To discern whether a historical, theoretical, methodological, contextual, chronological, or thematic literature review is the most appropriate for informing the research design, focus, and questions.

- To appreciate the ethical and political considerations of conducting research.

Introduction

Comprehending the research process is not as easy as it may seem. There are rules and procedures that help ensure that we find the most accurate answers possible. Although the parts of this process are discussed in separate chapters, they are all interrelated in the sense that decisions made at one stage affect decisions in later stages.

Consequently, we cannot skip any of the research steps. Think of it in terms of a recipe. Reading a recipe shows you how others have made the dish and what they've concluded in terms of the best way to proceed. The ingredients are your data and the directions, such as oven temperature, are your methods. Your data analysis involves tasting the final product and making an assessment based on various criteria. Deciding that the dish tastes great or that it's not what you expected represents your conclusion. If you don't complete all these steps, you cannot confidently ascertain whether the recipe is truly good or not.

What we believe to be true is subject to change over time. Can we work from the assumption that trained researchers consistently conduct research properly? The answer partly depends on how we define the term *properly*, as not all crime and justice research is of equivalent quality and some topics are easier to investigate than others. For instance, quantitative research investigating crime rates over time is different from quantitative research investigating recidivism, which can be measured in a variety of ways—number of new offences, type of new offences, or the length of time between offences. Likewise, qualitative research on the work of correctional officers may be easier to conduct than would work on a member of the Hells Angels. Thus, we need to examine a study's research methods if we are to assess the accuracy of the claims to knowledge.

The ability to identify methodological strengths and weaknesses in previous research—which allows us to evaluate contributions to knowledge on the subject accurately—is critical when beginning a new study.

The purpose of research shapes the research questions, which influence the methods used to collect and analyze data. The scientific method provides a road map for navigating the research process. However, this method is an ideal of "perfect" or "excellent" research. In practice, achieving this ultimate standard can be challenging, but the closer we get, the stronger our claim to knowledge. Furthermore, it can be difficult, or verging on impossible, to completely adhere to a study's original research design. Conducting research on all facets of human behaviour is often methodologically messy. The research design can adhere to the scientific method on paper, but once data collection starts, even the best-laid plans are modified because they don't work in the real world as anticipated. In some cases, you will be aware of possible problems beforehand; in others, you won't realize things are awry until the research is underway.

Methods in Action

The Freedom of Information Act as a Methodological Tool

As a criminal justice master's student at the State University of New York at Albany (SUNY), Yeager (2006) was interested in the class and ethnic composition of individuals involved in the drug trade. In 1976, he filed a Freedom of Information Act (FOIA) request to the Drug Enforcement Administration (DEA) for a copy of its data codebook (a description of codes for each variable; e.g. 1 = male, 2 = female) and access to data from four government databases with all personal identifiers removed.

The trial court granted access to only one database and stated that the remainder fell under Exemption 7 of the FOIA, which applies to data that relate to ongoing police investigations, interfere with criminal proceedings, disclose investigative techniques or the identity of confidential sources, or invade privacy. The DEA was ordered to use disclosure-avoidance techniques, meaning that the data are collapsed into larger categories to ensure anonymity. Yeager took his case to the US Court of Appeals, which ruled that the DEA could not be required to use these techniques. Thus, Yeager lost his bid to use the most appropriate data for addressing his research questions.

Continued

During his PhD studies at Carleton University, Yeager wanted to examine determinant sentences, which require that a person serve his or her entire sentence. Yeager requested access to the Offender Management System (OMS) and the 1992–1993 Correctional Service Canada (CSC) release cohort with all personal identifiers removed. The OMS contains data such as intake and risk management assessments. The CSC release cohort dataset tracks reoffending by following parolees for a period of several years.

For a variety of reasons, CSC denied the data request. In 2001, Yeager once again found himself in court. The CSC was ordered to release the data and provide a codebook. It appealed; in 2003, the court upheld the original ruling. However, since the agency would need approximately forty days to fulfill Yeager's request, the appellate court saw the process as an unreasonable burden and denied disclosure. An appeal filed with the Supreme Court was unsuccessful.

Yeager's experiences provide an excellent example of the best-laid plans failing in practice. Once research questions are developed, the issues of what data are required and how they can be accessed must be carefully considered when structuring a research project. As for Yeager, not only did he fail to gain access to the data he wanted but he also incurred over $20,000 in personal costs with the case against CSC alone.

Research designs can also be affected by restrictions on the scope and access to quantitative data. For example, information such as an individual's sex may be suppressed to ensure the participant's anonymity. Qualitative researchers can be denied access to a research site, leading to constraints on addressing the research questions, inconsistent findings, stronger caveats when stating conclusions, or specific suggestions for future research. No research design is perfect. The trick is to become cognizant of the limitations, the best response, and the impact on the validity of your findings and conclusions. Every research project has limitations that you need to recognize when reviewing their findings and respond to when conducting your own research. Even though your topics and questions will vary by study, there are two initial required tasks: state what you want to investigate as clearly as possible and determine the best way to go about finding the answers.

This chapter introduces the concepts, procedures, and skills required to structure a research project. To start, the scientific method and methodological theory are discussed in terms of the research process and design. This section is followed by the more practical matters of choosing a topic, writing a literature review, deciding on a quantitative or qualitative approach, and following ethical principles. Together, these elements structure a research study and pave the way for the methodological tools discussed in later chapters, such as measurement and sampling.

Scientific Method

As discussed in Chapter 1, the scientific method is a series of steps used to increase confidence in conclusions about the social world. If a crime investigation looks for the facts and the judicial process searches for the truth, the scientific method seeks knowledge. Whether with a qualitative or quantitative research design, the method starts with a research purpose and research questions. The researcher collects and analyzes the appropriate data for addressing the research questions and makes inferences that provide insight or describe or predict human behaviour and events.

However, crime and justice research is a dynamic and iterative process (i.e. circular), as illustrated in Figure 2.1 by the broken arrow. Contrary to assumptions, iterations between theory and method occur in both quantitative and qualitative research. How is this possible when quantitative research is consistent with the hypothetico-deductive method, which intuitively is anything but circular?

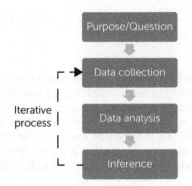

Figure 2.1 Scientific method in quantitative and qualitative research

Hypothetico-deductive Method

Based on the principles of falsifiability and deductive reasoning, the **hypothetico-deductive method** is seen by quantitative researchers as *the* scientific method. You start with a general theory, develop testable hypotheses, create predictions based on these hypotheses, collect empirical observations, and then formulate conclusions that support or disprove the theory (Popper, 1959). If the findings disprove the theoretical proposition, you develop a new hypothesis. Yet quantitative research is also iterative. As the data are analyzed and evaluated, the findings are used to refine theories, research questions, and hypotheses.

Theory and the scientific method go hand in hand, as the latter's procedures provide the framework for testing theoretical propositions by adhering to five principles:

1. Empiricism: Observing with our five senses.
2. Skepticism: Always looking for, and not dismissing, disconfirming evidence.
3. Objectivity: Being unaffected by researcher preferences or biases.
4. Accuracy: Recording observations exactly as they occur in the real world.
5. Precision: Articulating the subcategories or dimensions of a concept.

Theoretical perspectives and worldviews inform all aspects of the research process. The scientific method is frequently referred to as the hypothetico-deductive method with five guiding principles to test theoretical propositions. The next step is to examine how quantitative and qualitative research is conducted using the scientific method.

Research Process

Within the scientific research process, "criticism is not directed first to what an item of information says about the world, but to the method by which the item was produced" (Wallace, 1971, p. 14). We use this scientific process because it has the most sophisticated methodological controls and techniques to guide the collection of qualitative or quantitative empirical evidence. In Figure 2.2—the Wallace Wheel—theories, hypotheses, observations, and empirical generalizations are informational components. Logical deduction, research design, data analysis, and logical induction are methodological controls.

Informational Components

Theoretical ideas use **concepts** to classify objects or behaviours and to provide meaning. Concepts can often be measured in multiple ways. Let's say that we have a theory suggesting that teenagers are more likely to engage in antisocial behaviour than adults are. Conceptually, we could define teenager as "a person in his or her teens" and antisocial behaviour as "delinquency." Our research question asks, "In what way are teenagers more likely than adults to engage in antisocial behaviour?"

hypothetico-deductive method a research method that formulates a testable hypothesis to explain a social phenomenon, deduces predictions from the hypothesis, and, when the prediction is falsified by observable data, rejects the theory and develops a new hypothesis.

concept an abstract, general idea inferred or derived from particular instances or occurrences; describes the general characteristics or the essential features of something.

Key Thinker

Charles R. Tittle

Born on 26 March 1939, Charles R. Tittle received a BA in history from Ouachita Baptist College in 1961 and an MA and a PhD in sociology from the University of Texas–Austin in 1963 and 1965, respectively. According to Tittle (2002), criminology is a substantive area dependent on scholars from a variety of disciplines. Throughout his career, he saw four trends: accurate claims to knowledge about the causes and control of crime are limited; the scientific method is the best approach to investigate these types of problems and issues; researcher bias is far too prevalent in published research; and public policy recommendations are made without a sufficiently strong knowledge base or strong standards of evidence.

How do we ensure that crime and justice research adheres to the scientific process? Tittle (2002) says to start by rejecting personal experience and intuition as data sources. Researchers must use empirical evidence that can be measured and replicated, look for the causes of crime, and organize empirical generalizations within general theoretical explanations addressing the questions of how and why. Descriptive research is still important but as a first step to identify and describe empirical patterns in events and behaviours. The bottom line is an understanding that science is not a value-free enterprise but "absolutely committed to a value system—the values of science" (pp. 33–34). From this standpoint, Tittle explains deviations from the scientific process as the result of impatience, ad hoc research, and personal bias.

Scientific knowledge is a slow and cumulative process. Researchers are sometimes impatient and jump to conclusions based on limited or weak evidence. Explanations for crime and criminal behaviour differ, and this limited evidence doesn't reasonably allow us to judge these disparate findings. Making matters worse, policy recommendations are problematic as researchers "ignore the fact that no piece of research means anything except in context with all that has gone before, and no piece of research can be taken seriously until it has been subjected to repeated replication and scrutiny of critical scientists" (Tittle, 2002, p. 35).

In other words, there is a misplaced research focus on one issue or type of crime as if it's distinctive from all others. Applied researchers criticize basic research on the grounds of little practical application. Tittle challenges us to consider that serendipitous findings can lead to insights on an unrelated problem or issue. In fact, science should be separate from practical concerns because we can't predict usefulness or applicability in real life.

Despite the scientific ideal, Tittle finds that conclusions support the researcher's expectations, minimize contradictory evidence, and are sometimes unsupported by the data. He imparts a commitment to knowledge in which researchers "have a moral obligation to oppose inhibitions on truth seeking, to resist claims from incomplete knowledge, and to counter inappropriate applications of actual knowledge" by adhering to the scientific method (2002, p. 39).

---

hypothesis an untested statement or proposition that specifies the relationship between two theoretical concepts and their indicators.

A **hypothesis** is a testable statement of a specific relationship that we can observe empirically. Hypotheses are developed with deductive reasoning (i.e. logical deduction). For a hypothesis to be an empirical statement, it must use **variables** and not concepts. How will we know that a person is in his or her teens? How will we recognize a delinquent behaviour in our

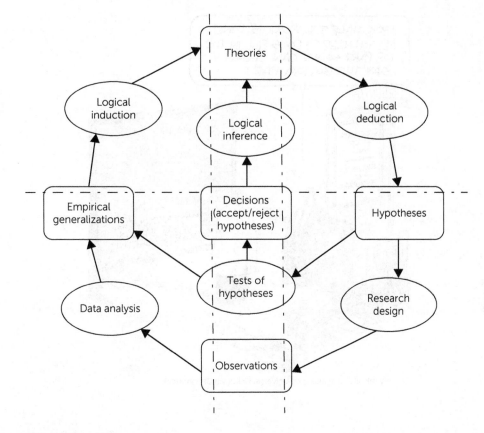

Figure 2.2 Wallace Wheel

Source: Adapted from p. 18, Wallace, W.L. (1971). *The logic of science in sociology*. Hawthorne, NY: Aldine de Gruyter.

observations? Variables can change in numerical values from case to case. A teenager (concept) could be a person between the ages of 12 and 17 (variable), an adult (concept) someone 18 and over (variable), and delinquency (concept) any behaviour resulting in a criminal charge (variable). Our hypothesis is the following: Anyone between 12 and 17 years of age is more likely to be charged with a criminal offence than those 18 years and over.

Empirical observations are highly specific and represent unique pieces of information. For the teenager variable, the empirical observations would document age so that a person can be identified

as a teenager or an adult. Similarly, the variable of illegal behaviour requires observations that tell us whether the person was charged with an offence under the *Criminal Code of Canada*.

Once the observations are analyzed, they are organized into **empirical generalizations** that represent factual statements to address the hypotheses. A finding is a generalization of the

variable something that can be observed and measured at different levels, amounts, or strengths in the real world.

empirical generalization a statement based on a pattern or regularity across different empirical observations that is not necessarily occurring in all circumstances.

© Wiley Ink, inc./Distributed by Universal Uclick via Cartoonstock

data, but the connection to theoretical propositions is not definitive at this point. Empirical generalizations are conclusions about reality based on repeated patterns in the empirical observations that do not necessarily have an accompanying explanation. Stating that 14-year-olds are more likely to be charged with a criminal offence than adults is an empirical generalization. It tells us what but not why.

Methodological Controls

Methodological controls connect the informational components and increase the accuracy of claims to knowledge. Logical deduction is the process of moving from a theoretical proposition to an empirically testable hypothesis. This technique involves the use of an additional

statement to prevent errors in deductive reasoning. For example, "Teenagers engage in more antisocial behaviour than adults do. Therefore, teenagers will have higher rates of being charged for criminal offences."

Research design is the stage where the methodological decisions are systematically mapped out to determine the best approach to address the research questions, including measurement of concepts and selection of cases, type of data, and type of analysis. In quantitative research, logical induction represents evaluating the accuracy of a theoretical proposition based on the empirical generalizations. In qualitative research, the empirical generalizations contain concepts that inductively create theory based on themes found in the observational data.

Components and Controls

In the centre of the Wallace Wheel in Figure 2.2, hypothesis testing is a methodological control that involves comparing the regularities in the observational data to the theoretically expected relationship. Our hypothesis is that teenagers are more likely than adults to be charged with a criminal offence. We find a pattern in the data showing that teenagers between the ages of 12 and 17 are more likely to be charged than are persons 18 and over. By way of logical inference, this pattern provides support for the hypothesis, conceptual research question, and the related theoretical proposition. Hypothesis testing and logical inference are steps between creating and testing theory and highlight the interconnectedness of theory and research.

The research steps are circular, with no fixed starting or ending point, as the research process is flexible, fluid, and dynamic. At the same time, it is structured by rules and principles to increase the accuracy of our claim to knowledge. If we look on the left side of the wheel and start the research process at the bottom, we are inductively creating theory. We start with gathering information (observations), then identifying themes, patterns, or categories (empirical generalizations), and, finally, using inductive reasoning to create or refine theory that future researchers can use to test deductively with hypotheses. On the right side of the Wallace Wheel, the goal is to apply theory deductively by testing its theoretical propositions. Research questions and hypotheses are developed through logical deduction, variables are defined, appropriate methods are selected, and empirical observations are gathered to test the hypotheses and address the research questions.

In qualitative, quantitative, or mixed methods crime and justice research, logical induction, deduction, and inference are equally important in the research process. Did you notice a line breaking the wheel into a top and bottom half? If you follow the informational components and methodological controls in the top half, you theorize both inductively and deductively. If the research follows the steps on the bottom half of the wheel, it is divorced from theory and is strictly empirical.

A nomothetic explanation best fits the right side of the circle and the pathway leading up the centre. These types of explanations are more general and, in our example of teenagers' delinquent behaviour, won't necessarily be true for all teenagers. A nomothetic explanation depicts a pattern uncovered through logical deduction, such as measuring intelligence with an IQ test constituting a deductive application of theory. In contrast, idiographic explanations best fit the left side of the wheel and can provide a thorough understanding of one teenager's behaviour, such as stating that a teenager is intelligent or unintelligent. Neither of these explanations is necessarily accurate, as it depends on the use of methodological controls situated between each informational component.

The Wallace Wheel is a straightforward representation of the scientific method ideal to conduct research and test or create theoretical explanations. In practice, research is sometimes an unpredictable process. The fact that conducting research can be messy should not necessarily be interpreted negatively. Studying the causes and control of crime requires methodological flexibility.

In fact, your research findings can present an idiographic explanation based on either deductive or inductive reasoning. Your explanation of why your date left in the middle of your first dinner together is idiographic (an explanation for behaviour within a particular context) and inductive (ideas based on observational data). However, if you got ready for this date based on everything you managed to figure out about this person, you anticipate the effects of your actions on his or her behaviour. This approach is also idiographic but is based on deductive reasoning (your theory about your date and testing these ideas).

This duality can also occur with nomothetic explanations. If more first dates end this way and you find other people with the same experiences, the result could start to represent a general principle or pattern (nomothetic). What should you do? Teach others how to avoid this situation based on these collective experiences and see if the results turn out better (deductive). Or, using inductive reasoning, look back at your prior decisions to arrive at an explanation for this pattern of behaviour.

There is a trick to all this. Remember that no type of explanation, reasoning, research method, theoretical perspective, worldview, or approach is superior. An explanation of why your date left may be no more accurate in its knowledge claims than another explanation. We can be more confident about our claims to knowledge with methodological controls. Using an appropriate method, you may discover that it's not you. Your dates might not have the money or simply don't want to pay for the meal!

Vignette: Breaking It Down

Police Work: The Racial Profiling Controversy

Our knowledge of racial profiling depends on whom you ask and the type of data and research methods. The methodological controversy concerns the definition of the term, the nature of police work, and the types of data used to address the research questions.

The *Toronto Star* used six years of data (1996–2002) from the Toronto Police Service, obtained through a *Freedom of Information Act* request, to investigate the issue. The report found that, compared to whites, more black drivers are stopped, twice as many blacks are arrested for simple drug possession, and twice as many are likely to be detained for a bail hearing (Abbate, 2003). Then-police chief Julian Fantino commissioned an independent inquiry by Harvey and Gold, who argued that the previous findings of systematic racism were "sensational quackery." Gold states: "the *Star* work was junk science, so flawed in methodology . . . that its conclusions were simply false," while Harvey describes the methodology as "incomplete, inconsistent, and in some regards impossible to replicate" (Blatchford, 2003). The last charge is particularly serious, as replication is an important scientific test of claims to knowledge.

In another example, Wortley (2005) had Kingston police officers collect quantitative data on the age, sex, and race of every person involved in a traffic stop. He found that young black males and Aboriginal people were 3.6 and 1.4 times, respectively, more likely than white people to be stopped by the police. In response, Melchers (2003) argued that there aren't enough black residents in Kingston and that the differences are too small for these conclusions to be reliable. Wortley countered that this criticism has "more to do with politics than social science" (Porter, 2005). Yet Melchers correctly points out that not all data are created equal and scientific reasoning includes skepticism, as statistically significant findings are not necessarily substantively significant.

Beyond political implications, why have these studies caused such controversy? According to Wortley (2005), "profiling exists when racial characteristics—rather than behaviour—contribute to surveillance decisions." However, the variables used for the concept of racial profiling do not distinguish racial bias from law enforcement practices dictated by local crime rates. The nature of police work creates a Catch-22 as higher crime rates are often in impoverished, minority neighbourhoods. Racial profiling research fails to acknowledge that, when "more police efforts are focused on one ethnic community, the more crimes they are likely to uncover in that community, and consequently, the more statistics available to support profiling techniques" (Killey, 2003; see also Batton & Kadleck, 2004). When using official police statistics, research should provide evidence of a "disproportionate emphasis on minorities or minority communities, in a particular context, as unwarranted" (Gabor, 2004, p. 463).

In contrast, qualitative research designs provide ideographic explanations of routine police work. Satzewich and Shaffir (2009) interviewed 18 police officers in the Hamilton Police Service and found that officers define racial profiling in the context of their police culture and that the practice can occur unintentionally. Pratt and Thompson (2008) interviewed sixty Canadian border officers and concluded that the concept of race is too abstract to reflect the complexity of discretionary decision-making.

Despite the methodological muddle, these debates are vital to increasing the accuracy of claims to knowledge. After considering all relevant factors, differences may still exist, but they aren't necessarily evidence of actual discrimination. "The best research can conclude in such cases is the modest statement that the possibility of discrimination cannot be excluded. In the absence of compelling evidence, to make any more ambitious statement goes against the scientific ethic" (Melchers, 2003, pp. 362–363).

Cross-Sectional and Longitudinal Research Designs

The theory behind the scientific method reinforces the circular nature of the research process and the artificial demarcation between quantitative and qualitative research (given the fact that both employ deductive and inductive reasoning). The next dimension to consider in a research design is the concept of time. If the research questions reflect characteristics of individuals, behaviours, or events, a cross-sectional research design can work. If the research problem occurs over time, a longitudinal research design is a better choice. The examples in this book illustrate that both quantitative and qualitative research can be cross-sectional or longitudinal. Thus, we need to have a better understanding of the circumstances in which each design element is appropriate.

Cross-Sectional Research

Cross-sectional research collects data at a single point in time, creating a snapshot of a crime and justice problem or issue.

> **cross-sectional research** a research design in which data are collected at a single point in time.

This approach is a good choice if your research questions concern the investigation of opinions, attitudes, or retrospective data. Retrospective data is a double-edged sword. On one hand, it documents what you did in the past, such as victimization experiences and your current fear of crime. Researchers therefore have to be acutely aware of the fallibility of human memory and information recall. On the other hand, the advantage of cross-sectional research is the relatively low cost in terms of money and human resources, which allows you to gather a large amount of data on several different concepts.

time-series research (or trend study) a research design in which given characteristics of a population are analyzed at regular intervals over time.

longitudinal research a research design in which data are collected more than once over a period of time.

One variation of cross-sectional research is **time-series research** (or **trend study**), which analyzes cross-sectional data on the same concepts from similar samples at different points in time. The events, cases, or individuals are not the same at each point. This disparity is not terribly problematic as the research purpose is to identify trends over time (e.g. Uniform Crime Report). Alternatively, a researcher can administer a survey more than once over a period of time to a different sample of individuals each time (e.g. polls, censuses). The problem with such studies is that any trends could be due to the different people in each sample, not an actual change in behaviours or attitudes.

There are two overall disadvantages to cross-sectional research. These designs can provide only indirect evidence of change or processes over time. Let's say you conduct a survey on tax evasion because you suspect that more people cheat on their taxes than the Canada Revenue Agency uncovers. You find that respondents between the ages of 45 and 55 are more likely than those between 25 and 35 to falsify their income tax returns. Based on this data, it would be incorrect to conclude that we become more deceitful as we age or that those between the ages of 45 and 55 were more honest on their tax returns when they were younger.

Cross-sectional research designs are most effective for descriptive research. Although a considerable amount of explanatory research is cross-sectional, this design significantly decreases the strength of conclusions about cause-and-effect relationships as data are collected at one time for all variables. The criteria for a causal explanation (empirical association, temporal order, and non-spuriousness) are what make longitudinal research designs more desirable for explanatory research.

cohort study longitudinal research in which data are collected at different points in time from individuals who belong to a particular group or category

Longitudinal Research

In a **longitudinal research** design, data on a particular event, behaviour, or group of people are collected at different points in time. This research design is ideal when the purpose is to detect and predict social changes, compare similar groups, investigate behaviours and attitudes, or understand processes over time. All types of research—including exploratory, descriptive, explanatory, and evaluation—can be longitudinal.

Don't fall into the trap of assuming that all longitudinal research is quantitative. Much qualitative research is longitudinal by the nature of the data collection method. For instance, ethnographic research involves immersing oneself in the research setting over long periods of time. It's not uncommon for an ethnographer to be "in the field" for a year or more. Similarly, historical or legal research involves chronological time and is by definition longitudinal.

Longitudinal research is divided into two general categories: cohort and panel studies. The primary disadvantages of both are that they take longer to produce findings and are more expensive than cross-sectional research.

Cohort studies collect data from individuals who belong to a particular group or category. The most common cohort in crime and justice research is individuals from the same age range or birth year. But one can use any type of cohort, such as those in the same grade or those released on parole at the same time. The key distinction is that data collected at subsequent points in time are not from the same people—the different samples from the population are individuals in a particular cohort. The research questions involve analyzing a group as a whole and do not try to draw conclusions about individuals. This longitudinal research design is ideal if you are interested in patterns of behaviour or the impact of life events or if you are conducting evaluation research. A cohort study can be qualitative by conducting interviews or quantitative by using surveys.

Three interrelated effects can impact the accuracy of findings and conclusions in cohort studies.

First is the possibility of age effects, a consequence of natural changes that occur by growing older. Regardless of your current age, it's easy to see how you changed physically, mentally, and socially since you were 16 years old. Second, cohort effects are elements common to all those born in that period of time. The easiest way to think about cohort effects is to reflect on how different generations, such as yours and your grandparents', can think and act differently. Finally, period effects are shared experiences of historical events, such as the 9/11 terrorist attacks. These changes are experienced by everyone, not only those within the cohort.

Panel studies collect data from the same people, groups, or organizational entities at different points in time. Unlike cross-sectional research, panel studies do not rely on retrospective data to link past experiences with current thoughts and behaviours. Collecting data from the same individuals provides direct evidence to establish temporal order and minimizes risks associated with an individual's memory of events. Panel studies are ideal for exploring the relationship between life events, cohort, and period effects. But they are extremely expensive and must contend with research subject fatigue (from repeated data collection) and with respondents dropping out of the study.

To place longitudinal research in perspective, consider a situation where prior cross-sectional research data contradict confidence in the police and concerns about crime. The contradiction lies in which of these factors is the cause and which is the effect. Research finds support for the accountability model, which states that, as individuals become more concerned about crime in their neighbourhoods, their confidence in the police decreases. On the other hand, an equivalent body of research supports the reassurance model: the more confidence people have in the police, the less concerned they are about crime in their neighbourhood. To address this contradiction, Skogan (2009) used data from a two-wave panel study (the same individuals at two different points in time). Any prior victimization experiences or interactions

with the police were captured in the first survey and the effects from subsequent experiences in the second survey. Skogan found little support for the accountability model, providing a possible answer to the temporal order debate. Using panel data, he concluded that more confidence in the police leads to fewer concerns about crime.

Practical Considerations: The Initial Steps to Designing a Research Project

In criminology, researchers conduct basic research, investigating topics such as the incidence of certain crimes, the display of criminal behaviour, or the explanation of theories. In criminal justice, applied research topics are equally varied and examine the responses to crime by law enforcement, courts, and corrections. Topics of interest could be trends in case law, changes in the use of criminal sanctions, or differences in the causes and responses to crime in different countries, provinces, or jurisdictions.

> **panel study** longitudinal research in which data are collected from the same individuals at different points in time.

Choosing a Research Topic

Choosing a topic may seem easy; nonetheless, "I have yet to see any problem, however complicated, which when looked at the right way, did not become still more complicated" (Shapiro, 2006, p. 19). Although researchers build their careers on conducting research in a subtopic area or by using particular research methods, they are affected by the socio-political climate, including their graduate school training, popular topics, access to data, and funding opportunities. Researchers change subject areas, theoretical foci, and types of data over time as the socio-political circumstances support these changes (Savelsberg & Flood, 2004). But the bottom line remains that all methodological decisions are related to the research topic.

Pauling had it right when he said, "You aren't going to have good ideas unless you have lots of ideas and some sort of principle of selection" (Root-Bernstein, Berstein, & Garnier, 1993, p. 339). Ideas for research topics can come from a variety of sources. You could be reading a newspaper article that praises the municipal licensing of escort services for legitimizing sex work and facilitating safer work conditions. Lewis and Maticka-Tyndale (2000) conducted research in Windsor, Ontario, to see if this relationship was true. They found that the potential for these municipal policies to increase the health and well-being of sex workers exists; however, these benefits are far from realized and can actually place escorts at even greater risk of social, physical, legal, and psychological harm. Another possible source is course material that you want to learn more about.

You might also get an idea for a research topic from your personal experiences, such as understanding why your sibling is always in trouble with the law and you are not. In short, ideas for research topics stem from personal or professional interest and curiosity.

etic an outsider perspective; the researcher interprets the events and behaviour under investigation.

One caveat that must be kept in mind at all stages is feasibility. You must be able to investigate possible research topics scientifically. As intriguing as the topic of Canadian prisoners' last thoughts before execution might be, it's not the most practical. The death penalty existed from 1892 to 1976 in Canada, with the last hanging occurring in Toronto on 11 December 1962 (Amnesty International, 2000). Even if there is some written documentation or surviving witnesses, this topic is problematic.

Choosing a Research Method

Quantitative and qualitative research are often depicted as opposite ends of a continuum and philosophically incompatible within the same research study. This dichotomy is overly simplistic. Carefully constructed research designs allow for both in one study, providing that the methods are consistent with different types of research questions. To better understand how this combination works, we need to examine the assumptions and elements in each approach to see how mixed methods research can be philosophically and methodologically consistent.

Quantitative Methods

Quantitative research reflects positivistic epistemological assumptions. Recall that positivistic research wants to uncover statistical regularities by counting and measuring the extent to which events and behaviours occur. Thus, a quantitative approach is appropriate when research questions involve validating a theory, identifying what factors affect an outcome and to what extent, assessing the utility or effectiveness of an intervention, or determining the best predictors of a particular phenomenon. Quantitative research can also be described as etic in nature. The **etic** perspective is nomothetic and typically quantitative as the focus is on "universal aspects of human behaviour, namely general laws and causal explanations, by imposing on it a general knowledge-structure created by the researcher" (Sabbagh & Golden, 2007, p. 373). Elements of the research process are all determined prior to data collection and are not amendable to modifications based on unique settings or behaviours.

In much the same way that you might be more comfortable driving an automatic car than one with a manual transmission, the quantitative–qualitative dichotomy may have more to do with personal, political, and social orientations of researchers. Although the prevalence of mixed methods research in criminology and criminal justice has increased over the years, the trend in monomethods prevails. Of all the articles published in the top five criminology and criminal justice journals between 1998 and 2002, 73.1 per cent were quantitative, 20.3 per cent were qualitative, 5.2 were evaluation research, and 1.4 per cent were mixed methods (Tewksbury, DeMichele, & Miller, 2005). Justifiably, Tewksbury and colleagues argue that "crime, deviance, and law are broad enough social phenomena that research can implement diverse methodological approaches to better define, explain, understand, and intervene in these issues" (p. 278).

Qualitative Methods

Qualitative research involves interpretive epistemological assumptions. If we want to understand events and behaviours, we have to do so from the point of view of those involved and their interpretations. Theories created explain behaviour based on the observations and statements made by the social actors. A qualitative approach is appropriate when research questions involve topics we know little about, the topic hasn't been investigated with this group of people, or the existing theoretical explanations do not seem to apply to the group.

Qualitative researchers argue that this approach may not be an exact fit to the scientific method but is scientific nonetheless. Quantitative methods don't capture non-measurable factors such as social and interpretive processes. Therefore, the traditional interpretation and application of the scientific method derived from the natural sciences may not help us fully understand human behaviour.

Strict adherence to objectivity isolates us from our research subjects and causes us to lose access to in-depth knowledge. A qualitative approach emphasizes trustworthiness, dependability, and credibility. Trust is created by presenting the evidence in sufficient detail that readers feel as though they share these lived experiences. Dependability is achieved by using different perspectives to validate knowledge, detailed notes, and verbatim descriptions. Credibility is presenting an in-depth understanding so that readers can see the degree of verstehen gained about the research subjects.

Qualitative researchers also argue that no research method can guarantee objectivity. For instance, the accuracy of quantitative and qualitative self-report data is sometimes questioned because people may not remember what they did, know why they do what they do, or accurately predict what they would do in certain situations

(Sechrest & Sidani, 1995). Hence, subjectivity is inherent in all social research, including objective observation. Subjective decisions are made on the questions to ask, data interpretation, and correspondence between a person's actual behaviour and the researcher's description. Research objectivity may not be linked to a research method but to the individual researcher. This stance is due to the adoption of an **emic** perspective, which uses language, concepts, and expressions that social actors use to describe the events and behaviours being investigated. Adopting an emic perspective uses qualitative methods as they assume that "human acts are shaped within socio-cultural contexts, adopt the viewpoint of a cultural insider and attempt to understand the culture in its own frame of reference" (Sabbagh & Golden, 2007, p. 373). The researcher's language and interpretation is not imposed.

> **emic** an insider perspective; events and behaviours under investigation are interpreted based on what they mean to the social actors involved.

With mixed methods research, we can see both etic and emic perspectives within the same research study. For instance, a researcher might begin with an etic perspective and then employ an emic perspective to see the specific conditions under which these events and behaviours occur according to those within the specific social group.

Mixed Methods

The choice of research design must be appropriate for the research topic and allow you to address the research questions. However, there may be situations where neither approach in isolation is sufficient to investigate the topic. Under these circumstances, researchers consider a mixed methods research design (covered in more detail in Chapter 12). As illustrated in the Wallace Wheel, the research process will involve both inductive and deductive reasoning in all three cases (see Table 2.1 for a comparison of the three designs).

Table 2.1 Quantitative, mixed, and qualitative methods

Quantitative methods ──────▶	Mixed methods ◀──────	Qualitative methods
• Nomothetic	• Can be one or both	• Ideographic
• Etic	• Can be one or both	• Emic
• Researcher is objectively separate from the research	• Researcher is both objective and subjective	• Researcher becomes subjectively immersed
• Classify, count, and construct explanatory models	• Both numerical and descriptive	• Complete and detailed description
• Know in advance what to look for	• May or may not know in advance	• May know in advance what to look for
• Predetermined—study designed prior to data collection	• Both predetermined and emerging methods	• Emerging—design details often emerge during the research process
• Instrument based	• Both instrument- and researcher-based	• Researcher is the data collection instrument
• Close-ended questions (e.g. multiple choice)	• Both open- and close-ended questions	• Open-ended questions
• Performance, attitude, observational, and census-type data	• Multiple forms of data drawing on what works	• Interview, observation, document, and audio-visual data
• Statistical analysis	• Statistical and text analysis	• Text and image analysis
• Statistical interpretation	• Quantitative and qualitative interpretations	• Interpretation of themes and patterns

Source: Adapted from Creswell (2014, pp. 17–18).

In mixed methods research designs, we can combine two nomothetic methods, two ideographic methods, or one nomothetic and one ideographic method. For instance, an idiographic explanation can provide insight into quantitative results. Surveys can combine close- and open-ended questions in the same instrument. Once again, the key is that the research question drives the method and that nomothetic and ideographic approaches operate from different worldviews—positivistic and interpretivistic, respectively. The research questions on a given topic are consistent with each of these research goals, which is what necessitates a mixed methods approach.

Let's say you want some clarity on the assignment of letter grades. In formulating your research questions, you conclude that a mixed methods research design is the most appropriate. You use an etic perspective to create a survey with closed questions to investigate the views of students and professors and, perhaps, how often certain letter grades are received by students and assigned by professors. As these are close-ended questions, you are pre-determining the dimensions and conditions under which a particular letter grade is defined and applied.

Once you have your results, you adopt an emic perspective. You conduct interviews to see what language and concepts are used to describe what a particular letter grade means, under what conditions it is used, and how it is interpreted in terms of academic achievement. The last point may be important. For one student, anything less than an A is devastating. For another, a B represents one of his or her highest grades. The findings are not directly compared but create a more holistic explanation as the etic and emic perspectives in this example address different types of research questions on the same research topic.

When does one adopt qualitative, quantitative, or mixed methods? The research question is the determining factor in choosing a design. Qualitative methods are best used when the question concerns the nature of human actions and experiences, a small number of research subjects, or a single case.

Quantitative methods are amenable to questions about patterns of behaviour and descriptions of populations. Researcher preference is also an important element because, when we think about a research topic, we typically develop research questions in line with our preferences, be they qualitative or quantitative.

Conducting a Literature Review

Once you select a research topic, finding related theory and prior research increases your sensitivity to primary concepts and relationships. Doing so initiates a process of specifying the research questions to structure a more refined and feasible research project. One research study cannot address all facets of a problem or issue. Research is always incomplete and produces new unanswered questions. As Thorstein Veblen points out, "the outcome of any serious research can only be to make two questions grow where only one grew before" (Daintith et al., 2000, p. 484).

Purpose of a Literature Review

The purpose of a **literature review** is to specify the problem, issue, event, or behaviour under investigation. Delving into past research informs and refines our thinking to create a clear topical focus and provide methodological information on the best way to answer the research problem. Literature reviews published in crime and justice academic journals are not a shopping list summarizing one research study after another. Their aim is to synthesize theory, themes, and trends by evaluating the findings in connection with a research problem and questions.

There are three overall purposes for conducting a literature review. First, the review summarizes, compares, and evaluates key research findings on a subject. The goal is to ascertain which conceptual relationships are supported across different research studies. Equally important is making comparisons to identify any inconsistencies that leave unanswered questions and gaps in our knowledge, justifying the need for further research.

Second, identify the important theories, concepts, and variables, including the descriptive or explanatory factors, and whether they explain the event/behaviour. Despite one or more studies finding them meaningless or statistically insignificant, they shouldn't necessarily be omitted from consideration in the current research.

Finally, literature reviews are an excellent way to identify research designs, data sources, and analytical techniques. For example, if you are conducting a survey, look at previous survey questions. Taking note of the methodological designs and associated limitations help to anticipate and account for them in your research design. Conducting crime and justice research can be challenging and might not translate perfectly from research design to practice. You don't need to reinvent the wheel if you don't have to and you can avoid repeating the mistakes (e.g. survey respondents understanding a question in multiple ways or being unable to match their opinion to an answer choice) of previous studies.

If the literature review is thorough, the conclusions highlight why the current research study is needed to further our understanding of this topic. The review demonstrates how theoretical explanations and prior research lead to the development of your research objectives and the rationale for the methods chosen. In many ways, literature reviews create a research framework (or bread basket), inform the research focus and involve a desire to

> **literature review** the systematic summary, synthesis, classification, and comparison of scientific knowledge published on a topic.

- replicate research in a new setting or with different individuals;
- challenge previous findings and conclusions;
- test theoretical ideas with a different group, event, or behaviour;
- investigate a topic we know little about;
- build on previous findings by asking different types of research questions requiring a different approach; and
- resolve gaps in knowledge or inconsistent findings.

historical review
a systematic presentation of key developments in theory and research over time.

theoretical review
a systematic comparison and assessment of theoretical explanations of crime and criminality.

methodological review a systematic summary of research methods adopted in prior research; used to assess the methods' effects on findings and conclusions.

contextual review a systematic summary, synthesis, and comparison of theory and research to provide the rationale for new research.

Types of Literature Reviews

Literature reviews differ based on the scope of topic coverage and the depth of discussion. Researchers consider the type of literature review that is the most appropriate given the topic and research questions.

Literature reviews in criminology and criminal justice vary by objective and include four types—historical, theoretical, methodological, and contextual. Much like the scientific process depicted in the Wallace Wheel, all four styles are ideal types. Scientific reviews of relevant theory and research do not fit neatly into each category. More often than not, reviews incorporate two or all four types.

Historical reviews present the evolution of a research topic over time. They are not necessarily only about tracing key developments or attitudes. Historical, theoretical, and methodological reviews frequently provide a framework of changes in conceptual definitions, theoretical propositions, and the research methods used by prior researchers. An excellent example is Sprott and Doob's (2009) comparative research on youth justice system responses to female offenders, which focused on the continuity and changes in concepts such as paternalism, social control, and law reform.

Qualitative and quantitative research use **theoretical reviews** to highlight the similarities and differences in the explanations and conditions under which specific events and behaviours occur. Theoretical reviews systematically examine the underlying philosophical assumptions, worldviews,

logic, parsimony, and the scope or extent of application to the specific topic and related subjects. For instance, Braithwaite's (1989) theory of reintegrative shaming uses a theoretical review to set the stage for the use of social bond, strain, and labelling theories to explain recidivism in a manner contrary to the criminal justice system's philosophy and responses.

With **methodological reviews**, the goal is to summarize the strengths and weaknesses of the data collection and analytical techniques adopted in prior research on the subject. The review assesses the impact that different research designs have on findings and conclusions, particularly the connection between the methodological limitations and the associated constraints on generalizability and interpretation of the findings. In his methodological review, Klinger (1996) examined traditional approaches to investigate police actions. He found that the previous methods and techniques limit our ability to test legal theoretical propositions, such as how much law is applied in a police–citizen encounter. This result led to his development of a new quantitative measure of police behaviour.

Contextual reviews are the most common in all types of research, but their absence in quantitative studies is noticeable. In this type of review, the current research is placed within the larger framework of theory and prior research to show where it fits in our quest to increase our understanding and knowledge of the subject. The synthesis of information helps to identify the gaps in knowledge and any inconsistent findings that can inform the research questions. Contextual reviews can be an entire study when there is little evaluation or synthesis of research and theory on a topic. For instance, Farrington and Welsh (2007) reviewed an astounding 473 prior research studies to synthesize our knowledge of life course criminology and developmental trajectories of criminal behaviour into adulthood (e.g. chronic offending, effectiveness of preschool programs).

Structure of a Literature Review

The last consideration is how to structure a literature review. If you are conducting a historical review, the choice is quite logical: chronological in time. You can approach methodological, theoretical, and contextual reviews from either a chronological or thematic style. **Chronological reviews** present theoretical and empirical trends on a topic over time. More common is the **thematic review**, which groups themes (theories, methods, or findings) into subsections to demonstrate the links and importance to the current research project.

Finally, there are many sources that can be incorporated into a literature review, including periodicals, scholarly articles and monographs, theses and dissertations, government reports, criminal justice agency reports, Internet sources, and conference papers. The websites listed at the end of this chapter provide guidance in identifying criminology and criminal justice journals and suggestions for research topics in crime and justice. Appendix A, on writing a research proposal, provides information on the logistics of writing a literature review. Appendix B, on reading and interpreting published research, offers tips on how to evaluate and synthesize past research.

Methodological Tool Box

Research design is a road map that allows the research process to come as close as possible to acquiring valid knowledge claims. In quantitative and qualitative research, some of the most challenging decisions stem from the research questions and concern measurement, sampling, data collection methods, and analytical techniques.

Measurement

Discussed further in Chapter 3, measurement is far from a simple task. Concepts that may seem intuitively obvious can be measured in a variety of ways. The decision on how to analyze the data is not only influenced by the nature of the research questions but also by the definition of concepts. In quantitative research, measurement involves breaking down concepts into variables and elements that can be assigned a numerical value. If we measure age as young, middle-aged, and elderly, the numerical values could be 1, 2, and 3, respectively. A yes–no question could have values of $0 = $ No and $1 = $ Yes.

In many cases, a concept from a qualitative research question is defined so as to sensitize the researcher to recognize data related to the concept. Theoretical and methodological approaches such as grounded theory define and measure concepts using the data itself. Qualitative researchers let the data speak rather than impose a definitional structure on them. This and similar approaches to measurement are consistent with qualitative research's common purpose to develop idiographic explanations.

> **chronological review** a literature review that presents theory and prior research on a subject in order of chronological time.

> **thematic review** a literature review that presents theories, methods, or findings on a subject in groups related to future research endeavours.

Sampling

Sampling is the process of choosing observations to describe facets and elements of society articulated in the research questions. Sampling decisions attempt to overcome limitations in prior research by selecting cases that can provide better data on a problem or issue. Yet, once again, quantitative and qualitative research is distinguishable in their approach to sampling.

In quantitative research, we could easily include everyone in the population of interest. However, this approach is problematic for a few reasons. We don't need to collect data from everyone to reach a valid conclusion. In fact, doing so is an exercise in diminishing returns. In most cases, it simply isn't feasible because of financial costs, access, or logistics such as time. Instead, a representative sample allows for accurate empirical generalizations of the findings to a larger group while reducing the time and associated costs. The probability of a random sample's results being similar to what would be obtained from the entire population is high.

Qualitative research studies sample fewer people than quantitative studies do. The objective is not to have a representative sample of a larger population but to use a smaller number of cases that can provide in-depth data on the issue or problem. The purpose of sampling is to choose subjects that can clarify and expand on our knowledge within one specific context. The different types of sampling techniques are covered in detail in Chapter 4.

Data Collection

Presumably, a literature review provides insight on how other researchers approached the same research topic. Sampling and data collection go hand in hand as certain data collection methods necessitate using different sampling techniques. At the same time, certain methods are best suited to either quantitative or qualitative approaches by virtue of philosophical and methodological consistency.

Experiments, surveys, secondary data analysis, and meta-analysis are primarily used in quantitative research. Experiments are the gold standard for research questions and hypotheses testing causal explanations (see Chapter 5). Whether a survey is conducted by mail, telephone, face-to-face, or online, it is more likely to be within a quantitative research design. Surveys are administered to a subset of a population for the purpose of capturing attitudes and behaviours about the larger population (see Chapter 6). Secondary data analysis—in which administrative data or data from previous research is reanalyzed to address different research questions—is one of the most common quantitative data collection methods in criminology and criminal justice. Similarly, statistical meta-analyses use the results from previous research to ascertain an overall conclusion, such as the effectiveness of a criminal justice program to treat juvenile

sex offenders. Although not appropriate for all research questions, meta-analysis is a very cost-effective and timely approach to data collection (see Chapter 9).

Interviews, focus groups, participant observation, and case studies are more common for qualitative inquiries. Unstructured and semi-structured interviews are on a continuum of how fixed the questions are prior to conducting the interview. Unstructured reflects general topic areas that will be discussed, whereas semi-structured provides a series of questions that give the respondent latitude to drift between subjects or discuss one in greater depth than anticipated by the researcher. Thus, interviews are an ideal choice to address a variety of qualitative research questions. Focus groups—interviews with small groups of respondents—attempt to gather in-depth information but also to capture group dynamics on forming and maintaining opinions. Participant observation, field research, and ethnographic research involve immersion in the lives of the research subjects for extended periods of time. Case studies collect data on one substantively relevant research site, group of individuals, or even one person to better understand a social problem or issue. All these methods (discussed further in Chapters 6 and 7) allow researchers to collect data conducive to holistic descriptions and explanations within a specific context.

Evaluation research designs and unobtrusive methods are used in both qualitative and quantitative research designs. Evaluating a program could involve participant observation of the program delivery and interviews with key informants or analysis of numerical data to determine program outcomes (see Chapter 11). Unobtrusive measures, such as content analysis, can constitute examining the meanings of words, phrases, and images or creating numerical data on the frequency and types of words, phrases, and images (see Chapter 8).

Data Analysis

Data analysis is the process of giving meaning to empirical observations and producing empirical generalizations that are then summarized to form conclusions. Quantitative research statistically analyzes numbers (see Chapter 9) and qualitative research analyzes verbal descriptions, observations, field notes, documents, photographs, images, and narratives (see Chapter 10).

In general, data analysis is a four-step process. First, the raw data are organized into an analyzable format to produce empirical generalizations. Quantitatively, this step involves coding the data into variables; qualitatively, it could entail transcribing an interview recording into a text document. Second, initial analyses are conducted to verify data quality (e.g. a case coded as male and pregnant) or an error made in transcription that doesn't accurately reflect the respondent's statement. Third, the chosen analysis technique is used to generate findings addressing the research questions. Finally, follow-up analyses may be done to explore analogous findings, indicate the need to collect additional data, or verify that the analytical technique was implemented appropriately.

Ethical and Political Considerations

Ethical dilemmas occur in all areas of our personal and professional lives. Conducting research on human subjects is no exception and there are usually no clear-cut answers. We like to believe that we act ethically and do the right thing. The logistical reality in crime and justice research is that ethical dilemmas are not always obvious until it may be too late. Interviews with 142 criminologists revealed that 62.5 per cent reported having to work through an ethical research dilemma (McSkimming, Sever, & King, 2000). According to Merriam-Webster's *Dictionary of Law* (1996), ethics are the rules or standards governing the conduct of a person or the members of a profession. **Research ethics** establish

boundaries for our research and professional decisions and are mandatory in criminology and criminal justice. Despite these imperative ethical and political considerations, a review of research methods textbooks finds glaring omissions in the coverage of topics such as scientific misconduct, research ethics boards, and order of authorship (McSkimming et al., 2000).

In practice, there is no such thing as perfectly ethical or harmless research. But we are expected to make a concerted effort to anticipate and minimize any risks to human research participants. This awareness of ethical responsibility has not always existed. Prior to the *Nuremberg Code* (1947), there was no generally accepted code of conduct for the ethical aspects of human research. Many medical experiments conducted during World War II had an average mortality rate of 25 per cent. As a result of the Nuremburg trials in 1946, the *Code* introduced principles such as voluntary consent without coercion of any kind, avoidance of unnecessary suffering and accidental death, termination of research if harm is likely, the requirement of highly qualified researchers, and the principle that research findings should be for the good of society and unattainable by any other means. Article 5 of the *United Nations Universal Declaration of Human Rights* (1948) states: "No one shall be subjected to torture or to cruel, inhuman or degrading treatment or punishment." The Declaration of Helsinki (1964) is a set of ethical principles regarding human experimentation and is widely regarded as the cornerstone document of human research ethics codes in force today. All the major sections and principles in the disciplinary codes of ethics and the *Tri-Council Policy Statement* (*TCPS2*) used in Canada are within the Declaration of Helsinki.

Code of Ethics

The American Sociological Association, Academy of Criminal Justice Sciences, and the British Society of

> **research ethics** ethical standards that are accepted by the scientific community and hold researchers responsible for their professional conduct.

Criminology have ethical codes for its members. These documents emphasize the purpose of research (the pursuit of truth and knowledge), scientific values, and mechanisms to hold researchers accountable to the public and the scientific community (e.g. research ethics board, peer review). In short, they contain ethical standards outlining the right and wrong ways to conduct research. These codes are not without controversy. As Bloomberg and Wilkins (1977, p. 443) point out, "the responsibility for safeguarding human subjects ultimately rests with the researcher...A code of ethics may provide useful guidelines but it will not relieve the scientists of moral choice."

In Canada, all research is governed by the standards and procedures within the *TCPS2*, a joint policy of the Canadian Institutes of Health Research (CIHR), the Natural Sciences and Engineering Research Council of Canada (NSERC), and the Social Sciences and Humanities Research Council of Canada (SSHRC). The policy's goals are to articulate shared values and ethical norms across disciplinary boundaries and to harmonize the ethics review process. As with all ethics codes, the *TCPS2* (2014, p. 6) does not provide researchers with definitive answers on how to handle ethical dilemmas:

No single document can provide definitive answers to all ethical issues that may arise in an undertaking as complex as research involving humans. This Policy aims to assist those who use it—researchers, sponsors, members of research ethics boards (REBs), participants, and the public—to identify ethical issues in the design, conduct and oversight of research and to point the way to arriving at reasoned and ethical responses to these issues.

All proposed research involving human subjects must be reviewed and approved by a research ethics board (REB). REBs, which exist within all research institutions, have a mandate to approve, reject, propose modifications to, or terminate research based on ethical standards, principles, and procedures.

During an ethics review, decisions are guided by eight principles within a subject-centred framework that focuses on the views of research subjects and the potential harms and benefits of the proposed research. Ethical principles represent commonly held standards and values of the scientific community.

The *TCPS2* contains the following ethical principles:

- The overarching principle is respect for human dignity. It is unacceptable to objectify or treat a person as a means to an end (in this case, the production of knowledge). Crime and justice researchers are required to keep the welfare and integrity of their research subjects paramount throughout the research process.

- A respect for free and informed consent is premised on the assumption that we have the capacity and fundamental right to make free and informed decisions, including the decision to participate in a research study.

- High ethical standards are expected, based on the principle of respect for vulnerable persons with diminished competence or decision-making. Vulnerable persons can include children, youth, or institutionalized individuals. Particularly in criminal justice, certain groups of participants, such as prison inmates, people with a mental illness, gang members, and serious, violent, or sex offenders, are "difficult populations" (Trulson, Marquart, & Mullings, 2004, p. 451). Hence, special protections and procedures are required to prevent abuse, exploitation, or discrimination.

- A respect for privacy and confidentiality protects the psychological and physical state of research subjects by adhering to standards that protect access, control, and dissemination of personal and identifying information.

- The ethics review process is to be independent and procedurally fair to respect justice and inclusiveness. This principle also includes ensuring that the possible benefits and harms of research do not disproportionately affect a segment of the population.

- Balancing harms and benefits requires ethical justifications that the anticipated benefits from the research outweigh possible harms to participants.
- Minimizing harm involves a duty to avoid and prevent harm to participants by not subjecting them to unnecessary risks.
- Maximizing benefit is a duty in conducting research, which benefits research participants, other individuals, society as a whole, or claims to knowledge.

Researchers consider the ethical aspects of the proposed research from the beginning of the research design stage. REBs are to adjudicate the ethical standards and procedures within the specific context and disciplinary conventions. However, institutional ethics oversight of qualitative research is not without difficulties. REB requirements can pose ethical problems for qualitative researchers at all stages, including informed consent. In fact, many classic works in criminology and criminal justice—particularly those on secrecy, criminal activities, or deviant groups—would not be possible with today's ethical oversight of the research process. To ensure that their projects adhere to ethical principles, researchers include provisions for minimal risk, informed consent, voluntary participation, and confidentiality or anonymity.

Minimal Risk

It goes without saying that minimal risk of harm should be a reasonable expectation. The potential to harm participants in crime and justice research is always present and must actively be avoided and minimized. These risks can be in the form of physical harm, psychological abuse, and legal ramifications for the participants or researcher.

Sometimes the principle of no harm is difficult to follow in absolute terms. For instance, research on the relationship between neighbourhoods and

crime could lead to an increased fear of crime. Most research involves some risk; researchers need to weigh the relative risks against possible benefits in relation to the importance of the findings.

Physical Harm

The ethical expectation is that a research project will be terminated when there is a high potential for or actual physical harm to participants. Highlighting this imperative is the Stanford prison experiment, conducted by Philip Zimbardo in 1971. More than 70 college students responded to an advertisement for participants in a study of the psychological effects of prison life. After holding diagnostic interviews and personality tests to eliminate candidates with psychological or medical conditions and a history of crime or substance abuse, Zimbardo recruited a sample of 24 students and assigned them as either "guards" or "prisoners."

The guards were not trained or given specific instructions other than to do what they felt necessary to maintain order in the prison and respect from the prisoners. The prisoners expected a certain degree of discomfort and harassment but were instead denigrated, humiliated, and tortured physically and psychologically. For instance, using the toilet was a privilege that guards could grant or revoke. After lights out, prisoners were forced to urinate and defecate in buckets and, at times, were not allowed to empty them. By the fifth day of the two-week experiment, the inmates were acting pathologically, the guards sadistically, and five prisoners were removed (due to emotional breakdown, erratic behaviour, or entire body rash). The experiment was terminated after only six days. Zimbardo later admitted that the experiment was unethical as "people suffered and others were allowed to inflict pain and humiliation on their fellows over an extended period of time" (Zimbardo, Maslach, & Haney, 1999, p. 14).

Psychological Abuse

We all feel moments of stress in everyday life. But it is a completely different matter to experience psychological stress from participating in a research study. Some research focuses on how we respond to stress and anxiety in a variety of settings. Zimbardo's experiment investigated this topic within a simulated prison environment. Other research has the sole purpose of manipulating and inducing psychological stress, which can cross the line into abuse.

Milgram (1963) reported that anxiety and stress induced in his obedience experiment was evident, as subjects were observed to sweat, stutter, tremble, and dig their fingernails into their arms. He writes: "I observed a mature and initially posed business-man enter the lab smiling and confident. Within 20 minutes, he was reduced to a twitching, stuttering wreck, who was rapidly approaching a point of nervous collapse" (p. 376). Is it ethical to conduct research such as this study? Although the participants were informed of the research purpose at the end of the experiment, does this step compensate for the short- and long-term psychological stress?

Legal Ramifications

Ethics codes create possible conflicts between ethical principles and the law. Crime and justice researchers have an ethical responsibility to ensure that information about study participants is not used against them. Researchers can face legal dilemmas regarding mandatory reporting of certain crimes (e.g. child abuse), gaining knowledge of possible future crimes where there is civil liability for harm caused, or being subpoenaed to court (Lowman & Palys, 2001). Even if you delete identifying information from field notes or interview transcripts, you can't delete it from your memory.

Laud Humphreys' (1975) *Tearoom Trade* brought possible unethical practices and the associated legal implications to the forefront. His highly controversial study examined impersonal and anonymous homosexual encounters in public park restrooms. The men in these meetings were unaware that they were part of a research study. Furthermore, they were not openly homosexual and their actions were not known to others, even family members.

The controversy here is not substantive but concerns the research design. As a lookout, Humphreys alerted participants of impending danger, such as an unsuspecting stranger or law enforcement, thereby breaking the law on repeated occasions. He also recorded participants' licence plate numbers without the men's knowledge or consent and used them to obtain names and home addresses. With this information, he later interviewed participants face-to-face under the guise of a public health survey. Was the balancing act between scientific and societal benefit and the participants' right to privacy enough to justify covert observation? As a result of the study, Humphreys almost had his doctoral degree revoked and faced personal legal implications from his refusal to identify research subjects. He states: "After my research became a public controversy to protect human subjects I spent some weeks early in the summer of 1968 burning tapes, deleting passages from transcripts, and feeding material into a shredder" (Galliher, Brekhus, & Keys, 2004, p. 41).

This problem is not exclusive to crime and justice researchers. For instance, a master's student from Simon Fraser University was charged with contempt of court for refusing to disclose confidential data about the identities of interviewees who participated in assisted suicides of AIDS patients (Palys & Lowman, 2000). When designing their studies, researchers in Canada must bear in mind that they do not have specific legal protection or privilege.

Informed Consent

The degree of **voluntary participation** hinges on **informed consent**. Simply asking someone if he or she wants to participate in your research study is insufficient. For informed consent, a potential research subject is provided with enough information to make a

---

voluntary participation a person's informed consent to participate in a research study; gained without coercion, manipulation, or other controlling influences.

informed consent agreement to participate in a research study after being made aware of the purpose, process, risks and benefits, and intended use of the data.

voluntary decision about whether to participate in the research study. Most REBs require information on the following elements: research purpose, research questions, potential risks and discomfort, anticipated benefits, data collection and analysis, length and scope of participation, data storage, treatment of participants' identity, dissemination of the results, and contact information for the researcher and the REB associated with his or her university. The ethical standard of voluntary participation stipulates that potential research subjects be competent to provide informed consent without any type of coercion or manipulation. That is, they must be able to appreciate the potential consequences of their decision to participate.

Even after someone provides informed consent, he or she maintains the right to withdraw from the study at any time without penalty. Informed consent should be seen as a dynamic process that isn't restricted to the beginning of a research project. As circumstances change, informed consent to participate should be reaffirmed. Consent is not required, per se, from organizations such as a police service but is needed from individuals. Natural observation in public places where there is no expectation of privacy (e.g. shopping malls) does not require informed consent from everyone present.

Potential research subjects must have the opportunity to ask any questions and weigh the pros and cons of participating in the study. Researchers provide information in a format that is comprehensible and consistent with the cultural and social setting to which the potential participants belong. For example, the *TCPS2* (2014, pp. 113–114) points out that "In the case of Aboriginal peoples, abuses stemming from research have included: misappropriation of sacred songs, stories and artefacts; devaluing of Aboriginal peoples' knowledge as primitive or superstitious; violation of community norms regarding the use of human tissue and remains; failure to share data and resulting benefits; and dissemination of information that has misrepresented or stigmatized entire communities." Therefore, obtaining informed consent from and conducting research

with Aboriginal participants can pose unique ethical challenges, including language differences. Chapter 9 of the *TCPS2* (2014) makes the following recommendations for obtaining informed consent from Aboriginal peoples (these guidelines should be followed throughout the research project):

- Respect the culture, traditions, and knowledge.
- Conceptualize and conduct research with Aboriginal peoples and their communities as a partnership.
- Consult members of the group who have relevant expertise.
- Involve the group in the research design and ethical considerations.
- Structure the research to address the needs, concerns, and different viewpoints of the group.
- Provide the opportunity for the group to respond to the research findings.

Figure 2.3 is an example of an informed consent form; however, the format for written informed consent varies.

Confidentiality and Anonymity

An integral component of informed consent is that potential participants understand how the researcher will protect their right to privacy. Crime and justice research frequently asks participants for information that they would not share with anyone else and/or that could identify them. **Confidentiality** or **anonymity** protects research subjects from harm caused by unauthorized use of their personal information or characteristics, including culture, age, life experiences, and medical, criminal, or employment histories.

If identifiable personal information is collected, the REB requires additional information for approval. If it is collected using interviews,

confidentiality the guarantee that the identities of a study's subjects are known to the researcher but will not be revealed.

anonymity the guarantee that no one, not even the researcher, can link the study's data to the identity of a research subject.

The Dynamics of Antisocial Behaviour: An Investigation of Responses to Youth Crime

Please mark the "Yes" and "No" boxes with your initials to indicate whether you are providing consent to each of the consent and privacy options outlined below.

	Consent and Privacy Options	YES	NO
1	I understand and willingly agree to participateina face-to-face interview to be scheduled and conducted at my convenience.		
2	I agree to have the interview tape recorded.		
3	I would like to review a copy of my transcript.		
4	I am willing to allow the researcher to use quotations from the interview providing they are cited anonymously (the quote does not identify me).		
5	I am willing to allow the researcher to use quotations from the interview that are not completely anonymous as long as I am contacted by the researcher so I can review the quotation and give my consent to use it.		
6	I would like to review and have the opportunity to comment on a draft report before it is published.		
7	I would like to receive a copy of the executive summary.		
8	I would like to receive a copy of the final report when it is published.		
9	I agree to be contacted at a future date if the researcher would like clarification on my answers to any of the interview questions.		

I have read the information presented in the attached Letter of Information about a study being conducted by Jennifer L. Schulenberg of the University of Waterloo. I have had the opportunity to ask questions about my involvement in the study and to receive any additional details I wanted to know about the study. I understand that I can choose to withdraw from the study at any time and I voluntarily agree to participate in this study.

_____
Name of Participant (please print) –Date (dd/mm/yyyy)

_____
Signature of Participant

_____
Email address

In my opinion, the person who has signed this informed consent is agreeing to participate in this study voluntarily, understands the nature of the study, and any consequences of participation.

_____
Signature of Researcher or Witness

Figure 2.3 Sample informed consent form

the questions must be approved by the REB. Surveys require approval for one or all of the following: type of data to be collected; intended use of the data; limits put in place for data use, disclosure, and retention; safeguards for securing and maintaining confidentiality; anticipated use by other researchers; and the possibility of linking data to a person's identity.

Secondary data analysis may require accessing data that reveals a person's identity. To obtain the data, a researcher must demonstrate to the REB that the identifiers are essential, that appropriate steps are taken to protect the individuals' privacy, and that the research subjects do not object to their information being used for secondary research purposes.

When collecting original data for crime and justice research, it is often difficult to ensure respondents' anonymity. Thus, confidentiality becomes even more critical. Individuals, especially those in conflict with the law, might be unwilling to disclose personal information or secrets if they think such details could be disclosed and detrimental to their psychological, social, or legal well-being. According to Israel (2004), three ethical dilemmas associated with confidentiality are quite common for researchers in criminology and criminal justice:

1. Third parties pressure researchers to disclose data.
2. The data reveals past injustice or the potential for future harm.
3. Popular opinion is that certain participants (e.g. child molesters) do not deserve the protection of confidentiality.

How do we work around these problems to ensure confidentiality? Under certain circumstances, the researcher can, in good conscience, guarantee only limited confidentiality given the relationship between ethics and the law. For instance, a research subject's information cannot be kept confidential if he or she discloses information that falls under mandatory reporting laws or indicates that he or she is a danger to himself or herself or to others (see *CIHR, NSERC, & SSHRC*, 2014, p. 60).

Legal and ethical approaches to confidentiality can result in different courses of action. "Researchers shall maintain their promise of confidentiality to participants within the extent permitted by ethical principles and/or law" (*CIHR* et al., 2014, p. 60). To alleviate or prevent a possible conflict, do not record names or identifying details. If necessary, remove the identifying information as soon as possible. Create pseudonyms for individuals and store the codebook in a separate location. Limit geographical details by disguising the research location or community.

Conflict of Interest

A trust relationship is expected between the researcher and participants, sponsors, institutions, professional associations, and society. Conflicts of interest could be in the form of research sponsors wishing to suppress findings, undue influence on research design (particularly in evaluation research), financial benefits for the researcher, or different expectations that restrict access to data. Researchers must disclose any actual, perceived, or potential conflicts to the REB and in publications.

Let's look at an example. You submit a data request to a government organization that requires both REB approval and a separate application with the following: project title, researcher name and qualifications, research purpose, research design and methods, number of youth and time anticipated, provisions for confidentiality, projected amount of staff time, benefit to the agency or profession, and the amount and source of funding. Gaining approval seems simple enough, but there are so many external research requests that approval is granted only if the results are likely to have a direct benefit for the agency in terms of policies or procedures. Otherwise, the use of government resources is not seen as cost-effective but disruptive to daily operations.

Jeffords (2007, p. 97) conducted a survey of research directors at correctional facilities across the United States and found that "what may be viewed as an advance to the general body of delinquency literature does not necessarily mean it is of direct benefit to a participating agency. Thus, what may be important in academe may have little bearing on an agency itself or the probability of research approval." The likelihood of approval also increases if any requested research design modifications are completed and the researcher agrees to allow the agency to review and comment prior to any type of publication.

Scientific Misconduct

Ethical violations and professional misconduct always depend on definitions and the specific context in which the offence occurs. **Scientific misconduct** is not honest error or differences in research design or interpretation but an intentional misrepresentation, misappropriation, or deception in professional activities (Canadian Association of University Teachers, 2003; Weed, 1998). Policies and procedures are in place at colleges and universities to handle student misconduct such as plagiarism (i.e. using someone else's words or ideas without proper credit) and dishonesty (e.g. cheating on an exam, using a paper mill). Professors' teaching and scholarly activities aren't always straightforward, as codes of ethics tell us what we cannot do but not what we ought to do (Frankel, 1998).

Unfortunately, scientific misconduct is neither new nor as rare as we would all like to believe. Why would an academic risk his or her career? Reasons include pressure to publish (i.e. the "publish or perish" manta linked to promotion), competition, demands from research sponsors, fewer opportunities to mentor students effectively, personal financial gain, and ego and vanity (Sardar, 1998; Weed, 1998).

scientific misconduct intentional fabricating, falsifying, or plagiarizing of research data or other means of violating commonly accepted practices within the scientific community for proposing, conducting, and reporting research.

What constitutes scientific misconduct, questionable practices, and sloppy science varies greatly (Swazey, 1998). In the initial research stages, these actions could include conducting a literature review that fails to acknowledge contradictory prior research, submitting funding proposals for research that is already complete, or delegating research tasks to students and not giving authorship credit. During data collection, unethical practices can include inappropriate measurement or statistical techniques to enhance the findings, significant departures from the research design approved by REB, or data fabrication to produce the desired results (Smith & Godlee, 2005).

There is no systematic or consistent monitoring of the research process outside of data collection. Hence, disseminating the findings is the point in the research process at which scientific misconduct enters a larger gray area. Let's look at one example, the order of authorship. The order is meant to represent the degree of intellectual contribution, which can be a sensitive topic when it involves researchers of different ranks (McSkimming, et al., 2000). The implicit suggestion is that, the earlier a name appears, the larger the contribution. Guest authors are listed according to their status to increase the probability of publication (Morgan, Harmon, & Gliner, 2001). For instance, should a professor's name be included as a secondary author to a student paper? Or when a professor is first author but the student did most of the work? Alternatively, should a professor add a student as a secondary author to boost his or her publication record, increasing the likelihood for scholarships, employment, and tenure? Ghost authors are those "who did make a significant professional contribution but are not included as authors" (p. 1477). Unfortunately, students are often ghost authors. The ghost author phenomenon also raises the issue of whether one can drop co-authors who aren't pulling their weight. Think about the struggles you may have when completing group work assignments and a member doesn't complete his or her assigned tasks.

To place scientific misconduct into context, consider two cases. Cyril Burt's research was instrumental in measuring intelligence with IQ scores (Willmott, 1998). He argued that variations in IQ are largely genetic. Unfortunately, some results were "so surprising that they could only have been invented or improperly manipulated" (p. 372). Wilmott found that Burt reported the average IQ to be 153.2 in 1943 and 139.7 in 1971, when almost all other research placed it at around 100. Burt provided little information on his data sources, published much of his research in a journal he edited, and added non-existent co-authors.

Ranjit Kumar Chandra was a professor at Memorial University and Officer of the Order of Canada. In 2001, he published an article showing that a specific multivitamin and mineral supplement improved cognition function for those over 65 years of age—an incredible finding that could help delay the onset of Alzheimer's disease (White,

2004). Unfortunately, the paper was identical to one Chandra submitted in 2000 but was rejected because of serious methodological problems and strong evidence of fabricated data. One suspected finding was that the average number of digits remembered was 50; most of us can't remember more than 8. Chandra had published over 200 articles, largely in a journal he edited. Because of the scandal regarding the 2001 article, these others became suspect (Smith & Godlee, 2005). Chandra resigned from the university in 2002.

Research integrity is extremely important for researchers of all ranks, including students. Beyond the human and financial resources squandered, scientific misconduct severs the trust required to create knowledge based on prior research. It provides a negative model for students and junior faculty in an increasingly high-pressure work environment. Finally, scientific misconduct greatly erodes public confidence in scientific research and the use of evidence-based practices in criminal justice.

Summary of Important Points

Introduction

- The scientific method is an ideal, or model, for perfect research.
- No research design is perfect.

Scientific Method

- The scientific method is an iterative process between theory and method.
- The hypothetico-deductive method is based on the principles of empiricism, skepticism, objectivity, accuracy, and precision.
- The perception of quantitative and qualitative research as dichotomous is false.
- Mixed methods research is philosophically consistent, as quantitative and qualitative approaches are adopted based on a particular research question.
- The etic (outsider) perspective is nomothetic and the emic (insider) is idiographic.

Research Process

- Informational components include theories, hypotheses, observations, empirical generalizations, and decisions to accept or reject hypotheses.
- Concepts express general characteristics or the essential features of an individual, behaviour, or event. Hypotheses are untested statements about a relationship between two theoretical concepts. Variables can be observed and measured at different levels in the real world. Empirical generalizations are statements about patterns in the data.
- Methodological controls include logical deduction, research design, data analysis, logical induction, hypothesis testing, and logical inference.
- Both quantitative and qualitative research employ logical inference and deductive and inductive reasoning.

Research Design

- Cross-sectional research collects data at a single point in time and is limited in creating causal explanations.
- Longitudinal research, a stronger design for establishing causality, collects data more than once over time.
- Cohort studies collect data from individuals within a particular group over time. Age, cohort, and period effects negatively impact the findings.
- Panel studies collect data from the same individuals at different points in time.

Practical Considerations: The Initial Steps to Designing a Research Project

- Research topics stem from personal and professional interest and curiosity, but need to be feasible for scientific investigation.
- Literature reviews specify the problem, demonstrate the need for research, and inform the research design.
- Literature reviews are historical, theoretical, methodological, or contextual and are organized chronologically or thematically.
- Quantitative methods reflect an etic perspective, while qualitative methods are consistent with an emic perspective.
- Research designs also include measurement, sampling, data collection, and data analysis.
- Experiments, surveys, secondary data, and meta-analyses are often used in quantitative research.

- Interviews, focus groups, participant observation, and case studies are frequently used in qualitative research.
- Evaluation research and unobtrusive methods are used in both quantitative and qualitative research.

Ethical and Political Considerations

- Research ethics are standards and procedures accepted by the scientific community that hold researchers responsible for their professional conduct.
- The *TCPS2* governs all research conducted in Canada. Ethical principles include respect for human dignity, informed consent, respect for vulnerable populations, privacy and confidentiality, fair ethics review process, and a balance of risks and benefits to reduce harm to research participants.
- If more than minimal risk of physical, psychological, or legal harm exists, research should be terminated.
- With confidentiality, the identity of participants is known to the researcher but not revealed. Anonymity means that even the researcher cannot link a participant's identity to his or her personal information.
- Conflicts of interest are actual, perceived, or potential compromises due to the relationship between the researcher and participants, sponsors, or society.
- Scientific misconduct includes fabrication, falsification, and other actions that violate accepted practice in the scientific community.

Key Terms

anonymity 55
chronological review 49
cohort study 42
concept 35
confidentiality 55
contextual review 48
cross-sectional research 41
emic 45
empirical generalization 37

etic 44
historical review 48
hypothesis 36
hypothetico-deductive method 35
informed consent 54
literature review 47
longitudinal research 42
methodological review 48

panel study 43
research ethics 51
scientific misconduct 58
thematic review 49
theoretical review 48
time-series research (or trend study) 42
variable 37
voluntary participation 54

Review Questions and Exercises

1. Describe the scientific method depicted in the Wallace Wheel for quantitative and qualitative research.
2. What is the relationship between a literature review and the structure of a research project?
3. Using the criteria for causality, compare and contrast cross-sectional and longitudinal research designs.
4. Choose any crime and justice journal article and draft an informed consent form for its participants.
5. Suppose that you collected interview data from an individual working on an organized crime case. The interviewee read the transcripts and signed a form stating that she had read them. But, during data analysis, she tells you that she wants to delete some of the things she said because she fears repercussions from her supervisor. You have to decide whether to restate what was said in a way that would be less threatening, delete the information entirely, or leave everything as it is. What ethical issues are raised in this situation? What would you do, and why?

Online Exercises and Websites of Interest

Codes of Ethics

www.acjs.org/pubs/167_671_2922.cfm
www.britsoccrim.org/docs/CodeofEthics.pdf
Using either the Code of Ethics from the Academy of Criminal Justice Sciences or the British Society of Criminology, identify any ethical standards that are unique to research in criminology and criminal justice.

Crime Spider

www.crimespider.com/
This online resource canvasses crime- and law-related websites to assist in choosing and narrowing down a research topic.

Criminal Justice Resources

http://staff.lib.msu.edu/harris23/crimjust/index.htm
This website contains excellent coverage of over seventy topics, with annotations for the online and print sources.

Ethical Research in Canada

www.pre.ethics.gc.ca/pdf/eng/tcps2-2014/TCPS_2_FINAL_Web.pdf
The current version of the Canadian *TCPS*, known as *TCPS2*, is found online.

The Literature Review: A Few Tips on Conducting It

www.writing.utoronto.ca/advice/specific-types-of-writing/literature-review
https://ctl.utsc.utoronto.ca/twc/sites/default/files/LitReview.pdf
The University of Toronto provides two resources with step-by-step guidance on writing a literature review.

Additional Resources

Bechtel, H.K., & Pearson, W. (1985). "Deviant Scientists and Scientific Deviance." *Deviant Behavior, 6,* 237–252.

If you are curious about scientific misconduct, this article discusses it as a form of elite occupational deviance.

Creswell, J.W. (2014). *Research Design: Qualitative, Quantitative, and Mixed Methods Approaches* **(4th ed.). Thousand Oaks, CA: Sage.**

This text is an excellent step-by-step guide and provides checklists for all stages of the research process.

Leauvilt, F. (2001). *Evaluating Scientific Research: Separating Fact from Fiction.* **Upper Saddle River, NJ: Prentice Hall.**

Pay particular attention to Chapter 4 ("Finding Research Problems") and Chapter 6 ("Research Design Choices").

Vaughn, M.S., Del Carmen, R.V., Perfecto, M., & Charand, K.X. (2004). "Journals in Criminal Justice and Criminology: An Updated and Expanded Guide for Authors." *Journal of Criminal Justice Education, 15,* 61–128.

This entire issue of the *Journal of Criminal Justice Education* provides an annotated list of all scholarly journals in criminology and criminal justice, including submission guidelines.

Part II
Nuts and Bolts of Conducting Research

Chapter 3

Quantitative and Qualitative Measurement

"If you cannot measure it, then it is not science." Lord Kelvin (1824–1907)
"Speech created thought which is the measure of the universe." Percy Bysshe Shelley (1792–1822)

Learning Objectives

- To understand the measurement process by using deductive and inductive logic.
- To create conceptual and operational definitions.
- To identify different types of variables and create hypotheses.
- To understand the criteria for causality and errors in causal reasoning.
- To appreciate the importance of tests for reliability and validity.
- To articulate the levels of measurement and the differences between indexes and scales.

Introduction

Measurement is a part of our everyday lives. When you use a recipe, you measure the ingredients. When you drive, you check your speedometer every time you see a police cruiser. When you go to the ATM, your receipt measures how much money you withdrew and how much remains in the account. Measurement is everywhere; it tells us how things change and how too much or too little of something can have profound effects.

Hubbard (2010) argues that absolutely everything in life can be measured. If we can observe something, there is a way to measure it. The measurement may be imprecise, but Hubbard claims that, as long as it tells you more than you knew before, it's still measurement. Although this view may be adequate for daily life, it is insufficient for scientific inquiry.

In the scientific method, the measurement process typically starts with an objective. For instance, you might want to ascertain the nature or extent of a particular phenomenon's existence. Yet, even when you have an objective, what should be measured may not be clear. If you want to measure the process of saving money, would you measure how much you spend or how much you don't?

Researchers in criminology and criminal justice have additional measurement issues to consider. For example, to assess the effectiveness of a domestic violence program, researchers must make several decisions. Do they measure the success of program components or the reoffending of participants? Is success defined by a participant not being rearrested for spousal assault or by an improvement in the interpersonal dynamics between two individuals, such as fewer verbal altercations? Is failure defined as a rearrest for any kind of crime? There is no perfect measurement, but there is a process within the scientific method that allows us to measure concepts and ideas more accurately. This chapter examines this process and its components, including variables, hypotheses, causality, and levels of measurement.

The Preliminary Steps of Measurement

One can think about the measurement process as a series of four preliminary steps: articulating the topic, research problem, purpose statement, and research questions. Regardless of whether you plan to conduct quantitative, qualitative, or mixed methods research, these tasks begin the process. To contextualize this logic, each stage is illustrated by O'Beirne, Denney, and Gabe's (2004) study on the fear of violence as an indicator of risk for probation officers.

The first step is deciding on a topic. You could be intrigued by an event or pattern of behaviour. After familiarizing yourself with past research, you discern gaps in knowledge. Topics appropriate for qualitative research are frequently exploratory and start with a broadly defined central research question. In other words, the research question comes first and the nature and scope of the topic often emerge as the study progresses. In contrast, quantitative research has a clearly delineated topic that is broken down into discrete research questions and hypotheses.

In their work on probation officers, O'Beirne et al. (2004) conducted a mixed methods study. Upon reviewing the literature, they found that "quantitative researchers have tried to understand the social patterning of fear of crime including violence, qualitative researchers have sought to disentangle the meaning of fear and its origins in order to make sense of why it exists and how it can be managed" (p. 115). They felt that incorporating both perspectives was the most appropriate choice for their study.

The second decision is determining the research problem, which is not to be confused with creating research questions. Here, you clearly articulate the issue or problem under investigation. This step represents the foundation for developing your research questions and helps to determine why the study is important. O'Beirne et al.'s (2004) problem statement focuses on practitioners wanting to know the risks they will be exposed to when trying to control dangerous offenders.

Third, the **purpose statement** builds on the research problem to explain why you are conducting the research and what you want to accomplish by doing it (Locke, Spirduso, & Silverman, 2007). In doing so, you are able to articulate how the findings will contribute to our understanding of the topic. For instance, the purpose statement for the study on the fear of violence was to ascertain the nature and extent of probation officers perceiving the danger and risk of violence.

purpose statement
a statement outlining a research study's objectives.

Finally, researchers develop research questions. The journey from a topic to research questions is not always easy, but developing good questions is integral for conducting quality research. Certain questions, using terms introduced in Chapters 1 and 2, guide you through this process: Will you use basic or applied research? Does the topic suggest an exploratory, descriptive, or explanatory research design? Is your topic going to focus on a particular time, place, or people? (In our example, the type of people is probation officers.) Taking cues from earlier research may also be helpful. Most articles have a section with suggestions for future research. If you formulate research questions from one of these ideas, you may find contradictory results, replicate the original study, or apply a new theory to the topic or type of behaviour.

Research questions have to be realistic, clear, and testable using empirical data. They are not questions of morality, such as whether a particular approach to punishment is "right" or "just." They are not vague but specify the concepts of interest. A good research question is relevant, feasible, concise, and ethical. For example, the research question "What can we do to prevent crime?" is too ambiguous. A better question would be, "Does the mandatory arrest policy prevent domestic violence?" The main concepts are arrest policy and domestic violence. Certain terms are associated with different types of research questions. In exploratory research, words such as *do* or *what* appear. Research questions for descriptive studies can start with *how* or *in what way*. In explanatory studies, examples include *factors affecting*, *likelihood*, *to what extent*, and *influence*.

In quantitative research, the research questions state the relationships among concepts. Qualitative research features a broad research question exploring the main concept or social phenomenon. This type of question sets the stage for investigating various perspectives and meanings, where it's common to see a series of subquestions that narrow the study focus. In mixed methods research, there is one or more central questions that are separated into qualitative and quantitative research questions.

O'Beirne et al. (2004) used two data sources in their study. For the quantitative portion, they administered a victimization survey to probation officers to measure the extent and prevalence of work-related violence. The qualitative data consisted of interviews with a subset of the survey respondents to explore their perceptions on the nature and impact of violence and fear on their personal and professional lives. The researchers developed four central questions: Who felt fear of violence at work? How did individual probation officers handle fear? How was fear recorded? How did management support staff who were fearful or worried about violence? As you can see, the topic, problem, purpose, and questions are consistent and logical in their progression. This example shows precisely what we do before engaging in the measurement process.

Reasoning in the Scientific Process

To appreciate the measurement process, we need to revisit the scientific method and its use of deductive and inductive reasoning. Measurement can occur while reasoning both deductively and inductively. In this way, the expected relationships can be tested similarly for all data collected.

As discussed in Chapter 1, deductive reasoning involves moving from the general and abstract to the specific. Thus, a researcher uses a theoretical explanation to make a specific prediction about relationships that are then tested empirically. The logic of a deductive explanation requires that every variable, concept, and theoretical proposition have a consistent meaning throughout the research process. An example is Skogan's (2009) examination of the relationship between concerns about crime and confidence in the police. The study's two key concepts were crime and confidence. The research problem was the ambiguity in existing theoretical explanations of whether perceptions on crime come before or after confidence in the police. Moving from general to specific, the purpose statement tested the assumptions about causal order posited by three theoretical models: accountability, reassurance, and reciprocal causation. Finally, Skogan's research question centred on causal order: Do concerns about crime come before confidence in the police? Hypotheses developed for each theoretical model were based on how crime and confidence are defined. In this case, confidence in the police was defined as performance and crime concerns as worries about specific offences. The hypotheses tested whether the causal order suggested by each theoretical model was correct. As should be evident, Skogan went from a broad topic and, by completing the preliminary steps of the measurement process, deductively

Key Thinker

Malcolm W. Klein

Malcolm W. Klein is one of the most well-known and respected gang researchers in the field. He earned his PhD in social psychology at Boston University and served as the director of a project to reduce street gang violence in Los Angeles. He is currently professor emeritus at the University of Southern California, where he continues to serve as the director of the Social Science Research Institute. Reflecting on his career, he makes several observations that are akin to measuring the world around us.

Klein (2002) became a criminologist entirely by accident when he became the director of the gang project. As a result, he asks the pertinent question of how one defines oneself as a criminologist. This question can be seen as a measurement problem. Criminology is multidisciplinary, encompassing political science, sociology, anthropology, biology, psychology, geography, history, and other fields. A criminologist doesn't necessarily get his or her PhD in criminology or criminal justice. Klein argues that the result is an absence of a central focus or unifying theories and methodologies. Criminology is very much a "cosmopolitan discipline" (p. 49). Criminologists use both quantitative and qualitative methods and have an appreciation of both.

In his research endeavours, Klein has learned that a researcher's favourite topic may not be the audiences' choice. "The issue is similar to newsworthiness in journalism. Dull doesn't sell; normal doesn't sell; complexity doesn't sell. What sells is drama, exotica, excitement" (Klein, 2002, p. 50). Although Klein has conducted research in many areas, including international juvenile justice and survey methodology, he is recognized for and receives funding for work on gangs, a topic of political and sensationalistic interest.

When it comes to measuring crime, Klein strongly encourages future researchers to update their methods regardless of how methodologically sophisticated they may be when entering the field. Until the 1960s, estimates on the prevalence of crime were based almost entirely on official records, particularly police arrest data. Unfortunately, this practice underestimates the extent of crime and overestimates the nature of crime based on class, ethnicity, and sex. The result is that arrest data may reflect police behaviour better than it does criminality. Now victimization and self-report surveys can be used to measure the nature and extent of crime. Klein played an instrumental role in the development of the International Self-Report Delinquency (ISRD) scale, which is used in 28 countries. He suggests that it is more valid than police data in terms of getting to the extent of criminal offending and is reliable in comparison to other instruments that measure attitudes and behaviours.

Regardless of the topic, problem, purpose, research question, or methods, there is a common thread. According to Klein, this thread is more of an implication or consequence of shoddy measurement. He states: "Sloppy research allows greater claims to success than does careful research" (Klein, 2002, p. 60).

moved from theory to hypotheses. Theory informs the research question that specifies the hypotheses, which are then tested against the data.

Inductive logic starts with empirical observations and moves to identifying patterns, developing tentative hypotheses, and then informing theory with general conclusions. For example, Dunham and Alpert's (2009) research topic explored the dynamics within a police–citizen encounter and each person's reaction to the demeanour of others. The research problem was not the role of behaviour on the outcome of an encounter but how the words and actions of one person affected those of another during the encounter. The purpose statement was to provide a better understanding of what occurs within encounters by examining the demeanour of everyone at the beginning and any changes that occur over time. Prior to data collection, the concept of demeanour was broadly defined based on past research. During data collection and analysis, this definition was modified and refined based on the actions and words of suspects versus officers. These characteristics created a multi-pronged definition of demeanour to assess change throughout the encounter.

Peterson-Badali and Broeking (2010) explored the nature of parental involvement in relation to the *Youth Criminal Justice Act (YCJA)*. Their topic asked this question: Does the enhanced parental involvement stipulated in the *YCJA* occur in real life? Their research problem was based on the fact that little research exists to evaluate the nature and extent of parental involvement in the youth criminal justice process. The purpose statement was to explore the perceptions of youth justice officials to provide insight on parental involvement in youth court. This understanding could facilitate more effective and meaningful involvement and affect the tangible outcome of the court case. In the study, the key concept of parental involvement was open-ended and defined as parents' presence in court. As data collection progressed, it was expanded to include the type and effect, which was no role, general support, socialization, and legal advantage.

The Research Question Drives the Method

The rule of thumb is that, the further removed from direct observation or the more abstract a concept is, the less agreement you will see in definitions. The question we need to ask ourselves is, "Why?" The answer is that research uses or tests different theoretical perspectives, different substantive foci, and multiple interpretations of key concepts varying by time, context, place, method, and available data.

Qualitative purpose statements use action words such as *describe, understand, develop, examine the meaning of,* or *discover* (Creswell, 2014). Meaning is derived from the data inductively. Definitions

that begin the measurement process are developed and refined as data collection and analysis progress. They are non-directional and represent the working definition of the central issue or problem under investigation. Quantitative purpose statements identify a theory or model and may state a directional relationship between concepts. A mixed methods purpose statement indicates the study's central focus and intentions and explains why combining quantitative and qualitative research is appropriate. For a summary of the differences in measurement logic between quantitative and qualitative research, see Table 3.1.

Above all, we have to remember the mantra that the research question drives the method. Measurement not only guides data collection but also drives every stage in the research process to remain consistent when addressing the research question.

The Measurement Process

Measurement redefines an abstract concept into something we can detect empirically using our five senses. To measure concepts, we use empirical indicators that are observable and can tell us the presence and variation of our concept of interest. Our goal is to capture the full range of what a concept means, use multiple indicators, and ensure variability. We go back to the literature and see how others define and measure the object, event, or behaviour in your research question. Developing anticipated

Table 3.1 Deductive and inductive measurement logic

	Quantitative research	Qualitative research
Logic	Deductive	Inductive
Topic	Clearly defined; used to develop research questions and hypotheses	Research questions broadly defined, outline the topic's scope
Research problem	Specifies the issue or social problem that requires further research	Explores a relationship and why it requires further research
Purpose statement	Overall intent and study objectives (specifying the nature and direction of the relationship)	Overall intent and study objectives (non-directional; exploratory or descriptive focus)
Key concepts	Predetermined prior to data collection	Emergent; broadly defined and modified through data collection and analysis
Research question	Specific and fixed	Flexible; develops based on preliminary data collection
	States the relationship between variables; "To what extent do legal and situational factors affect police discretion in youth-related incidents?"	Central question explores the main concept(s) or relationship; "How do police officers decide when they are going to use their discretion?"

meanings is an important step in both quantitative and qualitative research.

As depicted in Figure 3.1, the measurement process starts with conceptualization, the process of taking imprecise ideas in the form of concepts and making them clear and concise. In other words, it is the process of defining a concept. Recall that a concept is an abstract term that describes an aspect of the empirical world. It's a general definition and open to multiple interpretations. Concepts can't be observed in the empirical world because they represent the mental images we have about an event, behaviour, or interaction. With deductive reasoning, we translate abstract ideas into something that is testable and can ultimately be subdivided into variables. With inductive reasoning,

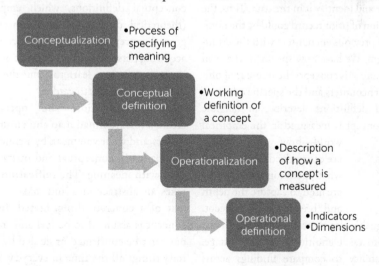

Figure 3.1 The process of measurement

conceptualization forms part of the analytical process of understanding the data. So, if we are to conceptualize prior record, it could be a record of experiences with an event, object, or behaviour. As you can see, the concept is still abstract, but it does tell us the topic of interest and the meaning of record.

The next task is to create a **conceptual definition**, which explicitly states the interpretation of the concept. Think of a conceptual definition as a dictionary definition. For instance, the conceptual definition of prior record could be a person's criminal history. We have now narrowed the focus from any type of record to one that involves criminality.

conceptual definition an explicit, working definition of a concept, resembling a dictionary definition.

Operationalization takes this process one step further by creating **operational definitions** that specify how a variable will be measured and thereby detected. The concept can then be understood in the same way by other people. Operationalizing a concept helps us describe exactly how to measure and identify it in the data. Thus, the operationalization of prior record could be the number and type of previous encounters with the criminal justice system. We have now specified what will be used to measure this concept: the number of officially recorded encounters and the specific crimes.

operational definition a definition that specifies the operations or criteria used to identify and empirically measure a concept.

Operational definitions describe, in tangible terms, how a concept is measured in the empirical world—how observations are categorized (criteria) and what operations (indicators) are used to capture the depth and breadth of a concept. This step is arguably the most controversial in the measurement process. Definitions vary at this stage, affecting our ability to compare findings across

empirical indicator an exact indication of how a concept is recognized and measured.

reification the practice of treating a concept as though it has a material existence.

studies. You can't reasonably make a comparison when the results are based on measuring different aspects of a concept. For example, the operational definition of prior record could be the number of previous arrests for criminal behaviour. However, we could just as legitimately measure this concept as the number of previous convictions for an offence. We can't directly compare the results from prior convictions to arrests because someone can be arrested for an offence but not be convicted.

We next go from a concept to a variable and specify **empirical indicators** such as the number of prior arrests. Virtually every concept has more than one meaning; therefore, researchers use multiple indicators to better ensure capturing the range of meaning. A cluster of related indicators is known as a dimension. Think of a dimension in terms of intelligence. The indicators of IQ scores and a person's GPA measure the dimension of academic intelligence. The number of times a person is not convicted for an offence and the amount of illicit money earned represent the dimension of street intelligence.

Quantitative research, by its very nature, requires operational indicators and criteria. However, the conceptualization and operationalization process is vital for qualitative research. The difference is that the inductive process relies on nominal, conceptual definitions, which employ domains (theoretical dimensions of a concept) to create general conceptual categories. The research is about acquiring perspectives on a concept. In other words, it concerns how we learn to define the world around us and our attitudes toward it.

Conceptualization and operationalization create a research road map and ensure that others understand what you mean by a concept. But they do not instill conceptual and operational definitions with meaning. The **reification** of a concept takes an abstract idea and makes it the equivalent of a concrete thing. Stated differently, the concept is assumed to be real and treated as such but can't be confirmed or denied by the data. We reify things all the time in everyday life. We treat

Research Highlights

The Tricky Business of Measurement

Depending on your topic and research problem, the measurement process can become a minefield. To further contextualize the differences between conceptualization, conceptual definitions, operationalization, operational definitions, and indicators, let's look at a few research examples. In their own way, these studies raise questions as well.

Female Violent Offenders

Kruttschnitt and Carbone-Lopez (2006) examined female offenders' narratives of their violent offending. The research question was "whether the existing portrayals of women's violence do justice to the range of circumstances and reasons for women's violent encounters" (p. 329). The conceptual definition of female violence included the domains of media accounts, the courts, and scholarly research, which reproduce stereotypes of female violent offenders. The researchers found that the media characterize female violence as inherently evil, the courts represent it as black and white, and scholarly research demarcates it into public and private spheres. Meanwhile, the first-person narratives suggest disrespect, jealousy, self-defence, and self-help as common reasons for the women's behaviour. These qualitative findings create the operational definition that shows us the dimensions of the concept of violence as it pertains to motivation.

Perceptions of Risk and Fear of Violence

Recall the O'Bierne, Denney, and Gabe (2004) study exploring probation officers' fear of occupational violence. The authors argued that researchers are acutely aware of the difficulty associated with finding the best operational definition of fear of violence. The conceptual definition was complex, which led to problems with developing good indicators on the nature of fear. Even though qualitative studies can uncover what fear means to people and the factors that lead to their definitions, it can't shed light on the extent or pervasiveness of fear. Doing so requires quantitative data. Once again, we are left with the quandary of an operational definition.

Active Offenders

Jacques and Wright (2011) focused on the nature and extent of victimization of active offenders who participate in research. Their purpose was to develop a theory of violent victimization in active offender research and to specify definitions, measures, and distinctions from unrelated violence. The intent was to develop and test theories that would reduce the likelihood of victimization so as not to impede scientific progress in this unique area of research.

Let's take the abstract concept of violence. The conceptual definition incorporates "causing damage or destruction." Jacques and Wright's (2011, p. 505) operational definition is the "use of physical force against people or property, including threats and attempts." Possible indicators include the number of murder threats, shots fired, and punches thrown.

The concept of active offender research may seem relatively simple on the surface, but it is deceptive. The conceptualization is the process of "obtaining information about criminals through conversation with, or observation of, unincarcerated persons involved in crime" (Jacques & Wright, 2011, p. 505). The conceptual definition clarifies this process by saying that

Continued

active offender research entails the processes of recruitment, remuneration, and data collection. Using recruitment as an example, the operationalization is interacting with criminals and
convincing them to provide data. The operational definition is "the amount of social interaction spent convincing criminals to participate in the study." The hypothesis being tested is
that, the more times an offender is asked to participate, the greater the recruitment. Thus, the
indicator is the number of times the request to participate is made.

Mother Nature as if she is real, yet her existence can't be confirmed or denied by any data. Not everyone will conceptualize and operationalize a concept in the same way. To some extent, measurement is a creative process and inherently subjective. However, building on the work of others can help support your measurement decisions.

attribute a representation of a variable's categories or numerical values.

The measurement process is an integral component of conducting research. Decisions made at this stage affect all subsequent sampling, data collection, and analytical conclusions. Much like social control constitutes "all the processes by which people define and respond to deviant behavior," so too does measurement (Black, 1984, p. 34). How we define our topics and concepts affects how we design our research study and respond to and analyze our data.

dependent variable the effect or outcome of one or more causes whereby their values are altered by a change in an independent variable.

independent variable the cause that changes, influences, or predicts the values of a dependent variable.

Variables

Variables can be observed and measured at different levels, amounts, and strengths. This is why they are part of the operational definition. Hypotheses incorporate variables and are developed on the basis of the research question. Why? Because we want to find empirical support that will provide a causal explanation for the anticipated relationship between concepts.

Variables give concepts measurable characteristics. Recall that variables operationalize concepts and change in value. All variables have **attributes,** which represent the different levels or categories. For instance, the variable sex has the attributes of male and female. The key point to remember is that most variables are not simply present or absent but vary in degrees.

Dependent and Independent Variables

Two fundamental types of variables are dependent and independent. A **dependent variable**—symbolized by the letter Y—represents our concept of interest or what we are trying to explain. The **independent variable** is known as the effect, predictor, or criterion variable and is symbolized by the letter X. Variation in an independent variable causes a change in the dependent variable. In other words, a dependent variable is the behaviour, attitude, or condition that changes in response to variation in an independent variable. For example, suppose that you are tired but you can't figure out why. You operationalize tired as the number of hours you need to sleep, which represents your dependent variable. A possible independent variable, or cause, is the amount of sleep the previous night.

A dependent variable in one study could just as easily be an independent variable in another. It simply depends on the concept that the research is trying to explain or understand. You might want to understand the factors that affect fear. Here, the dependent variable would be some measure of fear. You could also conduct research on fear's impact on behaviour. Now a measure of fear becomes your independent variable. Remember, whether fear is a dependent or independent variable, it must be operationally defined.

Control Variables

The other major type of variable is a **control variable**, one that does not vary but is held constant. They are symbolized by the letter X to distinguish them from the dependent variable.

Control variables can affect both the independent and dependent variables but are not what the study is trying to understand. If you are measuring various factors that affect the likelihood of becoming pregnant, a good control variable would be sex. In fact, much research in criminology and criminal justice uses sex as a control variable to see if there are any differences between offending by men and offending by women. Sex could be a control variable in our previous example; men and women might not need the same amount of sleep (see Figure 3.2).

Where: X_1 = Bedtime (Time a person goes to bed)
              Independent variable
          X_2 = Sex (male, female)
              Control variable
          Y = Sleep (Time a person needs to sleep)
              Dependent variable
Relationship:

Figure 3.2 The relationship between variables to investigate fatigue

Hypotheses

Hypotheses were introduced in Chapter 1 as untested statements, or propositions, that specify the relationship between two theoretical concepts in the form of variables. Furthermore, they are empirically testable predictions about experiential reality. According to Kraska and Neuman (2012), hypotheses

- can be logically linked back to the research question,
- are written as a prediction of a future outcome,
- contain at least two variables,
- clearly express a cause–effect relationship, and
- are falsifiable (i.e. can be shown to be true or false).

Hypotheses typically contain words or phrases such as *causes, leads to, influences, associated with, produces, results in, is higher or lower,* or *affects the likelihood of.* One can also write a hypothesis using an if–then statement. Whatever the wording, hypotheses make a causal statement.

The **alternative hypothesis (H_A)** is the anticipated outcome or relationship expected between two variables. The more important type is the **null hypothesis (H_0)**, which is the exact opposite of the relationship suggested by theory and past research. This hypothesis states that there is either no relationship or one that is inconsistent with the prediction in the alternative hypothesis.

The alternative and null hypotheses provide the researcher with a restatement of the research question in a testable format. When properly worded, these hypotheses state the expected and unexpected relationship between two variables that guide the collection, analysis, and interpretation of data. Both types of hypotheses make a relational statement that is verifiable and falsifiable, but we actually test the null and hope to reject it.

The alternative hypothesis can be directional or non-directional. As illustrated in Figure 3.3, a directional hypothesis specifies the anticipated direction of variation in the independent variable

control variable a variable that does not vary but can affect independent and dependent variables.

alternative hypothesis an empirically testable statement that specifies the relationship expected between two variables.

null hypothesis an empirical and falsifiable statement that specifies no difference between two variables that are expected to vary in a predictable way.

Research question

Does the severity of a substance abuse problem influence the likelihood of future criminality?

Independent variable:	Substance abuse
Operational definition of X:	The number of times a week a drug is consumed
Dependent variable:	Committing a crime
Operational definition of Y:	The number of arrests for a criminal offence
Where indicates a change:	$\Delta X \rightarrow \Delta Y$

Directional

H_1: If the severity of substance abuse increases, the likelihood of committing a crime increases.

Positive relationship: $\uparrow X \rightarrow \uparrow Y$

H_0: An increase in the severity of a substance abuse problem does not increase the likelihood of committing a crime.

H_1: If the severity of substance abuse decreases, the likelihood of more serious crimes increases.

Negative relationship: $\downarrow X \rightarrow \uparrow Y$

H_0: A decrease in the severity of a substance abuse problem does not increase the likelihood of committing more serious crimes.

Note: The negative relationship between X and Y can be in the opposite direction.

Negative relationship: $\uparrow X \rightarrow \downarrow Y$

Non-directional

H_1: The extent of a substance abuse problem is associated with the likelihood of committing a crime.

Non-directional: $\Delta X \rightarrow \Delta Y$

H_0: The extent of a substance abuse problem does not affect the likelihood of committing a crime.

Poorly written hypotheses

H_1: With a large increase in the severity of a substance abuse problem, a person is more likely to commit a crime.

H_0: There is no relationship between a substance abuse problem and the likelihood of committing a crime.

Problem with the null hypothesis: If there is a small increase in the severity of the substance abuse problem associated with an increase in the number of arrests, you can neither reject nor accept the null hypothesis.

Figure 3.3 Developing hypotheses: Substance abuse and crime

and the resulting change in the dependent variable. If we were researching the effects of a substance abuse treatment program, a directional hypothesis would state that increased participation in the program increases the likelihood of abstinence from drugs.

A directional hypothesis can posit a positive or negative relationship. A positive relationship occurs when the independent and dependent variables vary in the same direction—an increase in the length of treatment time increases the likelihood of abstinence. A decrease in wait times for program admission decreases the program drop-out rate. In a negative relationship, the independent and dependent variables vary in opposite directions. For example, an increase in the program's length decreases the likelihood for rearrest. As you can see, the expected relationship is that an increase in the independent variable causes a decrease in the value of the dependent variable. Stating the direction of the effect may not always be possible. A non-directional hypothesis simply states that a relationship exists between two variables, but the direction in which they co-vary is not specified because it's unclear in theory or past research.

There are two key points to remember about hypotheses. First, be specific and careful in the wording of the null hypothesis to avoid a situation in which neither the H_0 nor the H_A are supported or rejected by the data. If the H_0 states that there is no difference in how two groups respond to treatment but it turns out that there is a change in one group, neither hypothesis can be rejected nor accepted. Second, the null hypothesis cannot be proven true or false. You can only reject or fail to reject the null hypothesis based on the data. If you were to collect new data, you wouldn't be able to eliminate the possibility that the results will reject the null hypothesis again.

The Language of Causality

Explanatory research wants to find a causal explanation for why something happens and under what conditions. A simple causal explanation identifies an earlier event or condition (cause) that leads to a particular event, occurrence, or behaviour (effect). In most crime and justice research, the findings infer a multiple causal explanation in which an event or combination of events results in the same effect.

Criteria for a Causal Explanation

In order for an explanation to be causal, it must meet three criteria: empirical association, temporal order, and non-spuriousness. The conditions of mechanism and context also help to specify the causal relationship.

Empirical Association

The first step to establishing causality is an empirical association between two variables. In essence, an association means that two events, conditions, or behaviours interact in a patterned way. For instance, the amount of time you spend studying isn't necessarily the cause of your high grades; having a good professor could explain this relationship. In an empirical association between substance abuse and criminal behaviour, the hypothesis could state: As the severity of a person's substance abuse problem increases, the more likely he or she is to commit a crime.

Temporal Order

The second criterion of causality is temporal order. The problem is that we may not know which event, condition, or behaviour comes first. Does drug use cause people to commit crime, does crime cause drug use, or do they occur together? Considerable research in criminology is dedicated to unravelling criminal behaviour in terms of the order of variables. For instance, with an independent variable of homelessness and a dependent variable of mental illness, can you rule out that mental illness comes before homelessness? Having a mental illness could increase someone's chances of losing his or her job, which increases his or her likelihood of becoming homeless. By establishing temporal order, you eliminate potential causes that occur after the effect.

Suppose that the individual in our substance abuse and criminal behaviour example began using drugs at 14 years of age and committing crime at 17. We can establish temporal order because the cause (drug use) started at an earlier age than the effect (criminality). Yet confirming an empirical association and establishing temporal order are still not enough to infer that a causal relationship exists between substance abuse and future criminality.

Non-Spuriousness

In addition to establishing an empirical association and temporal order, we need to ensure that the relationship is not caused by an alternative, unrecognized cause. The condition of **spuriousness** refers to a relationship in which the variation in the independent and dependent variables is caused by a third variable. Suppose you want to identify the cause of acting drunk (although absurd, this example demonstrates spuriousness well). On one occasion, you drink beer and water. The second time, it's wine and water. On the third, you switch to martinis and water. On all three occasions, the effect was drunken behaviour. Water was consumed every time, but the other liquids were different. Consequently, you conclude that drinking water causes drunken behaviour. You have an empirical association between water and drunken behaviour. You have established temporal order as the water was consumed prior to the drunken behaviour. Yet you haven't established non-spuriousness.

In fact, the empirical association between water and drunken behaviour is false—the alternative unmeasured variable of alcohol causes the drunken behaviour. Alcohol is a **confounding variable** that represents an alternative explanation for the cause–effect relationship.

spuriousness the situation of a possible causal relationship being caused by a third, alternative, and unmeasured variable.

confounding variable a variable representing an unmeasured factor that, when it causes a change in the independent and dependent variables, creates a spurious relationship.

intervening variable a variable that explains a causal relation between others by accounting for how an independent variable affects the dependent variable.

Mechanism

Specification is not mandatory for causality; however, when we identify the causal mechanism, we identify how the connection between two variables is created (Cook & Campbell, 1979). A causal mechanism states how the relationship works by articulating the connection between the cause and the hypothesized effect. In other words, it shows the reason that the relationship between substance abuse and future criminality is causal. In our example, the mechanism could be the motivation for breaking the law.

Our example includes an **intervening variable**, symbolized by the letter Z. This type of variable is caused by the independent variable and qualifies the causal explanation by showing why the association between the independent and dependent variables occurs in the way it does. Intervening variables don't have to cause a change in the dependent variable but can affect the nature and degree of variation in the independent variable. The need for money to purchase drugs influences the relationship between two variables; therefore, we call it an intervening, or moderating, variable.

At this stage, there is an unwritten assumption that causal explanations need to make intuitive sense or fit within a theoretical framework. Seeking to identify the causal mechanism will help to ensure that the causal explanation makes sense.

Let's review our example so far:

- Empirical association: A patterned relationship exists between substance abuse and criminal behaviour.
- Hypothesis: As the severity of a person's substance abuse problem increases, the more likely he or she is to commit a crime.
- Temporal order: The individual began using drugs at 14 years of age and first committed an offence at 17.
- Non-spuriousness: We assume that the possible alternative explanations are taken into account.
- Causal mechanism: The individual needs money to purchase drugs.

Context

Nothing in life happens in a vacuum, which is why researchers strive to identify a causal relationship's context—the set of circumstances about the event, situation, or behaviour. We can't reasonably argue that only one independent variable is responsible for all the variation in the dependent variable. No cause has an effect divorced from the larger context or other contributing factors. In practice, identifying context entails specifying a set of interrelated variables, temporal or spatial effects, and characteristics of individuals or groups. An example of this contextual effect is the difference between the decision-making factors for police and those for probation officers. These two groups work and interact with offenders in different contexts.

Returning to our example, a number of other factors could explain why drug users use crime to support their habit. The type of drug consumed (alcohol versus methamphetamines), the type of access to drugs (friends versus strangers), the length of time the person has used drugs, or the availability or completion of a drug treatment program are all possibilities. There could be differences based on a particular drug's addictive properties, parental drug use, parental criminality, or situational stress. Specifying the context is an important step as it can help to detect a spurious relationship. That said, in all research we can confidently say only that a prior event or circumstance influences, predisposes, or increases the likelihood of a future event, occurrence, or behaviour (see Figure 3.4). Although causality is implied in theoretical explanations whenever we see terms such as *determine, influence, produce, generate,* or *effect,* we have to be vigilant in qualitative research as well (DiCristina, 1995).

Causality in Qualitative Research

Despite initial assumptions, qualitative research is equally able to ascertain and test causal relationships (Miles & Huberman, 1994; Seawright, 2002; Seawright & Gerring, 2008). Idiographic explanations include the conditions related to a series of events that result in a particular outcome or causal effect. Careful attention is paid to temporal order and causal mechanisms. These explanations are viewed as more holistic than nomothetic ones, which are probabilistic and inherently incomplete.

A causal explanation doesn't have to be true for all cases. In real life, there are always exceptions. It becomes a question of what is more or less likely and whether qualitative research can add insight to causal inferences made using other methods. Qualitative research is concerned with understanding an outcome's context as part of a larger set of interrelated factors or circumstances. In other words, it focuses on how a series of events in a certain set of conditions leads to a particular outcome.

The perceptions of individuals within a field setting are important contextual factors in a causal explanation. As Maxwell (2004a, p.7) argues, "meanings, beliefs, and volitional actions constitute processes that can't be converted to variables, even 'intervening variables,' without fundamentally concealing and misrepresenting the nature of the process." It's not simply about uncovering general patterns but understanding particular situations, events, and behaviour contextualized within the beliefs of the individuals observed.

According to Maxwell (2004b), qualitative researchers approach causal explanations in several ways. To account for variation, researchers make comparisons within and across groups. To ascertain the process, context, and mechanism, intensive long-term engagement in the field and detailed data collection provide evidence for causal statements. Finally, to assess alternative explanations and eliminate rival explanations, look for the counterfactual, perform triangulation, and check interpretations with participants.

Controlled comparisons across different time periods or within a setting confront the criticism that qualitative research is inappropriate

Empirical association

Hypothesis: If drug use (X) increases, the likelihood of committing a
                               crime (Y) increases.

Empirical association: $\Delta\,X \leftrightarrow \Delta\,Y$

Established: A Δ X or Y is associated with a Δ in the other variable.

Temporal order

Temporal order: Δ X occurs before a Δ Y

Established   Age of onset for drug use occurs before committing crime. The
                               average age of starting drug use is 14, and the arrest for the first
                               crime occurs (on average) at the age of 16.

Spuriousness

Spurious relationship:

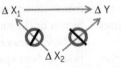

Rejected: The type of drug (X_2) does not affect when drug use (X_1) or
                               criminal behaviour (Y) occurs.

Mechanism

Mechanism:

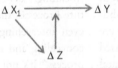

Established: The need for money to buy drugs (Z) explains how drug use
                               causes a person to commit crime (motivation for offending).

Context

Context:

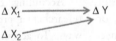

Established: Engagement in drug use (X_1) and length of time addicted (X_2)
                               cause variation in the likelihood of committing a crime (Y).

Figure 3.4 Establishing a causal explanation: Drug use and crime

> **counterfactual** a conceptualization of alternate conditions, factors, or outcomes.

for causal inferences. Qualitative research examines processes, conditions, and behaviours from the perspective of those being studied. The data is ideal for capturing variance and identifying confounding factors. In this way, it complements quantitative research.

The **counterfactual** compares the observed and unobserved to target what causes the effect. Researchers ask themselves how actors anticipate different outcomes. Alternatively, the task is to identify what would happen under different circumstances. Thus, the counterfactual is a conceptualization of alternate conditions, factors, or outcomes. The process involves four generic steps:

1. Identify the outcome of interest.
2. Identify negative cases that don't result in the anticipated outcome.
3. Identify the various causal conditions connected to the outcome.
4. Interpret the combination of conditions. How well does it compare to the cases or individuals studied?

To eliminate alternative explanations, qualitative researchers look for evidence on how processes generate the anticipated outcome. The primary activities are looking for contradictory evidence and conditional exceptions and determining whether they offer a more plausible explanation for the effect. Triangulation can have a variety of meanings, but you collect data from a variety of different people or settings with multiple data collection methods. For instance, you can observe life as it occurs and conduct interviews with key informants. This approach reduces the likelihood of systematic bias from a singular source or method (Maxwell, 2004b). Finally, alternative explanations can be eliminated by checking your interpretations with the research participants. Doing so can be illuminating, as they may provide alternative explanations that the data didn't suggest.

Errors in Causal Reasoning

Causal reasoning is inferred and not directly observable. Additionally, our common sense understandings only go so far. Can we really demonstrate that the groundhog seeing his shadow will result in another six weeks of winter?

Researchers can make one of four causal reasoning errors. When they argue that a causal explanation is due to some force or common sense, they commit the fallacy of **teleology**. Either the cause does not definitively precede the effect or it cannot be measured empirically. In the first case, the post hoc fallacy assumes that a prior event is sufficient evidence to cause a later one, which creates a question of temporal order. The possibility of reverse causation is ignored. The second case is an appeal to anecdotal evidence. To say that stealing is part of human nature is teleological reasoning because human nature is not measurable.

A **tautology** is circular reasoning. With this error, the statement is logically true, but the cause is impossible to verify or falsify because it's indistinguishable from the effect. Put another way, the cause is the effect by definition or description, as the statement is logically true. Further, there is no association between the antecedent (cause) and the consequent (effect). By using different words to say the same thing, the claim becomes redundant. Two examples are "Survival of the fittest is fitness" and "The cause of crime is breaking the law." In both cases, the causal logic is circular and true by definition.

The fallacy of **reductionism** occurs when causal explanations at the individual level are overgeneralized to explain larger societal-level processes. Individual-level data cannot describe group-level processes. Reductionism takes a complex phenomenon such as why some areas of the city have a high crime rate and explain it by analyzing the behaviour and characteristics of individuals.

The **ecological fallacy** is the inverse of reductionism. In this case, macro-, societal-, and community-level trends are attributed to micro-level relationships. The conclusion

teleology a type of faulty causal reasoning that cannot be empirically tested or falsified.

tautology circular reasoning; employed when the causal statement is true by definition.

reductionism overgeneralization of individual-level data to make statements about societal-level processes.

ecological fallacy overgeneralization of group-level data to describe individual-level processes, behaviour, or attitudes.

isn't necessarily wrong, but the data from groups can't support causal relationships for individuals. Let's say your research project seeks to understand the factors that affect arrest rates for violent crime. This study is at the community level. Suppose you find that crime rates are higher in urban areas. If you were to conclude that people who live in urban areas are more likely than people in rural areas to commit violent crimes, you would commit the ecological fallacy.

Necessary and Sufficient Cause

Babbie (2013) raises important issues about causal interpretations: necessary cause and sufficient cause. A necessary cause is an independent variable that must be present for the dependent variable to change. For instance, being gainfully employed is a necessary cause to receiving a paycheque. Babbie's example is that you need to take specific courses to fulfill your degree plan requirements. To get credit for the course, you have to pass it.

A sufficient cause is a condition that ensures the effect. This doesn't mean that the independent variable causes the variation observed in the dependent variable. For example, skipping work one day is sufficient cause but not necessary to reducing your paycheque as you probably have a number of sick days. Returning to Babbie's example, missing a mid-term is sufficient cause to fail the course, but it is not necessary. You can fail the course in other ways, such as by not demonstrating sufficient mastery of the material.

The ideal, which virtually never happens, is an explanation that is both necessary and sufficient. In nomothetic explanations, it is rare to find a single independent variable that explains virtually all the variation in the dependent variable. The same problem arises with ideographic research. You can have a thorough explanation of a causal relationship, but the outcome could change when studying different people on the same subject. Thus, you have demonstrated sufficient, but not necessary, cause.

Quality of Measurement

For a reliable measure, the indicator derives the same score each time it is administered. You minimize **random measurement error** by testing for reliability. This error occurs when unpredictable external factors cause inconsistent scores. For example, a person's mood could affect how he or she responds to a survey, but not all respondents are in the same mood or are affected in this way.

Similarly, you can never know how close the empirical indicators match the conceptual definition. You can, though, minimize **systematic measurement error** by testing for validity. Systematic measurement error creates bias and erroneous findings because the indicators do not properly measure the breadth or depth of the concept. Alternatively, there is an external factor, such as the room being too cold, that affects everyone answering the question. The point is that the measurement of the concept is biased in the same way for all participants. Developing reliable and valid measures is critical for making strong causal inferences and drawing meaningful conclusions.

However, creating operational definitions and measures is far from easy or consistent in the literature. According to Farrington (2010a), establishing the measurement reliability and validity, and thereby reducing the chances for random and systematic error, is a common problem. In reality, researchers can't agree on the best way to measure factors such as parental supervision or discipline. Even with multiple indicators, the data are possibly biased from self-reports of parents and youth.

random measurement error an error that is always present to some degree, is unpredictable, affects reliability, and varies from one measurement to the next.

systematic measurement error an error that affects the validity of the measure, represents an inaccuracy in the instrument, and impacts the results in a predictable way.

Quantitative Research

Reliability

Unreliable indicators can be interpreted in more than one way; hence, they do not portray a consistent frame of reference for the concept. **Reliability** refers to measurements producing the same score each time the instrument is administered. As with other aspects of nomothetic and ideographic research, the tests or criteria for reliability differ. Yet, for both, we look for consistent results each time we measure the concept. Researchers look at a measure's reliability from the perspectives of stability, equivalence, and internal consistency. For each of these perspectives, there are techniques used to test a measure.

Determining the stability of a measure refers to acquiring similar scores with repeated testing of the same research subjects. As mentioned, reliability can be reduced by factors that affect how a person responds to the measurement instrument. A reliable measure is not sensitive to factors such as time of day and has little variation in the results. A test–retest method measures stability across time by comparing scores from repeated testing on two different occasions. The higher the level of agreement between a person's responses to the instrument, the more stable the measure. There should be little variation regardless of the length of time between administrations.

Equivalence of a measure, or parallel-forms reliability, represents the amount of agreement between two instruments. The cross-test compares the degree of association between the scores from two different operational measures of the same concept. The greater the similarity, the more reliable the instrument.

Internal consistency, or homogeneity, is the extent that an instrument's items measure the same thing. This type of reliability evaluates individual questions in relation to one another. The split-half test divides an instrument into two parts that are administered to the same people and compares the responses to find the degree of association. The split-half is frequently used when it's impractical or unfeasible to create two instruments and when you want to ensure that all the indicators measure the same theoretical construct.

Sometimes more than one person codes the data. In these cases, equivalence is assessed by calculating the interrater reliability score. This approach measures the consistency of researchers' judgments on classifying cases, assessing meaning, or assigning scores. Evaluating reliability across different people is calculated with the following formula: (# of agreements/# of opportunities to agree) × 100. The score ranges from 0 to 1, where 1 is perfect agreement and 0.8 is the goal.

> **reliability** the extent to which repeated testing of a concept produces the same result.

To summarize, the test–retest method administers one instrument to the same people at two different times. The cross-test administers two different instruments at the same time to the same people. The split-half test gives different questions from one instrument to the same people. The interrater test involves the same instrument coded by different people. To improve reliability, follow these four steps: develop a clear conceptual definition; use more than one indicator to measure a concept; consider using a measurement that is as precise as possible, such as continuous variables; and pilot test your measurement instrument to better ensure that you get the same results every time.

Validity

Determining whether a measure has validity means ascertaining if it measures what it intends to and how much truth there is to the results. Validity comes down to how well a construct is operationalized. Thus, we can define the term as the extent of "congruence of the researcher's claims to the reality his or her claims seek to represent" (Garaway, 1997, p. 2).

face validity a validity test in which a person's judgment validates a measure based on its appearance and appropriateness.

content validity a validity test in which a knowledgeable person's judgment validates a measure by concluding that it covers the range of the concept.

criterion validity a validity test that compares a measurement's scores to an external, established instrument or criterion.

concurrent validity a validity test that determines the extent to which the scores from one measure correspond to those of an existing measure.

predictive validity a validity test that examines the degree to which a measurement instrument can predict a future behaviour or event.

construct validity a validity test that finds the extent to which scores on multiple indicators are related to one another as predicted by theory.

convergent validity a validity test that assesses whether two measures associate in a manner consistent with theoretical predictions.

discriminant validity a validity test that determines whether two concepts differ from one another as predicted by theory.

Face validity is the least precise but often the first measurement test that researchers use. This test involves a knowledgeable person reviewing the instrument and concluding whether it adequately measures the concept. Unfortunately, judgment depends on the assessor's expertise. Face validity is never sufficient by itself, as validation is based on common-sense rules. When using a person's GPA to measure intelligence, it isn't difficult to conclude that the measure has face validity; common sense tells us that high grades reflect smartness.

Content validity is the degree that an instrument measures all facets of a concept. A knowledgeable person reviews the measure for readability, clarity, and comprehensiveness. Content validity can ensure that the concept's important aspects aren't omitted and that irrelevant indicators don't contaminate the instrument. Using GPA, attendance, and memory as indicators of intelligence creates two possible problems. First, attendance is irrelevant to the concept of intelligence and hence contaminates the measure. Second, aspects of intelligence such as degree completion are absent. As with face validity, content validity is insufficient as the only test of congruence with real life.

Criterion validity compares scores on a specific conceptual domain to an external, established criterion. The objective is to determine how well your measure corresponds with external empirical evidence or predicts the external criterion. There are two types of criterion validity. **Concurrent validity** compares scores from the current instrument to an external measure to predict the current status. The closer the scores are to each other, the higher the validity of your measure. For example, if you are measuring intelligence with GPA, an external measure could be IQ scores. When measuring the success of a program geared at helping at-risk youth graduate high school, scores are compared to the criterion of a standardized test administered to all students. A measure with **predictive validity** predicts a future level using the current instrument. Examples include a measure of political preference and public opinion polls predicting votes in an election.

An instrument with **construct validity** measures the intended theoretical construct using multiple indicators. This validity test is well-suited to deductive hypothesis testing. Without construct validity, it's garbage in, garbage out. As a measure of intelligence, the size of a person's skull has low construct validity.

There are two subtypes of construct validity. **Convergent validity** occurs when two measures associate with one another in the anticipated way. For example, you have high convergent validity for education when the number of years in school, grades, and courses completed are all connected to one another. In contrast, **discriminant validity** tests whether measures of two constructs differ as expected theoretically. That is, it establishes that two measures that should not be related are in fact unrelated. An example is the concept of self-esteem. You have convergent validity with confidence and self-worth, which are related to one another and to self-esteem. You have discriminant validity when self-esteem and intelligence are unrelated, as would be expected.

Methods in Action

Is It Science? The Reliability and Validity of Crime Lab Evidence

A report by the Committee on Identifying the Needs of the Forensic Sciences Community argues that fingerprint, bite mark, ballistic, and other types of forensic evidence presented in court have "little or no basis in science" (Felch & Dolan, 2009). The report finds insufficient evidence to suggest that forensic methods reliably connect the crime scene to specific people. Further, the validity of conclusions is questionable: "The simple reality is that the interpretation of forensic evidence is not always based on scientific studies to determine its validity" (Committee on Identifying, 2009, p. 8).

Following the release of the report, a US Court of Appeals judge stated that, if we claim that something is a science, we should be able to test its methods and measurement (Felch & Dolan, 2009). For example, the claim that there is a zero rate of error for fingerprint matches isn't scientifically possible. The report includes an analysis of a thousand fingerprint matches in which two were false positives (i.e. they did not match the suspect's prints). A potential for bias also exists as many crime labs are not independent from the investigatory process but are run by law enforcement agencies. This relationship can lead to expedient rather than valid interpretations.

As this example illustrates, ensuring that measurements are reliable and valid is of critical importance. In criminal justice, the consequences of using measurements that do not meet these criteria have profound effects for legal system actors and suspects alike. The admissibility of fingerprint and other forensic evidence often plays a significant role in the likelihood of a conviction. The quality of measurement can mean the difference between protecting society and convicting the innocent.

Qualitative Research

Qualitative reliability is similar to the quantitative type but uses paradigm-specific criteria to assess rigour. Researchers disagree about whether the quantitative criteria of reliability has any meaning for assessing the accuracy of qualitative measurements and findings; therefore, reliability should be judged by its own paradigmatic terms (Golafshani, 2003; Lincoln & Guba, 1985; Morse et al., 2002; Shenton, 2004). Rigour becomes a question of the stability of a researcher's data and findings over time. Lincoln and Guba (1985) outline four alternative criteria that better reflect the underlying assumptions in qualitative research. Dependability is the equivalent of reliability. Credibility, transferability, and confirmability are the qualitative equivalents of assessing validity.

Dependability

Many qualitative researchers dispense with the quantitative concept of reliability in favour of **dependability**, which involves documenting and tracing the development of the findings so that they are consistent and repeatable. Replicability means repeating the same study at a different time, with different people, and with the same methods. This process is achieved by employing an audit trail, which records in detail the data collection and analysis procedures. An audit trail is an inquiry that documents the research process and inductive measurement logic so that they're traceable by others. In this way, another researcher can repeat the work and use the research design as a prototype model (Shenton, 2004).

Interrater reliability can be assessed by having two people code the same set of observations to ensure that the interpretation is dependable. Similarly, intra-coder reliability involves one

> **dependability** the consistency of qualitative findings, along with the ability to replicate them, trace their methods, and develop their findings.

researcher coding the same segment of data at two different time periods to ensure similar assessments of meaning. Ultimately, the objective of dependability tests is to examine the process and research product for consistency and rigour.

Trustworthiness

With **credibility**, the objective is to establish that the results are believable. Qualitative research strives to describe or understand the phenomena of interest from the participant's eyes. The participants are the only ones who can legitimately judge credibility. Thus, they act as their own point of reference. The question is whether the evidence is a good fit between the research subjects' views and the researcher's interpretation or reconstruction of events. Credibility can be assessed in several ways:

credibility the trustworthiness of interpretations based on the research subjects' perspective.

transferability an assessment of trustworthiness that determines the degree to which research findings can be generalized or transferred to other settings, situations, and people.

confirmability an assessment of trustworthiness referring to the degree that research findings can be confirmed or corroborated by others.

reflexivity a process in which a researcher considers his or her role and how it influences or is influenced by the data and research participants.

- prolonged engagement in the field, which opens the researcher up to contextual factors that affect the problem or issue
- persistent observation, which brings depth of knowledge
- triangulation, which enhances credibility when the results are similar from different sources or methods
- a member check, which involves conferring with research subjects to see if the interpretations make sense and are valid from the participants' perspective
- a peer debriefing, which can uncover any biases that have impacted data collection and analysis
- a deviant case analysis, which involves determining whether the explanation fits most cases (The data are probed for instances or patterns that do not fit the emerging hypothesis.)
- referential adequacy, which involves archiving a portion of the data and analyzing it after the remaining data (Credibility is established when the results are similar.)

Transferability exists when the results can be generalized or transferred to other contexts or settings. The researcher enhances transferability by describing the research context and related assumptions. This assessment requires enough information about the events and individuals to establish how similar the particular case is to other settings, situations, and people. The person who wants to transfer the results is responsible for judging the sensibility of the generalization. Although there is disagreement as to the extent of description to be provided, researchers agree that a full accounting of the setting and any contextual factors is needed (Shenton, 2004).

Qualitative research assumes that each researcher brings a unique perspective to the study. **Confirmability** is the degree to which results can be confirmed or corroborated by others. In other words, we need to provide enough evidence of objectivity so that the reader can determine that the results are not fabricated or caused by researcher biases, preferences, or characteristics. One technique is **reflexivity**, a researcher's examination of his or her decisions and role in the construction of knowledge.

Confirmability can be enhanced in three additional ways. First, the researcher documents the procedures for revisiting the data throughout the research process. Another researcher then takes the role of devil's advocate and records this verification process. Second, the researcher actively seeks and describes disconfirming evidence that contradicts prior observations. Finally, after the study is complete, an audit trail judges possible bias or distortion. All these steps involve a careful recording of the links among assertions, findings, and interpretations.

The Connection between Reliability and Validity

The ability to address your research question depends on measurement quality. A measure must be reliable for it to be valid, although reliability is not the sole requirement. However, a measure can be reliable and not valid. Suppose your bathroom scale consistently measures you two pounds heavier than you really are. It's reliable because it always measures an excess of two pounds, but the weight displayed is inaccurate and, therefore, not valid. Thus, a valid instrument is always reliable, but a reliable measure is not necessarily valid.

Figure 3.5 highlights the relationship between measurement reliability and validity. In Figure A, the shots are reliable because they are all clustered together, but they have low validity because none are in the bull's eye and a portion are not even on the target. In Figure B, the shots have higher validity as all of them made it onto the target, but they are far from reliable as they are not clustered together. The shots in Figure C are clustered together, establishing high reliability, and they are inside the bull's eye, representing high validity. Practically, reliability is much easier to establish than validity, but for causal inferences and meaningful conclusions you need to get as close as possible to the bull's eye.

More Logistics for Quantitative Measurement

Quantitative research seeks to understand a larger, objective reality by measuring its components, which are removed from the larger contextual setting. The inherent problem here is the difficulty in adequately defining concepts or accurately measuring the event or behaviour's pertinent variables. Numbers play a role in our everyday lives, but we don't always need them to perform mathematical operations. Sometimes, all we need is for them to identify a person, object, and event or to establish a sequence (e.g. serial numbers or numbered assembly instructions).

A	B	C
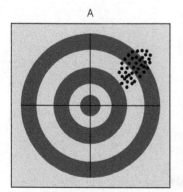	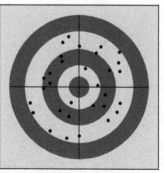	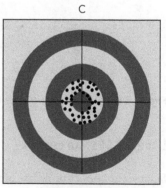
Reliable but not valid	Valid but not reliable	Valid *and* reliable

In Figure A, the shots at the target are reliable because they are all clustered together but have low validity because none are in the bull's eye and a portion are not even on the target. In Figure B, the shots have higher validity as all of them made it onto the target but they are far from reliable as they are not clustered together. In contrast, in Figure C they are clustered together establishing high reliability *and* they are inside the bull's eye representing high validity.

Figure 3.5 Can you hit the measurement bull's eye?

Source: Adapted from Babbie, E. (2013). Figure 5-2: An analogy to validity and reliability (p. 153). *The Practice of Social Research* (13th Ed.). Belmont, CA: Thomson Wadsworth.

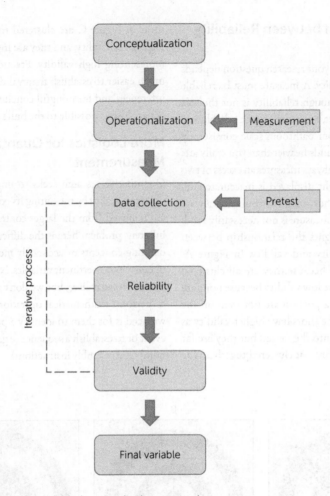

Figure 3.6 Finalizing a variable in quantitative research

Level of Measurement

In some cases, we can do only so much with numbers when examining the nature of a social phenomenon. Rooted in our existing knowledge about a concept as we see it in the real world, the level of measurement describes the mathematical characteristics of variables. Determining the level is a logical deductive process from conceptualization onwards (see Figure 3.6). We clarify the empirical indicators, variable attributes, and determine the level of measurement during operationalization. The variable is tested for reliability and validity through preliminary data analysis. Then the variable is finalized and data collection proceeds.

Variables differ from one another in terms of the type of variation and their existence in the real world. Quantitative variables are categorical or continuous. A **categorical variable** (or **discrete variable**) has a fixed number of unchanging categories or classes to

> **categorical variable (or discrete variable)**
> a variable that can adopt a value of two or more fixed categories.

which you can assign a value. With a **continuous variable**, any score on a range of numbers is possible.

Let's look at a concrete example. Religious affiliation is categorical; you are one religion or another. Affiliation does not vary on a range of values. In contrast, height is a continuous variable; you could, for example, be 154 centimetres tall, but you could just as easily be 176.4 centimetres. Flipping a coin may seem continuous because you can count the number of times you get heads or tails, but it is categorical—it is impossible to get 1.5 heads out of 3 coin tosses.

A **dichotomous variable** is a special type of categorical variable. Dichotomous variables have only two categories in which a score can fall. A pass/fail credit system is an example. Dichotomous variables can occur naturally, as is the case with sex, or represent a continuous variable that has been collapsed into two categories, such as your percentage grade into pass/fail.

Categorical Variables

There are two types of categorical variables: nominal and ordinal. Creating **nominal variables** is a naming process; numbers are assigned to a category strictly for the purpose of distinguishing cases from one another. Thus, the scores are categorical and you can compare only the size of each category. For example, sex is a nominal variable with the attributes of male and female. These cannot be ranked, added, subtracted, multiplied, or divided. Being male or female is not inherently more/less or higher/lower.

With an **ordinal variable**, scores or categories can be ranked. People can be compared by their placement in a category. However, the score represents only a relative position because we don't know the exact distance between each category. For instance, assigning a letter grade allows us to rank academic performance from high (A) to low (F), but we can't determine the exact distance between an A or B. Socio-economic status has the categories of upper, middle, and lower class. We know that the upper class is higher than the lower class but not by how much.

There are three requirements for categorical variables. First, they must be homogeneous (i.e. all cases assigned to a category must have the same characteristics) and be logically comparable. A categorical variable doesn't include apples and oranges. Second, the categories must be mutually exclusive, whereby a case can be classified into only one category. There can be no ambiguity as to which category or classification applies. Finally, a variable must be exhaustive so that every case can be classified into one of the categories. In other words, a category exists for every person, thing, or idea. Researchers often include an "other" category to be exhaustive.

Continuous Variables

There are two types of continuous variables: interval and ratio. **Interval variables** have all the characteristics of an ordinal variable with the addition of a meaningful difference between two scores. The intervals are evenly spaced and interpretable, and mathematical operations of addition and subtraction are possible. The only characteristic that an interval variable does not have is a true zero. For instance, temperature has a range of evenly spaced numbers that are organized in a sequence. The distance between 5 and 15 degrees is the same as that between 20 and 30 degrees, but 0 degrees Celsius does not mean the complete absence of all heat.

continuous variable a variable that adopts any of a range of values, thereby allowing a researcher to find an intermediate value between any two given numerical scores.

dichotomous variable a type of categorical variable that adopts one of only two possible values.

nominal variable a variable that distinguishes categorical names by assigning numbers to them.

ordinal variable a variable in which data are organized in rank order with no numerical difference between categories.

interval variable a variable that organizes data in order and includes a discernable numerical distance between data points.

Ratio variables have all the characteristics of interval variables but contain a true zero. All mathematical operations are possible and meaningful. In social research, most variables that you can count, such as the number of prior arrests, are ratio variables. Weight is a ratio variable because there is such a thing as no weight. You could earn $60,000 a year or you could earn nothing—in which case zero becomes very meaningful! If you get 50 per cent on one test and 100 per cent on another, you can say you did twice as well on the second one.

> **ratio variable** a variable that includes ordered data, an equivalent numerical distance between points, and a true zero.

To summarize, the attributes of nominal variables are simply names. Ordinal variables have a rank order or sequence. Interval variables have all the qualities of an ordinal variable except that the distance between values is meaningful. Finally, ratio variables are like interval variables but also have a true zero.

Choosing Levels of Measurement

There is no such thing as a perfectly measured concept, but there are three rules to bear in mind when choosing the right level of measurement. The first is to create variables with as much precision and accuracy as possible. Precision is based on how well variations can be detected. When you are asked the time, it's less precise to say, for example, "Just past one" than "Nine minutes and 37 seconds past one o'clock in the afternoon." Granted, the highest level of precision isn't always necessary. Accuracy is important because extremely precise measurements may not be valid. For instance, your watch may be running slow.

> **index** the total score of two or more variables; used to create a numerical score measuring a single construct.

The second rule when considering the level of measurement is to determine how you plan to analyze the data. You need to anticipate the type of analysis as certain analytical techniques can be performed using only continuous variables. In general, the type of statistical procedure is determined by three criteria: the number of independent and dependent variables; the number of groups of cases/participants; and the variable's level of measurement.

The third rule is to be aware of the implicit hierarchy in the levels of measurement. Based on the amount of information conveyed about the differences between variable attributes, the range goes from nominal as the weakest variable to ratio as the strongest. You can discern the most variation when analyzing interval/ratio variables. At the lower levels of measurement, the analyses are less sensitive to degrees of change. Thus, the higher the level of measurement, the more precise you can be. Although it is not always possible to have interval/ratio variables, don't fall into the trap of treating a categorical variable as a continuous one. If you are measuring attitudes toward life sentences with an ordinal variable, you can't analyze the data as though there is a meaningful difference between support and strong support.

Composite Measures

Composite measures combine more than one variable to measure a concept that is too complex to be captured by a single indicator. They typically measure an attitude or behaviour and include ordinal variables. Scales and indexes are both composite measures; however, there are key differences based on their purpose and structure.

Index

An **index** is a tally of scores from two or more variables. As a ratio variable that measures the quantity of a social phenomenon and combines categorical variables, an index is ideal when conceptual definitions have considerable variance. Overall, indexes are used to explore the causes or underlying traits of concepts such as alcoholism or psychopathy. Kupchik (2007) used several indexes while examining the correctional experience of youth housed in adult and juvenile facilities. One was the Fairness Index, which contained questions regarding whether the rules were fair and if the staff acknowledged a resident's good behaviour.

The first step in constructing an index is selecting items. Each item should have face validity and

Research Highlights

What Does *Recidivism* Mean?

In conceptual terms, *recidivism*, or *reoffending*, refers to a person committing subsequent offences that bring him or her to the attention of the criminal justice system. Conceptually, it seems straightforward, but this is far from the case for operational definitions. There are errors of commission in the sense that an arrestee may not be convicted for the offence. There are errors of omission; a person could be guilty but not convicted. These problems led Maltz (2001) to argue that rearrest is a better indicator of offender conduct than convictions. However, there is considerable room for error in measuring offending and the predictors for reoffending (Hollin, 2001). Piquero (2009) suggests that researchers should consider using more than one data source when measuring recidivism over a person's criminal career and should recognize the inherent limitations. For instance, official records capture only those offences that come to the attention of the police; self-report surveys underestimate serious offending; and victimization surveys do not cover drugs or victimless crimes well.

Recidivism features several possible empirical indicators. At the nominal level, a dichotomous variable of yes or no for an arrest, conviction, or incarceration can be an indicator. At the ordinal level, it could be classified by the severity of court sanction. The rank order could range from withdrawal of charges to absolute or conditional discharge, probation, and incarceration. You can also use categories for the number of arrests such as none, one to two, and three or more. It is not possible to create an interval variable (there is a true zero), but a ratio variable can be the number of rearrests.

In Tille and Rose's (2007) comparison of first-time and repeat female offenders, the former were those incarcerated for the first time, regardless of how many prior offences without conviction they had. Recidivists were girls who had been incarcerated at least twice. Recidivism was used to compare two groups and was operationalized based on sentences to custody. The researchers found that female recidivists between the ages of 13 to 18 had more emotional and behavioural problems, unstable lifestyles, and less predictable home environments than first-time offenders did.

Using arrest records and victimization data, Labriola, Rempel, and Davis (2008) found nearly identical rearrest rates between offenders who were assigned to a batterer program and offenders who were not. They operationalized recidivism as rearrest for any crime, domestic violence, or offences against the administration of justice, such as breaching probation conditions. Cortoni and Hanson (2005) used official records and victimization surveys to examine the prevalence and likelihood for recidivism of female sex offenders. They found that 20 per cent of female sex offenders reoffended for any crime versus 36–37 per cent of male sex offenders. Guay (2012) compared 172 offenders serving over six months in provincial correctional facilities, of which half were gang members. Recidivism was operationalized as rearrest and reconviction. Overall, gang members were found more likely to recidivate than non-members were. Gang members were more likely to be rearrested for all types of crimes but reconvicted for violent offences.

These studies show the great variety in how researchers operationalize reoffending. There is no perfect measurement of recidivism. However, researchers adhere to the hierarchy of measurement and use ratio measures whenever possible.

Methods in Action

Measuring Crime in Canada

The crime rate measures the volume of crime but tells us little about the seriousness. As a result, the Canadian Centre for Justice Statistics developed the Crime Severity Index (CSI), which uses court data to measure the amount of police-reported crime while accounting for the seriousness. Each crime is assigned a seriousness weight based on the actual sentence received by those convicted for the offence.

The weight consists of two parts. The incarceration rate is the proportion of those convicted for a particular offence and sentenced to a prison term of any length. The average length of the prison sentence is measured in days. The conceptual logic is that, the more serious a crime, the more likely one is to be incarcerated for it. The incarceration rate is multiplied by the average sentence length to get the seriousness weight. Finally, the number of police-reported incidents for that offence is multiplied by the seriousness weight to get a score for each offence. Here are some examples of offence seriousness based on the incarceration rate and length of custodial sentence.

Because there is little fluctuation in sentencing patterns between any two years, the CSI is updated every five years (Wallace et al., 2009). The next index is set for release in 2019.

Crime Severity Index

Offence	CSI score
First- and second-degree murder	7,042
Manslaughter	1,822
Robbery	583
Sexual assault—Level 1	211
Break and enter	187
Possession of a weapon	88
Theft under $5,000	37
Assault—Level 1	23
Failure to appear	16
Possession of cannabis	7

Source: Data from Wallace et al. (1999, p. 28).

be unidimensional (i.e. measure only one dimension of the concept). Second, examine the empirical relationship. If the score from one variable in an index predicts the scores from another, the two variables are associated and might represent the same concept. Third, determine the range of scores and whether each item has equal weight based on its importance. Unless there is a compelling reason, items should be weighted equally. Fourth, decide how missing data will be handled. Researchers often treat missing data as one of the possible responses or assign the average score as its value. Finally, validate the index. Validation can occur in two ways: an item analysis provides an assessment on whether each item makes an independent contribution, and an external validation compares the scores to those from an external measure. By taking these steps, the index should have face, content, and convergent validity.

Scale

In **scales**, items are arranged logically in order of intensity or importance when compared to index items in no particular order and accumulated scores. A scale represents a singular dimension or conceptual domain of behaviour, attitudes, or emotion. Thus, scales are always unidimensional with content and construct validity. There are five types of scales used in criminology and criminal justice research: the Likert, semantic differential, Guttman, Bogardus social distance, and Thurstone.

The Likert scale, one of the scales most commonly used to measure attitudes, is typically high in reliability. It has a five-point structure with response categories of strongly disagree, disagree, neutral, agree, and strongly agree. Occasionally, "don't know" or "not applicable" will be included. The latter category can indicate that a respondent is aware of the question's topic but has no experience with it (Lee, Altschuld, & White, 2007). For instance, if you weren't enrolled in the program being studied, it is difficult to express your feelings about participation. In their examination of the reasons behind female officers' passive and assertive responses to sexual harassment, Chaiyavej and Morash (2009) used several Likert scales to assess perceptions of and factors affecting responses to gender harassment, unwanted sexual attention, and sexual coercion. The Fairness Index referred to earlier is another example of a Likert scale.

The semantic differential scale is similar to the Likert scale except that it asks respondents to rate something on the basis of two adjectives reflecting the extreme reactions to a stimulus. The stimulus—a word, phrase, statement, or image—is placed at the top of the scale. The ratings are usually on a continuous scale from –3 to 3, thereby producing interval-level data. The adjectives can be grouped into three categories: evaluation (worthless/valuable, clean/dirty, mean/kind, love/hate); potency (strong/weak, hard/easy, submissive/dominant); and activity (active/passive, relaxed/tense, calm/agitated). It is not uncommon for the adjectives to be reversed in the scale so that the positive ones are not all on the same side.

Guttman scaling is also quite common in criminology and criminal justice research. Originally designed to be used after data collection, it checks whether index items can be organized into a scale. Guttman scales measure the degree to which a person agrees with a position or concept. From a series of statements provided by the researcher, the participant selects the ones that align with his or her opinion. Each item is a dichotomous variable, and the statements increase in specificity. The idea is that people will agree with the statements up to a certain point. For example, a scale with the statements "Criminals should be punished," "Sentences need to be harsher," and "Violent offenders should be given the death penalty" is ideal for measuring the extremes of a person's opinion on punishment.

The Bogardus social distance scale helps a researcher determine people's willingness to socialize with others who are unlike them in some way. Furthermore, it measures the degree of closeness a person can tolerate. This scale is a variant of the Guttman scale; the only difference is the statement content. Let's say the stimulus is a sex offender. The statements for a Bogardus scale could be "I'm okay with a sex offender living in my city," "in my neighbourhood," "next door," "as friends," and "as a romantic partner."

Thurstone scales assess the intensity of different indicators. Respondents answer survey questions and rank them to determine each statement's perceived importance. In other words, the respondents act as judges and assign weights to each item based on a particular concept. This scale approximates an interval-level variable. The judges are asked to sort the statements by indicating the order on a line that spans the entire range of attitudes from extremely unfavourable (1) to extremely favourable (11), with neutral

> **scale** a logical arrangement of scores on the variable that represents patterns of responses and captures the intensity of emotions or attitudes.

as 6 on the scale. For example, respondents judge a series of twenty statements on punishment that vary in degree, nature, and severity. Thurstone scaling is not very popular; the problem is finding judges with an adequate understanding of the concept that allows them to rank it according to their feelings.

Conclusion

Researchers are concerned with precisely and accurately measuring concepts, reducing error, identifying sources of bias, and following ethical practices. Reliability and validity, which tend to increase when more than one indicator, method, or source of data is used, help to achieve these goals. Furthermore, triangulation allows one method or data source to compensate for the weakness of another. Triangulation and multiple indicators help a researcher cover conceptual breadth and depth, allowing for stronger causal inferences and conclusions about relationships posited by the data or theory.

There is no perfect measure, especially once ethics are considered. Concepts are social constructions that vary by time and place and are influenced by power, class, and sex. For instance, IQ tests have long been criticized for having culturally biased questions that introduce systematic measurement error. Culturally sensitive measurement ensures that instruments are equally accessible to all.

Political considerations are of equal concern. Political processes and pressure can influence research outcomes. Succumbing to politics results in findings that, not surprisingly, reify decisions. For instance, measuring recidivism in a certain way may not cover the concept's variability. Measuring a continuous variable as a dichotomy or using incarceration instead of arrest as a cause of lower recidivism rates can yield flawed results because not everyone convicted of an offence is incarcerated. Alternatively, an organization may provide data that allows operationalization in only their preferred way. The implication is that an improper definition of recidivism can result in funding ineffective programs.

Vignette: Breaking It Down

What Is Police Decision-Making?

Decision-making is a processual concept. For example, the police make decisions about when and how to intervene in a situation; more specifically, police discretion is the decision not to invoke formal social control even when the circumstances warrant or legally allow it. Schulenberg (2014) argues that quantitative research helps us to understand the decision to arrest but is less successful at explaining informal action. Qualitative findings provide insight into the process and beliefs but provide little evidence that attitudes and values are key factors to explain police behaviour.

Systematic social observation (SSO) is a field research method that captures the dynamic aspects of police decision-making as an outcome and process. The essence of what encounter-based SSO accomplishes is the combination of a structured survey with the descriptive accounts of police work. Data are collected on the officer, encounter, and all citizens involved. All forms of police action are captured, from providing assistance, advice, warnings, and referrals to arrests and charges. Field notes capture temporal order and contextual detail on the social and interactional processes of decision-making. Within this structure, the measurement of decision-making varies both methodologically and substantively.

No two encounters are the same, and responses depend on a variety of factors. Stroshine, Alpert, and Dunham (2008) analyzed SSO field notes that included debriefing details with officers to understand the decision-making rationale or working rules. Debriefing occurred after a police–citizen encounter to understand the officer's decision-making process. Using inductive measurement logic, the researchers conceptualized decision-making as factors that arouse suspicion and subsequent police action. Their findings included factors such as time, place, behaviour, appearance, safety, and "pissing off the police" (p. 328).

Spano (2003) used SSO data to examine the impact of the observer's presence on police arrest behaviour for non-traffic-related encounters. He operationalized discretion as a dichotomous arrest variable. He found that, when officers worry about observer safety, they are less likely to arrest suspects.

Tillyer and Klalm (2011) used traffic stop data to investigate the relationship between an officer's use of discretion when conducting a search for contraband drugs. Their dependent variable was dichotomous, measuring whether drugs were found. Mandatory searches are dictated legally or by departmental policy. Discretionary searches occur when there is probable cause, drugs in plain view, or the officer detects an odour of drugs. With discretion conceptualized as the decision to search, the study revealed that citizen characteristics were not related to mandatory searches, but minority citizens were more likely to be found with contraband with discretionary searches.

Finally, Boivin and Cordeau (2011) looked at the decision to record an encounter in the official records. Recording rates were presumed to be stable except for proactive initiatives that temporarily target certain types of crime. The researchers found considerable bias in official records based on officers' decision-making to record an incident. Officers were more likely to take a report upon complainant request if they wanted to end disruptive behaviour and were less likely when the infraction caused little damage to person or property.

With these four examples, we see decision-making operationalized inductively as factors influencing police action or deductively as the decision to arrest, search, and file a police report. This operationalization suggests conceptual variability and multiple theoretical domains. It also highlights the importance of measurement transparency to ensure an understanding of what and how decision-making is measured.

Summary of Important Points

Introduction

- The research problem articulates the issue under investigation and highlights the importance of the study.
- The purpose statement clarifies the study objectives and how the findings contribute to our knowledge.
- Research questions are testable using empirical data. They state the relationship between concepts or broadly explore the main concept.

- Deductive measurement logic requires that every variable, concept, and theoretical proposition has a consistent meaning throughout the research process.
- Inductive measurement logic is an active, emergent process in which data collection refines concepts and research questions to better address the event or behaviour under investigation.

The Measurement Process

- Conceptualization takes imprecise ideas and defines what the concept means. A conceptual definition interprets and provides a working definition.
- Operationalization redefines a concept so that it is empirically observable. An operational definition specifies the empirical indicators.
- A dependent variable (effect) is the behaviour, attitude, or condition that changes in response to variation in an independent variable (cause).
- Control variables do not vary but affect the independent and dependent variables.
- Hypotheses are linked to the research question, contain at least two variables, predict a causal relationship, and are falsifiable.
- The alternative hypothesis is the anticipated causal relationship and the null hypothesis is the opposite of the prediction. We test the null hypothesis.
- A directional hypothesis has a positive or negative relationship, whereas a non-directional hypothesis predicts that two variables are associated.

The Language of Causality

- The criteria for a causal explanation are an empirical association, temporal order, and non-spuriousness. The mechanism and context specify the relationship.
- In qualitative research, causal relationships are tested using controlled comparisons, the counterfactual, and triangulation.
- The four types of faulty causal reasoning are teleology, tautology, reductioninsm, and ecological fallacy.
- Most causal explanations provide sufficient but not necessary cause.

Quality of Measurement

- The goal is to minimize random and systematic measurement error.

- A reliable measure produces consistent results each time, whereas a valid measure accurately represents the concept.
- Quantitative researchers assess the stability, equivalence, and internal consistency to establish reliability and face, content, criterion (concurrent, predictive), and construct (convergent, discriminant) validity.
- Qualitative researchers assess dependability in lieu of reliability and the trustworthiness criteria of credibility, transferability, and confirmability instead of validity.
- A valid instrument is always reliable, but a reliable measure is not necessarily valid.

More Logistics for Quantitative Measurement

- Categorical variables have a fixed number of categories. A dichotomous variable has only two categories. Continuous variables have a range of values or numerical scores.
- There are two types of categorical variables: nominal variables name attributes and ordinal have a rank order.
- There are two types of continuous variables: interval variables have an equal distance between values and ratio has all these characteristics plus a true zero.
- Researchers must measure with as much precision and accuracy as possible and at the highest level of measurement possible while considering the anticipated analysis.
- An index adds scores together from two or more categorical variables to create a numerical score.
- Scales represent response patterns based on the intensity of emotions or attitudes.

Conclusion

- Triangulation, multiple indicators, culturally sensitive instruments, and political savvy improve measurement.

Key Terms

alternative hypothesis 73

attribute 72

categorical variable 86

conceptual definition 70

concurrent validity 82

confirmability 84

confounding variable 76

construct validity 82

content validity 82

continuous variable 87

control variable 73

convergent validity 82

counterfactual 78

credibility 84

criterion validity 82

dependability 83

dependent variable 72

dichotomous variable 87

discriminant validity 82

ecological fallacy 79

empirical indicator 70

face validity 82

independent variable 72

index 88

interval variable 87

intervening variable 76

nominal variable 87

null hypothesis 73

operational definition 70

ordinal variable 87

predictive validity 82

purpose statement 65

random measurement error 80

ratio variable 88

reductionism 79

reflexivity 84

reification 70

reliability 81

scale 91

spuriousness 76

systematic measurement error 80

tautology 79

teleology 79

transferability 84

Review Questions and Exercises

1. You have been hired to create a survey. For each of the key variables below, describe how you will ask the question and determine the attributes and level of measurement.
    a. sex
    b. income
    c. marital status
    d. prior victimization
    e. satisfaction with the criminal justice system
2. Create directional, non-directional, and null hypotheses for the following research question: What is the relationship between fear of crime and contact with the criminal justice system?
3. For each scenario, identify the different types of variables, classify their level of measurement, and discuss the criteria for causality.
    a. The province is considering raising the highway speed limit but wonders if an increase will affect the number of accidents. Data are collected on accidents, fatalities, time of day, and number of cars over a three-month period before and after the change.
    b. A researcher is studying harassment and asks 250 women if they have experienced these behaviours. Each woman is asked to estimate the frequency of harassment. Other data collected are age, occupation, marital status, and opinions.
    c. A campus bar is closed due to liquor licence violations and bar fights. Students are surveyed about their reactions, support, number of times they frequented the bar, and whether alcohol causes fights. Other data include sex, age, major, religious affiliation, and contact with the police.

Online Exercises and Websites of Interest

How Do You Measure Sexual Orientation?

American Institute of Bisexuality: The Klein Measurement Scale
http://bisexual.org/wp-content/uploads/2014/08/Modified-Klein-11x17bi-fold.pdf

Kinsey Institute

www.indiana.edu/~kinsey/research/ak-hhscale.html
Alfred Kinsey developed the seven-point Heterosexual-Homosexual Rating Scale in 1948 to capture variation in sexual orientation. In 1978, Fritz Klein created the Sexual Orientation Grid, which is a seven-point scale on seven variables measured in the past, present, and ideal. Review both scales at the website addresses provided. What are the strengths and weaknesses of each scale? What are some other ways that the concept of sexual orientation can be measured?

Research Methods Knowledge Base

www.socialresearchmethods.net/kb/measure.php
Providing further information on measurement, this website has links for reliability, validity, scales, and levels of measurement.

Additional Resources

Carmine, E.G., & Zeller, R.A. (1979). *Reliability and Validity Assessments*. Quantitative Applications in the Social Sciences, vol. 17. Thousand Oaks, CA: Sage.

This text is a methodological classic for understanding reliability and validity in quantitative research.

Creswell, J.W., & Miller, D.L. (2000). "Determining Validity in Qualitative Inquiry." *Theory into Practice, 39,* 124–130.

Outlining paradigm-specific tests of validity, this article is the qualitative research counterpart of Carmine and Zeller's work.

Maxwell, J.A. (2004). "Using Qualitative Methods for Causal Explanation." *Field Methods, 16,* 243–264.

This article provides comparisons to deductive logic, the rationale for qualitative methods as appropriate to develop causal explanations, and practical techniques that can be used.

Chapter 4

How Do I Find My Research Subjects?

"Sampling is a major problem for any type of research. We can't study every case of whatever we're interested in, nor should we want to. Every scientific enterprise tries to find out something that will apply to everything of a certain kind by studying a few examples, the results of the study being, as we say generalizable." H.S. Becker, *Tricks of the Trade* (1998, p. 67)

Learning Objectives

- To distinguish the following parts of a research study: sample, population, target population, sampling elements, sampling frame, and sampling error.
- To appreciate the benefits of Central Limit Theorem, EPSEM, and random selection for representative samples and generalizability of results.
- To recognize the differences between probability and nonprobability sampling

  techniques, as well as the appropriate uses, strengths, and limitations of each method.
- To articulate the relationships among sampling error, sample quality, sample size, confidence levels, and confidence intervals.
- To create a sampling design appropriate for given research objectives and questions.

Introduction

Like measurement, **sampling** in one form or another is part of daily life. Suppose you conclude that your research methods course is the worst class you have ever taken. Perhaps the professor or subject is boring, the material is too hard, your grades are low, or it's a combination of these factors. You ask a few others in the class what they think. By not asking everyone in

sampling the process of selecting a number of individuals, objects, or observations from a larger group.

the class, you are sampling. The larger group is all of your classmates; the ones you choose are the **sample**. This chapter focuses on how we select individuals or objects that can inform our research objective.

sample a subset of individuals or objects selected from the population and used to draw conclusions about the larger group.

The problem with everyday life sampling is that it's often biased and distorts the results and conclusions. If you are irritated with having to take this course, you may ask only those who have a higher likelihood of sharing your opinion or who you believe are not doing well. Scientific research is as methodical about the sampling process as possible to better ensure meaningful results and valid knowledge.

The Sampling Process

When undertaking a study, researchers must decide on the goal of the sampling process, the selection method, and the number of cases required. The mantra guiding this process and all research design decisions is "the research question drives the method." In other words, a study's sampling technique is a function of the research purpose and questions and is the starting point for making these decisions.

Sampling uses a systematic technique to select a subset from a larger group (referred to as the **population**)—the former should be as similar to the latter as possible. In most cases, it's neither practical nor possible to gather data from everyone. Even in smaller groups, you may not have time to gather data from all members. However, with very small groups (usually defined as under fifty cases), it is best to include all members (Kitchenham & Pfleeger, 2002).

population theoretically, all individuals, groups, or objects that share particular characteristics.

probability sampling random sampling techniques in which each individual or observation has the same chance of being selected.

nonprobability sampling sampling techniques in which individuals or observations are not randomly selected and do not have the same chance of selection.

By this point, it should not surprise you that quantitative and qualitative researchers have different goals for the sampling process. Quantitative researchers have two sampling objectives: to select a subset as similar as possible to the larger group and to relate the findings from the sample back to the population. Using this approach, researchers produce statistics that estimate how close the sample and its characteristics are to the population from which they came. Researchers can then say with a certain degree of confidence that the results describe the larger group, even though they analyzed just one subset.

Qualitative researchers attempt to identify individuals who can provide the best information possible about the concepts of interest. They are less concerned about relating the findings back to a larger group, an approach that is inconsistent with the ontological and epistemological assumptions of qualitative inquiry. Instead, their objective is to gain an in-depth understanding of the concepts and to produce findings that meet the criteria of credibility and transferability.

Just as there are two major types of research, there are two types of sampling approaches. **Probability sampling** is typically associated with quantitative research and involves randomly selecting cases. When probability sampling is done correctly, the sample has a similar composition to the larger group and reflects its variations. In other words, the characteristics of the selected cases resemble what you would find if you were to collect data on every member of the population.

Sometimes, randomly selecting cases may be inappropriate in light of the research question or be impossible given the population. **Nonprobability sampling** is any sampling technique that does not select cases at random. Thus, the chances of being included in the sample differs for every individual of the larger group. This approach to sampling is useful when, for example, a characteristic or behaviour of interest occurs infrequently or little is known about it. In such studies, researchers won't have enough cases or be able to identify individuals in the population with any degree of confidence. Therefore, it doesn't make sense to select cases randomly. To select cases randomly, you need to be able to identify everyone that belongs to this larger group. There are circumstances and topics where this isn't possible.

Before we dive into greater detail, we need to see how the parts of the sampling process fit together. Figure 4.1 outlines the four steps in general terms. Step one is to define the population by considering the research objectives and research questions. By defining the population, you identify all relevant cases from which you will choose your sample. Let's

return to the example given in the introduction. The research question for your study could explore students' feelings about research methods. You define the population as all students taking a research methods class. Your goal would be to make conclusions based on analyzing data from your sample and thereby understand the population better. However, if your research question is about understanding the opinions of students in CJ304 Research Methods, the population is all students who took or are taking this particular course. If your research question focuses on a particular professor's teaching style,

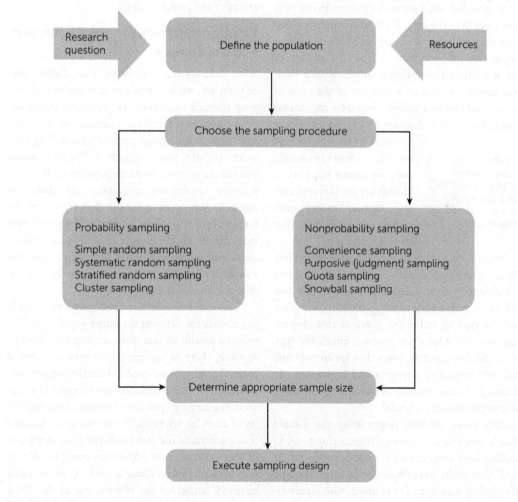

Figure 4.1 Steps to creating a sample

your goal with a nonprobability sampling technique would be to draw conclusions that apply to your sample rather than some larger population.

The next part of this step is to assess the scope of the research. If the individuals are geographically dispersed or the population is large, probability sampling is appropriate. You should also decide how much knowledge about the population you need. If considerable knowledge about the characteristics of the group is required, nonprobability sampling techniques are a better option. If you are unable to compile a complete list of the population, probability sampling is difficult. Furthermore, consider how you plan to analyze the data. If you anticipate conducting a statistical analysis, many analytical techniques require random selection of cases, which means you need to use probability sampling. This decision involves an honest assessment of the amount of time and money available. Resources are another consideration when choosing a sampling technique; you need to ask whether you have the resources to identify everyone in the population. Probability samples cost a lot more time and money; nonprobability sampling is less resource intensive.

target population the group of individuals or cases that provide data to best address the research questions and to whom the findings will apply.

Step two is to choose your sampling procedure. There are several factors affecting this decision. How you defined your population clarifies whether you will adopt probability or nonprobability sampling and the type of technique. Later in this chapter, you will learn what these methods entail, the type of sample they generate, when they are appropriate, and their respective strengths and limitations. At this stage, the key is to discern where in the sampling process this decision is made.

Step three involves determining the sample size. As you will see, various elements play a role in deciding how many cases you need to conduct your study. One of the more important factors is the type of sampling technique. For example, with nonprobability samples, the size is not as critical because

you're applying your findings to the cases within your sample or similar situation only, not the population. The final step is to execute your sampling design and choose cases.

Learning the Lingo

This section looks at the logistics of step one, the relationship between the population and the sample, and key terminology. Learning the lingo helps you to understand how the techniques work. At the end of the chapter, you will be a more knowledgeable, critical consumer of information, both in your everyday and professional life.

Relationship between the Population and the Sample

After defining the population, you identify who or what you want to study so that you can address your research questions. As previously stated, we can almost never include everyone in the study and large samples make probability sampling even more expensive than it already is. The trick is how you select the subset from the population. Whether you are conducting quantitative or qualitative research, you create a sample that represents the **target population**—the portion of the population that will specifically pertain to the research objectives, that can provide the desired information for addressing the research questions, and that will be affected by the conclusions.

The research objectives and questions provide the criteria for defining the target population. You must be specific so that those reading the results or applying them to different situations understand them. But why do we need to identify a target population? Why is a population not enough? In a nutshell, the target population determines the eligibility of cases for selection. If your research objective is to understand the factors affecting the likelihood of incarceration, your population could be all persons incarcerated in Canada. Let's say the research question centres on the effectiveness of the *Youth Criminal Justice Act* to achieve its goal of reducing the use of incarceration. You would then use inclusion and exclusion criteria to define the target population.

Inclusion criteria specify the target population's main characteristics. In our example, inclusion criteria includes persons between the ages of 12 and 17 who receive dispositions of open or secure custody. Exclusion criteria are characteristics that do not apply or will compromise your ability to make inferences back to the target population. We can base the exclusion criteria on rare events such as murder (where incarceration constitutes the minimum sentence). You may also decide to exclude cases that are difficult to access without incurring considerable additional costs, such as youth who are on intensive supervision orders (which involve serving a portion of the custodial sentence in the community). Alternatively, you can exclude youth who are held in custody awaiting trial, as they have not been convicted of an offence.

Researchers must identify all the specific qualities that are common for the group. Think of the population as the conceptual definition and the target population as an operational definition. Our target population would be all youth between the ages of 12 and 17 who receive a disposition of open or secure custody or intensive supervision, have not committed offences with mandatory custodial sentences, and are not incarcerated awaiting trial. There is one caveat: the target population is still theoretical in the sense that you can never be 100 per cent certain that you identified all the cases in the population.

As depicted in Figure 4.2, the sample is drawn from the target population. The underlying assumption is that studying the sample will provide valid information on the target population. In other words, the findings based on the sample are intended to show the characteristics, processes, and behaviours of the target population or the population as a whole. The sample should be a microcosm of the target population. If it isn't, the findings will be invalid and misleading when inferences are applied to the target population.

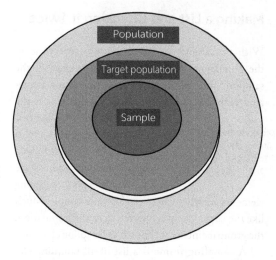

Figure 4.2 Where does the sample come from?

Parameters and Statistics

Before you panic about the term *statistics*, keep reading. When we discuss probability theory, the terms *population parameter* and *sample statistic* are important. These terms are introduced now to facilitate learning and to simplify each step in the sampling process.

A **population parameter** is a population characteristic that is estimated based on findings from a sample. A parameter is unknown because we analyze just a subset of this population. We have to estimate the population parameter but can never be absolutely certain about its true value. A **sample statistic**—a numerical value calculated from sample scores—summarizes the data and provides us with information on the unknown population parameter. The quality of a sample statistic depends on the type of sampling technique adopted and the extent of error associated with creating the sample.

population parameter a characteristic of the population whose value is unknown and is estimated based on findings from the sample.

sample statistic a characteristic of the sample used to estimate an attribute of the population (the population parameter).

Making a List and Checking it Twice

With probability sampling, a list of everyone in the population is mandatory at some stage in the sampling process. There are two key terms associated with this process. A **sampling element** is the object you want to describe or understand and is essential to provide the information required to address the research question. Sampling elements are what you select for your sample. Much like the larger group is referred to as the population, the group members are known as sampling elements.

A **sampling frame** is a list of all sampling elements in the target population. An accurate sampling frame is critical for a good sample that resembles the population. Unfortunately, researchers run into several problems, despite their best efforts. When using probability sampling techniques, elements are often missing from the sampling frame. Using more than one source when listing elements can help minimize this problem, but it's still impossible to eliminate entirely. Anticipating this problem is important because a truly representative sample includes as many elements from the target population as possible. Although sampling frames are not perfect, the point is to minimize the number of missing elements, thereby reducing the amount of error associated with the sampling process.

Do not make the mistake of drawing conclusions about the target population that the sampling frame does not support. You can make inferences only to a population that the sampling frame accurately represents. In reality, researchers usually start with a population and then look for appropriate sampling frames, such as voter lists, telephone directories, or records from schools or criminal justice organizations.

We simply have to be cautious, as the sampling frame defines the target population. If we want to generalize to the target population, the sampling frame and its constituent elements must resemble the aggregate population characteristics. It is extremely difficult to produce a sampling frame that exactly matches the population, but probability sampling gives us our best chance at resembling the population.

> **sampling element** a person, group, organization, document, or event sampled from the population.

> **sampling frame** a list of the elements from the target population that are used to create a sample.

Key Thinker

Travis Hirschi: A Criminology Legend

Born in rural Utah in 1935, Hirschi completed his BA and MA at the University of Utah and his PhD in Sociology at the University of California–Berkeley. He has worked in the Department of Sociology at the University of Washington–Seattle and the University of California–Davis. Feeling like a "fish out of water in sociology," he moved to the School of Criminal Justice at the University of Albany–SUNY and then to the University of Arizona (Morrison, 2010, p. 221). Hirschi's philosophy "is founded on [his] observation of the world, not on anything so trivial and irrelevant as personal history" (p. 221).

Hirschi adheres to the premise of methodological individualism, which sees behaviour as a function of a person's relationship with society. He also transforms our way of thinking about underlying assumptions. Most theories ask why people commit crime. Hirschi flips this question on its head and asks, "Why don't people commit crime?"

In *The Causes of Delinquency*, his dissertation project and seminal work, Hirschi (1969/2009) compares his social control theory to the work of Edwin Sutherland and Robert Merton, the two most prominent theoretical explanations for criminality at that time. The results support his theory that a strong social bond to society created by attachment, involvement, commitment, and belief explains why we don't break the law. His research used three types of data: school records (his sampling frame), self-report surveys, and police data that provide information on the total number of offences, offence type, age at first offence, and date of most recent offence. The police data were used to check for sampling bias in the survey responses as well. The target population was 17,500 students entering eleven schools in the fall of 1964. Hirschi sampled based on the attributes of race, sex, school, and grade. Using a probabilistic sampling technique, his sample was 5,545 students. After survey administration, he had complete data for 4,077 students.

Since its publication, this study has been cited 8,478 times. Few theories have sparked as much empirical attention and debate as Hirschi's social control perspective. When asked why he believes his work has been cited so frequently, he provides four reasons: the theory his work advocates, the contextualization of findings in the correlates of delinquency, the type of data on which conclusions are based, and the methodology he adopts (Hirschi, 1980).

Hirschi's work influences sociologists and criminologists in numerous ways. For example, the process of theoretical development has been sloppy overall (Gibbons, 1994). But Hirschi revolutionized how we conduct research. He introduced the comparative test by using empirical data to test competing criminological theories within the same study. He developed operational measures of key concepts that are still used today. His work sparked tremendous interest and more replications of social control theory than any other theory. His research is methodologically rigorous and meticulously structured, so his findings can be traced back to the data and the inferences about the population back to sample statistics.

Sampling Error: How Good Are My Population Parameter Estimates?

Sampling error is a product of the sampling process and the inability to know the population parameters. It is the difference between the value of the sample statistic and the true value of the population parameter. When we make inferences about the population based on the results from our sample, a margin of error is inevitable. The larger the error, the less representative the sample and the less able we are to make accurate inferences. Even the most carefully designed samples will always have some degree of sampling error.

There are two reasons why a sample statistic does not represent a population parameter well. The first is **random sampling error**, which means that any discrepancies between the sample statistic and the true value of the population parameter occur completely by chance. If you were to collect multiple samples from the same target population, any variations in a statistic from one sample to another would occur randomly. One cannot prevent this type of error, but increasing the sample size minimizes it.

The second reason is **systematic sampling error**, or **sampling bias**. This error is introduced by the sampling method adopted and is arguably much more problematic than random sampling error. Whereas the latter is to be expected for every sample, the same cannot be said

sampling error the difference between the value of the sample statistic and the value of the population parameter.

random sampling error error that occurs by chance and affects the accuracy of the sample statistic.

systematic sampling error (or sampling bias) errors—resulting from mistakes or deficiencies in how the sample is created or how the data are analyzed—that affect the accuracy of a sample statistic.

about the former. Here, elements are selected for a sample that is not representative of the population. When systematic error occurs, it creates an under- or overestimate of a characteristic in the sample that is strictly due to how sampling elements are chosen. Any differences between the population and the sampling frame are a facet of sampling bias, as is processing the data incorrectly.

Having systematic error gives us a distorted view. For instance, our friends would be a biased sample with high levels of systematic error. Why? The people we know are typically similar to us. If they constitute our sample, we may believe that everyone thinks as we do because, each time we ask for our friends' opinion, they usually agree with us. We may think it's better to carefully pick people with different or specific traits. Yet probability sampling involves randomness and not intentionally selecting certain cases. If we deliberately choose certain elements, our choices may reflect our biases about what sort of people are likely to have certain opinions, thus creating an unrepresentative sample. We also need to be acutely aware of systematic error when using institutional records as our sampling frame. Such documents are only as complete and accurate as the organization needs them to be for its own purposes. Much research in criminology and criminal justice uses official records from the police, courts, and corrections, making this source of systematic error a real concern.

Figure 4.3 illustrates the various sources of random and systematic sampling error. Random error is based on not observing a certain number of elements in the population, which can happen for two reasons. First, the sampling elements were not included in the sampling frame. This occurs in every research project to varying degrees; however, the likelihood of exclusion is entirely random. Second, an element in the sample could not be contacted or refused to participate. Both circumstances are beyond your control and occur randomly because you cannot predict whether a particular element falls into this category. Refusals are usually the result of not answering a question because it's on a sensitive topic or having no motivation to participate in the study.

Systematic sampling error is the result of faulty observation. The manner in which the sample is created and how the data are collected and analyzed contribute to systematic error. Sources of this error, which include sampling technique, data entry, analysis errors, or researcher bias, are preventable. Creating a sample from your group of friends is the result of the sampling technique and researcher bias. By strategically choosing the sampling technique, being aware of its limitations, and carefully processing the data, systematic error can be minimized and the total sampling error reduced.

Probability Theory

Probability theory exists everywhere, be it forecasting the weather, gambling, or even investing in stocks, mutual funds, or RRSPs. Think of probability theory in relation to games of chance. If you flip a coin enough times, you will be closer to getting heads or tails 50 per cent of the time. If you choose cards from a deck, you will eventually have a one in four chance of drawing a particular suit.

Probability is the chance, or likelihood, that something will randomly occur. It is the ratio of actual occurrences to the number of possible occurrences and is expressed as a number between 0 and 1, where 0 represents impossibility and 1 absolute certainty. (The ratio can be expressed as a percentage as well.) If you toss a coin 250 times and get heads 110 times, you have a 0.44, or 44 per cent, chance of getting heads (calculated by dividing 110 by 250).

The **sampling distribution** is a statistic based on every possible sample of a given population. To find the statistic, researchers draw multiple samples until every possible combination of elements is achieved within all the samples. They then calculate a sample statistic, such as the average for a characteristic. The

sampling distribution
a statistic based on multiple samples of a given population and the probability of it occurring.

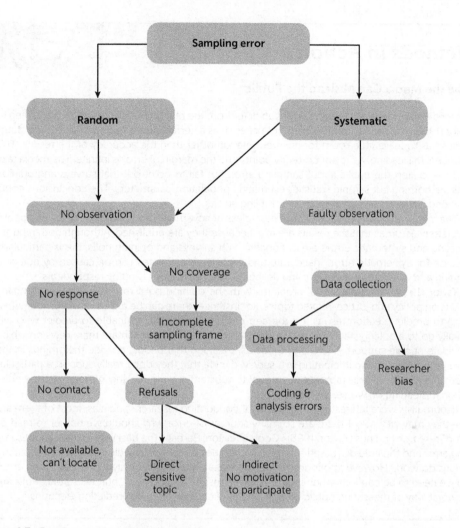

Figure 4.3 Random and systematic sampling error

probability of the value of this statistic occurring given a sample of a particular size is the sampling distribution. The variability in the sampling distribution is affected by the number of observations in the population and sample as well as the sampling technique chosen.

Central Limit Theorem

Since we don't have the resources to create multiple samples, the **Central Limit Theorem** allows us to calculate the probability of our sample being accurate and representative of the population. If we were to take multiple independent random samples, the distribution will be normal (assuming that we have a large enough sample size). The larger the sample size, the more likely the sampling distribution will approach the population parameter. The Central Limit Theorem implies that, with a fairly

Central Limit Theorem a theory stating that, with an infinite number of samples from a population, the sampling distribution will be normally distributed around the population average for that characteristic.

Methods in Action

How the Media Can Mislead the Public

The media's portrayal of sampling error can differ from the reality of social research. According to Taylor (1998), the media reports the margin of error as a certain percentage and words the statement so as to leave little room for an interpretation other than the accuracy of the results. This practice is misleading. As Taylor correctly points out, the margin of error is infinite. The media take the time to alert the public about sampling error, but fail to point out that surveys and opinion polls are nothing but sample statistics estimating population parameters. The conclusions could be wrong if there is a large amount of sampling error.

The media often publish the findings regardless of how much sampling error exists. The public then falsely assumes that the results are true because they are published. Although both random sampling and systematic errors are of concern with surveys and opinion polls, this is particularly the case for systematic error. Inaccurate and misleading estimates can be caused by question wording and order, sample design, and deliberate or unconscious lying by respondents.

Taylor (1998) raises additional problems with the opinion polls that frequently accompany reports on policy and justice-related topics. For instance, there can be a differential turnout when trying to predict election results. It's the age-old problem of being unable to predict who will actually go to a polling station and vote, which is much harder to estimate than views on which candidate people support. A late-swing occurs, meaning that people change their minds in the eleventh hour or, after participating in a survey, decide that they don't really support a particular piece of legislation. These factors can amount to substantial error, making inferences to the population misleading or, worse, incorrect.

If journalists were interested in the reality of conducting research "and alas, most of them are not—they may well ask, if there are so many sources of error why should we bother to read or report" research findings (Taylor, 1998)? Good question. Perhaps the best way to think about sampling error and the little discussed sampling techniques is to say that well-thought-out sampling designs do work. However, polls and marketing research are notoriously high in sampling error, and we need to be cautious when interpreting the results. As Winston Churchill stated, "Polls are the worst way of measuring public opinion and public behavior, or of predicting elections."

large sample size, the sampling distribution resembles a normal distribution centred on the population average. A normal sampling distribution exists when the centre point, being the most frequent value, is the same for the sample and the population. Figure 4.4 depicts a normal distribution. As you can see, the normal distribution forms a bell-shaped curve.

The normal distribution—and its relationship with the Central Limit Theorem—highlights the importance of sample size and probability sampling techniques. Probability sampling ensures that, if the study were repeated with different samples, the sample mean wouldn't differ significantly from the population mean. We cover the mean in Chapter 9; for now, it is enough to know that it is the average score within a distribution. Your GPA is an example of a mean. The population mean is a standard deviation of zero.

With repeated random samples, sample statistics are distributed around the population parameter, creating a normal curve. We estimate how close sample statistics are to the population mean by using the standard deviation, which measures the variation or distance between the sample and population mean in a distribution. In other words, it gauges the range of a sample statistic's scores.

Based on the Central Limit Theorem, we can estimate just how close the sample statistics are to the population parameter without drawing multiple samples. Look at Figure 4.4 again. With one standard deviation in either direction, 68 per cent of the sample means fall within this range. At two standard deviations, the number increases to 95 per cent; and, at three, to 99 per cent. The second illustration shows how this frequency distribution statistic works.

Within one standard deviation from the mean, 68 per cent of the population has an IQ between 85 and 115. If your IQ is 130, it is higher than 95 per cent of the population's.

The EPSEM Principle

A sample is more likely to be representative if all elements of the target population have an equal chance of being selected for the sample. A sampling

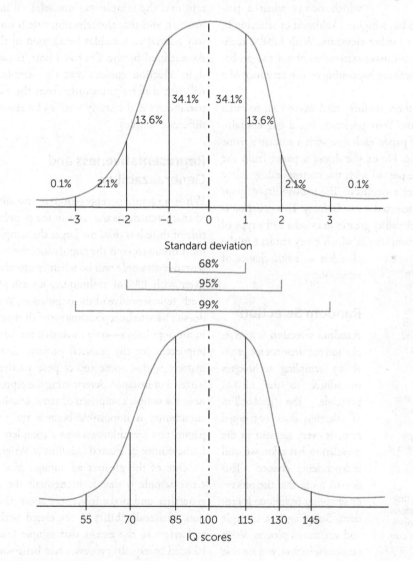

Figure 4.4 The normal distribution

technique adhering to the **equal probability of selection method (EPSEM)** principle means that element selection occurs by chance and is independent of any other events in the sampling process. There is no discernable pattern to how cases are selected. EPSEM sampling designs reduce selection bias, which occurs when a person or group has a higher likelihood of selection in comparison to other elements. With EPSEM techniques, you can make statements about the probability of something happening or the existence of a relationship.

Let's say there are forty students in your research methods class. Your professor has a bag containing pieces of paper, each one with a student's name written on it. He or she draws a paper from the bag, and the person with the corresponding name has to answer a question. The probability of your name being selected is one in forty. This situation is a known probability greater than zero and a type of probability sampling in which every student in the class has an equal chance of selection.

Random Selection

Random selection is a strategy and requirement for probability sampling techniques to adhere to the EPSEM principle. The probability of selection does not equal zero, as every element in the population has a known and independent chance. This doesn't mean that the process or sampling technique is random. Sampling is a strategic and structured process. With random selection, you are able to minimize systematic error.

The key connection between a sample and population is similarity, which can best be accomplished using random selection. Choosing 25 of your friends or acquaintances is not a random sample because the chance of selection is not equal. Your findings cannot be generalized back to the target population. Tansey (2007, p. 768) states: "Without randomness that probability sampling entails, it would be impossible to be certain that the sample was not selected in a biased manner, and that the selection rule is not in some way related to variables being used in the study." As outlined by the Central Limit Theorem, random selection ensures that the sample statistics will not differ significantly from the population parameters if the study were to be repeated with different samples.

Representativeness and Generalizability

When a sample is **representative**, the distribution of characteristics is the same in the population. The rule of thumb is that, the larger the sample and the more homogeneous the population, the more representative a sample will be when randomly selected. Even with EPSEM techniques, no sample is perfectly representative of the population. Yet a sample doesn't have to be representative of all characteristics in the population—only those that are substantively important for the research project. Complicating matters is that some topics pose particular challenges. For instance, determining the representativeness of a sample comprised of active criminals in the community is impossible because the population parameters are unknown and a complete sampling frame cannot be created (Mullins & Wright, 2003).

One of the greatest advantages of a representative sample is that it strengthens the ability to generalize and make inferences about the population. **Generalizability** is associated with validity and refers to the extent that sample findings can be used to explain processes and behaviours in the population. Generalizing is "an act of reasoning that

equal probability of selection method (EPSEM) the theory that each element in the sampling frame has a known, equal, and non-zero probability of sample selection.

random selection the process of creating a representative sample in which the elements are randomly selected and have a known and independent chance of selection.

representativeness the quality that occurs when sample characteristics important to the study resemble what is found in the population.

generalizability the process of extending a study's findings and conclusions to the population; occurs after analyzing data from a sample.

involves drawing broad conclusions from particular instances" (Polit & Beck, 2010, p. 1451).

While generalizability involves applying the findings to a larger population, transferability (the qualitative equivalent) is the ability to extend findings to related situations and concepts that are not the focus of the current study. Qualitative researchers strive to generalize to an area of understanding. Inductive logic and confirmatory strategies are used to address the credibility of their conclusions, allowing for generalizations about the phenomenon under study (Polit & Beck, 2010).

Probability Sampling

Probability samples adhere to the EPSEM principle and are one way to minimize sampling error. Subjectivity is removed from the sampling process to obtain an unbiased sample that is more representative of the target population. Unless you have a probabilistic sample, you cannot make statistical inferences. There are four types of probability samples: simple random, systematic random, stratified random, and cluster.

Simple Random Sampling

Simple random sampling (SRS) is an EPSEM technique that uses a lottery method or random number table to choose elements. There are five steps to SRS:

1. Define the target population.
2. Identify an existing sampling frame or create a list of all elements in the target population.
3. Sequentially number each element in the sampling frame.
4. Determine the sample size.
5. Randomly select the required number of elements.

An example of the lottery method is randomly drawing names from a hat until you reach your desired sample size. The disadvantages of this approach are that it is time-consuming and is only a realistic option with small target populations. The alternative is a random number table. In this type of table, the numbers are not arranged in any particular order and are read either horizontally or vertically. You match the number from the table to the same number assigned to an element in the sampling frame. As with the lottery method, this process can be arduous and time-consuming. Thus, it is not recommended for large target populations.

Stoddard-Dare, Mallett, and Boitel (2011) used a random number table to explore the

> **simple random sampling (SRS)** a probability sampling technique that uses a lottery or random number table to select sequentially numbered elements randomly from a sampling frame.

Methods in Action

Using a Random Number Table

Imagine that you are conducting a job satisfaction survey for correctional officers. Your population is all correctional officers, your target population is 8,000, and the government contract specifies a sample of 800.

With SRS, all elements in the target population are assigned a number. As the maximum number of digits in the sampling frame is three (8-0-0), you are looking for possible values in the table from 001 to 800. Appendix C provides a random number table, with combinations randomly chosen from 00001 to 10,000.

You're probably thinking, "How do I use the table when the sample size involves three digits but the table values have five?" You simply need to decide which three numbers to use. You

Continued

can use the first three (1-2-3-4-5), the middle three (1-2-3-4-5), or the last three (1-2-3-4-5). Whatever you decide, this pattern is used throughout the sampling process. We are going to use the last three digits.

The second decision is whether you will move down or across the list of numbers. Either option is acceptable. We'll move down the columns.

The third decision is choosing a random start. You have two options. You can close your eyes and randomly point to a spot in the table. Note the column and row number. Or you can randomly choose a column (A–H) and row number (1–90). Both methods create a random starting point. You go to the particular column and row and start with that number, then continue until you have 800 elements in your sample.

In this example, we'll choose Column B, Row 13 as the random starting point. Looking at Appendix C, our starting number is 11366. Our first element selected, then, is 366. Working down the column, we find that the next two numbers are 27433 and 88282; we select cases 433 and 282. The next number, 07986, is problematic. Whenever you run into a number above the total number of cases (here, 800), ignore it and go to the next row in that column. Because the numbers in the table are random, you may also run into the same number more than once. The same principle applies: ignore it and keep going.

effect of mental health disorders on delinquent behaviours. Their target population was all adjudicated youth in one courthouse who were under probation supervision. Over a period of three years, this group equalled 6,900. Calculations indicated that, for a margin of error of 5 per cent, a sample size of 360 was required. Using a random number table for each population year, the researchers created a final sample consisting of 342 youth.

Simple random sampling is used frequently, but there are advantages and disadvantages to consider. The technique requires no detailed information about the population, is conceptually easy to understand, and convenient if you are able to create a sampling frame of the target population. On the other hand, it is unmanageable with large populations, does not account for researcher knowledge or subgroups in the population, and is resource intensive. Table 4.1 provides a summary of SRS.

Table 4.1 Simple random sampling

Technique	• Create a sampling frame. • Assign a number to each element. • Randomly select cases using the lottery method or a random number table.
Advantages	• Does not require information on population characteristics. • Adheres to the EPSEM principle, improving representativeness and generalizability. • Is easy to understand. • Is convenient when a sampling frame exists.
Disadvantages	• Requires a complete sampling frame. • Is cumbersome to create sampling frames with large populations. • Does not account for researcher knowledge of the population and its characteristics. • May not include sufficient numbers of subgroups of interest to conduct a meaningful analysis. • Is expensive and time-consuming, especially if elements are difficult to locate.

Systematic random sampling

A simpler and cheaper technique than SRS, **systematic random sampling** involves randomly selecting a starting point exactly as you would for simple random sampling. However, you do not use a random number table but choose every k^{th} element in the sampling frame. Results are almost identical to SRS but can potentially produce a more representative sample.

One component of systematic random sampling is the **sampling ratio**, a numerical value representing the proportion of sampling elements in the target population to be selected for the sample. To calculate the sampling ratio, you need the target population size (symbolized by "N") and the projected sample size (designated as "n"). The calculation is simple: sampling ratio = n/N. If your target population is 660 and your sample size is 50, you divide 50 by 660 for a sampling ratio of 0.075. Round up or down to the nearest whole number, which in this case makes the sampling ratio 8. Using the sampling ratio, we randomly pick our first element between the first and eighth case in the sampling frame.

The **sampling interval** is a crucial component for systematic sampling as it determines the numerical distance between each element selected. The interval represented as "k" is calculated by dividing the population size by the sample size (k = N/n). Thus, you divide 660 by 50, giving you a sampling interval of 13.2. You then round down and have k = 13.

Our sampling frame includes 660 cases and we want a sample size of 50. With a sampling ratio of 8, we randomly choose 5 as our random start. The sampling interval is 13, so our first case is 5, the second is 18, followed by 31, 44, and so forth until we have 50 cases.

Sampling bias is present when the sampling interval coincides with periodicity in the sampling frame. **Periodicity** occurs when elements are listed in a systematic order (e.g. alphabetical order, by birthdate). For instance, if you use two newspapers that are always listed one after another and your sampling interval is two, you would always select the same newspaper. Therefore, we carefully examine the sampling frame for patterns. If we find any, we randomize the list or use a different sampling technique. To summarize, the steps for systematic random sampling are:

1. Define the target population and locate or create a sampling frame.
2. Examine the sampling frame for any evidence of clustering or periodicity.
3. Determine the sample size.
4. Calculate the sampling ratio and interval and round to the nearest whole number.
5. Randomly select every kth case based on the numerical value of the sampling interval until the desired sample size is reached.

Due to a large target population size, Herzog (2004) adopted systematic random sampling for his exploration of whether the law's lack of recognizing motive when assessing seriousness also occurs when the public forms their opinions. The data were collected from the adult Israeli population using telephone directories as the sampling frame. Systematic random sampling was adopted because of the large target population. Listing the phone numbers randomly ensured that each household had an equal probability for selection. The final sample included 805 households.

Weinrath (2009) used systematic random sampling to understand why the number of

systematic random sampling a technique in which a sampling interval is calculated and, with a random start, every k^{th} element is selected until the desired sample size is reached.

sampling ratio the proportion of elements to be selected from the target population; this numerical value determines the range for a random start.

sampling interval the standard distance between each sampling element selected.

periodicity a phenomenon that creates sampling bias when elements in the sampling frame are listed cyclically and the pattern coincides with the sampling interval.

people held in pre-trail custody has dramatically increased in Canada. The target population for this study included 668 inmates held in a provincial correctional facility. The sampling frame was administrative data listing every inmate in the general population. With a sampling interval of two, every second inmate was selected (n = 334). Weinrath compared the sample to the target population on key characteristics and found that the sample was representative of the general inmate population.

Systematic random sampling has the advantage that you do not have to number each element in the sampling frame. Providing that a random start is used, the sample is similar to one created with SRS and adheres to the principle of EPSEM. Of concern with this technique is sampling bias when the frame is systematically ordered. Additionally, using a sampling interval means that the first element chosen predetermines all the other elements selected. However, it is the use of the interval that makes this method less cumbersome and costly than SRS. See Table 4.2 for a summary of systematic random sampling.

Stratified Random Sampling

When a researcher wants to isolate a subgroup in the population or examine the relationship between two or more groups, the most appropriate technique is **stratified random sampling**. The researcher divides the population into subgroups, or **strata**, based on values of a relevant characteristic and then randomly selects an equal number of elements within each stratum. Each stratum and element within are chosen randomly using simple random or systematic random sampling. The most commonly used strata are age, sex, race/ethnicity, socio-economic status, and rural/urban.

Strata are independent, and an element can fit in only one stratum. The rule of thumb is that you want strata to be heterogeneous, or different from each other, and the elements within a stratum to be homogenous. The number of strata is determined by the number of categories within a stratification

stratified random sampling a probabilistic technique that divides the target population into homogenous subgroups (strata) and randomly chooses elements within each subgroup (stratum).

strata subgroups within the target population.

Table 4.2 Systematic random sampling

Technique	• Define the target population and create a sampling frame. • Examine the sampling frame for clustering or periodicity. • Determine the sample size. • Calculate the sampling ratio and interval. • Select every kth element randomly until the desired sample size is reached.
Advantages	• Is less resource intensive than SRS. • Does not need numbered elements in the sampling frame. • Resembles SRS sample (with randomly ordered elements). • Ensures elements selected are from beginning to end in the sampling frame. • Is generally considered an EPSEM technique, providing that a random starting point is chosen.
Disadvantages	• Results in periodicity, a form of sampling bias, if the elements are in a systematic pattern. • Uses the first sampling element to determine the subsequent elements selected. • Is challenging to create a sampling frame with geographically dispersed or hard-to-locate elements.

variable. If your stratification variable is sex, you will have two strata: male and female. Here, the objective is to maximize the sample size within strata.

Employing this technique, Coupe and Blake (2006) examined the factors affecting the decision to commit burglary at night or during the day. At one police agency, the sampling frame consisted of 5,768 burglaries that occurred over a six-month period. The stratification variable was detected or undetected, that is, whether the offenders were seen by victims or witnesses. SRS was used to select elements within each stratum for a sample of 704 cases.

In their study of high comorbidity rates among incarcerated youth diagnosed with psychiatric disorders, Abram and colleagues (2003) had a target population of approximately 8,500 youth detained at one facility over a three-year period. They used stratified random sampling to create a sample of 1,829 youth. The stratification variables, in order, were sex, race/ethnicity, age, and legal status; they were used to obtain sufficient numbers to compare substantively important subgroups.

Proportionate and Disproportionate Stratified Sampling

When researchers use **proportionate stratified sampling**, the number of elements chosen from each stratum is the same as the proportion in the target population. This method requires knowledge of the stratification variable's distribution in the target population. With **disproportionate stratified sampling**, the researcher deliberately oversamples within a stratum. As the proportion of elements from each stratum is not equivalent to what is found in the population, the probability of selection is known but unequal.

Researchers opt for disproportionate samples when they want to make sure that elements in the smaller strata have sufficient numbers to make comparisons among strata. If you are interested in female crime, you might use a disproportionate stratified sample to ensure that you have enough women to make meaningful comparisons to men. Yet this approach is not without a disadvantage, as the sample's representativeness is reduced. A full discussion of weighting is beyond the scope of this book—what essentially happens is that certain elements are oversampled and then weighted to once again represent the proportion in the population.

A **sampling fraction** is the ratio of sample size to stratum size. If the sampling fraction is the same for each stratum, representativeness increases. Recall that stratified sampling has strata of equal size. With proportionate samples, the sampling fraction is different for each stratum. The elements chosen match the proportion of the stratum in the target population, which also increases representativeness. With disproportionate samples, the sampling fraction is different as elements do not correspond with the proportion found in the population. EPSEM requires the same sampling fraction, revealing a particular limitation of proportionate and disproportionate samples.

To contextualize disproportionate sampling, let's take a brief look at an example. Hays, Regoli, and Hewitt (2007) wanted to understand the alienation that police chiefs experience while doing their job. The sampling frame was over 10,000 names created from each state's police chief association membership lists. The researchers used a two-stage disproportionate stratified sampling technique in which departments were first stratified by city size. At the second stage, the stratification variable of race/ethnicity resulted in oversampling Latino chiefs, creating a sample of 1,500.

Another situation with an insufficient number of minorities is the Guevara, Herz, and Spohn

> **proportionate stratified sampling** a sampling technique in which each stratum is proportional in size to what exists in the target population.

> **disproportionate stratified sampling** a sampling technique in which the proportion of each stratum is intentionally different from the proportion in the target population.

> **sampling fraction** the ratio of sample size to stratum size; used to determine the number of elements selected from the strata.

cluster sampling a sampling technique that selects groups from the target populations (clusters) and then randomly selects members within each group to create a sample.

clusters naturally occurring groups in a population, such as schools, neighbourhood blocks, or police agencies.

(2008) study, which investigated the impact of race, gender, and type of legal counsel on court outcomes for young offenders. The researchers collected data from files at two courthouses over a four-year period, creating a target population of 22,553 cases. They stratified based on race and sex and then used SRS in each stratum to produce a sample of 7,872 cases. A disproportionate sample was chosen to ensure sufficient minority youth in the sample for the comparison of subgroups.

Here, then, are the key steps for all types of stratified random sampling:

1. Define the target population.
2. Identify the stratification variable(s).
3. Identify or create a sampling frame that includes information on each stratification variable.
4. Divide the target population into the strata and create a sampling frame for each stratum.
5. Determine whether elements in a stratum will be chosen in equal numbers or proportionate or disproportionate to the target population.
6. Using a sampling fraction, randomly select elements from each stratum.

Strengths and Weaknesses

Providing that the information on the strata is correct, stratified samples are more representative of the population than samples created using simple random or systematic methods. This technique allows for a higher degree of precision when compared to SRS because the variability in the groups is low. With homogenous subgroups, a smaller sample is needed, saving time and money. Randomly selecting elements from homogenous groups also minimizes the amount of sampling error.

One disadvantage is that this technique requires knowledge about the strata in the target population. Strata variables are determined both practically and substantively by available information on the population and those you want the sample to represent accurately. For all types, a complete sampling frame with stratification variables is required, which can be challenging. Further, a degree of subjectivity exists as researchers are determining which characteristics are important. Similar to simple random and systematic, this technique doesn't work well with large samples. See Table 4.3 for a review of stratified sampling.

Cluster Sampling

Cluster sampling randomly selects naturally occurring groups from the target population, known as **clusters**, and then members within each group. Each element belongs to no more than one cluster. If your target population consists of clusters of schools, you randomly select a certain number of clusters using simple random, systematic, or stratified sampling. Once you have the desired number of clusters, you again use one of the other random sampling techniques to select elements within each cluster until the desired sample size is achieved. The key thing to remember is to use a technique that gives each cluster and element an equal probability of selection.

Why use cluster sampling? With large and geographically dispersed populations, creating a sampling frame can be difficult. However, elements can be grouped into primary sampling units and a sampling frame of these clusters is possible. A complete sampling frame is required only for elements within each of the randomly selected clusters, known as secondary sampling units. Hence, the clusters are sampling units and the elements are those within each cluster.

How Many Clusters?

If the secondary sampling units are police officers and the population is 15,000, the first step is to determine the sample size. Let's say you want to sample 25 per cent, or 3,750 officers. The most logical cluster would be a police service.

Table 4.3 Stratified sampling

Technique	• Define the target population. • Identify the stratification variable for each element. • Locate or create a sampling frame that includes information on each stratification variable. • Divide the target population into strata and create a sampling frame for each stratum. • Determine whether stratum elements will be chosen in equal numbers or be proportionate or disproportionate to the target population. • Use a sampling fraction to select elements from each stratum randomly.
Advantages	• Is more representative than SRS and systematic, as elements from each subgroup are included in the sample. • Is able to use other sampling techniques to choose elements in each stratum. • Uses the researcher's knowledge about population characteristics. • Allows for analyses between and within strata. • Has a lower sampling error with homogeneous strata. • Has the possibility of a smaller sample size without increasing the sampling error.
Disadvantages	• Requires information on the stratification variable for each sampling element in the population. • Requires information on the proportion of a population's characteristic for each subgroup in proportionate and disproportionate samples. • Choosing an appropriate stratification variable is challenging substantively and logistically if there are a large number of possibilities. • Requires a sample size large enough in each stratum for meaningful analyses. • Requires weighting of strata elements (with disproportionate stratified sampling). • Is more complex and resource intensive than SRS.

Using the most recent Statistics Canada Police Administration Survey, you create a sampling frame of all agencies in Canada. Suppose there are 1,500 police agencies. Although the size of each cluster varies, the average number of officers in each agency is 150. The number of clusters is calculated by dividing the sample size by the average cluster size (3,750/150 = 25). Thus, you randomly select 25 police agencies out of the 1,500 in the sampling frame. All the officers in each cluster can be selected or a sampling frame can be created and simple random, systematic, or stratified sampling used to select elements.

Rainone and colleagues (2006) employed cluster sampling to examine the impact of substance abuse on deviant and delinquent behaviour. The target population consisted of all secondary school students drawn from 136 clusters using simple random sampling. Within each of the school clusters, four classes from each grade (7 to 12) were selected using SRS, for a sample of 14,977 students. A survey was administered to all students present, resulting in a final sample of 10,383.

To recap, cluster sampling involves the following steps:

1. Define the target population and determine the sample size.
2. Identify or create a sampling frame of the clusters in the target population.
3. Calculate the number of clusters to be sampled.
4. Randomly select clusters.
5. Develop a sampling frame for each cluster or use all elements within the cluster.
6. Randomly select an equal number of elements from each cluster.

Rules of Thumb and Sampling Error

Each stage in cluster sampling has its own sampling error and, when totalled, the error will likely be higher than with other probabilistic techniques. Sampling error increases as the number of clusters decrease. It is reduced by increasing the number and homogeneity of clusters.

When cluster sampling, it is best to have an equal number of elements from each cluster. Sampling elements are closer to the target population values if you maximize the number of clusters and minimize the number of elements selected within each cluster. The more homogeneous the clusters are, the fewer elements needed from each cluster. More clusters better represent population diversity. Thus, you want to have heterogeneity between the clusters and homogeneity within. Although this practice reduces sampling error, it makes sampling more expensive.

Another option to reduce sampling error is to use stratified random sampling to select clusters. This approach reduces sampling error because it increases the homogeneity in clusters from which elements are drawn. For instance, Kirk and Matsuda (2011) tested the proposition that a lot of crime in minority neighbourhoods goes undetected. The cluster sampling frame was 343 Chicago neighbourhoods. A sample of 80 clusters was randomly selected and stratified by ethnic composition and socio-economic status. Within each cluster, SRS was used to select 1,329 households.

Probability Proportionate to Size (PPS)

Probability proportionate to size (PPS) is a type of cluster sampling in which each cluster is selected based on the number of secondary sampling units. Whenever clusters differ substantially in size, PPS is appropriate. The sampling error is reduced by increasing the chances that an element is chosen from a larger cluster. Hence, each element has an equal chance of selection. PPS sampling increases the representativeness of the sample, but there is no guarantee that it

> **probability proportionate to size (PPS)** a type of cluster sampling in which clusters are chosen proportionately based on their size in the population.

will be representative of all population characteristics of interest. The steps involved are as follows:

1. Define the target population.
2. Create a sampling frame of the clusters including data on the size of each one.
3. Calculate the sampling interval and random start.
4. Select a random number between 1 and the sampling interval.
5. Choose subsequent clusters by adding the sampling interval to the random start number.
6. Ensure that the number of chosen clusters is approximately equal to the target number of clusters.

To see how this process works, let's use a hypothetical example. The population of clusters are police agencies across Canada (N = 1,500), and we want to select 10 per cent for the sample (n = 150 clusters). If we divide the sample size by the population size, there is a 10 per cent chance that a police agency will be selected. The problem is that police services vary in size based on the population size of their jurisdiction. By not accounting for population variation, the secondary sampling units selected can be unrepresentative. With PPS, the chance of selecting each cluster is proportionate to its size. A police service with 100 officers has twice the likelihood of selection than one with 50.

Next, we create a sampling frame of all 1,500 police services. If Agency A has ten officers, Agency B has five, and Agency C eight, we would list ten elements for Agency A, five for B, and eight for C. The process continues until all agency elements are listed.

We then calculate the sampling interval, which should sound familiar from systematic random sampling. We divide the population size by the sample size (SI = N/n). Next, we select the random size (a number between 1 and the sampling interval) and a random start (the sampling interval). We then choose cases by counting down the list based on the sampling interval increments. Therefore, larger

Table 4.4 How to create a PPS sample

Sampling frame			
1	Agency A	13	Agency B
2	Agency A	14	Agency B
3	Agency A	15	Agency B
4	Agency A	16	Agency C
5	Agency A	17	Agency C
6	Agency A	18	Agency C
7	Agency A	19	Agency C
8	Agency A	20	Agency C
9	Agency A	21	Agency C
10	Agency A	22	Agency C
11	Agency B	23	Agency C
12	Agency B	24	Agency D and so forth
	Sampling interval (SI)		Random size
	SI = N/n		Random number between 1 and 10 = 7
	SI = 1,500/150 = 10		
	Random start (RS)		Cluster selection
	SI = 10		10 + (0 x 10) = 10 (Agency A)
			10 + (1 x 10) = 20 (Agency C)
			10 + (2 x 10) = 30 (e.g. Agency E)
			Continue until 150 clusters are selected.

clusters have the same probability of selection as smaller ones. Table 4.4 illustrates this process.

Advantages and Disadvantages

Cluster sampling is an efficient sampling technique when populations are large and a sampling frame is unavailable. When a researcher does not have a lot of resources, this technique is ideal as only the clusters and the elements within the selected clusters require sampling frames. Unfortunately, this type of sample is the least representative of the population. With homogeneous clusters, you may have over- or under-representation of certain population characteristics. There is also a higher degree of sampling error as it is cumulative with each stage of sampling. Table 4.5 summarizes cluster sampling.

Nonprobability Sampling

The distinguishing characteristic of nonprobability sampling is that the researcher's decision-making and subjective judgment determines element selection. The advantage is greater control over the sampling process; however, these techniques limit the generalizability of the findings. Nonprobability sampling techniques are chosen because respondents are accessible or there is a reason that they are representative of the population under examination. In most cases, the population is hard to locate or is very specific, a sampling frame is not available, or the project is a pilot study. These techniques can lead to sampling bias and lack representativeness. Thus, caution must be exercised.

Due to difficulties associated with sampling frames and the EPSEM principle or a lack of financial

Table 4.5 Cluster sampling

Technique	• Define the target population and determine the sample size. • Identify or create a sampling frame of clusters in the target population. • Calculate the number of clusters to be sampled. • Randomly select clusters. • Develop a sampling frame for each cluster or use all elements within the cluster. • Randomly select an equal number of elements from each cluster.
Advantages	• Is ideal for large populations when sampling frames of all elements in the target population are not available. • Requires a sampling frame for only the clusters and elements within the selected clusters. • Is less expensive (with geographically defined clusters). • Is able to use other sampling techniques to choose clusters and elements. • Requires less information prior to selecting elements than stratified sampling.
Disadvantages	• Sampling error exists at each stage of sampling, increasing total sampling error. • Increases precision by maximizing the number of clusters and minimizing elements within a cluster but increases the costs. • Has a lower precision of the estimates, requiring a larger sample size of clusters to be equivalent to stratified sampling. • May not be as representative as an SRS sample of equal size. • Is more complex, making analysis and interpretation difficult.

resources, many criminology and criminal justice studies use nonprobability samples. A strong argument exists that we shouldn't assess these techniques with representativeness and generalizabilty but with other criteria. Qualitative research operates under a different paradigm and assumptions, suggesting different sampling, data collection, and analytical techniques.

Convenience Sampling

Convenience sampling is also known as haphazard or accidental sampling. Research subjects are chosen based on accessibility and convenience (see Table 4.6). This technique is ideal for exploring a setting we know little about, probing attitudes and behaviours of group members, conducting exploratory research, or pretesting a survey.

In convenience sampling, there is no definable target population to sample and no systematic technique or selection rules for choosing elements.

convenience sampling
a sampling technique in which cases are selected because they are convenient, regardless of their characteristics.

Therefore, it is easy to implement. Many surveys reported in the media are based on convenience samples. You can quickly find instant online polls asking for opinions on various topics.

Convenience sampling has several strengths and weaknesses. One cannot gauge representativeness or generalize the findings to a larger population. The results apply solely to those in the sample or to the concept of interest. Nonetheless, research using convenience samples has provided us with findings that are meaningful and useful and that present new knowledge.

For example, Piquero and Piquero's (2006) study tested the ability of control balance theory to explain white-collar crime. A convenience sample was the most appropriate for this research because it was exploratory, required respondents with business experience, and represented a hard-to-reach population. A survey with various hypothetical scenarios was given to 87 students taking university business courses.

Similarly, Taylor, Kowalyk, and Boba (2007) conducted an exploratory study on how crime analysts

Table 4.6 Convenience sampling

Technique	• Select cases based on what is accidentally or haphazardly available and convenient.
Advantages	• Is ideal for a setting we know little about or an undefinable population.
	• Is the least expensive nonprobability sampling technique.
	• Is often an effective way to find participants to pretest a survey.
	• Is a quick and easy way to select a sample.
Disadvantages	• Has no controls for representativeness of the sample, thereby increasing sample bias.
	• Has no systematic selection process.
	• Can apply findings to sample participants only.

perceive patrol officers' attitudes on the nature of their work. The sampling frame consisted of all analysts who were members of any three listserves geared toward law enforcement. The goal was not to gain a representative sample of all US analysts but to access those with sufficient knowledge on the key issues that hinder the crime analyst's job. Online surveys were sent to all 3,307 members; 238 responded.

Purposive Sampling

Purposive sampling requires appropriate judgment and adequate knowledge about the population to select cases. Sample elements are chosen based on the research problem and knowledge of the population to identify a small subset of a relatively accessible population that is very specific or hard to reach. For example, deviant cases are purposely selected to gain a better insight into that setting or situation.

Researchers decide who has certain characteristics of interest. For instance, when sampling homeless persons under the age of 25, the judgment is age. As research progresses, the sample is reviewed and sampling criteria are modified to

purposive sampling
a sampling technique in which elements are selected based on the researcher's judgment, knowledge, and substantive criteria.

Research Highlights

The Case of Student Samples

According to Payne and Chappell (2008), students are involved in the research process in several ways. They are co-authors when they actively participate in all stages of the research process. Given the ebb and flow of the academic schedule, however, this participation rarely occurs. They serve as research assistants at various stages of the research process. Some very large-scale studies would not have been possible without collecting data from students. Students can be passive participants when researchers gather data about them but not directly from them, such as official transcripts. The most common role is active research subjects, which usually involves completing surveys during class.

The typical substantive area in student samples is behaviours, be they criminal, deviant, or victimization experiences, or attitudes on topics such as theft, binge drinking, or cheating.

Continued

Second is testing theories and determining risk factors. The most common risk factor investigated is alcohol consumption patterns and its relationship to deviant and criminal behaviour. Third, student samples are used to refine methodological approaches, such as pilot testing a survey and using the feedback for modifications. Lastly, comparisons are frequently drawn among criminal justice majors and other majors, the general population, students in other cultures, criminals, and criminal justice professionals.

Student samples are extremely accessible and cost- and time-effective. They can measure change easily (as students are in the program for four years), provide information on people who are close in age to the majority of criminals, and can serve as a learning experience about the research process. But there are four limitations. Validity concerns exist when students fill out multiple surveys in a term. They may no longer take them seriously or provide socially desirable answers. The ethics of forced participation are another concern. Students may feel an obligation to participate by virtue of their "student status." There is also a stigma associated with student samples. The importance of the findings is regularly minimized. Finally, we have the issue of generalizability. Students are younger, with different life experiences, interests, and income brackets than other groups and are part of a unique subculture.

Payne and Chappell (2008) have a few recommendations about using students in criminological research. Universities should develop policies governing how students are involved in research studies. Professors need to demonstrate to students how their participation fits into the research process and ensure that students are not taken advantage of by any implicit or explicit forced participation. The authors advocate for the continued use of student samples. Many research studies using student convenience samples are published in leading criminology and criminal justice journals, suggesting there is value and knowledge gained from using this technique.

ensure inclusion of elements with different characteristics and experiences. Sampling continues until the researcher has a sense of a concept's meaning and saturation, where nothing new would be learned with additional research subjects.

There are many examples of purposive sampling in the literature. Kohm and colleagues (2012) examined the impact that exposure to the media has on the fear of crime. A purposive sampling strategy was adopted to capture the diversity of students. Professors in different departments were approached and classes at all levels were sampled. Surveys were administered to 397 Canadian students. The authors stated that this sample could not be generalized to all students but was consistent with other exploratory research in criminology and criminal justice. Lewis and Maticka-Tyndale (2000)

examined the relationship among municipally licensing escort agencies, the law, police practices, and the well-being of female escorts. This Canadian case study used purposive sampling to maximize sample diversity in terms of experiences and relevant situations. Thirty-six in-depth interviews were conducted with escorts, agency personnel, community workers, and city officials.

Purposive sampling is appropriate when focusing on deviant cases and when conducting in-depth examinations of specific cases, exploratory research, or hard-to-reach populations. However, the quality of the sample depends on the researcher's ability to make decisions. Nonetheless, these samples are useful if the objective is not to generalize but to gain a deeper understanding about a characteristic or setting (see Table 4.7).

Table 4.7 Purposive sampling

Technique	• Choose cases based on the research problem, population characteristics, and researcher's knowledge and judgment.
Advantages	• Is ideal when a sampling frame doesn't exist but a subset of the population is easily identifiable.
	• Is advantageous when conducting exploratory research or case studies, targeting hard-to-reach populations, or examining deviant cases.
Disadvantages	• Cannot generalize findings but can achieve a deeper understanding.
	• Is a more systematic selection process but remains subjective with no controls for representativeness.
	• Can lead to oversampling of more accessible subgroups in the population.

Quota Sampling

Quota sampling creates a sample with certain characteristics in the same proportion as found in the population. Therefore, you need to know the proportions to set the right quotas. Suppose 50 per cent of the homeless population is above and below 25 years old, 60 per cent are male, and 40 per cent are female. For a sample size of 40, you need 12 males and 8 females for each category. Table 4.8 presents a quota frame of population proportions. Each cell has a proportion assigned, and research subjects who have all the characteristics in each cell are recruited. The quota for males under 25 is 12; thus, sample until this cell has 12 subjects. Sampling continues until a predetermined number of cases for each cell is selected. This method is the nonprobability version of stratified sampling, where a sampling frame doesn't exist and elements are not randomly selected.

Quota sampling helps to represent certain characteristics when a sampling frame is unavailable (see Table 4.9 for a summary). Simultaneously, there are several challenges. Researcher bias can lead to overrepresentation of subjects. Even when the sample is representative based on the characteristics chosen, there is no way to assess representativeness for other characteristics. You can determine quotas for only a small set of characteristics, making it marginally better than convenience sampling. Accurate information is needed when calculating the proportions for each cell, which is difficult without a sampling frame. If one existed, you would use stratified random sampling.

> **quota sampling** a sampling technique in which elements are selected based on predetermined characteristics that are proportionately similar in the population.

Snowball Sampling

This technique is an excellent way to study deviant or insular populations and controversial or marginal attitudes and beliefs. With **snowball sampling**, or **respondent-driven sampling**, a few participants

> **snowball sampling** a sampling technique in which researchers begin with one informant, who refers them to other participants who possess the required knowledge.

Table 4.8 Quota frame

	Under 25 years old		Over 25 years old		
Sex	**Proportion**	**Number**	**Proportion**	**Number**	**Total**
Male	0.6	12	0.6	12	24
Female	0.4	8	0.4	8	16
Total	1.0	20	1.0	20	40

Table 4.9 Quota sampling

Technique	• Select cases based on a combination of two or more population characteristics. • Sample until sufficient numbers are obtained in the different categories.
Advantages	• Ensures that some population characteristics are controlled for in the sample. • Can deliberately oversample a characteristic. • Reflects population diversity better, as the researcher controls key variables.
Disadvantages	• Dictates that sample quality depends on the accuracy of proportions on population characteristics. • Features possible bias due to unaccounted-for characteristics. • Has quotas for only a small subset of characteristics. • Involves researcher subjectivity when selecting population characteristics.

are studied and then asked to refer the researcher to others who also coincide with the research purpose (Korf, van Ginkel, & Benschop, 2009). A set of knowledgeable informants provide information on the group and serve as gatekeepers by vetting the researcher and introducing them to group members. Referrals are requested to other group members with similar characteristics who can provide relevant information on the concepts of interest. You stop sampling when you are learning nothing new, have a good idea of what the concepts of interest mean to group members, or a predetermined number of individuals is reached. Researcher's judgment and repetitive referrals are other reasons for stopping.

Two key considerations in this type of sampling are that trust is essential for access and that the first set of informants must be sufficiently diverse and knowledgeable about the group as a whole to avoid skewing the sample toward a population subgroup. The initial informants largely shape the sample. It's like the expression "guilty by association." You may end up being blocked from accessing certain members. You don't want the equivalent of deviant cases as the first group, as it biases information and structures your access. You may discover only the nature and extent of atypicality as the research progresses. As data collection continues, it becomes more evident that certain types of individuals will provide key information to understand the social phenomenon of interest.

Baron and Forde (2007) tested control balance theory's ability to explain the problems of crime and adversity among 400 homeless youth in Vancouver. Potential respondents were approached, told about the project, and recruited. New contacts were established with referrals or youth who had heard about the study from others. After the interview, participants received $20 in fast-food vouchers.

Jacobs, Topalli, and Wright (2003) explored active carjackers' decision-making and motivations to offend. Interviews were conducted with 28 carjackers, using snowball sampling. Offenders were located with assistance from a street-based field recruiter who was part of the criminal underworld and who tapped into his social networks. Participants received $50 after the interview was complete.

This nonprobability technique is appropriate for conducting exploratory research and case studies, investigating hard-to-locate populations, and understanding the dynamics of social networks. Although not ideal, if your initial informants are deviant cases, you will still gain knowledge on a hard-to-reach population. According to Rubin and Rubin (1995), the rules of snowball sampling are to ensure that you choose initial informants who are knowledgeable about the group, situation, or behaviour under investigation, who are participating of their own free will (which can be easier said than done in certain subcultures), and whose views represent the group to which they belong. The findings must apply exclusively to the group sampled and not to a larger population. See Table 4.10 for a summary of this approach.

Table 4.10 Snowball sampling

Technique	• Identify initial cases and informants, who then make referrals to others in the group (chain referral, reputational sampling).
Advantages	• Is ideal for exploratory research and members of hard-to-locate or insular groups. • Provides an opportunity to collect in-depth information on controversial or marginal attitudes and beliefs. • Can gain an understanding of social networks and identify key stakeholders. • Increases credibility as individuals are involved in the research process.
Disadvantages	• Is shaped by initial informants' structuring access to group members. • Requires trust and rapport for continued access. • Includes a time-consuming sampling process. • Features a compromised anonymity of participants due to the referral process.

Logistical Considerations

This section focuses on sample quality and size. The generalizability of research findings is contingent on sample quality. The representativeness of the sample is related to sample size. Both sample quality and size are affected by the extent of sampling error. The more sampling error that exists, the less representative the sample and the less generalizable the findings.

Sample Quality

We cannot assess quality if we don't know the population or how elements were selected. Quality does not depend on which sampling technique is chosen but on the sample itself.

Research Highlights

Can Sampling Approaches Be Combined?

The answer to this question is, "Absolutely." Recall that cluster sampling uses other probability sampling techniques to choose the clusters and the elements within selected clusters. Stratified sampling uses simple random or systematic sampling to select elements within each stratum. What we know less about is how research combines probability and nonprobability sampling. A couple of examples illustrate the process well.

Kupchik's (2007) research objective was to explore the experiences of youth serving their sentences in youth versus adult correctional institutions. Kupchik used purposive sampling to select one city and five institutions, based on housing the highest number of eligible respondents and proximity to the city. Out of four youth facilities, two were chosen and, of the fifty adult facilities matching the selection criteria, three were selected.

Each institution created a sampling frame of eligible youth from the inmate population. SRS was used by correctional staff to select 95 interviewees randomly and then prison counsellors approached each inmate about participating. Convenience sampling chose 18 key staff members to complete a survey on available programming, disciplinary practices, program

Continued

participation, physical condition of the facility, staff training, and the extent of misbehaviour and violence at the institution.

Wolfer and Friedrichs (2001) were interested in students' perceptions of justice at a Jesuit university. Sixteen criminal justice and 12 sociology courses were purposively sampled based on the research objectives. From these 28 courses, 2 criminal justice and 2 sociology courses were selected using simple random sampling. This process resulted in a sample of 33 criminal justice majors and 53 non-criminal justice majors who completed a survey during class. The researchers made clear that the "statistics are not generalizable to other schools or to students beyond this sample due to our sampling techniques and the exploratory nature of the study" (p. 326).

Probability and nonprobability sampling techniques are, in principle, oppositional to one another, much like the paradigms underlying quantitative and qualitative research. However, this relationship does not mean that they cannot be combined if the research objectives and questions deem this approach appropriate. For marginalized and hard-to-reach populations, a multimethod approach to sampling can be more effective. The key to these combinations is the acknowledgement that one cannot guarantee the representativeness of the sample or the accuracy of any generalizations made to the population.

For meaningful conclusions, we have to estimate how close the random sample is to the population values and how confident we are of that closeness. The extent of sampling error depends on the heterogeneity of the population, sample size, and **confidence level**. The easiest way to indicate sampling error is to provide two numbers, being a lower and upper boundary, along with the probability that the population parameter falls between these two values. Confidence levels give you the ability to estimate the extent to which the findings would be obtained if you were to analyze all elements in the population. In other words, given a certain level of probability, a statement is made that the true population parameter lies within a specified range of values. The level is the probability and is frequently expressed as a percentage rather than an alpha level of probability (if α equals 0.05, the significance level equals 95 per cent).

The **confidence interval** is the range of values that the population parameter lies within. The larger the sample size, the narrower the confidence interval. You have likely seen an ad claiming that a certain percentage of people prefer one product over another. In the fine print, it will say plus or minus a certain number, known as the **standard error**. This measure estimates the standard deviation value for a particular sample (as in Figure 4.4) and tells us the variability in the sampling distribution for a statistic.

Let's say 72 per cent of lawyers believe that the people they represent are deceitful. You want to determine with 95 per cent confidence (the level most commonly used) that the population parameter falls within a certain confidence interval. Think back to Figure 4.4, where the population parameter equals a standard deviation of zero. If the population parameter is estimated to be 72 per cent and the standard error is +/- 3, the confidence interval allows you to say with 95 per cent confidence that the population parameter falls between 69 per cent and 75 per cent.

confidence level an indication of how confident one is about the accuracy of a sample statistic's estimation of the true population parameter.

confidence interval a range of values—including the value of the population parameter—with a specific probability.

standard error the measurement of the total sampling error and of the sample mean's ability to estimate the population mean.

Based on the Central Limit Theorem, the confidence level depicts how often you can expect to get similar results or how often the findings will be outside the margin of error. A 95 per cent confidence level has a 5 per cent margin of error. This means that the results will be in the margin of error 5 per cent of the time, or once every twenty times. You can then state with 95 per cent certainty that the sample statistics are representative of the population parameter within a range of values. With this confidence level, there is a 95 per cent certainty that the sample is representative of the population. The confidence level and interval form the basis for calculating the sample size.

Sample Size

The obvious question is, "How big does my sample need to be?" Well, as large as possible. The better question to ask is, "What is the minimum number of cases needed for my sample?" There are two reasons why determining sample size is important: inadequate size can compromise conclusions and limit generalizability back to the target population, and too few elements within clusters or strata hinder the ability to compare subgroups in the population (Kitchenham & Pfleeger, 2002).

When determining sample size, several factors require consideration: sampling technique, degree of accuracy for sample statistics (confidence level), heterogeneity in the population, number of subgroups, and available resources. The more characteristics, selection criteria, or variation in the population, the larger the sample. Yet the required sample size does not depend significantly on the size of the whole population, even if it is large.

There is always a margin of error between the values of sample statistics and population parameters. When you don't know the population value, you statistically estimate the margin of error by using confidence intervals. With the confidence level, we estimate how confident we are about the interval values. For a more heterogeneous population, a larger sample is required to get a similar degree of

confidence and standard error than in a homogeneous population. The larger the sample, the lower the random sampling error (see Figure 4.5). Smaller samples are to be expected and are appropriate with exploratory and descriptive studies, as the same type and level of precision are not required. This is also the case for homogenous populations, such as those created within strata. However, it doesn't matter how large the sample is if it isn't representative of the population.

Three pieces of information are required to calculate the sample size: the degree of accuracy needed, the extent of heterogeneity in the population, and the number of variables to be examined. Further, consider the research purpose and your intended use of the results. The problem is that estimating population variability is harder than it looks. As a last resort, researchers make educated guesses based on the information they are able to gather. Thus, with increased heterogeneity, subgroups, variables, confidence levels, and statistical precision, the larger the sample size.

Recall that the sampling ratio is the number of cases in the sample divided by the number of cases in the population. If your target population is 1,000 cases and you have a sampling ratio of 28 per cent for a 95 per cent confidence level, you sample 300 elements. The calculation requires the population size, sample size, confidence level, and interval. For illustration purposes in Table 4.11, the conventional

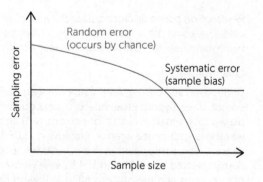

Figure 4.5 The relationship between sampling error and sample size

Table 4.11 Appropriate sample sizes at a confidence level of 95 per cent (0.05)

Population size	Minimum sample size	% of the population	Population size	Minimum sample size	% of the population
10	10	100	1,000	278	28
20	19	95	1,500	306	20
50	44	88	2,000	323	16
70	59	84	4,000	351	9
100	80	80	5,000	357	7
150	108	72	10,000	370	4
200	132	64	15,000	375	3
250	152	61	20,000	377	2
300	169	56	25,000	378	2
400	197	49	50,000	381	1
500	218	43	100,000	383	0.003
750	254	34	1,000,000+	384	0.0004

Source: Adapted from Poulin, Orchowsky, & Trask (2011).

95 per cent degree of confidence is used. Consider these sample sizes as rules of thumb, but remember that they are only minimums that must be amended when considering the research objective, sampling technique, and other factors previously mentioned. These rules do not apply to nonprobability sampling.

Vignette: Breaking It Down

Sampling in Police Discretion Research

Research on police discretion uses all types of sampling strategies because the research method differs based on the research question. Quantitative, qualitative, and mixed methods research are highlighted here to illustrate how the research question drives the method.

Quantitative

Godfredson and colleagues (2010) examined the factors affecting discretion after officers viewed one of three hypothetical videos on encounters involving people with a mental illness, people without a mental illness, or persons with an ambiguous mental state. The target population was the largest police agency, employing 11,000 sworn officers, in the largest state in Australia. Officers who participated in the mandatory operational safety tactics training course were randomly selected (n = 310), and 304 surveys were completed. Responses were linked to the severity of symptoms and the officer's attitude toward mentally ill persons. The authors concluded that officers face considerable obstacles when resolving these types of encounters.

Cihan and Wells (2011) examined citizens' perceptions on the appropriate amount of police discretion by considering factors that influence opinions (e.g. fear of crime, criminal victimization experiences). The sampling frame consisted of 4,966 phone numbers, created using SRS. After removing business and fax lines, there were 3,055 numbers; 1,300 interviews were completed. Sample size declined due to refusals, non-contact, or disconnection during the interview. Weighting increased representativeness and generalizability for groups such as low-income families. The researchers found that about 50 per cent of citizens believe that the police use the right amount of discretion.

Qualitative

Landau (1996) investigated the nature and extent of police work within the context of social service and security needs. A purposive sampling strategy selected four remote, fly-in, Canadian Aboriginal communities. The study included 120 interviews with community leaders, service providers, police officers, and community members. The findings suggested that alcohol is the most serious social problem and is perceived as the root of most other community problems. Police were seen as the social agency that can best deal with social problems and those related to alcohol use.

McKillop and Pfeiffer (2004) examined the factors used—and the importance of each—in police decision-making in youth-related encounters. A convenience sample of seventy police officers were invited to participate by completing a survey after each youth encounter. Thirty-two officers provided voluntary, informed consent to participate. Findings suggested that extra-legal factors, such as demeanour, are secondary to offence seriousness and that older youth are less deserving of leniency. Finally, an officer's prior knowledge of factors such as a minimal offending history, non-criminal family, or a disadvantaged background affected disposition decisions, where the tendency was toward diversion from the youth criminal justice system.

Mixed Methods

Schulenberg and Warren (2009) investigated whether the factors affecting discretion differ between patrol officers and specialized youth officers in Canada. Proportionate stratified random sampling was used to select 98 police agencies in every province and territory while ensuring representation by location and population size. The 202 interviewees within agencies were selected using purposive sampling to include all ranks, shifts, duty assignments, and years of service. The researchers found that agencies with specialization were more likely to make referrals, less likely to charge, more likely to detain when charged, and to consider situational factors related to the particular youth and offence when using their discretion.

Conclusion

Researchers have options when choosing a sampling strategy. The first step is examining the research purpose and questions, a process that informs the decision between probability and nonprobability sampling. The choice of a particular sampling technique also depends on the research objectives and sampling frame availability, population characteristics, accessibility, anticipated analysis, existing resources, and the possibility of random selection.

There is one last thing to consider, which is how ethics fit into this stage of the research process. The ethical considerations fall into four general areas. Participation must be voluntary, and each participant must provide informed consent (which can be revoked at any time). When individuals agree to participate, they must do so with an understanding of what the study entails overall and in regards to their participation.

Great care must be exercised when conducting research on special and vulnerable populations. These groups can include youth, captive populations (such as inmates or students), Aboriginal peoples, persons with a mental illness, or active criminals. Confidentiality, anonymity, and informed consent are even more important in such cases, so that these populations are not implicitly or explicitly taken advantage of or harmed in any way.

As seen with snowball sampling, some techniques compromise the researcher's ability to guarantee anonymity. When referrals and introductions are made by participants, their identity is likely to be known to the person they suggested.

Finally, ethics plays a role in the analysis and writing up of results. We must be completely transparent about potential sampling error, sampling frame weaknesses, representativeness, and generalizability. For example, with nonprobability samples, do not take differences among sample elements as indicative of differences in the population. Doing so commits the error of overgeneralization.

Summary of Important Points

Introduction

- We sample to make inferences about a population, concept, or similar situation.
- The difference between probability and nonprobability sampling is random selection.
- Research questions inform decisions about the population, sample, and choice of sampling technique.

Learning the Lingo

- Sampling elements are selected from the target population.
- The target population is defined by using inclusion and exclusion criteria.
- Sample statistics estimate population parameters of characteristics, processes, and behaviours.
- Sampling frames, which list all elements in the target population, are used to select cases.
- Sampling error consists of random and systematic errors.

Probability Theory

- With a large enough sample, Central Limit Theorem suggests that, with repeated sampling, the sample statistics will be the same as the population parameters and form a normal distribution.
- The EPSEM principle states that each element in the target population has a known, equal, and nonzero probability of selection.
- Random selection increases representativeness and improves generalizability of the findings.

Probability Sampling

- Using a lottery method or random number table, simple random sampling randomly selects elements numbered sequentially.
- Systematic random sampling uses a sampling ratio, interval, and random start to select every kth element in the sampling frame.
- Stratified random sampling divides the target population into strata based on key characteristics,

and an equal number of elements are selected from each stratum.

- Proportionate and disproportionate stratified random sampling purposefully uses a different sampling fraction to resemble or differ from the proportion found in the target population.
- Cluster sampling randomly selects naturally occurring groups (clusters) and elements within chosen clusters.
- PPS is a type of cluster sampling in which clusters are selected based on the number of elements in each one.

Nonprobability Sampling

- Convenience sampling chooses cases based on accessibility.
- Based on relevant research criteria, purposive sampling employs the researcher's knowledge and judgment to select cases.
- Quota sampling selects cases based on characteristics proportionate to what exist in the population.
- Snowball sampling uses informants to make referrals to the next set of participants.

Logistical Considerations

- The degree of sampling error depends on the heterogeneity of the population, sample size, and confidence level.
- The confidence level indicates the probability that the true population parameter lies within the confidence interval values.
- Standard error calculates the standard deviation value, telling us how well the sample mean estimates the population mean.
- Larger samples reduce random sampling error.
- A larger sample is needed with heterogeneous populations, higher confidence levels (if the research question involves comparing subgroups), or a large number of variables.

Conclusion

- Ethical considerations include providing voluntary and informed consent, exercising care when working with special and vulnerable populations, guaranteeing anonymity, and being transparent when reporting results.

Key Terms

Review Questions and Exercises

1. Propose a sampling design on a topic that interests you. Include the following information:
   a. the research question
   b. the population definition
   c. the most appropriate sampling technique (and explain why it is so)
   d. the sampling frame (if applicable) and the elements
   e. the sampling process as it applies to this study
   f. the advantages and disadvantages of this approach
2. Propose a sampling design to conduct research on the following:
   a. judges' decision-making
   b. convicted sex offenders
   c. Hells Angels' members
3. Why is randomness an important feature of probabilistic sampling? Isn't it better to create a balanced sample based on certain characteristics? Give reasons to support your answer.
4. Locate an example of a research study covered by the media and identify the population, sampling technique, sampling error, confidence level, and interval.
5. Choose a journal article on a topic of your choice. Answer the following questions:
   a. Is the sampling technique chosen appropriate, given the research question?
   b. How is the sample selected?
   c. What are the advantages and disadvantages of this approach?
   d. What does sampling error mean in this case?
6. What ethical concerns require attention when researching hidden or hard-to-locate populations?

Online Exercises and Websites of Interest

Random Number Table

www.randomizer.org
This site allows you to create your own random number table and export it into Excel.

Research Methods Knowledge Base: Sampling

www.socialresearchmethods.net/kb/sampling.php
This site provides a summary of key terms, statistical terminology, probability, and nonprobability sampling.

Sample Size Calculator

www.surveysystem.com/sscalc.htm
This online tool automatically calculates the ideal sample size based on a study's population size and the desired confidence level.

Statistics Canada: Selection of a Sample

www.statcan.gc.ca/edu/power-pouvoir/ch13/sample-echantillon/5214900-eng.htm
This site offers an excellent summary of sampling design, population, frame, elements, size, and technique.

Additional Resources

Falco, D.L., & Martin, J.S. (2012). "Examining Punitiveness: Assessing Views toward the Punishment of Offenders among Criminology and Non-Criminology Students." *Journal of Criminal Justice Education,* ***23*(2), 205–232.**

This article provides a good discussion of the advantages of convenience samples with students and the use of comparisons.

Levy, P.S., & Lemeshow, S. (2008). *Sampling of Populations: Methods and Applications* **(4th ed.) New York: Wiley.**

This text is a great resource if you are looking for more advanced coverage on sampling techniques and related logistical concerns.

Chapter 5

Experimental Research Designs

"No amount of experimentation can ever prove me right; a single experiment can prove me wrong."
Albert Einstein (1879–1955)

Learning Objectives

- To appreciate the benefits of conducting experiments in exploratory and explanatory research.
- To create an experiment appropriate to the research question and hypotheses.
- To distinguish between a true experiment and pre- and quasi-experimental designs.

- To differentiate the threats to internal and external validity and their links to an experiment's components.
- To articulate the relationship between experiments and ethical principles as well as practical challenges facing researchers.

Introduction

The word *experiment* is used to describe both scientific and unscientific endeavours. For example, we conduct an unscientific experiment whenever we attempt to eliminate alternative explanations for a problem or find causes of a predicament. As film director David Cronenberg (2012) argues, "Everybody is a mad scientist, and life is their lab. We're all trying to experiment to find a way to live, to solve problems, to fend off madness and chaos."

We can find examples in the media associated with the effectiveness of a change in the criminal justice system. However, the method of collecting evidence lacks the characteristics of a scientific experiment needed to support a causal explanation. For instance, the headline to a *Winnipeg Sun* article on incarcerating young offenders reads, "Youth Justice Act experiment failing us" (Brodbeck, 2012). In this article, the reporter draws on the scientific usage of the term while citing inadequate findings to support a causal argument. He mentions that a group of teenagers involved in the death of a cab driver in 2008 received little or no jail time, despite the severity of the offence. He also refers to the statistic that, in 2011, 56 per cent of young offenders who completed a sentence in the community were convicted of a new crime. The conclusion is that "despite all the talk about how incarceration doesn't work and that community sentencing is the preferred option, we now have over-whelming evidence that this social experiment has failed." This experiment is unscientific because the first piece of evidence is anecdotal and the criteria for causality have not been met. There could be a variety of different reasons for the percentage of young offenders who reoffend, reasons that may or may not have anything to do with youth justice legislation or sentencing practices.

From a scientific perspective, an **experiment** is a research design appropriate for conducting explanatory research or evaluating a program or intervention. The first documented scientific experiment was performed by Galileo in the sixteenth century. To test his theoretical proposition about acceleration, he timed how long it took for balls to roll down an inclined slope (Levitt & List, 2006). Considered the gold standard of the scientific method, an experiment controls a situation to varying degrees and records changes to assess an intervention's impact on a particular behaviour, belief, or attitude. The goal is to demonstrate the existence of a causal relationship and to specify how it works. In other words, the study seeks to determine or predict the impact of an action.

Experimental research assesses whether a certain outcome occurs when a stimulus is introduced. An observed result could be caused by several factors other than the intervention. To demonstrate a cause-and-effect relationship, the research findings must address an additional dimension: if a program is administered, a certain outcome occurs and, if it is not delivered, the outcome does not occur. Only in this way can you isolate the independent effect of par-ticipating in the program. Returning to our example on the youth justice social experiment, only then can we make causal inferences that community-based sentences lead to increased rates of reoffending.

Experimental research can test an everyday version of truth. Valla, Ceci, and Williams (2011) investigated the common stereotype that we can identify a person's character—or whether a person is a criminal—by what he or she looks like. Their results may surprise you. Research subjects were shown pictures of 32 males in their twenties with-out any scars, tattoos, or excessive facial hair (16 were convicted criminals and 16 were non-criminals). Subjects were asked whether they thought each male was a criminal and, if so, what type (e.g. drug dealer, rapist, or thief). The subjects were relatively accurate in spotting the actual criminals, but they could not consistently iden-tify the type of criminal.

> **experiment** a research design that isolates, con-trols, and manipulates an independent variable to measure its effect on the dependent variable.

Appropriate Topics and Research Questions

Four guidelines determine if an experimental research design is appropriate for a given topic and research question. First, the research purpose is to establish causality, that is, to generate findings to support a causal explanation. Recall from Chapter 3 that, with causality, we assume that everything in life is ordered and patterned. We are trying to explain why, how, and to what extent an intervention affects an outcome. Thus, the research design must be struc-tured so as to satisfy the three criteria of causality. There must be an empirical association, whereby the cause and effect are both present and vary in conjunction with one another. The researcher must establish temporal order by demonstrating that the cause precedes the effect in time. Spurious relation-ships must be eliminated. The researcher has to rule out alternative explanations by isolating the variables of interest so that no other possible cause can affect the predicted result.

Second, experiments are appropriate when the researcher can manipulate the cause (independent variable). This manipulation is possible only when you can control whether a person receives the treatment.

Third, only one causal variable can be tested, but more than one effect variable can be assessed. For instance, if you are evaluating the value of an anger management program, you could have two dependent variables: violent reoffending and the frequency of verbal conflict with others. Finally, the researcher must be able to address the research question with a reasonably small group of research subjects. Experiments are not appropriate when the goal is to generalize the findings to a larger population and/or from sample sizes greater than a hundred people.

What if your topic is the criminal behaviour of burglars and your research question asks, "How do burglars rationalize their criminal behaviour?" The topic may be amenable to an experimental research design, but the research question is not. It would be very difficult to operationalize rationalization into an observable variable and to manipulate this potential cause for criminal behaviour.

Alternatively, the research question "Do boot camps reduce the likelihood of reoffending?" meets all four parameters for experimental research. It is explanatory research because the objective is to determine whether boot camps are effective and to what extent. The researcher can select subjects based on whether they were sent to boot camp or received a different sentence, thereby manipulating the causal variable of boot camp participation. The topic has only one independent variable of interest. The concepts of boot camp programs and reoffending are clearly definable, and the variables of participating in boot camps and committing new crimes are directly observable. The researcher can ensure that participating in a boot camp occurs prior to measuring the dependent variable. He or she does not necessarily need a large number of research subjects to address the research question.

The Logic behind Experiments

One way to decide if experiments are appropriate is to establish whether the proposed research is descriptive, exploratory, or explanatory. Research that tries to describe a process is not appropriate for

experimentation; therefore, this section focuses on the other types.

Researchers consider three factors when determining the best way to address the research question and hypothesis and to draw valid inferences from the data. First, an experimental design allows the researcher to make conclusions about the relationship between an intervention and outcome. Testing a hypothesis yields findings that centre on a causal relationship and how it works. Second, this research design allows the experimenter to eliminate spuriousness by ruling out alternative explanations. Experimenters are active participants in the research process because they exercise varying degrees of control over the experiment's setting. Controlling the treatment conditions is one way to control for possible external factors that might explain how and why an outcome occurs. Third, experiments help researchers to control variability in how the treatment is administered. Thus, you can have more confidence that the same treatment actually caused the effects and the differences between those who received it and those who did not.

Explanatory Research

Experimental research designs are most commonly associated with explanatory research. In criminology, researchers test the applicability and effectiveness of a theory to explain a particular event or behaviour. In criminal justice, experiments are used to test a program's success and to inform policy-making. Determining the degree to which one thing causes something else and how or why it happens is far from easy, but explanatory experiments can help accomplish this goal.

Exploratory Research

Although less common than explanatory research, exploratory research was used in some of the most famous criminological experiments, including the Stanford prison experiment. Exploratory experiments address the question "What would happen if?" and develop testable theoretical propositions and hypotheses. They are sometimes referred to as hypothesis-generating because researchers try to determine if a particular intervention is related to a particular outcome. Exploratory experimentation is appropriate when theories provide conceptual propositions, not specific expectations.

Exploratory experiments restrict the intervention's variability. For instance, limiting the subject matter taught by more than one instructional method allows the researcher to focus on more promising methods and to work from the perspective of theories on effective teaching practices. However, exploratory experiments are rarely self-sufficient. They can be viewed by the scientific community as fishing expeditions. Thus, the next step is to conduct a hypothesis-driven, explanatory experiment. For example, an explanatory experiment hypothesizes that lecture-based classes are less successful than discussion-based in terms of final grades. The exploratory experiment clarifies how discussion-based techniques are defined and ideally operationalized.

Experimental Settings

Once researchers determine whether the research is explanatory or exploratory, they must decide whether it should be a laboratory, field, or natural experiment. The decision is driven by the research question, but researchers are also constrained by their degree of control over treatment administration, by the availability of data on the dependent variable, and by ethical constraints such as the ability to assign subjects to groups randomly. Choosing an experimental setting is a critical decision as the conclusions drawn from an experiment can apply only to conditions similar to those that occurred in the study (Stoeffer, 1950).

Laboratory Experiments

Building on the natural sciences, a **laboratory experiment** occurs in an artificial environment created by the researcher. In a controlled environment, you can reduce the influence of external factors and manipulate the independent variable in a consistent manner. Hence, laboratory experiments are the strongest at measuring the cause–effect relationship.

Unfortunately, experiments in a laboratory are not without limitations. The validity of the conclusions is threatened because participants may not necessarily behave as they would in a natural setting. The idea that a laboratory can simulate real-life situations is questionable. Can we accurately recreate the adrenaline or panic associated with criminal behaviour, victimization, or witnessing a crime? Criminologists argue that field experiments are a better approach if we truly want to understand human behaviour.

laboratory experiment an experiment conducted under highly controlled conditions in an artificial environment.

Field Experiments

Field experiments take place in real-life settings, but the researcher still controls the treatment, intervention, or program administration. These experiments are common in policy-related research examining the effectiveness of a criminal justice intervention and attempting to better understand the causes of criminal behaviour. Working in the field allows you to conduct an experiment in a more realistic setting, but you lose control over factors that might also contribute to the outcome. In other words, field experiments are more limited than laboratory experiments in their ability to isolate and focus on the variables identified in the causal relationship and to eliminate spuriousness.

field experiment an experiment conducted in a real-life setting where the researcher controls the administration of the treatment, program, or event.

An example of a field experiment is Castillo and colleagues' (2012) investigation of the opportunistic behaviour that occurs when delivering mail. Envelopes that looked like they contained birthday cards were sent through the United States and Peru postal services. Each contained a card and either two $1 bills folded in half or no money. Eighteen per cent of the mail did not arrive at its destination; envelopes containing money were twice as likely to be lost. In another experiment, Lane (2006) investigated whether drug use and delinquent behaviour increase the fear of crime. Youth between the ages of 12 and 18 sentenced to probation were randomly assigned to either participate or not participate in a program. The results showed that those less involved in delinquent behaviour are more afraid of crime regardless of assignment to the program.

natural experiment an experiment conducted in a real-life setting where the researcher does not control the administration of the treatment, program, or event.

Natural Experiments

Natural experiments observe behavioural changes as they occur in real life, such as what happens after legislative change. The difference with this type is that the researcher does not control the incidence of the treatment or cause or the variability in its administration. Furthermore, the researcher usually uses pre-existing groups. Researchers look for a naturally occurring context that allows them to observe a number of groups over a sufficient length of time in order to measure the dependent variable. Although randomly assigning participants to groups is not possible in natural experiments, it must still be reasonable to assume that subjects in each group do not vary in a systematic way. Finally, the intervention is successful or unsuccessful for one or more groups.

true experiment a design that randomly assigns participants to one of two groups and measures the dependent variable before and after the independent variable is administered.

The weakness of natural experiments is that it lacks baseline data on the participants prior to the event. You cannot be sure that a change in behaviours or attitudes is produced by the naturally occurring event or other factors. Consequently, testing a causal relationship is rarely the rationale for natural experiments, which are appropriate for exploratory research or hypothesis development.

True (Classical) Experiments

A **true experiment** is the most powerful research design that a researcher can use to investigate a causal relationship. True experiments have three unique characteristics: the researcher compares two

Methods in Action

Research Informing Evidence-Based Practice

Hot spot policing is generally accepted as a useful approach to controlling street violence. Yet the best way to implement and sustain this police mobilization strategy remains unknown. Within an urban area, crime typically clusters in small high-crime-rate areas. These hot spots account for a disproportionate amount of criminal behaviour and public disorder. For instance, Sherman, Gartin, and Buerger (1989) found that 3 per cent of addresses account for approximately half of the calls for service. Basically, this result is an enforcement approach; more officers are directed to patrol the streets, alleys, and other locations in neighbourhoods where crime is most prevalent.

Taylor, Koper, and Woods (2011) conducted a ninety-day randomized experiment with the Jacksonville Sheriff's Office (JSO) to assess the success of problem-solving and directed saturation patrol strategies. Problem-solving involved officers identifying and addressing the primary factors behind the prevalence of crime in these areas. Tactics included situational crime prevention, public order offence enforcement, community partnerships, and targeted enforcement practices. Directed saturation patrol involved assigning officers working on overtime in hot-spot areas, where they targeted offences and crime patterns identified by crime analysts.

groups; research subjects are randomly assigned to each group; and the dependent variable is measured before and after the intervention is administered. In other experimental designs, one or more of these characteristics are missing.

Two Groups

In true experiments, researchers compare the scores on the dependent variable (outcome) for two types of groups. Participants in the **experimental group** receive the intervention, stimulus, or program. In other words, the researcher administers the cause (independent variable) to the experimental (treatment) group only. By controlling when this group receives the intervention, the researcher establishes temporal order.

The **control group** resembles the experimental group as much as possible; the only difference is that it is not exposed to the stimulus or intervention. By comparing the scores from the subjects in both groups, we can isolate the independent variable's effect on the dependent variable. For example, we could assess whether a person's participation in an anti-shoplifting program impacts his or her reoffending. Administering the treatment to the experimental group and withholding it from the control group allows us to detect effects of the intervention rather than other factors.

Assigning People to Groups

There are two ways to assign individuals to the experimental and control groups: random assignment and matching. Regardless of the method selected, you need enough research subjects in each group to make them equivalent to one another and to ensure that any differences do not occur systematically (e.g. the experimental group has more males than the control group). The rule of thumb is fifty subjects in each group (Weisburd, 2000; Welsh, 2007).

experimental group in an experiment, the group exposed to the stimulus or intervention.

control group in an experiment, the group that is not exposed to the stimulus or intervention (independent variable) and is therefore expected to remain unchanged.

Eighty-three violent crime hot spots were randomly assigned to receive these strategies; the remaining areas continued to use established patrol practices. Crime declined in both the problem-solving and directed patrol hot spots, but the effects were the stronger in the former. To build on these results, the JSO assigned officers to 19 hot spots from the original experiment that were previously assigned directed patrol or no change and again assessed the value of the problem-solving strategy.

The Sheriff's Office realized that an officer's definition of problems in these hot spots directly affects his or her effectiveness. Officers appeared to be overly reliant on crime analysis data instead of their law enforcement training and experience. They required specialized training in the problem-solving strategy to be more effective. In August 2010, officers were not provided with the crime data but were instructed to conduct observational periods in their assigned hot spots. They received informal and formal training at the individual and group levels, leading to a further decrease in crime and disorder within these hot spots.

This example demonstrates that evidence-based policing and findings from an experiment can have far-reaching effects. The JSO dedicates resources and assesses the results from modifications in practice. The experiment also shows that, although there are challenges in translating research into practice, it can and does happen.

Random Assignment

Random assignment, also referred to as **randomization**, ensures that similar types of people are in the experimental and control groups. Using this selection method, assignment to each group is by chance; there is an equal probability of assignment to any particular group, reducing the likelihood of bias and limiting over- or underrepresentation in any one group. Randomization arbitrarily assigns numbers to each person and then uses a random number table to select participants or uses every odd number for one group and every even for the other. This process makes random assignment an effective way to control testing of unrelated factors because the groups are not systematically different from one another. Any subsequent differences observed between the groups can be attributed to the treatment's effect.

random assignment (or randomization) a selection method that uses probability sampling techniques to assign participants to experimental and control groups.

matching a selection method in which participants are assigned to the experimental and control groups based on similar individual or aggregate characteristics.

We frequently confuse random sampling with random assignment. Random sampling is a method for selecting research subjects to participate in a study. EPSEM techniques increase the findings' generalizability and the sample's representativeness of the population. In contrast, random assignment describes how we assign study participants to groups. Remember, a random sample with less than a hundred cases is usually not representative of the population. For this reason, random sampling is rarely used to select subjects for an experiment.

Although random sampling is rarely used to select experiment subjects, there is precedent for it aiding in participant selection prior to randomization or matching. Anderson, Sabatelli, and Trachtenberg (2007) hypothesized that youth who participate in police programs exhibit more positive changes in personal adjustment, social competencies, and relationships with others. Their experimental group consisted of 367 youth participating in a police program. The comparison group was recruited, using cluster sampling (n = 337), from local high schools and was matched to youth in the experimental group. The equivalency test showed no significant differences based on race, family structure, GPA, or grade level.

Matching

Matching is a poor substitute for randomization but is sometimes the only option available. Similar to quota sampling, subjects are matched on individual characteristics. Once pairs are created, each person from the pair is randomly assigned to the control or experimental group. Without random assignment, the likelihood that these comparison groups are unequal is much higher. Unfortunately, quota sampling and matching share the same weaknesses, namely the inability to identify the relevant characteristics and to match on more than a few characteristics. Thus, the two groups may have differences that could affect the outcome.

Choosing relevant characteristics depends on the research question and those most likely to affect the dependent variable. Subjects are assigned based on characteristics such as age, prior criminal history, and sex. The more confident we can be about the similarity of the two groups on these key characteristics, the more confident we can be that the treatment causes different outcomes in the experimental group.

Equivalency of Groups

An equivalency test should be used regardless of whether subjects are allocated to groups using random assignment or matching. After randomization, members of each group are tested for comparability. When matched at the individual level, subjects are deemed similar based on key characteristics and are then assigned to different groups. At the aggregate level, groups are selected on the basis of similarity in the distribution of characteristics, such as the average number of males and females. At either level, subjects in both groups should be as similar to each other as possible.

Experimental studies use both randomization and matching to assign individuals or geographic areas to groups. Exum (2002) used the former to look at the effects of alcohol and anger on violent decision-making. Eighty-four male students were recruited through classroom announcements and flyers. Members of the experimental group were randomly assigned and exposed to alcohol or situations in which a false accusation induced anger. The control group did not receive alcohol or an anger stimulus.

In their assessment of community policing as a strategy to combat violent crime, Connell, Miggans, and McGloin (2008) used matching. The killing of a youth served as a catalyst for residents to demand more police presence and a crackdown to be initiated. The researchers created two comparison groups, matching participants on the key areas of financial resources, number of patrol officers, access to departmental resources, and population characteristics.

Another matching example is from Miller and Miller (2010), who investigated whether a prisoner re-entry program successfully reduces reoffending. The experimental group consisted of 73 program participants. As is often the case in criminal justice research, random assignment was not possible. The comparison group consisted of 72 subjects that were eligible for the program but denied admission. They were matched on sex, age, race, current offence, criminal history, and diagnosis of a substance abuse disorder, all representing possible external factors that could affect recidivism.

Measuring the Dependent Variable

Although we discussed hypotheses in Chapter 3, it is important to be clear on their role in experimental research. Experiments are designed to test a hypothesis, which proposes a relationship between variables. The independent variable is identified in the hypothesis as causing a change in the dependent variable.

When creating a hypothesis, following a few guidelines can make the difference between valid and invalid conclusions. According to Goode and Hatt (2002), operational definitions should be clear in terms of language, measurement, and other concepts and variables. There should be no judgments or language suggesting morality, such as *should* or *ought*. A legitimate hypothesis has empirical indicators that are directly observable in the real world. It is very specific and testable, avoids general predictions, and clarifies the association between variables and direction of the relationship. Theory and method are not oppositional; hypotheses refute, qualify, or support existing theory. Failing to keep these guidelines in mind will affect your ability to measure the variables, consistently administer the intervention, and test for changes in the dependent variable.

In an experiment, we control when and to whom the independent variable is administered. The dependent variable is measured to discern if any changes occurred as a consequence of the treatment. In a true experiment, subjects in both groups are given a **pretest** to gather baseline data on the dependent variable before the intervention is administered to the experimental group. After administration, both groups are given a **posttest**, using the same instrument, to again gather data on the dependent variable. Any difference in the dependent variable can be interpreted as the effect of the independent variable.

In an experiment on the effectiveness of instructional techniques, the independent variable is the type of instructional strategy. The dependent variable is mastery of the subject matter, demonstrated

pretest a test administered before a subject is exposed to a treatment; used to collect baseline data on the dependent variable.

posttest a test—the same as the pretest—administered after a subject is exposed to a treatment; used to assess any changes in the dependent variable.

Key Thinker

Joan McCord: The Journey of a Female Academic (1930–2004)

Born in Tuscan, Arizona, Joan McCord was "one of the most brilliant, inspiring, and enthusiastic researchers that criminology has ever seen" (Farrington, 2010b, p. 184). She completed her BA in philosophy (1952) and her PhD in sociology (1968) at Stanford University. She became the first female president of the American Society of Criminology (1989–1990) and received numerous prestigious awards and honours for her research contributions employing experimental designs.

McCord's journey was far from easy. While her first husband studied at Harvard University (under the supervision of Sheldon and Eleanor Glueck), she became an elementary school teacher and, as an education research assistant, studied child development. Her husband became an alcoholic and abusive during her graduate studies. He objected to her having an independent career at a time when teachers could be fired for becoming pregnant (McCord, 2002). After her divorce, she had to support herself and her two sons, which meant that she couldn't continue her studies until the National Institute of Mental Health gave her a three-year fellowship. During the fellowship, she published 18 journal articles and co-authored 4 books.

McCord was a researcher in the longitudinal Cambridge-Somerville Youth Study, which combines the two best research methods to understand criminal behaviour, incorporates risk factors over time, and examines the effectiveness of criminal justice intervention programs. It was the first large-scale randomized experiment in criminology and the first evaluation to find harmful effects from a promising program (Farrington, 2010b). The hypothesis tested whether helping families of young males in troubled neighbourhoods reduces delinquent behaviour. The males were matched based on background characteristics, family structure, parental behaviour, early aggressiveness, intelligence, and physical strength. Tossing a coin, one member of each pair was randomly assigned to the treatment group and the other to the control group. The intervention was a program involving tutoring, counselling, social skills, and pro-social leisure activities. McCord failed to find any benefits to the treatment and admitted that the researchers never considered the possibility that the program could increase delinquency. She reported that those in the treatment group died five years earlier (on average) and were more likely to be repeat offenders, become alcoholics, and have psychiatric disorders (McCord, 2002).

Another of McCord's landmark studies tested whether males from broken homes engaged in more serious offending. She found that the number of parents is less important than family functioning, such as parental conflict and maternal affection. Since she was a single parent for much of her life when this family structure was stigmatized in society, she was pleased that she could report these results (Farrington, 2010b).

David Farrington (2010b, p. 183), an equally influential criminologist, describes McCord as having an "infectious enthusiasm for research questions," demonstrating an "intellectual curiosity," and being brilliant, determined, and competitive. Prior to her death, she offered future scholars two pieces of advice. She urged them to obtain the credentials needed to choose "interesting things to do, activities that will not be heavily dependent on events over which [you] have little control" (McCord, 2002, p. 107). To anyone considering academia as a profession, she advised: "It is better to work on projects you believe to be important than to select with an eye to winning praise or prizes" (p. 107). We have much to learn from this exemplary researcher!

in the form of grades. A pretest is administered to all students at the beginning of the course, testing their knowledge on the subject matter. The experimental group is taught using the discussion-based technique. The control group receives lectures with no discussion questions. The posttest is administered to both groups at the end of the term. If only the students in the experimental group get higher grades than they did in the pretest, we can say that discussion-based instruction results in better grades than does learning the material with the traditional lecture approach.

Let's look at two examples of true experiments. Berk and colleagues (2003) tested whether a new inmate classification system (other than the usual low, medium, and high security) is more accurate in terms of space allocation and the likelihood of inmate misconduct. All new felony offenders within a six-month period were selected and followed for two years. Prisoners with odd ID numbers were randomly assigned to the experimental group, which was classified with the new system (n = 9,662). Even-numbered prisoners formed the control group, which was classified using the existing system (n = 9,656). The equivalency test found similar composition in terms of gang affiliation, age, and relevant background characteristics. The results suggested that the new classification system was better at predicting institutional misconduct and used better risk factor predictors, such as gang affiliation versus marital status.

Gottfredson, Najaka, and Kearley (2003) investigated whether specialized courts reduce reoffending for drug-addicted offenders. Everyone eligible for drug court was randomly assigned to specialized court (n = 235) or treatment as usual (n = 96). No significant differences based on background characteristics were found. The two-year follow-up showed that drug treatment court reduces reoffending. Participants who received treatment were much less likely to reoffend than were untreated drug court subjects and control group members. However, there is a problem with the causal explanation. Some of the experimental group subjects did not receive treatment as part of their sentences; therefore, the reduction in offending could have been caused by unmeasured external factors.

Methods in Action

Does Having a Place to Live Affect Criminal Behaviour?

As part of a five-year, $110-million project investigating whether providing housing and social services reduces criminal behaviour, victimization, and costs to society, At Home/Chez Soi offered housing to homeless people with a serious mental illness. The program was a randomized field experiment that adopted a mixed methods approach to measure the prevalence and process of implementing the intervention and the perceptions of program participants. The sample included 2,149 homeless people in Winnipeg, Toronto, Vancouver, Montreal, and Moncton to see what works, at what cost, for whom, and under what conditions. The intervention was based on evidence-based practice from New York City's Pathways to Housing and Toronto's Streets to Homes programs. Interviews were conducted at the start of the study to gather baseline data (pretest) and then every three months for a two-year follow-up period (posttests).

Homeless persons face multiple life challenges. For instance, 56 per cent of the study's sample did not finish high school, 90 per cent had at least one chronic physical health problem, and 100

Continued

per cent had one or more serious mental illness (part of the study eligibility criteria; Goering et al., 2012, p. 9). The outcomes measured included housing stability, visits to emergency rooms, hospital admissions, social service agency visits, nights spent in jail or prison, and—in the longer term—health status, social functioning, and quality of life (p. 20). The September 2012 interim report found that the health, criminal justice, and social services' systems saved $9,390 per person annually (p. 19). Thus, every $1 spent on the Housing First program saves $1.54 on shelter, health, and justice services (p. 6).

An associated chronic offender program facilitating drug treatment and housing in Vancouver operates on the principle that change is not possible until addiction and homelessness are addressed. Since the program's inception in 2007, property crime in Vancouver has dropped 29 per cent and violent crime 12 per cent. Vancouver Police Department Chief Jim Chu says, "The good news is [it's] dropping faster than any place in Canada. The not-so-good news is we are still higher than the Canadian average" (Matas, 2012). Police, criminologists, and the business improvement association attribute the decrease to effective policing strategies, societal change, and better housing for the homeless.

What role do the police play in this experiment? The shift is from the crime to the criminal. Detectives prepare a detailed biography, outline every contact with police, courts, and corrections, list all available social services, and give this information to the Crown attorney prior to sentencing. Once the criminal is released from jail, detectives ask what he or she needs to leave the criminal lifestyle behind and take an active role in directing him or her to the needed resources, including At Home/Chez Soi. At 12 months, 73 per cent of those in the experimental group were still in stable housing and doing well in comparison to 30 per cent in the treatment as usual group. Such preliminary findings suggest that having a place to live reduces criminality.

Learning the Symbols

Experimental research designs use a notation system to indicate the key characteristics associated with a true experiment. In this way, we are able to distinguish between a true experiment, its components, and experimental variations. "R" refers to the random assignment of research subjects into the experimental and control groups. "O_1" signifies administering a pretest. Similarly, "O_2" refers to participants completing a posttest. "X" denotes the administration of the treatment, or exposure to the independent variable. Variations from the true experiment will lack one or more of these elements. The notation for a true experiment is depicted in Table 5.1.

How Do You Conduct a True Experiment?

Conducting a true experiment still involves the preliminary steps associated with other research approaches. You start by isolating a topic, formulating a research question, and developing a testable hypothesis. Creating a hypothesis requires stipulating the causal relationship and operationalizing the concepts in the research question. Valid and reliable measures are needed for the independent and dependent variables. Once they are obtained, you can move to the next series of steps.

Returning to our example on education, suppose you are investigating the effectiveness of discussion-based instruction on increasing student learning. You operationalize the treatment of discussion-based learning as a question-driven instructional style and the effect as the grade received on the final exam. You need to determine how the treatment will be administered. For example, will the control and experimental groups be taught in the same classroom by the

Table 5.1 True experiment

		Pretest	Treatment	Posttest
Experimental Group	R	O_1	X	O_2
Control Group	R	O_1		O_2

same instructor? You also need to control the content and timing of exposure to the independent variable.

Next, you identify your research subjects. This stage is often based on convenience sampling by advertising for volunteers or using intact groups. Once you have a sample, assign the research subjects to the control and experimental groups with random assignment. Check for equivalency between groups and, finally, anticipate and take steps to deal with ethical problems and sources of bias.

After all these steps are complete, you are ready to conduct the experiment. For a true experiment, pretest the control and experimental groups and then introduce the treatment to the experimental group. After administering the independent variable, test both groups again. Once the posttest is finished, debrief the research subjects if any element of deception was used to mask the study's real purpose.

Now analyze the data. Since the control group did not receive the treatment, their pretest scores should be the same or very similar to the posttest scores. In this case, you would expect a degree of increased knowledge but not to the extent of the experimental group. It is the pretest and posttest scores from the experimental group that are of particular interest. Students' knowledge of the subject matter is assessed by the pretest and should be similar for both groups. If discussion-based instruction is more effective than traditional lectures, the posttest scores of students' knowledge after exposure to discussion-based instruction would be higher than the control group's posttest scores.

Variations on the True Experiment

Experiments are subject to various threats to internal and external validity, which we will discuss later in the chapter. For now, we will focus on a threat to the true experiment: the pretest can impact posttest scores on the dependent variable due to familiarity with the instrument. To assess and control for this possibility, researchers adopt two elaborations on the true experiment.

Two-Group Posttest Only

The **two-group posttest only** research design is a type of experiment used to combat the potential bias associated with administering a pretest. This problem is more likely to occur when there is a short period of time between the pretest and posttest. As seen in Table 5.2, the only difference between this type of research design and the true experiment is that neither group receives a pretest.

As participants continue to be randomly assigned to either the experimental and control groups, a researcher can assume that the groups and, by extension, their pretest scores, do not differ systematically. But it is important to remember that experiments lacking a pretest cannot eliminate the possibility of differences in the dependent variable prior to treatment. The fact remains that there is no baseline data and, consequently, you can't establish causality with much confidence. The only way to infer that the independent variable produced the changes in the

> **two-group posttest only** an experimental research design that adopts all elements of a true experiment, with the exception of a pretest.

Table 5.2 Two-group posttest only

		Pretest	Treatment	Posttest
Experimental Group	R		X	O_2
Control Group	R			O_2

dependent variable is to use random assignment so that there are no differences between the groups.

Solomon Four Group

The **Solomon four group** experimental research design combines the true experiment and the two-group posttest only. It is appropriate when you suspect that the pretest is potentially impacting measurement of the outcome variable. This bias can come in two forms: subjects are alerted to the nature and intent of the treatment or subjects perform better on the posttest because they have taken it before.

The most important interpretation in this design is examining both experimental groups. If the two

Solomon four group an experimental research design in which subjects are randomly assigned to two experimental and two control groups and one of each group does not receive a pretest.

treatment groups have similar results, any learning associated with the pretest has no effect on the outcome and changes in the dependent variable at the posttest are more likely caused by the treatment. Figure 5.1 illustrates the scientific notation and the multiple comparisons made to interpret the data.

Similar to a true experiment, the preliminary step is to check for equivalency between all four groups. You then compare the dependent variable pretest scores for Experimental Group 1 and Control Group 1 to ensure equivalency on the dependent variable. Next, assess if the pretest created a bias and influenced the posttest scores for Experimental Group 1 and Control Group 1. If the scores differ between Experimental Group 1 and Experimental Group 2 as well as Control Groups 1 and 2, you can assess the intervention's effectiveness based on the posttest scores from Experimental Group 2 and Control Group 2 only. If there is no

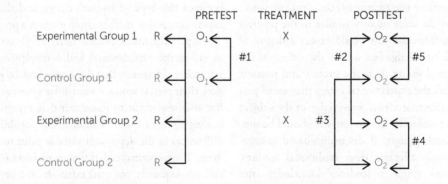

Figure 5.1 Solomon four group

pretest effect, the results from Experimental Group 1 and Control Group 1 can be interpreted with more confidence. The control group scores for the pretest and posttest should be similar as they were not exposed to the treatment stimulus. The change in posttest scores should occur for the experimental group. You then compare the posttest scores and draw conclusions on the treatment's impact on behaviour or attitudes.

The Solomon four group's limitations are the increased human and financial costs. The findings are hard to interpret given the multitude of comparisons that are made to assess the independent variable's effect on the dependent variable. At the same time, this design is arguably the strongest and the one with the most controls for threats to internal and external validity.

Research Requires Creativity

Sometimes researchers must be creative in their research design in order to address the research question. Salazar and Cook (2006) evaluated the success of a five-week program administered to African-American adolescent males convicted of intimate partner violence. Interestingly, they used two independent variables: time and treatment.

The two dependent variables were a person's knowledge of intimate partner violence and patriarchal attitudes. One pretest and two posttests were administered. The two control variables were prevalence of witnessing parental violence and prevalence of committing violence (psychological, physical, and sexual). They found no significant differences between groups for the two dependent variables based on the pretest scores. Table 5.3 provides the notation for their experimental research design. Experimental Group 1 received the program immediately after the pretest, whereas Experimental Group 2 waited two weeks before program admission.

Salazar and Cook's findings are encouraging. The intervention successfully increased a person's knowledge on intimate partner violence and reduced patriarchal attitudes. These effects remained three months later. The prevalence of violent behaviour did not impact outcomes; however, the program's effectiveness was greater for those exposed to higher levels of parental violence. The real limitation to this design is not the structure itself but the sample size. Generalizability is reduced as the experimental groups consisted of 21 participants and the control groups had 16.

Table 5.3 Testing for the effectiveness of an intimate partner violence program

		Pretest (immediate)	Treatment (5 weeks)	Posttest 1 (immediate)	Posttest 2 (3 months)
Experimental Group 1	R	O_1	X	O_2	O_3
Control Group 1	R	O_1		O_2	
Experimental Group 2	R	O_1	X	O_2	O_3
Control Group 2	R	O_1		O_2	

Research Highlights

The Santa Cruz Experiment

The Santa Cruz Experiment was a six-month randomized true experiment that fundamentally changed how the Santa Cruz Police Department responds to crime. The study investigated the effectiveness of data-driven predictive policing, a way to prevent crime by predicting when and where crimes will occur and proactively dispatching officers to the location. Predictive policing takes the CompStat approach—which uses crime data to hold police management accountable for their performance based on subsequent crime activity in designated areas—to the next level (DeLorenzi, Shane, & Amendola, 2006). It is based on four principles: accurate and timely crime analysis data; successful tactics and planning; rapid deployment; and follow-up assessment.

Building on an algorithm used to predict earthquakes, the researchers targeted property crime, which had increased by 25 per cent over a six-month period (Thompson, 2011). This new intervention strategy identified hot spots where future property crime was likely to occur. In the experiment, additional officers were dispatched to patrol the experimental areas for one hour. In the other half of the hot spots, no additional officers were dispatched.

In predictive policing, criminals are viewed as no different as consumers. Property crime is largely opportunity driven and not random. In a previous experiment in Los Angeles' San Fernando Valley, 20–95 per cent more crimes were successfully predicted using this method than by using crime maps generated for CompStat meetings (McCue & Beck, 2009). In Santa Cruz, property crime in the experimental hot spots dropped by 27 per cent after only thirty days (Thompson, 2011).

Adopting the true experimental research design is critical for criminal justice agencies. The findings can form evidence-based practice and directly impact the real world. For this reason, we want as much confidence as possible that the intervention strategy is more effective than what is used in the control group. The reality is aptly summarized by Los Angeles Police Chief Charlie Beck: "I'm not going to get more money. I'm not going to get more cops. I have to be better at using what I have and that's what predictive policing is about" (PredPol, 2012).

Pre- and Quasi-Experimental Designs

There are times when random assignment or pretest data collection is not feasible. Alternative experimental research designs exist, but their ability to provide causal explanations is limited. In the seminal work on experimental research, Campbell and Stanley (1963) present 16 variations on the true experiment. This section presents only those that are commonly adopted in criminological research.

Pre-Experimental Designs

Frequently used in exploratory research, **pre-experimental designs** do not adhere to the characteristics of a true experiment. Their defining characteristic is the absence of randomization and pretests or control groups. Remember, when results for a single group are interpreted, alternative explanations can't be ruled out and causality can only be implied.

> **pre-experimental design** an exploratory research design that does not control for alternative explanations or use random assignment.

One-Shot Case Study

A **one-shot case study** is associated with exploratory research and is not appropriate for establishing cause–effect relationships. The notation for this research design is as follows:

$$\text{Experimental group } X\,O_2$$

A one-shot case study has two characteristics. There is no control or comparison group exposed to different intensities or duration of exposure to the independent variable. The only requirement is introducing the independent variable to one group. There is also no random assignment. Therefore, this design cannot meet the criteria for causality.

The one-shot case study has low internal validity (see pp. 152–153) as there is no definitive way to determine whether the posttest scores are caused by the introduction of the independent variable. It is conceivable that other factors influenced the outcome. Alternatively, the behaviour measured by the posttest existed at the same level and frequency before exposure to the independent variable, which means that you cannot discern if a change occurred. Although this type of design is easy to employ, the results are essentially meaningless at worst and misleading at best.

One-Group Pretest–Posttest

A **one-group pretest–posttest** is better than a one-shot case study because it can demonstrate that a change occurs after an intervention. At the same time, without a control group, how do you rule out alternative explanations for any changes in the dependent variable? This research design is depicted as

$$\text{Experimental Group } O_1\,X\,O_2$$

Rowe and colleagues (2012) used this design to evaluate an educational policing strategy to reduce alcohol-related violence, public disorder, and drunk driving of patrons leaving licensed bars and restaurants. Their field experiment was conducted over a four-month baseline period and included a follow-up one year later. They found that the number of police-recorded incidents decreased but admitted that, without a control group, this finding is tentative. The research design limited the researchers' ability to conclude that the reduction in crime was a direct product of the policing strategy. They couldn't eliminate the possibility that it could be attributed to trends over time in recorded crime rates. Yet the one-group pretest–posttest was the most appropriate design given the research question and that the initiative was implemented across the entire city, eliminating the possibility of selecting a comparison group.

Another study using this design looked at the effect of participating in a school program aimed at reducing violent, aggressive behaviours and increasing empathy (Sprinkle, 2008). The experimental group consisted of 310 students in grades 4 to 6. Preliminary findings suggested a degree of success; however, the lack of a control group meant that the researchers couldn't exclude the possibility that students had acclimatized to the school routine and were calmer by the time they completed the posttest. Further, a time series design with more than one posttest would indicate whether these effects are short- or long-term.

Static Group Comparison

In a **static group comparison**, there is no random assignment or pretest administered. Hence, pre-existing differences can exist between groups for the dependent variable and in terms of

one-shot case study a pre-experimental design that observes one group at one point in time after a treatment is introduced.

one-group pretest–posttest a pre-experimental design that measures one group before and after an independent variable is introduced.

static group comparison a pre-experimental design that does not randomly assign paritcipants to the two groups and that measures the dependent variable with only a posttest after exposure to the independent variable.

Table 5.4 Static group comparison

	Pretest	Treatment	Posttest
Experimental Group		X	O_2
Control Group			O_2

background characteristics. Any posttest differences between groups could be due to nonequivalence. Table 5.4 depicts a static group comparison.

Let's say that you have two groups—you show a violent film to one and not the other. After the film, participants complete a survey to assess their fear of crime. The problem is, without randomization and a pretest, you cannot be sure if both groups had an equal degree of fear. The experimental group may have had more fear even before exposure to the film. You won't know if they differed in any way if you don't randomize or match participants into groups. So why would a researcher use this design? The short answer is when there is no other choice, the findings must be interpreted within the context of the limitations, that the criteria for causality cannot be met.

quasi-experimental design an exploratory research design that does not use random assignment but measures the dependent variable before and after the intervention and gives the researcher some control over the independent variable.

nonequivalent control group a quasi-experiment design that lacks randomization but includes pretests, posttests, and two groups.

Quasi-Experimental Designs

With **quasi-experimental designs**, research subjects are not randomly assigned to groups, but the dependent variable is measured before and after the intervention and the researcher exercises some control over the independent variable in most cases. In essence, it is a compromise between the ideal and the feasible but lacks the causal inference power of the true experiment. Quasi-experimental research designs can be field or natural experiments and, in criminology and criminal justice, are often used in evaluation research.

Nonequivalent Control Group

Nonequivalent control group design is the most commonly used approach in criminal justice evaluation research (Moskowitz, 1993). This type combines a static group comparison and the pretest–posttest control group design. Unfortunately, it lacks random assignment and, sometimes, will not use matching. Table 5.5 depicts the structure of this research design.

Table 5.5 Nonequivalent control group comparison

	Pretest	Treatment	Posttest
Experimental Group	O_1	X	O_2
Control Group	O_1		O_2

With a pretest, the equivalency of groups on the dependent variable can be determined prior to administering the treatment. This step eliminates the possibility that any change in the dependent variable is the result of pre-existing differences between groups. Yet there is no guarantee that the two groups have similar background characteristics. By using intact groups, one cannot state that any differences exist purely by chance. Using matching is one way to strengthen this design, as some alternative explanations can be eliminated based on the characteristics chosen for the matching process and the inclusion of a control group.

McGarrell and colleagues (2001) used a nonequivalent control group to test the effectiveness of directed patrol on firearms-related violence. The authors conceded that selecting comparison beats was very problematic as "no two areas are alike and they are likely to be influenced by a myriad of demographic, economic, neighborhood, and police processes" (p. 128). The comparison areas "appeared to be the most similar"; however, they had a higher violent crime rate than the city overall and a significantly lower rate than the target areas (p. 129). Thus, the experimental and control groups are nonequivalent, as are the two comparison groups. Nonetheless, if we take the methodological caveats into account, the study showed that violent gun crime decreases when directed patrol focuses on suspicious activities.

Wells and colleagues (2006) took a different approach by using three posttest measurements of the dependent variable. They tested the value of a shock incarceration boot camp to a matched control group of youth with traditional dispositions and measured reoffending 4, 8, and 12 months after program completion. They found that recidivism was lower for the treatment group. Control group subjects were matched on age, race, prior offences, and release date. The researchers pointed out that equivalence between comparison groups could not be achieved without random assignment. Although individual-level matching can control for the main

variables that could affect the outcome, there is still no guarantee that extraneous factors did not cause the observed changes.

Before-and-after Design

Before-and-after designs use multiple measurements of the dependent variable over an extended period of time. There is no control group; if there is a baseline comparison group, random assignment is not used. Consequently, participants may change between the pretest and posttest even if they didn't receive the stimulus.

> **before-and-after design** a quasi-experiment design that measures the dependent variable several times before and after the intervention for intact groups.

The most common before-and-after design is a time series analysis. A simple time series design uses repeated measurements of the dependent variable over equal increments of time. It is based on the principle of propinquity, which states that observations closer together in time are more related than those farther apart. Researchers adopt this design to examine trends over time, test the impact of an intervention, or predict future trends. The key components are looking for an overall trend, cyclical patterns, and normal, random fluctuations. For example, if you are looking at crime rates over time, you would ask the following questions: Is there an overall pattern showing a reduction in crime in the city? Are there any peaks at certain times of the year? Or does the rate appear to go up and down at random?

An interrupted time series design investigates whether a change in one group occurs over a period of time once an event occurs. Researchers conduct a series of observations on the dependent variable to gather baseline data and an additional series after the stimulus occurs (see Table 5.6). Finally, they compare the pretest and posttest data. If changes occur after the stimulus is introduced, researchers can assume that the change is caused by the introduction of the independent variable. The primary weakness

Table 5.6 Simple time series

	Time 1	Time 2	Time 3	Treatment	Time 4	Time 5	Time 6
Experimental Group	O_1	O_1	O_1	X	O_2	O_2	O_2

is that an unmeasured event might have occurred at the same time as the treatment (a confounding variable). This other event could be the cause of the changes in the dependent variable.

Carrington and Schulenberg (2008) conducted an interrupted time series analysis to determine the *Youth Criminal Justice Act's* effectiveness in reducing the number of youth referred to court by the police. The intervention was the enactment of the legislation in 2003. The number of referrals to court was measured annually with 17 pretest years and 2 posttest years. The researchers concluded that the *YCJA* was successful in achieving this objective. The before-and-after research design was appropriate as the study investigated the effects of an event over time.

A variation on the simple time series is a control group time series, which strengthens internal validity by including a control group. As seen in Table 5.7, two intact nonequivalent groups (one of which is not exposed to the event) are observed over a period of time. If an external event occurs at the same time as the exposure to the independent

ex post facto control group a quasi-experimental design in which a researcher creates a comparison group and examines the impact of an intervention but conducts the study after the event has occurred.

variable, it would presumably be detectable and affect both groups.

Ex Post Facto Control Group

An **ex post facto control group** design is the weakest of the types discussed here. Technically, it isn't even an experiment because the study is conducted after the event has occurred. By using existing data, the researcher has no control over manipulating the independent variable but usually has enough information on when, where, and to what intensity the independent variable was administered. There is a posttest, but it may not be possible to collect any pretest data. Researchers compensate by statistically controlling for variables that may have affected the outcome. They can use pre-existing groups or divide the sample into two groups based on the research subjects' previous experience or pre-existing condition (under the assumption that it could influence the outcome). Again, the important thing to remember with ex post facto research is that you are unable to manipulate the independent variable.

Criminal justice agencies often look for a researcher to conduct a study after they have already implemented a new strategy or program. The researcher does not have the ability to manipulate

Table 5.7 Control group time series

	Time 1	Time 2	Time 3	Treatment	Time 4	Time 5	Time 6
Experimental Group	O_1	O_1	O_1	X	O_2	O_2	O_2
Control Group	O_1	O_1	O_1		O_2	O_2	O_2

the independent variable or use randomization. The agency provides statistical data from their administrative records, which typically do not include all the key variables suggested by theory and past research. Matching becomes problematic, and the researcher is left to use an existing intact comparison group. The intervention's effectiveness can still be assessed, but there are additional limitations for tests of a cause–effect relationship and the conclusions that can be drawn from the data. A summary of pre- and quasi-experimental designs is provided in Table 5.8.

Threats to Internal and External Validity

A true experiment is strong in internal validity but weak in external validity. Internal validity refers to any causal factors other than the experimental stimulus that affect

Table 5.8 Experimental research design summary

True experimental designs

True experiments randomly assign subjects to experimental and control groups in conjunction with pretests and posttests to measure the effects of the independent variable on the dependent variable.

True experiment	Experimental Group	R	O_1	X	O_2
	Control Group	R	O_1		O_2
Two-group posttest only	Experimental Group	R		X	O_2
	Control Group	R			O_2
Solomon four group	Experimental Group 1	R	O_1	X	O_2
	Control Group 1	R	O_1		O_2
	Experimental Group 2	R		X	O_2
	Control Group 2	R			O_2

Pre-experimental designs

Pre-experimental research designs lack at least two characteristics of a true experiment.

One-shot case study	Experimental Group		X	O_2
One group pretest–posttest	Experimental Group	O_1	X	O_2
Static group comparison	Experimental Group		X	O_2
	Control Group			O_2

Quasi-experimental designs

Quasi-experiments do not use random assignment but incorporate all other characteristics of a true experiment.

Nonequivalent control group	Experimental Group		O_1	X	O_2	
	Control Group		O_1		O_2	
Simple time series	Experimental Group	O_1	O_2	X	O_3	O_4
Multiple time series	Experimental Group	O_1	O_2	X	O_3	O_4
	Control Group	O_1	O_2		O_3	O_4
Ex post facto	Researchers can use any pre- or quasi-experimental research design. The researcher is unable to manipulate the independent variable, and the study is designed and conducted after the intervention has occurred					

the outcome. Stated differently, strong internal validity depends on how well a researcher can demonstrate that a treatment affected outcome. External validity refers to the extent that the findings can be applied to other people, events, circumstances, or settings. The following discussion is informed by Campbell and Stanley (1963), the first to outline the threats to internal and external validity that are of concern for all experimental designs.

Internal Validity

A threat to internal validity exists anytime something other than the intervention affects the dependent variable. Thus, we look for the counterfactual by having a control condition that allows us to see what happens to subjects when the treatment is not administered. To get a valid estimate on any changes, the experimental and control groups have to remain the same throughout the experiment. Maintaining this balance is a real challenge. Participation in a research study is voluntary and a researcher can't realistically control the attention a person pays to completing the pretest or posttest. Experimental designs are vulnerable to 12 threats to internal validity that are categorized as noncomparable groups, endogenous change, history, contamination, and misidentification.

instrumentation a threat to internal validity in which different outcomes are caused by variations in the experimental conditions or the measurement of the dependent variable.

selection bias a threat to internal validity in which characteristics of experimental and control group members differ prior to independent variable manipulation.

compensation a threat to internal validity that occurs when researchers compensate control group members for being deprived of the treatment.

experimental mortality (or attrition) a threat to internal validity that occurs when groups differ because the subjects in one are more likely to drop out than those from the other.

Noncomparable Groups

The threat of **instrumentation** concerns changes in how the stimulus is measured, which leads to changes in scores even if behaviour stays the same. Any changes in the experimental group could be attributed to how the tests are administered (e.g. different instructions). If your posttest involves grading short answer questions, your assessment of an answer could change from the first test to the last one. This difference means that the outcome may not be the product of the instructional technique but of the instrument measuring the dependent variable. With an intervention, subjects could feel greater pressure to respond to the posttest in a socially desirable way regardless of how it is structured or administered. Instrumentation is most likely to occur right after program completion; the chances of it happening dissipate with time (Moskowitz, 1993).

Selection bias occurs when members of the experimental and control groups systematically differ. There could be differential selection for the comparison group, whereby the researcher ends up comparing apples and oranges. Research subjects self-select by volunteering to participate in an experiment. If the researcher does not use random assignment, he or she may inadvertently stack the deck in favour of one characteristic or another. In this case, the groups will differ before the study begins. Whenever you randomly assign subjects to groups, you eliminate this threat. Further, you must analyze the pretest data to determine equivalency on a range of variables, not just the dependent variable.

Compensation is a concern because the control group is deprived of a treatment in a real-life situation. The researcher may feel pressure to compensate control group members with an alternative treatment. If you succumb to this temptation, you no longer have a legitimate control group.

Experimental mortality, or **attrition**, represents a serious threat to any experiment and can affect the external validity of the findings as a result. Having experimental or control group members drop out of a study between the pretest and posttest undermines the comparability, or equivalence, of the two groups. If the dropouts are systematically different from those who complete the experiment, the assumption of randomness is violated and the groups are no longer equivalent.

Attrition is a greater problem under one or more of four conditions. Subjects may drop out of a study if they aren't interested in the intervention or if they receive low pretest scores. The more time required from a participant, the more likely he or she will quit. Finally, if there is a long period of time between the pretest and posttest, subjects may be hard to find or may withdraw, move, or become unavailable for some other reason. When attrition occurs equally across groups, the threat to internal validity is not a problem. However, this is rarely the case.

Differential attrition occurs at a higher rate under certain conditions. For instance, in an experiment on women undergoing substance abuse treatment, single mothers are more likely to drop out because finding appropriate daycare becomes more difficult as time goes on. That is why a pretest is so important in determining whether attrition is an equivalency problem.

Endogenous Change

Endogenous change refers to threats that occur during a study. These are natural changes, other than the manipulation of the independent variable, that occur between the pretest and posttest. With a **testing effect**, a pretest makes the subject more aware and sensitizes him or her to the treatment or posttest. In this case, the treatment might not be the cause of any changes between the pretest and posttest tests. If a study looks at increasing a person's vocabulary, subjects may look up the meaning of words after they take the pretest and get them correct on the posttest, irrespective of the program delivered. In a true experiment, the testing effect is not a serious problem, as both the experimental and control groups complete a pretest and a posttest. But it is still a possible threat if there is a short period of time between tests. If the testing effect is a concern, a Solomon four group is the best experimental design to adopt.

The threat of **maturation** involves natural biological or psychological changes in subjects during the experiment, such as being tired or hungry or maturing over time. Although these changes are unrelated to the independent variable, they can affect the measurement of the dependent variable. Maturation is more of a threat for longer experiments because (presumably) people are continuously changing. Randomly assigning subjects and ensuring that they are roughly the same age reduces this threat to internal validity.

Statistical regression is particularly acute if the research question involves selecting participants with extreme scores (e.g. poverty, failing grades). Those with extreme scores on the pretest may have less extreme posttest scores as a result of random error, such as a lucky streak. Average scores based on probability theory are much more likely. A person who has extreme scores on the pretest probably won't perform to the same level on the posttest. The odds are greater that he or she will score near the average. Even without the intervention, the subjects in both groups will show some improvement over time. The good news is that, if subjects are randomly assigned to groups, this threat should affect both groups equally.

Demoralization is a threat to internal validity that is difficult to control. It occurs when control group members are aware that they are not receiving the program or intervention and feel deprived. This situation leads to attrition because they give up or don't see the point in participating. They ultimately feel

testing effect a threat to internal validity in which the completion of a pretest affects posttest scores.

maturation a threat to internal validity that occurs when posttest scores are affected by biological or psychological changes within subjects.

statistical regression a threat to internal validity in which extreme scores on the pretest are less extreme on the posttest.

demoralization a threat to internal validity that is a form of attrition caused by control group members feeling deprived.

that they aren't gaining anything from the experiment. Offering incentives to participate, such as gift cards or a raffle, can help mitigate this threat.

History

With the threat of **history**, an external event that occurs at the same time as the intervention makes it difficult to detect any differences between the experimental and control groups. It is important to know local history once the experiment is underway so that you can rule out alternative explanations for any outcomes observed. Let's say you are conducting an experiment on the effectiveness of anti-drinking-and-driving presentations. You show a video to a group of high-school students; meanwhile, the quarterback of the school's football team is hospitalized for alcohol poisoning. If you observe fewer drunk-driving charges after your experiment, you can't be sure whether the result was instigated by the video or the quarterback's hospitalization.

By its very nature, experiments take place over time and other events can impact the outcome or even offer a more viable explanation for changes in the dependent variable than the treatment does. By including a control group, an event other than the intervention will presumably affect both groups and there should still be a difference in the posttest scores.

Contamination

When experimental and control groups communicate with each other, there can be a contamination problem. Experimental group subjects might inform control group members of the intervention. If the control group uses this information to imitate the treatment, **diffusion** occurs. The control group is also affected by the stimulus to varying degrees and, by definition, is no longer a control group. Careful administration of the experiment reduces this threat to internal validity.

If your control group members realize that they are not receiving the treatment, you may be dealing with **compensatory rivalry**. This threat to internal validity involves the control group subjects trying harder in an effort to perform as well or better than the experimental group. They are no longer a true control group, as their posttest scores will potentially rival those of the experimental group whether the treatment is successful or not.

Misidentification

Misidentification reflects an unknown intervening process affecting posttest scores. **Causal time order** concerns the dependent variable causing changes in the independent variable. This threat to internal validity is quite rare. But it can still arise when conducting any type of experimental design and needs to be addressed prior to commencing an experiment. Table 5.9 summarizes the threats to internal validity and experimental components that address them.

External validity

External validity deals with the generalizability of the findings. In experiments, this type of validity involves generalizing the cause–effect relationship to nonexperimental settings. The concern is that a treatment may have a positive or negative effect for only certain people or under certain conditions. In this case, the experiment has low external validity.

Reactivity

The threat of reactivity is primarily the interaction effect of testing and treatment. The pretest increases or decreases respondent sensitivity to the stimulus, thereby making the results unrepresentative.

---

history a threat to internal validity in which events external to the experiment affect the posttest scores.

diffusion a threat to internal validity in which treatment information is passed from the experimental group to the control group.

compensatory rivalry a threat to internal validity that involves control group members trying to perform as well as or better than the experimental group.

causal time order a threat to internal validity involving the violation of the temporal order criterion of causality.

Table 5.9 Threats to internal validity

	Pretest & posttest	Control group	Random assignment	Additional groups	Procedures
Causal time order	Yes	No	No	No	Yes
Compensation	No	No	No	No	Yes
Compensatory rivalry	No	No	No	No	Yes
Demoralization	No	No	No	No	Yes
Diffusion	No	No	No	No	Yes
Experimental mortality	Yes	No	No	No	No
History	No	Yes	No	No	No
Instrumentation	No	Yes	No	No	Yes
Maturation	No	Yes	No	No	No
Selection bias	Yes	Yes	Yes	No	No
Statistical regression	No	Yes	Yes	No	No
Testing effect	No	Yes	No	Yes	No

Source: Adapted from Leedy (1997, pp. 232–233).

Subjects behave atypically because they are participating in an experiment. The treatment is effective only because of the conditions created by the experiment. Unfortunately, the true experiment cannot reduce this bias, but the Solomon four group design can assess the nature and extent of the threat.

In such a situation, participants are active, not passive. They pick up subtle unintended cues from the researcher, try to guess the purpose of the study, and modify their behaviour accordingly to help the researcher. The crux of the reactivity problem is known as the **Hawthorne effect**, which refers to subjects changing their behaviour simply because they know they are participating in a study. The name of this threat to external validity comes from experiments conducted from the late 1920s to the early 1930s at the Western Electric Company's Hawthorne plant. In these experiments, researchers tested whether worker productivity is affected by changes to the physical working environment. Workers ignored the changes in physical conditions, such as less

light, and were more productive because they knew they were participating in an experiment. When a Hawthorne effect exists, the control subjects respond as if they are experimental subjects, despite not receiving the stimulus. Consequently, the posttest does not truly measure the intervention's influence, which affects the generalizability of the results.

Interactions

There are several interactions between threats to internal validity that impact the findings' external validity. A history and treatment interaction occurs when the conditions under which the treatment is administered do not represent future conditions. There is also the selection and treatment interaction, whereby two groups are different and lead to differential treatment effects.

Hawthorne effect a threat to external validity in which control group members are aware that they are participating in a study and modify their behaviour accordingly.

Table 5.10 Threats to internal and external validity by experimental research design

	One-shot case study	One-group pretest–posttest	Static group comparison	True experiment	Posttest-only control group	Solomon four group	Non-equivalent control group	Simple time series	Control group time series
Causal time order	(−)	(+)	(−)	(+)	(−)	(+)	(+)	(+)	(+)
Compensation	x	x	?	?	?	?	?	x	x
Compensatory rivalry	x	x	?	?	?	?	?	x	x
Demoralization	x	x	?	?	?	?	?	x	x
Diffusion	x	x	?	?	?	?	?	x	x
Experimental mortality	(−)	(+)	(−)	(+)	(+)	(+)	(+)	(+)	(+)
History	(−)	(−)	(+)	(+)	(+)	(+)	(+)	(−)	(+)
Instrumentation	x	(−)	(+)	(+)	(+)	(+)	(+)	?	(+)
Interaction of factors	x	(−)	(−)	(+)	(+)	(+)	(−)	(+)	(+)
Interaction selection/X	(−)	(−)	(−)	?	?	?	?	?	(−)
Interaction testing/X	x	(−)	(−)	(−)	(+)	(+)	(−)	(−)	(−)
Maturation	(−)	(−)	?	(+)	(+)	(+)	(+)	(+)	(+)
Reactivity	x	?	?	?	?	?	?	x	x
Selection bias	(−)	(+)	(−)	(+)	(+)	(+)	(+)	(+)	(+)
Statistical regression	x	?	(+)	(+)	(+)	(+)	?	(+)	(+)
Testing effect	x	(−)	(+)	(+)	(+)	(+)	(+)	(+)	(+)

Source: Adapted from Campbell & Stanley (1963, pp. 8, 40, 56).

Notes: (+) = The threat is controlled for by the research design; (−) = A weakness of this experimental design; ? = A possible concern, especially when related to the administration of the experiment (see Table 5.9); and "x" = The threat is not applicable.

Additionally, the experimenter's expectations can affect measuring the dependent variable. For example, if you expect to see more aggressive behaviour in the control group, you might score borderline cases as more aggressive than subjects in the experimental group who underwent an anti-violence program. A double blind experiment can reduce experimenter bias as the subjects and researcher are both unaware of who is receiving the treatment. To review, Table 5.10 summarizes the threats to internal and external validity by type of experimental design.

The Trade-Off

Random assignment, pretests, posttests, and control groups increase a study's internal validity. Whenever these characteristics are present, one can control for most threats to internal validity, particularly testing, selection, mortality, maturation, and statistical regression. Whereas internal validity is linked to the design, external validity is associated with the administration. Increasing an experiment's external validity is much more challenging, but field experiments are better in this regard than a laboratory setting.

There is a trade-off: increases in internal validity reduce external validity and vice versa. With high internal validity, you can be more confident that any changes in the dependent variable are caused by the introduction of the independent variable. However, by increasing the control in an experiment, the results can become harder to generalize to another setting. Use your judgment in your experiments. Whenever possible, use randomization and a control group and remember that, unless you can generalize the findings to other groups, the utility of your study is limited.

Practical Aspects of Conducting Experiments

Even a well-designed and well-executed randomized experiment can resemble more of a quasi-experiment because of real-life events. It is critical for researchers to provide sufficient evidence that there was no history

threat to validity and that the true experimental design was maintained. Ensuring treatment integrity, an integral part of this process, entails dealing with implementation problems, random assignment, differential attrition, and contamination.

Does the Type of Experiment Matter?

Weisburd, Lum, and Petrosino (2001) pose an excellent question: Does the type of experimental design used in criminal justice research affect the results observed? Quasi-experimental designs do not use random assignment, making it difficult to create equivalent groups and more likely to produce biased findings. Nonrandomized experiments require considerable insight and knowledge on factors that influence the treatment; the data must then be available to measure and control for these elements. Additionally, volunteers may be more motivated to change—creating the threat of self-selection—or a researcher may have to compensate for agencies' decisions on who is more amenable to treatment, which influences who is assigned to the experimental group. For this and many other reasons, the research design systematically affects evaluation outcomes. Weaker designs with lower internal validity are more likely to find treatments effective and less likely to identify harmful program effects.

Strengths and Weaknesses

A true experiment is the best experimental design to control for threats to internal validity. This design is considered the gold standard for several reasons. It is the best research design available to test causal relationships. It allows researchers to manipulate and measure the impact of the independent variable. True experiments are easily replicated because they have a very specific focus, the methods are recognizable, and the procedures are described in detail. When compared to other research designs, true experiments require fewer research subjects, making them less expensive in time and money.

All experiments have weaknesses. Without random sampling, they are weak in external validity.

The artificial environments created in laboratory experiments may or may not induce behaviour found in real-world situations. As previously mentioned, there is the problem of self-selection. It is common for university professors to recruit student volunteers for their experiments. Students represent only one portion of the population, which limits the generalizability of the findings to other people, settings, or conditions. There is also the potential for systematic differences between volunteers and those who choose not to participate.

Experiments in Criminal Justice Research

Researchers face unique challenges when conducting experiments in a criminal justice setting. True experiments are uncommon, often because the experimental design is not an appropriate way to address the research question. For example, the research purpose and question might be to generate findings that are generalizable to a larger population or are descriptive in nature, such as a process evaluation.

Another problem is the inability to use random assignment, possibly for ethical reasons (see the next section). The type of program or policy may make it difficult to identify an appropriate control group, especially if the program being investigated affects an entire community or jurisdiction. Additional problems include securing and maintaining institutional support and participant co-operation and anticipating external events that could impact the outcome. Although they might have less confidence in the results, criminological researchers will frequently conduct quasi-experimental research. When assessing the strengths and appropriateness of a research design, always ask yourself why the researcher(s) adopted this type of experiment. In many cases, ethical and practical constraints played a role.

For instance, Kent and colleagues (2000) investigated the success of a program targeting incarcerated repeat gang offenders. They were unable to conduct a true experiment for two reasons. First, there were practical obstacles to creating a control group. Many factors affect the likelihood of reoffending, which makes it extremely difficult to match on all the pertinent characteristics. The correctional agency would not allow the researchers to randomly assign some inmates to a treatment-as-usual group because withholding treatment conflicts with the ethical and legal obligation to take measures to improve public safety and therefore places the community at risk. Second, even though a quasi-experimental design incorporates a pretest and posttest, it doesn't provide information on intervening factors associated with how a program works. The researchers instead examined one outcome variable and conducted a simple time series.

Another group of researchers evaluated a Persistent Violent Offender program but were unable to include a legitimate untreated control group (Serin, Gobeil, & Preson, 2009). Why? "Correctional Service Canada is legislatively mandated to provide offenders with rehabilitative programming" in line with their criminogenic needs to promote successful reintegration upon release (p. 70).

Lawton, Taylor, and Luongo (2005) also used a simple time series to evaluate Operation Safe Streets' effectiveness in reducing violent and drug crime. Although they had 12 months of pretest data, they had only 4 months of posttest data. Repeated requests for additional police data were denied. Thus, it is unclear if the positive effects were short- or long-term.

Greene et al. (2010) adopted a quasi-experimental design to examine youth on their first court appearance. The study found that youth who experienced an environment filled with confusion and perceived unprofessionalism viewed the entire justice system as less legitimate than youth who had a better experience. The researchers make clear that they cannot say with certainty that the courtroom atmosphere affects views on legitimacy, as they didn't measure other events that could cause this result, such as type of sentence or judge's attitude. The only option to account for alternative explanations was controlling for characteristics such as prior record, race, age, and so forth.

Vignette: Breaking It Down

Police Patrol Experiments

Several experiments examine elements of police work by manipulating deployment strategies to assess their effectiveness at reducing crime. The Kansas City Preventive Patrol Experiment investigated whether increased routine patrol reduces crime (Kelling et al., 1974). Fifteen beats were matched based on crime rates, calls for service, and population characteristics and were randomly assigned to five experimental, five reactive, and five routine patrol control groups. Simply driving a vehicle on targeted patrol has little effect on crime; hence, they argued that scarce resources should be allocated elsewhere. This claim paved the way for experiments assessing problem-oriented policing (POP) and targeted foot patrol and reducing geographic areas to smaller high-crime-rate areas allowing for more focused interventions.

In New Jersey, a randomized block field experiment matched 24 violent crime areas into 12 pairs and randomly assigned one of each pair to treatment conditions by flipping a coin (Braga et al., 1999). The treatment areas received aggressive order maintenance tactics using POP. Crime incident data and calls for service were used as indicators of crime. The treatment areas showed a significant reduction in most violent crimes, with no evidence of displacement (i.e. crime moving to adjacent areas).

Another randomized block field experiment assessed the value of POP by matching 34 hot spots into 17 pairs. Areas were randomly assigned to experimental and control groups based on quantitative and qualitative indicators of crime, including officer perceptions of crime (Braga & Bond, 2008). Participant observation of CompStat meetings and field observers were used to ensure treatment integrity and collect pretest and posttest data on physical and social disorder. The experiment found significant reductions in crime and disorder calls for service, with no evidence of displacement.

Ratcliffe et al. (2011) also used hot spots (specifically, sixty violent crime areas) to assess the effectiveness of targeted foot patrol. Violent crime reports were used to identify the hot spots, as calls for service in large metropolitan areas were too large and weren't used to inform patrol activities. The researchers found a 23 per cent drop—a significant reduction—in violent crime in the treatment areas (p. 809). Using this data, Sorg and colleagues (2013) explored whether displacement occurs and if reductions in violent crime are short term. Every two weeks for three months, they measured reported crime in zones surrounding the treatment areas. They saw no differences in violent crime between experimental and control groups.

Piza and O'Hara's (2014) quasi-experimental study examined foot patrol in four areas: experimental, surrounding area, routine patrol, and another control group matched on experimental area characteristics. They found that violent crime decreased, with no evidence of displacement. In this case, practical constraints prevented the researchers from conducting a true experiment. They were unable to assign subjects randomly, as the deployment strategy called Operation Impact targeted police-defined areas. Moreover, they couldn't test whether the effects decreased over time because funding was cut, redirecting many officers back to routine patrol. Thus, there was no definitive end date for the intervention and no way to maintain treatment integrity.

Methodologically, none of these experiments were able to control for specific patrol strategies in the experimental areas. Although it did not occur in the examples, controversy about the long-term benefits versus short-term risks, such as crime increasing in the control areas, can arise (Kelling et al., 1974). Agencies can maintain experimental conditions but not without challenges. Nevertheless, they are slowly becoming more open to experimental research.

Ethical Considerations

Ethical concerns vary from one experiment to another based on the topic and research design. In Canada, the *Tri-Council Policy Statement 2* (CIHR et al., 2014), introduced in Chapter 2, establishes guidelines for ethical conduct based on the principles of respect for persons, concern for welfare, and justice. Respect for persons entails ensuring that a person is free to make an informed and ongoing choice to participate. "An informed choice is one that is based on as complete an understanding as is reasonably possible of the purpose of the research, what it entails, and its foreseeable risks and potential benefits" (p. 7). Participants are free to withdraw from the study at any time without penalty. As demonstrated in this chapter, participant withdrawal can be particularly problematic when conducting experiments.

It may be impossible to address the research question without a degree of deception about the research purpose. Article 3.7B of the *TCPS2* mandates that a debriefing—which informs subjects of the experiment's true purpose, explains why they had to be misled temporarily, and includes the researcher ensuring them of their well-being—occur as soon as possible. For instance, deception was required to study whether interacting with a weapon increased testosterone levels and aggressive behaviour (Klinesmith, Kasser, & McAndrew, 2006). Subjects were informed that the study was on taste sensitivity and that saliva samples were required. None of them were suspicious of the actual research purpose at any time. Upon debriefing, subjects were assured that they needn't feel bad about displaying aggressive behaviour. Researchers must debrief subjects if there is even the slightest amount of deception about the true purpose and research questions.

Concern for welfare involves providing participants with enough information to assess the potential risks and benefits of participation. Researchers must ensure that participants are not exposed to unnecessary risks and take steps to minimize risks while maximizing benefits (CIHR et al., 2014). For example,

in their study on testing a new inmate classification system, Berk and colleagues (2003) acknowledged that there were risks to prisoners and administrators. The risks were weighed against the potential benefits of adopting a safer and more cost-effective system. The correctional system decided that the benefits exceeded the potential human and financial costs. All stakeholders reviewed the research design in full and agreed to move forward.

Finally, the principle of justice is a thorny issue when conducting experiments. Researchers have an obligation to treat participants in an equal and fair manner and to take special precautions for vulnerable populations because an inherent power imbalance exists between the researcher and the participant (CIHR et al., 2014). Article 4.7 of the *TCPS2* states that participants, particularly institutionalized people, are vulnerable when they may not be able to safeguard their own interests (p. 54).

Does random assignment adhere to the principle of justice? The point is to test whether a treatment is beneficial. When you employ the scientific method, you can't assume that the treatment gives the experimental group some type of advantage. Random assignment, then, is ethical. There is another way to approach the ethical problem of random assignment. To reduce the potential for violating the principle of justice, you can create an equal distribution of benefits where even the control group members receive the treatment at some point in time (Boruch, Victor, & Cecil, 2000). This is accomplished by randomly delaying the treatment for some participants, who then temporarily form a control group. From a practitioner perspective, an experiment testing the effectiveness of a scarce resource is ideal, as random assignment can serve as a mechanism for equitable resource distribution (Boruch et al., 2000).

Conclusion

An anonymous quotation states, "In the spirit of science, there really is no such thing as a failed experiment. Any test that yields data is a valid

Table 5.11 Principles to guide criminology and criminal justice researchers

1.	There are fewer ethical barriers to experimentation when interventions involve the addition of resources.
2.	There are fewer objections to experiments that test more lenient sanctions than existing criminal justice penalties.
3.	Experiments with lower public visibility will generally be easier to implement.
4.	In cases where treatment cannot be given to all eligible subjects, there is likely to be less resistance to randomization.
5.	True experiments are easier to develop if the subjects of intervention represent less serious threats to community safety.
6.	Experimentation will be more difficult when researchers try to limit the discretion of criminal justice agents who traditionally act with significant autonomy and authority.
7.	It is easier to develop true experiments in systems with a high degree of hierarchal control.
8.	When treatments are relatively complex and involve multiple actions on the part of criminal justice agents, they can become prohibitively cumbersome, expensive, and less feasible to develop.

Source: Weisburd (2000, p. 191). Copyright © 2000, SAGE Publications.

test." This argument even applies to studies that find the intervention has no effect! Numerous criminologists advocate for researchers using more experiments when evaluating criminal justice policies and practices. Table 5.11 outlines eight principles that can help researchers determine the feasibility of adopting an experimental research design.

Despite the obstacles of ethics, agency cooperation, feasibility, and practical concerns, experimental research designs have been successfully used and have informed policy and evidence-based practice.

Summary of Important Points

Introduction

- Experiments are appropriate to test causal relationships.
- Experiments are more commonly used in explanatory research than in exploratory research.
- Researchers conduct experiments in laboratory, field, and natural settings.

True (Classical) Experiments

- The experimental group is exposed to the independent variable while the control group is not.

- The pretest and posttest measure the dependent variable. The scores indicate the intervention's effect.
- Randomization ensures that groups are equivalent so that any differences in the dependent variable are not pre-existing.
- Matching assigns participants to groups based on similar characteristics.
- A true experiment manipulates the independent variable, administers a pretest/posttest, and assigns participants to experimental and control groups using randomization.

- With all components in a true experiment, you can infer that any changes in the dependent variable for the experimental group are caused by the treatment.
- A two-group posttest only design has all components of a true experiment except a pretest.
- The best experiment to use when you suspect that the pretest is impacting posttest scores is the Solomon four group, which combines the true experiment and the two-group posttest only designs.

Pre- and Quasi-Experimental Designs

- A one-shot case study, one-group pretest–posttest, and static group comparison are pre-experimental designs and are the weakest tests of cause–effect relationships.
- The quasi-experimental nonequivalent control group has all elements of a true experiment except for random assignment.
- Before-and-after designs assess the impact of an event on intact nonequivalent groups over time.
- An ex post facto control group investigates the impact of an event after it has already occurred.

Threats to Internal and External Validity

- A true experiment is strong in internal validity and weak in external validity.

- Experiments in which causal factors other than the treatment affect the outcome are low in internal validity.
- Experiments in which the applicability to other people, events, circumstances, or settings is questionable are low in external validity.
- Types of internal validity are instrumentation, selection bias, compensation, experimental mortality (or attrition), testing effect, maturation, statistical regression, demoralization, history, diffusion, compensatory rivalry, and causal time order.
- Types of external validity are reactivity (such as the Hawthorne effect) and interactions.

Practical Aspects of Conducting Experiments

- Weaker designs with low internal validity are more likely to find treatments effective and less likely to identify harmful effects than are stronger designs with high internal validity.
- Practical challenges to conducting true experiments include random assignment, agency co-operation, treatment withdrawal, and access to data on the dependent variable.
- Experiments pose ethical challenges regarding respect for persons, concern for welfare, and justice.

Conclusion

- Criminologists advocate for more experimental research whenever appropriate and feasible.

Key Terms

Review Questions and Exercises

1. How do experiments provide the evidence required to support a causal explanation?
2. In what ways can a researcher affect an experiment's outcome?
3. What are the advantages and disadvantages of laboratory versus field experiments?
4. How do quasi-experiments differ from true experiments?
5. Why is the true experiment considered the gold standard in terms of threats to internal and external validity?
6. What ethical and practical challenges do researchers face when adopting experimental research designs?

Online Exercises and Websites of Interest

At Home/Chez Soi Experiment

www.youtube.com/watch?v=CY155hbKcbE&feature=youtu.be
This video provides an overview of this randomized trial.

QuickCalcs and Research Randomizer

http://graphpad.com/quickcalcs/randomize1.cfm
www.randomizer.org
Both of these websites provide an online tool to assist with randomly assigning subjects to an experimental and control group.

Sociosite: Identifying Experimental Research Designs

http://sociosite.net/
Select a subject area (crime, criminology, deviance, or police) from this site and, from the list of links, select an empirical article. Answer the following questions about the article you chose:

1. What is the purpose of the research? Specify the research question.
2. Identify the type of experimental research design.
3. Illustrate the research design, using the appropriate scientific notation.
4. What are the strengths and weaknesses of this type of experiment?

Additional Resources

Campbell, D.T., & Stanley, J.C. (1963). *Experimental and Quasi-Experimental Designs*. Chicago: Rand McNally.

This book is the seminal work on conducting experiments in the social sciences. It reviews the different types of experimental research designs and the threats to internal and external validity.

Key, J.P. (1997). Experimental Research and Design. Retrieved from www.okstate.edu/ag/agedcm4h/academic/aged5980a/5980/ newpage2.htm

This website provides an excellent summary of the steps, components, and types of experimental designs, as well as the threats to validity and ways to control them.

Part III
Data Collection Techniques

Chapter 6

Surveys and Interviews

"Every method of data collection, including the survey, is only an approximation to knowledge. Each provides a different glimpse of reality, and all have limitations when used alone."
D.P. Warwick and C.A. Lininger, *The Sample Survey* (1975, pp. 5–6)

Learning Objectives

- To determine when surveys, interviews, and focus groups are the most appropriate data collection method.
- To differentiate between different types of surveys and interviews.
- To create survey and interview data collection instruments.
- To describe the characteristics of effective surveys and interviews.
- To appreciate ethical considerations when conducting survey, interview, and focus group research.

Introduction

The words *survey* and *interview* should bring to mind your personal experiences with both of these data collection methods. Have you ever bought or subscribed to something and received an unsolicited telephone call a few weeks later for a customer satisfaction survey? Perhaps you didn't answer the phone. If so, the agency conducting the survey would have continued to call until you became so frustrated that

you answered. (And, by the way, the survey typically takes longer than promised.)

Consider what happens at the end of a course. The professor walks in with a large envelope full of course evaluation surveys, reads a preamble with instructions, asks for a volunteer, and promptly leaves the room. Do you feel obligated to complete these surveys for your courses? Do you scan the items and answer all questions in a similar way? Do you feel compelled to express your views in more detail by answering one of the written questions? Have you ever wondered if anyone takes your answers seriously? Although most professors and universities do care what their students think, such evaluations may seem like a necessary evil to you.

We are exposed to surveys, interviews, and focus groups for a variety of reasons; each time, there is a reason for collecting data in this way. Some experiences with these methods are positive, some negative. We might be ambivalent about participating or dread the prospect to the point that we decline. This chapter examines the three methods, including their types, structures, advantages, and disadvantages. We will unpack why these data collection methods are used, how they collect data, and their strengths and weakness. You will gain an appreciation for why surveys and interviews are so popular in research and everyday life, along with why you keep getting those customer satisfaction calls!

Research Applications

Surveys contain a series of questions that are asked in the same way and the same order to the largest sample possible. Certain types of research problems in criminology and criminal justice are more appropriate for surveys than others. Let's look at two examples where using surveys makes sense.

Police interrogation and interview strategies are based on identifying individual characteristics associated with the likelihood of confessing to a crime. Beauregard and Mieczkowski (2012) conducted face-to-face, computer-assisted surveys with 624 inmates convicted of a sex crime and serving at least two years in a maximum security facility. They found that the chances of a confession vary by context, whereby offenders weigh the costs and benefits of confessing and the potential for a shorter sentence. A person's criminal career has no impact,

but providing a partial confession satisfies the need to confess while balancing the discomfort associated with discussing the crime.

Another study used a life course perspective to investigate the frequency, onset, and duration of behaviours in stalking perpetrators and victims. A simple random sample of 48,237 university students resulted in a 19.4 per cent **response rate** to a web-based survey (Nobles et al., 2009). Twenty-seven per cent of the respondents were victims of stalking and 6 per cent perpetrators, of which the majority of victims were female and perpetrators male. There were no differences in frequency and few gender differences in the seriousness of the behaviours.

Interviews are face-to-face social interactions guided by a series of questions aimed at getting a person to describe a topic's meaning in his or her life. The interviewer engages in a dialogue to understand someone's story, experiences, and formation of opinions. For example, the police conduct interviews with informants, who have access to a criminal network and can provide information in exchange for special sentencing treatment. Dodge (2006) chose interviews as the most appropriate data collection method to examine the police perspective of using youth informants. Snowball sampling was adopted, due to the reluctance to discuss the topic. Data from 21 semi-structured interviews revealed that officers view the practice as an end that justifies the means. Dodge's conclusion was that it negates rehabilitation, places the youth in danger, reduces accountability for his or her actions, and questions the legitimacy of the youth criminal justice system.

> **survey** a data collection method used to gather information from individuals on facts, opinions, or experiences.

> **response rate** the percentage of the survey sample that completes the survey; the item response rate is the percentage of respondents who answer a particular question.

> **interview** a conversation with structure and purpose eliciting a person's point of view and the meaning he or she gives to life experiences.

Methods in Action

Navigating the Job Interview

Interviews in everyday life involve a structured conversation, process, and dynamic interplay of controlling the impression that parties have of each other. The difference between a research interview and other types, such as a job interview, is what's at stake. In the former, the researcher requests the interview, participation is voluntary, and you have nothing to lose. With a job interview, you make the request by submitting a resumé, you are expected to ask questions as well, and you may not receive a job offer.

Prior to an interview, job candidates should conduct background research on the organization, anticipate potential questions, and imagine the impression they will make (Youth Canada, 2012). Traditional job interview questions include the following: Why do you want this position? What can you offer the company? What are your strengths and weaknesses? Where do you see yourself in five years? How did you deal with a past challenge? You might also be asked questions meant to assess your personality, disposition, temperament, and potential impact on the work environment, such as "If both a taxi and a limo were priced exactly the same, which one would you choose?" "In what situation did you attempt to do something, but failed?" or "Who do you admire the most, least, and why?" Be aware that it is illegal for employers to ask questions regarding your citizenship, age, marital status, disabilities, religion, or criminal history.

A poll by the Society of Human Resource Managers finds that 54 per cent of interviewers base their hiring decision on their chemistry with the candidate during the interview (Dobrzynski, 2010). How you answer questions can be the deciding factor on whether you are hired (Jerome Young, 2010). Schachter (2011) states that weaker candidates tend to generalize their experiences, are less open about learning experiences, focus more on what happened instead of why, are less able to analyze failure, overstate strengths, and are unable to judge their limitations.

Effective impression management includes dressing professionally, being punctual, exuding confidence, thinking before you speak, and monitoring body language (e.g. firm handshake, eye contact, good posture). In contrast, research subjects worry about providing relevant information and the impression their answers make; they are less concerned about how they are dressed.

By asking questions, job candidates take a more active role in interviews than research subjects do. This step in the process is your opportunity to turn the tables and gather information on the company, position, and potential job satisfaction. Howard (2010) suggests asking how the interviewer would describe the ideal candidate so that he or she pictures you in this position. Asking how success is defined for this position can give insight into the type of supervisor you would be working for, as well as the company culture.

The job interview is only one real-life example of this data collection method. When we think about the purpose of structured conversations, the employer's use of an interview makes perfect sense. Conducting a survey would not yield the type of interpersonal information that employers need to make informed hiring decisions. Navigating this rite of passage is integral to professional success, just as the research interview process is essential to collecting the data needed to address the research question.

Surveys provide researchers with a breadth of information, while interviews are an opportunity to gather in-depth information. Surveys are the predominant data collection method used to gather data on crime, criminals, and intervention strategies. A review of research published in the leading journals finds that 45 per cent of empirical research used some kind of survey-based data collection method: face-to-face,

21 per cent; telephone, 9 per cent; mail, 11 per cent, other self-administered, 22 per cent (Kleck, Tark, & Bellows, 2006, p. 150). Why are surveys so popular? They are versatile, as they can investigate a variety of topics and address many research questions. They are efficient because they are quick and inexpensive in comparison to other data collection methods. Their findings are usually generalizable, as one can collect data from a representative sample.

When choosing to conduct interviews, researchers select participants who represent a range of perspectives. This method is ideal for collecting detailed information in a timely manner, and it allows researchers the opportunity to access hard-to-reach populations. Unlike a survey, participants use their own words to express their opinions and experiences. Approximately 12 per cent of empirical research used interviews to investigate crime or criminal justice-related research problems (Kleck et al., 2006).

Surveys

As surveys are so common, it is increasingly necessary to understand the design and the collection of data if we are to make sense of what appears in newspapers and on television. Often the goal is to describe or better understand a population that is too large for methods such as interviews or participant observation. Because the data are largely analyzed quantitatively, the ability to administer some types of surveys to a representative sample is an important consideration.

The When and the Why

Designing and conducting survey research is both an art and a science. The extensive instructional literature on the topic comprises the scientific aspect. Surveys using an interviewer constitute the art aspect, as interviewing skills strongly impact the reliability and validity of the data collected.

Appropriate Topics

Although surveys are amenable for a host of different research problems, they are the most appropriate

data collection method for certain topics. For example, surveys are used to count the frequency of criminal behaviour, to assess the nature of criminality and perceptions or attitudes on crime, and to better understand victimization patterns. Surveys provide an alternative estimate of criminal activity, as official records represent only crime reported to the police.

One of the most common reasons for conducting surveys is to assess attitudes, behaviour, experiences, or beliefs. When investigating people's attitudes, you look to understand what they want from or feel about a given subject. Behaviour involves what people do in everyday life. Experiences are the life events that are the focus of the study, such as offending, the criminal justice system, or victimization. Beliefs concern what people think is true or right.

Surveys are also appropriate for exploring a person's expectations. Consider a research study evaluating a treatment program for drug users convicted of prostitution or theft-related crimes. Surveys elicit data on what the participants expect from the program, if they anticipate that the program will lead to a drug-free lifestyle, and whether they believe it will target the underlying causes of their addiction.

Virtually every survey includes questions on personal characteristics, background, and demographic attributes, such as age or education level. These attributes help the researcher describe the sample and gain an appreciation for who the respondents are and any potential connection between their characteristics and experiences. Overall, surveys are appropriate to investigate research questions on

- personal characteristics,
- factual information,
- ways in which individuals self-identify and describe themselves,
- behaviour and experiences,
- attitudes, values, and opinions, and
- nature and extent of knowledge and understanding.

Strengths and Weaknesses

There are three primary strengths of surveys. First, they are effective for collecting information from a larger group of people. Second, surveys provide flexibility—you can ask many questions on the same topic. Third, survey questions are standardized so that everyone who completes the survey is asked exactly the same questions in the same order and is given the same response options, thereby increasing the reliability of the data.

As with every data collection method, surveys are not without their weaknesses. Although standardization has its benefits, questions can lead to inadvertently missing information that is important to the respondents. Thus, standardized questions increase reliability but can simultaneously reduce the validity of the data. Similarly, there is another dimension to flexibility. With standardized questions and administration, researchers are unable to change the survey at any point. Finally, surveys are not appropriate for understanding the context in which attitudes form or behaviour occurs.

Types of Surveys

Surveys can be administered in several ways. One can gather information by interviewing the respondent in person or on the telephone. Alternatively, the survey can be self-administered, whereby respondents complete the survey by themselves without the assistance of an interviewer. These types of surveys are administered by mail, to groups, or online. To appreciate why researchers choose one mode over another, let's take a closer look at each of these options.

Face-to-Face Surveys

When conducting **face-to-face surveys**, an interviewer travels to the respondent's location, is physically present throughout the entire process, and provides any assistance needed to help respondents understand and answer the questions. With face-to-face surveys, a researcher reads the questions and audio records or handwrites responses.

face-to-face survey
a survey administered by a researcher, who asks respondents questions in person.

Researchers can also use computer-assisted personal interviewing (CAPI) or computer-assisted self-administered interviewing (CASI) to collect the data. CAPI displays the interview questions on a laptop or tablet screen and the interviewer records responses on the spot. Post-survey data entry is no longer required; the program does not allow interviewers to skip questions (but makes asking a series of complex questions easier), and data entry errors are minimized. CASI involves the respondent completing the survey on a computer, without an interviewer administering each question. By answering directly on the computer, the respondent may feel more comfortable and be more truthful in his or her responses. CASI tends to elicit candid responses, particularly to sensitive questions that might embarrass the respondent or be difficult to verbalize. In fact, this is one of the main reasons that researchers strongly consider adopting CASI.

Face-to-face surveys are more responsive to the participant than other types, despite the element of standardization in the question structure, order, and delivery. If the respondent does not understand the question, he or she can ask the interviewer to clarify or repeat the question. This possibility translates into a more personalized interaction between two people. In addition, the survey can last up to an hour, allowing researchers to ask more questions, seek more detailed responses, and elicit information in the respondent's own words.

Due to the type of interaction, researchers can access a population that might not otherwise be able to participate, such as illiterate persons who would experience great difficulty completing a written survey. One can also ask questions in more than one way. For example, questions can include images or videos. Questions are asked one at a time, preventing people from looking at later questions, which might influence their responses to earlier questions. Unlike other types of surveys, the researcher can select the right person to answer the survey. If the research focuses on adults, he or she can ensure that a teenager in the household is not completing the survey. Finally, face-to-face surveys have the highest response rates. Rates can be as high as 85 per cent, probably because it is difficult for people to turn down someone who is at their front door.

Four disadvantages lead researchers to opt for alternative formats. First, the face-to-face survey is the most expensive and time-consuming type. It can cost twice as much as telephone surveys because it takes time to collect the data and there are travel costs. Second, all research has budgetary constraints limiting the sample's representativeness and geographic coverage. Third, collecting data in person creates the possibility of reactivity, whereby the respondents and their answers are influenced by the interviewer's characteristics or demeanour. Lastly, although CASI can increase the likelihood of honest answers to sensitive questions, this advantage does not necessarily exist with direct interaction or CAPI. An element of anonymity is lost, and people are put on the spot, negating the possibility to think about their response.

Telephone Surveys

Telephone surveys are a reliable way to gather data on the general population's attitudes, opinions, and experiences. Collecting data over the telephone is considerably less expensive than gathering information in person. In this type of survey, the impersonality of a self-administered survey is combined with the personal connection of the face-to-face format.

Almost all of us have participated in a telephone survey at some point. Several things happen before you get that phone call. The first challenge for researchers to overcome is being able to contact you. A common technique is random digit dialling (RDD). The researcher specifies the area codes of interest and the computer program randomly generates and dials phone numbers within that geographic area. Although RDD increases the likelihood of reaching those with unlisted phone numbers, it includes both households and companies. Multiple follow-ups are often required to make contact with a respondent. However, the clear advantage is that researchers can reach a more geographically disperse population than is possible with face-to-face surveys.

Telephone surveys use computer-assisted telephone interviewing (CATI), which is similar to CAPI and CASI. Interview questions are displayed on a monitor and the interviewer enters the data as the respondent answers a question. Questions are asked in the same way each time, increasing the data's reliability. Many universities have data research centres that provide the facilities and human resources for telephone surveys. For instance, the Institute for Social Research at York University (2013) uses CATI and selects respondents using RDD. Once verbal contact is made, household members are randomly selected to complete

telephone survey a survey in which an interviewer asks respondents questions over the telephone, reducing the costs in comparison to face-to-face surveys and enabling a representative sample.

NEW RESEARCH ON STREETCRIME

DO YOU DO THIS :
A: WEEKLY
B: DAILY
C: SEVERAL TIMES A DAY ?

CANARY PETE

the survey. To increase the number of completed surveys and representativeness, the RDD makes up to 12 attempts to make contact from a given phone number. Follow-up calls are made at different times of the day and on different days of the week.

One advantage to telephone surveys is that the researcher can monitor interviewers, their performance, and how questions are asked because the surveys are conducted at a central location and audio recorded. As the interviewer is not in direct contact with the respondent, there is less reactivity. Providing that there are sufficient follow-ups and the survey is short enough, the response rate is sometimes as high as 70–80 per cent. Data can be collected rapidly because no travelling is required. Adopting CATI reduces the time required to process the data, and there is an additional layer of anonymity for respondents. It is much easier to assure potential participants that their responses are confidential as there is no visual contact and the interviewer is not aware of where they live or their first and last name.

self-administered survey a survey completed without interaction between the researcher and respondents; respondents receive the surveys in the mail or via an e-mail or a hyperlink directing them to a website.

Representativeness is both an advantage and a disadvantage of telephone surveys. It can take up to a thousand phone calls to secure 200–300 responses, which means that response rates can be as low as 25 per cent (Bernard, 2013). In such cases, one wonders whether respondents are truly representative of the general population. Another drawback is call screening—a common practice, particularly for certain segments of the population, such as those trying to avoid creditors and collection agencies. There are also constraints on the number of questions and the time required to complete the survey. The phone call interrupts a person's routine and personal life, which is why most researchers suggest that the survey should be no more than 15–20 minutes in length. Moreover, distractions and interruptions by others in the household, especially young children, are more likely with this format. With the rise in marketing surveys, opinion polls, and telemarketers, potential respondents are leery of the call's true purpose and are tired of receiving unsolicited phone calls, which increases the chances of quick refusals or hang-ups.

Self-administered surveys

In many ways, Dillman's (1999) prediction that **self-administered surveys** would become the primary type of survey in the twenty-first century was correct. We encounter these surveys in multiple contexts, including mid-terms, course evaluations, customer satisfaction cards, and even credit card applications. Such surveys are completed when it is convenient for the respondent and any reactivity effect is obviously not a concern. This format can potentially lead to more honest responses and therefore more valid data. Mail and online surveys share characteristics; however, their differences affect the choice of one over the other. Decision-making factors include the amount and type of information needed, the target sample, and the amount of time and funding available (Burns et al., 2008).

Mail Surveys

Mail surveys allow researchers to ask more questions than they can in a face-to-face or telephone survey. At the same time, this format requires a different approach in terms of structure, layout, and procedures to increase response rates. There are also additional factors to consider.

For example, the researcher cannot control how a question is interpreted. Some populations, such as people who are homeless or visually impaired, are largely inaccessible. Respondents can scan the entire survey, which could influence their decision to participate and how they answer the questions. By far the biggest concern is the lower response rate, which averages 20–30 per cent. This rate reduces the chances of a representative sample; that is, it increases the likelihood that those who complete the survey are different in some significant way from those who do not.

Researchers can achieve up to a 70 per cent response rate by taking additional steps to address non-response. Follow-up mailings encourage non-respondents to complete the survey while emphasizing its importance and the value of their perspective. A personalized cover letter establishes the researcher's credibility, explains that participation is voluntary, and provides assurances of confidentiality and anonymity. An effective cover letter increases the response rate and the likelihood that answers are complete and honest. A reminder postcard is often sent two weeks after the initial mailing, followed by a new cover letter and survey two to four weeks later and again six to eight weeks after the initial survey distribution. Researchers find that, the more time that passes after the initial mailing, the less likely the person will complete the survey. Survey non-completion may be partially attributable to respondents thinking it's too much work, is unimportant, or irrelevant to their lives.

Consider these examples. Wehrman and de Angelis (2011) investigated citizen willingness to participate in community policing initiatives. Data were collected as part of a municipal government project to assess citizen satisfaction with public services. Anonymous surveys were mailed to 16,193 residences, yielding a 37 per cent response rate. Follow-up telephone surveys with some of the non-respondents determined no differences compared to those who completed the survey. Based on the results, it appears that African Americans were more willing to participate than white citizens were.

Jackson (2004) conducted a mail survey with no follow-ups, yielding a low response rate of 18 per cent. He found that mail survey research exaggerates the extent to which the public fears crime, as perceptions of risk are embedded in the meanings associated with vulnerability, neighbourhood characteristics, and societal attitudes and values. Remember, surveys (especially mail surveys) are not the most appropriate data collection method if we want to understand the context or development of opinions.

Online Surveys

An online survey can be part of an e-mail message or an attachment. E-mail surveys are not ideal if the questionnaire is longer than three or four pages. Web-based surveys direct respondents to websites such as Survey Monkey to complete the questionnaire. A PIN or unique alphanumeric identifier can be used to monitor the response rate and facilitate follow-up e-mails.

Web surveys are more flexible, inexpensive, and interesting and are easier to tailor to the respondent than e-mail surveys. To enhance the survey, researchers can use multimedia content when asking questions. For example, they can include videos or pop-ups that define a term or provide a point of reference. Although representative samples are less likely, response rates are higher for people working in organizations, the middle class, and university students.

Online surveys increase the chances of getting honest answers about behaviour defined as unacceptable by society and about unusual experiences. There are fewer data entry errors because the respondents enter the data themselves. They find it easier and quicker to complete online surveys than mail surveys—the former shouldn't take longer than 10 to 15 minutes. Researchers can also provide selected results after the survey is finished (to satisfy a respondent's curiosity) and offer a token of appreciation for participating.

Patchin and Hinduja (2006) took a novel approach to online surveys to explore the nature of cyberbullying. They placed a survey link on a popular music artist's official website and entered all participants in a draw for one of three autographed photographs of the artist. Within 31 days, 571 individuals completed the survey, of which 384 were under the age of 18. As with other online surveys, this one was a convenience sample because respondents self-selected to participate. Informed consent was implied by respondents checking a box to indicate voluntary participation. The researchers make two points: as with all surveys, respondents may have lied about their age, and the impact of survey length remains unclear because the entire survey was on one screen (evidence suggests that this format increases response rates).

Which Is Better: Mail or Online?

Schaefer and Dillman's (1998) experiment found that both approaches have approximately the same response rate (58 per cent). Other researchers argue that online surveys have lower response rates; however, electronic surveys are completed faster than the self-administered paper version (Burns et al., 2008).

Online surveys also elicit more responses to individual questions, especially those asking for written explanations, with longer and more detailed answers. Ultimately, debate remains as to which approach yields higher response rates and data validity.

Peak, Barthe, and Garcia (2008) compared the findings from mail surveys conducted in 1986 and online surveys using Survey Monkey from 2006. Both surveys contained questions on officer attributes, campus police agency characteristics, and relations with local law enforcement. With 915 agencies in the sample, 243 had invalid e-mail addresses and, despite four follow-ups emphasizing the study's importance and that the message wasn't junk mail, the researchers achieved only a 34 per cent response rate. They concluded that online surveys may not be viewed as credible when compared to mail surveys and that researchers battle against the high volume of e-mails received on a daily basis.

Navigating the Survey Landscape

As we have seen, the factors involved in choosing a survey format revolve around the research topic, sample, desired response rate, and available resources. Depending on your research question,

one type of survey format can be more appropriate than the others. For instance, asking sensitive questions is better suited for self-administered surveys because the sense of privacy leads to higher levels of disclosure (Tourangeau & Smith, 1996). However, even this is not a foregone conclusion. When comparing face-to-face and self-administered survey results, Klinkenberg and colleagues (2003) found no differences when people with a severe mental illness reported the frequency of socially stigmatizing behaviours. If you are interested in the fear of crime among retired individuals, a face-to-face or telephone survey is more appropriate than an online one.

Response rates vary by type of survey. For example, face-to-face surveys will have higher response rates with less educated people or those for whom English is a second language. There is also that omnipresent problem of available time and money. Although self-administered surveys have lower response rates, they are far cheaper and quicker than other survey formats. There is always a trade-off when choosing one type of survey over another, but understanding the strengths and weaknesses of each approach will lead to more informed decision-making. Table 6.1 summarizes the characteristics of each type of survey.

Table 6.1 Comparing different types of surveys

Factor	Face-to-face	Telephone	Mail	Online
Financial cost	Expensive	Moderate	Inexpensive	Least expensive
Data collection speed	Slow	Fast	Moderate	Fastest
Response rate	High	Moderate	Low	Low to moderate
Sampling information	Address	Phone number	Address	E-mail address
Respondent burden	Low	Moderate	High	Moderate
Researcher control	Varies	Varies	None	None
Survey length	Long	Moderate	Short	Short
Social desirability bias	High	Moderate	Low	Low
Reactivity effect	High	Moderate	None	None
Response option length	Moderate	Moderate	Short	Short
Use of their own words	High	High	Poor	Moderate
Survey complexity	High	Good	Poor	High

Source: Adapted from Miller (n.d.), the Duke Initiative on Survey Methodology.

Methods in Action

Surveys and the Media

The media set the agenda for what the public should be thinking about. When it comes to crime, the media play a significant role in publicizing survey results within the context of a newsworthy event.

For example, the *Globe and Mail* reported on an Angus Reid poll's findings that most Canadians agree bullying is a serious problem, compared to 43 per cent of university students (Baluja, 2012). This article is unusual in that it included the poll's margin of error (in this case, "plus or minus 3.1%, 19 times out of 20"). With university students, then, the average could be as low as 39.9 per cent or as high as 46.1 per cent. Another key feature of opinion polls is the small sample size—in this case, 1,006 respondents—raising questions of representativeness.

Another poll focused on public perceptions of police enforcement tactics at the 2010 G20 Toronto Summit. Angus Reid conducted a telephone survey with 1,003 Canadians and 503 Torontonians to conclude that 67 per cent of Canadians and 73 per cent of Toronto residents felt that police actions with protesters were justifiable (Gillis, 2010a). The sample size wasn't always provided but was included more often than the response rate, making it virtually impossible to determine the extent that the findings represent the general population.

The media also conduct surveys to measure public perceptions. For instance, *Cosmopolitan* conducts an annual online sex survey on attitudes and preferences. In terms of crime-related topics, the *Toronto Star*'s website often solicits readers' opinions. One survey explored why victims do not report crimes to police (Gillis, 2010b). Unfortunately, no information was provided on the questions asked or the number of completed surveys. The results suggested that people think the crime is too insignificant for police involvement or nothing will be done about it if they do file a report.

Less commonly, the media publish academic research findings. In 2008, the *Houston Chronicle* published the results of a survey on nearly 3,500 incarcerated youth in Texas. About half had emotional disorders, just under 60 per cent had substance abuse problems, and nearly 20 per cent had severe emotional problems (Viren, 2008). The *Edmonton Journal* reported on Duxbury and Higgins's survey of 4,500 officers working for 25 police agencies. They found that the police are stressed from long hours, constant shift changes, understaffing, caseloads, family pressures, and limited career opportunities (Quan, 2012). Although the latter survey tells us the average characteristics of officers, neither article gives any information on the response rate nor type of survey used.

Government surveys are frequently reported. Statistics Canada publishes police-reported crime rates annually. The media then focus on specific information, such as changes in crime rates for particular offences. For instance, there were fewer hate crimes in 2010 than in 2009 and the most common victims of violent hate crime were homosexuals and blacks (Ha, 2012).

It is wise to exercise caution when interpreting surveys reported in the media. Be critical and look for information on the sample, type of survey, and response rate to assess representativeness. Not all surveys are created equal. However, critically assessing media reports influences the extent to which your opinion is affected.

Survey Structure and Design

Researchers spend considerable time writing survey questions and almost as much time structuring the survey. Structure and design is all about survey layout. A poorly structured questionnaire increases the chances that respondents won't bother answering the survey or will skip questions or answer too few questions to make it usable for analysis. Before we look at survey parts, methods, and logistics in more detail, here are some overall tips. The title should indicate the survey's topic. The use of space influences the amount and nature of responses. Use easy-to-read fonts and underline or bold any words integral for understanding a question and responding appropriately. Do not put too many questions on the same page and make sure that a question doesn't spread over two pages. You want the survey to be user-friendly and visually appealing.

Introduction

Survey introductions emphasize the significance of the research endeavour, why the respondent is the most appropriate participant, and why his or her perspective is important for understanding the topic. Therefore, clearly outline the research purpose, research questions, and any sponsor or funding agency. The introduction should be written or spoken in a professional tone as it sets the stage for the survey to be taken seriously.

Equally critical is stating that participation is voluntary and all responses are confidential. Making these ethical parameters crystal clear decreases item non-response rates (Singer, 1978). In order to provide a measure of anonymity, informed consent is implied with self-administered surveys. In other words, if the person completes the survey after reading the introductory letter, he or she has consented to participate. When signatures are required, sensitization effects can occur and response rates decrease because the stipulation itself is interpreted almost as a sensitive question (Alwin, 1977; Singer, 1978). This situation is particularly problematic for face-to-face surveys.

Instructions

Surveys are broken into thematic sections and questions are presented in different formats (e.g. check all that apply, choose only one response). Thus, you need to provide clear instructions for each section and type of questions. Always include an introductory statement for each section, outlining the purpose and content. This practice helps respondents see the logic behind the survey. Don't forget to thank the respondent at the end of the survey and reiterate the importance of his or her perspective.

Question Order

The order of survey questions creates a logical progression from beginning to end. View a survey as one integrated data collection instrument. Each thematic section and question is there for a reason. There are links among the research purpose, objectives, and other sections.

List questions in a sequence that will make sense to the respondent. In other words, they should be in a logical order and resemble a conversation. Avoid randomizing the question order because respondents will be forced to switch topics constantly, making it difficult for them to focus. Instead, organize questions thematically, from general to specific.

Start with interesting questions to grab the respondent's attention and, if possible, focus on subjects that the respondent would want to answer. The first question should tell him or her the purpose and topic of the survey. Dillman (2004) argues that it is the most important question in the entire survey. It plays a large role in whether the survey is completed because it can illustrate that completing the survey will be easy. Therefore, ensure that the question applies to everyone taking the survey, piques his or her interest, and encourages him or her to continue answering questions.

Never ask sensitive questions at the beginning of the survey. They raise "concerns about disapproval or other consequences (such as legal sanctions) for reporting truthfully or if the question itself is seen as an invasion of privacy" (Tourangeau & Smith,

1996, p. 276). Sensitive questions are best placed in the middle or close to the end of the survey. In this way, respondents are more likely to answer and have already invested their time. For instance, many people interpret a question on their income as sensitive. Demographic questions are best placed at the end of the survey, except in face-to-face surveys; with this type, beginning with demographic questions can help put the respondent at ease and facilitate the development of **rapport**.

Finally, when two questions ask for similar information, you can run into context effects. It's human nature to try to be consistent so as not to come across as deceitful. As a result, one question can affect how subsequent ones are interpreted and answered. This situation highlights the importance of question sequencing within thematic sections.

Total Design Method

Much of what has been discussed so far is part of Dillman's (2004) total design method, an approach aimed at increasing response rates for self-administered surveys. Widely adopted by researchers, this method consists of the following advice:

- Include a one-page cover letter outlining the nature of the study, the reason subjects were selected, instructions, a guarantee of confidentiality, and the importance of completion.
- Use professional presentation and language.
- Include eye-catching front and back covers.
- Ensure that the layout is easy to read and attractive.
- Use an appropriate question sequence.
  ▷ Make the first question directly related to the topic of interest and easy to answer.
  ▷ Place sensitive questions in the middle to end of the survey.
  ▷ Save demographic questions for the end of the survey.
- Limit survey length (the rule of thumb is that response rates decrease with surveys over 12 pages).

- Package the survey professionally and use prepaid return envelopes.
- Increase response rates by offering incentives, even if their value is only a dollar.
- Follow-up with non-respondents one week, three weeks, and then four to five weeks after the initial mailing.

Applegate and Davis (2006) adhered to Dillman's model. They mailed surveys to a random sample of 967 Florida residents to explore perceptions regarding the appropriate severity of punishment for juvenile murderers. They sent a personalized cover letter, postage-paid return envelope, and a $1 financial incentive. A thank-you postcard was sent one week later, and the entire survey package three and seven weeks after the initial mailing. This process yielded a 48.6 per cent response rate.

> **rapport** an open and trusting relationship between a researcher and subjects, which fosters mutual understanding.

Castellano and Schafer (2005) used a variation of the total design method in their comparison of current and historical criminal justice education models. To understand professors' views, they mailed surveys on the purpose and content of criminal justice education, sent reminder postcards two weeks after the initial mailing, resent the entire survey package four weeks later, and e-mailed a request after six weeks.

Survey Question Content

A survey should include only questions integral to addressing the research questions. For instance, ask just those demographic questions that are necessary, or the survey may be interpreted as too intrusive. If possible, provide a rationale for including various survey questions. One example is from Schulenberg (2013a), who evaluated the effectiveness of a forum on police complaints systems that brought together community members, the police, and policy-makers. The rationale provided for the demographic questions was

Responses to Questions 16 to 22 are important and will be used to:

(1) improve the composition and structure of any future Forums so we can collectively and meaningfully contribute to the process of improving Ontario's police complaints system; and (2) assess the success of our goal to ensure equal representation from the community. Please check off the appropriate category.

When feasible, use questions from existing survey instruments. There is no need to reinvent the wheel and your results will be comparable to previous research. Reliability and validity are high as the questions have been tested and any problems have been addressed by the original researchers. With pretested questions, you can be more confident that questions are understood correctly. The downside is that these questions may not perfectly measure the concepts of interest in your study.

In general, questions about a person's attitudes and beliefs are the most common. The quality of answers increases if these questions are related to concrete circumstances and behaviours. Providing a context improves a respondent's competency to answer the question. When testing for factual information, include preliminary questions that ensure only those respondents with the requisite knowledge are asked the question.

Close- and Open-Ended Questions

Close-ended questions consist of fixed responses from which respondents choose the answer that best describes their opinions, beliefs, understandings, or experiences. These questions are extremely common and respondents find them easier to understand and quicker to answer. Moreover, response options can clarify the question. Close-ended questions are basically multiple choice

close-ended question
a survey question in which respondents select an answer from a pre-defined list of options.

open-ended question
a survey question in which respondents answer the question in their own words.

questions. They can be yes/no, 0/1/2/3+, most to least, agree/disagree, or another rank order format.

Close-ended questions may seem like a perfect solution, but there are disadvantages to consider. As response options are determined in advance, you might miss an issue important to the respondents. Too many response options can create confusion. Further, people are forced to choose answers that might not reflect everyday life or that provide ideas they never thought of before. Thus, close-ended questions are inappropriate for complex issues because of the need to simplify and target just one aspect at a time.

Open-ended questions elicit detailed responses and allow respondents to clarify what they are trying to say. They provide insight into how a person thinks and his or her frame of reference, which can produce unanticipated findings. These questions, then, are ideal for complex, interrelated issues and sensitive questions. For example, instead of simply asking for the number of previous arrests, an open-ended question could ask what it feels like to be arrested.

Coding these questions is difficult because the researcher needs to interpret responses and might misunderstand them. Open-ended questions take longer to answer and require more effort than close-ended, thereby increasing respondent fatigue. There is also the possibility that an answer has little to do with the question.

Survey Question Logistics

People have to want to share their views if they are to become survey participants. Following certain guidelines will help you to write effective questions and to facilitate this willingness. Always keep four criteria in mind: short, simple, specific, and objective.

Unambiguous

When we are knowledgeable about a subject, we can inadvertently make assumptions about others' understanding of it or its related terminology. Direct and short survey questions that use short words and sentences will reduce any possible confusion and enable respondents to answer, even if they are less familiar with the topic. However, when questions are too simplistic, what is being asked may be unclear. The question "Where do you live?" could refer to the type of dwelling, the street, the city, or even the country. A better question would be, "In what city is your current residence?"

Vague and confusing questions have a few characteristics. They are long, neglect respondent's characteristics or ability to answer, use words that are too subjective and open to multiple interpretations, or incorporate other question errors (which we'll discuss in the next pages). Use words that a respondent would understand and avoid slang, acronyms, or technical language. Aim for questions at an eighth-grade level.

Doubling up Questions

Double-barrelled questions include more than one idea within a single question. They are confusing because you could have different answers for each part but are forced to choose a single response. Consider the question, "Do you support hiring more police officers and longer sentences for criminals?" If you agree with the first part and disagree with the second, how do you answer? Double-barrelled questions lead to ambiguous, unreliable, and invalid data. The best way to avoid this error is not to use the word *and*.

One sure way to muddy the meaning of a question is to use two negative words. **Double negative questions** make it difficult for respondents to figure out which response matches their sentiments. Even experienced researchers unintentionally make this mistake while trying to prevent other wording problems. For example, "Do you *disagree* that there should be *no* standard minimum wage?" is a double negative question. A better question would be, "Do you think that there should be a minimum wage?" Double negative questions can usually be fixed with some minor rewording.

Biased Questions

Even the most seasoned researchers find it hard to detect biased questions, which encourage respondents to answer in a certain way. **Leading questions** neglect to give equal weight to opposing perspectives or suggest a preferred response. For instance, leading questions can start by saying, "Don't you agree that . . . ?"

Alternatively, question wording can induce a **social desirability bias**, in which respondents choose the socially acceptable answer in order to avoid embarrassment or an image of irresponsibility, prejudice, or incompetence. A personal interpretive framework analyzes what makes us look good to others, and leading questions are triggers for this bias. An example is, "Most people support drinking and driving laws that increase punishments for all offenders. What are your thoughts on drinking and driving?" Avoid value-laden words such as *racist* or *horrible*, as definitions vary based on the respondent's social location and personal experiences. Remember, the interpretation of a question is largely determined by how it is worded.

To eliminate **loaded questions**, neutralize the action and ensure that the question applies to that person. Words may have negative connotations or focus on controversial subjects. For instance, a question that asks how often you take drugs assumes that you are a drug user. Similarly, asking someone if they have stopped drinking and driving assumes they have done so in the past. Include preliminary screening questions to avoid this error.

double-barrelled question a question that includes two or more ideas, resulting in more than one possible answer.

double negative question a question that includes two negative words, making it difficult to understand.

leading question a question that indirectly encourages respondents to answer in a certain way regardless of their true opinion.

social desirability bias the tendency for respondents to answer questions in a manner that makes them look socially acceptable; particularly common with sensitive questions on deviant and criminal behaviour.

loaded question a question that assumes the respondent has experienced or done something.

Mutually Exclusive and Exhaustive

mutually exclusive response options that do not overlap, allowing respondents to choose only one answer.

exhaustive response options that represent every view or experience.

skip pattern a set of filter and contingency questions used to ensure that the appropriate respondents are answering the questions.

filter question a question that identifies whether a respondent should answer the contingency questions or be directed to a question later in the survey.

contingency question a question that respondents answer solely on the basis of their answers to a filter question.

matrix question a series of questions with the same response options.

response set effect the tendency for respondents to answer multiple matrix questions in the same way.

If response options are not **mutually exclusive**, distortion occurs because respondents can choose more than one answer. Therefore, avoid overlapping response options. Let's say your question is, "How many times have you been arrested?" Your response options are not mutually exclusive if they are 0, 1–2, 2–3, and 3 or more. Respondents who have been arrested twice could choose 1–2 or 2–3. A mutually exclusive question eliminates the possibility of selecting more than one answer.

An **exhaustive** question provides response options that represent all possible views and experiences. A common strategy is to include an "other," "no opinion," or "not applicable" choice. If you are trying to find out how old someone is and you provide response options up to 45 years old, the question is not exhaustive because anyone 46 or older cannot answer. When using an "other" option, provide space for the respondents to insert their responses.

Special Types of Questions

Some question formats improve validity and make sure that respondents have enough knowledge to answer the questions. These tools are valuable, as your conclusions are only as good as your data and quality data is based on collecting accurate answers.

Skip Patterns

A **skip pattern** sorts respondents into groups so that only those with the knowledge to answer a question are directed toward it. This approach increases survey completion rates and reduces respondent fatigue because people answer questions that apply to them. In a skip pattern, a **filter question** determines whether a person is qualified to answer one or more subsequent questions. If the filter question doesn't apply to the respondent, he or she is directed to skip the question and move to one later in the survey. If the person is knowledgeable on the subject, he or she is directed toward one or more **contingency questions**. Thus, responding to these questions is contingent on how the filter question is answered. Let's put this process in the context of an example:

1. Have you ever been arrested? (Filter question)
   a. No (go to question 3)
   b. Yes (go to question 2)
2. Has a police officer ever used force to handcuff you? (Contingency question)
   a. No
   b. Yes
3. Have you ever been diagnosed with a mental illness?
   a. No
   b. Yes

Matrix Questions

Matrix questions are a series of questions with identical response options. Grouping these questions together uses space efficiently, allows respondents to answer them quickly and easily, and helps the researcher compare answers from different questions. Often in the form of a Likert scale, response options are listed across the top of the page, with the questions placed down the side.

There are two things to consider when using matrix questions: respondents may read the questions too quickly or answer questions in the same way. The latter creates a **response set effect**. Matrix questions are ideal for detecting this problem, but they can also cause it. By listing the questions in a row, respondents may choose the same response option regardless of the topic or their opinions. Consequently, responses are motivated by factors unrelated to perceptions on question content. A response set occurs more frequently with respondent fatigue, social desirability, boredom, or laziness. To avoid this pattern, vary the order of response options and include less than ten statements for each matrix question.

Vignette Questions

Vignette questions elicit how a person would feel or respond in a given set of hypothetical circumstances. This question type is an option for asking sensitive questions in a non-threatening manner. Instead of using generalities or questions about respondents' behaviour to solicit opinions, you ask a set of questions on the basis of hypotheticals. These questions create a distance between the respondents and the situation so that they feel freer to respond without fearing negative judgment or succumbing to social desirability bias. Keep vignettes as brief as possible while providing enough detail for respondents to answer the follow-up questions. It is best not to ask more than five follow-up questions. An example is describing a hypothetical situation in which someone commits a crime. The survey would include questions about the seriousness of the crime, the reason it should be illegal, or the most appropriate sentence.

Survey Obstacles

Every data collection method has obstacles affecting the validity and generalizability of the findings, as well as ethical principles to consider. These issues can be viewed through two lenses. Floaters, fence-sitters, and memory recall are problems related to the respondent. Response rates and ethics are associated with collecting survey data.

Floaters and Fence-Sitters

Approximately one-third of respondents are **floaters**, who choose an answer even when they know little about the topic. "Respondents may infer that the middle response option represents the typical value and use this option as an anchor for their own answers" (Tourangeau & Smith, 1996, p. 284). Ninety per cent of floaters will choose "don't know" if they are given this option (Schuman & Presser, 1981).

Fence-sitters consistently have a neutral opinion. Approximately 10–20 per cent of respondents will choose the neutral option, as they are ambivalent or don't feel strongly about the subject (Schuman & Presser, 1981). Many researchers argue that offering a "don't know," "neither agree nor disagree," or "no opinion" option is the best way to go. Others point out that doing so gives participants a way out from thinking about how they truly feel or from revealing their true sentiments. If you are concerned about floaters and fence-sitters in your surveys, include an open-ended question that asks respondents to elaborate on their opinions.

Memory Recall

Most of us are better at remembering things from the recent past or significant life events. Memory problems can create difficulties in conducting surveys. **Telescoping** refers to respondent recall problems that lead to under- or over-reporting behaviour. The most common type is forward telescoping, where events are remembered as occurring more recently than they actually did. Backward telescoping occurs when more recent events are remembered as occurring later than they did.

The best way to combat this problem is to create a reference period or bounded recall time frame. The tendency is that, the longer the reference period, the more likely that behaviour will be underreported.

vignette question a question placed in the context of a hypothetical scenario.

floaters respondents who choose a response option to a close-ended question even though they are not sure how to answer or what their views are on the issue.

fence-sitters respondents who choose neutral response options because they do not have a definitive opinion on the topic.

telescoping a recall problem in which respondents have trouble accurately remembering when, for how long, or how often something occurred in the past.

For mundane everyday behaviour, it is better to use a shorter reference period. Rarer events such as victimization can have longer reference periods, bounding recall to the last 6 to 12 months.

Response Rates

Response rates are one of the biggest challenges in surveys. There are two different types of response rates. The overall response rate is the percentage of completed surveys or the number of people who completed the survey divided by the number of sampling elements. The item response rate is the percentage of answered and usable responses or the number of people who answered a question divided by the number of people who completed the survey.

Response rates vary widely for all types of surveys. Carlan and Lewis (2009) assessed the relationship between individual characteristics and police professionalism. They mailed 1,953 surveys and 1,114 were returned, for a response rate of 57 per cent. Renauer (2007) examined whether residents

87% OF THE 56% WHO COMPLETED MORE THAN 23% OF THE SURVEY THOUGHT IT WAS A WASTE OF TIME

think informal social control or police intervention is a better explanation for the fear of crime. A random sample of 1,550 households yielded a 50 per cent response rate. Even when half of the sample responds, you need to be cautious when generalizing the findings. However, as Reanuer states, it is not as concerning when the research purpose is testing theoretical propositions versus drawing inferences about a specific population.

The type of target population can affect response rates. The lower the respondents' educational level, the more you'll see "don't know" answers; the wealthier the respondent, the less likely he or she is to answer questions about income and buying habits. You'll get lower response rates when surveying the general population compared to targeting a specific group. To investigate the characteristics and frequency of animal cruelty in an incarcerated population, Tallichet and Hensley (2009) used 2,093 self-administered surveys, of which 261 (12.5 per cent) were returned. The researchers pointed out that "although this response rate appears low, most prison studies dealing with sensitive issues attract 25% or fewer respondents" (p. 601). Even though the sample is representative of the prison population based on race, age, and type of offence committed, there are still significant generalizability limitations.

Response rates also vary by categories within the target population. For example, Gill and Taylor (2004) investigated financial companies' perspectives on reducing money laundering. A question asking respondents to identify the type of company had a 12 per cent item non-response rate. Although the survey response rate was 35 per cent, just 10 per cent of the insurance companies contacted participated, compared to 65 per cent of the banks. Overall, be aware that you have to state explicitly the limitations that non-response imposes on representativeness and generalizability.

Ethics

In some ways, there are fewer ethical challenges to overcome with surveys than with other data collection methods. Anonymity is difficult to guarantee because identifying information is needed to establish contact and to follow-up with non-respondents. In addition, survey researchers need to address the two interrelated concerns of confidentiality and potential harm. Recalling victimization experiences can cause further emotional trauma and disclosing illegal activities can lead to legal implications. Potential harm makes confidentiality important, as questions may elicit responses that could be damaging if an individual and his or her responses are identifiable.

Several tactics help guarantee the confidentiality of responses. Using alpha numerical codes for respondents makes it difficult to link answers to a particular person. Only researchers should have access to linkage information and it should be stored in a separate secure location from the data itself. Encryption technology can provide additional safeguards for online surveys.

Interviews

Interviews directly access personal experiences and the ways that people make sense of the world around them. The interview is a behavioural event. Interactions are a structured conversation that creates a partnership between the researcher and interviewee. Accurate information on sensitive topics is possible once rapport is established. Subjects can describe their attitudes, feelings, behaviours, and interpretations of the world in their own words and in a manner that creates meaning for them. Moreover, interview questions may lead people to think about their views and experiences in a new way.

Interviews are flexible because interviewees can say something that is important to them, even if it is unexpected. When a person starts talking about a topic covered later in the interview, the interviewer can shuffle questions to capitalize on the connection made by the interviewee. In this way, the interviewer does not interrupt the interviewee's train of thought.

Similar to surveys, the more abstract the question, the more likely the interviewee will not know how to answer or not understand what the answer should be. The interviewer also has to interpret the respondent's answer accurately. Ask for more information to confirm that you have correctly understood the response. Finally, researchers are cognizant of contradictions in responses. Even though they are in the process of data collection, they are simultaneously analyzing what is being said to ensure that they seek clarification when inconsistencies arise. Questions are open-ended, seeking to elicit detailed responses. Unlike surveys, questions are not standardized and can vary from one person to another.

Interviews about criminal behaviour carry the risk of participants embellishing their answers—offenders may glamourize their crimes to give the researcher what they think he or she wants or to make themselves look like a better criminal. This problem was a concern for a study that conducted interviews with 28 active carjackers to understand their motivation to offend (Jacobs et al., 2003). Each was offered $50 to participate and extra assurances of anonymity and confidentiality were required. The researchers had to use external sources of data as much as possible to assess the validity of statements on the nature and frequency of offending and contacts with the criminal justice system (e.g. police, courts, or corrections).

Appropriate Topics

Interviewing representative samples is not the goal. The data are analyzed inductively to create, inform, and refine theoretical explanations. For example, Copes and Tewksbury (2011) conducted 42 interviews with auto thieves on probation or parole to understand their motivation to offend and their perceptions on the risks associated with stealing cars. The authors acknowledge that they could not determine how the sample was related theoretically or substantively to the larger population. However, this inability is not problematic as representativeness is not a goal for exploratory research, thereby making interviews an appropriate data collection method.

People who are caught and convicted (i.e. captive populations) arguably represent unsuccessful criminals. Faupel (1987) interviewed thirty heroin addicts to unpack the relationship and dynamics of criminal behaviour. Multiple interviews ranging from 10 to 25 hours were conducted to capture their life histories. One could argue that most incarcerated participants are less sophisticated criminals, but comparisons were made to heroin addicts on the streets, and the responses of the two groups didn't differ significantly. Therefore, it is possible to achieve conceptual generalizability with interview data.

Another study focusing on theory development investigated how adopting adult roles and responsibilities at an early age leads to a methamphetamine addiction (Carbone-Lopez & Miller, 2012). Thirty-five interviews were conducted with women enrolled in a correctional drug treatment program to inform theoretical explanations for a new target population. The researchers offered the women $20 to participate, which raises the issue of using financial incentives.

Finding research participants is always an obstacle and this data collection method is no exception. Interviews are appropriate for research on hidden or hard-to-reach populations. Financial incentives are common because convincing people in these populations to participate, especially when they can have more to lose by doing so, is difficult. The question is whether offering such inducements renders true voluntary consent impossible.

An example of this problem is Zhang and Chin's (2002) exploratory research on operating Chinese human smuggling organizations. Formal interviews were conducted with 72 individuals. When formal meetings were not possible or feasible, spontaneous, unstructured interviews in the form of social conversations were conducted with 18 people. Snowball sampling was adopted due to the nature and secrecy of smuggling operations. A $75 financial incentive was offered, but some people felt that the money wasn't worth the risk of participating. Those who chose to participate typically declined payment. Further, the researchers had to spend months in the field before guarantees of anonymity and confidentiality were taken seriously.

Types of Interviews

The three interview formats—structured, semi-structured, and unstructured—collect different types of data better suited to different types of research projects. Although rarely used in criminology and criminal justice research, **structured interviews** use both open- and close-ended questions that are read in the same way each time. The order of questions is exactly the same for every person. Researchers use an **interview schedule**, which stipulates precise wording for all questions, provides instructions to the interviewer, and lists **probes** to gather more information.

Semi-structured interviews are the most common in criminology and criminal justice research. They are less procedurally stringent than the structured format but also use an interview schedule that lists the topics and questions in a specified order. The difference between the two types is that, in a semi-structured interview, you can change the order or skip questions based on how interviewees answer previous questions. Probes can be used at any time to delve into unanticipated directions or to clarify responses, but they are not necessarily scripted in advance.

The purpose of **unstructured interviews** is to get the participants to open up and express their viewpoints in their own words and in the order

structured interview an interview in which questions are read verbatim to all respondents and are asked in the same order.

interview schedule a list of interview topics and questions; depending on the type of interview, the question order may change, questions may be skipped if they are no longer relevant or repetitive, and probes may be inserted.

probe an interview technique used to get respondents to elaborate on their answer.

semi-structured interview a type of interview that, when responses are substantively significant, gives the interviewer the flexibility to ask questions that are not on the interview schedule.

unstructured interview a type of interview in which the question content, wording, and order vary each time.

in which they think about the subject. Thus, control over the interviewee's responses is minimized. Questions are open-ended and conversational, and prompts stimulate further discussion. Unstructured interviews are appropriate for understanding lived experiences in a given context. An additional benefit is that the data can be used to develop an interview schedule for semi-structured interviews.

Unstructured and semi-structured interviews are advantageous when you are confronted with contradictory evidence or have problems establishing rapport with participants. To combat these difficulties, Wilkinson (2007) interviewed 159 violent males from 16 to 24 years of age to better understand youths' perceptions of responses to criminal behaviour contextualized by geographic location. Interviewers challenge respondents when inconsistencies emerge by using probes for clarification. In some cases, researchers increase rapport and shared meaning by modifying the question or substituting slang words for deviant and criminal behaviours.

Interview Questions

A well-designed interview schedule takes respondents on a thematic journey. Interviewers adopt the role of outsider and novice, placing the interviewee as an insider with knowledge only he or she can provide. It may be useful to think of your role as a socially acceptable incompetent (Lofland et al., 2006). You don't understand the situation and you need the interviewee's help to grasp even the basics and obvious aspects of the situation.

The difference between a guided and normal conversation is that the interviewer does not share his or her point of view. Good interviewers listen more than they talk. The interview schedule serves as the journey's road map and is organized in the shape of an hourglass, going from general to specific and back to general questions. When conducting interviews, actively engage interviewees in the process by allowing them to develop arguments, link topics together, and elaborate on their responses.

Questions should focus on the individual's experiences. No one is in a position to know the feelings or rationale behind other people's actions. Questions can focus on personal background, opinions and beliefs, feelings and perceptions, behaviour, factual knowledge, and perspectives on life experiences. Like a survey, the first few interview questions should be easy to answer, which is why you can ask demographic questions at this point.

Give careful thought to the last question as it can lead to unanticipated findings. I have conducted over 350 interviews with police officers and some of the most interesting information came with the last question. One example is, "I don't do what you do for a living but developed these questions based on what I think might be relevant to your experiences with youth crime. Is there anything we haven't talked about that you would like to add?"

There are a few techniques that can elicit truthful answers while avoiding any social desirability bias. Questions with illustrative examples in the preamble provide a context depicting all sides of a topic. For instance, Patton (2002) was interested in the experiences of juveniles in group homes. Prior to asking, "What about you—how have you been treated in the group home?" the following illustration was provided:

> Some kids have told us they were treated like one of the family; some kids have told us they got knocked around and beat up by the group home parents; some kids have told us about sexual things that were done to them; some of the kids have told us about fun things and trips they did with the parents; some kids have felt they were treated really well and some have said they were treated pretty bad. (p. 367)

This context helps interviewees focus on relevant responses, gives them time to reflect on their answer, and diffuses any uncomfortable feelings that develop if they are to answer truthfully. Another way is to use vignette questions, which prompt interviewees to visualize themselves in a hypothetical situation.

When drafting an interview schedule, keep the following rules of thumb in mind. Use conversational language and avoid technical terms or jargon, unless it is used in the subjects' occupations. Don't start questions with *why* but *how*. Using the former could make interviewees feel that they must justify their perspective, whereas the latter provides flexibility to describe the process and context for their views. To collect in-depth narratives, avoid close-ended questions. Be aware, though, that even open-ended questions can inadvertently prompt yes/no responses. If this problem occurs, use probes and ask yourself how you might answer a question. Finally, as in surveys, avoid leading, loaded, or double-barrelled questions.

Interview Process

The process of interviewing can be broken down into three parts: preparation, interview, and post-interview activities. Each stage plays a role in successful interviews and the quality of data collected. Not only are you selecting interviewees who are knowledgeable and represent a range of perspectives, but you also need the skills to make the interview a conversation with a purpose.

Preparing for the Interview

The first consideration when preparing for an interview is location. In most cases, interviews are conducted in the interviewee's environment, be that at work, home, or a location of his or her choice. If such a location is not possible, the interview should be held in a neutral space, with as little background noise and as few interruptions as possible.

With the interviewee's consent, interviews are audio recorded to ensure accuracy and to facilitate data analysis. However, don't rely solely on this recording. Err on the side of caution and take notes in case something goes wrong with the audio equipment. These notes should record body language in conjunction with the substantive content of responses, information that can provide

valuable clues as to the interviewees' comfort level (e.g. whether the question made them defensive). Since you are not recording verbatim statements, your notes can remind you of follow-up questions or probes. An interviewee might ask what you are writing down or want to see your notes. Save any observations that you would not want him or her to read for after the interview is complete.

Take steps to make a good impression. Dress in a way that is consistent with interviewee expectations. For example, when interviewing in a formal environment, such as a courthouse, wear business clothes. If you're interviewing a homeless person, wearing jeans and a T-shirt is more appropriate. Always be punctual and schedule enough time so you don't rush through the interview schedule. Remember, people are sacrificing their time to participate in an interview. Be respectful by ensuring that they have enough time to share their thoughts but that the interview doesn't take longer than you said it would.

As with all data collection methods, ethics must be considered in interview preparation. Choose what you will ask respondents to elicit specific types of information consistent with your research purpose. You have an ethical responsibility to maintain guarantees of confidentiality and to ensure that the process doesn't cause respondents any harm. If the potential for psychological harm exists, you must be able to provide the interviewee with the contact information of appropriate support personnel.

Conducting the Interview

There are five things to do before asking any questions:

1. Review the informed consent, secure a signature, and reaffirm the confidentiality and anonymity parameters.
2. Describe the research purpose.
3. Clarify that the interview is meant to better understand what the interviewee knows and thinks about the subject. This step reinforces why his or her perspective is important.

4. Ask if the interviewee has any questions about the study or his or her participation.

5. Review the parameters for control over the interview. In my research, I emphasize that participants are free to refuse to answer any or all questions without penalty, to withdraw their consent at any time, and to turn the audio recorder off at any point.

Remember to treat the interviewee as an expert in his or her own lived experience. Your primary role is to define the focus, not the content, of responses. Allow the person to explain what aspect of the topic is important to him or her.

Developing rapport creates a comfortable atmosphere for the interviewee and a mutual trust between two people. Be patient and enthusiastic about the topic and the opportunity to interview the person. Know your substantive area well, as interviewees may ask you questions or test your knowledge. (I have experienced this situation in numerous interviews with police officers.) Your credibility is determined by your ability to answer these questions.

Probes

Interviewers listen very carefully to responses, as they can inform subsequent questions. Probes are neutral, and it helps if possible probes are identified for each question when creating the interview schedule. Six types of probes are used to get interviewees back on topic, to reaffirm that you are paying attention, or to ask for additional information. You may even find them helpful in everyday conversations!

The silent probe is one of the hardest things to master. When you use this probe, you ask a question and remain silent until the interviewee responds. By doing so, you create an uncomfortable silence, and human nature dictates that we want to fill that silence. Don't fall into the trap of restating the question. It confuses the interviewee about what you are asking or changes his or her response. In most cases,

silence is indicative of the interviewee thinking about an answer.

If you want people to elaborate on their response, use an echo probe. Repeat a portion of their answer to trigger a continuation of their narrative. Although this approach demonstrates that you understand what they are saying and are encouraging them to continue, you may sound like a parrot or frustrate them. Therefore, use this probe sparingly.

The uh-huh probe is simple to use. It involves uttering affirmative statements such as "yes," "right," or "I see what you mean" to show the person that you are listening to what he or she says. By inserting positive probes, you can increase the length of the interviewee's responses to your questions.

You will frequently run into situations in which you sense that the interviewee has provided only a partial answer or you aren't entirely sure you understand what he or she means. The tell-me-more probe invites the person to go into greater depth or to expand on additional facets of the topic. Common probes include, "Could you tell me more about that?" or "What do you mean by ... ?"

Long question probes elicit more focused responses. They are ideal as a preamble to sensitive questions, as you saw with the illustrative question. The difference is that this probe does not involve providing detailed examples but does explain what the question is about. For instance, "Can you describe ...?" or "Can you tell me about ...?"

Probing by leading reiterates a portion of an interviewee's previous response with a follow-up question. Researchers use this probe to get the interviewee to talk about knowledge they take for granted. It is a directed probe based on previous interviews in which you start to see a dimension of the topic as important or you learn something new through unexpected findings. This probe helps you test this knowledge by asking a direct question about your hunches.

Probes effectively detect deception and assess the extent to which accounts of behaviour are embellished. Any of these probes can be used to explore response inconsistencies. For example, Jacques and Wright (2011) conducted fifty interviews with unincarcerated drug dealers to understand the drug dealing process, prices charged, and the ways conflict is resolved. Probes played an integral role in sorting out the truthfulness of active criminals.

Active Listening

The effectiveness of verbal communication isn't based entirely on how words are spoken but also on how words are heard. Every day we devote, on average, 45 per cent of our time to listening, 30 per cent to speaking, 16 per cent to reading, and 9 per cent to writing (Schulenberg, 2008). Effective listeners are constantly reviewing and mentally summarizing the speaker's points. Active listening helps you understand what the speaker is feeling and what the transmitted message really means.

There are three benefits for listening actively: demonstrating professionalism, as others see that you are paying attention; helping both the speaker and listener clarify information; and increasing memory recall for emotional topics.

transcript a written version of an interview, documenting verbatim responses to the questions.

There are four common active listening techniques. First, paraphrase what was said to get feedback from the speaker about your understanding of his or her message. If you can't paraphrase, either the message wasn't clear or you weren't listening carefully enough. This technique improves rapport and establishes a mutual understanding. A sense of empathy is created, as reiterating the words suggests you are genuinely trying to understand what the other person is saying. To initiate this process, statements such as "What I hear you saying ..." work well.

impression management the act of controlling and manipulating the impression left on others.

Second, emotion labelling shows others that you are listening to their words and feelings. Examples that validate feelings include "You sound upset ..." or "I hear your frustration." This technique is a good way to de-escalate tense situations that can occur when discussing traumatic experiences.

The last two strategies work together. Effective pauses involve you taking a break in speaking to facilitate further communication or to emphasize a point. By pausing, you indirectly place the other person in a position to fill in the blanks created by silence. Minimal encouragers are words or actions that indicate you are listening without interrupting the speaker. Good examples of minimal encouragers include "oh," "uh huh," or "right." Nonverbal communication strategies include leaning forward, nodding your head, and maintaining eye contact.

Post Interview

A **transcript** is a word-for-word written account of an audio recorded interview. Be forewarned: it takes an average of six to eight hours to transcribe one hour of an interview. This time estimate is based on having some transcribing experience, working with a clear recording, and having only one interviewee on the recording. There are two benefits for transcribing your own interviews. You gain insight into how the interview schedule can be improved for subsequent interviews, and you can assess your strengths and weaknesses as an interviewer, including how you ask questions.

Interviewer Characteristics

The interviewer's role is to build rapport while remaining neutral and objective in words and actions by not revealing personal opinions on the topic or responses. Good interviewers are skilled at **impression management**, controlling the impression left on the interviewee (Goffman, 1959). Interviewers can come across as more approachable based on how they are dressed, how they speak and carry themselves, and how professionally they act.

How we dress projects an image of our personality and attitudes. Dressing inappropriately can bias responses, affect response rates, or impact interviewees' degree of honesty. A non-threatening and

Vignette: Breaking It down

Police Misconduct: Uncovering Hidden Secrets

There is little agreement on how best to define police misconduct (Frank, 2009; Maher, 2003). This lack of consistency creates problems for measuring police deviance and comparing results across studies. Further complicating the matter are the challenges involved in assessing the nature and extent of misconduct, a consequence of the low visibility of street-level policing, the police culture that discourages reporting peers' questionable behaviour, and the fact that just a portion of citizens file a formal complaint (Frank, 2009; Son & Rome, 2004; Waters & Brown, 2000).

Considerable research uses official records of filed complaints; however, this approach has the inherent weakness of capturing only reported behaviour. Victimization surveys are used to measure the prevalence of misconduct, but they may be an artefact of attitudes toward the police. In other words, perceptions on people's interaction with the police are affected by previously formed attitudes (Son & Rome, 2004). Thus, researchers also use interviews and surveys either as the sole method or in conjunction with one another.

Using a random sample, Weitzer (1999) conducted telephone surveys with citizens to investigate the relationship between race and type of neighbourhood. Respondents were asked about their perceptions and experiences with unjustified traffic stops, verbal abuse, and excessive use of force. The data suggested that the class and racial composition of neighbourhoods is an important factor in shaping attitudes on police misconduct.

Employing the same methodology, Son and Rome (2004) conducted telephone surveys with 988 citizens and 665 police officers to shed light on the prevalence of misconduct. RDD selected citizens, a stratified cluster sample selected agencies, and simple random sampling chose officers within those agencies. The researchers found that the prevalence and visibility of misconduct varies by the type of behaviour and that experiences differ by citizen characteristics.

Self-administered surveys are also common. Seron, Pereira, and Kovath (2006) used an experimental design to investigate the factors affecting citizens' perceptions of appropriate punishments for misconduct. Vignette questions asked respondents to make judgments on the severity of different types of officer behaviour and the best way to respond. The experiment randomly varied the situations described in the vignettes. The findings suggest that citizens consider the type of behaviour and the degree of civilian injury as key factors in determining severity and fair punishments.

In another study, patrol officers chose what they believe would be an appropriate use of force given a certain level of citizen non-compliance (Paoline, III & Terrill, 2011). Over 2,000 officers were present at roll call; the researchers achieved a 96.5 per cent response rate, representing 67.5 per cent of all sworn officers at eight police agencies. Officers reported being conservative in their use of force, leading the authors to argue that additional interviews are needed to gain more in-depth information on rationales for the use of force.

Becoming equally prevalent is the use of mixed methods. Schulenberg (2013a) conducted pre- and post-test surveys to evaluate the success of a forum aimed at improving Ontario's police complaints system. Focus groups were conducted several months later to better understand survey responses. Waters and Brown (2000) conducted 30 unstructured interviews and

Continued

51 mail surveys to explore complainants' perceptions and experiences with police complaints systems. With a 26 per cent response rate, a bias—whereby dissatisfied citizens were more likely to participate—may exist in this study. In general, interviews and surveys are effective techniques for illuminating actions and perceptions on a host of sensitive topics, including police misconduct.

polite demeanour displays a genuine interest in the respondent's answers. Knowing the interview schedule and being able to ask questions without stumbling over your words allow you to modify questions and better reflect the interviewee and his or her personal circumstances.

> **focus group** a group of respondents who are interviewed together in order to facilitate discussion.

Interviewer bias

Data quality highly depends on the researcher's interviewing skills. Interviewers are the data collection instrument and need to know what, how, and when to ask questions or insert probes. Interviewer characteristics might affect responses. The extent and likelihood of bias varies by person and research subject. Characteristics such as age, gender, race, or education can all increase or decrease responsiveness, depending on the situation. To minimize bias, match interviewers to interviewees with similar characteristics whenever possible.

Gender can be an advantage or disadvantage. Female interviewers are more effective when investigating sensitive subjects, for example, domestic violence or sexual violations. However, females encounter challenges in male-dominated settings, such as interviewing the police. Stereotypical gender roles embodied in the police culture may make it difficult for women to be taken seriously or to establish rapport (Schulenberg, 2014). Honing interview techniques can make a significant difference in such situations.

Interviewer expectations can create problems as well. Researchers have extensive knowledge and are looking for certain types of information. Bias is introduced if assumptions are made about right and wrong answers or what responses should entail. Receiving adequate training and conducting mock interviews can neutralize this effect.

Focus Groups

A **focus group** is an interactive interview of multiple people simultaneously. Researchers are interested not only in interviewees' responses but also in group dynamics and how meaning is socially constructed by group members. The interview isn't solely about a person's opinions; the debates between participants and the subsequent shifts in opinions are important as well. Despite the reduced generalizability of focus groups, you can use them to develop hypotheses, survey questions, and understanding on a range of opinions. Focus groups are not a substitute for interviews or surveys but can be used to enhance the outcomes of these methods. Researchers contextualize survey results and discover how respondents interpret questions, why people feel a certain way, and how they came to feel that way.

Advantages and Disadvantages

Focus groups capture data in real life, increase the validity of findings, and are cost-effective. They are especially good at gathering data to inform the development of other data collection instruments. Focus groups are appropriate when research seeks to understand group behaviour, attitudes, or shared meaning. For example, Honkatukia, Nyqvist, and Pösö (2006) conducted 15 focus groups with reform school residents between the ages of 12 and 17 to understand perceptions on violence and the reform school experience. The researchers emphasized that the focus was not on

Research Highlights

Mixed Methods: Approaches to Complex Questions

A mixed methods approach adopts a combination of data collection methods to inform subsequent data collection and analysis or to gain a more holistic perspective. Multiple methods help to communicate findings to appropriate audiences and to develop recommendations for evidence-based practice (Westheimer & Kahne, 2004). The specific methods and their order is determined by the nature and complexity of the research problem under investigation. There are two rationales for combining interviews and surveys.

One reason is to provide a comprehensive explanation. To understand the factors affecting police officers' perceptions of legislative directives to divert youth from court for minor offending, Marinos and Innocente (2008) administered surveys to seventy officers and conducted interviews with a subset of respondents (n = 64). The surveys used vignette questions to explore attitudes toward structuring police discretion. The interviews were used to discern how and why officers decide to charge or divert youth and what informs their attitudes.

A large-scale study commissioned by the Department of Justice Canada used surveys and interviews to provide a comprehensive understanding of the criminal justice system from the perspective of victims and criminal justice professionals (Prairie Research Associates, 2004). Researchers conducted interviews with 112 victims and 214 professionals to collect detailed information on their experiences. In addition, 1,664 respondents across Canada completed self-administered surveys to capture the perspectives of as many criminal justice professionals as possible and to complement the in-depth qualitative data.

Mixed methods are also used to gather data from different types of respondents. Rose, Reschenberg, and Richards (2010) evaluated a college course delivered in a correctional facility. Their surveys resembled course evaluations targeting assessments of the course and instructors. Focus groups explored prisoner experiences taking the course. Finally, the instructors were interviewed to explore perceptions of the program's educational benefits.

The second rationale is to inform the development of other data collection instruments. Read and Tilley (2000) used surveys to inform interview and focus group questions when investigating how 43 police agencies approach crime reduction initiatives. To examine the perceptions and effects of graduated sanctioning guidelines for parole officers, focus groups and interviews were used to develop mail survey questions (Steiner, Travis, & Makarios, 2011). Using four follow-up reminders, the researchers achieved a 76 per cent response rate, with surveys as the last data collection method. Unsurprisingly, they found that officers are typically dissatisfied with the restrictions that currently limit their decision-making discretion.

Adopting a similar approach, Taylor and Norma (2011) attempted to understand what motivates a woman's decision to report sexual violence to the police. Focus groups were conducted to develop relevant survey questions that were then distributed to a larger population. Interestingly, the study found that women decide not to report as a form of symbolic protest against a criminal justice system that they view as not serving sexual assault victims. The same combination was used to explore the experiences and perceptions of correctional officers who participated in a solution-focused training program geared to overcoming

Continued

obstacles associated with offender rehabilitation (Jen Der Pan, et al., 2011). Once again, focus groups were used to inform the development of self-administered survey questions.

In all cases, the research purpose and questions drive the methodological choice to adopt more than one data collection method, which ones to use, and in what order they are administered. Surveys, interviews, and focus groups are complementary ways to collect data. Using only one of these methods can provide detailed information; however, mixed methods are appropriate for comprehensive investigations into complex and multi-faceted research problems.

the participants' personal experiences but on their understanding of violence. For this reason, focus groups were more appropriate than conducting interviews.

However, there is less control in the guided interaction than in conducting an interview. It takes longer for everyone to answer a question, which means you have to ask fewer questions. You need to manage group dynamics, such as individuals who dominate the conversation or who rarely offer their opinions. There is also the issue of groupthink and conformity, in which everyone consistently agrees with one another. Focus groups are challenging to schedule, require a well-trained moderator, and complicate data analysis. You can't analyze the responses of a single person in isolation. Participants consider their own opinions in the context of other's views. A focus group lasting 1 to 1.5 hours produces more data than an interview does and creates transcripts of forty to sixty single-spaced pages.

Focus Group Logistics

Although rarely a representative sample, focus group participants embody key characteristics of the target population. The ideal focus group is one to two hours long and contains six to eight people. They should not know each other prior to the focus group but be relatively similar to help reduce any inhibitions about participating or volunteering their views. Heterogeneous groups will give you a broader spectrum of opinions, but they inhibit participation. Researchers typically want homogenous groups representing categories of characteristics. Analyses typically compare one group's responses to those of another.

Running a Focus Group

The first step in running a focus group is to ensure that the moderator is nonjudgmental and creates a safe environment. Ground rules for engagement—respecting others' opinions, not talking over each other, and not interrupting—are established. An icebreaker is then used to introduce everyone. The moderator can administer a short survey before the focus group starts to get people thinking about what they are going to talk about and to keep the discussion on topic. An assistant facilitator records an identifier for each participant, along with the first few words of each contribution, to help the transcriber link statements in the audio recording to specific people. He or she also notes any group dynamics as these won't be captured on the audio recording.

Characteristics of a Good Focus Group

Quality focus groups share certain characteristics. The moderator has genuine respect for participants, listens well, redirects from those who dominate the conversation, and draws quiet participants into the discussion. Potential bias is reduced if the moderator is not vested in the outcome

Key Thinker

Robert Merton (1910–2003)

Robert Merton profoundly impacted public policy and academic discourse in criminology and criminal justice. His theory of anomie and the innovation mode of adaptation most associated with delinquency are included in virtually all criminology textbooks. Yet many don't know that, by the age of 14, he worked as a magician at birthday parties and Sunday schools (Jock Young, 2010). After taking a position at Tulane University in 1939, he earned his full professorship in only two years (Jones, 2003). In 1941, he relocated to Columbia University, where he taught for the rest of his academic career.

Building on the work of Émile Durkheim, Merton argued that, in periods of societal upheaval, new rules or the lack of rules creates strain for an individual. His strain theory informed other explanations for delinquency, such as Cloward and Ohlin's (1960) differential opportunity theory. A little-known fact is that labelling theorists did not develop the concept of a self-fulfilling prophecy. In 1948, Merton argued that this concept refers to "a false definition of the situation, that is, it is a prediction that is false, not true, but then becomes the basis for a new behavior which makes the originally false conception come true" (Jones, 2003, p. 8). Merton's methodological contribution is also largely unknown. In their quest to observe the reactions of small groups to a radio program, Merton and Paul Lazersfeld—co-founders of the Bureau of Applied Social Research—unintentionally created the data collection method now known as focus groups and used in commercial marketing, political campaigns, and social science research.

What advice does Merton have to offer researchers? He strongly advocated reading the original works of the great criminology thinkers. He argued that students need to read the classics because doing so "(1) avoids reinventing the wheel; (2) aids in the clear formulation of ideas; (3) ensures that ideas will stand up to previously issued challenges; (4) provides a model for theory development; and (5) the reader gleans something different each time a classic work is read" (Jones, 2003, p. 7).

In 1994, Merton became the first sociologist to receive a National Medal of Science. After a battle with cancer, he died on 20 February 2003. He continues to be known for his methodological and theoretical innovations, as well as "founding the sociology of science and pioneering contributions to the study of social life, especially the self-fulfilling prophecy and the unintended consequences of social action" (Jones, 2003, p. 9).

(Stitt, Leone, & Jennings-Clawson, 1998). The questions are clear and understandable, focus on what you really want to know, and can be answered by participants. There should be no power differentials between participants because heterogenous groups inhibit participation.

In a successful focus group, researchers send interviewees reminders about where and when the focus group will occur and offer incentives for participation. The ethical wrinkle is how to ensure confidentiality. A common approach is to include an instruction in the informed consent form that participants are not to discuss individuals or responses with anyone outside the group.

Conclusion

Surveys and interviews are frequently used to collect data on people's experiences and perceptions of crime, punishment, rehabilitation, and deviant behaviour. Although focus groups are found infrequently in the literature, this method has potential for understanding important questions in criminology and criminal justice. Whether it is exploratory, descriptive, explanatory, cross-sectional, evaluative, or longitudinal research, interview and survey data are often the only way to collect the data required to address the research question.

The trick, as always, is to figure out whether these data collection methods are the most appropriate for your research project. As the relevance of survey questions are determined in advance, the data collected reflects the researcher. Yet interviews aren't much different when the researcher is the data collection instrument.

Some researchers argue that interviews are superior to surveys because they allow "for an in-depth, spontaneous outflow of pointed information" (Sengo & Dhungana, 2009, p. 127). Others advocate using surveys, as they provide a breadth of information simply unattainable from other data collection methods. I am of the view that no singular method is superior to another, simply because the research question drives the method. Data collection methods produce different types of data, of which some are more appropriate to address a research question than others. Thus, each research project is unique and methodological decisions should be oriented around the research problem, not convenience or researcher preferences.

Summary of Important Points

Introduction

- Surveys ask questions in the same way to gather information on facts, opinions, and experiences.
- Interviews are structured conversations exploring perspectives and meaning on issues, context, and life experiences.

Surveys

- Face-to-face surveys are more personalized, are longer, and have higher response rates than other types but are subject to reactivity effects.
- Telephone surveys are more representative, less expensive, and quicker but have lower response rates and ask fewer questions.
- Self-administered surveys are best for sensitive topics and are the cheapest type but have the lowest response rates.
- The total design method outlines key strategies for structuring, designing, and executing self-administered surveys.

- Surveys use either open- or close-ended questions.
- When writing survey questions, avoid ambiguous, double-barrelled, double negative, and biased questions, but make the questions mutually exclusive and exhaustive.
- Skip patterns, matrix, and vignette questions are techniques to increase validity and response rates.
- Consider floaters, fence-sitters, response rates, memory recall, and ethics when designing surveys.

Interviews

- Structured interviews use standardized questions and probes determined in advance.
- Semi-structured interviews are the most common type and provide flexibility to change the question wording, format, and order.
- Unstructured interviews vary with each interviewee and are usually topic, not question, driven.
- When preparing for interviews, consider location, introduction information, and ethics.

- During the interview, act professionally, develop rapport, engage in impression management, probe, and use active listening.

Focus Groups

- Focus groups collect data from multiple people simultaneously to understand personal opinions, group dynamics, and develop survey questions.

- Ideal focus groups are homogeneous, are one to two hours long, and have six to eight people.

Conclusion

- Each study is unique, and the methodological decision to conduct surveys, interviews, or focus groups is based on the research question.

Key Terms

close-ended question 178
contingency question 180
double-barrelled question 179
double negative question 179
exhaustive 180
face-to-face survey 170
fence-sitters 181
filter question 180
floaters 181
focus group 190
impression management 188
interview 167
interview schedule 184

leading question 179
loaded question 179
matrix question 180
mutually exclusive 180
open-ended question 178
probe 184
rapport 177
response rate 167
response set effect 180
self-administered survey 172
semi-structured interview 184
skip pattern 180
social desirability bias 179

structured interview 184
survey 167
telephone survey 171
telescoping 181
transcript 188
unstructured interview 184
vignette question 181

Review Questions and Exercises

1. Using a topic of your choice, discuss why a researcher would choose to administer a face-to-face, telephone, mail, or online survey.
2. Identify five aspects of survey structure, design, and administration that affect overall and item response rates.
3. For each of the following open-ended questions, create appropriate close-ended survey questions.
   a. How do you feel about shock incarceration and boot camp programs?
   b. How do people in your neighbourhood feel about the police?
   c. What do you think is the main reason for offenders continuing to break the law?
   d. How do you protect your home from burglary?
4. In research involving active criminals, what are some of the factors you need to consider when designing the interview schedule and conducting interviews?
5. For the following research topics, identify whether a survey, interview, or focus group is the most appropriate data collection method. Explain your choices.
   a. Nature and extent of alcohol and drug use by teenagers.
   b. Motivation to commit a crime.
   c. Evaluation of an intervention program.
   d. Perceptions on punishments for repeat offenders.

Online Exercises and Websites of Interest

Express Scribe

www.nch.com.au/scribe/index.html

This is a free transcription software program that allows you to adjust volume, background noise, and speed.

StatPac Survey Design Tutorial

www.statpac.com/surveys

This tutorial reviews the latest survey techniques, what works, and what doesn't.

Survey Monkey

http://surveymonkey.com

You can use this site to design an online survey and analyze data for up to 10 questions and 100 respondents for free.

UK Data Service: Variable and Question Bank

http://discover.ukdataservice.ac.uk/variables

Go to this website and choose a survey that interests you. Pick five different types of questions and discuss the effectiveness of each one.

Additional Resources

Fink, A. (2013). *How to Conduct Surveys: A Step-by-Step Guide* (5th ed.). Thousand Oaks, CA: Sage.

Geared toward students, this guide covers suitable topics for surveys, question formats, data analysis, and other related issues.

Gubrium, J.F., Holstein, J.A., Marvasti, A.B., & McKinney, K.D. (2012). *The Sage Handbook of Interview Research: The Complexity of the Craft* (2nd ed.). Thousand Oaks, CA: Sage.

This text provides comprehensive coverage of theoretical and practical aspects of interview research.

Krueger, R.A., & Casey, M.A. (2009). *Focus Groups: A Practical Guide for Applied Research* (4th ed.). Thousand Oaks, CA: Sage.

This book offers practical advice on conducting focus groups, from design to recruitment, data collection, and analysis.

Chapter 7

Ethnographic Field Research

Ethnography is "the peculiar practice of representing the social reality of others through the analysis of one's own experience in the world of these others."
J. Van Maanen, *Tales of the Field on Writing Ethnography* (1998, p. ix)

Learning Objectives

- To describe how researchers prepare, design, and access field settings and how they conduct participant observation.

- To appreciate different field roles and identify when each is appropriate.

- To develop skills for collecting observational data, writing field notes, and managing interpersonal dimensions.

- To understand alternative field research techniques, including systematic social observation, netnography, and ethnomethodology.

- To demonstrate understanding of the ethical challenges involved in ethnographic field research.

Introduction

As a criminology and criminal justice doctoral student, Peterson (1999) had a unique perspective and access to the field. To understand the student–professor mentorship process, he conducted 120 hours of participant observation in locations where faculty members and students congregate. As data collection progressed, it became clear that mentoring styles had distinct differences from one situation and one professor to another. Not surprisingly, the findings indicate that students are almost exclusively responsible for, and the initiators of, mentoring relationships. Could the process of developing and maintaining mentor relationships been studied using other data collection methods? Perhaps. Was field research the most appropriate for addressing the research question? Potentially.

We are constantly conducting field research as we go about our lives. At every point of the day, we observe the people and events around us and draw inferences and conclusions about what we see and experience. When you walk into a coffee shop, you may unconsciously scan everyone sitting down as you wait in line. Although you are not purposely observing social life, you nonetheless notice what people say and do in your presence. Every time you sit in a lecture hall, you might check out who or how many sit in the front or back rows. You will listen to what the professor says and take notes. These are all components of field research. The only difference lies in how systematic the process of observation and recording becomes. For instance, you may not realize that the person two rows down from you has missed every class until now or that your professor is wearing white tube socks with black shoes. A good field researcher will notice all these things.

ethnocentrism an interpretation of the world based on one's own understanding and not from the participants' perspective.

Some History

Collecting data through direct observation is as old as recorded history. Many religious texts and historical accounts document experiences. Maps that we take for granted today were developed on the basis of collecting data through direct observation. However, it was not until the early twentieth century that field research was consciously employed in the social sciences.

Anthropological Roots

At the turn of the twentieth century, anthropology matured as a discipline. Using observational data, the famous ethnographer Boas (1911) amalgamated his theories on the history and development of culture and called for a greater tolerance of civilizations different from our own. Malinowski (1961) argued that the facts

ethnography a research method that uses the research subjects' perspective to describe a culture and alternate way of life.

recorded by an observer are infinite but remain only a selection of social reality. Thus, the more conscious the researcher becomes of this process, the greater the scientific nature and relevance of selected facts. These anthropologists are credited with establishing fieldwork as a legitimate activity to address questions about culture and society. The goal they advocate for "is to grasp the native's point of view, his relation to life, to realize his vision of his world" (p. 25).

Researchers collect observational data as actions, events, and behaviour occurs. Although researchers strive to maintain a degree of objectivity, early anthropological field research was criticized for being ethnocentric. **Ethnocentrism** refers to imposing one's worldview onto the data. Unfortunately, this interpretive framework based on personal understandings is seen as superior to others' views.

The Chicago School

In the 1920s and 1930s, researchers at the University of Chicago strived to gain a better understanding of social processes that occur in urban areas. They literally viewed the city of Chicago as one big laboratory waiting for exploration. Their methodological position was that, if we truly want to understand human behaviour, we have to experience the research subjects' activities and everyday lives. Ethnographic research is a way of gaining access to the meaning of social action and social relationships through empathetic identification with cultural, linguistic, and symbolic norms in that group or subculture.

The Chicago School forged a new path by producing the first **ethnographies** of deviant populations. Classic studies include Shaw's (1930) *The Jack-Roller*, on the lives of young offenders; Whyte's (1955) *Street Corner Society*, a recount of how he lived in a slum neighbourhood inhabited by Italian immigrants to investigate the racketeering business and the formation of local gangs; and Becker's (1963) *Outsiders*, which established the foundation for the labelling theory of deviance through his field research on the two deviant groups of musicians and marijuana users.

Historically, there are two stages in the development of field research methods. From 1910 to about 1930, researchers at the Chicago School adopted a case study or life history approach using interviews, documents, official records, and direct observation in conjunction with one another. A good example is Thrasher's (1927) study on Chicago gangs. Using multiple data sources, he documented how the urban landscape shaped gangs and their culture, codes of honour, and power dynamics. In the second stage of development for field research (1940–1960), participant observation grew in stature. The methodological principles involved using natural settings and direct interaction and capturing the participant's perspective to understand a social phenomenon. Some of the greatest insights on responses to crime and criminal behaviour developed from this approach.

What is Field Research?

It's easy to think that ethnography, field research, and participant observation are all the same thing, but they are not. Ethnography is a research orientation that employs a variety of data collection techniques. As ethnographic data is collected outside of a laboratory, it is a type of field research. Think of ethnography much like a research design. Ethnographies collect data using participant observation, semi- or unstructured interviews, or some combination of other techniques. Fieldwork is how the researcher develops a cultural understanding, whereas an ethnographic text is how this culture is portrayed to others.

Another distinction is that between field research and participant observation. **Field research** is much broader and denotes the process of collecting data in a natural environment. In contrast, **participant observation** is a type of data collection method. Although much ethnographic field research collects data using participant observation, it is important to remember the distinction between these three terms. Ethnographies describe a culture or way of life from the participants' point of view. Field research occurs in a natural setting where one or more data collection methods are used to collect data. Participant observation is a data collection technique.

Purpose

Field research involves observing behaviour as it occurs and asking questions, often in an unstructured and normal but guided conversation. The objective is to understand daily life from the subjects' perspective and definition of concepts. Members of the culture are viewed as experts in their everyday reality. The researcher tries to understand motives and actions, as well as to discover the range of behaviour within that setting and its meaning to participants.

Field research and participant observation is embedded within social constructionism. Reality, meaning, and definitions of situations are socially constructed through our use of language and interactions with others. To understand a social context, you look for explicit knowledge (conscious actions or speech) and implicit or **tacit knowledge** (unconscious or unspoken). By doing so, you develop an insider point of view while maintaining an analytical perspective.

Participant observation involves the researcher immersing himself or herself in the field for an extended period of time, developing an empathetic understanding through shared experiences, and uncovering meanings and definitions constructed by participants to make sense of their social world. This flexible, inductive data collection method is used to understand how people give meaning to their social lives and environment. As pointed out by Becker

field research a research approach that collects data to understand a natural setting in which the behaviour being investigated actually occurs.

participant observation a data collection technique in which researchers immerse themselves in the culture and collect observational data to produce descriptions of everyday life and how it is understood by participants.

tacit knowledge a person's unconscious or unwritten knowledge.

and Geer (1957), events and experiences occur in daily life that go virtually unnoticed and would never be brought up in an interview. However, with enough time in the field, you can detect distortion (compare verbal descriptions against observations), observe changes in behaviour over time, and discern the order of events. More important, a researcher can direct attention to "what has happened and on what the person says about what has happened" (p. 32).

Research Instrument

In field research, the researcher is the data collection instrument in every meaning of the term. The quality of the data depends on observational skills and how well the events and behaviours are recorded. Not only is the researcher the data collection instrument, but the field research also personally impacts him or her. There is self-imposed pressure to capture as much observational data as possible and to write field notes consistently and well. Personal relationships are affected, as the researcher spends extensive amounts of time in the field and contends with feelings about his or her field experiences. Being the research instrument entails that his or her reactions and feelings constitute data in and of themselves.

Popularity

The prevalence of ethnographic field research and participant observation is difficult to assess for three reasons. It is increasingly common for ethnographies to use interviews and participant observation in conjunction with one another. Moreover, their use depends on which journals are included in the study. Much ethnography is not published as journal articles but as research monographs.

Despite the potential for rich and detailed information, participant observation data collection is rare. Of the articles published in the seven highest-ranked criminal justice journals in 2001–2002, 6.2 per cent collected data using direct observation (Kleck et al., 2006). Less than 4 per cent of all research published in the top 16 criminal justice journals between 2000 and 2009 (190 out of

4,743 articles) used ethnographic methods (Copes, Brown, & Tewksbury, 2011). Of those articles with ethnographic techniques as secondary, the main methods were interviews (68 per cent), quantitative methods (13.6 per cent), fieldwork (12.8 per cent), and focus groups (5.6 per cent) (p. 350). When employing only one method, 7.7 per cent of published research uses interviews, 3.4 per cent focus groups, and 9.1 per cent fieldwork (p. 351). What may surprise you is that the trends are quite different for non-American-based journals. *The British Journal of Criminology, Australian & New Zealand Journal of Criminology,* and the *Canadian Journal of Criminology and Criminal Justice* show more than a quarter (27.2 per cent) of published research is qualitative (p. 343).

Appropriate Topics

Without question, field research is inappropriate for large social settings. On the other hand, this approach is highly suitable if you are interested in what people do, how things work in everyday life, and what practices, customs, and beliefs exist in the culture. Ethnographers seek to document lives, events, and behaviour within a social context while understanding experiences from the members' perspective and the ways in which behaviour is shaped by culture. To uncover deeply held assumptions of daily life within this worldview, researchers need to "prioritize the social actor and his/her subjective orientation and immerse themselves in a host society in order to try, as far as possible, to see, feel and even act as members of that society" (Marks, 2004, p. 870).

According to Lofland and colleagues (2006), field research methods are most appropriate for nine types of research:

1. Meaning: The importance of beliefs, social norms, and cultural practices and the ways in which they are interpreted. Similarities and differences likely exist between social actors in that setting.
2. Practices: An interest in behavioural patterns.

3. Episodes: Routine or exceptional events.
4. Encounters: A focus on interactions between two or more people (e.g. content and how the interaction occurs).
5. Roles: The types of roles taken on by subjects and their associated behaviours.
6. Relationships: Interactional behaviour between two individuals who have similar or different roles.
7. Groups: An understanding of the behavioural and interaction dynamics of small groups.
8. Organizations: Formal organizations, such as the police, that consist of more than one small group (e.g. platoons).
9. Settlements: Groups within larger settings (e.g. city neighbourhoods).

Where Do I Start?

Discovering the interpretations, meanings, and activities that constitute people's worlds is no easy task when observing participants in their own environments. Selecting a topic and formulating one or more research questions is nothing new. Developing a research statement and description becomes important in field research. A research description is a short statement describing the research purpose and the researcher's preferred involvement in the field setting. You use the description with group members and those who grant you access. The key is to ensure that it's simple and uses everyday language so you can remember it and participants can understand what you are doing in their world.

Key Thinker

Howard Becker (1928–)

Very few would argue about Howard Becker's impact on how we understand crime and deviance. Becker is credited with developing labelling theory and conceptual frameworks (e.g. moral entrepreneurs) and with expanding our horizons in the sociology of deviance. He is known as an exemplar of clear and easy-to-understand academic writing. Ethnographic fieldwork requires clear writing to make the readers feel as though they were in the field as well.

Becker started playing piano at 14 to 15 years of age and performed at dances and other celebrations; he went on to become a professional jazz musician (Snyder, 2010). However, at the advice of his father, he started graduate school at the University of Chicago in 1949. "I was beginning to see that I was probably not going to be a great jazz pianist. And so, I'll keep on going to school" (Molotch, 2012, p. 433). As the saying goes, the rest is history.

His experiences as a jazz musician informed his later work on marijuana use and the social construction of deviance. For instance, smoking marijuana was common among jazz players and was socially accepted within the community. He sought to understand how this activity was defined as deviant by the majority of society. Becker conducted participant observation—he was, after all, part of the subculture—which helped to inform his opinion. His conclusion was that "the presence of a given kind of behavior is the result of a sequence of social experiences during which the person acquires a conception of the meaning of the behavior, and perceptions and judgments of objects and situations, all of which make the activity possible and desirable" (Becker, 1953, p. 235).

Becker says he doesn't "like to take anything for granted . . . you have to find out what really happens" (Molotch, 2012, p. 439). The challenge is not to accept participants' evaluation that "nothing is happening" but to analyze what is occurring when "nothing's happening" (Becker, 1998). To accomplish this goal, concepts should be based on continuing interaction with empirical data.

Continued

In his seminal work, *Outsiders* (1963), he focuses on deviant groups rather than on how and why individuals deviate from social norms and expectations. He found that behaviour doesn't have to be deviant or criminal to be labelled as such—it just has to be unconventional. Thus, it's not the nature and quality of the act but a function of being labelled. There isn't a single behaviour that is inherently deviant. Instead, "the deviant is the one to whom that label has been successfully applied; deviant behavior is behavior that people so label" (p. 9). Through participant observation, he is able to say that, once this deviant labelling occurs, a person is treated as an outsider by society.

Becker is skeptical of a lot of criminological theory because it is developed on data that is not grounded in everyday life experiences. Yet the theory purports to explain behaviour. How can this make sense or really describe the how and why of human behaviour? He feels strongly that, particularly with deviant and criminal subcultural groups, researchers have to spend time with the people whose behaviour they seek to explain (Snyder, 2010).

Once you have a better idea of the research purpose and questions, you need to dive into the scholarly literature. You do not want to go into the field without knowing as much as possible about the community and substantive area. Look for advice and experiences from other researchers as well. They can not only help you avoid pitfalls and potential disasters but also provide you with information that can be used to gain access, develop rapport, and handle conflict.

You are the research instrument. Thus, it is important to work on your observational and note-taking skills. Although you may have an innate ability to retain information, these skills take practice and we all have to work on improving our memory if we are to collect quality data. Go to a public place, such as a coffee shop, shopping mall, or church. Look around the setting for five minutes, then leave and write down everything you remember about it. You will probably realize that you recorded little information on certain aspects of the setting, such as what people are wearing. Walk by a storefront window and record all the details you can recall. Then walk by it again and see how you did.

I can't emphasize it enough: know thyself. When you place yourself in a setting out of your comfort zone,

you need to know your limits, the potential impact of previous personal experiences, and ways to overcome self-doubt. Part of preparing for data collection is determining your ethical boundaries and the lengths you are willing and comfortable to go to when in the field. Assess the risks and potential dangers in the field, for example, what could happen and what you will do when an officer responds to a gun call. Some argue that researchers must share the risks and dangers faced by participants to develop better rapport and must share common experiences to truly understand them. We will delve into this idea further when we talk about what to do once we are in the field.

One of the most important decisions researchers make is choosing a field site. Some settings are easier to access but all carry varying ethical and personal challenges. The easiest are public places. Entry into organizations is moderately difficult. However, the most challenging are closed communities, dangerous settings, and active criminal groups. You develop a plan on how you are going to access the community and, once you have entry, group members. For example, what field role will you adopt? To what extent will you participate in daily activities?

After getting over the initial hurdles, researchers have to develop **field relations**. From beginning to end, the impression you leave on others based on

field relations the logistics, procedures, ethics, and personal dimensions related to informants, gatekeepers, and social actors in the field setting.

your appearance, actions, and words is carefully managed. To increase the authenticity of data, you have to develop rapport with participants and cultivate relationships. The heart of data collection involves observing and documenting field experiences in the form of field notes, which are continuously reviewed to help direct your ongoing participation. At some point, you will leave the field. Doing so is easier said than done. Disengagement can be gradual or quick, but the group and setting largely determine the exiting process.

Field Roles

A **field role** determines the extent that a researcher is actively involved in the everyday activities of research participants. The role adopted is influenced by the setting, members, ethics, and comfort level. Consider the situations you might run into while in the field. Be cognizant of your own background and personality. Do you see yourself being comfortable with having knowledge of criminal activity or with participating peripherally in deviant or criminal behaviour, such as being a lookout or smoking weed? As Ferrell (1997, p. 19) points out, "before you can tell a criminal who you are and make it stick, you have to know yourself . . . you need to decide beforehand, as much as possible, where you wish to draw the line."

Field roles are not mutually exclusive or fixed throughout the research process. They are fluid and can change on a given day, based on the member you interact with or the activity in question (Williams et al., 1992). That is, field roles can shift, stay the same, or hover between two different roles during data collection.

Take Van Maanen's (1973) study as an example. He wanted to understand how police officers are socialized into the police culture. He completely immersed himself in the culture and completed the three-month training course at the police academy. Once in the field, he took on the role of participant as observer on ride alongs by declaring his researcher status. He achieved credibility because "a recruit would introduce me to veteran officers as 'Van Mannen, he's OK, he went through the academy with us'" (pp. 416–417).

Good field researchers maintain flexibility in their roles while in the field. You may have no alternative but to participate more than anticipated if you are to demonstrate trust, commitment, and credibility. An example is doing small favours for police officers, such as reading the description for a dispatched call off the computer screen while they are driving or carrying a suspect's belongings after an arrest.

Field roles are on a continuum of least to most participation by a researcher. The roles range from absolutely no interaction with setting members to covert research, in which research participants do not know a person's status as researcher and researchers participate in all group activities and are seen as full-fledged members. Based on the research purpose and questions, one or more roles—complete observer, observer as participant, participant as observer, or complete participant—may be the most appropriate.

> **field role** a role that defines the degree to which a researcher participates in the research setting's activities.

Complete Observer

Some argue that a **complete observer** role should not be considered participant observation but a type of unobtrusive research that should be discussed with other techniques covered in Chapter 8. Despite the lack of interaction, most see this role as field research because data is collected in a natural setting. A complete observer has no interaction at all with members of the research setting but observes everyday life and nonverbal behaviour in the context of cultural rules. Although commonly used in public places and Internet communities, the complete observer role can be adopted when

> **complete observer** a field role in which the researcher is an unobtrusive observer (i.e. does not interact with group members in any way).

starting any field work project because it orients you to the patterns of social life in the group or community of interest.

There are two disadvantages that make this field role inappropriate for a lot of crime-related research. First, you have to rely solely on observations, which raises the possibility of misinterpretation. Unless multiple methods, such as interviews, are used, you can't interpret what is happening with any degree of certainty. Second, adopting this role captures behaviour, but it provides no insight into the meaning associated with the actions. To appreciate the lives of criminals and crime control agents, criminologists "must share to whatever extent possible in the dangers, pleasures, emotions, and experiences" (Ferrell, 1997, p. 13).

Observer as Participant

The **observer as participant** makes his or her role as researcher known and is minimally involved in group activities. An advantage of this field role is that it becomes easier to take on the role of needing to be taught about everyday life and activities. The researcher can "observe and interact closely enough with members to establish an insider's identity without participating in those activities constituting the core of group membership" (Adler & Adler, 1994, p. 380). However, he or she may not be accepted as a member or be trusted to observe certain behind-the-scenes activities or to interpret accurately what is observed. Although the researcher has more access than a complete observer does, some aspects of group

life remain inaccessible and may even be invisible (i.e. the researcher has no knowledge that these interactions or behaviours exist).

At the same time, this field role gives you extended exposure that leads to adopting at least some of the group members' values and beliefs. Objectivity can actually be a barrier, as what the subjects have to say cannot be understood without a degree of immersion and shared life experiences. The researcher relates to those investigated, affecting both parties. "The knowledge thus gained from these relationships, not only changes the knower, it becomes part of the knower" (Clarke, 1975, p. 118).

Participant as Observer

The most common field role adopted by researchers is **participant as observer**. In this role, the researcher reveals his or her identity to community members and participates in group activities to varying degrees to understand the group through mutual personal experiences. This role becomes easier to adopt when the researcher has similar characteristics or experiences as community members. Although still viewed as an outsider, the researcher has greater access to what actually occurs and to participants' meaning associated with these events and behaviours by personally experiencing the emotions, dangers, and situational meanings of the setting.

In observer as participant and participant as observer roles, researchers are not forced to participate in unethical, criminal, or dangerous activities and can more or less assume the role of an **acceptable incompetent** (Lofland et al., 2006). The researcher pretends to have less knowledge or fewer skills than is actually the case to learn more about the setting. However, it is a delicate balance because you don't want to appear too incompetent and frustrate participants when they have to explain everything to you. The acceptable incompetent in these field roles maintains some distance, works on developing an empathetic understanding, and increases rapport while not making assumptions or completely

observer as participant
a field role in which the status of researcher is known to group members and the researcher participates minimally in group activities.

participant as observer a field role that involves the group's members knowing the status of researcher and the researcher actively participating in group activities.

acceptable incompetent
a field role in which a researcher learns more about the setting by portraying himself or herself as being less knowledgeable than is truly the case; can be used in observer as participant and participant as observer roles.

identifying with the culture. Think of it as dual citizenship: you are a member of your own world and your subject's world.

A researcher might have restricted access to an insider understanding. To overcome this problem, he or she may start to increasingly identify with the group and risk **going native**. At that stage, the researcher develops too much empathy for and personal connection with the participants. Additionally, the researcher is in more personal danger, has a greater chance of being categorized into one role, risks losing objectivity, and data collection is more demanding psychologically.

Complete Participant

A **complete participant** becomes or already is a full-fledged member of the community. Typically associated with covert research, this role involves keeping the research purpose and researcher status hidden from community members. Researchers who have been complete participants have directly participated in illegal activities, witnessed criminal behaviour, or been accomplices. Due to ethical concerns, such as voluntary participation and informed consent, covert research is rare.

Some researchers walk a fine line between upholding the law and capturing authentic and valid observational data. Controversially, Ferrell (1997, p. 9) states: "To put it bluntly, for the dedicated field researcher who seeks to explore criminal subcultures and criminal dynamics, obeying the law may represent as much of a problem as breaking it." However, you can just as legitimately argue that being a complete participant changes the role of researcher from academic to criminal.

This field role yields the highest level of cultural immersion and therefore the richest data. Although rarely used, it can be appropriate with extremely marginalized groups stigmatized in society, groups that would never be willing participants if the researcher status was known. Prior to becoming a complete member or studying your own subcultural group, you need to consider carefully the ethical challenge of the members' inability to provide informed consent. You also need to actively take steps to avoid overidentification and going native. It may be impossible to assume the role of acceptable incompetent and ask questions, as doing so would create suspicion among members. Lastly, publishing the results from covert research can reduce the public's trust of researchers and make it more difficult for future researchers to gain access to certain communities.

> **going native** the situation of a researcher becoming too immersed in the research setting and losing objectivity by adopting the participants' worldview.

Gaining and Maintaining Access

To access the field setting, researchers consider the quality of the data available—the chances for meaningful interactions, researcher familiarity, and suitability to investigate the research topic and address the research questions (Lofland et al., 2006). Field sites can be open or closed settings and, even within one site, parts may be open or closed to the researcher. A common tactic to gain access to any site is hanging out in open settings. As we'll see, this strategy is not always possible, particularly with formal organizations.

> **complete participant** a field role that involves the researcher adopting an active role as a full-fledged group member and participants being unaware of his or her researcher status.

Many recommend choosing a site where the participants are strangers to you. Think of it as situating yourself in an environment and observing people, events, and conversations as if you were an alien. The advantage of this approach is that everything is new; thus, the chances of taking knowledge for granted are less. However, the odds of being overwhelmed by the volume of data and suffering from culture shock are much greater. Access becomes easier when the research objective coincides with issues that members feel have not received enough attention and are worthy of exploration. Let's take a closer look at how you gain access.

Gaining Access

A **gatekeeper** is someone who is in a position to grant or deny a researcher access to the setting. This person is a formal leader or a person with informal authority recognized by group members. Researchers often need both formal and informal gatekeepers. Formal gatekeepers help you gain initial access and informal gatekeepers assist gaining access to members once you are in the field.

> **gatekeeper** a person who has informal or formal authority that influences or controls whether a researcher has access to the research site.

The way you pitch the research to a gatekeeper has a great deal of influence on the likelihood of gaining access. To increase the odds for success, you need to do several things. Provide a general description of the study, research purpose, questions, and potential benefits and risks to the organization and members. At the same time, it is not advisable to give too much detail about the research questions. I am not suggesting you lie; just be general so as not to influence the areas you can access and use accessible language to avoid frustration or misunderstandings. In a lot of ways, you need to become a salesperson but simultaneously always be honest in the information you provide and in your responses to gatekeeper's questions. Offer something in return, such as a copy of the final report. Lastly, be abundantly clear about how much time you expect is required from research participants.

Gaining access to formal criminal justice organizations is best done top-down. If at all possible, identify a sponsor who can endorse the project and vouch for you. This support will help pave the way for the organizational head, such as the chief of police, to respond to your initial query. Write a letter with an introduction and a brief description of the research study, purpose, and type of access requested. Identify the sponsor and what actions (e.g. phone call, meeting) you are requesting. Make that phone call or write a follow-up e-mail.

A meeting with a gatekeeper is the most critical juncture for gaining access.

You need to be flexible, as there is often a negotiation process prior to being granted access to the setting. Ethical considerations usually arise as a concern, especially guaranteeing confidentiality. The agency may explicitly request that it be identified solely by a pseudonym and that specific parameters be established for using the data, reporting certain findings, and reviewing manuscript drafts prior to publication. With the exception of the pseudonym, you need to be careful that you don't give away so much of your autonomy that the agency controls what the outcomes will be and which ones will be released. If confidentiality of members and the organization are assured, this situation should be less of a concern.

The negotiation process for access continues because formal organizations will almost always have more than one gatekeeper. Think of it in terms of accessing a police service. You first need permission from the police chief at the top of the hierarchy. To access patrol officers, you need to secure the co-operation of platoon staff sergeants and road sergeants who structure your access. Don't be discouraged. Even if you do everything to the best of your abilities, the process can take months, depending on the type and number of gatekeepers.

Finally, don't be fooled. Most gatekeepers are not really concerned with the findings. Operational concerns, the meaningfulness of results, and the potential for them or the organization to be viewed in a negative light are more important. In other words, gatekeepers are more likely to grant access if the research can potentially assist their mandate and create a favourable impression of the organization.

Maintaining Access

Your first entry into the setting is the most sensitive time period. The participants don't know you, you don't know them, and (more important) you are not familiar with group norms, language, or practices. Members may view you as a spy for upper management and fear that their words and actions will get back to their supervisors. If you are conducting field research with the police, they may take fewer coffee breaks or meet-ups with other platoon members or may handle proactive encounters differently based on their perceptions of researcher expectations. Prepare to be tested on your subject matter competence, credibility, and personal characteristics. In the field, trust and respect is earned. It's not something you can expect will be given to you because you are a researcher. In fact, this status can make it harder to earn trust as an outsider.

One technique to maintain access is the notion of **reciprocity**. Provide small tokens or do small favours for members. It will be interpreted as an indicator of your commitment and your desire to understand. Why? Shared experiences are catalysts for discussions more so than are retrospective accounts. By experiencing the event, both parties share a commonality that can be used as a basis to maintain access and further develop the relationship. Volunteering or agreeing to assist a participant in a small way will speak volumes and increase the sense of shared experiences.

For example, as a way to give back to the police service I conducted interviews and ride alongs with, I gave the inaugural address at their Cops and Youth program. One officer told everyone about our calls for service and having to "babysit a dead body on New Year's Eve." To the officer, this experience was proof that I was "cool, can be trusted, and get it" when it comes to what the police do. Although this endorsement occurred six months after I left the field, it reaffirms that shared experiences and reciprocity can mean much more to members than you may initially believe.

That said, sharing experiences means that you will need to navigate the feelings associated with conflict-laden situations and the consequences for taking a side. The problem is that, when you take a side, you may inadvertently alienate yourself from other members, cutting off your access and making it hard to maintain access in other areas. The bottom line is to stay neutral whenever possible.

> **reciprocity** a give-and-take relationship of sharing information and doing small favours for the privilege of gaining access to a social world.

Research Highlights

Field Research in Deviant and Criminal Subcultures

Despite the challenges, field research is conducted in closed subcultures. However, researchers don't enjoy a privileged relationship with participants in the same way that a lawyer and client are allowed. A researcher's presence or knowledge of illegal activities can make him or her an accessory to the crime. When studying criminals in their natural settings, researchers must decide whether they are willing to break the law (Jacobs, 1998).

For many reasons, studying institutionalized criminals might seem like a more attractive alternative. Unfortunately, these research subjects might not be representative of active offenders. For example, one study found that one-quarter of 105 active offenders were never arrested and, on average, "offended more frequently and had committed more lifetime

Continued

burglaries than their arrested counterparts" (Wright et al., 1992, p. 160). In other words, those incarcerated are more representative of unsuccessful criminals.

Gaining Access

Gaining access involves hanging out in areas where criminals congregate. Adopting the role of a complete observer can help give you a lay of the land; interactions with the police on the scene may even give you credibility. You need to establish a street reputation as trustworthy, something that is easier said than done. Even after you get to know members of these hard-to-locate populations, they are reluctant to reveal information about themselves and their activities.

Another viable approach is to hire an ex-offender who still has ties to the criminal subculture and street credibility to vouch for the researchers (Wright et al., 1992). With gatekeepers, Hopper and Moore (1990) quickly realized that they couldn't tell the members of outlaw motorcycle gangs their true research purpose of understanding the role, motivation, and background of gang-affiliated females. The description was intentionally vague; otherwise, access would have been impossible and would have focused on the club as a social organization.

Field Relations

As with all research settings, offenders will test researchers. Ethnographers are encouraged to immerse themselves in the culture; at the same time, they can't pretend to be an active criminal. They'll either end up breaking the law or being exposed as a liar because they don't back up their claims (Jacobs, 1998).

The field is much more dangerous than other research settings. Jacobs (1998) was robbed at gunpoint by his primary gatekeeper—a crack dealer who felt slighted because he couldn't make any more referrals and so was not contacted anymore. Thus, Wright and colleagues (1992) made sure to let offenders know that they had only just enough money to pay for their participation. Hopper and Moore (1990) witnessed activities that dramatically clashed with their values. It was too dangerous to make this situation an issue and, if they had, their access would have ended. Researchers depend on their subjects for access and data, which has new dimensions in this context.

Final Thoughts

The more illegal the behaviour, the more members have to lose and the harder it will be for researchers to gain access (Jacobs, 1998). This type of fieldwork requires a high commitment of time and energy—Hopper and Moore spent 17 years studying female bikers! There is also a big difference between access and safe access. You may gain access to the setting through the wrong person, putting you at greater risk. Inevitably, all fieldwork is unpredictable to varying degrees, and this is certainly more the case with active offenders.

Entering the Field

Although it might feel overwhelming, don't despair or believe you couldn't possibly conduct participant observation. How one enters the field affects all subsequent interactions. Three things to consider at this stage are sampling, using informants, and managing interpersonal dimensions. Depending on your research purpose, adopting a participatory action research design may be appropriate and enhance rapport and trust with group members.

Sampling

You may think that sampling, which we discussed in Chapter 4, isn't applicable to field research, but it is no different than any other data collection method and extends beyond selecting the research site. In fact, sampling occurs throughout the data collection process. To increase authenticity, researchers sample different activities and people to gather as much information about the social phenomenon of interest as possible. Two nonprobabilistic sampling techniques are used by most researchers.

The first is theoretical sampling. As you become more acclimatized to the group, you start to see certain issues, interpersonal dynamics, or events as significant for addressing your research question. You then seek out circumstances or participants that allow you to test these hunches. In essence, you are looking for typical and deviant cases. Think of it this way. You are interested in understanding how and why individuals become involved in drugs, ultimately become addicted, and then start dealing. With the help of a gatekeeper, you initially target homeless drug users. You realize that some drug dealers are gainfully employed, so you add them to the sample. As data collection continues, you become aware that your sample consists mostly of individuals in their mid-twenties. Hence, you seek out older participants to see if your preliminary inferences still apply. You discover that one pathway to addiction is common, but it is unclear how it leads some to deal drugs. You then sample group members that could shed light on this matter.

The second technique is snowball sampling, or respondent-driven sampling. Remember, this method is ideal and effective for subcultures or hard-to-reach populations. In many cases, researchers use both techniques when conducting participant observation. Snowball sampling is used to find group members, and theoretical sampling is used to flush out ideas that are developing during data collection.

Informants

Gatekeepers among the group members you interact with in the field can also serve as **informants** to help navigate the setting and develop an insider understanding. From an everyday perspective, think of informants as tour guides who show you what they feel is important and answer questions to help you understand. Spradley (1979, p. 34) describes the researcher's approach to an informant as follows:

> I want to understand the world from your point of view. I want to know what you know in the way you know it. I want to understand the meaning of your experience, to walk in your shoes, to feel things as you feel them, to explain things as you explain them. Will you become my teacher and help me understand?

The cultural aspects of the group are important to learn as quickly as possible. When entering the field, the biggest challenge is to fit into the group. Learning the culture is how you will know when to speak and what is acceptable or appropriate under certain conditions and with different types of people. This situation is like learning street smarts within a cultural milieu. For example, the way you interact with a patrol officer will differ from that of a staff sergeant. Yet each platoon is a subculture within the larger police culture. Learning this social and behavioural etiquette will be your first order of business.

There are three characteristics of good informants. They are completely integrated within the setting, have solid relationships with other members, and know the culture. Obviously, they have to be accessible. (If you have trouble getting in touch with an informant, they are of little use to you when you need assistance.) Finally, they do not think like a researcher but describe the setting and individuals from their own perspective. This quality is why informants are one of the most lucrative ways to gain insider knowledge.

As helpful as informants are to the research process, you still need to be careful and not let your guard down. Frequently ask yourself a few questions: Do your observations match what the informant says? What are possible reasons for any discrepancies? We all

informant a person in the field setting who the researcher develops a relationship with and gains insider knowledge as a result.

have our own understanding and memory of events. Questioning what you hear and see and then unpacking discrepancies will yield important insights.

Interpersonal Dimensions

Impression management is just as important in field research as it is when conducting interviews. In fact, it may be even more important because of the extended time spent in the field. The first impression you make will be remembered by group members throughout your stay in the field. Dress, behaviour, and demeanour should be appropriate for that setting. Taking on the role of complete observer before entering the field can be invaluable. Keep in the back of your mind that sticking out in the crowd is probably not going to do you any favours. Similarly, emphasizing your credentials or expertise isn't necessarily going to increase your access or acceptance by group members. Portraying yourself as approachable and nonjudgmental gets you a lot further. Yet you will need to be distinct enough so you are not mistaken for a group member. As discussed, there can be some serious consequences if this happens while researching active criminals.

Developing Rapport

Developing trust and rapport is a process that occurs over time with shared experiences, conversations, and nonverbal communication. Without rapport, it is difficult to achieve credibility or gain an in-depth understanding of the people, events, and actions within a setting. Even when you feel you have achieved rapport, you often need to reaffirm that you have as new situations arise. The good news is that your outsider status will decrease the longer you are in the field. The more time you spend with members, the more likely they are to forget that your role as researcher is your primary identity. Your everyday interactions become the focus.

Researchers decide how much personal information they reveal to participants when trying to establish rapport. The timing and type of information is largely dictated by the setting, social actors, researcher judgment, and comfort level. Examples of personal information include personality characteristics, experiences, hobbies, family, and background. This information varies with each participant, and personal disclosures may increase over time as the relationship with members develops and intensifies.

Sharing personal information can help break the ice and develop trust, as it represents two-way communication. The question is whether the personal information you reveal or the favours you do for members compromise or influence what they share and do in your presence. The longer you are in the field, the better sense you will gain as to whether this situation occurred in the early stages of data collection. However, many agree that practising reciprocity is more likely to build rapport than to threaten data validity. As previously mentioned, doing small favours and sharing information when asked build trust and demonstrate a genuine interest in learning and understanding the participant's world.

One final piece of advice: our everyday lives will always have some measure of conflict, and a field setting is no different. Although it can be difficult to do so, make neutrality your goal whenever conflict occurs in the field (Wolcott, 2005). It may be very tempting to agree with a group member while trying to build rapport. You may feel so uncomfortable and be almost desperate enough to do just about anything to fit in. The conflict you become aware of is the tip of the iceberg. Taking sides, no matter how much you want to build rapport, will shape future data collection and potentially introduce bias and limit access.

How Close?

Maier and Monahan (2010) interviewed 29 crime and deviance researchers to uncover the crux of the debate on developing rapport and practising reciprocity. They found that there is no universal rule for what constitutes a close enough relationship with participants. Your relationships have to be close enough to gather meaningful data but not too close; they should not blur boundaries, affect your reputation in the field, impair decision-making, or compromise your ability to analyze and report data objectively.

Strong rapport creates an environment for sharing intimate personal details, but these close relationships introduce complications. Many researchers feel compelled to engage in reciprocity because participants give their time, talk about sensitive topics, and are expected to welcome the researcher as a "de facto member of their social world and grant them the freedom to observe their behaviors and document their interactions" (Maier and Monahan, 2010, p. 16). These favours often resemble what you would do for close friends. For instance, when Adler (1985) conducted research on drug dealers and smugglers over a six-year period, she loaned subjects her car, babysat for them, attended social functions, and wrote letters for them when they got into trouble with the authorities.

How do you ensure data collection and analysis is unaffected by the degree of intimacy or detachment? Adler subjected her data to the logic of common sense and looked at everything with a degree of suspicion. She attempted to verify her interpretations by bouncing ideas off informants, gathering alternative interpretations of members' behaviour, and comparing data to alternative sources such as arrest records or personal possessions. Field research is an unpredictable and messy endeavour. Once you enter the culture, you will consistently revisit your decisions and position on this issue.

Participatory Action Research

In reflecting on *Street Corner Society* (1955), Whyte (1993) argues for adopting a **participatory action research (PAR)** design, which builds rapport and bridges the gap between researcher and group member. PAR directly tackles the issues of status and power between participants and researchers. The rationale for this research design is that research subjects are invariably affected by participating in research; therefore, they should play an active role.

In a PAR design, the researcher invites members to participate throughout the research process. In this way, he or she goes above and beyond interpersonal reciprocity, as members are committed to research outcomes and are less concerned with personal or organizational gains. Participants are empowered when defining the problem and its investigation. Participatory action researchers serve as a resource, allowing members to work actively to induce beneficial change for their group.

There is a delicate balance when negotiating who is in charge and what constitutes knowledge. Whyte (1993, p. 296) makes a valid point when he says, "We may agree that no outsider can really know a given culture fully—then we must ask whether any insider can fully know his or her culture." We focus almost entirely on building rapport and the importance of insider knowledge, but Whyte urges us not to forget that outsiders can and do make important contributions in all field research endeavours.

Field Notes

Researchers can easily become overwhelmed by the volume of information and observations every time they go into the field. In the beginning, they are not familiar enough with the setting or participants to discern which observations are important and which ones are not. Enter the heart and soul of ethnographic research: field notes.

Field notes organize your thoughts about what you see and hear in the field so you can understand what observations mean. In other words, these notes are the data that help you discern the forest from the trees. They will guide you when interacting with participants in the field.

To improve the reliability and validity of your participant observation data, follow these general principles. Be vigilant about recording dates and times to establish a chronology of

> **participatory action research (PAR)** a research design that empowers a community through collaboration at all stages in the research process in order to create change and understand social reality.

events. Approach writing field notes systematically and include as much detail as possible. You never know what will be meaningful later in the research process. Memory fades quicker than you think once you leave the field. Ensure there is a clear distinction between recording observations (events, words, behaviours) from your reactions and interpretations. Some field researchers find it helpful to divide the page in half. One side is reserved for descriptive notes about the setting, activities, conversations, and events. The other half contains reflective notes (thoughts, feelings, and any problems that occurred while in the field). During data analysis, compare all your types of notes to see if any potential bias is affecting what you observe (e.g. reactivity) and how you recorded it (e.g. selectivity).

As the previous paragraph suggests, field notes fall into two groups: data and reflection. Data include jotted notes made in the field and the full field notes you write after leaving the field for the day. Reflection notes include personal notes that document your feelings and reactions to observations and analytical notes that assign meaning to observations.

Jotted Notes

When writing **jotted notes**, record phrases, key words, and quotes to jog your memory. At this stage, you are trying to capture what has happened and not your interpretation of events. These notes are called jotted notes because you don't have a lot of time to record information if you are going to see what continues to happen in the setting. Therefore, you develop abbreviations and shorthand notations so you can keep up. Record even those things that you think

are irrelevant because, as was already stated, you can't be sure that they won't be important once you start analyzing the data, particularly in the early stages of data collection.

In most settings, researchers use small pocket notebooks, but it's not unheard of for them to use anything that is readily available, such as napkins or newspapers. There will likely be many times when you have to wait to write your jotted notes. Believe me; you can escape to the restroom to write your notes only so many times. Some find using mnemonics—including acronyms, sentences with each word representing something, and songs—helpful in recalling important information.

Jotted notes are unique to each individual; however, the ability to write them is largely determined by the type of research setting. Because jotted notes are created in the field, remember the maxim of not recording anything you wouldn't want a participant to read. If necessary, use code words to create reminders.

Full Field Notes

Once you leave the field, your jotted notes are used to construct **full field notes**. You document complete descriptions of the setting (e.g. physical layout), individuals (e.g. their clothes), body language, and any unique words that are part of the group's language. These notes involve **thick description**, whereby you capture as many details from the setting and participants as possible to create a depiction that makes the reader feel as if he or she has personally experienced the events and participated in the conversations.

Full field notes avoid generalities by recording concrete examples with the detailed descriptions. Recording dates and times is important because it creates a step-by-step narrative of everything that occurs while you were in the field. Ensure that you can differentiate between direct quotations and paraphrased words. Whether you use italics or quotation marks, stay consistent throughout. Make note of any questions that arise as you are writing. This

---

jotted notes field notes that are written while still in the field and use cue words to increase memory recall for writing the full field notes.

full field notes field notes documenting, in as much detail as possible, what the researcher hears, sees, and does while in the field setting.

thick description description that explains behaviour, the context in which it occurs, and understandings that make it meaningful to participants.

practice will orient you to seek answers the next time you are in the field, inform theoretical sampling, and provide clues to possible interpretations and meanings.

Some researchers do not create separate notes for personal reactions and feelings, as they also constitute data. The trick is to clearly distinguish these notes from the observational data. I often use italics or square brackets for this purpose.

Reflection Notes

What do you record in **personal notes**? Note the days that you didn't feel on top of your game because such feelings affect your attention span and the data you capture. Include your personal feelings and reactions to observations. For example, I record how I feel about disturbing calls for service and how they affected me. Processing trauma I saw in the field occurs in my personal notes as well. Using reflexivity, I record this information to control for any observer bias. Personal notes are one way to cope with stress in the field, particularly if ethics prohibit you from sharing your thoughts, feelings, and experiences with anyone else.

Analytical notes are the starting point for assigning meaning to observations and mapping out how things are organized within the cultural group of interest. These tentative conclusions are constantly revised as data collection continues. You record the methodological problems you encounter in the field, consider the context, and brainstorm possible reasons. Analytical notes literally document your personal growth as a research instrument.

The Logistics of Field Notes

If you take anything away from the logistics of field notes, it should be to write your field notes as soon as possible after you leave the field. You can forget up to 90 per cent of the pertinent information by the next day; therefore, don't wait more than 24 hours to write full field notes. There are times when taking notes in plain view sticks out in the field. I make it a practice to write additional jotted notes once I leave the field to ensure that I have triggers for as much information as possible if I can't write the full field notes right away.

I can't emphasize enough that you must record absolutely everything you can remember. Subsequent events or interactions can shed light on previous notes. Many argue that social life and participants' meanings associated with their social world can be appreciated only by observing mundane and sometimes trivial events and behaviours. We typically ignore this aspect in everyday life, but a good field researcher records it all.

Writing your field notes can take just as much time as you spent in the field. Estimate the process of writing your full field notes as three times longer than the time you spent observing activities in the field. Finally, back up, back up, and back up again. Save your field notes on your computer hard drive and USB stick, as a printed copy, and in different secure locations. There will be no way to recreate the data if it is compromised or lost.

> **personal notes** field notes on the researcher's feelings while in the field and his or her personal reactions to observations.

> **analytical notes** a researcher's notes on ideas and themes that develop when reviewing data.

I'm in the Field—Now What?

Don't get too comfortable and think that, once you gain entry and develop rapport, data collection is easy. There are logistics to consider, such as the impact of your presence, the need to learn the lingo, and culture shock. Finally, at some point, all field research ends. You will have to determine when and how to leave the research setting.

Understanding Group Relations

Not only is the researcher observing group members in field research, but the group members are also observing the researcher. Based on interactions, impressions are shared with other members.

You do the same thing with your friends after meeting someone new or when particular words are spoken and actions occur.

In most languages, the same word can mean different things. For instance, in North America the word *flat* denotes a level surface, but in the United Kingdom it refers to an apartment. When conducting field research, you quickly realize that every group and organization has its own lingo, known as **argot**. Groups create new words for experiences and events or take ownership of a word by defining it in a different way. For example, the police use 10 codes, such as 10-4, to let others in their group know they are okay and use code green in a hospital to denote a violent patient. Usually, *lunch* refers to a midday meal, but to officers on the late afternoon shift, it's their meal break at 11:00 p.m.

Becker and Geer (1957, p. 29) write:

> Any social group . . . will have to some degree a culture differing from that of other groups, a somewhat different set of common understandings around which action is organized, and these differences will find expression in a language whose nuances are peculiar to that group and fully understood only by its members.

The argot illuminates how members interact with one another and their interpretation of the world and helps the researcher fit into the setting. Learning the lingo is one of the best ways to understand tacit knowledge. Sometimes group members are not necessarily cognizant of this knowledge because they take it for granted. I can attest that learning the culture's argot made my field experiences easier, as I understood communication nuances and, based on members' reactions, felt much more like an insider.

Culture shock is a state of distress upon exposure to new and strange social environments. It occurs after the first few weeks in the field, when the initial

argot shared terminology, which signals group membership.

adrenaline wears off. Take comfort knowing that you are not alone. Unless you go native, this problem will always exist to varying degrees. In fact, the field research experience and culture shock may become so intense that leaving the field is very tempting. Breathe . . . this too shall pass.

Impact on the Researcher

Researchers often experience stress from the volume of data and embarrassing or uncomfortable interactions. There are times when researchers are made to feel like insiders and others when outsider status prevents engaging in the insider in-depth personal conversations (Sword, 1999). Researchers are also away from their normal lives and routines for long periods of time.

To reduce some stress, recall the golden rule of fieldwork: don't do anything in the field that you can't live with personally or professionally or that you don't want others to know about. Practice reflexivity and document any possible ways that your presence or characteristics such as age, gender, academic status, or marital status might affect what you record and how you interpret what you observe.

Marks (2004) attributes her success as an ethnographer to projecting a matter-of-fact, bold, engaged, and interesting persona. Yet she was still concerned that being white and female in a male- and black-dominated environment could affect access to data, which it did. However, this effect can be positive. Marks explains that "being a woman seemed to innately mean that I was trustworthy and understanding. Members would talk to me about both their work and personal dilemmas . . . I would listen, share my own experiences with as much openness as I felt was necessary" (p. 881). Her experience is a good example of using reciprocity to maintain rapport. This type of reciprocal disclosure contributes to the depth and quality of the data while diminishing the hierarchical relationship between researcher and participant (Sword, 1999).

I Can't Cope . . . Yes, You Can

There is no right or wrong way to manage and cope while navigating the research setting and developing relationships. How you cope depends on personality, confidence, and background characteristics. There are a few guidelines to help you survive fieldwork:

- Just be yourself. At some point, you will no longer be able to keep up a façade and will lose participants' trust.
- Don't disrupt. Questions are expected, but don't make asking them a constant activity as it will alter how group members behave in your presence.
- Employ active listening skills. Be cognizant of body language, communication methods, argot, and meanings.
- Show up and be on time. I was late for the briefing the first time I went to a new police division. Each division starts their shifts at different times, and I neglected to confirm the details with my gatekeeper. It was embarrassing, and I was the butt of jokes for the day.
- Be alert. Pay attention to everything in the field, regardless of whether you are exhausted or bored or whether you think something is routine and unimportant.
- Protect your sources. Word gets around; if you have loose lips, the trust you have worked so hard to earn can disappear.

Leaving the Field

Participant observation research is an extremely personal and intense experience. Leaving the field can be hard and result in something that feels like withdrawal symptoms. Disengagement is as carefully planned as the other stages in the research process. It's usually not a good idea just to stop going to the research setting. Leaving under good terms allows you to maintain relationships with key informants, to perform member checks, and to avoid burning bridges for future researchers.

When do you know it's time to leave the field? Unless your field setting is an organization that limits the time in the field or prematurely ends your access, you will exit when you reach saturation, as you will learn nothing new with repeated observations. When you are in the field, writing your field notes and reviewing them, you will realize that behaviour and events are largely predictable. You will not be left with unanswered questions. At this point, you have reached saturation and will prepare an exit strategy.

With each fieldwork project, the exit strategy is unique and only the researcher can determine if a quick or gradual exit is appropriate. Circumstances affecting the exit strategy include researchers suffering from burnout caused by the types of observations and the frequency and duration of data collection. Family or other personal reasons may also dictate ending fieldwork.

Typically, you leave the field gradually. You reduce the number of visits and hours over a period of time, which allows both you and the participants to prepare for this eventuality and deal with any associated feelings. However, this can backfire; when they realize engagement is coming to an end, participants might freeze you out as a coping mechanism. To manage this process, provide informants and members with a rationale for disengagement.

The emotional labour associated with disengagement is sometimes surprising. These emotions include guilt, loss, disorientation (when you spend more time in the field than in your own personal life), culture shock, depression, and readjustment to everyday routines. To give you an example, I spent forty to fifty hours per week in a patrol car for six months. I also had to spend time writing my field notes and maintaining all the duties associated with my full-time job. In reality, I spent more time with patrol officers every week than I did on any other activity or with anyone else. I left the field due to burnout, saturation, and operational necessity. I felt utterly lost on so many different levels, depressed, and empty. These feelings are rarely talked about but truly need to be considered in an exit strategy.

Alternative Approaches

Three variations of field research are systematic social observation, which collects quantitative and qualitative data simultaneously; netnography, which uses field research methods to understand online patterns, content, and behaviour; and ethnomethodology, which seeks information on how social reality is constructed.

Systematic Social Observation

Systematic social observation (SSO) is a mixed methods approach that combines participant observation and surveys to collect observational data. For example, in policing research, the focus is on the patrol officer. When researchers study behaviour in a natural environment, "the ways in which the numerous situational, organizational, individual, and environmental factors play on the choices made" are more evident (Mastrofski & Parks, 1990, p. 42). By merging the behavioural (quantitative) and cognitive (qualitative), SSO builds on the strengths of both.

> **systematic social observation (SSO)** a mixed methods structured observation that uses explicit rules for observing, categorizing, and recording behavioural data.

Adopting the observer as participant field role, the researcher observes and interacts with group members closely enough to gain an insider's identity but not full-fledged member status. Divisions, patrol zones, shifts, and officers are sampled as randomly as possible, given the operational constraints of the police agency. Standardized data collection instruments increase reliability, officers can verify the validity of the data, and observer interpretation is as limited as possible.

Data Collection Instruments

The data collection instruments are developed prior to entering the field. For close-ended questions, the researcher identifies the specific behaviours to be documented based on the research questions. Similar to developing surveys, the questions have to be mutually exclusive and exhaustive. Clear coding instructions are developed to reduce ambiguity, and observers undergo up to two weeks of extensive training to increase reliability.

SSO data is hierarchical; the quantitative data are collected in ride along, encounter, and citizen sheets. Each type contains standardized open- and close-ended questions combined with qualitative narratives for each encounter and citizen. The field notes are for the ride along as a whole.

Time use sheets are also used. For instance, Liederbach and Travis (2008) used an encounter activity instrument that accounted for every minute of the patrol shift to test what enforcement style is used by agencies. Similarly, Famega and colleagues (2005) wanted to know if officers have sufficient time to engage in proactive activities during unassigned patrol time. With a time use instrument and narratives, they were able to determine that officers respond to 911 calls for only 19 per cent of the shift. Only 6 per cent of the remaining time involved proactive activities directed by a supervisor.

Typically, data are collected using handheld computers in a CAPI format. Alternatively, the data can be handwritten onto sheets (see Table 7.1 for examples of variables). The data are entered at the end of an encounter to minimize operational disruptions, while the officer completes his or her notebook entries.

One way to deal with the ethical aspects of recording data is to allow the participating officer to review all data and notations at any time. Data validity increases because the researcher can verify answers with the officer during a debriefing after each police–citizen encounter. A good example is determining if the officer feels the citizen was disrespectful of his or her directives and authority.

Debriefing an officer in the field is more effective than conducting an interview removed in time and place. The officer can feel more confident that the observer understands because both have experienced the encounter. Think of the debriefing as a conversation designed to obtain background information on what the officer knows, believes, and perceives as important, what influenced his or her responses,

Table 7.1 Examples of SSO quantitative variables

Data level	Type of information	Examples
Ride along	General information	Shift start and end times, patrol zone, weather
	Officer	Sex, years of service
Encounter	Background information	Length of time, source of call (dispatch)
	Description	Type of call, larger problem (high-crime-rate area)
	Particulars	Number of bystanders, number of units dispatched, percentage observed
	Police actions	Charges, use of force, personal assistance, warnings
Citizen	Personal identifiers	Sex, age, criminal history
	Indicators of behaviour	Under the influence, mental health, demeanour
	Citizen actions	Weapon, requests of officer, response to police authority
	Police actions	Referrals, detention, legal actions, discretion

what he or she hoped to accomplish, and how he or she feels about the interaction once it's over.

The narratives are written in the field and completed (preferably) within 8–12 hours of a patrol shift. To contextualize the quantitative data, they contain a chronology of all events and conversations during the encounter and by a particular citizen. Ideally, field notes are written within 24 hours of an observation shift. They contain thick description so that, as previously mentioned, the readers feel as though they have lived the experience. In my research, the field notes ranged from 8 to 17 pages single-spaced. Within the field notes, you find setting details, encounter events/interactions/conversations, non-encounter interactions between calls, details on the percentage observed, debriefing information, and researcher perceptions and reactions to observed events, as well as unanticipated information not captured in the quantitative instruments.

Limitations

SSO has three potential limitations. Reactivity occurs when an observer's presence alters the nature of events and what is observed. Altering behaviour in real-life interactions is difficult, as the officer is responding to citizens' actions. Building on this premise, the concern of reactivity is less with 911 calls and more with proactive activities such as vehicle or person stops. Researchers find that reactivity occurs in less than 0.002 per cent of the observed activities and police–citizen interactions (Liederbach & Travis, 2008). As time progresses, officers adjust to the presence of an observer and act normally in the execution of their duties (Mastrofski, Parks, & McClusky, 2010; Schulenberg, 2014; Spano, 2003). The longer the observer is in the field, the more desensitized officers become and the less likely they are to change their everyday behaviour.

SSO may not be the best data collection method for investigating why individuals respond in a certain way. However, if combined with semi-structured interviews and a debriefing after every encounter, it may not pose as much of a concern. By its very nature, SSO collects small bits of data that can create challenges for discerning the big picture from the specific concepts when interpreting the data.

Netnography

Online communities include interest groups, members-only websites, newsgroups, and chat rooms. Public conversations develop personal relationships and subcultures that ordinarily wouldn't be possible

Vignette: Breaking It Down

On Patrol with the Police

Quantitative research helps us understand the arrest-and-charge decision but is less successful at explaining informal action such as verbal warnings; qualitative findings provide insight into process and beliefs but little evidence that attitudes and values are key factors explaining police behaviour (Schulenberg, 2014; Worden, 1989; Worden & Brandl, 1990). Collecting quantitative and qualitative data simultaneously is the best of both worlds because you can investigate aspects of the police decision-making process and the impact of citizen characteristics, words, and actions on officer behaviour. Thus, SSO is ideal for capturing the full spectrum of police mobilizations and the context in which encounters occur. It can also evaluate the street-level decision-making impact on policy initiatives. In particular, SSO data collects non-crime-related activities and encounters and is a much more valid measure of the frequency of police behaviour than other methods (Liederbach & Travis, 2008).

There are three large SSO studies that have brought forth the majority of quantitative research results. The qualitative analyses and smaller SSO endeavours in this research are interesting. Dunham and Alpert (2009) conducted a primarily qualitative analysis of the narratives and field notes from traffic stops. They examined a sequence of events in which the actions of one person in the encounter affected those of someone else. In particular, they wanted to know how demeanour affects the interaction process. They found that the suspect's and officer's demeanours change throughout the encounter.

To investigate whether officers formulate any rules that shape how they do their job, Stroshine, Alpert, and Dunham (2008) asked them to think out loud. The focus was on the officers' acknowledgement and description of these rules. Seventy-three per cent of the encounters elicited a description of working rules. The outcomes suggest that officers have informal rules on issues such as appearance, information, behaviour, police aggravation, busyness, and safety that guide their reactive and proactive activities.

Rossler and Terrill (2012) conducted a primarily quantitative secondary data analysis of SSO and interview data when examining how police respond to citizen requests within an encounter. These researchers raised some very valid points to consider when using SSO instruments. First, the data are not representative of all patrol officers or agencies. Second, it is cross-sectional data that doesn't capture the long-term outcome of the encounter, such as a court disposition. Finally, the data do not directly address citizen requests for assistance during an encounter or the impact of situational and officer characteristics on the officer's willingness to comply. Of note, they found that the majority of officers did comply with citizen requests for assistance and offered an explanation when they didn't.

Much SSO data is used to understand the factors affecting police discretion and the decision-making process. However, the studies discussed here offer a different dimension. This form of field research occurs in a natural environment, captures data on behaviour as it occurs, and is an excellent way to move above and beyond the information available in official police records.

in a face-to-face environment. The former offers a degree of anonymity, leading to more open communication. Conducting a **netnography** involves employing field research in a natural environment to understand online behaviour and content. Typical field research depends on observational skills. This method uses documentary techniques and the complete observer field role.

Internet-related crime is increasing, yet we still know little about it. The Internet is "increasingly recognized as a powerful tool for research and a website in and of itself can be an extremely useful form of observational research" (Demetriou & Silke, 2003, p. 215). A good example of documentary netnography is Demetriou and Silke's (2003) work. Over a period of 88 days, these researchers observed 803 visitors to a members-only website to examine behavioural patterns online when accessing legal and illegal pornographic material. They found that illegal and deviant material is accessed by virtually everyone.

A clear advantage to this variation is the ability to investigate hard-to-reach groups or groups that have only the topic under investigation in common. Despite netnography's time- and cost-efficiency, it is a good idea to combine Internet-based field research with other data collection techniques. Without nonverbal communication cues, it is much harder to discern meaning. Similarly, it is virtually impossible to account for differing levels of participation in discussions.

There are also specific ethical challenges to the approach. Do you reveal your researcher identity at the beginning or at another point in the data collection process? Is netnography a form of covert research? How would you secure informed consent? What if some people in the discussion forums agree and others do not? With only partial participation, an approach is to record data solely from those who agreed to participate. However, doing so may restrict access to relevant data or cause a reactivity effect.

Ethnomethodology

Instead of focusing on what people do, **ethnomethodology** studies how participants create social meaning about the world. The assumption is that one cannot remove definitions of meaning from everyday life. The process involves addressing questions on how the world is experienced and seen as real by individuals, how a person's reality is created and sustained over time, and how participants view the social world around them and come to view it in this way.

> **netnography** the use of field research methods to study online communities.

> **ethnomethodology** a field research method focusing on how social actors create meaning in everyday life.

Field research focuses on the individual or the organization. At the individual level, research examines how and why deviant behaviour is normalized, ignored, or justified by community members. Social reality is negotiated when norms are violated. Ethnomethodology attempts to discern whether acts are planned or spontaneous. Data from participant observation seeks to understand accounts, and the meaning, of problematic behaviour in face-to-face interactions. A good example is Anderson's (1999) *Code of the Street*, for which he conducted field research to understand the street culture and the informal rules used in young black male communities to regulate deviant behaviour. At the organizational level, ethnomethodologists argue that accounts of deviance reflect organizational priorities and routine behaviour exhibited by agents of social control.

Ethics

Field research presents considerable ethical challenges. A field researcher is alone in the field and must make moral and ethical decisions on the spot. These ethical concerns vary with each research study and differ in formal organizations. The research topic affects the precautions that researchers take to ensure anonymity and confidentiality. For example, there will likely be more steps when researching controversial subjects, such as euthanasia, than when researching everyday occupational practices. Ethical challenges change over the course of the research project, by participant, and with circumstances that arise during data collection.

Voluntary Participation

With other data collection methods, ensuring voluntary participation is quite straightforward. You provide participants with a letter of information describing the study, data collection method, risks and benefits, analytical strategy, and ethical protections such as confidentiality. Participants are given a verbal overview and sign an informed consent form.

With participant observation, is it sufficient to secure voluntary participation from only those members whom you interact with the most? Some argue that it is not, that doing so doesn't constitute voluntary participation. Determining whom you will interact with most frequently can be extremely difficult, especially in the beginning, and the degree of interaction can change throughout data collection. Many researchers get informed consent from key informants and handle the rest on a case-by-case basis.

This practice raises the issue of primary versus secondary participants. Primary participants are those whom you interact with frequently and have provided informed consent to participate. Secondary participants are those on the periphery who have not voluntarily consented to participate.

For example, when collecting SSO data on policing, your primary participant would be a police officer. You would therefore obtain informed consent from this key informant. The people the officer interacts with, such as citizens at a call for service, would be secondary participants. As an observer as participant, you are not interacting with citizens. Do they need to be informed of

the study and consent to participate? The approach I and other researchers take is to allow the officer to explain our presence if asked by the citizen. The explanations range from a ride along and researcher to partner and detective.

The practice of covert research is controversial. Most researchers are adamant that there are no circumstances under which this method is ethical. A minority believe that it can be appropriate in a very small number of circumstances when studying certain deviant or criminal groups. The decision to conduct covert research is one that must be considered extremely carefully, as it violates the ethical principle of voluntary participation. However, when the motives for overt research are not always clear and seldom documented, it becomes difficult to assess when a covert strategy is necessary (Homan, 1992). Meaningful consent may not be appropriate in a given setting. Thus, "it is neither an 'anything goes' nor a 'one size fits all' policy but what is appropriate in that setting" (Calvey, 2008, p. 908).

Protection from Harm

Nonmaleficence and protection from harm, such as legal consequences, is directly related to guaranteeing confidentiality. Pseudonyms may be insufficient to protect the identity of a participant when collecting this extent of detailed information on participants, interactions, and encounters. The information you are collecting about the person is largely unique to him or her, which by definition means that the person could be identifiable. Participants assume, to varying degrees, that their experiences and conversations with you are in confidence. This presumption should always be in the back of your mind when writing up the results.

It is entirely possible that you will have guilty knowledge of criminal activities. You need to decide how you will deal with requests for your field notes from law enforcement or the courts. You run the risk of being subpoenaed or charged with obstructing justice if you refuse to divulge the requested information. Once again, each researcher must make this choice for himself or herself before entering the field. When researching the police, Van Maanen (2003) decided to deal with this "moral fix" by refusing compliance and risking possible sanction to protect his research subjects.

There is no hard and fast rule. With guilty knowledge and protecting participants, "there is the possibility that the researcher's personal morality will force him to violate implicit or explicit research agreements or perhaps even to abandon the study itself. To suggest the contrary would be to make a machine of the researcher and to dehumanize fieldwork" (Van Maanen, 2003, p. 370).

Conclusion

Although participant observation is as systematic as other methods, this data collection technique has certain strengths and limitations.

Strengths

Field research designs are flexible. The underlying complexity of everyday behaviour is acknowledged and the results can inform subsequent qualitative or quantitative research. Researchers are allowed access to parts of social life that are typically inaccessible to outsiders. They gain an in-depth understanding from the members' point of view. They are also able to examine social life holistically and to look at how various patterns of group life fit together.

This method is inexpensive and high in validity. Participants describe what their world means to them in their own language, and researcher observations can be compared to these descriptions. When in doubt, you can conduct a member check and ask participants if the findings make sense to them and truly reflect their world. These strengths are compelling, as field research allows you to investigate groups of people and topics that are inaccessible with any other method.

Limitations

A disadvantage to field research is that, when compared to experiments or surveys, the researcher has less control over the data collection process. Reactivity and ethical challenges must be considered as well. This method is very time-intensive, with extended engagement in the field, field note writing, and large amounts of data analysis.

The trade-off for high validity is questions of generalizability. A different researcher can't replicate the study, even in the same field site. This method is truly personalized, as the researcher is the data collection instrument. Researcher biases, attitudes, and beliefs need to be bracketed in order to collect quality data and produce accurate interpretations.

Another trade-off for high validity is low reliability. How observations are interpreted can differ by researcher. There are thousands of pieces of data; by necessity, there is always selectivity in the data recorded. One tactic that helps is to provide thick, detailed description. In this way, readers have sufficient information to see how the researcher derived his or her conclusions. Threats to reliability also include evasion (e.g. switching topics, giving vague responses) and lies (intentionally not revealing information to the researcher in order to mislead). These threats can be overcome by cross-checking interpretations with other types of data and reducing the interpretation required (e.g. SSO).

We can separate the limitations into five concerns. First, there is reactivity in which participation affects group behaviour. Many argue that group members' behaviour will return to normal only once a researcher has been accepted in the group. Spending extended periods of time in the field will help to desensitize participants.

Second is the concern of distortion. Triangulation of methods helps to counteract this limitation. For example, interviews can illuminate perceptions on life, but they provide very little information on actual behaviour. Combining

Methods in Action

Walking the Tightrope: Ethnography and the Media

Ethnographies present observations of actions and interactions within a context. According to do Mar Pereira (2013), "ethnography has the capacity to redefine the social landscape, to explode received categories . . . the capacity to develop different ways of thinking about a social universe that [people] often take for granted." The problem is that, when trying to create a public ethnography, the relationship with the media is not straightforward.

Gans (2010) argues that developing a public ethnography is an important endeavour. However, it "must be *relevant to* and *accepted by* the lay public" (p. 99). The public and, by extension, the media are interested in topics, not theoretical problems. The first stage is to gain acceptance from the media gatekeepers with publishers, editors, and producers as primary members and reviewers, columnists, and talk-show hosts as secondary members. The second stage, which is critical, is acceptance from the public. It is obtained by writing in non-technical language relevant to the public, not the researcher.

Media coverage allows researchers the opportunity to take part in public debate, potentially influence public policy or institutional practices, and make social inequalities visible (do Mar Pereira, 2013). However, the underlying problem is that ethnographers have control over how the setting, participants, and observations are described but limited control over media portrayals. Conclusions can be inadvertently misinterpreted and have unintended consequences in the public arena or on one's research participants. In fact, it could have "irreversible destructive effects on relations of trust within the field which made it difficult or even impossible for them to do future research in that context" (p. 2). Even when researchers are cautious, there is always the chance that the rapport and trust they worked so hard to build in the field will be threatened. Media coverage is an ethnographic process in and of itself, "to the extent that it has effects on life in the field and an impact on those within it" (p. 8).

When Adler (1984) published his study on a very successful university basketball team, he achieved celebrity status in the media, which played a central role in minimizing his outsider status despite the barricades players built to insulate themselves from media and public scrutiny. This media attention affected his sense of self and the research project. On the one hand, it allowed him greater access, and peripheral members in the group sought him out. As he describes it, his "role had the effect of drawing the data to me" (p. 323). He gained a deeper understanding of members' experiences but was at times overwhelmed by the "tightrope effect" of being afraid to say the wrong thing or break confidences.

Vannini (2013) argues that journal articles are not enough and journalists can be our friends. They are concerned with generating content, whereas ethnographers want to share content. If a mutual understanding is reached, the two groups have much in common. Radio is better than TV, as you lose less control and maintain a measure of depth in the coverage. That said, there is no such thing as big versus small media; "no ethnographer can afford to be a snob about audience size." Vannini advises thinking carefully about the potential audience of each medium. The Internet is great, but you have to work hard to get even ten to sixty visitors a day. Mainstream books may be tempting but average a distribution of 5,000, whereas a magazine article can potentially reach 50,000–250,000 readers.

participant observation and interviews can complement each other well by compensating for the weakness of each data collection method. That is, each method uncovers different aspects of social activity and communication patterns.

The next disadvantage is the imposition of beliefs and opinions. Researchers must avoid ethnocentrism and the imposition of their cultural beliefs. Depending on your field role, you learn and appreciate the group's beliefs, actions, and thoughts. This is a process of resocialization; you need to prevent imposing your own cultural interpretations and beliefs, as they will affect data interpretation.

Fourth, as beneficial as gatekeepers and informants are to the research process, they are also a limitation. You need gatekeepers to gain access to the field site. The gatekeepers may become informants who guide you through the resocialization process and gain access to members in the group. But a gatekeeper's social status in the research setting affects his or her ability to access certain group members. Finally, there are the demands on the researcher. As mentioned, this method is intensive, affects one personally, and takes its toll over time. Moreover, the quality of the data hinges on the researcher's skills.

Writing up the Results

When analyzing data, researchers look for patterns in the events, behaviour, activities, communication, and relationships. This is an inductive analytical strategy. Thus, field notes should be reviewed throughout the data collection process as a means of orienting you to look for specific things in the field and thereby clarify emerging patterns and explore relationships. Be sensitive to your role as the research instrument. You become part of the social world and the processes that occur; therefore, it is important to document your actions in the setting and your reactions to what you experience and witness.

Ensure that you include the following types of information in your report, journal article, or research monograph:

- the rationale and process of choosing the field site
- the process of securing access and the ways that gatekeepers were identified.
- the type of field role, the rationale for adoption, and comments on whether the role was consistent or in transition during the data collection process
- the process of entering the field, including impression management and rapport development
- methodological issues such as responses to conflict and challenges that potentially affect data collection or interpretation
- ethical considerations, particularly steps taken to ensure confidentiality
- the research findings, supported with quotations and concrete examples of observations
- implications of the results, limitations, and acknowledgement of reliability, validity, and generalizability (transferability)

Start writing early, while you are still collecting data. Force yourself to clarify the research purpose. If you can't complete the sentence "The purpose of the research is to . . ." you have a problem that will undoubtedly affect your data collection, as you don't know what it is you are looking for or why you're looking for it. Remember to write using thick description because ethnographies tell a story.

Personal Journey

Field researchers do not simply conduct a study but undertake a personal journey. I am not the same person I was before I entered the field. One grows personally and professionally when operating as the research instrument. Each field setting is different, and you will find the effect on you differs. What I can say is that the journey is very rewarding. I learn as much about myself as I do about the group members.

Summary of Important Points

Introduction

- Ethnographies capture participants' understanding of their social world; field research collects data in a natural setting; and participant observation is a data collection method.
- To understand a social setting, you immerse yourself in it for an extended period of time and capture explicit and tacit knowledge.
- In field research, the researcher is the data collection instrument.
- Field research is appropriate when you are interested in people's actions, everyday life, behavioural patterns, customs, and beliefs.

Where Do I Start?

- Develop a research statement on your purpose and your involvement, using everyday language.
- Be knowledgeable on the substantive area, the community, and plan for field relations.
- Develop observational and note-taking skills.
- Know yourself to prepare for challenges in the field.

Field Roles

- The complete observer does not interact with group members.
- The observer as participant participates minimally and researcher status is known.
- The participant as observer actively participates in group activities and researcher status is known.
- A complete participant is a full-fledged member and conducts covert research.
- Going native involves adopting the group's worldview and losing objectivity.

Gaining and Maintaining Access

- Access varies on a continuum from open to closed field settings.
- Gatekeepers have the informal or formal authority to grant access to settings.

- Access in formal organizations depends on organizational concerns, utility of the findings, and a favourable impression of the agency.

Entering the Field

- Theoretical and snowball sampling occur throughout data collection.
- Key informants help researchers learn the culture, have solid relationships with members, are accessible, and share an insider perspective.
- Impression management, rapport, personal information, reciprocity, and neutrality are important components of successful field research.
- Participatory action research collaborates with members to create positive change for the group.

Field Notes

- Jotted notes are written in the field to record details and jog memory.
- Full field notes constitute the observational data.
- Memory fades quickly; researchers must be timely, systematic, and detailed when writing full field notes.
- Personal notes record reactions and feelings about observations and are considered data.
- Analytical notes capture developing ideas and themes.

I'm in the Field—Now What?

- Argot is terminology symbolizing group membership and illuminating tacit knowledge.
- Practice reflexivity because fieldwork impacts the researcher personally and professionally.
- Researchers leave the field for many reasons, including burnout, operational necessity, and (most commonly) data saturation.
- Exit strategies are typically gradual.

Alternative Approaches

- Systematic social observation combines participant observation and surveys to collect quantitative and qualitative data simultaneously.
- Netnography uses field research methods to study online content and behaviour.
- Ethnomethodology uses field research methods to understand how meaning is created in everyday life.

Ethics

- Securing informed consent and ensuring voluntary participation is complicated, particularly with the issue of secondary participants.
- Covert research is controversial and violates ethical principles.

- Protecting researchers and participants from harm of legal consequences is a concern.

Conclusion

- Participant observation is high in validity but low in reliability.
- Strengths of field research include an in-depth understanding and accessibility not possible with other methods.
- The limitations of reactivity, distortion, bias, differential access from informants, and demands on the researcher can be overcome.
- Recognizing them as an iterative process, ethnographies document every aspect of the research process and findings.

Key Terms

acceptable incompetent 204
analytical notes 213
argot 214
complete observer 203
complete participant 205
ethnocentrism 198
ethnography 198
ethnomethodology 219
field relations 202
field research 199
field role 203

full field notes 212
gatekeeper 206
going native 205
informant 209
jotted notes 212
netnography 219
observer as participant 204
participant as observer 204
participant observation 199
participatory action
research (PAR) 211

personal notes 213
reciprocity 207
systematic social
observation (SSO) 216
tacit knowledge 199
thick description 212

Review Questions and Exercises

1. Imagine you are conducting participant observation on a topic of your choice.
   a. What methodological problems do you anticipate?
   b. How would you negotiate access?
   c. Are there any perceived problems based on personal characteristics?
   d. What would be stressful for the researcher in the field?
   e. What ethical considerations exist?
2. Under what circumstances do you believe covert research is justified? Why?
3. What are some of the steps that researchers can take to increase the chances of collecting quality observational data?

4. Select a picture that has you in the background. In five minutes, write down everything you possibly can about your picture. Working with a partner, switch pictures. Now write down everything you can about his or her picture. Compare your field notes. What is similar and what is different? Why?
5. Argue for and against conducting an ethnographic study using only participant observation.

Online Exercises and Websites of Interest

Ethnography Blog

www.ethnography.com
This blog is devoted to ethnography with a category for research methods. Go to the site and click on the category of research methods. Choose a blog on a topic of your choice and discuss what you have learned above and beyond the chapter material.

Guidelines for Ethical Conduct In Participant Observation

www.research.utoronto.ca/wp-content/uploads/2009/03/Participant-Observation-Guidelines.pdf
This resource, prepared by the University of Toronto, outlines practical issues and ethical challenges.

Internet Ethnography: Online And Offline

www.ualberta.ca/~iiqm/backissues/3_2/pdf/sadebeck.pdf
Researchers from the University of Alberta discuss methodological issues with online research and ways to overcome these challenges.

Additional Resources

Gobo, G. (2008). *Doing Ethnography*. Thousand Oaks, CA: Sage.

This guide is designed for novice researchers and covers ethnographic research design, data collection, logistics, ethics, and analysis.

Gray, P.S. (1980). "Exchange and Access in Field Work." *Urban Life,* 9, 309–331.

Gray offers a frank discussion on barriers faced by researchers who want to access organizations, evolving field roles, and ways to develop rapport.

Miller, J.M., & Tewksbury, R. (Eds.). (2001). *Extreme Methods: Innovative Approaches to Social Science Research*. Boston: Allyn and Bacon.

This edited collection provides guidance on research with populations such as drug dealers, gangs, outlaw motorcycle gangs, pornographers, strippers, and witches.

Chapter 8

Unobtrusive Methods and Secondary Data

"What we observe is not nature itself, but nature exposed to our method of questioning."
W. Heisenberg, cited in King, *Explorations beyond the Machine: A Philosophy of Social Science for the Post-Newtonian Age* (1994, p. 53)

"We are the recipients of the scientific method ... but we can each of us be a creative and active part of it if we so desire." K. B. Mullis, *The Benefits of Science* (2009)

Learning Objectives

- To describe the use of unobtrusive methods that collect and analyze nonreactive data (physical trace, historical, content, secondary, official statistics, legal, meta-analysis, online).
- To appreciate when unobtrusive methods are the most appropriate for addressing a research question.

- To develop the methodological skills to conduct historical and content analyses.
- To understand the relationship between secondary data, agency records, and evidence-based practice.
- To articulate how unobtrusive measures can further our understanding of criminal offences and responses to crime.

Introduction

Webb and colleagues (1966) were the first to name the set of data collection methods that do not include direct researcher–subject interaction unobtrusive measures, oddball measures, or what I refer to here as **unobtrusive methods**. The distinction between unobtrusive measures and other approaches is that the individual "is not aware of being tested and there is little danger that the act of measurement will itself serve as a force for change or elicit role-playing that confounds

unobtrusive methods
research methods in which the researcher does not directly interact with research subjects, thereby removing the threat of reactivity possible with other data collection methods.

the data," thereby compensating for the weakness of other methods in which participants can potentially be influenced by direct interaction (p. 175). While some researchers use data collected by someone else, other unobtrusive measures collect evidence that is created without the person intending or even thinking it would ever be analyzed by researchers. Potential data sources include government or agency datasets, newspapers, graffiti, dumpsters, diaries, court records, television shows, commercials, movies, magazines, and crime scene forensics.

This chapter begins with a summary of nonparticipant observation and physical trace, followed by a brief overview of historical, content, and secondary data analysis.

Nonreactive Data

Nonparticipant Observation

Researchers conducting nonparticipant observation have no direct interaction with research subjects or collect data at a distance from a neutral location. This unobtrusive form of participant observation is ideal when you have limited access to a subcultural group, are interested in a dangerous setting, are investigating patterns of behaviour, or have concerns of a potential reactivity effect.

An example of no interaction is Piff and colleagues' (2012) study of drivers' behaviour at a busy four-way stop. Those who obeyed the stop sign, cut someone off, or failed to yield were compared by social class (based on the type of car), sex, approximate age, time of day, and traffic volume. The researchers conducted six additional tests, including experiments and surveys, to conclude that, when the motivation and opportunity exist, individuals from an upper-class background are more likely to behave unethically whether they are in a naturalistic or laboratory environment.

Theft under $5,000 is a very common offence, yet we have limited knowledge of the characteristics or motivations of typical shoplifters. Dean,

Hollinger, and Dugan (2004) conducted nonparticipant observation from a neutral location to develop demographic and behavioural profiles of the average shoplifter. They coded live closed-circuit television observations for every third shopper whose clothing could conceal merchandise. In addition to shopper characteristics, observers geographically mapped the individual's entire trip throughout the store. They found that behavioural indicators (e.g. scanning the store, leaving without a purchase) are stronger predictors than demographic characteristics.

Digital media is a new variant of rich data that can depict aspects of daily life, is open access, and (due to anonymity) can lead individuals to be frank in their opinions posted online. Although digital media is rarely used in crime and justice research, it is an important data source to consider. Google Trends (www.google.ca/trends/) generates log files that can be used as proxies for social behaviour if you are documenting Internet users' websites and information of interest (Hine, 2011). Social science researchers conduct keyword searches and analyze discussion forum postings (Holt, Zeoli, & Bohrer, 2013; Seale et al., 2010). For example, one study analyzed web forum postings by individuals interested in participating in sex tourism (Holt et al., 2013). The data allowed the researchers to explore the decision-making process that leads to committing deviant and illegal sexual behaviour; more commonly used methods, such as interviews, would have made the research virtually impossible and have likely yielded little valid data.

Physical Trace

Examining physical evidence left behind by humans (e.g. arrowheads, bones, pottery shards) has strong roots in the discipline of archaeology. You need to think much like a detective or Sherlock Holmes when collecting and interpreting trace data. Some argue it is as much a science as it is an art.

There are two types of physical evidence denoting human activity: accretion and erosion. **Accretion** occurs when something that wasn't in a setting before is now present or when there is a

accretion the addition of an object or substance to a setting once an individual leaves.

build-up of a material due to human activity within the setting. Think about a typical homicide crime scene. Physical accretion evidence includes blood spatter patterns, hair strands, fingerprints, and damaged property. Another example is assessing how popular different types of fish exhibits are by counting the number of fingerprints or nose prints on the glass. One could assess how busy a soup kitchen is on various days of the week by counting the number of dirty plates. You might be interested in the extent and nature of drug use within a neighbourhood and document the drug paraphernalia in alleys and garbage cans.

In crime and justice research, graffiti is the most common accretion data analyzed. To better understand socialization patterns, Klofas and Cutshall (1985) examined the graffiti left behind at an abandoned youth custodial facility. General population rooms were analyzed in conjunction with official reports, interviews with former staff and inmates, and newspaper articles in the three years prior to the institution closing. The researchers found changes in the graffiti, concluding that sentence length and conditions of confinement have an impact on youth. The authors noted limitations—as with all data collection methods—including the inability to know anything about the youth, the representativeness of the sample, and, by extension, the generalizability of the findings.

Physical trace evidence of **erosion** involves data on what is missing or selectively wearing away or was removed from a setting due to human

> **erosion** the wearing away or removal of an object once an individual leaves the setting.

activities. At a crime scene, a detective may notice that one knife is missing from a set, suggesting that it might be the murder weapon. If you want to see how popular certain literary genres are, you could go to the library and record whether the corners of relevant books are bent or the floor in that section of the building is worn. You might also document accretion, such as the number of dog-eared pages or underlined and highlighted passages.

Although physical trace data can support inferences based on other types of data, researchers must exercise caution. If you are interested in the prevalence of smoking cigarettes in certain segments of the population, you may try to count cigarette butts discarded on the street and sidewalks. However, depending on the neighbourhood, the streets may be cleaned more frequently, thereby distorting your conclusions. The same phenomenon can occur with graffiti. Graffiti may be removed quicker in residential areas than in industrial locations. If you see grass worn away on certain parts of campus, you might conclude that more students use the building or that there should be a path there. Yet construction activities or lawn treatments may have caused more rapid erosion.

Research Highlights

Sneaky Measurements

Crime occurs more frequently in some areas. If we know that we are in a high-crime area, we organize our activities based on this knowledge (e.g. travelling at night, walking quickly). A hot spot of crime is "an area that has a greater than average number of criminal or disorder events, or an area where people have a higher than average risk of victimization" (Eck et al., 2005, p. 2). One question regarding hot spots is, "On what type of evidence and analysis are personal and police policy-related decisions made—word of mouth, media crime reports, police-reported crime statistics, or the state of disorder in a neighbourhood?"

Continued

Some argue that crime hot spots are poorly identified when they are defined solely on the basis of quantitative data from police agency records, as not all crime is known to the police and not all police activities are recorded as calls for service (Garwood, Rogerson, & Pease, 2000; Klockars, 1999). Such researchers question the reliability of location records, depending on the type of crime investigated. Additionally, there is the problem of not having sufficient information on the circumstances of the case to support evidence-based practice (Klockars, 1999).

Unobtrusive data sources are appropriate for supplementing other data sources. Garwood and colleagues (2000) refer to these methods as a "sneaky measurement of crime and disorder." Using unobtrusive measures in addition to the quantitative data increases the validity of the inferences. For example, patterns in public nuisance behaviour were associated with crime in Kelling and Wilson's (1982) famous broken windows theory, which argues that maintaining physical and social order in a neighbourhood can stop offences such as vandalism from escalating into more serious crime. Unobtrusive methods are arguably more appropriate for measuring physical and social disorder. For instance, documenting physical trace evidence and conducting nonparticipant observation of the "minutiae of every-night life may permit areas under 'stress' to be identified" (Hadfield, 2007, p. 179).

Skogan (1999) defines physical disorder with indicators such as trash in vacant lots, rundown buildings, vandalism and graffiti, or abandoned cars. Social disorder can be

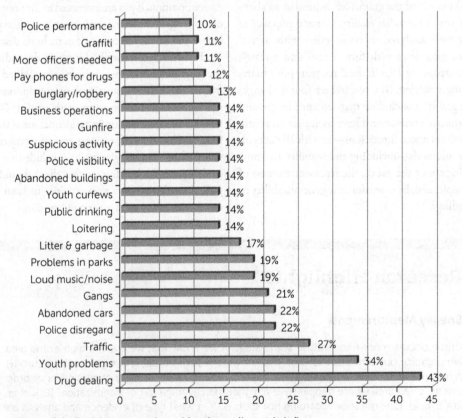

Figure 8.1 Problems mentioned by the police at briefing

Source: Skogan, W.G. (1999). Measuring what matters: Crime, disorder, and fear. In R.H. Langworthy (Ed.), *Measuring what matters: Proceedings from the Policing Research Institute meetings* (pp. 37–54). Washington, DC: National Institute of Justice., p. 42.

measured by the number of youth congregating on street corners, prostitutes, panhandlers, public intoxication, and drug use. In short, physical disorder concerns signs of "negligence and unchecked decay" and social disorder refers to a question of behaviour (p. 42). Even the police mention problems at briefing before a shift, many of which can be measured using nonparticipant observation and physical trace evidence (see Figure 8.1).

Garwood and colleagues (2000) take a similar approach. Their research measured alcohol consumption in public locations by the number of beer bottles or cans in parks, alleys, and garbage cans. Vandalism was recorded with damage to bus shelters or (the now almost obsolete) phone booths. Evidence of physical disorder included indicators of property damage and illegal drug use, such as used needles; the condition of public washrooms; or high water sales at clubs, as indicative of amphetamine use.

A point to remember is that researchers can measure crime-related concepts in more than one way. Some concepts, such as public disorder, are well-suited to unobtrusive measures such as physical trace evidence. The results from these types of investigations can contextualize the nature of social activity that occurs in hot spot locations and is identified using data on crime known to the police.

Historical

Historical data, or **archival data**, include documents and pictures from a particular period in history. Data are in one of three forms. Running records, such as organizational meeting minutes, financial documents, judicial records, or police-reported crime statistics, are chronological. Alternatively, archival data (e.g. media accounts) can be episodic, reflecting a particular period instead of continuous documentation. Finally, personal documents can be a running record (e.g. diary) or episodic (suicide notes or photographs).

Let's say you are assessing the erosion patterns around campus buildings. An additional unobtrusive measure that you could use is aerial photos—both current and historical—to gain a different perspective on pedestrian traffic. To understand the life course over time, you could collect archival data from tombstones. Documenting age at the time of death, family relations, tombstone descriptors (e.g. size), and time period can illuminate the health of the population across generations.

Content Analysis

A **content analysis** is unobtrusive because the data are written, spoken, or pictorial communications previously created by one or more individuals. The

analysis is inductive or deductive and can be quantitative or qualitative. A quantitative content analysis uses coding categories determined in advance, much like survey questions. The data are systematically coded and analyzed to detect predominant ideas and patterns in documents or images. Objective coding procedures produce findings based on numerical descriptions of the communication content. Comparisons are made across sources to uncover aspects of the text or imagery that are not easily recognizable when looking at a few sources.

> **archival data** existing records that contain information on the past; usually stored in libraries and depositories.

Qualitative content analysis isn't about counting words or images. Instead, the analysis tries to identify underlying patterns and themes. The analysis is inductive and coding categories are derived from the data itself. The goal is to provide an explanation for how ideas are part of a meaningful larger context that shapes our experiences and how we make sense of the world around us. Just remember: whether the content analysis is quantitative or qualitative, it is bound within a given time and place.

> **content analysis** the systematic analysis of communication found in text, audio, video, or images.

Secondary Data Analysis

The final unobtrusive method is **secondary data analysis**—researchers analyze data collected by someone else for a different purpose than the current study. It makes little sense to reinvent the wheel when a dataset with the concepts of interest on the right target population already exists. Researchers can replicate previous findings, perhaps with a slightly different approach, or use the data for a different research purpose. Remember, individual researchers lack Statistics Canada's resources in terms of access, quality control, sample size, financial resources, and the ability to collect certain types of data, which all makes secondary data a viable alternative.

secondary data analysis analyzing, reclassifying, and interpreting data collected by other researchers.

Why Use Unobtrusive Methods?

Due to certain limitations, indirect methods aren't used in crime and justice research very often. A key consideration is the fact that you can only make observations. You can't question people to understand attitudes or motivations for offending or the use of discretion. Thus, for many research questions, direct methods such as surveys, interviews, and participant observation are more appropriate.

Lee (2000) argues that there are three primary reasons to use unobtrusive methods. First, all data collection methods have methodological weaknesses. The data and findings are always going to be shaped and constrained by the data collection method. With interviews and surveys, researchers acknowledge that the data collection instrument can "create attitudes in part because respondents commonly try to manage impressions of themselves in order to maintain their standing in the eyes of the interviewer" (p. 2). For example, there are concerns about a reactivity effect when conducting interviews and experiments. Similarly, a social desirability bias concerns survey researchers. These factors reflect the dynamic interplay between researcher and research subject, which (by definition) is not an issue with unobtrusive measures.

Second, Lee points out that Webb and colleagues (1966) are strong advocates of mixed methods and that unobtrusive measures are complementary to other methods, as their strengths and weaknesses overlap. An alternative perspective on the mixed methods approach is held by researchers adhering to the principles of discourse or narrative analysis, phenomenology, or semiotics, who approach research seeking to understand social phenomena within an interpretive framework. Thus, as Lee (2000) points out, everything is culturally, socially, and temporally situated. All forms of data are important, whether we initially see them as relevant or not. In practical terms, nonreactive data are ideal and should not be overlooked. It's not a question of using multiple methods but of collecting data that illuminate cultural meaning that other data collection methods are unable to do adequately by themselves.

Lastly, unobtrusive measures are adaptable. Hard-to-reach populations where snowball sampling is appropriate are ideal candidates for collecting nonreactive data. For instance, consider repeat violent young offenders. Interviewing probation or police officers will certainly provide valuable information, but it must be interpreted within the context of their job duties and potential biases. Conducting participant observation would be challenging indeed based on researcher characteristics, access, and subcultural values that are highly distrustful of outsiders. However, you can use unobtrusive measures, such as physical trace of gang activity (e.g. graffiti, tagging), which is often associated with violent offending.

Advantages and Limitations

One of the most important strengths of unobtrusive methods is that reactivity is no longer a concern. Unlike what we see with interviews or participant observation, researcher characteristics or gaining and maintaining access are not challenges that have to be considered or overcome. There are also fewer ethical concerns when there is no contact with research subjects. At the same time, researchers must still deal with issues of anonymity when analyzing secondary data at the individual level of aggregation. Yet it may not be an issue for all secondary datasets. For instance, some of the secondary data sources outlined in Appendix D have been anonymized, whereby a case cannot be linked to an individual because potential identifying information, such as birthdays, was removed. Lastly, concerns can arise because data is always produced in a political, organizational context, particularly when working with criminal justice agencies. As we'll see with evaluation research, this type of secondary data can reflect the agency's need to demonstrate effectiveness to support continued program funding.

Although cost-efficient, unobtrusive methods data collection can actually take a lot of time. For physical trace evidence, having sufficient data available impacts the length of time required. It will take a researcher longer if there are challenges to overcome when accessing the required historical, archival, or agency data. Variation occurs based on sampling technique and sample size when conducting content analysis. Similarly, the number of variables and dataset complexity affect the length of time researchers need to familiarize themselves with the data prior to analysis.

Despite the fewer ethical concerns, new ones arise with nonreactive data. There are potential concerns about a presumption of privacy. For example, diaries were not written for analysis. Similarly, people can become uncomfortable or irritated if they see someone going through their garbage.

Finally, physical evidence and analyses of documents can provide valuable information and insight on social phenomena. However, one cannot presume to understand anything beyond the observation or attribute meaning to social processes. Thus, it is advised to combine unobtrusive measures with other data collection methods to investigate people's motivations and ideas further.

Historical Research

In this context, the word *historical* doesn't have a fixed or specific definition beyond a time period prior to the researcher's own experiences. Historical research is like a case study that looks at a limited set of prior events. This type of unobtrusive research adheres to **historical specificity**, whereby the research is bound to a particular place and period of time.

> **historical specificity** an examination of past events that are specific in time and space.

The purpose of historical research is to develop theoretical explanations for patterns of behaviour and events. It's not simply a fact-finding exercise. For example, a common form of historical research is to conduct a case study on an important event to explore participants' life experiences, the implications of historical events that continue to the present day, or (more commonly) past successes and failures as they pertain to current social problems. Historical data analysis can also form part of an ethnographic inquiry to illustrate the development or genesis of a behavioural practice or reoccurring event (e.g. court trial). This unobtrusive measure can be used to test theoretical propositions on the basis of a select number of prior events. Researchers adopt this method to investigate whether cultural trends or institutional change exists. Finally, historical data is appropriate for understanding the present by making comparisons to the past.

When we talk about historical data sources, we refer to two different types of documents. **Primary data** are the original documents collected by the researcher, such as eyewitness accounts, original copies of letters, or interview recordings. As referred to earlier, **secondary data** constitutes information and datasets collected and created by someone else. They are not to be confused with secondary sources, which borrow knowledge from primary sources to explore others' narratives of the events, the interpretation, and the arguments. An easy way to distinguish the two types of sources is to think of a theory textbook as a secondary source that presents the authors' interpretation of the primary

> **primary data** original sources and data collected by the researcher.

> **secondary data** data collected by someone other than the researcher.

texts written by the theorists. Historical research relies on primary data and sources.

Public records and legal, personal, and government documents are frequently available online. Researchers benefit from the transfer of primary data to an electronic format, making historical research more cost-effective. Archival databases have powerful search engines that allow for keyword searches to narrow down potential sources, retrieve relevant data, or place requests so that the data are ready when a researcher arrives at the archive. Furthermore, data collection can occur entirely online, without a researcher having to travel to archives.

Methods in Action

Library and Archives Canada

Located in Ottawa, the Library and Archives Canada (LAC) contains primary sources on Canada's cultural heritage. It is the country's largest archive, with over 20 million books, periodicals, newspapers, microfilm, and government publications; 3 million maps, plans, and architectural drawings; 350,000 hours of film and musical items; 24 million photographs; and every thesis and dissertation written at any time across Canada. Many sources have been digitized and are available online. However, there is even more material that is not in electronic format. The only way to access it is to travel to Ottawa, and even the online search engine Amicus may not include these sources.

You may be wondering if the LAC is really an option in criminological and criminal justice research. Absolutely! Historical research using primary sources is conducted more frequently, to gain a better understanding of how we got to where we are today. To give you some context, a basic keyword search yielded the results shown in the following table. As you can see, there is a wealth of information simply waiting to be analyzed, with primary sources from as early as the 1750s. Naturally, you would use the advanced search and select parameters based on the research question when searching the LAC or any archive.

Amicus keyword searches

Keyword	# of sources	Keyword	# of sources
Corrections	3,408	Murder	2,035
Courts	2,549	Parole	1,271
Crime	3,014	Prostitution	116
Police	50,014	Sex offender	80
Policing	307	Theft	902
Prison	1,484		
Probation	76		

The LAC (2008) offers several suggestions for successfully conducting archival research. It encourages prospective users to take enough time to do background research, determine what is held at the archives, and develop a realistic time schedule given the volume of material they expect to consult. Your ability to find relevant data depends on your grasp of the secondary material in your subject area, as "secondary sources help you develop parameters for your project and provide a context for assessing the primary sources you use." The LAC uses the analogy of a successful detective, someone who can find clues and leads after an initial investigation.

The book stacks at an archive are closed, which means you can't browse the shelves as you would at your local library. You must request the sources—onsite retrievals take 24–48 hours and offsite online requests take up to one week, for a maximum of ten sources. Documents are viewed in supervised reading rooms. At the LAC, you need to provide your name, address, telephone number, and photo identification and to complete a reference interview. Your job is to be as concise as possible on your topic, research question, what you have done so far, what you need, and your research deadlines. The regulations and responsibilities for handling archival material are then explained. For instance, only pencils or a laptop can be used for note-taking. You can't bring any personal belongings into reading rooms and, occasionally, you are required to wear white cotton gloves when handling the material.

Personal Documents

Personal documents include diaries, letters, and autobiographies. They are selectively preserved and the authors have a variety of reasons for presenting themselves in this way. Researchers are aware of this and use three evaluation criteria.

First, there is the question of authenticity. Is the person who is identified as the author actually the one who wrote the document? Second, researchers determine the credibility of the source. Famous individuals may omit information or frame it in such a way so as not to jeopardize their reputation if the document is read by others. Ask yourself if you can be reasonably sure that the facts are accurate and express the author's perspectives and feelings. What personal documents omit can be just as important as what they explicitly state. Third, representativeness or generalizability must be assessed. Historically, literate people typically came from the upper classes and were male. As a result, these documents are more likely to survive over time. Finally, remember that determining something's meaning can be hard because you lack the larger context. In other words, each picture or diary entry represents a puzzle piece, and you are missing the picture that

emerges when all the pieces are there and put in the right place.

Life Histories

Life histories are autobiographies that capture a micro perspective on an individual's experiences while situating them in a historical, social, environmental, and political context. The goal is to relate a person's life story to their actions as well as their reactions to life experiences.

> **life history** an account of a person's life story, told using his or her own words and placed within a specific larger context.

Researchers take one of two approaches with life histories. Some focus on the way stories are told—what is said, not said, and how. Others are interested in the facts. The research presents the information holistically with little separation between public and private, placing all facts within a specific context. Life histories are often written in the style of a novel and discuss critical life events, such as marriage or war, and how they shaped the writer's perceptions about the world around him or her.

For example, Kruttschnitt and Carbone-Lopez (2006) examined incarcerated women's narratives to uncover motivations for violent offending. A life events calendar chronologically documented women's experiences as victims and perpetrators in the three years prior to incarceration. Popular opinion and media reports typify female violent offending as the result of an evil streak, mental illness, or prior victimization. The researchers found this dominant narrative problematic; although not representative of all offenders, their results suggested varied motivations for a larger range of violent offences. In this case, using personal documents addressed questions of gendered stereotypes that other data sources couldn't adequately address.

Photographs

Photographs provide a rich data source but are not without their challenges for historical researchers. They often reflect ceremonial occasions and not routine life (e.g. the difference between wedding photos, mug shots, and candid pictures). According to Scott (1990), there are three different types of pictures: idealization (formal portraits); natural portrayal (informal pictures capturing behaviour as it occurs); and demystification (candid shots showing a person in atypical situations, such as being under the influence of alcohol and standing on the hood of his or her car).

Regardless of the type of photograph, the analysis can be challenging. Without the advantage of additional information and knowledge of the context, one has little choice but to take the picture at face value. Let's say you are looking at an old wanted poster. Under what conditions was the picture taken? Is it a mug shot? How old is the picture in relation to the date of the poster? Is it a personal picture? If so, what type? None of these are easy questions to answer. Thus, when using photographs, be sure to question your interpretation.

Like personal documents in general, the issue of representativeness applies, as pictures are selectively retained. Someone decided that the picture is worth keeping because a behaviour or event is worth memorializing. Finally, what is not captured in pictures potentially gives you information about the photographer.

Official Documents

Official documents are potentially appropriate for an endless number of topics in criminology and criminal justice. There are two sources of official documents: private and public. Examples of private official documents include corporate annual reports, press releases, newsletters, meeting minutes, and written or electronic communication. Documents from private sources may or may not be publicly available. Public official documents usually originate from government sources, such as Statistics Canada and Public Safety and Preparedness Canada, or are in the form of case law and secondary datasets.

When using either private or public documents, be cognizant of credibility and representativeness. Documents are written and distributed to communicate a particular point of view or goal, which raises the question of authenticity and objectivity, particularly with private source documents. Are only certain documents retained, and why? Further, it may be that even the intended recipients interpret the messages differently than the writer intended. Just think about the misunderstandings that can occur with Tweets.

Comack and Seisha (2010) used private official documents to collect data on the nature of violence in the sex trade, a research topic that is extremely difficult and can be dangerous for a researcher. They collected data from newsletters published between 2002 and 2007 by two Winnipeg inner-city agencies that provide health, outreach, and resources to female sex workers. They found 222 incidents of "bad dates" and "street hassles." Although we don't know the true extent of violence against sex trade workers, these official private source documents shed light on a population highly susceptible to victimization. Comack and Seisha (2010) found that, along with violence, victimization from the stigma attached to street prostitution is a risk for sex workers, creating a discourse of disposal that perceives these actions as justifiable.

Historical Comparative Research

The purpose of **historical comparative research** is to develop a more holistic and broader understanding than is possible when studying a single event or location. By comparing different countries or cultures to investigate topics such as the circumstances for certain court sentencing decisions, you can map shifts in societal views over time and place. Alternatively, historical comparative researchers want to understand the causes of events. Data are collected on a large number of cases and analyzed quantitatively to explain the factors affecting the likelihood of various outcomes. Finally, this type of research can also be a qualitative study when you want to understand how a group of events produce various outcomes within a cultural-historical context.

Understanding the domain of comparative research requires distinguishing between the different types of historical research: events, process, cross-sectional comparative, and comparative historical (Neuman & Robson, 2012). Here is a brief explanation of each:

- Historical events research investigates events or processes that occurred over short periods of time. Methodological concerns include incomplete information and shifts in understanding and meaning attributed to the event or process.
- Historical process research examines how a sequential series of events occurred and why they might have occurred in this way. Methodological considerations include shifts in definitions over time, selective retention of documents, overemphasis on specific people's interpretations or decisions, and difficulties in determining general patterns.
- Cross-sectional comparative research compares two or more settings or groups (usually countries) at one particular point in time. A methodological problem is the comparability of the measures from one country to the next.
- Comparative historical research combines historical process and cross-sectional comparative

research to understand the processes working within certain groups and to identify historical patterns across time and place. Methodological problems include the

> **historical comparative research** a research approach that compares two or more countries, time periods, or different social groups in one country.

accuracy of information, difficulty establishing causality, and tough decisions on how to deal with exceptions in terms of measurement differences across countries.

An example of historical comparative research is Lappi-Seppälä's (2011) study comparing the imprisonment rates in thirty European countries, Canada, Australia, and New Zealand. He found that countries that have relatively low levels of economic disparity, allocate more funds to social welfare, score high on citizen well-being and prosperity, and have citizens with high levels of trust in each other, the police, and the justice system tend to have relatively low imprisonment rates. On the other hand, if a large proportion of the population feels unsafe and reports intolerance toward various groups, such as offenders, the country typically has higher imprisonment rates. On the basis of these cross-national comparisons, the findings suggest that imprisonment rates are not necessarily a reflection of criminal justice policy; they are also influenced by values and approaches to governance in each country.

There is a strong connection between interpretivism and historical comparative research, resulting in unavoidable subjectivity. Much like what you see with field research, researchers have to immerse themselves in the data. Further, any pre-existing opinions and biases need to be bracketed prior to data collection and analysis.

Historical Research Process

The first step in historical research, as with all research, is to conceptualize an idea or research problem. Developing research questions is important but impacts the process somewhat differently because it leads the investigator to certain types of data rather than determining the data collection method. This type of research becomes easier when the research question is as specific and focused as possible, making it clear what you are trying to understand, at what point in time, and where.

After conducting a literature review, the second step is to locate, evaluate, and organize the evidence. The documents must be assessed, as not all are created equal. Every piece of data is situated in a particular context bound by time and place. As each document is produced by a particular person or organization, you must establish authenticity. You will increase the validity every time you can cross-reference with other data sources from this time period.

The third step is to develop a deductive or inductive explanation. The quantitative or qualitative findings are usually presented in a type of narrative that acknowledges cultural shifts and changes over time in people's everyday experiences.

Reliability, Validity, Generalizability

Working with historical archival data raises unique problems of reliability and validity. How confident can you be in the evidence? The closer we are to the events, be it temporally or individually, the more validity that can be asserted from the data. Is there any additional outside information that can be used to corroborate the accuracy of the event description? To produce a narrative of an event is, by definition, situated within the person's perceptions and understanding of the situation. Much like a journalist writing a newspaper article, every statement is written from a specific perspective or for a particular purpose and audience. To assert credibility, you need to discern the potential motivation and identify any information on the intended audience. Finally, generalizability is affected, as this form of unobtrusive research is embedded in historical specificity. In other words, the causes and patterns in historical events may also be unique.

Various other factors affect reliability, validity, and generalizability. Documents can be hard to locate or are lost over time. Researchers may be unable to gather sufficient evidence from documents that are damaged from water, fire, or mould. The sample may be biased due to selective survival of documents. The researcher's data selection process may not be transparent. (It's the researcher, after all, who defines whether a source is significant to address the research question.) It is impossible for historical research to be value-free because researchers have to frame, categorize, and select the evidence used to derive conclusions from the data. Inferring feelings about events is difficult, even if the researcher is able to establish a context for the document and its message. Finally, how researchers organize the evidence in a narrative can make definitions of concepts and discerning selection criteria even more challenging.

Content Analysis

Quantitative content analysis objectively and systematically describes the content of a message, numerically assessing its frequency (number of times) and intensity (positive or negative). The advantage here is that these categories permit analyzing a large amount of data and detecting patterns and trends. The numerical values are meaningful and subjectivity in coding is reduced.

Peelo and colleagues (2004) analyzed editions of three national newspapers published between 1993 and 1997 to investigate media portrayals of 2,685 homicides in England and Wales. Articles were coded on a wide range of quantitative variables, including the type of homicide, region, victim characteristics (age, sex, number, ethnicity, and occupation), method of killing, suspect characteristics, and the circumstances of the crime. The findings suggest a theme of distorted coverage: the circumstances and those acts lacking motive are more likely to be reported, as are cases involving young children. The researchers concluded that the narrative presented by the media is not necessarily based on empirical facts.

In contrast, qualitative content analysis systematically describes the content with more of an emphasis on meaning. For example, Muschert (2007) conducted an ethnographic content analysis on the media coverage of the 1999 Columbine school shootings by examining 683 newspaper articles over a one-month period. A thematic content analysis was appropriate because Muschert was interested in the social construction of the juvenile superpredator. With these analyses, researchers immersed themselves in the data and repeatedly analyzed them until patterns and themes emerge. Overall, the findings suggest four themes in media coverage: identification and description of the victims, details on how death occurred, coverage of memorial services, and related social issues such as gun control. The thematic reporting reifies the myth of juvenile superpredator, which is an inference that would be difficult to conclude with a quantitative analysis.

The combination of print and visual sources is not uncommon in crime and justice research. One Canadian study investigated how the police administer the right to remain silent and legal counsel cautions by conducting a qualitative content analysis of 37 videotapes and 89 interview transcripts (Snook, Eastwood, & MacDonald, 2010). These interviews, conducted between 1995 and 2009, were on all types of criminal investigations. Visual material can be tricky if contradictory messages are embedded within images and speech, as many words have multiple meanings. Images are culturally bound and time specific. The only quantitative findings presented in this study were the percentage of coded text, a typical technique to demonstrate the prevalence of codes and themes. The researchers found that the average rate of talking was too quick to reasonably assume that the cautions were understood. Few attempts were made to ensure that a person interpreted their rights correctly. In this non-random sample from an Atlantic police service, only 25 per cent decided to remain silent and 31 per cent requested a lawyer.

Manifest and Latent Content

Manifest content is most associated with quantitative content analysis. Words, phrases, and images that appear explicitly in the communication medium are coded and counted. A list of key words and symbols, developed prior to data analysis, guides the researcher throughout this process. Manifest content is high in reliability because the data are countable, avoiding any interpretations of the meaning of words or images. The problem is that the same word or image can have multiple meanings. Enter latent content.

Identifying and coding for **latent content** is a type of semantic analysis; the meaning is implied and generally does not appear explicitly visually or within the text. This type of content requires researchers to use common premises when deciding whether a latent theme exists. In terms of the coding categories, the context provides indicators of potential meaning much in the same way as we figure out what someone means by the topic, where the conversation occurs, tone of voice, or facial expressions. The coding manual establishes the criteria for coding words and images to potential meanings and categories. Although less reliable than manifest content, latent meanings may be more valid. However, if the two types of coding lead to similar interpretations, the conclusions are strengthened.

> **manifest content** the words, phrases, and images in a communication that illustrate themes with a concrete, explicit meaning.

> **latent content** a subjectively derived theme implied from underlying and implicit content in words, phrases, and images.

Research Steps

Content analysis is appropriate when the objective is to understand the motivation, intention, or beliefs expressed by the author or a certain type of source, such as newspaper articles, on a type of crime or event. Prior research finds that depictions of events or social problems in print media are directly or indirectly related to personal or institutional ideologies. Further, it's important to assess sources of information. Traditionally, law enforcement is quoted and serves as the primary definer of crime to further the police agenda and newspapers are selective, sensationalizing coverage in order to sell newspapers (Schulenberg & Chenier, 2014). Thus, content analysis studies can investigate relationships to larger social problems or the impact of communications on the audience.

Content analysis can be a lucrative approach when conducting cross-cultural historical comparative research. Using newspaper articles from the *Globe and Mail* and the *New York Times* from 2003 to 2008, one historical comparative study looked at the social construction of responsibility in relation to fish contaminated by mercury. Of the 230 articles, 69 per cent came from the *Times* and 31 per cent from the *Globe* (Fitzgerald & Baralt, 2010). Although the quantitative characteristics, such as page number, were recorded, the authors conducted a qualitative content analysis on the themes of what causes mercury contamination and who is portrayed as responsible for mitigating the impact. The findings are interesting. Both Canada and the United States focus on the role of the state, not corporations, in taking responsibility and on warnings to consumers.

Overall, the objective of a content analysis is to address the five *W* questions: Who is the reporter or the author of the communication? Where is the issue or problem reported? What is the nature and scope of the content? When is the event or behaviour reported and for how long? Why is it considered to be news? In addition, content analyses address what is omitted from the coverage and how the information is packaged for the reader in terms of both manifest and latent content.

Where Do I Start?

Again, we always start with formulating a research problem, questions, and hypotheses. Part of specifying the research problem includes determining the appropriate type of data required to address the research questions and how it will be used to accomplish the research objectives. Is it magazines, books, TV shows, newspapers, radio broadcasts, personal documents, or more than one type of nonreactive data?

The unit of analysis must be determined. Will it be words, phrases, themes, or images? Measurement

plays a key role in content analysis. The coding themes in qualitative and the coding categories, manual, and sheets in quantitative all require the researcher to go through the process of conceptualization and operationalization.

You must also decide whether probabilistic or nonprobabilistic sampling is appropriate and choose the size of your sample. Collect the data, code, analyze, and interpret the results. Note that part of the analytical process is to assess the validity and reliability of the coding categories and data process.

Sampling

The first order of business is to determine the unit of analysis. This unit can be words, sentences, phrases, paragraphs, images, or even articles. In other words, you define the amount of text or images that are assigned within a coding category. This process can get complicated. For example, the unit of observation could be a TV show, whereas the unit of analysis could be a commercial. Both represent how you identify the universe and sample population.

Let's think of sampling in the context of an example. Your research question asks how female true-crime authors portray male crime victims. In terms of the universe, you probably can't identify or access all the true-crime novels written by women throughout the world and across time. If you did, your study would never be finished! Obviously, the population of sources can include only female authors of books classified as true crime. Is the unit of analysis the entire book, chapter, or each male crime victim?

Now, do you want to restrict the population to female authors who published on Canadian cases? Should the true-crime novels be in English only? What range of years should the sample be restricted to? The answers to these questions are dictated by the research question. If you are interested in how portrayals have changed since the advent of the women's movement, looking at 1960 onwards makes sense. However, if the interest is more contemporary, a shorter time frame would be more relevant.

Once you have defined the universe, choose a sampling technique. Again, the type depends on the research question. You might use a purposive sampling technique when substantive criteria dictate the relevance of sources. For instance, a content analysis was conducted on newspaper reports of executions between 2006 and 2011, to understand family members' feelings after the execution in areas such as justice, closure, and healing (Burton & Tewksbury, 2013). Purposive sampling was used to ensure relevance by selecting only those articles that included the victim's family members' feelings about the executed person. In our example, if you adopt a probability sampling technique, create a sampling frame by making or obtaining a list of all true-crime novels published by the five largest publishers in North America. Record the time of publication as anything from 1960 onwards and then use simple random sampling to select a hundred novels.

Do you have to sample? The answer is, in most cases, yes. Although some studies, such as Schulenberg and Chenier's (2014) analysis of media portrayals of police and protesters at Toronto's 2010 G20 Summit, use the universe within a bounded period of time, it is typically unwise to analyze the universe due to an impossibly large sample size. With that said, circumstances can result in analyzing the universe because the population is too small. You can imagine that, within a specific period of time, an investigation into the nutritional value of death row inmate's last meal requests would be small and the analysis of the universe appropriate. Wansink, Kniffin, and Shimizu (2012) conducted such a study and found that the average last meal is high in calories (2,756) and 2.5 times the recommended intake for protein and fat; 40 per cent of requests include name brand food or beverages (p. 837).

Coding Categories

A **coding system** represents the process of conceptualization and operationalization and needs to be meaningful in relation to the research questions and theoretical concepts. The coding method is determined in advance, with decisions made on the specificity of coding. For both quantitative and qualitative analyses, the researcher creates a coding manual outlining coding rules for the words, symbols, images, and (in qualitative research) the themes. Think of it as the difference between a priori and emergent coding. In both cases, it's in the form of a data collection sheet that lists all the categories and dimensions to be coded for each unit of analysis.

For example, one content analysis used a stratified sample of over 650 police agencies to examine the prevalence, predictors, website content, and extent that information is disseminated versus collected online (Rosenbaum et al., 2011). The coding system was based on two types of information: output (information from the police to the public) and input (ways the police gather information from the public). Here are two examples from the coding manual for output and input measures:

Output: Links—Both the content and number of links to external websites about social, legal, city, and other law enforcement services were quantified and recorded. Only links on the home page of a site, accessible through a single portal on the home page, or provided in a site index were considered. For agency sites housed within city or county sites, links offered through the overriding site were categorized as agency links only if accessible from the agency's home page (p. 32).

Input: Contact mechanisms—To measure mechanisms on the sites that allow citizens to contact or communicate with the police (apart from reporting incidents and surveys), we looked for the presence of email addresses for the agency and individual officers, feedback forms, sign-in books, message boards, and listservs (p. 34).

Quantitative content analysis can measure four communication aspects. Categories can measure the frequency, that is, whether it occurs and

> **coding system** a classification system or set of rules to code words, phrases, symbols, sounds, or images.

the percentage out of the total number of articles. It can measure the direction of the message along a continuum, such as supportive and unsupportive or positive and negative. The intensity can be assessed in terms of the strength and importance given to the message. Finally, researchers record the space allocated to the message in centimetres, paragraphs, or minutes. Coding buzz words and the frequency in which they appear is one way to demonstrate the salience of ideas. The importance of a message in respect to manifest and latent content could be assessed based on the newspaper article's size or location (e.g. front page, Section A, or specialized sections).

Concise coding definitions allow you to recognize the category in the data consistently. As with survey questions, each category must be mutually exclusive and exhaustive. Further, as the number of categories increases, so do the analytical possibilities, but this change may be at the expense of the reliability and validity of the coded data. Once the categories are established, use empirical and theoretical ideas to list the dimensions of each category (e.g. types of behaviour, ideas, symbols, characteristics, sex).

Quantitative categories and dimensions can be complex, be it identifying certain words, phrases, or images in advance or counting their frequency or position. Qualitative content analysis takes a different approach: themes are identified in advance, but their meaning and dimensions are defined during coding and analysis. Thus, some argue that coding how messages are presented in a larger context can be easier and potentially more meaningful. For instance, the theme of types of crime for youth versus adults in television shows initially requires a less complex coding manual.

Consistent with survey research, it's important to conduct a pretest by having others code the same

intra-rater reliability the extent to which assigned codes for the same text are equivalent and stable when coded by the same person at two different periods of time.

inter-coder reliability the extent of agreement between two or more coders to ensure that the code is assigned in the same way.

data and to compare their judgments for consistency. Coding reliability needs to be high to ensure accuracy and valid inferences. People can code the same text differently and "reliability problems usually grow out of the ambiguity of word meanings, category definitions, or other coding rules" (Weber, 1990, p. 15). This problem is particularly of concern with latent content because there is no definitive way to avoid subjective judgments. Such intersubjectivity only increases the importance of making the case that these subjective judgments are consistent across coders (Lombard, Snyder-Duch, & Campanella-Bracken, 2004). The fewer decisions and interpretations a coder must make, the higher the reliability. With content analysis, you assess two types of reliability.

The first type is stability reliability, also known as **intra-rater reliability**. If coding extends over a period of time, a coder recodes text examined earlier to determine the extent to which similarity exists for the coding categories. If the researcher is the only coder, a test–retest will assess the degree of consistency and measurement error. Recall that this reliability test involves coding the same section of data by the same person at two different periods of time.

The second type is reproducibility, or equivalence reliability. To test for **inter-coder reliability**, also known as interrater reliability, multiple coders work with the same text and calculate the extent to which their coding is consistent with each other. Snook and colleagues' (2010) content analysis of police cautions had an interrater reliability coefficient of 0.93, which is above the minimum level required for valid inferences. For intra- and interrater reliability, the minimum degree of agreement should be 0.90, or 90 per cent, and higher; 0.80 or greater is acceptable but not preferred (Lombard et al., 2004).

Strengths and Limitations

As with all unobtrusive methods, content analysis removes the possibility of any reactivity bias. Other data collection methods can be difficult to use without collaborators or research assistants, but that is not true for content analysis. This method is ideal for gauging values and testing preliminary ideas as part of a pilot study; it can also be combined with other methods to check and enhance the validity of inferences and conclusions.

On the other hand, content analysis is not ideal for testing causal relationships because there is a real risk of making incorrect inferences. The results can describe only the content of the communication, not the author's motivations or intentions or the audience's reaction and interpretation. In other words, content analysis can tell us what is there but not the effect or causes of a particular interpretation. It is, by definition, limited to recorded information. This unobtrusive method is reliable in terms of manifest content, but there are threats to validity in respect to attributing meaning through latent content. Finally, remember that culturally bound communications and sample limitations both reduce the generalizability of the findings.

Secondary Data Analysis

Secondary data is popular in crime and justice research and is used to investigate virtually all topics. For example, one criminological study confronted the problem of conceptual inconsistences when testing routine activities theory by using two waves of longitudinal data from the Mobile Youth Survey (Spano, Freilich, & Bolland, 2008). With a sample of 9- to 19-year-olds in high-poverty neighbourhoods, the dataset was exactly what was needed, as prior research had not investigated this population and it contained variables for key concepts. The researchers' findings have methodological implications because the previously identified relationship between being in a gang and carrying guns may be due to measurement differences and to not analyzing a sample of high-poverty cases.

Statistics Canada is a valuable source of secondary data. *The Daily*, published every week since 1932, provides an overview of available data and new datasets released; it can also include summary tables and charts, all searchable by keyword. Available through your university library, E-STAT allows researchers to display, in tabular or graphical format, summary data using variables of their choosing. The results can then be exported into a statistical software or Microsoft Office program. If what you are looking for isn't available through E-STAT, you can purchase customized datasets directly from Statistics Canada or submit a research proposal and use a dataset available in Research Data Centres across the country.

The research steps for secondary data analysis are similar to those for other unobtrusive measures. The first step is to clarify the research problem, questions, and hypotheses. Next is the thorny issue of measurement, as you are not the person who designed the data collection instrument and cannot control operationalization. Explore what datasets are available in your substantive area. In each case, ask yourself the following questions: How were the data collected? What variables are included? Are you able to measure key concepts adequately? What are the dataset's strengths and limitations? Finally, you need to access the data, prepare it for analysis, code new variables, and analyze and interpret the results.

Official Statistics

The primary sources for official statistics are government and criminal justice agencies. In respect to the latter, researchers often need a sponsor or gatekeeper to gain access to the data. This requirement is a main reason why they use official statistics. Criminal justice agencies across the country submit their data to Statistics Canada, where the information is amalgamated, analyzed, and made available to researchers. For example, Webster and colleagues (2009) used Statistics Canada data on imprisonment rates to understand why the rate of holding people in custody while awaiting trial continues to increase despite the decrease in the crime rate. Using official statistics, they found that cases involving offences against the administration of justice (e.g. breach of probation, failure to appear in court) are much more likely to result in a police decision to detain for a bail hearing. This and other findings led them to conclude that there is a risk ratio in the decision-making process. The criminal justice system is seen as responsible when an accused reoffends upon release, resulting in the "get tough on crime" approach.

Cross-cultural, cross-sectional, and longitudinal research is possible with official statistics. For instance, the National Longitudinal Survey of Children and Youth (NLSCY) records the development and well-being of a sample from birth to 25 years of age. Data include social, emotional, and behavioural factors and their impact on the child's development over time. The International Youth Survey is Canada's contribution to the International Self-Report Delinquency Survey of youth in grades 7 to 9 in the United States, Canada, and over thirty European countries (see Appendix D). Specialized surveys are also available. For example, the Conditional Sentencing Special Study from Statistics Canada allowed Roberts and Gabor (2004) to examine the effectiveness of conditional sentences. They found a significant drop in admissions to custody, with changes to the criteria for using this disposition. The final advantage is that official criminal justice statistics are often based on the entire population, not a sample, as would be the case when using records from one agency in a particular province.

Vignette: Breaking It Down

The Uniform Crime Reporting Survey: What Do We Know about Crime?

The Uniform Crime Reporting Survey (UCR) measures the number of crimes reported to the police, the disposition, and the people involved (Statistics Canada, 2012). Only substantiated cases (i.e. ones with sufficient evidence to determine that an offence occurred) are included. Summary data are provided on almost 100 different criminal offences. The aggregate UCR 1.0 began in 1962. Despite the long history, it is difficult to use this survey to make direct comparisons over time for some offences due to varying definitions (stability reliability) and reporting practices (equivalence reliability) in the early years. Introduced in 1988, the UCR 2.2 is incident-based, providing individual-level data on the crime, victim, and accused.

One argument regarding the UCR is that police statistics are systematically biased and poor indicators of crime. As Skogan (1999, p. 38) points out, the traditional law enforcement framework produces "a torrent of data on crime and disorderly conditions; these data were sometimes of dubious quality, and now they are becoming increasingly unreliable." Low levels of police-reported crime could be a reflection of public confidence in the police and could say little about how crime is experienced (Kelling, 1999). Mischief is considered a minor crime, but stomping on an elderly person's garden could affect the victim differently than it would a corporation. Questioning public confidence is valid, as the extent of minor criminal offending is higher when using data from self-report surveys (Bruce & Desmond, 1998; Weisner, Capaldi, & Kim, 2007). Of concern is that these statistics serve as a measure of official crime and provide a framework for the media, public, and government to understand this social problem.

Stephens (1999) summarizes three criticisms launched against the UCR. To become educated consumers of police crime statistics, it is important to recognize these limitations.

There are those who argue that official crime statistics are some of the most unreliable numbers because of the difference between the reported crime rate and the actual amount of criminal activity. Only crime known to the police is captured in official statistics. Therefore, researchers must be aware of the dark figure of crime when drawing conclusions based on the analysis of official statistics. Further, certain types of crime, such as sexual assault, have lower reporting rates; methods of measuring variables change over time; and reported crime based on proactive police initiatives can increase. By the same token, the police may not enforce particular laws as stringently in certain neighbourhoods.

Crime statistics point to a larger issue of using official statistics. The data are not collected by the researcher and are often gathered for administrative purposes. Always look for the potential differences between reported and actual rates of behaviour and events or whether the characteristics of those in the sample are representative of the population. Also, remember that all data collection methods collect information that is subject to varying degrees of error and threats to validity, reliability, and generalizability. The trick is to acknowledge this fact and take steps to minimize the impact on inferences.

One criticism is that the likelihood that a crime will be reported to the police reflects the size of the agency, whereby the reporting is less likely with larger agencies. Using three different surveys, Levitt (1998) found a degree of reporting bias with five

1. Whether it is the aggregate or incident-based UCR, it reflects only police-reported crime. This limitation is magnified by how the information is used by others. It is not unheard of for media coverage to neglect this fact, leaving the audience to assume that these statistics reflect the actual level and nature of crime in a community.
2. The aggregate UCR survey follows a hierarchy rule that only the most serious offence is counted. This rule underestimates minor offending when more than one offence is substantiated in the same incident. The incident-based UCR offers an excellent alternative, as it records the four most serious offences.
3. Despite stringent reporting regulations, it is still the police who classify data. Concerns of potential manipulation, mistakes made despite the quality control measures taken by Statistics Canada, and the impact of proactive activities are raised. Thus, official crime statistics are perhaps a better reflection of police practice than criminal behaviour.

In Montreal, Boivin and Cordeau (2011) found differential recording practices by type of offence rather than increases in the number of crimes from reports by the public or proactive initiatives. Brennan (2012) confirms that police-reported crime statistics are influenced by police policies and procedures; demographic and social factors; jurisdictional differences; and public perceptions. The volume of crime known to the police is also affected by shifts in alcohol consumption and employment rates in a community (Pottie-Bunge, Johnson, & Baldé, 2005). Interviews and systematic social observation can help illuminate potential reasons for the impact of these factors on recording crime. The bottom line is to be aware of what your data can and cannot tell you.

of the more serious violent offences. This problem is why some researchers choose to use self-report or victimization surveys instead of official statistics based on police-reported incidents.

Advantages and Limitations

When compared to original data collection, secondary data are cost- and time-efficient. Samples, non-response, data collection procedures, generalizability (e.g. national samples), and experienced researchers developing the data collection instruments contribute to high-quality data. In addition, you have more time for analysis when you don't have to collect your own data. Cross-sectional, longitudinal, and cross-cultural research are possible because different waves of data collection recycle questions, giving you data on the same variables at different points in time. Due to the larger sample size, there are enough cases to analyze subgroups in the population.

Yet comparative research can pose challenges. One cross-cultural study used secondary data from the World Health Organization and the International Social Survey Program to investigate the hypothesis that people who live in high-crime-rate countries are more likely to believe in punitive approaches (Stack, Cao, & Adamzyck, 2007). The researchers encountered a problem: measuring the frequency of crime was not comparable across nations because of operationalizating crime differently. However, the researchers used homicide data, considered the most accurate crime data. Incidentally, they found support for their hypothesis.

Sampson and Laub (2003) conducted a unique study that not only used secondary data but also collected new data to expand and update the dataset. They used secondary data collected by the Gluecks in the 1950s and conducted a 35-year follow-up on the individuals who participated in the original longitudinal survey. A dataset with information from the age of 14 to 70 was created. Sampson and Laub investigated whether a distinct group of offenders who offend at a stable frequency and seriousness throughout their lives exists. They found that this is not the case and that there are also no specific individual, childhood, or family background characteristics unique to desistance from crime.

In terms of limitations, consider the fact that the data were collected for a different purpose and are almost exclusively quantitative. This limitation can create measurement problems because you may not be able to operationalize your concepts in the most appropriate way. Considerable time is needed to learn the dataset and what each of the variables actually means. For one research study, I used a dataset on a national sample of men and women on probation to look at their noncompliant behaviour (Schulenberg, 2007b). The secondary data available didn't allow me to operationalize this in terms of breaching various conditions but I could use the proxies of missing a payment, a reprimand due to rule violations, and appearing before a disciplinary hearing. I could not generalize to the more serious offenders because the dataset included only those whose probation wasn't revoked as a result of noncompliant behaviour. Further, I easily spent fifty hours learning the dataset and preparing the data for analysis, a short period of time in comparison to longitudinal datasets.

Larger datasets (particularly longitudinal) are often complex, with many variables, cases, and levels of aggregation. As previously discussed, this complexity opens you up to the risk of committing the ecological fallacy, whereby conclusions are made about individuals when the data are at a higher level of aggregation, such as groups or the community. For instance, let's say the crime rate is higher in areas with a larger concentration of youth. You commit the ecological fallacy if you say that teenagers are more likely to break the law and get arrested.

There are also concerns about validity. Just because something is appropriate for the original study's research purpose does not mean it is for yours. Does the data provide measures that can adequately operationalize your key concepts? As I have found in my own research, the answer is often no. Yet, even when you collect your own data, you work with imperfect measures due to the threats to validity, reliability, and generalizability associated with each data collection method.

Key Thinker

Peter J. Carrington

Peter J. Carrington completed his undergraduate degree in philosophy at Harvard University (1970) and earned a MA (1975) and PhD (1981) in sociology from the University of Toronto. He joined the University of Waterloo faculty in 1984 and, using secondary data, established himself as an authority in the areas of youth crime, criminal careers, and social networks. I had the opportunity to ask Peter a few questions about his work (Carrington, personal communication, 18 July 2013).

> **JS:** What types of research problems interest you?
>
> **PC:** I study networks and criminal careers, which intersect as criminals have careers and are also involved in networks formed by committing crimes with other criminals. I also look at changes in crime rates and seriousness over time to assess trends and the impact of new legislation. For instance, Figure 8.2 uses data from the incident-based UCR to demonstrate the Youth Criminal Justice Act is effective at structuring police discretion since less youth are charged and referred to youth court since 2003.

For criminal careers, I use the incident-based UCR and the Youth Court and Adult Criminal Court Surveys. For crime rate trends, I use the aggregate UCR. In the past, I also used the Homicide Survey, the National Longitudinal Survey of Children and Youth, and the victimization module of the General Social Survey.v

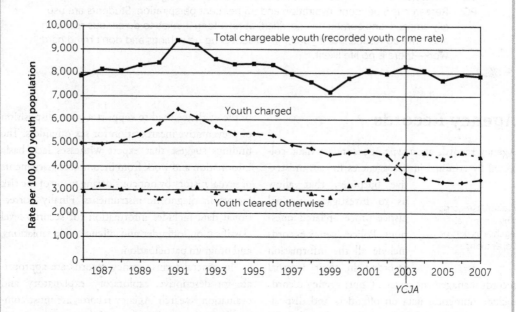

Figure 8.2 The effect of legislative change on police responses to youth crime

Source: Statistics Canada Canadian Centre for Justice Systems.

continued

JS: In your opinion, what are the advantages of using secondary data?

PC: First, these datasets provide comprehensive national or quasi-national coverage, eliminating the need to rely on statistical significance tests. Second, they have very large sample sizes, allowing for sub-group analyses and precise statistical estimates. Third, the data are extremely inexpensive and faster (at least in principle) than collecting one's own data. Finally, retrospective data are available for longitudinal research, whereas it is not feasible to collect one's own data unless one is willing to wait many years while subjects age!

JS: What do researchers need to consider [when] accessing this data?

PC: Accessing aggregate data is fairly straightforward and there's a growing amount of it available free from the university library and the Statistics Canada's website. For incident-based (individual-level) data, many projects are possible in the Research Data Centres (RDC). Each RDC has at least one Statistics Canada analyst who helps users access and use the facilities. I have found them very helpful. It's also possible to pay for custom datasets but I haven't found that to be a very fruitful approach.

The big drawback of secondary data is that the variables needed are not necessarily in the dataset. So the first thing to do before committing to using a dataset is to make sure it has the variables one needs and that they were collected and coded in a way that satisfies one's needs. Another drawback is that access to the data—whether public use or through the RDCs—is not nearly as straightforward as I may make it sound. It becomes fairly straightforward with experience, but getting that experience can be painful and time-consuming.

JS: What would your advice be to students about conducting research?

PC: Research is 5 per cent inspiration and 95 per cent perspiration. Students are usually amazed (and sometimes horrified) at how long it takes to do serious research and write up results. But if you enjoy discovering new things and don't mind hard work—there is no life like it.

Agency Records

Agency records are a type of secondary data, collected by criminal justice agencies for administrative purposes, that allow us to investigate criminal justice process-related questions. Police agency records include all the information recorded in their internal records management system. Court agency records include numerical data on offenders and dispositions. For example, Habermeyer and colleagues (2009) analyzed expert witness testimony and judge statements from court records in their exploration

agency records records created by a criminal justice agency as part of normal operations.

of the evidence used to support a court disposition of preventative incarceration for sex offenders. The findings suggest that expert witnesses lack basic information and work from incomplete assessments of sexual history by not considering many of the risk factors in diagnostic instruments. Finally, correctional data includes information for security-level classification, offender and offence, rule violations, and program participation.

In general terms, agency records are appropriate for descriptive, exploratory, explanatory, and evaluation research. Agency records are most commonly used in exploratory and descriptive research and are ideal for applied research, such as evaluating policies, developing evidence-based practice, or being part of a mixed methods study. While official crime statistics are appropriate for investigating aggregate trends or patterns, agency records can provide greater contextual detail. However, the only way to determine if this type of data is suitable for addressing the research question is to look at how the records are created.

Types of Agency Records

Crime and justice researchers use two types of agency records: non-public and new data collected by the agency. In the first case, criminal justice agencies usually make administrative data available to researchers who submit a proposal, providing that individuals are not identifiable or the information is not legally restricted. Avoid time-intensive data extraction requests, or the agency may not be willing to devote the human resources necessary to create the dataset. The other thing to keep in mind is the possibility of record-keeping problems. Unexpected findings could be linked to the validity or reliability in record-keeping practices. Criminal justice and government agencies are often more concerned about efficiency and costs associated with data collection than they are about rigour, reliability, and validity (Haggerty, 2001).

With the second type, agency personnel create or modify forms and collect information for a specific research purpose. To investigate racial profiling, Wortley and Marshall (2005) asked patrol officers to complete contact cards recording the race of people they stopped in Kingston, Ontario. In the United States, the Arrestee Drug Abuse Monitoring (ADAM) project is administered four times a year. Arrestees at county jails voluntarily provide an anonymous urine sample to correctional personnel so that researchers can understand the prevalence of drug use by type of offence (National Institute of Justice, 2013).

The advantages of agency personnel collecting new data is that it costs less than if the researchers collect the data themselves. There is also more control over measurement, as it is no longer entirely dependent on how the agency defines a concept.

The disadvantages include challenges associated with securing agency co-operation. The likelihood of co-operation varies by the degree of additional work and operational disruptions. Further, agency personnel may place less priority on data collection than on their regular duties.

Methodological Concerns

Many of the methodological concerns regarding agency records can be understood in two ways. The first category focuses on various research design logistics, such as measurement, reliability, and validity. The second concerns the social construction of knowledge for organizational purposes.

Considering the Logistics

If the agency records are longitudinal, changes in procedures or operational definitions affect reliability and validity. Think of it this way: you want to avoid claiming that a change occurred when it was actually caused by changes in how the agency collects and records data. Similarly, a threat to reliability is based on human nature. Errors increase with the volume of data; the more data the agency collects and stores over time, the harder it becomes to detect errors or duplicate records.

This all boils down to the fact that researchers have no control over how the data are collected or recorded. The vignette on pages 244–245 gives a few good examples of this general problem in relation to the Uniform Crime Reporting Survey (UCR). Stability reliability is compromised with longitudinal datasets when changes in definitions occur over time. For example, amendments to the *Criminal Code* of Canada changed the offence of rape to three levels of sexual assault in 1981. Making comparisons on the prevalence of this type of criminal behaviour is unwise due to the absence of stability reliability. Equivalence reliability is lacking when there are differences in how agencies define or record information.

Using law enforcement as an example, you may wonder how it is possible that police services can record solved crimes differently. A clearance rate is the proportion of incidents that result in laying a criminal charge or dealing with the offence in other ways (e.g. warning). According to Mahoney and Turner (2012), different criteria are used for determining if sufficient evidence exists to clear an incident. Factors affecting the choice to record an incident as cleared include policies and practice when deciding on minor offences and the reporting technologies used (e.g. phone, in person, or online).

Social Construction

Agency records are as much a reflection of decision-making by criminal justice personnel as they are about behaviour. Recall that the UCR secondary data are created based on agency record submissions to Statistics Canada. An analysis that compares data from the self-report NLSCY to the UCR finds "official measures of offending by youths in Canada are best seen as reflections of the behaviour of adults in responding to youths rather than of the behaviour of youths" (Sprott & Doob, 2008, pp. 634–635).

Further, the data's validity and recording method is an artefact of an agency's organizational capacity to capture and track data. As seen with the discussion on equivalence reliability, systemic differences exist in terms of how certain types of behaviour are recorded, and even small data entry mistakes can compound when summary statistics are produced. For instance, entering 99 instead of 9 will skew the average when the majority of individuals score between 5 and 20. No matter how flawed criminologists believe agency records can be, the law requires the police, courts, and corrections to collect data. The technical difficulty is that these records are not intended to be measures of the prevalence and nature of crime or the effectiveness of the police service to respond to criminal behaviour (Klockars, 1999).

For instance, Rojek and Decker (2009) investigated the disciplinary process for minority police officers by analyzing internal affairs case files over a five-year period. A total of 2,239 allegations of misconduct were lodged against officers; however,

the researchers had to remove 533 of them from the analysis. These files did not contain the officer's numerical identifier, meaning that the allegation couldn't be linked to the database on officer characteristics with the key variable of race. The researchers discovered that this situation wasn't an accident; department policy dictates that the police service not maintain records on "officer information [for] allegations that were eventually withdrawn by the complainant, where the finding of the allegation was unfounded, or the officer was exonerated" (p. 394).

From a different perspective, criminal behaviour narratives are written in a way that aids the prosecution (Alison, Snook, & Stein, 2001). Court case documents must not only establish the facts but also present a convincing argument that a particular person has committed the crime. Alison and colleagues point out that information on the situational context that may be of interest to researchers is not included. Overall, researchers who use agency data are encouraged to "pay considerable attention to potential oversights, inaccuracies, embellishments, and constructions" (p. 250).

Not all is lost with organizational data. Bear one thing in mind when approaching an agency to access the data or have it collect new data: if the data and anticipated findings are useful for making operational decisions, organizations are much more attentive to data quality and are willing to release data.

GIS and Crime Mapping

Agency records are used internally by police services and externally by researchers to explore the spatial distribution of crime through Geographic Information Systems (GIS) analysis. When people think of crime mapping, the first thing that comes to mind is hot spot policing. Recall that hot spots are defined as small geographical areas where crime frequently occurs. This mapping began in 1989 with a study using spatial data on over 323,000 calls for service at 115,000 addresses and intersections (Sherman et al., 1989). The key finding was that a small number of hot spots produces the most calls for service (i.e. 50 per cent of calls originate from 3 per cent of the places).

The process of crime mapping is beyond the scope of this textbook. What is important to know is that GIS analyses use dispatch data to study how space interacts with the criminal justice processes and behaviours we are trying to understand. For instance, the GPS latitude and longitude coordinates for each incident are plotted in conjunction with specific crime correlates such as age, type of offence, or neighbourhood characteristics. Using census data, Map 8.1 shows the distribution of visible minorities in Toronto. Maps 8.2 and 8.3 depict crime maps using incident-based UCR data supplied by the Toronto Police Service to Statistics Canada.

Crime maps are now available on some police service websites. They are also appearing in media reports more frequently. For instance, a CBC (2012) report featured an interactive map using crime data for 140 Toronto neighbourhoods, broken down into assaults, sexual assaults, break-ins, robberies, drug charges, stolen vehicles, thefts over $5,000, and homicides. Neighbourhoods are ranked for each offence category. The Toronto Police Service advises that these maps be interpreted with caution because resources are deployed after accounting for many factors, including criminal intelligence, history, and demographics. One example given is that higher downtown crime rates could be explained by the higher concentration of bars and nightclubs in the area.

Agency records are used for spatial analyses in exploratory, descriptive, explanatory, and evaluation research. Crime-mapping studies are ideal for supporting community policing initiatives by identifying crime patterns within patrol zones. Mapping calls for service can assist agencies with resource allocation and officer deployment

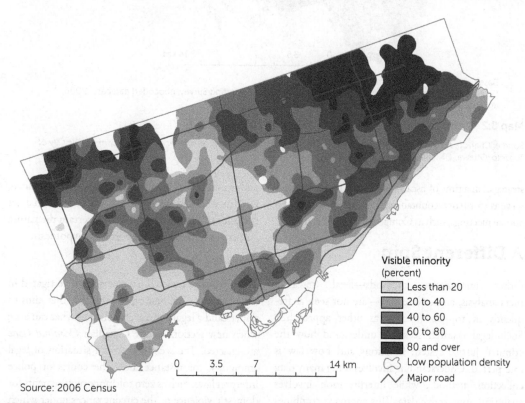

Visible minority
(percent)
- Less than 20
- 20 to 40
- 40 to 60
- 60 to 80
- 80 and over
- Low population density
- Major road

0   3.5   7   14 km

Source: 2006 Census

Map 8.1 Percentage of visible minorities in Toronto, 2006

Source: Charron, M. (2009). *Neighbourhood characteristics and the distribution of police-reported crime in the City of Toronto*. Ottawa, ON: Statistics Canada, p. 9.

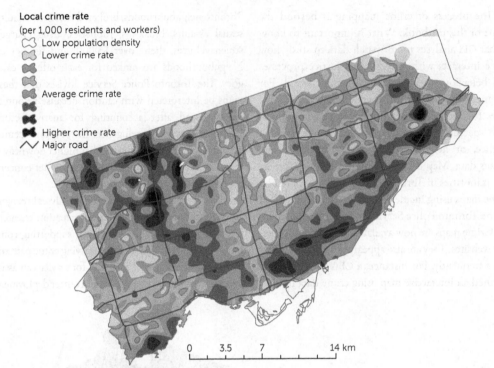

Local crime rate
(per 1,000 residents and workers)
- Low population density
- Lower crime rate

- Average crime rate

- Higher crime rate
- Major road

0   3.5   7   14 km

Based on 26,040 violent crime incidents,
Sources: Statistics Canada, incident-based Uniform Crime Reporting Survey, geocoded database, 2006;
and 2006 Census.

Map 8.2 Mapping the youth violent crime rate in Toronto, 2006

Source: Charron, M. (2009). *Neighbourhood characteristics and the distribution of police-reported crime in the City of Toronto*. Ottawa, ON: Statistics Canada, p. 12.

strategies in a time of fiscal constraint. Crime maps also serve as a form of accountability for effectiveness at operational meetings, such as CompStat.

A Different Spin

Other unobtrusive methods—legal research, meta-analysis, and online data—are not seen as frequently in top-tier journals as other approaches. Socio-legal research seeks to understand how the criminal justice system functions and how law is interpreted. Understanding involves using many data collection methods, while interpretation involves analyzing nonreactive data. This approach combines social science data collection methods with a legal case law analysis; the researcher uses "inductive methods to compare cases and laws across groups, institutions,

and jurisdictions" (Nolasco, Vaughn, & del Carmen, 2010, p. 17). Researchers who conduct meta-analyses use prior research as their data to ascertain the nature and extent of empirical support for a hypothesis.

Legal Research

Three types of research problems are investigated in legal research. The first type is research that aims to understand a legal controversy, such as what can arise when new sections of the Canadian *Criminal Code* are enacted. The second type is a situation of legal ambiguity, for instance, how the courts or police interpret laws, such as zero tolerance requirements for domestic violence or the circumstances under which evidence is considered admissible in court. Finally, legal research examines the implementation of the law, which could entail analyzing police practices

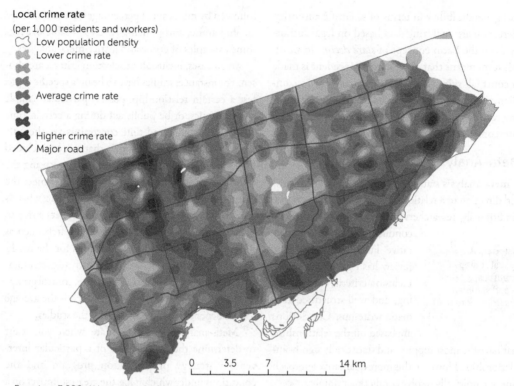

Local crime rate
(per 1,000 residents and workers)
- Low population density
- Lower crime rate

- Average crime rate

- Higher crime rate
- Major road

0   3.5   7   14 km

Based on 3,926 violent crime incidents,
Sources: Statistics Canada, incident-based Uniform Crime Reporting Survey, geocoded database, 2006;
and 2006 Census.

Map 8.3 Mapping major assault incidents committed by youth in Toronto, 2006

Source: Charron, M. (2009). *Neighbourhood characteristics and the distribution of police-reported crime in the City of Toronto.* Ottawa, ON: Statistics Canada, p. 46.

used with prostitution or understanding the genesis of proposed legislative change. For example, Hyshka (2009) conducted a legal analysis of various bills to decriminalize cannabis. The findings led her to conclude that, despite best intentions, "what is clear is that Canada's 'saga of promise, hesitation, and retreat' in cannabis-law reform continues today" (p. 86).

The first step in conducting legal research is to select a research problem and formulate the research question(s) within the parameters of a specific and feasible objective. If the research question isn't specific enough, you will be lost for days, months, and years in case law files available on Westlaw or LexisNexis. As with all other approaches, plan in advance for every stage in the research process, from measurement to sampling and data analysis. A clear

research design will make achieving your goal—to understand trends or historical events—much easier. Once you have collected your case law or other forms of legal documentation (e.g. court transcripts), you approach data analysis much in the same way you would historical or content analysis. It is an inductive approach that requires you to learn the argot because the legal system has its own language, phraseology, and logic.

In terms of legal analysis, there are some important general guidelines. To analyze legal meaning, you want to understand the facts of the case, identify the legal issue or controversy, uncover the legal principles framing the case, and describe the legal reasoning used in the case (Kraska & Neuman, 2012). To this point, we have talked about validity, reliability, and generalizability in terms of scientific authority. Here, you are analyzing data based on legal authority from the Latin concept of *stare decisis*. In short, this term means that, once a legal precedent is made in court, all subsequent decisions are to be in compliance with this precedent unless there is a compelling reason for a deviation. Thus, legal research is an interconnected, iterative process.

Meta-Analysis

A **meta-analysis** statistically determines the strength and direction of a relationship across multiple studies. Traditionally, researchers synthesize past research by conducting a systematic, narrative literature review. The review has explicit objectives, inclusion criteria, careful coding, and well-structured thematic write-ups. Conclusions are based on the relationships that have the most support and statistically significant relationships. However, this more qualitative approach cannot empirically resolve conflicting findings.

> **meta-analysis** a systematic analytical strategy used to statistically combine and summarize the results from more than one study.

A meta-analytic review is "combining the results of many different studies, analyzing the patterns of variation and agreement across studies, and triangulated to a more precise and reliable estimate of the common patterns" (Wells, 2009, p. 270). Pratt (2010) uses the analogy of a batting average, which doesn't simply count the number of base hits but the number of hits per game by the number of times the player was at bat per game. Other factors, such as runners in scoring positions, the stadium, and left- versus right-handed pitchers, are taken into account. Meta-analysis does the same thing, except with research findings and the methodological characteristics of the study.

Meta-analysis is not used as frequently in criminology and criminal justice research as it is in other disciplines. However, this appears to be slowly changing. Wells (2009) conducted a meta-analysis of 176 meta-analytic studies between 1978 and 2005, of which over half were published from 2000 to 2005. Thirty-eight per cent were in the area of crime and delinquency and 31 per cent in corrections,

followed by much small percentages in courts, drug/alcohol abuse, and policing (p. 279). Table 8.1 lists some examples of crime and justice meta-analyses.

In all cases, inclusion or selection criteria are chosen. For instance, studies have to be on a specific topic, test a certain relationship, possess particular sample characteristics, or be published during a certain time frame. Availability and time constraints are the only limits to the number of studies that can be included in a meta-analysis. Databases are searched using the same keywords, and only those studies that meet the selection criteria are included. To combat what is known as a file-drawer problem, researchers strive to include published and unpublished research, such as dissertations. A meta-analysis accounts for the methodological rigour or quality of the study (e.g. randomized controlled experiment, sample size, control group) and then calculates an effect size, which is the average for the dependent variable across all the studies.

Meta-analyses are appropriate when you want to determine the effectiveness of a particular intervention strategy or prevention program and the conditions under which it has the greatest impact on a person's behaviour. As seen in Table 8.1, another topic is determining if the relationship between risk factors is large enough to explain behaviour theoretically. Conducting a narrative review on a substantive topic and finding mixed and conflicting results is a perfect situation for conducting a meta-analysis. The ability to clarify this ambiguity strengthens the argument that it should be a normal part of criminal justice research rather than an "alternative methodology marginal to mainstream research and to evidence-based policy development" (Wells, 2009, p. 289).

Pratt (2010) outlines several advantages and limitations of meta-analysis. This type of analysis provides one numerical estimate of the size and direction of a relationship between two variables, which is intuitively appealing and compelling evidence. Second, you can control for the research design of each study and any possible impact it may have on the conclusions. Third, it is easy to replicate because the studies are listed and the coding is made explicit. Finally, when new research is published, it

Table 8.1 Examples of meta-analysis research

Author	Title	Sample	Findings
Campbell, French, and Gendreau (2009)	"The Prediction of Violence in Adult Offenders: A Meta-Analytic Comparison of Instruments and Methods of Assessment"	88 studies 1980–2006	Static risk factors (e.g. prior record) are better predictors of institutional violence and dynamic (e.g. employment status) of violent recidivism.
Kochel, Wilson, and Mastrofski (2011)	"Effect of Suspect Race on Officers' Arrest Decisions"	40 studies 1966–2004	Minority suspects are more likely to be arrested.
Leschied et al. (2008)	"Childhood Predictors of Adult Criminality: A Meta-Analysis Drawn from the Prospective Longitudinal Literature"	38 studies 1994–2004	Dynamic risk factors in childhood and adolescence are better predictors of adult criminality than static (e.g. aggression, attention-seeking, anxiety, negative parenting strategies, family conflict).
Tong and Farrington (2006)	"How Effective is the 'Reasoning and Rehabilitation' Programme in Reducing Offending? A Meta-Analysis of Evaluations in Four Countries"	16 studies 1988–2003 Canada US UK Sweden	The 36-week program seeks to teach youth not what to think but how to think. Fourteen per cent fewer program participants than non-participants reoffended.
Welsh and Farrington (2009)	"Public Area CCTV and Crime Prevention: An Updated Systematic Review and Meta-Analysis"	44 studies 1978–2007	Crime decreased in areas with CCTV by 16 per cent, primarily due to a decrease of 51 per cent when cameras were placed in parking garages.
Wilson and Lipsey (2000)	"Wilderness Challenge Programs for Delinquent Youth: A Meta-Analysis of Outcome Evaluations"	28 studies 1967–1992	Twenty-nine per cent of program participants reoffended compared to 37 per cent of non-participants. The largest decreases in delinquent behaviour were with programs featuring intense physical activity and a therapeutic component.

can easily be added to the database and a new effect size calculated. However, researchers need to be cognizant of potential journal bias toward publishing research with statistically significant findings.

Online Data

Online data may represent a new frontier in crime and justice research. Such data does not fit neatly into the traditional categories for unobtrusive methods and nonreactive data. The use of the Internet, e-mail, social networking, discussion forums,

e-commerce, and virtual communities has grown exponentially. The impact on criminal networks and communities is assumed but not well understood. We have unique forms of offending under the category of cybercrime, but how do we learn more about electronic communications between criminals?

Holt (2010) explores this very issue in an article on strategies for conducting qualitative research using online data. Discussion forums have threads, where postings are made by multiple members on a given topic, that resemble a form of social interaction. The less problematic forums are open (i.e. they don't require a password). Ethical dilemmas arise with closed forums, when access is restricted to those with a username and password. Should you actively engage or conduct covert observations of the threads? As with participant observation, there is no easy answer to this question.

E-mail and instant messaging can be a type of criminal activity. Just think of all the lovely spam mail on bank transfers from Nigeria or elsewhere that you receive. Some researchers have analyzed these messages and found that the words used and the message's structure are similar regardless of the recipient, to increase the chances of someone responding (King & Thomas, 2009).

The logical sources of online data are websites and blogs. However, Holt (2010) raises some excellent methodological concerns centring on the representativeness of information and websites. For example, is the data generalizable when "criminal groups, such as burglars and robbers, may not utilize the Internet as a means of planning and executing the offence" (p. 475)? Search engines are not perfect either. Thus, triangulate and validate results using more than one key word, multiple search engines, and, if necessary, country-specific ones. How valid is the information online? As Holt (2010, p. 477) points out, "it is possible that the information posted in certain sites may be falsified in order to attract offenders. Alternatively, individual users may over exaggerate their actions or lie for the sake of status or clout within a community." This problem is no different from the challenges that researchers face when conducting interviews, content analysis, or participant observation.

Conclusion

Unobtrusive methods and nonreactive data may not initially be on your radar screen, but they represent a rich source of data that can provide context when used in mixed methods research designs. Unobtrusive methods use data that is not subject to reactivity bias, as researchers do not interact with research subjects. However, coverage may be incomplete and the accuracy, authenticity, and credibility difficult to assess. Nonreactive secondary data may be time- and cost-efficient, but access, measurement, reliability, and validity remain concerns. Despite the methodological issues, these are a valuable set of methods and sources of data. They can address important crime and justice research problems and will likely be used more frequently in the future.

Summary of Important Points

Introduction

- Using unobtrusive methods to collect nonreactive data, such as historical, nonparticipant observation, physical trace, content, and secondary data, does not involve interacting with research subjects.
- Physical trace, historical, content, and secondary analysis are ideal for providing context for findings based on other types of data.
- Unobtrusive methods have no reactivity bias, are complementary to others in a mixed methods research design, are adaptable, have fewer ethical concerns, and are cost-efficient.

Historical Research

- Historical research uses archival data to develop theoretical explanations for behaviour and events adhering to the principle of historical specificity.
- Personal documents, photographs, and official documents are evaluated for authenticity, credibility, and representativeness.

- Historical comparative research compares two or more countries, groups, or time periods.

Content Analysis

- Quantitative content analysis focuses on manifest content and numerically assesses the frequency, intensity, direction, and importance of messages.
- Qualitative content analysis emphasizes meaning and thematic coverage and pays attention to latent content.
- Manifest content is explicit in a message and higher in reliability, whereas latent is implied and higher in validity.
- Measurement and sampling decisions are based on the research question and are consistent with a quantitative or qualitative approach.
- Content analysis is not ideal to test for causality as it describes only recorded information.

Secondary Data Analysis

- Official statistics are commonly used in cross-sectional, comparative, and longitudinal research.
- Some argue that official statistics are better indicators of criminal justice practice than behaviour because only crime reported to the police are recorded, some offences have lower reporting rates, and the measurement and recording of variables change over time.
- Secondary data is cost- and time-efficient, is of high quality with large samples, and can allow for longitudinal and subgroup analyses.

- Limitations of secondary data include an inability to measure key concepts, data complexity, and restrictions to (largely) quantitative datasets.

Agency Records

- Agency records are kept as part of normal operations and are most often used in applied research.
- Limitations include concerns about stability and equivalence reliability, access, the data reflecting criminal justice personnel decision-making, and the social construction of crime.
- Crime mapping uses the geographic location of crime incidents with correlates, such as neighbourhood characteristics, to identify crime patterns and inform evidence-based practice.

A Different Spin

- Legal research focuses on understanding legal controversies, ambiguity in the law or its interpretation, and the implementation of law.
- Meta-analyses statistically combine and summarize the strength and direction of a relationship from the results of multiple studies.
- Online data include discussion forums, e-mail, social networking sites, blogs, instant messaging, and websites, all of which have similar limitations of reliability, validity, and generalizability as other nonreactive data.

Conclusion

- Unobtrusive methods and nonreactive data are valuable, address important research problems, and will likely be used more frequently in the future.

Key Terms

Review Questions and Exercises

1. We have all heard about secret diaries written by teenagers. Based on what you have learned, what are the strengths and limitations of using this data source? Would these be any different if the author of the diary was an adult? Why or why not?

2. Watch a thirty-minute television show of your choice. What types of commercials are played? Next, watch thirty minutes from a daily news broadcast. In the context of the material covered in this chapter, what similarities or differences do you see? How might they impact data collection and analysis?

3. Choose an empirical journal article that presents the findings from a content analysis of print, visual, audio, or online communications. Answer the following questions:
   a. What are the research problem and research questions?
   b. Is the research quantitative or qualitative? Why is this approach the most appropriate?
   c. What is the unit of analysis?
   d. How did the researchers select their sample?
   e. How was the data coded?
   f. Do the researchers identify any limitations with this method or sample?

Online Exercises and Websites of Interest

Content-Analysis: Resources on Content and Textual Analyses

www.content-analysis.de/
This site provides a wealth of information, including bibliographies, research studies, software (quantitative and qualitative analyses), and how-to guides.

Content Analysis of Newspaper Articles

www.theglobeandmail.com/search/?q=crime
www.nationalpost.com/search/index.html?q=crime
For no longer than one month, examine the newspaper coverage of a topic of your choice from *The Globe and Mail* or the *National Post*. When conducting your search, limit the number of articles to a maximum of ten. Specify the research problem, define your coding categories and dimensions, develop coding rules, and provide examples of manifest and latent content in your sample of articles.

Inter-University Consortium for Political and Social Research

www.icpsr.umich.edu/index.html
Maintained by the University of Michigan, this site contains quantitative data sets available for download to conduct a secondary data analysis. It includes thousands of datasets on all criminological and criminal-justice-related topics.

Statistics Canada

www.statcan.gc.ca/

Aggregate data tables and publications on all areas of social life, including crime, are available for download from this site. Crime-related publications and data are managed by the Canadian Centre for Justice Statistics.

Additional Resources

Geerken, M.R. (1994). "Rap Sheets in Criminological Research: Considerations and Caveats." *Journal of Quantitative Criminology, 10, 3–21.*

This article explains the production of police arrest records and the implications for researchers in detail.

Krippendorff, K. (2012). *Content Analysis: An Introduction to Its Methodology* (3rd ed.). Thousand Oaks, CA: Sage.

This sourcebook covers the principles of content analysis and provides an introduction to collecting and analyzing print, visual, voice, Internet, and social media communication.

Lee, R.M. (2000). *Unobtrusive Methods in Social Research*. Philadelphia, PA: Open University Press.

This book provides a comprehensive overview of unobtrusive methods and nonreactive data collection and analysis procedures.

Part IV
Interpreting and Making Sense of the Data

Chapter 9

Interpreting Quantitative Data

Statistics can be defined as a "body of methods for making wise decisions in the face of uncertainty." W. Allen Wallis, in Wallis and Roberts, *Statistics: A New Approach* (1956, p. 3)

"An approximate answer to the right problem is worth a good deal more than an exact answer to an approximate problem." John Tukey, in Cochran, Mosteller, and Tukey, *Statistical Problems of the Kinsey Report on Sexual Behavior in the Human Male* (1954, p. 1335)

Learning Objectives

- To recognize which univariate, bivariate, and multivariate techniques are appropriate based on the nature of the data and the research question.

- To interpret common statistical findings, including measures of central tendency, dispersion, tests of significance, cross-tabulations, scattergrams, correlations, and regression.

- To understand Type I and Type II errors and tests of statistical significance.

- To appreciate the role of the elaboration model in making causal inferences.

- To understand how to conduct ethical research and not lie with numbers.

Introduction

Numbers are everywhere; we can't escape them. Whether you feel you are allergic to them, simply tolerate their existence, or love them, a degree of pride comes along with not skimming over numbers in newspaper articles or academic publications.

Statistics don't need to be intimidating. The ability to understand the basics and interpret what is transmitted in everyday sources of information will pay off for years to come. The goal of this chapter is to make learning quantitative analytical techniques as painless as possible and to place you in a position of being an informed consumer of the common statistics that you will encounter in both academic and everyday life.

As discussed in Chapter 2, quantitative data analysis is hypothetico-deductive and premised on the principle of falsifiability and deductive reasoning. Quantitative research adheres to a positivistic epistemological standpoint, where the goal is to uncover statistical regularities when investigating causal relationships and measuring the extent that events and behaviours occur (see Table 2.1). Thus, the purpose of statistics is to use numbers to describe the data and then draw conclusions. In other words, statistics help us understand information in a simplified way.

Two types of quantitative analytical techniques are discussed in this chapter. **Descriptive statistics** describe the characteristics of one or more variables. **Univariate analyses** summarize data from one variable, using tables, graphs, frequency distributions, and statistical measures of central tendency, dispersion, and association. Descriptive statistics that are **bivariate** include cross-tabulations, correlations, and regression. The chi-square and t-tests of statistical significance, which apply to both bivariate and multivariate descriptive statistics, are also introduced.

Whereas descriptive statistics summarize a set of observations, **inferential statistics** uncover relationships that are often causal and make inferences from the sample about the population. Researchers use sample statistics to make inferences about the values of population parameters. As previously discussed, sample statistics summarize characteristics or relationships in the sample. Population parameters, with their exact value unknown, reflect estimates based on findings from the sample. Inferential statistics can be used to conduct bivariate and **multivariate analyses**, which investigate the relationship between three or more variables.

Preparing for Quantitative Analyses

Data collection and analysis are driven by the research objective and questions. The conclusions drawn from the findings must be supported by the data. To this end, there are five factors to consider prior to engaging in a quantitative analysis (Statistics Canada, 2014):

1. What are the objectives of this research study? Consider what you need to accomplish, the issue under investigation, and the types of answers you need to address the research questions.
2. What is the rationale for conducting the study? An important consideration is why further understanding of this issue is important, how the findings can contribute to our knowledge, and why the findings are relevant theoretically and practically.
3. What type of data needs to be analyzed? This question goes beyond issues of data collection approaches and levels of measurement to questions about which data are the most appropriate to address which research question. In doing so, researchers consider the limitations of the data, as they affect analytical decisions.
4. Which analytical techniques are the most appropriate? For each quantitative analysis conducted, researchers must consider whether the findings will allow them to address the objectives and research questions.
5. Who is interested in this issue, and why? Will the findings be published in an academic outlet?

descriptive statistics
statistics that describe sample characteristics and relationships between variables.

univariate analysis
a statistical analysis that describes one variable.

bivariate analysis
a statistical analysis of two variables that assesses the empirical relationship.

inferential statistics
techniques that use sample observations to make inferences about the population.

multivariate analysis
a statistical analysis of three or more variables that assesses the empirical relationship between them.

If so, the use of advanced analytical techniques could perhaps be appropriate. Will the findings be geared toward practitioners? In this case, keeping the analyses and presentation of the data as simple as possible will go a lot further in the results' real-world utility.

Three additional tasks are entering, coding, and cleaning the data.

Data Entry

Unless you are working with a secondary dataset and engaging only in creating new variables (recoding), the data need to be entered into a statistical software program such as SPSS or Stata. You can enter this data in one of three ways. You can use optical scan sheets like those you see with end-of-term course evaluations. This data entry method is not restricted to surveys. When looking at changes in the scholarly influence and prestige of scholars cited in four international criminology journals, Cohn (2011) needed to count 48,033 citations from 2001 to 2005. To make this task manageable, she downloaded or optically scanned each reference page to capture the data.

Second, you can directly enter the information using computer-assisted telephone interviewing (CATI), discussed in Chapter 6. For example, Canada is one of thirty countries that participate in the International Crime Victimization Survey (ICVS). In addition to data on police-reported crime from the Uniform Crime Reporting Survey, self-report data were collected from a random sample of Canadians on their personal accounts of victimization and whether the crime was reported to the police. CATI was used to enter data directly into a spreadsheet during the interview. Incidentally, the ICVS revealed that 48 per cent of Canadian victims report incidents to the police; the country with the highest reporting rate was Austria, with 70 per cent (Sauvé & Hung, 2008).

Finally, there is the direct entry method, which is most prone to error. Despite this limitation, logistical constraints make it the most common approach. For instance, to make paper surveys accessible and to reduce response error, participants may have to circle their answers and complete the survey by hand. If direct entry becomes a necessity, careful data cleaning will be needed to catch as many data entry errors as possible. The exception is Internet surveys because the respondents enter the data directly into a spreadsheet.

Data Coding

Coding the data involves transforming them from a raw state into a format that can be analyzed with the level of measurement carefully considered (see Chapter 3). For example, a nominal variable for sex is straightforward and coded as 0 for female and 1 for male. On the other hand, you can enter age as an ordinal (0–5, 6–10, etc.) or as a ratio variable.

Decisions made at the data-coding stage affect data-manipulation options. The rule of thumb is to enter the data at the highest level of measurement possible. You can always collapse the interval/ratio data into categorical variables later, but you cannot do the reverse. You may also need to collapse categories if there are too few cases for a meaningful statistical analysis. When this situation arises, be sure to record that you have combined categories and adjust your coding documentation accordingly. Always create a new variable rather than recoding the original variable to protect your data. There are no options to "undo" data manipulation.

Not all coding is a straightforward process of transferring data from the question to the database. With open-ended survey questions, you need to identify patterns in order to create coding categories in much the same way you would approach content analysis (see Chapter 8). This process can involve creating an "other" category, in which respondents write their answer to the question. Read the data and assign a separate code for each unique response. If the results indicate insufficient cases for a category, they need to be collapsed thematically. The rule of thumb is to revise your codes when more than 10 per cent are classified as other.

Data coding in crime and justice research can be a demanding and detailed process. Blair and

> **codebook** a document outlining the structure, layout, and content of a data file; used by researchers for data entry and analysis.

colleagues (2011) used a video editing program to code data frame by frame in their quasi-experimental study on simulating reaction time in officer use of deadly force scenarios. Each frame was one-thirtieth of a second. The first researcher coded all 159 cases and a second coder independently coded 20 per cent, with an inter-coder agreement of 92 per cent. The coding rule was to note the time from when the suspect began to move the gun hand to when he or she began to fire.

A **codebook** is an integral document for data coding and analysis. For data entry purposes, codebooks contain the coding rules, definitions, and numbers assigned for each variable attribute. During data analysis, codebooks help researchers locate variables, especially in large datasets (50+ variables).

Variable names in the dataset can be cryptic; hence, researchers list the variable name, definition, description, and a coding example. In some cases, links are made to the actual survey questions. A code is assigned for each variable attribute, including a number for missing data, (e.g. 9 or 99) and numerical indicators for "Not Applicable" when using a skip pattern (e.g. 8 or 88). Figure 9.1 provides codebook examples of an ordinal variable and skip pattern, taken from a posttest survey used in an evaluation study of citizens, agencies, and the police collaboratively developing recommendations to improve Ontario's police complaints system.

Transforming observational to quantitative data makes a well-documented codebook exceptionally important. Myers and Dhillon (2013) examined the conditions attached to bail orders for accused young persons released into the community. These researchers captured observational data from four Toronto courts by using coding sheets created in advance. In some cases, variables were straightforward, such as the type of legal representation present. However, many of the bail conditions required detailed coding rules to ensure the validity and reliability of variables. Each release condition was coded as having a clear, ambiguous, or no apparent connection to the alleged offence. For instance, a curfew condition had the following coding rules (p. 196):

- Clear connection—if repeatedly committing at night.
- Ambiguous connection—if the offence occurs at night.
- No apparent connection—if there is no evidence that the offence took place at night.

Incidentally, for those youth who received a curfew condition, 57.9 per cent had no apparent connection to the alleged offence.

Data Cleaning

Data cleaning is important because data entry errors occur and lead to problems of validity, missing data, and misleading conclusions. However, I'm not suggesting that you put your coding sheets or USB drive in the washing machine. A few common techniques are used to detect data entry errors. First, recode 10 per cent of the data. If any mistakes are found, the entire dataset needs to be checked for invalid codes. Second, create a list of all values assigned to cases for that variable (frequency distribution) and look for entries that don't belong, as listed in your codebook. Third, check for impossible categories by comparing the coding for two variables (cross-tabulation). For example, an impossible code for sex and pregnancy would be a pregnant man. Another example is a person with no prior arrests being coded as having a three-month term of incarceration.

Univariate Analysis: What Does My Data Look Like?

Every quantitative analysis conducts univariate analyses to address research questions or, as required, preliminary steps before analyzing the data with more advanced techniques. Analyzing one variable at a time tells us what the data look

---

Ordinal variable

Name:	More_crime
Label:	More crime exists now than I remember as a child.
Measurement Level:	Ordinal
Value Labels:	1. Strongly disagree 5. Strongly agree
	2. Disagree 9. Missing data
	3. Neutral
	4. Agree

Skip pattern

Name:	PCS_involve
Label:	Whether the delegate has ever been involved in the police complaints system process or filed a complaint.
Measurement:	Nominal
Value Labels:	0. No
	1. Yes
	8. Prefer not to answer
	9. Missing data

Name:	Sat_compl
Label:	Whether the complaint was resolved to your satisfaction.
Measurement:	Nominal
Value Labels:	0. No
	1. Yes
	8. Prefer not to answer
	9. No prior experience with police complaints process.
	10. Missing data
Coding rules:	If PCS_involve = 8 then Sat_compl = 8.
	If PCS_involve = 0 then Sat_compl = 9.
	If PCS_invovle = 1 and no data for Sat_compl then code Sat_compl = 10.

Figure 9.1 Quantitative codebook

Source: Schulenberg (2013a).

like and whether we need to manipulate the data in some way to allow for further analysis. Techniques include frequencies, rates, graphs, central tendency, and dispersion.

Nuts and Bolts

In univariate analyses, researchers examine each variable separately. Information on the distribution of the data is then used to inform how data are summarized and used in bivariate and multivariate analyses.

Initial analyses involve examining frequency distributions and computing rates.

Frequency Distribution

A **frequency distribution** summarizes the number and percentage of cases that fall within variable categories. Tables 9.1–9.3 are frequency distributions of ride-along

> **frequency distribution**
> a distribution that summarizes nominal and ordinal variables in a table by presenting the total number and percentage for each score in the dataset.

Table 9.1 Frequency distributions for nominal variables

	Any signs of a mental illness		Under the influence	
	Frequency	Per cent	Frequency	Per cent
No	453	74.8	426	70.3
Yes	153	25.2	180	29.7
Total	606	100.0	606	100.0

Source: Schulenberg(2013b).

Table 9.2 Frequency distributions for ordinal variables

	How an officer requests information from a citizen			
	Frequency	Per cent	Valid per cent	Cumulative per cent
Not discussed	254	41.9	45.2	45.2
Conversational request	249	41.1	44.3	89.5
Verbal persuasion	54	8.9	9.6	99.1
Verbal command	5	0.8	0.9	100.0
Missing data	44	7.3		
Total	606	100.0	100.0	

Source: Schulenberg (2013b).

Table 9.3 Frequency distribution with a transformed continuous variable

	Officer months of service		
	Frequency	Per cent	Cumulative per cent
1 to 38 months	173	28.5	28.5
39 to 54 months	141	23.3	51.8
55 to 108 months	157	25.9	77.7
109 months or more	135	22.3	100.0
Total	606	100.0	

Source: Schulenberg (2013a).

data collected using systematic social observation. In the tables, the frequency is the number of cases that fall into that variable category and the per cent represents what percentage of the entire sample these cases account for in that category. By converting cell frequencies into percentages, interpretation becomes easier.

Frequencies containing missing data are included as a separate category. One normally collapses the data into five to eight categories to make interpretation easier. The range for the categories should be equal (e.g. 1–2, 3–4; not 1–2, 3–6). With the cumulative frequency and percentage, you can assess the proportion of cases above and below a certain category. Finally, each column will total 100 per cent, as every observation or case is included in a frequency distribution, even when data are missing for that variable.

For both nominal variables in Table 9.1, "no" is coded as 0 and "yes" as 1. The data shows that 25.2 per cent of the 606 citizens who interacted with the police exhibited signs of a mental illness. According to officers, 29.7 per cent of all citizens were under the influence of alcohol or drugs.

Table 9.2 is an example of a frequency distribution for an ordinal variable that contains data on how officers request incident-related information from citizens. The table is a good illustration of calculating a frequency distribution with missing data. There is no information on this variable for 44 observations, which represents 7.3 per cent of the sample. The valid percentage omits the missing data to tell us the per cent of cases for each category (n=562). Similarly, the cumulative percentage does not include the missing data. Officers asked for information conversationally in 44 per cent of the cases; for 90 per cent of all citizens, it was not a topic discussed or it was queried conversationally.

Table 9.3 brings us to a unique situation of collapsing a frequency distribution for continuous data into categories. Months of service for officers are coded as a continuous ratio variable. However, for the purposes of a frequency distribution, the information is broken into percentage quartiles: 0–25, 26–50, 51–75, and 76–100. Why? Frequency distributions can be used for any level of measurement but are most common with nominal and ordinal data. Interval/ratio variables are difficult to interpret unless there are less than 15 values. From the table, we see that 23 per cent of officers have 39 to 54 months of service and 52 per cent have between 1 and 54 months.

Computing Rates

Rates standardize the data so that it becomes comparable between groups and the comparisons are meaningful. Seeing the crime rate reported in journal articles or the media is common. Why is it used and how is it calculated? If City A has 1,000 assaults in a population of 50,000 and City B has 1,200 assaults in a population of 100,000, is it true that City B has more crime? The problem is that we can't compare them because they don't have the same population. To calculate the crime rate, the numerator is the number of assaults and the denominator is the population. For City A, we divide 1,000 by 50,000 and get 0.02; therefore, 2 per cent of the population committed an assault. For City B, we divide 1,200 by 100,000 and get 0.012, which is 1 per cent of the population. Thus, the correct answer is that City A has more assaults per capita than City B, despite the latter having 200 more assaults.

> **rate** a standardized value assigned to a frequency to allow comparisons between groups on the particular measure.

Visualizing the Data

There are four ways to present univariate data analyses graphically: bar chart, pie chart, histogram, and frequency polygon. Each is appropriate for certain types of data. Thus, some graphs are suitable for categorical data and others for continuous variables.

Bar Chart

A **bar chart** graphically represents data in discrete categories. For nominal variables such as religious affiliation, the order in which they appear is irrelevant. For ordinal variables, you organize the data in ascending or descending order. Bar charts are also used to discern the best course of action for creating new variables. For instance, when attempting to understand whether severe sanctions for violent behaviour at school prevent further crime, Maimon, Antonaccio, and French (2012, p. 507) used a bar chart to demonstrate why a dichotomous variable is necessary. The bar chart shows that just fewer than 70 per cent of students received a home suspension and approximately 25 per cent in-school suspensions; the balance is verbal warnings, minor actions, and expulsion. For this reason, the researchers combined

> **bar chart** a visual depiction using bars to represent the categories of nominal or ordinal variable frequency distributions.

home suspension and expulsion as a severe sanction and the rest as less severe.

Bar charts have spaces between each bar. As seen in Figure 9.2, the horizontal axis displays categories or groups and the other contains bars representing the quantity of the groups, expressed as frequencies, percentages, or rates. The numerical value is on the vertical axis with each mark labelled. If the bar chart is comparing the distribution of the variable for two or more groups, the bars for each group are different colours and a legend is included.

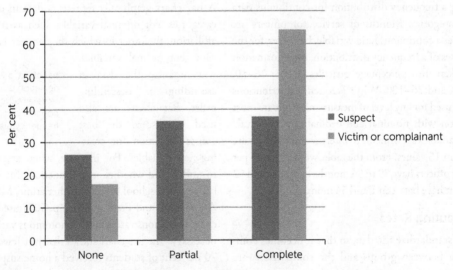

Figure 9.2 Bar chart: Nominal and ordinal variables

Source: Schulenberg (2013b).

Using data from Table 9.1, the second bar chart in Figure 9.2 compares two groups on the ordinal variable of citizen co-operation. You can see from the chart that the data suggest suspects appear just as likely to provide partial or complete information, whereas the majority of victims and complainants provide complete information about the incident when requested.

Pie Chart

Pie charts are ideal visual representations for highlighting an important point. Each attribute of a categorical variable is allocated to a slice of the pie based on the percentage it constitutes of the whole (i.e. per cent or valid per cent in a frequency distribution).

Figure 9.3 uses information from the frequency distribution on officer months of service (Table 9.3); you can see that the categories are relatively equal. The pie chart is not appropriate when this equality occurs because it doesn't depict a

> **pie chart** a circular graphic that visually represents a variable's frequency distribution, using percentages of the total.

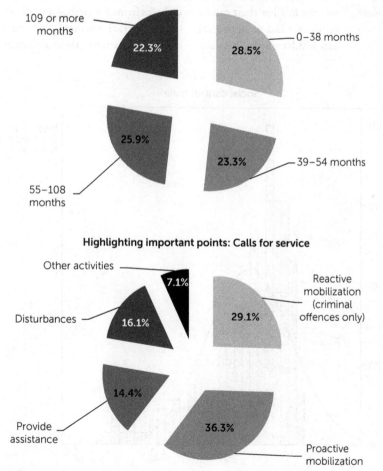

Not ideal: Officer months of service

- 109 or more months — 22.3%
- 0–38 months — 28.5%
- 39–54 months — 23.3%
- 55–108 months — 25.9%

Highlighting important points: Calls for service

- Other activities — 7.1%
- Reactive mobilization (criminal offences only) — 29.1%
- Disturbances — 16.1%
- Proactive mobilization — 36.3%
- Provide assistance — 14.4%

Figure 9.3 When do I use a pie chart?

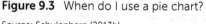

Source: Schulenberg (2013b).

salient point beyond what is delivered in a table. On the other hand, the pie chart on calls for service tells a story. We see that 64 per cent of officer activities were responding to different types of calls for service (disturbance, crime) and only 36 per cent of calls were initiated by the officer.

Histogram

A **histogram** graphically represents continuous variables. Due to the level of measurement, the bars touch each other and are always vertical. Each bar represents the number of cases for a value in the distribution. In contrast, the bars in a bar chart can be on the vertical or horizontal axis and have space between

> **histogram** a graph that uses vertical bars on the horizontal axis to represent a continuous variable's frequency distribution.

them, as the data is categorical. To understand the nature of a continuous variable, histograms are a better representation than frequency distributions.

Histograms provide information on the shape of the data to detect abnormal distributions that cause problems for bivariate and multivariate analyses. As seen in Figure 9.4, the frequency for scores on the social control scale appears on the vertical axis. The social control scale is a ratio-level variable that includes the informal and formal actions officers use to restore order in a police–citizen encounter. Informal action includes directives to modify behaviour, whereas formal social control includes items for tactical and dispositional actions such as verbal warnings, investigative detention, charges, and arrests. These actions are ordered on a

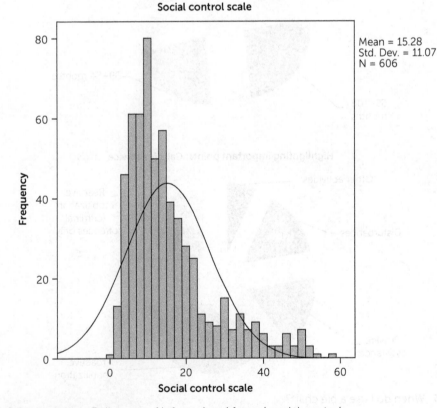

Social control scale

Mean = 15.28
Std. Dev. = 11.07
N = 606

Figure 9.4 Histogram: Police use of informal and formal social control

Source: Schulenberg (2013b).

continuum from least to most intrusive of citizen autonomy and the use of police authority. The variable values, being individual scores on the scale, are on the horizontal. All the bars are adjacent to each other, as the values vary along a continuum. Quite often, histograms are created with the normal curve superimposed on the distribution so that decisions on data manipulation can be made.

Frequency Polygon

Also known as a line graph, a **frequency polygon** graphically presents an interval- or ratio-level variable's frequency distribution by using a continuous line. The line connects the midpoints of the bars within a histogram, where the frequency of cases is

still on the vertical axis and the values of the variable are on the horizontal axis. A frequency polygon is a better option than a histogram when the highest and lowest values are far apart.

In Figure 9.5, the value of the dollar is on the vertical axis and the values of the variable year are on the horizontal axis. As you can see, our dollar doesn't go as far as it did in the past. Something that cost $1.00 in 1940 cost $3.65 in 1975, $7.83 in 1985, right up to $15.22 in 2013. The change is shocking when you look at it in a frequency polygon, which highlights a major

frequency polygon
a graph with a continuous line used to present the frequency distribution of interval/ratio variables visually; also known as a line graph.

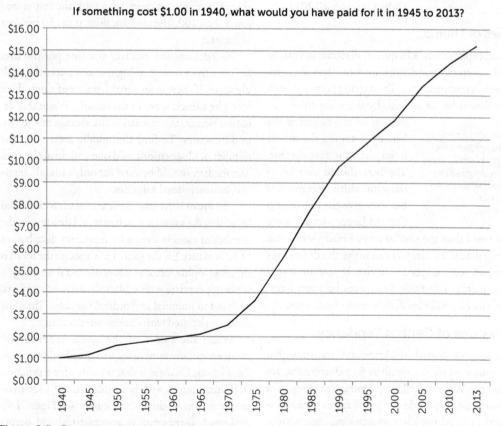

If something cost $1.00 in 1940, what would you have paid for it in 1945 to 2013?

Figure 9.5 Frequency polygon: Purchasing power of the Canadian dollar

Source: Bank of Canada (2013). Inflation calculator. Retrieved 22 October 2013 from http://www.bankofcanada.ca/rates/related/inflation-calculator/

mode a measure of central tendency that is the most frequent value found in a frequency distribution.

advantage of visualizing continuous data in this way.

A frequency polygon is often used for changes over time. For instance, a frequency polygon was used to represent graphically the frequency distribution of attempted hijackings globally and in the United States from 1931 to 2003 (Dugan, Lafree, & Piquero, 2005). Years were displayed on the horizontal axis (X) and the frequency on the vertical (Y) axis. The data suggest that, until about the mid-1980s, the trends were similar; however, from that point onward, such trends didn't occur in the United States until 2011.

median a measure of central tendency that is the middle point found in the distribution when the values are listed from lowest to highest.

Rules of Thumb

Visual depictions of a frequency distribution can be used incorrectly and distort the data. Thus, there are some rules to remember. The starting point for both axes should be set at zero. By the same token, do not cut off the height of the bars by changing the metric lower than the actual value. The bars should also be of the same width. Inconsistent bar sizes give the impression that the larger bars are more important than the smaller ones. Finally, when you manipulate the scale, you can make the differences in values seem bigger or smaller. If you use a very small metric with little differences between numbers, you can make small differences look large.

mean a measure of central tendency that provides the average score in a frequency distribution; calculated by adding the scores and then dividing the total by the number of cases.

Measures of Central Tendency

Measures of central tendency are statistics that summarize where the numbers in a distribution are clustered. When calculating central tendency, you measure the magnitude of a set of scores. Stated differently, central tendency statistics measure what is typical, or most numerous, in the data.

The **mode** is the most frequently occurring category in the data. It can be used with any level of measurement; however, it's the only one that can be used with nominal variables. The ideal situation is unimodal, where one value occurs the most often in the distribution. It can also be bimodal, where two values have the highest frequency in the distribution. Thus, the mode is the most imprecise measure of central tendency.

The **median** breaks up the frequency distribution into two equal halves. Fifty per cent of the distribution is above the median and 50 per cent is below when the observations are listed in rank order. A practical example is the comparison of standardized test scores. A raw score of 160 on the LSAT could be in the ninetieth percentile, which means that 90 per cent of those who took the test scored lower than 160. The median, then, is the 50 per cent percentile.

To calculate the median, you first put the data in order from lowest to highest and select the middle score. If there is an equal number of cases, there won't be a single score in the middle. When this situation occurs, the median is the average of the two middle scores. To find the middle score, take the number of observations, add one and divide by two. The median should be used for only ordinal-, interval-, and ratio-level variables.

The **mean** is the arithmetic average. It is calculated by adding the values for each case and dividing by the number of cases in the entire frequency distribution ($\Sigma X/N$, where Σ is the sum of). Although the mean is the most sophisticated measure of central tendency, it is not appropriate with arbitrarily assigned numbers, as found in nominal and ordinal variables. Thus, the mean can be used with continuous data only.

When the values of the mode, median, and mean are not the same, a skewed distribution occurs. Recall from Chapter 4 that we strive for a symmetrical distribution, with both sides virtually identical to one another—the normal curve (see Figure 4.4). A skewed distribution is asymmetrical and occurs frequently when analyzing criminological data. In

Vignette: Breaking It Down

Is Police-Reported Crime Rate Data Important?

We think of criminal behaviour either at the micro individual level or at the macro societal level. The aggregate crime rate gives us data that can be used within and across populations. However, the utility and validity of aggregate crime rates are challenged.

When discussing the Uniform Crime Reporting Survey (UCR) in previous chapters, we learned that some argue that police-reported crime rates are a better reflection of police behaviour than of criminal activity. One media columnist points out that lower crime rates could reflect fewer officers, more paperwork, or targeted enforcement efforts (Surette, 2009). For this reason, it is common to use data from multiple years to reduce the risk of making inaccurate conclusions on the basis of an anomalous year. This is exactly what Andreson and Felson (2012) did when examining data from the RCMP in British Columbia. They used data on all incidents from 2002 to 2006 and calculated averages across the years. They also used a frequency distribution to present the counts and percentage of each type of crime and a series of combined histograms and frequency polygons to present data on trends over time for violent and property crime co-offending.

Carrington (2013) used UCR data from 1984 to 2011 on chargeable youth to assess changes over time for various offences. He notes that 1984 is the first year that crime data categories were comparable! Taking a macro perspective, he concludes that, over this 28-year span, reported youth crime has declined and become more violent but less serious overall.

Recall that we calculate the crime rate by dividing the number of incidents of a particular crime known to the police by the population base, producing a standardized value that is comparable across time and place. By doing so, we accept the assumption that the residential population is an accurate denominator. Boivin (2013) questions this assumption and finds that residential population size isn't always an accurate measure of the number of potential offenders and victims in a given area because there are individuals in a region who do not live there. Thus, it is best if analyses include other measures of potential persons and opportunities for crime. For example, a more reliable approach to estimating crime rates could be demographics, whereby an increase in the youth population would likely lead to higher crime rates, as those under 24 commit most of the crimes (Whitton, 1999).

If our explanations are to be valid, they need to be current. Delaying the release of aggregate data for over a year hinders attempts to inform public policy. Individual police services report on a monthly basis and conduct analyses, such as hot spots, much more frequently. Real-time access is needed to ensure accurate evidence-based practice. For instance, Rosenfeld (2011, p. 21) argues:

> The first task of the policy maker is to place the local changes in the context of general trends . . . if the local rates are diverging from common trends, it is a good bet they are being driven by idiosyncratic local conditions . . . which would call for interventions specifically tailored to the local scene.

If we take this statement into account, the police-reported crime rate forms a breadbasket for evidence-based practice at the local level. It is in everyone's best interests to ensure timely access and accurate calculations.

positive (or right) skew distributions with a long tail on the right side, a large number of low scores, and—from lowest to highest—the mode, median, and mean.

negative (or left) skew distributions with a long tail on the left side, a large number of high scores, and—from lowest to highest—the mean, median, and mode.

Figure 9.6, the vertical axis is the frequency and the horizontal axis is the scores for the social control scale.

A symmetrical distribution has most scores in the middle of the distribution, leading to an equivalent length of tails on both sides. The mode, median, and mean are the same value. Figure 9.6 is an example of a **positively skewed** distribution, or a right skew. The largest number of scores is low, which leads to a longer tail on the right side. The mode is the lowest, followed by the median, and the highest value is the mean. With a **negatively skewed** distribution, or a left skew, one has the opposite problem. There are a greater number of high scores, which leads to a long tail on the left side. The mean has the lowest value, the median is in the middle, and the mode has the highest. Although a variety of transformations can induce normality in the distribution, the most common are a log transformation for a positive skew and a square root for a negative

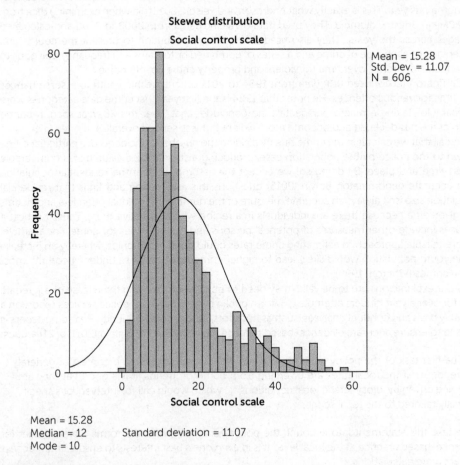

Skewed distribution

Social control scale

Mean = 15.28
Std. Dev. = 11.07
N = 606

Mean = 15.28
Median = 12   Standard deviation = 11.07
Mode = 10

Figure 9.6 Skewed frequency distribution

Source: Schulenberg (2013b).

skew. In the case of Figure 9.6, a log transformation was performed and now the mode, median, and mean are virtually identical. Always use the median with skewed distributions, or the results will be misleading.

Measures of Dispersion

Measures of central tendency provide information on the typical case. In comparison, measures of dispersion give us information on the variability within the distribution, as seen by the differences in the scores. Stated differently, they measure the extent to which the scores vary in a distribution around a central value, such as the mean. Large values of dispersion mean that the scores are widely distributed, whereas a smaller summary statistic suggests that the data are tightly clustered.

Range

The basic measure of dispersion is the **range**, the highest score minus the lowest score in a frequency distribution. If the highest score is 62 and the lowest is 7, the range equals 55. The range is calculated for interval and ratio variables, as it has more intuitive meaning. However, the range reveals only the spread of the data; it cannot tell us how dispersed the scores are within the distribution. The range is

> **range** a measure of dispersion that is the difference between the highest and lowest value found in a frequency distribution.

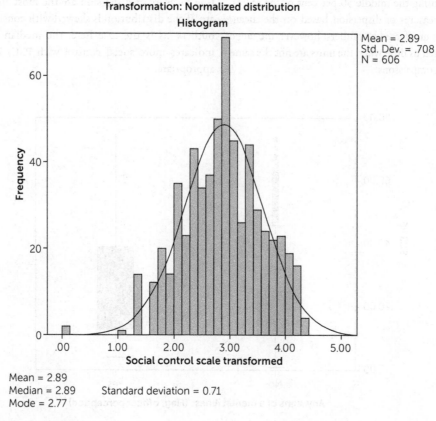

Transformation: Normalized distribution
Histogram

Mean = 2.89
Std. Dev. = .708
N = 606

Social control scale transformed

Mean = 2.89
Median = 2.89   Standard deviation = 0.71
Mode = 2.77

Figure 9.6 *Continued*

Source: Schulenberg (2013b).

interquartile range (IQR) in a frequency distribution, a measure of dispersion that is the distance between the twenty-fifth and seventy-fifth percentile.

box-and-whisker plot (or boxplot) a graphical representation of a distribution's shape, central tendency, and dispersion; based on the interquartile range.

also very susceptible to outliers (extremely low or high scores); therefore, it isn't always an accurate measure.

Interquartile Range

Due to the range's limitations, many researchers opt for the **interquartile range (IQR)**. The distribution is divided into the twenty-fifth, fiftieth, and seventy-fifth percentiles. In effect, you calculate the distance between the first and third quartile to remove the extreme scores at both ends of the distribution and summarize the data using the middle 50 per cent of the scores. Unlike measures of dispersion based on the mean, the IQR is unaffected by outliers; however, the range and IQR tell us little when the units are not the same between comparisons.

The IQR sounds quite abstract until you graphically represent it in the form of a **box-and-whisker plot**. Also known as a boxplot, it helps to detect a skewed distribution and the presence of outliers. It is ideal for large samples because it shows the shape of the distribution, middle value, and variability in the frequency distribution.

Figure 9.7 is a boxplot for persons with a mental illness (PMI) and the amount of social control used to restore order. The upper and lower quartiles (based on the IQR) are at each end of the box. The line inside the box is the median. The whiskers are the two lines that extend out from the box to represent the points where 95 per cent of the data are included. The asterisks represent outliers. If there are no outliers, the mean and the standard deviation measure of dispersion are the most appropriate. If the distribution is skewed with considerable outliers, as is the case here, the median (which indicates more social control with PMI) is more appropriate.

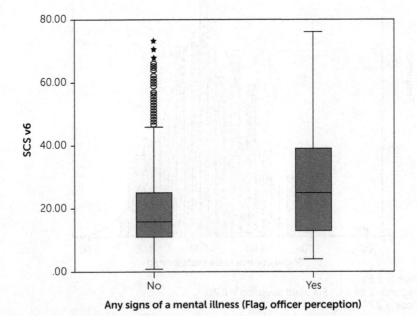

Figure 9.7 Box-and-whisker plot: The amount of social control by signs of a mental illness

Source: Schulenberg (2013b).

Standard Deviation

The **standard deviation** is the most commonly used measure of dispersion for continuous variables. As the average amount of distance between all scores and the mean, it illustrates the heterogeneous or homogenous nature of the data and estimates how much the average case in the sample differs from the population. A low value for the standard deviation means that the scores are close to the mean and a higher value indicates that scores are more spread out. Thus, when the standard deviation is small, the mean can be interpreted as an accurate measure of central tendency. However, the standard deviation is subject to the same limitations as the mean in that it is influenced by outliers or an extremely skewed distribution.

The equation and steps for standard deviation are as follows:

$$(\bar{x}). \quad SD = \sqrt{\frac{\sum\left(x - \bar{x}\right)^2}{n-1}}$$

1. Calculate the mean
2. Subtract the mean from each score (x).
3. Square the difference between the score and the mean $\left(x - \bar{x}\right)^2$
4. Add the squared differences to calculate the total of each squared difference (Σ).
5. Divide the sum of squares by the number of cases for the variance (n − 1).
6. Find the square root of the variance ($\sqrt{\ }$).

What does this all mean? Let's say there is a police crackdown on a group of drug dealers and, of the 18 arrested and charged, only 4 have no previous convictions for a drug offence. Three of them have one previous conviction and the others have two, three, four, five, six, or eight. The standard deviation tells us that the true mean in the population lies somewhere between 0.33 and 5.45 prior convictions (see Table 9.4).

Bivariate Analysis: Are They Related?

Although we touched on statistical significance in Chapter 1, we need to explore this topic further in relation to bivariate and multivariate statistics. An extensive look at the mathematical calculations is beyond the scope of this textbook. However, it's important to understand the nature, purpose, and interpretation of common analytical techniques, including contingency tables, scattergrams, correlation coefficients, and bivariate regression.

> **standard deviation** an estimate of how widely the scores are spread around the mean in a frequency distribution.

Statistical Significance

To estimate a population characteristic, you need to calculate whether the relationship you find between two variables in the sample actually exists and didn't occur by random chance. Tests of **statistical significance** tell you the chances of finding a random relationship in the sample that doesn't exist in the population. In an actual relationship, the value of the coefficient between two variables is larger or smaller than would be expected by chance.

> **statistical significance** a coefficient that indicates the chances of a relationship found in the sample occurring by chance and not existing in the population.

Logic and Assumptions

Statistical significance is stated as the level of confidence, or the probability, that the results are not caused by chance. There is no absolute certainty regarding the true differences between sample statistics and population parameters. For instance, we can only be 95 per cent certain that the results did not occur by chance. However, we do not interpret statistical significance as a measure of association wherein .01 (90 per cent) or .05 (95 per cent) is weaker than a .001 (99.9 per cent) probability that the results occurred by chance.

Table 9.4 Drug dealers' prior convictions

Previous convictions	$x - \bar{x}$	$(x - \bar{x})^2$
0	$0 - 2.89 = -2.89$	$-2^2 = 4$
0	$0 - 2.89 = -2.89$	$-2^2 = 4$
0	$0 - 2.89 = -2.89$	$-2^2 = 4$
0	$0 - 2.89 = -2.89$	$-2^2 = 4$
1	$1 - 2.89 = -1.89$	$-1^2 = 1$
1	$1 - 2.89 = -1.89$	$-1^2 = 1$
1	$1 - 2.89 = -1.89$	$-1^2 = 1$
2	$2 - 2.89 = -0.89$	$0^2 = 0$
3	$3 - 2.89 = 0.11$	$1^2 = 1$
3	$3 - 2.89 = 0.11$	$1^2 = 1$
4	$4 - 2.89 = 1.11$	$2^2 = 4$
4	$4 - 2.89 = 1.11$	$2^2 = 4$
4	$4 - 2.89 = 1.11$	$2^2 = 4$
5	$5 - 2.89 = 2.11$	$3^2 = 9$
5	$5 - 2.89 = 2.11$	$3^2 = 9$
5	$5 - 2.89 = 2.11$	$3^2 = 9$
6	$6 - 2.89 = 3.11$	$4^2 = 16$
8	$8 - 2.89 = 5.11$	$6^2 = 36$
$\Sigma = 52/18$	$\Sigma = 0$ (variance)	$\Sigma = 112$
Mean = 2.89		$90/(18 - 1) = 6.59$
		$\sqrt{6.59} = 2.56$

Instead, we test the null hypothesis, which says that there is no relationship between the two variables or that two categories/groups do not differ on some characteristic. This conclusion is based on the assumptions of probability sampling. All tests of significance assume that a sample is selected randomly; otherwise, estimates are inflated and inaccurate (see Chapter 4). In larger samples, there is less chance that a relationship is due to sampling error. However, there is no need to test for statistical significance if you are working with the entire population (e.g. UCR), as there is no potential for sampling error.

Decision-Making Errors

We can never truly know the answer to statistical significance or directly test the null hypothesis because it applies to the population and not the sample. Thus, we make inferences from the sample. There are two types of errors (summarized in Table 9.5) that can occur when calculating and interpreting statistical significance.

Table 9.5 Fitting it all together

		Action you are going to take	
		Accept the null hypothesis	Reject the null hypothesis
True nature of the null hypothesis	The null hypothesis is *actually true*.	Correct decision	Type I error
	The null hypothesis is *actually false*.	Type II error	Correct decision

Type I Error

Also known as an alpha (α) error, a **Type I error** occurs when we incorrectly conclude that two variables are related when the association actually occurred by random chance. If we set the level of significance at $p < 0.05$, we are saying that the probability (p) of rejecting a true null hypothesis is 5 per cent. When we don't commit the Type I error, we can be 95 per cent confident that the observed relationship exists in the real world and can conclude that there is a group difference, as it didn't occur by chance.

Type I errors are serious and of great concern because they produce conclusions that are not true—such as finding an innocent person guilty—and findings that claim there is a difference when one really doesn't exist. This error can have profound implications. For instance, you can end up falsely making the argument that saturated police patrol is effective; consequently, police services devote even more resources at great costs when, in reality, this approach makes no appreciable difference in reducing violent crime.

Type II Error

A **Type II error**, or beta (β) error, occurs when you assert that there is no relationship between two variables, yet one actually exists. It is the failure to reject a false null hypothesis. Returning to the previous example, a Type II error occurs when a guilty defendant is found not guilty.

Whereas the probability of committing a Type I error can be calculated, the exact probability of a Type II error is unknown. Further, as your sample characteristics become closer to the population, the probability of your accepting a false null hypothesis decreases. Finally, Type II errors are very sensitive to sample size. As the number of cases increases, the probability of committing a Type II error decreases.

The Balancing Act

There is a balancing act between committing a Type I and a Type II error. The more likely you are to make one type of error, the less likely you are to make the other type. Thus, you decrease the odds of a Type II error by increasing the sample size but increase the chances of accepting a false null hypothesis. As the level of significance increases, so do the chances of committing a Type II error, while lower levels of significance increase the likelihood of committing a Type I error. For this reason, the standard of $\alpha = .05$ (95 per cent confidence) is a balance between the risk of committing a Type I and a Type II error.

Statistical versus Substantive Significance

Henry Clay wrote that "statistics are no substitute for judgment." Two key questions to ask ourselves are, "What is the difference between statistical and substantive significance?" and "Why is this difference important?" A relationship between two variables can be statistically significant

> **Type I error** the rejection of the null hypothesis when it is true (i.e. the relationship found in the sample occurred by chance); also known as an alpha (α) error.

> **Type II error** acceptance of the null hypothesis when it is false (i.e. the relationship found in the sample did not occur by chance); also known as a beta (β) error.

chi-square a test of statistical significance determining the degree of confidence that an association between two categorical variables did not occur by chance (i.e. the null hypothesis can be rejected).

t-test a test of statistical significance determining whether the means for two groups differ from one another beyond what would occur by random chance.

but not substantively significant. Recall that virtually everything can become significant with very large samples, even meaningless or trivial ones. We know that statistical significance is the degree of risk we are willing to take that we will reject a true null hypothesis. Though statistical significance can tell us whether the observed values didn't occur by chance, it can't reveal whether it's something worth worrying about in the first place.

There is no objective test for substantive significance, but there are the measures of common sense, previous research, and theory. For instance, if two different drugs have statistically significant relationships with life span, this result can have substantive significance when one drug adds one hour to your life and the other adds five years.

Bear three things in mind regarding statistical significance. First, statistical significance derived from data mining is of less substantive significance. In contrast, research questions and hypotheses based on a theoretical and conceptual foundation help us interpret the results and make connections to the real world. Second, do not interpret the statistical significance of a relationship without the context in which it occurs. Otherwise, your interpretation will amount to assuming that we live in a vacuum and the only relationship that matters is between these two variables. Finally, remember that statistical significance is only one goal of quantitative scientific research.

Chi-Square

Is the joint variation between two variables above and beyond what exists by random chance? To determine the answer to this question, researchers conduct a test of independence to assess the null hypothesis that two variables have no relationship. The **chi-square** statistic can be a measure of association in descriptive and inferential statistics, but it is most commonly used with contingency tables.

The chi-square tests the probability that the difference between what is expected and what is actually observed is by random chance due to sampling error. The greater the value of chi-square, the less likely the distribution you are testing has a true null hypothesis. However, it is important to note that the chi-square statistic is sensitive to sample size. The larger the sample, the more likely you will find statistical significance. Similarly, fewer than five cases for each combination of the two variables leads to distortion and the risk of drawing faulty conclusions.

T-Test

The **t-test** statistic measures whether the difference between two means for two groups or two categories of the same sample is statistically significant. In this case, the null hypothesis is that the population means are equivalent. A statistically significant t-test tells us that the difference did not occur by chance; however, it sheds no light on why the groups are different.

There are two types of t-tests. A one-tailed t-test is used when you have a directional hypothesis. For instance, as the amount of illicit drugs consumed increases, the number of arrests increases. The hypothesis posits a relationship in one direction—up. Thus, the t-test assesses whether the higher average of one group is statistically significant. Sometimes researchers are not sure about the direction of variation and construct a non-directional hypothesis, assessed with a two-tailed t-test. Returning to our example, they would test whether an association exists between the average amount of drugs consumed and the mean number of arrests because they are unsure whether the amount of drugs increases or decreases the number of arrests. In a two-tailed t-test examining the effect of the media in different formats, the mean level of fear experienced by Canadian students is higher than

Americans overall and, specifically, for violent crime (Kohm et al., 2012).

You will see one of three patterns when testing the statistical significance of the variation between two continuous variables. First, the value of t increases as the difference between the two means increases. Second, as seen with the chi-square statistic, the value of t increases as the sample size increases. Third, the value of t increases when variation within a category decreases.

Cross-Tabulation

We can measure a bivariate relationship in several ways: cross-tabulation, scattergram, and correlation coefficient. Let's take a closer look at each. A **cross-tabulation** is ideal for examining the relationship between nominal and ordinal variables. Each cell in the table presents the joint frequencies and percentages of the number of cases falling into variable categories.

Cross-tabulations are known as contingency tables because the values of the dependent variable are contingent on the values of the independent variable. Simply using frequencies can be deceptive, which is why percentages are compared to investigate if variation in the independent variable categories relates to the dependent variable. Thus, cross-tabulations can tell you three things: they summarize the data

to ascertain whether the distribution varies between categories of the independent variables (association); they give some indication as to whether the values of the independent variable increase or decrease (direction); and they reveal the extent of variation in independent variable category values (strength).

Interpreting Contingency Tables

Table 9.6 is a contingency table with any signs of mental illness as the independent variable and under the influence as the dependent variable. In this example, we are analyzing how these two variables interact simultaneously to better understand any patterns of association. The independent variable is in the column and the dependent variable the rows, which means that we are looking at whether there is a higher percentage of those with a mental illness who are under the influence of either alcohol or drugs when interacting with the police. The column and row marginal are the totals at the side (rows) and bottom (column) of the table. The table shows that 50 per cent of those under the influence of alcohol or drugs exhibited signs of a mental illness, whereas 23 per cent did not. We can conclude that citizens under the influence

> **cross-tabulation** a contingency table that displays the frequencies and percentages for specific combinations of at least two categorical variables.

Table 9.6 Mental illness and under the influence

			Any signs of mental illness (MI)		
			No	Yes	Total
Under the influence of alcohol/drugs	No indication	Count	350	76	426
		% within MI	77.3%	49.7%	70.3%
	Yes	Count	103	77	180
		% within MI	22.7%	50.3%	29.7%
Total		Count	453	153	606
		% within MI	100.0%	100.0%	100.0%

$X^2 = 41.693$, $p \leq 0.000$

of alcohol or drugs are more than twice as likely to exhibit signs of a mental illness.

The chi-square statistic (χ^2) tells us whether the rows and columns of the cross-tabulation are independent. The greater the value of chi-square, the less likely the distribution tested occurred by chance. With a chi-square value of 41.693, there is less than a 0.001 per cent probability that the difference was caused by chance.

How do you interpret the table? You want to know how the dependent variable differs for each category of the independent variable. The rule of thumb is to percentage down (column) and then read across the rows (compare percentages on levels of the dependent variable). The first step is to read the title, row, and column headings. Second, determine whether the percentages are by row or column by looking at which direction adds up to 100 per cent. Third, compare the two variables in the opposite direction from the percentage, which means the rows. Fourth, interpret the percentages. If there is no relationship, the percentages in the cells are relatively equal in columns or in the rows. When there is a positive or negative linear relationship, the percentages are larger in diagonal cells. The last step is to look at the chi-square test of statistical significance to determine if the relationship between the two variables occurred by chance.

In Table 9.7, the independent variable is under the influence of alcohol or drugs and the dependent variable is use of police discretion not to charge. We can see that, when officers used their discretion, 70 per cent of citizens were under the influence compared to 66 per cent who were not. When looking at the chi-square, we see that the difference is non-significant; hence, the variation between these two variables is independent from one another and any covariation within the sample occurred by chance.

Limitations

Cross-tabulations have three primary limitations. They can show only the extent to which the relationship between two variables is linear and moving in the same direction. If you have too many categories, the cross-tabulation becomes unwieldy and extremely hard to interpret. Any patterns in the relationship between variables become unintelligible with more than 25 cells. Unless there are very few values, continuous variables are not suitable. For instance, if you were to cross-tabulate age by years of schooling, you would have over a thousand cells. The only solution is to collapse the values (and thereby sacrifice detail) or use a scattergram.

Table 9.7   Under the influence and police discretion

			Under the influence (UI)		
			No	Yes	Total
Use of police discretion not to charge	Charges laid	Count	73	42	115
		% within UI	33.6%	30.4%	32.4%
	No charges	Count	144	96	240
		% within UI	66.4%	69.6%	67.6%
Total		Count	217	138	355
		% within UI	100.0%	100.0%	100.0%

$X^2 = 0.396$, $p = 0.305$

Scattergram

A **scattergram**, also known as a scatterplot, is a graph that assesses the strength and direction of the relationship between two continuous variables. The dependent variable (Y) is on the vertical axis and the independent variable (X) on the horizontal axis. A scattergram shows the direction and shape of covariation, which can fluctuate (see Figure 9.8). Each x represents a data point of the combination

> **scattergram (or scatterplot)**
> a graphical representation of scores for two continuous variables distributed across the range of all possible values; used to indicate a relationship's strength and direction.

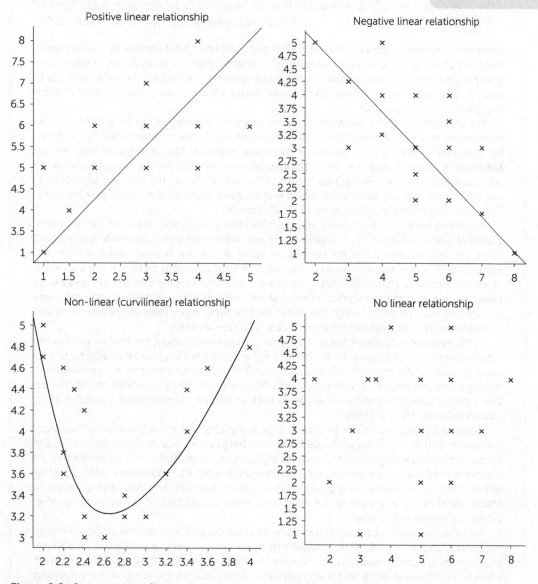

Figure 9.8 Scattergrams: Shape, direction, and precision of covariation

Source: Created using Alcula (2013).

Key Thinker

Adolphe Quetelet (1796–1874)

"We can assess how perfected a science has become by how much or how little it is based on calculation"

> A. Quetelet, 1828; quoted in Beirne, "Adophe Quetelet and the Origins of
> Positivist Criminology" (1987, pp. 1150–1151).

Adolphe Quetelet was born in Belgium in 1796 and completed his doctorate degree in mathematics in 1819. He is known as an astronomer, mathematician, sociologist, demographer, and criminologist who brought statistics to the social sciences. He applied statistical methods to discern social facts, such as crime, and became the leading authority in the new field of social mechanics (Amatrudo, 2010).

His thoughts on crime departed from the prevalent thinking of the time, that one can hypothesize that the volume of crime varies from one year to the next because crime is driven by individual opportunity. By analyzing aggregate statistics, Quetelet found that criminal behaviour is constant over time and resembles law-like patterns. He also became concerned with the relationship between crimes known to the authorities and the total number committed. He argued that this association would remain stable because the causes stay the same. Therefore, crime rates in official statistics are also stable.

According to Beirne (1987), Quetelet determined that poverty and lack of education are not causes of crime, despite these "dangerous" classes committing a disproportionate amount of crime. His research found that the correlation wasn't always true because some of the poorest regions of France had the lowest crime rates. He concluded that crime is more a question of wealth inequality (Amatrudo, 2010). By using cross-tabulations presented in contingency tables, he argued that the two factors most associated with the propensity to commit crime are age and sex. The data showed that males are four times more likely to commit crime and criminals are typically between the ages of 21 and 25 (Beirne, 1987).

At the same time, Quetelet became increasingly concerned about the limitations of crime data because their collection was not standardized or conducted in accordance with his understanding of scientific methods (Amatrudo, 2010). This concern extends to his caution when making causal inferences: "The causes which influence crime are so enormous and so diverse, that it comes almost impossible to assign to each its degree of importance" (Quetelet, 1831; quoted in Beirne, 1987, p. 1158).

Quetelet contributed much to criminological thinking and the application of statistical methods to crime-related research questions. Over the years, he examined trends in crime and its causes with increasing efforts for methodological rigour. Specifically, he is known for being a pioneer in the following areas: ecological crime analysis using aggregate crime rates; positivistic belief that human behaviour is governed by law-like regularities; and the use of government official statistics. He also created the Body Mass Index (weight/height^2) by quantifying mean values in a normal distribution.

Adolphe Quetelet was a progressive leader in criminological and methodological thinking. He did not take an individualistic approach by blaming crime on evil individuals. Instead, his explanations for crime were macro and environmental. Amatrudo (2010, p. 17) was correct when he said that Quetelet's "idea that crime can be scientifically understood through analysing statistics is (rightly or wrongly) still with us today."

of two values from the independent and dependent variables.

Figure 9.8 shows various scattergrams. A positive (direct) relationship is created when an increase in the value of one variable increases the value of the other. Thus, the x's on the graph go from the bottom left to the top right corner. If you were to draw a line from one corner to the other, you would see the strength of the relationship—the closer the dots are to the line, the stronger (and, by extension, precise) the relationship. An example of a positive relationship is height and weight: a taller person tends to be heavier. In a negative or inverse relationship, increases in one variable result in decreases in the other. For instance, the more cigarettes you smoke, the worse your health becomes, or the more you drive, the less gas you have in your tank. A non-linear, or curvilinear, relationship occurs when there is a positive linear relationship that becomes negative at a certain threshold (or vice versa). An excellent example is the age–crime curve. As age increases, so too does the amount of criminal offending. However, beyond the age of 25, the amount of criminal offending decreases. Finally, a scattergram of a no linear relationship has x's randomly scattered, indicating that the two variables don't co-vary in a predictable way.

A scattergram can tell us three important things about the dependent and independent variables. We can discern the type and form of the relationship. Is it a linear or curvilinear relationship? If the relationship is non-linear, certain statistical techniques, such as correlation coefficients, are poor measures of the association's strength. Next is the direction of the relationship. For example, a negative relationship yields a diagonal line in the x's from the top left corner to the bottom right, where higher values on the dependent variable are associated with lower values on the independent variable. Finally, the scattergram indicates precision in terms of how close the dots are to the line. The more spread out the dots, the lower the level of precision. The standard deviation provides a numerical indicator and the scattergram a

graphical indication of dispersion. However, the latter also reveals the presence of any outliers.

Correlation Coefficients

A **correlation coefficient** numerically summarizes the extent to which two variables are related with respect to the degree that a change in one changes the value in the other. Correlations can tell us the strength of the relationship for nominal variables. For ordinal, interval, and ratio variables, you can determine the strength and direction of the relationship. The **Pearson's product-moment correlation coefficient** is calculated by multiplying the z-scores of two variables (product) and then calculating the mean (moment). Z-scores are simply the distance of one observation from the group mean using standardized units. In practice, this z-score converts the raw score in a frequency distribution by the number of standard deviations from the mean.

> **correlation coefficient (or Pearson's product-moment correlation coefficient)** a statistic that describes the association between two variables in terms of strength and direction.

Interpretation

For the direction of the relationship, a positive correlation coefficient occurs when the values of two variables increase at the same time. For example, the more students study, the higher their grades in a course. The less sleep a person gets in a given night, the lower his or her ability to concentrate the next day. A negative correlation occurs when high values on one variable are associated with low values on another. For instance, the higher the level of education, the lower the probability of breaking the law.

There are two ways to determine what a correlation means and how to assess the strength of the relationship. The values range from zero to one; values closer to zero indicate a weaker relationship, and those closer to one indicate a stronger relationship between variables. To interpret the value, researchers can use the eyeball method or the coefficient of determination.

Eyeball Method

The eyeball method is a general interpretation of the size of the correlation or strength of the relationship. In most cases, this method is sufficient to assess correlation coefficients. Most research is written up to describe the data in terms of weak, moderate, or strong correlations, based on the following absolute values:

> **coefficient of determination (r^2)**
> a statistic summarizing the extent to which variation in the dependent variable can be explained by changes in one or more independent variables.

- .00–.20: Weak or no relationship (most common).
- .21–.40: Weak to moderate relationship (common).
- .41–.60: Moderate relationship.
- .61–.80: Strong relationship.
- .81–1.00: Very strong relationship (extremely rare).

In practice, be suspicious of correlations greater than .50, as they may indicate that two variables are so similar that they mean the same thing.

In Table 9.8, we see weak to moderate correlations between under the influence and mental illness (.262), mental illness and the use of social control (.172), and under the influence with social control (.378). The second number in each row is the chi-square test of statistical significance. In this example, the relationship between officer months of service and all other variables is not statistically significant. Due to their utility and diagnostic value, correlation coefficients are used prior to more advanced statistical analyses.

Coefficient of Determination

The **coefficient of determination** (r^2) is a sample statistic we use to determine how well one variable can explain variation in another variable. It is calculated by squaring the correlation coefficient. Table 9.9 transfers the correlation coefficients from Table 9.8 and presents the coefficient of determination.

To calculate the coefficient of determination for under the influence and the use of social control, square the correlation (.378 × .378 = .143). Thus, 14.3 per cent of the variance in one variable can be explained by variation in the other. In other words, 14 per cent of the increased use of social control is explained by whether or not a person is under the influence of alcohol or drugs. Further, Table 9.9 shows that those relationships that are not statistically significant also have very low coefficients of determination.

What to Remember

There are a few things to remember when using the correlation coefficient as a measure of association. First, we assume that the data are part of a random sample. Our conclusions and ability to generalize

Table 9.8 Correlation matrix

	Signs of a mental illness	Under the influence	Use of social control	Officer months of service
Any signs of mental illness	1.000	.262	.172	.033
		.000	.000	.412
Under the influence	.262	1.000	.378	−.008
	.000		.000	.847
Use of social control	.172	.378	1.000	.007
	.000	.000		.865
Officer months of service	.033	−.008	.007	1.000
	.412	.847	.865	

Table 9.9 Coefficient of determination

Variable combinations	Correlation (Pearson's r)	Coefficient of determination (r²)
Use of social control & under the influence	.378	.143
Use of social control & signs of mental illness	.172	.029
Use of social control & months of service	.007	.000
Under the influence & signs of mental illness	.262	.069
Under the influence & months of service	−.008	.000
Months of service & signs of mental illness	.033	.001

back to the population rests on how the data elements were chosen. Second, both variables under consideration have to be normally distributed. If there is little dispersion in the data, the correlation coefficient will be very small or close to zero. Third, if the relationship is curvilinear, a correlation coefficient can't provide an accurate estimate of that relationship. That is why it's important to always look at a scattergram to determine if the assumption of linearity is met. Finally, and most importantly, a correlation does not equal causation. Simply because two variables are associated does not mean one causes the other—other factors might affect the relationship. The correlation coefficient can indicate only the strength and direction of the relationship. For instance, it could be a spurious relationship between the use of social control and under the influence, where a third factor (such as mental illness) actually explains the relationship. Correlation coefficients can't tell us that interacting with an intoxicated person causes a change in the use of social control, only that an empirical association exists. This is where multivariate analyses and inferential statistics are required.

Bivariate Regression

Linear **bivariate regression** uses a correlation coefficient and researcher knowledge about an independent variable (X) to predict the value of the dependent variable (Y). We predict the value of a continuous dependent variable given a certain value for the independent variable. A higher correlation coefficient indicates

that the two variables share more commonalities. The more commonalities, the better able you are to estimate the variation in the dependent variable based on your knowledge of the independent variable.

While the primary purpose of bivariate regression is to predict values of the dependent variable, it is also used to explain causal relationships. To summarize the relationship between two variables, we produce a **regression line** that fits the data as closely as possible by minimizing the difference between the predicted and observed values (our actual data).

bivariate regression a statistical analysis used to assess the relationship between one independent (predictor) and one dependent (criterion) variable.

regression line the line running through points on a scattergram that shows the direction of the relationship; used to understand the relationship between an independent and dependent relationship.

Regression Equation

The regression line is the graphical representation of the regression equation:

$$\hat{Y} = a + b X_1 + e$$

where

$\hat{Y}$ = dependent variable (predicted)
X_1 = independent variable (predictor)
b = slope (direction of line)
a = intercept (point on Y-axis)
e = error (unexplained variance)

intercept the point at
which the regression line
intercepts with the Y-axis;
symbolized as *a*.

slope the angle of the
regression line; symbolized
as *b*.

To understand this equation, let's take another look at the positive linear relationship in Figure 9.8. The **intercept** is the point where the regression line intersects with the vertical axis. Although it plays no role in the interpretation of regression results, this point is the value of the dependent variable when the value of the independent variable is zero. Think of it as the starting point for salary with no years of education.

The **slope**, which starts at the intercept, is the angle of the regression line. The slope is what we actually interpret, as it estimates the amount of change we expect in the dependent variable given a one unit change in the independent variable. These changes are the regression coefficients. The error is the unexplained variance, or the difference between the predicted value of Y and the actual value of Y in the data. To clarify matters, let's look at some examples.

Interpreting Regression Coefficients

If you have an intercept of 50 and a slope of 2, each increment of X produces a two-unit increase in Y. Alternatively, let's say the independent variable is square footage and the dependent variable is the selling price of a home. You are trying to predict the selling price given the value of the independent variable. If the intercept is 0 square feet and the slope is 150, each additional square foot increases the home's price by \$150. If the value of X is 1,750 square feet with a slope of 150, the estimated selling price of the home is \$262,500.

If we look at Table 9.10, the dependent variable is police use of social control and the predictor variable is citizen age. The unstandardized coefficient (b) is in the original units of measurement (years, increment in social control), which is hard to interpret. The standardized coefficient, or beta (β), is used when you are comparing variables that are measured differently. In the case of regression, the coefficient of determination (r^2) tells us the variation in social control explained by citizen age. The standard error represents the error term and a t-test reveals whether the relationship is statistically significant. What can we conclude? As citizen age increases, the amount of social control used by an officer decreases and this relationship did not occur by chance. The independent variable of age is able to explain 12.9 per cent of the variance in the use of social control.

Multivariate statistics: Analyzing the Complexity of Life

Multivariate statistics build on univariate and bivariate techniques. These types of analyses are ideal for eliminating rival causal explanations and obtaining a more complete understanding of what affects variation in the dependent variable. We will look at a couple of techniques that build on the contingency table and bivariate regression.

Table 9.10 Does being under the influence affect the use of social control by the police?

	Unstandardized		Standardized		Statistical significance
	b	S.E.	β	t	
Constant (intercept)	3.122	.069		45.525	.000
Citizen age (years)	−.107	.002	−.150	−3.704	.000

$r^2 = 0.129$

Elaboration Model

The **elaboration model** introduces a control variable into a contingency table. To investigate the cause–effect relationship, we look at the relationship between two variables within the categories of another variable. The elaboration model is used when an empirical association exists between two variables. This association is determined by examining frequencies, contingency tables, and correlation coefficients. A third variable remains constant in the sense that its values do not vary. The cases from the original relationship are then separated into the categories of the control variable. For example, the independent variable is studying, the dependent is earning an A, and the control variable is sex. The elaboration model allows us to assess the causal relationship between studying and grades for males and females.

Remember the relationship between the use of discretion (Y) and being under the influence of alcohol and drugs in Table 9.7? In Table 9.11, sex (Z) has been added as a control variable. Officers issued warnings in virtually the same number of cases whether males were sober or under the influence of alcohol or drugs. However, officers appeared to issue more warnings to women under the influence than to sober women. This result isn't what one would intuitively expect. Using the elaboration model, we have specified the conditions under which the bivariate relationship operates.

Explanation

The trivariate contingency table provides an explanation when the original relationship between two variables disappears once a control variable is considered. Recall that one of the criteria for a causal relationship is a nonspurious relationship, which is exactly what we are testing for here. Once the third variable is introduced, the relationship between the independent and dependent variable either disappears or becomes significantly weaker. The control variable affects the values of the independent variable, resulting in the spurious association. For instance, the relationship between air conditioner use and ice cream consumption is spurious because it disappears once we control for temperature.

Specification

With specification, the original relationship is tested on subgroups of the population created by a control variable to specify the conditions of the relationship. In other words, the researcher specifies the conditions under which the bivariate relationship exists by seeing if the strength of the relationship varies within a particular category of the control variable. Thus, both the independent and control variable have an important impact on the dependent variable by explaining the strength and direction of the relationship within each category of the control

> **elaboration model** the model that examines the relationship in each category for two variables by controlling for the effects of one or more control variables (symbolized by Z).

Table 9.11 Sex, under the influence, and the use of discretion

		No indication (%)		Under the influence (%)	
		Female	Male	Female	Male
Use of discretion	No—Charges laid	25.5	36.1	18.2	34.3
	Yes—No charges	74.5	63.9	81.8	65.7
	Total	100	100	100	100

$\chi^2 = 4.801, p = 0.018$

suppressor variable
a variable that prevents a true relationship from appearing because the independent variable may not be associated with the dependent variable but correlated with one or more other independent variables.

distorter variable a third variable that reverses the direction of the relationship between independent and dependent variables.

multiple regression
a statistical technique used to assess the ability of two or more independent variables to predict variation in one continuous dependent variable.

variable. This effect is known as a statistical interaction.

Two types of control variables can be detected when using the elaboration model for specification. A **suppressor variable** tells us there is no relationship (even though we expected one) because a hidden third factor conceals the relationship between the two variables under investigation when its influence is uncontrolled. If we remove the suppressor variable, the correlation between the independent and dependent variable increases. For instance, education typically has a positive relationship with income. Higher incomes are associated with conservative attitudes. Here, income can be the suppressor variable because conservative attitudes are related to education.

Looking at things differently, a suppressor variable can have a positive effect on the independent variable and a negative one on the dependent variable, thereby cancelling out any causal relationship between X and Y even though one exists. For example, if studying (X) affects your grades (Y), getting enough sleep could be a suppressor variable (Z). Eight hours of sleep would reduce the time spent studying but increase grades because you are able to concentrate better.

In contrast, a **distorter variable** changes the direction of the two variables' relationship from positive to negative. Let's say you are investigating the glass ceiling phenomenon, which argues that women can climb only so far up the corporate ladder. Hypothetically, you find males (X) earn more money (Y) than females do. However, there is a distorter variable (Z) of having an undergraduate degree. Now women are earning more money because fewer men have an undergraduate degree.

Replication

With replication, the relationship between the independent and dependent variable remains unchanged after the introduction of a control variable. Thus, you learn no new information because the same relationship exists whether the third variable is considered or not. The bivariate relationship remains the same and is considered to be true.

Interpretation

The elaboration model can offer an interpretation when the introduction of a control variable mediates an independent variable's impact on variation of the dependent variable. In such a case, the original relationship disappears because the third variable interprets the relationship between the other two variables by connecting them. In a causal explanation, the third variable is known as an intervening variable. The variable is related to both the independent and dependent variables. Thus, it is possible to conceive of variable Z as a result of the independent variable (X), which is what affects the dependent variable (Y). When considering individual and situational factors that affect officer assaults, Rabe-Hemp and Schuck (2007) used a four-way contingency table to explore the relationship between female officers and family conflict calls. The findings suggest that this relationship is contingent on citizen impairment. Citizens who are under the influence are more likely to use violence against female officers in domestic violence calls.

Multiple Regression

The only difference between bivariate and **multiple regression** is the inclusion of two or more independent variables in the regression equation. Consider this example:

$$\acute{Y} = a + b\,X_1 + b\,X_2 + b\,X_3 + e$$

where
$\acute{Y}$ = Social control (predicted)
X_1 = Citizen age (predictor)
X_2 = Prior record (predictor)
X_3 = Disrespectful (predictor)

Research Highlights

Putting It All Together: Univariate, Bivariate, and Multivariate Statistics

Crime and justice research uses a variety of quantitative techniques to address the research questions. Some present the results from univariate, bivariate, and multivariate analyses. Others require only descriptive statistics, whether they are univariate or bivariate, to address

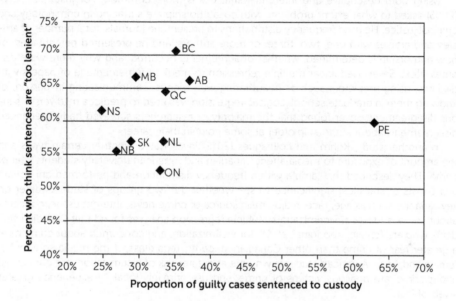

Relationship between perceptions of sentence leniency and the use of imprisonment

Source: Sprott, Webster, & Doob (2013, p. 284).

the research problem. Here are some examples to demonstrate that there is no set rule that you have to use both descriptive and inferential statistics.

Sprott, Webster, and Doob (2013) used only descriptive statistics to answer the question, "Is there a relationship between the severity of court sanctions and views on the criminal justice system?" They created a series of scattergrams, of which the following figure is an example.

We can see from the figure that there is no support for the "get tough on crime" approach, as harsher sentences don't lead to increases in public confidence in the criminal justice system. Instead, the more a province uses imprisonment, the more residents feel sentences are too lenient. Note the outlier of Prince Edward Island, where 63 per cent of

Continued

those found guilty are imprisoned and 60 per cent of residents feel sanctions are too lenient (Sprott et al., 2013).

White and Ready (2007) used descriptive statistics to examine taser use over a three-year period. The only quantitative technique used was frequency distributions on suspect, officer, incident characteristics, and behaviour (e.g. sex, race, suspect resistance, location, officer satisfaction with outcome). The effectiveness of Taser deployment was measured using the percentage of citizens taken into custody. Univariate statistics were sufficient to address the research questions; the findings were that officers consider Tasers an effective way to restore order.

Using both descriptive and inferential statistics is more common. For instance, Sever (2005) asked to what extent problems with co-authorship are surfacing in criminology and criminal justice. He used frequency distributions to present the journals, total number of articles, and articles with one, two, three, or more authors, and he presented percentages for how authorship is determined, whether disagreements occurred, and why there were disputes. Next, Sever used linear multiple regression to predict the percentage of papers with disputes, using predictors such as coauthoring with friends, communicating in-person, or knowing them in graduate school. Logistic regression was used to predict a mild versus serious disagreement. Sever found that the majority of researchers surveyed had experienced disagreements about authorship order at some point in their career.

In another study, Kohm and colleagues (2012) investigated whether certain types and the amount of exposure to media affect Canadian and American university students' fear of crime. They described the sample with a frequency distribution and performed chi-square and t-tests of statistical significance to see whether the two groups of students differ on key variables such as age, race, major, main source of crime news, Internet usage, concerns about crime, and risk of victimization. Multiple regression analyses found that Canadian students who are female, Aboriginal, at risk for victimization, and concerned about crime have a greater fear of crime than other Canadian students, regardless of the media source. Yet female and Asian-American students who are at greater risk of victimization, are concerned about crime, are previous victims of crime, and use primarily local TV experience greater levels of fear.

The most common approach is to conduct descriptive and inferential analyses using univariate, bivariate, and multivariate statistics. However, studies with inferential statistics often do not report the bivariate results. At other times, only descriptive statistics are needed to explore the research problem. The bottom line is that the research question drives the method and the choice of analytical techniques.

Table 9.10 presented the results of a bivariate regression with citizen age (X_1) and the use of social control (Y). Let's add two more variables and revisit citizen age in Table 9.12.

Multiple regression predicts variation in the use of social control by a one unit change in an independent variable while holding all other variables constant. In other words, given a prior criminal record and poor demeanour, what impact does a citizen's age have on the use of social control? The bivariate regression results found citizen age to be a statistically significant predictor. Once we account for a prior record and disrespect toward the officer, age is no longer statistically significant. r is the correlation of all variables in the model. r^2 is the coefficient of determination, indicating how well these three independent variables explain variation in using social control. I advise you to interpret the adjusted r^2, as it is the coefficient of determination after considering the number of independent variables included in the regression equation. The more variables included in the regression equation, the more variance explained.

Other Multivariate Techniques

It is beyond the scope of this textbook to discuss other multivariate techniques in detail. However, it is important to be aware that researchers have a multitude of tools at their disposal to analyze data quantitatively and address any research question. Let's look at some alternative techniques.

Alternate Forms of Regression Analyses

Having a categorical dependent variable, such as the use of police discretion, doesn't mean you can't perform a regression analysis. Logistic regression can be used to assess the independent variables' ability to predict values of the dependent variable. In other words, it is the odds of using discretion (yes/no) given a certain value for an independent variable, such as age, while holding the value of all other independent variables constant (the same).

Path analysis is a type of regression analysis that graphically presents the paths of causality. This type is a powerful tool for testing theoretical explanations deductively. The researcher specifies the causal model, temporal order, and direction of the relationship in advance. The causal order of the independent variables is assumed on the basis of theory and prior research. Path coefficients are the estimates of the strength or hypothesized direct and indirect relationships between independent and dependent variables. For example, family history of mental illness has a direct effect on suicidal thoughts and an indirect relationship with susceptibility to depression.

Factor Analysis

The goal of **factor analysis** is to identify latent factors from a group of correlated variables. A cluster of variables correlated with one another all load highly on a factor, which is some underlying unidentified theoretical construct. The factor is given a summary name based on the set of variables then included in regression analyses.

> **factor analysis** a statistical technique used to assess whether a number of indicators tend to group together and are interrelated to form a latent construct.

Factor analysis works well in the understanding of data patterns when you have many independent variables. The factor consisting of highly intercorrelated variables reduces a large number of variables to one or more factors that measure an underlying common theme. A word of caution: factors do not necessarily have any substantive meaning. The variables could be quite different and difficult to summarize. Think of it as the difference between statistical and substantive significance. For example, the latent construct of intelligence may load the grades from four out of five courses on this factor. You may find that they are all related to statistics

Table 9.12 Predicting the use of social control

	Unstandardized		Standardized		Statistical significance
	b	S.E.	β	t	
Constant (intercept)	2.857	.070		40.891	.000
Citizen age (years)	−.004	.002	−.094	−1.450	.115
Prior record	.200	.056	.140	3.586	.000
Disrespectful	.591	.068	.341	8.676	.000

$r = .418 / r^2 = .129 / \text{Adjusted } r^2 = .171$

and research methods. Thus, you label the factor for these four courses quantitative intelligence.

Analysis of Variance (ANOVA)

analysis of variance (ANOVA) a statistical technique that uses a continuous dependent variable to investigate whether the means of two or more groups are different from one another.

F-test a test of statistical significance determining the probability that differences between samples for two or more means are the result of sampling error.

A t-test is a good technique for comparing two groups; however, researchers use **analysis of variance (ANOVA)** for three or more groups. The dependent variable is interval or ratio, while the independent variable is categorical with three or more categories. With ANOVA, you assess whether there is more variation between groups than within groups.

Instead of using multiple t-tests, ANOVA uses an **F-test** to determine whether the differences between groups in the categories are statistically significant. The null hypothesis is that the means for all groups are equivalent. If statistically significant, the variance between groups didn't occur by chance. For example, do the ages and genders of the minor in child pornography and the offender affect university students' perceptions on the seriousness of possessing child pornography? To answer this question, Lam, Mitchell, and Seto (2010) presented a correlation matrix and several frequency polygons. They used a $2 \times 3 \times 2$ ANOVA analysis to compare participant sex, three age groups, and offender sex. The findings were that the offender's age and sex have no impact on perceptions of offence severity, but males are perceived as more likely to reoffend than females.

Conclusion

Statistics in and of themselves aren't capable of lying. It's how we use them and whether we hide information that is of concern. This isn't simply a question of ethics but also political considerations. Alvin Toffler is quoted as saying: "Political tacticians are not in search of scholarly truth or even simple accuracy. They are looking for ammunition to use in the information wars. Data, information, and knowledge do not have to be true to blast an opponent out of the water" (Statistics Canada, 2013a). Misinterpretation by personal bias, inaccurate analyses, or fictional data can all occur. Always assess the credibility of the information source and understand the methods, variable definitions, and statistical analysis.

You must also be critical and evaluate what you are reading. Is the data being analyzed and presented to the reader as objectively as possible? Statistics are not always right or comprehensible. Ethical researchers always report unexpected findings. Future research can use different samples to test whether these findings are anomalous or perhaps a trend.

Researchers can be dishonest when using numbers in several ways. An example is removing outliers from a dataset without disclosing a rationale for doing so. Similarly, it's unethical if researchers use an inappropriate statistical technique to enhance the significance of their findings. Statistical software will often not test whether the technique is appropriate. There is also the chance of committing a Type I or Type II error. The best defence is a large enough random sample. Finally, question any findings that are completely inconsistent with prior research because a Type II error may have occurred.

Be honest about data limitations and the potential for an unmeasured third variable affecting the results. Use the elaboration paradigm and report statistically insignificant findings. Check to see if your data are skewed, as a skew affects statistical analyses and leads to inaccurate findings. Watch the scale of your graph axes, as they can change the shape of the distribution. Finally, don't engage in a fishing expedition to find statistically significant relationships in the data. Guided by theory and prior research, the research question drives the method, and the statistical technique is no exception.

Methods in Action

Tips for "Statsy" Success

According to Newton and Rudestam (1999, pp. 290–295), there are ten tips for success when conducting quantitative research:

1. Get comfortable with the data. Before conducting any inferential statistics, be familiar with your data. What do the variables mean? What is the range? Are there any missing data? This point may seem obvious, but if you are not familiar with the data you can make critical mistakes when choosing the proper analytical technique for the type of data and research questions.

2. Explore your data in detail and then do it again. Conduct exploratory data analysis by pouring over graphs, box-and-whisker plots, and histograms to examine the distribution. Use the elaboration model to look for alternative explanations.

3. Pictures can speak louder than words. Graphical representations can give meaning to the data that might be concealed in a numerical table. Present the descriptive and inferential results with appropriate tables and graphs. However, use a graph only if it shows something special that cannot easily be summarized in a table.

4. Replication is underemphasized and overdue. Statistically significant results need to be replicated using a different sample; otherwise, the results may be untrustworthy and generalizations misleading. "In science, something worth doing is worth doing over and over again. Replicating a good study or improving on a flawed study is often a better choice than adding another trivial study to the literature" (p. 293).

5. Remember the difference between statistical and substantive significance. There is nothing sacred about statistical significance, particularly since it is so affected by sample size. The finding may have no theoretical or practical significance. Even a finding lacking statistical significance can have substantive significance.

6. Remember the difference between the size of the coefficient and confidence intervals. It's not just a question of statistical significance but also the size of the effect when assessing substantive significance.

7. Statistics do not speak for themselves. The goal is to present a coherent argument supporting or failing to support a particular position identified in theory and prior research. A common mistake is to present too much analysis with insufficient information and interpretation of the findings—what it all means in relation to the research questions.

8. Whenever possible, keep it simple. Complex quantitative analyses that are not needed to address the research question will create confusion. Always choose the simplest analysis, as it is also less likely to involve errors in the interpretation of the findings.

9. When in doubt, ask someone. Statistics can be confusing and frustrating, even for seasoned researchers. There is no shame in asking someone for help or for his or her opinion. We can't be experts in everything.

10. Don't be too hard on yourself. I know—easier said than done. Few studies find support for the hypotheses; if they do, the effects can be smaller than anticipated. Even with strong effects, we can't "prove" anything. Concepts are operationalized imperfectly, samples are not random or too small, and the theoretical explanations being tested are vague and incomplete. Don't be disappointed with small or non-significant findings because they are findings in and of themselves. They make a meaningful contribution to our understanding of the issue and can help develop new ideas for future research.

Summary of Important Points

Introduction

- Quantitative researchers conduct univariate, bivariate, and multivariate analyses classified as descriptive or inferential statistics.
- Preparing quantitative data for analysis consists of data entry, codebook creation, variable coding, and data cleaning.

Univariate Analysis: What Does My Data Look Like?

- Frequency distributions used with categorical variables present the number and percentage of cases for each category.
- Rates allow you to compare values on a variable for two different groups.
- Bar and pie charts are appropriate for categorical variables, while histograms and frequency polygons are used for continuous data.
- The mode is the most common score, median the middle score, and the mean the average of scores in a frequency distribution.
- A skewed distribution is either positive or negative and occurs when the mean, median, and mode are not equivalent.
- Measures of dispersion summarizing differences in scores include the range, interquartile range, and the standard deviation.

Bivariate Analysis: Are They Related?

- A Type I error occurs when you reject a true null hypothesis. A Type II error involves accepting a false null hypothesis.
- When testing for statistical significance, the chi-square statistic is used for categorical variables and t-tests for continuous variables.

- Substantive significance is as important as statistical significance.
- Cross-tabulations are displayed in a contingency table, with joint frequencies and percentages of cases falling into categories of the independent variable.
- Contingency tables are percentaged down columns (X) and read across rows (Y).
- Scattergrams show the shape, direction, and dispersion of the relationship between two continuous variables.
- A correlation coefficient summarizes the strength and direction of two variables and is interpreted using the eyeball method or a coefficient of determination.
- In bivariate regression, we predict the value of the dependent variable based on a one-unit change in the independent variable.

Multivariate Statistics: Analyzing the Complexity of Life

- The elaboration model tests causal relationships in a contingency table by examining the relationship in each category for two variables while controlling for the effects of a control variable.
- The elaboration model can result in explanation, specification, replication, and interpretation of the bivariate relationship.
- Multiple regression estimates how well two or more independent variables predict values of a continuous dependent variable.
- Logistic regression uses a categorical dependent variable.
- Path analysis specifies direct and indirect effects of independent variables on the dependent variable.
- Factor analysis reduces a large number of intercorrelated variables to one factor.

- Analysis of variance tests whether the means of two or more groups are different for a continuous dependent variable.

Conclusion

- Conduct quantitative research ethically by avoiding misrepresenting, omitting, or deleting data.

Key Terms

analysis of variance (ANOVA) 294
bar chart 267
bivariate analysis 262
bivariate regression 287
box-and-whisker plot (or boxplot) 276
chi-square 280
codebook 264
coefficient of determination (r^2) 286
correlation coefficient (or Pearson's product-moment correlation coefficient) 285
cross-tabulation 281
descriptive statistics 262

distorter variable 290
elaboration model 289
factor analysis 293
frequency distribution 265
frequency polygon 271
F-test 294
histogram 270
inferential statistics 262
intercept 288
interquartile range (ICR) 276
mean 272
median 272
mode 272
multiple regression 290
multivariate analysis 262
negative (or left) skew 274

pie chart 269
positive (or right) skew 274
range 275
rate 267
regression line 287
scattergram (or scatterplot) 283
slope 288
standard deviation 277
statistical significance 278
suppressor variable 290
t-test 280
Type I error 279
Type II error 279
univariate analysis 262

Review Questions and Exercises

1. Examine the following salary distribution and the measures of central tendency:

103 employees at $40,000 each	Mode income:	$40,000
9 managers at $75,000 each	Median income:	$40,000
1 CEO at $5,200,000	Mean income:	$88,451
Total annual salary payout = $7,195,000		

   In the real world, what is the implication of relying on the mean when describing salaries at this company? What would be a more realistic representation of this distribution? Why?

2. Sarah Achiever works at a restaurant near campus and wants to know whether there is some way to increase her tips. She conducts a little experiment: she randomly selects twenty cheques and writes "Have

an awesome day!" on them; she randomly selects another twenty and writes nothing on them. Here is the list of tips she received (presented in percentages):

"Have an awesome day!"	No message
17	45
28	21
41	27
33	34
27	34
44	25
22	31
24	28
65	21
27	36
34	31
72	30
25	20
47	39
21	8
30	22
33	23
29	30
40	28
21	28

Using this data, complete the following steps/questions:

a. State the minimum and maximum values. Calculate the range.

b. Calculate the mode, median, and mean.

c. Calculate the interquartile range.

d. Which measure of central tendency best represents both sets of bills? Support your answer.

e. What would you tell Sarah about the impact of writing a personalized positive message on the bill?

3. Examine one day's edition of your local newspaper and of either the *Globe and Mail* or *National Post*. For each newspaper, perform the following steps:

a. Record the frequency in which crime-related articles appear in the first section of each newspaper.

b. Note the number of crime articles in which statistics are included. Calculate the mean for each newspaper. What can you conclude from this data? What other statistical test(s) could be appropriate when comparing these two newspapers?

c. Present the results in a contingency table.

Online Exercises and Websites of Interest

Statistics in Academic Research

http://scholar.google.com

For this exercise, conduct searches for journal articles on Google Scholar.

1. Search for journal articles on a topic of your choice. For the first ten articles you find, how many address the research question(s) using descriptive or inferential statistics? Why do you think this is the case?
2. Choose three key terms from this chapter and conduct an article search for each of them. What types of relationships and questions are addressed in the articles? Write three methodological summaries (one for each key term) describing how the concept (key term) was used in the article.

Statistics: Power from Data!

www.statcan.gc.ca/edu/power-pouvoir/toc-tdm/5214718-eng.htm

This excellent online resource from Statistics Canada provides easy-to-understand explanations for data processing, graphs, central tendency, dispersion, the use of statistics, problems commonly encountered, and ethical considerations.

Additional Resources

Babbie, E., Haley, F.S., Wagner III, W.E., & Zaino, J. (2013). *Adventures in social research: Data analysis using IBM SPSS statistics* (8th ed.). Thousand Oaks, CA: Sage.

A practical hands-on guide with screen shots, this text offers guidance on how to conduct univariate, bivariate, and multivariate analyses in SPSS.

Best, J. (2012). *Damned Lies and Statistics: Untangling Numbers from the Media, Politicians, and Activists* (Updated edition). Berkeley, CA: University of California Press.

This book, which builds on Huff's (1954) *How to Lie with Statistics*, is an introduction to descriptive statistics. It also sensitizes the reader to how statistics can be manipulated to tell a story.

Coolidge, F.L. (2013). *Statistics: A Gentle Introduction* (3rd ed.). Thousand Oaks, CA: Sage.

This text is an introduction to common statistical techniques used in social science research. It focuses on step-by-step explanations rather than on formulas.

Finkelstein, M.O., & Levin, B. (2001). *Statistics for lawyers* (2nd ed.). **Statistics for social science and public policy. New York: Springer-Verlag.**

This book provides an often humorous explanation of descriptive and inferential statistical techniques in the context of examples such as the parking meter heist (descriptive), DNA profiling (descriptive), or creating a jury list (probability).

Morgon, S.E., Reichert, T., & Harrison, T.R. (2002). *From numbers to words: Reporting statistical results for the social sciences.* **Boston, MA: Allyn and Bacon.**

This book is a step-by-step guide on how to present descriptive and inferential statistics in tables and graphs, along with how to discuss the results.

Chapter 10

Interpreting Qualitative Data

"Data analysis is the process of bringing order, structure and meaning to the mass of collected data. It is a messy, ambiguous, time consuming, creative and fascinating process. It does not proceed in a linear fashion; it is not neat. Qualitative data analysis is a search for general statements about relationships among categories of data." C. Marshall and G. B. Rossman, *Designing Qualitative Research* (1990, p. 111)

Learning Objectives

- To understand the analytical process of moving from raw data to theoretical explanations.
- To differentiate between the analytical frameworks of ideal type, illustrative method, analytic comparison, and successive approximation.
- To articulate how to fracture data, code text segments, write memos, and identify relationships within and across concepts.

- To understand open, axial, and selective coding in grounded theory and other textual analysis techniques.
- To create a database and code data in NVivo.
- To appreciate the role ethics plays in qualitative data analysis.

Introduction

Two of my biggest fears during data analysis are, "What happens if I don't find anything interesting or can't identify any themes? Will my findings contribute to knowledge?" Don't panic. The data will speak to you. The key is not to test ideas with the same logic used in quantitative research or to enter the analysis with preconceived notions and ignore all unsupportive evidence.

It may seem like a mysterious and almost magical process, but there is a method to the madness. Qualitative data analysis is as systematic as what we discussed in Chapter 9 for quantitative research. You are just as likely to see bad examples of qualitative research as you are quantitative research, simply because the analysis depends on the data collected and the analytical abilities of the researcher.

The mantra "the research question drives the method" still applies. The research question and the social context influence the analysis. Accounting for the social context by no means suggests that the process is ad hoc. This flexible approach involves adhering to methodological guidelines and established techniques. Otherwise, it would be impossible to authenticate the findings.

Data analysis starts while you are still collecting data. The two processes are intertwined. It's not that you are coming to premature conclusions but documenting analytical insights as they occur. This approach allows you to collect additional data that can assess the validity of these preliminary hunches. Qualitative data analysis engages researchers in a sense-making process. You are not simply looking at the literal content but also the text's interpretive meaning to understand that person's perspective.

Analyzing Numbers versus Words

The structure of qualitative data analysis can be understood by the basic differences between quantitative and qualitative research. As we saw in Chapter 3, quantitative research engages in a process of conceptualization, creating nominal definitions and operationalization with variables as indicators of the concepts. Qualitative research takes an entirely different approach by letting the data create and refine conceptual definitions. The research question is broad, which allows the data to dictate relationships among key concepts. Concepts are defined during data analysis, not prior to data collection. The analysis is not geared around testing propositions but developing them by identifying patterns and themes. Any numbers presented are descriptive only, with quotations used to support interpretations.

In this case, it is the participant and not the researcher who is an expert on the subject matter.

These points are consistent with the assumptions of qualitative research discussed in Chapters 1 and 2. The goal is to represent the insider perspective, where events and behaviours are interpreted based on what it means to the social actors, not the researcher, involved. Reflexivity is practised by writing notes on the process, in relation to the researcher, during data collection and analysis. The researcher is the data collection instrument and the analysis must be sensitive to the potential for reactivity and other potential influences on the data and its interpretation. Acknowledging how the research process has affected the researcher increases the trustworthiness of the findings and confidence in the conclusions.

Finally, qualitative analysis is iterative and recursive. Data collection and analysis occur simultaneously versus the linear, deductive approach of quantitative research, which analyzes the data after collection is complete. As the Wallace Wheel demonstrates, qualitative research is both inductive and deductive (see p. 37). The process is inductive because concepts and theoretical explanations are created from the data. It is deductive because the researchers engage in this iterative process, whereby they check initial interpretations and conceptual definitions with new data until they stop learning anything new (i.e. achieve theoretical saturation).

Wilkinson (2007) conducted 159 interviews with violent males between the ages of 16 and 24 to understand the impact of social control efforts on drugs, violence, and property destruction. The analysis was inductive as it involved assigning text segments to categories based on what was found in the data; it was deductive as they were checked for consistency within and across categories. A data analysis software program was used to engage in two cycles of analysis: coding and determining relationships in the data between themes. Using this approach, the researchers discovered that local social networks undermine formal social control efforts involving the law unless age and space (offence location and neighbourhood) are taken into account.

The goal of qualitative data analysis is to create theoretical propositions and explanations that can apply to as many aspects of the event, situation, or process under investigation as possible. Engaging in **analytic induction**, researchers develop a working hypothesis early in data analysis and then assess whether each piece of data supports the preliminary hypothesis. If the data don't fit the hypothesis, it's revised to include this circumstance or redefined to exclude this situation. This is how negative cases are used to refine a theoretical explanation.

Analytic induction is a research strategy. You pay attention to evidence that either supports or refutes the themes identified from previously analyzed data. You compare events or cases to one another within a concept or theme and refine the concept further to better reflect social reality.

It is human nature to pay attention to evidence that is similar and supports the meaning of a theme you find in the data. However, think back a moment to quantitative research. When we test a deductive hypothesis, we actually test the null hypothesis (H_0), which says there is no relationship—not the alternative hypothesis (H_A), which expects the relationship to be true. In qualitative research, there is a parallel logic. Although evidence that supports our hunches is comforting and important, evidence that does not corroborate the definition or the content of a theme or a hypothesized relationship between concepts has more analytic importance. Analytic induction is how we understand what we are investigating, refine definitions, and elaborate on the basis of evidence that confirms but also disconfirms our developing understanding of this social reality. If you can't identify similarities as more data are collected, it means that your concept, category, or theme is too big or heterogeneous and requires reconceptualization for clarity.

Let's bring analytical induction to a more practical level. It is always a challenge to list an iterative process, but consider this list circular. When you get

to the end, you start again until you learn nothing new. The research question gives you the focus for data collection and a road map to the analysis. The next steps are as follows:

- Collect data and begin the analysis.
- Formulate tentative theoretical explanations during data analysis.
- Assess the adequacy of explanations by comparing segments of data within concepts and themes and to new data.
- Upon discovering disconfirming evidence, redefine concepts, and collect additional data to target this contradictory evidence specifically.
- Revise the explanation to incorporate all the evidence, including the negative, deviant cases.

> **analytic induction** an iterative process in which hypotheses develop early in the data analysis process and subsequent evidence is compared to either support or refute themes and relationships between concepts.

This process continues until you no longer find disconfirming evidence that indicates another facet of the theme. For instance, a theme of confusion can include dimensions on the basis of what causes confusion. The process for this theme ceases when you no longer find new causes or other aspects of confusion as perceived by respondents (e.g. impact of confusion on outcomes).

The Process of Analyzing the Data

So far, we have talked about the iterative and recursive nature of qualitative data analysis in the context of analytic induction. Figure 10.1 provides a graphical representation of how data analysis involves four simultaneous activities: data collection, reduction, display, and drawing conclusions. Although in simplified form, the figure depicts our thinking about the data.

Data reduction involves finding and choosing text segments, as well as simplifying and transforming the data into a format that can be analyzed

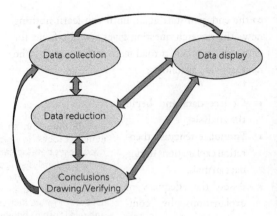

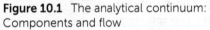

Figure 10.1 The analytical continuum: Components and flow

Source: Miles & Huberman (1984, p. 23). Copyright © 1984, American Educational Research Association.

further. The data display stage continues the organization of the data but in a way that allows for drawing conclusions by coding. This method could involve creating a map to represent visually the relationships among concepts and categories. As Miles and Huberman (1984, p. 24) suggest, "you know what you display." By drawing conclusions, you create meaning. Patterns, clusters, sequences of events, and theoretical propositions are identified from the data. These are then verified for plausibility and validity by comparing new data to these developing ideas.

There are two additional things to note. First, data collection is connected to all activities. You collect data; you reduce, display, and categorize them; you draw conclusions about them; and, consistent with analytical induction, you collect additional data and make comparisons to verify and modify the theoretical explanations. Second, there is movement back and forth at every point. For example, the data are displayed after data collection. However, interplay occurs between data reduction, display, and conclusions. When a conclusion is drawn, the data are displayed again and can be broken down within a theme or additional data are

ideal type an abstract description of the social phenomenon that is a model used to compare data.

collected to flush out nuances in the propositions and explore disconfirming evidence.

The Method to the Madness

Think of qualitative data analysis as a way to get behind the numbers. You are able to find out how people really feel about something at a given point in time. By its very nature, qualitative data is rich and detailed, which means the analysis will include thick description to present the findings that lead to a theoretical explanation. Meaning is negotiated through social interaction between research subjects. You have a similar relationship with the reader so that you communicate the intended meaning when you present the results. As Geertz (1973, pp. 25–26) points out, "the essential task of theory building here is not to codify abstract regularities but to make thick description possible, not to generalize across cases but to generalize within them."

Theory and method are interconnected—and nowhere more so than in qualitative data analysis. Based on the research objective, methodological theory informs the analytical framework, which articulates the goal of the analysis and provides a roadmap.

Ideal Type

An **ideal type** is an abstract depiction that creates a model to compare all of our data against. This term originates from the work of Max Weber (1904/1949, p. 90), whose definition is the basis for this analytical framework:

> An ideal type is formed by the one-sided *accentuation* of one or more points of view and by the synthesis of a great many diffuse, discrete, more or less present and occasionally absent *concrete individual* phenomena, which are arranged according to those one-sidedly emphasized viewpoints into a unified *analytical* construct. In its conceptual purity, this mental construct cannot be found empirically anywhere in reality. It is a *utopia.* (emphasis in original)

An ideal type is not meant to be a perfect picture but a way to highlight common features of that event, situation, person, or process. It becomes a comparison point across time, location, and culture.

Ideal types don't actually exist in real life but serve as a measuring rod during the analysis to identify similarities and differences between cases. For example, let's say we create an ideal type of a crime scene. This doesn't mean that all crime scenes look like the ideal type or contain all the characteristics. The characteristics that are included do not describe a particular crime scene, but data on specific crime scenes are compared to see how they measure up to this ideal type. Ideal types have characteristics of the social phenomenon instead of describing a particular type or case.

This model highlights the specific details in a case. It is one way to make us aware of the contextual factors and their impact on the phenomenon's features. We can see the uniqueness of the case as part of a generic process. It's a benchmark to our interpretation of the data. When ideal types are used in published research, analogies are made between events, situations, actions, or people similar to one another. In other words, a connection is made between a pattern in the data and familiar everyday experiences.

Illustrative Method

When using the **illustrative method**, you apply an existing theory to a situation, setting, group, or experience and use data as theoretical examples. Think of theoretical explanations as moving-day instructions. Each concept in a theory is an empty box. The analysis involves placing data inside each box to illustrate the conceptual meaning and order. Thus, the data can support, modify, or refute the theoretical explanation in that given setting.

This theory-driven framework is used to accomplish three things. First, the illustrative method results in understanding the social phenomenon better by applying existing theoretical explanations

in new ways. This is an important part of the scientific enterprise as theories have greater explanatory power when they are transferable across time, settings, and culture. Second, this framework explores whether the theory can explain the phenomenon across cases. Finally, it illustrates what a theory means and how it can be used. With additional circumstances under which a theory can offer an explanation, it has greater impact on our understanding of everyday life.

Analytic Comparison

With the illustrative method, data are used to *describe* the theory in a given context. When using **analytic comparison**, data are compared to an existing theory to *explain* an outcome in a given context. Clusters of factors are associated with a particular outcome and are inductively and deductively identified across cases. To ensure conceptual clarity, the factors have to be mutually exclusive and exhaustive, as they would be in quantitative research. Analytical comparisons are interpretive and not a type of nomothetic inquiry. They create a detailed, in-depth understanding of a few cases rather than generalizable patterns that apply to many cases.

How do you make analytic comparisons? You use the methods of agreement and difference to explore factors associated with outcomes. The **method of agreement** involves looking for commonalities across cases that have a similar outcome as predicted by theory. In this way, you isolate causal factors with key similarities for this outcome, regardless of other differences between cases.

illustrative method a qualitative method that applies an existing theory to a situation, setting, group, or experience and uses the data as theoretical examples.

analytic comparison the development of theoretical ideas, using the methods of agreement and difference, based on patterns in existing theories when compared to alternative explanations in a particular social context.

method of agreement an analytical technique that involves comparing data characteristics that are similar to other cases and results in the same or similar outcome.

method of difference an analytical technique that involves comparing data characteristics that are different for cases that have the same or similar outcome.

The **method of difference** is often used with the method of agreement as a different but related way to make comparisons to existing theory. Characteristics and factors are determined by the existing theory. Cases are then categorized for the same outcome, where one group is similar on important characteristics or factors and the other group has different ones.

The researcher uses the **constant comparison method**, in which the data describing a social phenomenon are compared for similarities and differences. This method is a key component in grounded theory but is applicable here as well. In grounded theory, the constant comparison method is used to create an inductive theory, while analytic comparisons involve assessing a theory's ability to explain an outcome in a given context.

constant comparison method a comparison of empirical indicators that describe people, events, and situations to other data for similarities and differences.

To clarify, you don't start with a theory in the way you would with the illustrative method. Analytic comparisons develop ideas about patterns in theories and compare them to explanations derived from the data. The data are used to make comparisons to existing theory rather than to illustrate and describe the theory, as is the case with the illustrative method.

"Thinking outside of the box is difficult for some people. Keep trying."

Source: Glasbergen Cartoon Service

a theoretical model starts to develop. The model becomes more and more accurate with each successive review of the data. Successive approximation is the theoretical framework for the analytic induction approach.

Not only do researchers become extremely familiar with the data but different insights are also inductively gained with each reading. When you proofread something the second time, you will find additional leaps in logic or grammatical mistakes. When you reread sections of a textbook chapter, you may understand the material better or in a different way. The same thing happens with successive approximation.

Successive Approximation

Successive approximation solidifies how repeated readings of the data define concepts and identify patterns. This methodological theory suggests that researchers move from general notions and specific pieces of data to larger thematic interpretations. With each reading of the data, concepts are clarified and

successive approximation iterative movements between data and existing theoretical concepts that guide further data collection, refine theory, and develop empirical generalizations.

Nuts and Bolts: Where Do I Start?

Now we are back to the mounds of data. If you conduct 25 interviews that range in length from 60 to 90 minutes, you will have between 625 to 1,000 single-spaced pages of data. As daunting as this volume may be, data analysis is doable by fracturing the data, writing memos, and engaging in several cycles of coding. The underlying story in the data will emerge piece by piece.

Methods in Action

An Art or a Science?

"It is a capital mistake to theorize before one has data."

Sir A.C. Doyle, The Penguin Complete Sherlock Holmes (2009, p. 27).

Life is a series of judgments made using insufficient data. If we are to tell a scientific story based on empirical data, can we get past this situation? Debate exists on whether qualitative data analysis is an art or a science. One can argue both ways. The analysis is an art because we transmit understanding in ways that promote insight, contextualize findings, and address questions left unanswered by quantitative research. It is a science because of the consistency with a worldview, epistemological, and ontological assumptions associated with qualitative inquiry, adherence to established analytical techniques, and the creation of theoretical explanations grounded in the data. However, the analysis is also a craft due to the skill required for data collection and analysis.

There is no universal approach to qualitative research. Adding to the confusion is the messiness inherent in data analysis, with varied, abstract, and perplexing instructions on how to conduct the research from beginning to end (Mellor, 2001). Students of research methods can find comfort in quantitative data analysis because of its nomothetic, law-like nature, where there is arguably a "right" and "wrong" way to analyze the data. On many levels, this idea is true; however, the art of interpretation applies to both quantitative and qualitative research. Not only does qualitative data analysis use established analytical techniques but the interpretations are also made within conceptual frameworks. From this perspective, all research is both an art and science.

There is no great divide between theory and method. Theories provide us with explanations about the world, while methods consistent with a paradigmatic worldview help us gather and interpret data through an iterative, recursive process. Brinkmann (2012) raises two related issues. First, the art is the development of an analytic awareness and the science concerns the awareness being informed by theory. Thus, theory and method are both tools in the quest to interpret qualitative data. Second, this marriage between theory and method is the craft of analysis. The intellectual craft constitutes a "practice that involves the whole person, continually drawing on past experience as it is projected into the future" (Mellor, 2001, p. 4). The art and craft of reflexivity is how we hone our awareness, acknowledge the researcher as the data collection and analysis instrument, and better ensure the trustworthiness of the conclusions we assess using appropriate scientific stands for this worldview.

Where does this leave us? I would argue that the craft of all data analysis is both art and science. However, as seen in Chapters 1 and 2, some argue that qualitative research is too subjective and does not measure up to the standards of reliability and validity as defined in quantitative research. Without unpacking the mess as Mellor (2001) advocates, these misconceptions regarding the contribution to knowledge from qualitative research are perpetuated. Therefore, it is even more important for qualitative researchers to document the data analysis process that leads to findings and theoretical explanations.

Fracturing the Data

Fracturing the data involves pulling it apart, organizing it, and then putting it all back together in a meaningful way so that we can tell a story (Glaser & Strauss, 1967; Strauss & Corbin, 1998). Participant responses or descriptions of events and actions are broken down into empirical units that can be assigned to a concept. In practical terms, you examine the data by word, phrase, sentence, line, or paragraph for any action, interaction, idea, or meaningful event. Richardson and Kennedy (2012) took the road less travelled and coded data word by word to understand the common use of the word *gang* and its underlying meanings in four Canadian newspapers. Although articles with higher word counts were overrepresented, it was preferable to thematically coding when the word *gang* has multiple interpretations within one article. Incidentally, they found the word ambiguous and, if left unquestioned, interpreted it in the hegemonic discourse that associates it with crime.

> **coding** a systematic process of categorizing groups of text segments together and assigning a term or phrase to summarize that topic, event, or person.

Fracturing the data and coding are essentially synonymous, but both processes require the development of different analytical skills (Neuman, 2011). To fracture data, researchers require the ability to recognize patterns and, in doing so, think about concepts and the relationships among them. In addition to having relevant knowledge on the research topic, the researcher needs sufficient background knowledge on the setting, people, or events to contextualize findings while coding. Finally, once initial codes are created, the last thing to do is to treat them as fixed entities similar to quantitative measurement practices. Qualitative data analysis and coding are fluid and emergent.

You also want to avoid analyzing at only the descriptive level. You code to develop

> **deductive coding** an approach to the data in which coding occurs with certain concepts and themes in mind.

an understanding of what is going on. Coding is not a mechanical or linear process conducted by a robot. If it is approached in this way, you will miss conceptual definitions and emerging connections.

Coding

When fracturing the data, you break it down into manageable chunks, which leads to the process of **coding**—organizing text segments into meaningful categories. A code can represent a concept of interest, a theme, or something appearing in the data that warrants further exploration. In other words, when coding data, a name is applied to groups of similar text segments. Once coded, the constant comparison method is used to refine these categories and determine how segments and concepts relate to one another. You are constantly making decisions on whether a concept is present in the data you are reviewing. It is just as important to code an idea or action that doesn't appear in a situation but in other contexts.

Coding is approached in three ways. First, data are sorted according to an analytical schema. In this case, it is content specific and determined in advance on the basis of prior research and theory. Second, a typology is created on the basis of common sense or substantive knowledge. Consistent with symbolic interactionism, this approach is non-content specific and determined in advance on the basis of a typology or ideal type. The final approach will be specifically discussed in the next section. Grounded theory is context specific and inductive. It is not developed a priori. Instead, the words of respondents generate codes and categories. The meaning in codes and categories are refined using the constant comparison method until theoretical saturation is achieved (i.e. nothing new is learned).

Deductive Coding

Data can be coded deductively and inductively. In many cases, the analysis uses both techniques. **Deductive coding** involves approaching the data with certain concepts and themes in mind. These could be based on prior research, theory, the research question, or interview questions. For instance, if your research topic is responses to youth crime and one interview question asks how respondents define inappropriate behaviour, a deductive coding theme would include antisocial behaviour. With this a priori code, you choose data based on their ability to describe and better understand this concept.

Deductive coding doesn't necessarily occur at the initial stages of data analysis. It can occur later during inductive activities, when a deductive process is engaged with the constant comparison method. Additionally, when "a researcher derives hypotheses from data, because it involves interpretation, we consider that to be a deductive process" (Strauss & Corbin, 1998, p. 22). This is why I want you to see qualitative data analysis as both inductive and deductive. Concepts and hypotheses are created from the data inductively; hypothesizing on how they are related to one another is assessed deductively.

Aligned with symbolic interactionism, these a priori codes are sometimes referred to as **sensitizing concepts**, which serve as a point of reference on where to look in the data. The definition tells us what the concept looks like and means within a given social setting or group of people. First discussed by Herbert Blumer (1969, p. 148),

> a sensitizing concept lacks such specification of attributes or benchmarks and consequently it does not enable the user to move directly to the instance and its relevant content. Instead, it gives the user a general sense of reference and guidance in approaching empirical instances. Whereas definitive concepts provide prescriptions of what to see, sensitizing concepts merely suggest directions along which to look.

Definitive concepts are what we use in quantitative research, where a nominal definition is operationalized in a way that we can precisely measure the concept the same way each time. Sensitizing concepts lead the qualitative researcher through the data much like a guide suggesting some interesting places to visit while in the area.

Inductive Coding

Everyday assumptions need to be unpacked so we can better understand the taken-for-granted knowledge of our research subjects. Are there words or phrases that the participants use frequently? What do these terms mean to them and how are they used to make sense of the social world around them? **Inductive coding** is used within concepts to elaborate on what they mean or to create a larger conceptual category. Based on the research question, researchers may code for patterns that occur in specific contexts. This is when the analysis uses inductive coding by starting to identify themes and patterns that emerge out of the data, not from predetermined concepts, as with deductive coding.

Codebook

A codebook is required for the same reasons it's used in quantitative research. The codebook serves as your road map during the multiple readings of the data to track the conditions under which a segment is assigned to one code over another. Table 10.1 shows an example from a research project that examined criminal justice responses to youth crime.

For each concept, there are five columns in the codebook. The first one is a label or name. It is a short descriptor—typically no more than two to three words—for the code. The second column provides a working definition of the concept, including a defining characteristic (in this case, the nature and degree of support youth receive from their parents). The third gives an indicator(s), which is an analytical trigger. Don't confuse indicator with its use in quantitative research. In this circumstance, the indicator

---

sensitizing concept a preliminary conceptual definition based on prior research and theory that is used to recognize this idea in the field and during the initial stages of data analysis.

inductive coding a type of coding that elaborates on meaning by creating larger conceptual categories.

Table 10.1 Qualitative codebook example

Label	Definition	Indicator	Parameters	Example
Parental involvement	Perceptions on the nature and degree of support from parents when responding to antisocial behaviour and youth crime.	Actions taken by parents; words exchanged during official communications with parents.	Exclude how parents' behaviour is compared to that of the youth (e.g. apple doesn't fall far from the tree).	"I think a lot of parents are exhausted or single parents don't have the energy . . . they wipe their hands of their parenting or look at the system . . . 'fix Johnny and then give him back to me. I can't deal with him any longer.'"

provides cues to identify applicable text segments. The fourth column stipulates the concept's parameters, such as qualifiers for inclusion, a characteristic that excludes a piece of data from being coded, or a clarification when certain words or actions are coded to this concept. Finally, the codebook provides an example. An excerpt from the data assigned to this code serves as an exemplar and helps you recognize additional data related to this concept.

Memos and Annotations

Memos and annotations are two different ways that researchers document the analytical process. Have you ever thought of something and then just as quickly forgot what it was? In the same way, not writing memos and annotations is a surefire way to lose important thoughts and connections. The difference between insightful analyses and merely descriptive ones are well-written memos and annotations.

Memos

We write memos to ourselves every day. When you underline something in a textbook or write a note in the margin, you create a memo. These "notes to self" serve

memo a document that explains coding, defines concepts, brainstorms theories, and records methodological issues that arise during data analysis.

as reminders as you study. **Memos** document any observations about the coding process, preliminary insights into the meaning we associate with a code, and connections between various categories. By recording this process, memos can provide evidence of the dependability (reliability) of coding and the trustworthiness (validity) of the empirical findings. Memos vary in length and detail depending on their purpose, but it's not unusual for the content to be incorporated in the findings as preliminary theorizing becomes supported by data.

There are a few rules to follow when writing analytical memos. I find it really helpful to create a new memo for each concept. When I discuss connections between concepts, I make a notation about the insight in both concepts' memos. Why? When using the constant comparison method, I may see additional connections that won't appear in other related concepts. These relationships would be missed if I hadn't made the cross-reference and created separate memos for each concept.

Let's say you have the concept of parental involvement and family risk factors for criminal behaviour. In both memos, you note a connection between the two concepts. With further analysis, you see that parental involvement is also related to whether a criminal charge is laid. However, when re-reading the segments coded to family risk factors, you see a different connection, one to the type and length of sentence. You hypothesize that the judge appears less influenced by the degree of parental involvement than by the parenting style when deciding on conditions of probation.

Every time you make an entry into a memo, insert the date so you can track the progression in your thinking for a particular conclusion. Memos are also data and serve as holding pens for important information used to create theoretical explanations. They should be included in the analysis.

Last but not least, add ideas to memos as soon as they come to mind. I sometimes make jotted notes to aid recall. Obviously, this practice means writing down absolutely everything that comes to mind. You can't predict which preliminary ideas about themes, definitions, and connections will turn out to be integral to your understanding of this social phenomenon.

Annotations

Memos are ideal for capturing your overall reflections on a topic, person, event, concept, or situation and on how they relate to one another. **Annotations** are associated with a specific text segment indicating a clarification, an idea to explore, reactions to this data, or a possible exemplar quotation. As data analysis progresses, the notes for text segments can inform memo content when drawing connections between codes and placing them in a theoretical order.

Research Example

Let's look at an example from my research. I wrote a memo on a code created with a respondent's own words: "agent of hope." In the memo, I made connections between transmitting positivity to youth who are in trouble to the respondents' motivations for doing so. I discussed how a segment of the population felt it was their goal and the purpose of their job. They felt no reason not to help because, when giving hope, there is always a chance for even a little bit of change. Another theme that developed in the memo was the perceptions of the "other"— those who did not work directly with youth. For instance, other people don't understand sympathy for youth because they don't know the background circumstances, such as abuse or drug addiction.

Annotations helped me to start seeing that the respondents viewed giving hope as a chance for the youth to show up differently. For instance, an annotation was linked to this text segment from a vice principal: "We have to be agents of hope. I'm always positive for the kids. Try not to give up even though sometimes you want to kill them." This quote refined the definition of the concept further by using the memo as data. To be an agent of hope involves being positive for kids even when you are frustrated.

In another case, I wrote an annotation connected to this text segment: "What do you want to bring to the fire? Do you want to bring a bucket of water or a bucket of gasoline? It depends on the outcome you want. And if you're dealing with antisocial behaviours, a bucket of gasoline really is an antisocial behaviour when you think of the norms in society." The memo for antisocial behaviour reflected on this exemplar further. I noted how interesting it was that this respondent felt that certain types of responses to youth can be antisocial behaviour in and of themselves. Thus, if you are not an agent of hope and lack patience and positive thoughts, your response to their behaviour may also be antisocial.

annotation a type of memo associated with a particular text segment rather than a larger concept.

First and Second Cycle Coding

Researchers typically read transcripts and field notes without coding anything to better familiarize themselves with the data and start figuring out what the data do and do not cover. Initial coding begins and memos start to be written to capture preliminary ideas about the data. At this point, researchers pay as much attention to what is missing from the data as they do to the ideas that create and fill out codes. During the second stage, researchers start thinking about the data in terms of the research questions and patterns within and across codes. These stages are known as first and second cycle coding, respectively.

First Cycle Coding

first cycle coding the coding cycle stage during which text segments are assigned to descriptive, process, in vivo, and emotion codes.

You are analyzing qualitative data when you start breaking the data into segments and assigning them to a code. This process is known as **first cycle coding**. The following sections examine the types of first cycle codes commonly used in criminology and criminal justice research.

descriptive coding a type of first cycle coding that assigns text segments to a code because they describe the concept or idea.

Although we do not want to focus solely on categorizing this type of data, **descriptive coding** is important contextual information because the segments describe the concept or idea. This type of coding is used for settings, events, objects, and people but is less useful when coding actions and sequences. These codes also articulate what participants perceive as important and how this information fits into the larger cultural milieu and social setting.

process coding a type of first cycle coding that assigns text segments to a code because they describe actions and sequences.

You will find evidence of **process coding** in virtually every qualitative study. Think of process codes as capturing anything that ends in an "–ing" (gerunds). A process code is an action; the data assigned to it reflect changes over time, strategies adopted by respondents, or the sequence of events. For instance, a process code could be complaining, and data assigned to this code could be related to when a person complains or how a person goes about complaining.

in vivo coding a type of first cycle coding that assigns text segments to a code because they describe a meaningful word or phrase used by a respondent.

Although most associated with grounded theory (see pp. 315–317), **in vivo coding** occurs in generic ways during first cycle coding by using a respondent's own phrase to describe an aspect of his or her social reality. The code uses these words as a label and the segments capture how participants make sense of their social world and experiences. An example of in vivo coding is the agent of hope concept previously discussed.

emotion coding a type of first cycle coding that assigns text segments to a code because they describe the nature, scope, and circumstances of emotions.

Information that helps us understand emotional sentiments and reactions to events, actions, situations, or people in participants' lives can arise. **Emotion coding** represents what constitutes an emotion, what produces the emotion, what it means to participants, and how they deal with it. For example, text segments assigned to the emotion code of frustration might include a police officer talking about being disrespected by citizens or their feelings about losing weekends because of their shift schedule.

Second Cycle Coding

second cycle coding the coding cycle stage that creates categories' grouping codes and identifies patterns in the data.

When you engage in first cycle coding, you fracture and organize your data into meaningful codes. In contrast, **second cycle coding** involves looking for patterns in the data within and across codes and amalgamating codes into larger categories. Categories can develop out of a single code when it becomes too heterogeneous or when similar codes explain a larger phenomenon.

Miles, Huberman, and Saldaña (2014) suggest that researchers examine the data for patterns in categories and themes, causes and explanations, relationships among people, and theoretical constructs. This type of coding is focused; you look for the most frequent or substantively significant first cycle codes. "Pattern codes can emerge from repeated observed behaviors, actions, norms, routines, and relationships; local meanings and explanations; common-sense explanations and more conceptual ones; inferential clusters and 'metaphorical' ones; and single-case and cross-case observations" (p. 88).

Putting the Pieces of the Puzzle Together

So far, we have talked about the coding process in pieces. Figure 10.2 brings this discussion together to present these analytical components visually. Throughout the data analysis process, we move iteratively from real and specific at the raw data level to abstract and general as we identify themes and develop theory. During first cycle coding, the data are fractured and text segments are assigned to codes. During the second cycle, related codes are combined to form categories. Patterns and themes are identified within and across codes. Comparisons

continue to specify relationships between categories (reflected by the dotted line) to form themes that develop into theoretical explanations.

Moving from Point A to B

To summarize, five interrelated strategies are used to analyze data. First, fracture the data, breaking the text into meaningful segments that are assigned to a code. Fracturing continues in second cycle coding. Comparisons within a code involve breaking up segments further into dimensions (e.g. the concept of frustration has dimensions of cause and type). If you were to remove or change a dimension, it would alter the concept. Imagine a course as a concept with the dimensions of grading components, type of instruction, and topics. Changing any of these alters the meaning of *course*.

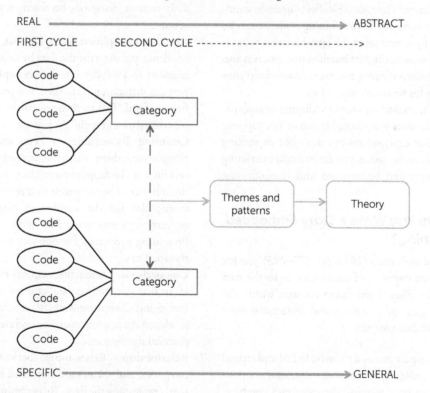

Figure 10.2 The process of first and second cycle coding

Source: Adapted from Saldaña (2013, p. 13).

Another strategy is identifying relationships among codes, concepts, categories, and themes. Are certain concepts related to one another in a specific way? Are there any patterns that place concepts in a particular order? For instance, when you look at the data coded to the category course, is there a relationship between each topic that leads to them being presented in this order?

The third strategy is using the constant comparison method. This method allows you to identify similarities and differences within and across concepts and themes. Researchers are constantly comparing previously coded data to other data from the initial coding stage right through to theoretical explanations.

Fourth, don't forget to look for disconfirming evidence. Are there any deviant cases? What makes them different? How does this affect our understanding of the concept? Disconfirming evidence can be manifest by appearing in the text. However, what is expected to be in the data but does not appear is also a form of disconfirming evidence. Always keep your eyes open for what isn't in the data.

Finally, researchers consider alternative explanations. Why does something happen or not happen? What other explanations can there be? By seeking alternative explanations, you are critically examining taken-for-granted assumptions and disconfirming evidence.

How Do You Write a Story Embedded in Meaning?

Miles and colleagues (2014, pp. 277–293) provide an excellent overview of tactics used to let the data tell a story. These eight tactics are used within the five strategies outlined above and characterize most qualitative data analysis:

1. **Noting patterns and themes:** In first and second cycle coding, you document potential relationships in your memos. The categories combine, creating patterns and themes within the context of a social setting. Be persistent about exploring

alternative explanations by constantly questioning your interpretations of predominant ideas and patterns.

2. **Plausibility of the story:** Does your interpretation of the data make sense? It can look plausible on the surface but, as you analyze the data further, alternative explanations can appear. It is important to avail yourself of as many techniques as possible because you may come up with what looks like a brilliant conclusion but in reality is untrustworthy.

3. **Clustering:** This process moves from the specific to the general. To create a cluster, aggregate codes into categories and conceptually link categories to one another. Assign a word or phrase that captures the meaning of all the data in that cluster. An example is several different types of daily routine categories becoming a cluster of actions.

4. **Creating metaphors:** Metaphors are a way to condense and describe the data by drawing connections to everyday life. For example, empty nest can include adult children, lost parents, and free as a bird. This tactic helps you to step back from the data and highlight patterns.

5. **Counting:** By definition, a theme and pattern reflects something occurring frequently in a certain way. To support these inferences, count the number of occurrences; that is, present the frequencies for the number of respondents or text segments associated with this idea. Presenting percentages is one way to promote transparency.

6. **Comparisons:** Conducting comparisons doesn't mean that you compare and contrast absolutely everything. Comparisons are chosen substantively to address the research questions and are based on practical significance.

7. **Relationships:** Relationships between codes, categories, and themes are identified by consistently examining the data. This examination will become second nature as part of the iterative process involved with the constant comparison

method and second cycle coding. Investigating relationships is a story-building activity.

8. **Conditions:** Are the relationships found in the data conditioned by the presence or absence of various factors or situations? Is there something that affects the relationship between categories or changes the pattern under certain circumstances? If so, conditions either initiate the process in a certain way or act as an intervening factor in a sequence of events, thereby changing the direction or outcome.

Grounded Theory

First developed by Glaser and Strauss (1967), **grounded theory** is both a method and a theory of systematically gathering and analyzing data inductively to create a theoretical explanation. It is "a specific, highly developed, rigorous set of procedures for producing formal, substantive theory of social phenomena" (Schwandt, 2001, p. 110). Induction and deduction are used simultaneously to develop insights that guide further data collection and analysis. A key element is using the constant comparison method to compare the emerging theory to new data. It's in this way that we say the explanation is *grounded* in the data.

Memos play a pivotal role here. They come in three different forms: code, theoretical, and methodological. Code notes are your reflections on the process of creating labels and definitions for concepts. Many of the labels are words that have taken-for-granted definitions in everyday life. The meaning needs to be clarified, as it is defined by the data and not our common-sense understandings. Theoretical memos document your thoughts on dimensions within a concept, relationships between concepts, propositions about conditions, and outcomes. Code memos help unpack data within a code, while theoretical memos are geared to record theorizing about relationships. Finally, methodological memos document things that occur during data collection that

might affect what data is collected and how it is interpreted in the analysis. For instance, potential bias is a marker to look for additional support that there is truly a deviant case uncovered in the analysis.

A theoretical model is built by using open, axial, and selective coding. Virtually all research projects use open and axial coding. Not conducting selective coding is perfectly acceptable if it isn't required to achieve the research objective or address the research questions.

Open Coding

When **open coding**, researchers assign labels to ideas, objects, actions, or situations. Text segments are then assigned to these preliminary concepts using sensitizing concepts, as in first cycle coding. The size of the text segments depends on the substantive content and the research questions. As you become more immersed in the data, you develop a heightened theoretical sensitivity that allows you to see more and more analytical insights—which you record in memos, of course. The open coding process is best described by Strauss and Corbin (1998, p. 102), who write that it starts with codes and then moves to category creation by breaking the data "down into discrete parts, closely examined, and compared for similarities and differences. Events, happenings, objects, and actions/interactions that are found to be conceptually similar in nature or related in meaning are grouped under more abstract concepts termed categories." A piece of data can be allocated to more than one code because it may be indicative of more than one concept. This situation may change as coding continues and categories start to develop, bringing these two codes together.

> **grounded theory** an emergent theory and method that uses constant comparison and coding procedures to develop a theoretical explanation grounded in the data.

> **open coding** the process of identifying and creating a label for ideas and assigning text segments to these codes to develop an initial framework for further analysis.

For grounded theory, in vivo codes are embedded in the characteristics of the social world under investigation, adopt the research subject's words to label a concept, and are an excellent example of grounding the findings in the data. In vivo codes are

> assumptions, actions, and imperatives that frame action. Studying these codes and exploring leads in them allows you to develop a deeper understanding of what is happening and what it means. Such codes anchor your analysis in your research participants' world. They offer clues about the relative congruence between your interpretation of participants' meanings and actions and their overt statements and actions. In vivo codes can provide a crucial check on whether you have grasped what is significant. (Charmaz, 2006, pp. 56–57)

axial coding analytical processes that combine two or more codes to form thematic categories and relationships across codes; categories are identified and specified.

These codes are advantageous because they can authenticate the findings and assess the plausibility of the explanation at later coding stages.

In a grounded theory analysis on antisocial behaviour, I created an in vivo code of "bank of patience." An analogy was made to explain why a youth has to be dealt with formally by the criminal justice system. They have run out of chances and do not simply receive a warning. This in vivo code was created based on the following text segment:

> I try to say okay there's what I call the bank of patience. You've been withdrawing and now you're overdrawn. Because they find it very unfair sometimes that they get kicked out when other kids are doing it. I said well it's 18,000 times you were doing it before, and Billy Bob just did it for the first time this time. So it's easy to sacrifice you. Sometimes they get it, sometimes they don't. Sometimes, they don't care.

Axial Coding

Instead of assigning data excerpts to codes, **axial coding** involves organizing these initial codes in terms of relationships to one another, creating larger categories. Codes are organized by comparing the content within and across concepts. By doing so, you address the research questions but can also create new ones in this inductive process. If you are still collecting data, further collection can be targeted to answer these new questions. The relationship between open and axial coding isn't a neat and tidy linear process. Depending on how saturated a concept becomes, you may be engaging in axial coding while still actively conducting open coding with other concepts.

Table 10.2 illustrates the different types of relationships that grounded theorists identify and specify

Table 10.2 Relationships identified through axial coding

Type of relationship	Format	Example
Strict inclusion	A is a kind of B.	Red is a kind of colour.
Spatial	A is a part of B.	Nunavut is part of Canada.
Cause–effect	A is a result of B.	A low grade is a result of not studying.
Rationale	A is a reason for doing B.	Being tired is a reason to drink coffee.
Function	A is used for B.	A pot is used to cook pasta.
Sequence	A is a step in B.	Putting on socks is a step in getting dressed.
Attribution	A is a characteristic of B.	Yawning is a characteristic of being bored.

Source: Adapted from Strauss & Corbin (1998).

during axial coding. When you start to understand how the concepts and categories are related to one another, you get closer to explaining the what, why, where, when, how, and with what consequences. You also position yourself to engage in selective coding.

Selective Coding

The third stage in grounded theory is **selective coding**, where a central concept forms the heart of a theoretical explanation. The central concept subsumes all other codes and categories developed in open and axial coding. Selective coding involves reviewing the data once again to look for thematic cases that, in combination with one another, elaborate on a larger theme or pattern in the data. Stated in a different way, selective coding creates a primary code that all the concepts relate to. The primary code is the story, while the other codes and categories take the reader to this final conclusion.

The findings are integrated instead of being presented as a group of interrelated categories or list of themes. With a central category, the researcher can make statements about when something occurs and under what conditions. Axial coding is still at the descriptive level. Selective coding moves to the level of explanation.

Corbin and Strauss (2007) provide criteria that can be used to assess a grounded theory explanation. A "good" grounded theory offers an appropriate explanatory fit with the social phenomenon under investigation. This point may seem obvious, but it is worth repeating. If the grounded theory doesn't provide an explanation grounded in the data and applicable in the real-world setting under investigation, it lacks utility. Another quality of a good grounded theory is that the understanding is developed from the data itself. In other words, the researcher hasn't approached the analysis deductively as you would see with the illustrative method. The grounded theory also has generality, whereby the theoretical model is sufficiently abstract that it allows for a potential application in a variety of contexts and situations and perhaps transferability to other research settings or parallel situations (e.g. a theory explaining police decision-making can help us understand probation officer decisions). Finally, the grounded theory is logical, as it specifies the conditions under which the model applies.

> **selective coding** the process of developing a theoretical explanation by creating a central concept that organizes all the other categories and codes developed in open and axial coding.

Key Thinker

Mark Pogrebin: Qualitative Research in Criminal Justice

Mark Pogrebin is internationally recognized in the areas of deviance, criminal justice organizations, policing, and qualitative research methods. In 1973, he received his PhD from the University of Iowa. After working at Florida State University and the University of Iowa, he joined the faculty in the School of Public Affairs at the University of Colorado Denver in 1976. Not only has he published eight books, such as *Qualitative Approaches to Criminal Justice: Perspectives from the Field* (2002), but he is also the author of over thirty book chapters and more than sixty journal articles. Having extensive research experience, he shared his thoughts on collecting and analyzing qualitative data to assist new researchers (Pogrebin, 2010).

Research Approach

Dr Pogrebin describes himself as a grounded theory ethnographer. He adopts an inductive approach, consistent with Glaser and Strauss (1967), by conducting research that generates

Continued

theory grounded in the data. This approach to data collection and analysis makes researchers "faithful to the understandings, interpretations, intentions, and perspectives of those whom they were conducting research on in their study subject's own terms as expressed through their words and actions" (Pogrebin, 2010, p. 542). Throughout his career, he experienced a battle against the dominant quantitative approach in the disciplines of criminal justice and criminology. For example, while he was a PhD student he was advised to put his qualitative instincts on hold until he had established himself as a quantitative researcher. Thankfully, he did not follow this advice.

Challenges

As we discussed in previous chapters, every research study must receive ethics clearance prior to the start of data collection. However, obtaining this approval is challenging, especially for qualitative methods. Only 5.5 per cent of doctoral courses in criminology and criminal justice are on qualitative methods (Pogrebin, 2010, pp. 557–558). Further, consistent with an inductive approach, many qualitative research studies are not linear endeavours and are not completely mapped out in advance. This poses difficulties with the deductive ethics approval process. As Pogrebin points out, there are many classic research examples that are ethical but would not receive clearance today. For instance, Whyte's (1955) *Street Corner Society* includes a 79-page appendix explaining that the study described in his proposal was not the data collected because the original idea turned out to be inappropriate for the community he was studying. Similarly, a study on humour in the police briefing room was not originally planned (Pogrebin & Poole, 1988). It was only after accompanying three patrol shifts for six months that it became clear that humour played a role in managing work-related tension and stress among the rank and file. Both are excellent examples of qualitative research as emergent and inductive.

Pogrebin also conducted a study on the sexualized work environment for female jail officers (Pogrebin & Poole, 1997). Their work environment was so problematic that, when the results were published, it was picked up by the media and considerable pressure was exerted to reveal the jails' and interviewees' identities. The need to protect practitioners when conducting research on sensitive issues in criminal justice agencies is a common challenge.

Pogrebin urges qualitative researchers to stay true to the presentation of social reality from the research subjects' perspective. In contrast to the deductive model of research, one should not defend one's work by justifying the use of methods for that research study. Data analysis and "academic research findings should be judged on the quality of the work produced" (Pogrebin, 2010, p. 558), not by the type of research design or analytical techniques.

Looking at the Analysis a Different Way: Some Alternatives

discourse analysis analysis that examines language to understand communication patterns that occur during social interactions.

Thus far, this chapter has presented qualitative data analysis as an overview and in terms of one specific approach of grounded theory. But there are other ways to approach the data. For example, ethnomethodologists seek to understand how social actors create meaning in everyday life. Different variations of **discourse analysis** are used to examine communication patterns and how language is used. The crux of the analysis is to examine strategies used by social actors to create different outcomes and interpretations during social interactions. In its basic form, a discourse is a theme in the text.

There are three assumptions in discourse analysis. First, a discourse is a topic in and of itself. We can conduct a research topic on a discourse and not simply as an analytical framework to uncover the meaning collaboratively created through social interaction. Second, the analyst remembers that language creates a particular understanding of reality. All language is socially constructed and has an organization to its content and flow. Finally, all discourse is a type of action. Even not actually speaking in a conversation is an action through omission, as we are not passive when we listen.

Discourse analysis is very much a bucket term that includes any analysis of language. Let's take a closer look at a few different alternatives: narrative analysis, conversation analysis, and semiotics.

Narrative Analysis

A **narrative analysis** demonstrates how stories play a central role in our interpretation and description of our lives. The focus is on the organization, development, function, and content of the narrative in that context. In crime and justice research, narratives are often high risk and neglected. Manning (1999, p. 297) explains that they are

reflective and interpretive, but are not ethnographies. They fail to set out a systematic framework for data gathering and analysis. Nor are they guided by abstract, general theory or theoretical questions. They describe in detail a microsegment of a culture [and emphasize] substantively the coping, muddling through ability of people, and illuminate the intrinsic and perhaps fundamental playful aspect of human conduct.

This type of analysis is appropriate when telling stories about stories, looking at the structure of an experience, seeking to understand the relationship between stories embedded in a cultural narrative, or unpacking how people create meaning in their lives through social interaction.

By focusing on the content of the story, the data are treated as an integrated whole without engaging in a fracturing process. The rationale is that the integrity of the narrative is required to understand the content adequately. Thus, coding the data involves reading the story and classifying its themes (e.g. justification, descriptive, or action stories).

This approach involves sampling one or more research subjects, collecting data in the form of stories, creating a story about the stories, and authenticating the interpretation of this new story with participants (Edmonds & Kennedy, 2013). The last step is important because one of the underlying assumptions of narrative analysis is that no absolute truth exists in social reality. By implication, this assumption means that there isn't one definitive way to interpret a person's narration of a story. Unstructured interviews are a common data collection method, used to encourage unrestricted dialogue by allowing the participant to decide content and topic order. With this open-ended approach, the researcher is free to deviate based on the person's dialogue and to encourage reflection and elaboration of ideas.

> **narrative analysis** an interpretation of stories in terms of organization, development, and function within the context of life experiences as they are described in the social interaction.

Edmonds and Kennedy (2013) outline three types of narrative analysis: descriptive, explanatory, and critical. For descriptive narratives, the researcher presents the life stories of specific events while accounting for contextual factors and any relationships between the story and the person's cultural background. He or she describes the social phenomenon in the context of an individual or group. Explanatory narratives are concerned with why something has happened in the story. Critical narratives seek to shed light on larger social issues and critique the status quo understanding of social reality. Unlike descriptive and explanatory, where this involvement may or may not occur, research subjects are actively involved in meaning construction and interpretation in critical narratives.

After the researcher identifies the topic, he or she collects data using nonprobability sampling. For critical narratives, data collection occurs in collaboration with research subjects so they are not marginalized further. Next, the researcher retells the stories, also referred to as restory. A summary story is then written about the participants' experiences. In a critical narrative, the story is meant to "empower participants through speaking on their behalf (non-neutral stance)" (Edmonds & Kennedy, 2013, p. 134). Finally, the researcher authenticates the narrative story. The connection among the situation, the larger context, and the retelling is double-checked with one or more research subjects.

Narratives focus on life events and how they are related to one another within a certain culture and temporal order. To accomplish this sequence, periods are established. The temporal order is theoretically broken into distinct time periods. The number and length of each time period is dictated by the research question and ongoing data analysis.

Path dependency is the process of tracing a series of events. Given a certain starting point, path dependency traces a series of events to create a sequence that shapes and limits the potential outcomes. The sequence is identifiable across cases and time; choices made at one point in time affect later decisions and available options. The analysis is typically presented with the outcome first and then the story, which outlines the sequence of events that have led to this point.

Another technique is historical contingency. A combination of factors are used within a specific context to help explain a process, experience, events, or action. This method usually involves looking for the exception to the rule. In other words, we identify the constellation of unexpected factors. When existing theories

conversation analysis
analysis that examines verbal interchanges to understand the structure of social interaction.

are unable to provide an explanation of the outcome, this technique can help shed some light.

Presser (2010) offers a glimpse into narrative research, an often neglected analytical approach in criminology and criminal justice, when conducting research on offenders. Consistent with human nature, it can be hard to get someone to tell his or her story when doing so evokes painful memories. However, the opposite is true for offenders' stories about crime once the people are officially labelled an offender. Telling a story can serve as a bragging mechanism or provide a means to explain oneself, and those sanctioned have a vested interest in doing so (Presser, 2010; Sandberg, 2010). Using unstructured or semi-structured interviews, Presser (2010, p. 437) warns that "the researcher who conceptualizes narrative as a shaper of reality should be disinclined to influence the speaker's articulation of the narrative."

In all research projects, Presser (2010) completes three tasks: coding for themes, creating a summary of each narrative as sequential events, and writing memos on the personal interactions between interviewer and interviewee. As part of a narrative analysis, the plot or meaning of the story is also told through its content and use of language. Specifically, the researcher looks for linguistic structures used to deflect the conversation and justify actions, as well as for delays in responding, repeating ideas and facts, inconsistencies, missing information, and awkward or unusual phrases (pp. 440–441). These are all presented in the individual, social, and cultural context because stories have a history and a location (i.e. where they are created).

Conversation Analysis

Conversation analysis is a type of narrative analysis that focuses on the story's structure rather than its content. We create a social order when we communicate with other people. Adopting a constructionist ontology, the findings present the words that are spoken before a response that is of substantive interest in the story being told. All talk is structured and situated in a given context. The conclusions are grounded in the data and presented using thick description.

Consistent with ethnomethodology, this analytical approach has three underlying assumptions (Silverman, 2013). First, all communication is organized in a specific order. Thus, we focus on the process of communicating and not on the content of what is spoken. For instance, we pay attention to implicit rules of behaviour, such as taking turns to speak. A person interrupting is of great interest. Second, when people speak with one another, this social interaction always occurs in a given context, be it an environment or for a particular purpose. The context shapes how the conversation goes and what things mean. For example, what you say in one context could mean something completely different in another (e.g. "I'm going home" to your professor when leaving class early versus when having an argument). Finally, all forms of interaction constitute part of a process where even the smallest of details can be important theoretically. For example, saying words such as *ah* can denote understanding or *um* and a pause can denote thinking about what was said or trying to come up with a response.

In a nutshell, conversation analysis looks at how talk is organized. Aspects of focus include adjacency pairs—or how the conversation moves between two people—such as question and answer rhythms, how people take turns to talk, or how preferences for certain types of responses are communicated. The key distinction of conversation analysis is the focus on the words and their structure in the process of social interaction. All words have a purpose in a conversation. What a word or a series of words means is determined by the role they play within that interaction.

Semiotics

Semiotics focuses on symbols, signs, and their associated meanings. From this perspective, language is but one way we communicate with each other. We also use gestures, such as a thumb pointing up to convey the message "A-Okay." A semiotic analysis can also detect mixed signals and contradictions by exposing hidden meanings in text.

A sign is anything with an associated meaning. For example, when it's 12:00 on the clock, it can mean lunchtime. Thus, when we talk about signs there are two parts to consider. As outlined by Gubrium and Holstein (2000), the signifier is the thing itself—the clock—which points to a latent meaning. The signified is the meaning of the signifier (e.g. you are late for your 11:45 class if it's 12:00).

Once the signifier and signified are identified, there are three different types of meaning (Gubrium & Holstein, 2000). A denotative meaning is the common-sense, obvious meaning of a signifier. Continuing with our example, the function of the clock is to tell time. The connotative meaning is the secondary meaning, which arises with the denotative meaning. In other words, hurry up and get to class before the test begins. Think of denotative as manifest meaning and connotative as latent meaning, with manifest being the object with its obvious identification and latent being the underlying message within a given context. Lastly, polysemy recognizes that signs may be interpreted differently by different people. At this point, semiotics can detect and unpack misunderstandings.

Computer-Assisted Data Analysis

The tools available for conducting qualitative data analysis have come a long way in the last twenty years. Gone are the days of cutting out quotes with a pair of scissors and putting them into piles or file folders. However, researchers may still conduct their analysis manually if they have a small amount of data or have narrowly focused projects. Computer-assisted data analysis, which can be done using a word-processing program or specialized analytical software, aids in sorting the data.

semiotics analysis that focuses on symbols, signs, and their meanings in social interactions.

Vignette: Breaking It Down

The Enterprise of Policing

Police decision-making and strategies used to create meaning for occupational experiences are ideal research problems for qualitative research. What types of conclusions and theoretical explanations develop from analyzing qualitative data on these topics? Using different analytical techniques, researchers have sought to contribute to our understanding of police behaviour by analyzing data in ways that produce trustworthy findings.

Haar and Morash's (2013) study is an excellent example of using successive approximation and of adopting multiple approaches to analyze the data. The researchers conducted interviews with 21 female officers to explore coping strategies for workplace discrimination and harassment. Transcripts were repeatedly reviewed for direct and indirect associations to coping practices in negative work environments in relation to years of service and rank (e.g. sergeant). The number and types of coping strategies were counted in connection with officer characteristics and the percentages were presented. For each coping strategy, distinctions were made based on career stage (i.e. in the academy, patrol work, and after promotion). The data were also examined for statements that indicated changes over time. Overall, the findings suggest that police departments remain highly gendered, with female officers confronting bias and harassment in different ways throughout their careers.

Campbell (2004) took a different approach to understanding police decision-making by conducting a narrative analysis of 206 case summaries. In an effort to understand the nature of administrative discourse, the analysis looked at the "cultural, spatial, temporal, social and textual-discursive relations of decision-making and the condition which created, sustained and produced an endemic series of negative policy outcomes" (p. 698). Despite negative commentary about administrative work, police officers recognize why paperwork is important for accountability. Unpacking this idea further, report writing is both an offensive and defensive practice that is quite standardized in structure. Based on comparisons made within and across criminal case summaries, police action is emphasized as part of a "police drama" with victims playing a supporting role (p. 704). Overall, "police-speak" is used to "mobilize a quasi-legal and esoteric language which, in turn, buttresses readers' sense of police 'professionalism,' 'expertise,' and their 'specialist' role as guarantors (and arbiters) of law and order, authority and control" (p. 705).

An interesting development in this research area is a movement toward contextualizing this process within the police culture. Police accounts of why they do what they do are not taken at face value but seen as a communication medium for values and subcultural priorities. Waddington (1999) found two dimensions to the police culture reflected in operational actions versus words found in oral and written narratives. This connection between behaviour, communication patterns, and culture highlights the use of language to make sense of decisions and incidents while reaffirming communal understandings. As Cockcroft (2013, p. 113) argues: "the challenge for police researchers whose work draws on the narrative accounts of officers is how to identify whether the phenomenon they are actually addressing is a factual account of what happened, where and to whom or a symbolically charged account aimed at perpetuating figurative themes."

Many excellent ethnographies and much research use grounded theory. In addition, more research conducts narrative analyses to understand how social reality is constructed and how participants make sense of the world around them through language. By critically examining police discourse as a theme, we enter largely uncharted territory.

Harnessing the Technology

Computer-assisted qualitative data analysis software (CAQDAS) is a powerful tool for analyzing relational databases. However, you may not have the financial resources or opportunity to purchase a student version of some of the more popular qualitative data analysis software, such as Atlas.ti or NVivo. If not, programs such as Microsoft Word are a viable option to consider when exploring a few relationships (La Pelle, 2004). It is inexpensive and involves a much lower learning curve.

Microsoft Word

The first step to using Microsoft Word for data analysis is to create a table and, copying and pasting from the original document, to insert each text segment

into a cell. Second, specify the source document and the role of the person speaking for each segment and assign a sequence number so that you can figure out where it came from after you have sorted by word or theme. As seen in Table 10.3, the third step is to assign numbers to each code, category, and theme to organize and search the data. In this case, 3.00 is the theme for factors affecting the use of police discretion; 3.11 is the category for attitude; 3.21 is the concept of parent demeanour; and 3.12 is the nature of the offence. Another category is meaningful consequences (3.20), of which informal action became 3.21.

Next, use the comment function to add annotations. It is much easier to create separate documents for each memo than to add comments for memos, as they can get quite lengthy. Finally, once you

Table 10.3 Tabulating qualitative data

Identifier	Role	Code	Question or response	Sequence #
P10	Interviewer	3.00	What factors do you take into account when deciding how to handle a youth-related incident?	14
P10	Officer	3.11	The offence is, their attitude, if it's to the point where I'm sitting on the fence and their attitude is okay I would contact Mom and Dad and see what their attitude is on things. If they've got a poor attitude and the child has a poor attitude, then I'll put them through the court system. If the kid has a so-so attitude, or a good attitude, and Mom and Dad have a good attitude, I would try and come up with some sort of punishment that would fit the crime.	15
P10	Interviewer	3.21	Yeah, meaningful consequence. So [an] extrajudicial measure of some kind.	16
P10	Officer	3.12	Exactly. So whether it would be to, you know, if they were egging somebody's house, for instance, well I think yard work at this particular house would be appropriate.	17
P10	Interviewer	3.00	If the homeowner agreed.	18
P10	Officer	3.21	Exactly. So I mean there are other factors, obviously, but you know we'd find something to, some sort of punishment to fit the crime. So whether it's cleaning a park, but then you'd have to have somebody from the city to, or township, who's doing that particular day to be out there with them to make sure that it's done properly. Or even have Mom and Dad who would be on board to supervise because we can't be there all the time.	19

have entered all the data and assigned segments to codes, you can use "Sort" to put the codes with their associated segments in numerical order or use the "Find" function to locate all instances of a certain word or phrase.

CAQDAS

CAQDAS automates the coding process. Relevant pieces of data are associated with one or more codes, categories can easily be created, and queries that quickly display all text segments within a code greatly facilitate the constant comparison method. Annotations are directly linked to the text and memos are stored within the database as separate files.

Specialized software programs allow researchers to analyze much larger amounts of data than can be reasonably done manually or with Microsoft Word. They are also more efficient at identifying and coding relationships such as those found in second cycle and axial coding. Along the same lines, coding video, audio, or pictures is possible with CAQDAS.

NVivo project: policing

Let's look at how NVivo analyzes the data in a qualitative research project. When you first open the program, you have the option of opening an existing database or starting a new project. For our example, we will create a new project file. You will then see a screen shot like the one in Figure 10.3.

On the top navigation bar, select "External data." This option allows you to import text data (.doc, .docx, .rtf, .txt, .pdf), visual (.bmp, .jpg, .gif, .tif), video (.mpg, .wmv, .avi), and audio (.mp3, .mp4, .wav). These file formats are only a few of the types that the program accepts—some CAQDAS allow you to import content directly from the Internet. Choose the type of data. A dialog box will appear; select the folder and file that you want to import into the database. You then have the options of entering a description of the source and coding the source to a classification and attribute. An example of a classification could be job role, with the attributes of patrol officer, detective, community service officer, and specialized unit.

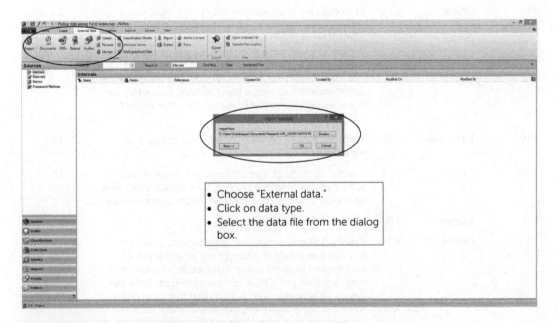

Figure 10.3 Starting a NVivo Project

Source: NVivo qualitative data analysis software; QSR International Pty Ltd. Version 10, 2012

Once you have imported all your data files into the program, you can create nodes. A **node** is a label representing an idea, concept, category, theme, situation, event, setting, or experience. All data that are related to one another along this substantive dimension are assigned to this code. Nodes can be determined in advance, inductively during the analysis, or in vivo by using the respondents' exact words.

One way to create a node is to click on the "Node" button on the navigation pane. As seen in Figure 10.4, a window appears; you enter the node name and a preliminary description or definition. If you create nodes during analysis, highlight the text segment and right click. One of the options is "Code to a new node." The same dialog box will appear.

Next, open a source document by clicking on "Sources" at the bottom left of the screen. A list of all sources will appear in the top half of the screen. In the example, I have opened Interview P02_v3 and it appears in the bottom half of the screen. Highlight the text you would like to code, right click, and select "Code selection at existing node" or create a new one as described above. If you are coding to an existing node, the dialog box in Figure 10.5 appears; you can check off which node(s) you would like to assign this text segment.

> **node** a coding unit used as a label for a concept, category, or theme in computer-assisted qualitative data analysis.

For each node that represents a concept, you can create dimensions and use "Highlight" and "Coding stripes" to assist you in keeping track of the data. Nodes and dimensions are assigned a colour. On the right-hand side, you can see the most recent codes assigned to text segments in this source document.

There are many different analytical options. Some of the more common are searches and queries. A text search looks through all sources, nodes, annotations, and memos for particular words, phrases, or themes. A word frequency query allows you to determine which words or phrases appear the most frequently in the data. You can specify the closeness of the match by including allowable synonyms. This type of query is useful for identifying or supporting inductively created themes or detecting patterns in how respondents describe a person, situation, or

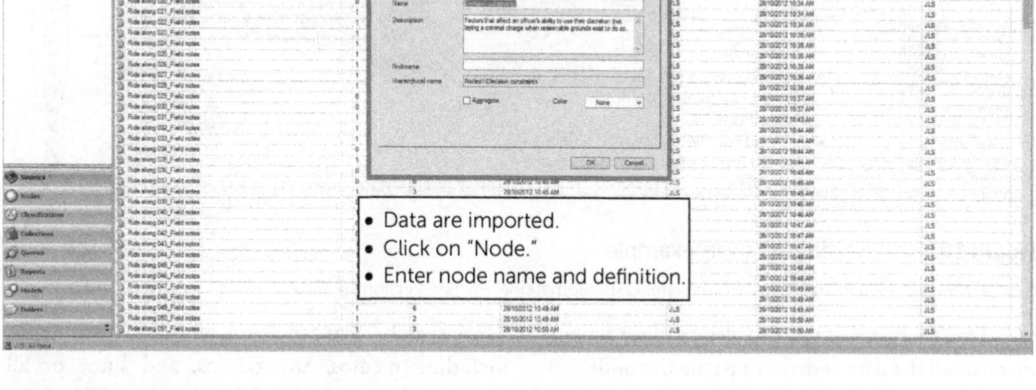

- Data are imported.
- Click on "Node."
- Enter node name and definition.

Figure 10.4 Creating a node

Source: NVivo qualitative data analysis software; QSR International Pty Ltd. Version 10, 2012

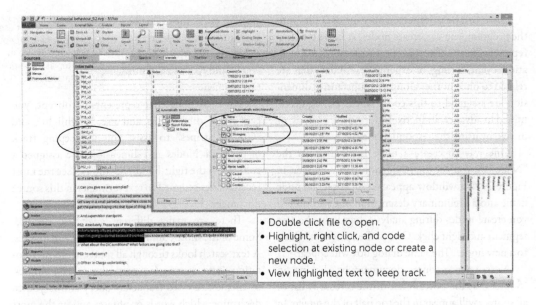

Figure 10.5 Coding text to a node

Source: NVivo qualitative data analysis software; QSR International Pty Ltd. Version 10, 2012

- Double click file to open.
- Highlight, right click, and code selection at existing node or create a new node.
- View highlighted text to keep track.

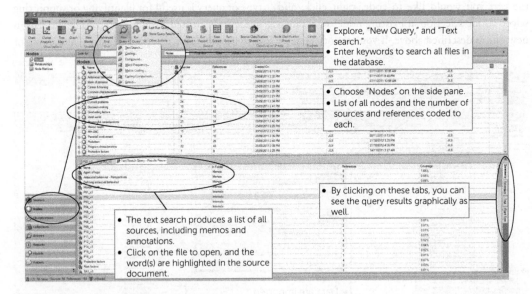

Figure 10.6 NVivo data analysis example

Source: NVivo qualitative data analysis software; QSR International Pty Ltd. Version 10, 2012

- Explore, "New Query," and "Text search."
- Enter keywords to search all files in the database.
- Choose "Nodes" on the side pane.
- List of all nodes and the number of sources and references coded to each.
- By clicking on these tabs, you can see the query results graphically as well.
- The text search produces a list of all sources, including memos and annotations.
- Click on the file to open, and the word(s) are highlighted in the source document.

idea. Don't forget that you can also produce a report that lists all the data coded to a particular node.

Select the "Explore" tab of the navigation pane (see Figure 10.6). Click on "New Query" and choose "Text Search." You can search all source documents, including memos, annotations, and some or all nodes. If you go to the left-hand side at the bottom of the screen, you can click on "Nodes" to display all the nodes created, the number of sources coded to each, and the number of text segments. Once you run the query, the results appear on the bottom half of the screen. Click on any of the source documents listed, and every instance of the words or phrase will be highlighted. Finally, on the right-hand side, you will see additional tabs that allow you to display your text query graphically.

Figure 10.7 is a visual representation of a cluster analysis conducted for a project that analyzed media representations of the police and protesters at the 2010 G20 Summit held in Toronto (Schulenberg & Chenier, 2014). Over 400 newspaper articles were coded from three major Canadian newspapers (*Toronto Star*, *National Post*, the *Globe and Mail*). This cluster analysis visually depicts patterns in the data. Sources with similar words or shared coding to nodes are grouped together, which helped discern relationships in the data prior to creating categories. For example, you can see that the Vancouver Olympics was used when presenting the police perspective to support the number of officers, the operation of the chain of command, and the need for these types of security measures at the Summit.

Authenticity: Evaluating Qualitative Research

There are no precise standards for authenticating the results from a qualitative data analysis. However, researchers carefully examine the analytical procedures followed. Are the respondents credible to speak on the issue or situation? Does any motivation exist to lie directly or by omission? To what extent is there a threat of reactivity?

Recall that everything seen and heard is interpreted through our own lens of social experiences and values. The researcher is the data collection and analysis instrument, and he or she is only human. Interpreting data is not only descriptive but also multi-faceted:

Interpretation means attaching significance to what was found, making sense of findings, offering explanations, drawing conclusions, extrapolating

lessons, making inferences, considering meanings, and otherwise imposing order on an unruly but surely patterned world. The rigors of interpretation and bringing data to bear on explanations include dealing with rival explanations, accounting for disconfirming cases, and accounting for data irregularities as part of testing the viability of an interpretation. (Patton, 2002, p. 480)

Although authentication is not standardized in the way we assess validity in quantitative research, there are assessment guidelines. The criteria for trustworthiness (credibility, transferability, dependability, confirmability) were initially introduced in Chapter 3 so will not be repeated. Here we add originality, resonance, and usefulness as criteria used to establish authenticity.

Table 10.4 presents questions to ask yourself when assessing qualitative research published in articles and books. Remember that strong evidence for originality and credibility will enhance resonance and usefulness (Charmaz, 2006). In combination, these qualities increase the contribution to knowledge in this substantive area and in any generic social processes.

Conclusion

We have covered a lot of ground in this chapter, moving from the more philosophical underpinnings of qualitative data analysis to the nuts and bolts of techniques used in crime and justice research. No research methods topic is complete without a consideration of ethics and addressing the "so what" question. The key to success may lie in remembering that we are concerned with understanding how research subjects go about their daily lives. Ensuring that their way of life, identity, and routines are respected is of utmost importance. "Researchers traffic in *understanding*. Most study participants are preoccupied with *action*—how to work and live better. It can be argued that if you approach your analytic work with a deeper sense of its action implications, your understanding will be deeper—and the

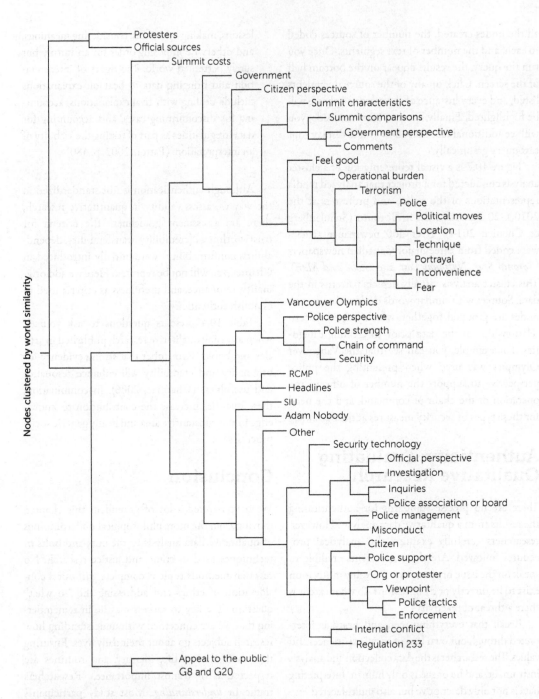

Figure 10.7 Visual representation: Cluster analysis

Source: Schulenberg & Chenier (2014).

Table 10.4 Measures of authenticity

Criteria	Questions to consider
Credibility	• Has your research achieved intimate familiarity with the setting or topic?
	• Are the data sufficient to merit your claims? Consider the range, number, and depth of observations contained in the data.
	• Have you made systematic comparisons between observations and categories?
	• Do the categories cover a wide range of empirical observations?
	• Are there strong logical links between the data and your argument?
	• Has your research provided enough evidence for your claims to allow the reader to form an independent assessment and agree with your conclusions?
Originality	• Do your categories offer new insights?
	• Does your analysis provide a new conceptual view of the data?
	• What is the social and theoretical significance of your work?
	• How do the findings challenge, extend, or refine current ideas, concepts, and practices?
Resonance	• Do the categories portray the fullness of the studied experience?
	• Have you revealed taken-for-granted meanings?
	• Have you drawn links between larger groups or institutions and individuals?
	• Does your theoretical explanation make sense to your participants or people who share their circumstances? Does your analysis offer them deeper insights about their lives?
Usefulness	• Does your analysis offer interpretations that people can use in their everyday world?
	• Do your analytic categories suggest any generic processes?
	• Can the analysis spark further research in other substantive areas?
	• How does your work contribute to knowledge?

Source: Adapted from Charmaz (2006, pp. 182–183).

benefits to participants more equitable" (Miles et al., 2014, p. 61; bold in original).

Although every stage in the research process has ethics to consider, three aspects of the ethical imperative are most pronounced in terms of data analysis. The first is confidentiality. When reporting the results, researchers will use fictitious names or alphanumeric codes, as I did in Table 10.3. However, this practice may not be enough to protect the research subjects' confidentiality. Those in the research setting may be able to recognize the words or position taken and link it to a particular person or group.

Having intimate and extensive background knowledge will help you detect this problem.

Researchers have to be especially careful to remove any information that could even remotely be an identifier. It goes without saying that this situation is of particular concern when the research is on illegal behaviour. Not only should it be made crystal clear in the informed consent that such information will be excluded, but some researchers will also request not to be told about reportable activities (e.g. intent to harm self or others) or future crimes when investigating certain research topics.

Research Highlights

Analyzing the Data on Youth Crime

While adhering to established analytical procedures, researchers are innovative when analyzing qualitative data because the process is anything but straightforward. Based on the research questions, the analysis may be complex, using multiple techniques that require different stages for data analysis. In other cases, strategies such as counting are used to support theoretical explanations grounded in the data. Still others take additional steps to ensure the authenticity of findings.

One research study investigated what violence means to youth in residential custodial facilities. Fifteen focus groups were conducted with youth between the ages of 12 and 17 in two reform schools. The use of focus group interviews was appropriate because the subjects could "not only voice their individual opinions but also discuss and even debate among themselves and thus present arguments for their opinions—or modify or elaborate them" (Honkatukia et al., 2006, p. 332). As discussed in Chapter 7, focus group data is very difficult to analyze. In this study, the researchers approached the analysis in two stages.

The first stage identified themes in different contexts and on the basis of different definitions of violence. The second stage involved examining the narratives within each theme and how youth described violence. The researchers found that violence is instrumental as a mechanism of belonging, creating social order, and solving problems. Violence is expressive of crazy individuals, emotions, and fictional depictions. The findings support the study's conclusion that it's important to identify the multiple meanings held for the concept of violence when considering how to respond through social and criminal policies.

Second, researchers have an obligation to report the analytical procedures. Think of it as a new stage of field work in which you observe yourself analyzing the data. Take your lead from the data and let it tell the story. Don't impose any preconceived frameworks or understandings when analyzing the data and writing up the findings. Further, it is unethical to use only the part of the data that agrees with what you want to find.

Finally, questions about a potentially biased interpretation can arise. Coding is arguably a subjective activity. Can you rule out the possibility that you are seeing what you want to see in the data? The entire process of writing up qualitative research is an exercise in ethical practice. It is impossible to include everything you have coded to a particular theme or idea. You can only use

exemplars and, if writing a journal article, you are often restricted to 25 pages or less. The process of selecting quotations is not always straightforward because the evidence and themes you decide to include and exclude as part of telling the story can manipulate the message. Awareness, reflexivity, and peer review can serve as a check and balance for this ethical concern.

The "so what" question is an important issue to revisit and address. One way to do this is to think in terms of generic social processes that move beyond this particular setting, and the findings can be applied to other substantive areas, settings, or situations (Prus, 1996). This practice is also referred to as transferability or cross-population generalizability. Ask yourself: Does prior research provide any clues? Do your findings apply to other similar

Anderson and Linden (2014) interviewed 43 youth with a history of auto theft to explore motivations to commit this crime and to discern the characteristics of a typical offender. Themes such as target selection, process, and attitudes toward the justice system, of which percentages were used to support the inferences made about predominant views, were identified in the data. For example, "the most common reasons to steal a car were joyriding (93%), for transportation (87%), and for the thrill of it (84%)" (p. 252). Quotes such as this one were used to elaborate on these thematic dimensions: "After you drive when you're not supposed to drive it's kind of like an addiction because the adrenaline rush is so powerful" (p. 254). These statements are one example of how counting and exemplar quotations are used to enhance credibility and to provide the reader with information to determine the authenticity of the theoretical explanation.

An example of steps taken to authenticate findings is seen with Payne and Button (2009), who wanted to understand how violence prevention plan committees are created and their perceptions on how best to prevent youth violence. The researchers conducted seven focus groups with 85 stakeholders. To increase the credibility and resonance of the findings, they created themes on the basis of implicit meanings in the data. As a result, they conducted a member check by sharing these themes with members of the committee and eliciting comments on the data assigned to a theme, its definition, and implications for telling the story.

As with quantitative research, not all qualitative research is created equal. However, in the majority of cases, researchers are very cognizant of their presentation of evidence, strategies employed to analyze the data, and their role as the data collection and analysis instrument. The next time you read the findings from a qualitative research project, think back to this chapter. Take note of the story, the evidence, structure of the findings (e.g. analytic comparison), and the authenticity of the theoretical explanation.

groups? What part of the findings and conclusion can you argue is new knowledge and significant in the real world?

Qualitative data analysis may not look straightforward on the surface, but there is a method when using this iterative and recursive approach. Just remember that you are giving a voice to your research subjects outside of their everyday social world. The responsibility is heavy, but the journey is very rewarding.

Summary of Important Points

Introduction

- Qualitative data analysis is an iterative and recursive process for interpreting social reality from the perspective of the social actors.
- Analytic induction is a process that compares hypotheses to newly analyzed data to better understand the topic under investigation, refine definitions, and elaborate on evidence supporting or refuting a theme or pattern identified in previously analyzed data.
- The analysis includes four simultaneous activities: data collection, reduction, display, and drawing conclusions.

The Method to the Madness

- Ideal types are abstract models used to identify similarities and differences between cases.
- The illustrative method uses data examples to describe a theory in a given social context.
- Analytic comparison uses the methods of agreement and difference to explore how a theory explains factors associated with an outcome.
- Successive approximation is the process of repeatedly analyzing the data to improve a theoretical model.

Nuts and Bolts: Where Do I Start?

- Fracturing the data is breaking the text into meaningful segments that can be assigned to concepts using deductive or inductive coding.
- Memos capture the development and overall reflections on concepts, people, events, or situations, while annotations are associated with a text segment instead of larger concepts.
- First cycle coding involves fracturing the data and assigning text segments to descriptive, process, in vivo, and emotion codes.
- Second cycle coding involves identifying patterns in the data and amalgamating conceptually similar codes into larger categories.

Putting the Pieces of the Puzzle Together

- General analytical strategies are fracturing the data, identifying relationships, using the constant comparison method, seeking disconfirming evidence, and considering alternative explanations.
- Qualitative researchers create stories by noting patterns and themes, assessing plausibility, clustering categories, creating metaphors, counting, making substantive comparisons, investigating relationships, and specifying the conditions affecting outcomes.

Grounded Theory

- Open coding creates labels, assigns text segments to preliminary concepts, and compares data for similarities and differences.
- Axial coding combines concepts into categories and specifies relationships in the data.
- Selective coding develops a theoretical explanation by creating a central category that includes all concepts and categories.

Looking at the Analysis a Different Way: Some Alternatives

- Descriptive, explanatory, and critical narrative analyses interpret stories in terms of content and function using techniques such as periods, path dependency, and historical contingency.
- Conversation analysis focuses on the structure of a story when communicating rather than on the content.
- Semiotics examines verbal and nonverbal language to identify the meaning of signs and symbols used to communicate.

Computer-Assisted Data Analysis

- Microsoft Word is suitable for analyzing a small number of relationships.
- CAQDAS is an efficient tool for specifying relationships in second cycle and axial coding and allows for complex searches, large databases, and visual representations of the data.

Authenticity: Evaluating Qualitative Research

- Authenticity of the findings and theoretical explanations can be established on the basis of credibility, originality, resonance, and usefulness.

Conclusion

- Ethical concerns during data analysis and reporting results include protecting confidentiality, describing analytical procedures, and presenting evidence equitably and without bias by using exemplar quotations and thick description.

• Address the contribution to knowledge in terms of generic social processes in which findings apply to other settings and situations.

Key Terms

analytical comparison 305
analytic induction 303
annotation 311
axial coding 316
coding 308
constant comparison method 306
conversation analysis 320
deductive coding 308
descriptive coding 312

discourse analysis 318
emotion coding 312
first cycle coding 312
grounded theory 315
ideal type 304
illustrative method 305
inductive coding 309
in vivo coding 312
memo 310
method of agreement 305

method of difference 306
narrative analysis 319
node 325
open coding 315
process coding 312
second cycle coding 312
selective coding 317
semiotics 321
sensitizing concept 309
successive approximation 306

Review Questions and Exercises

1. What are some of the challenges researchers face when analyzing non-numeric data?
2. Pick a topic of your choice and list all the relevant words that come to mind. From this list, select five words or phrases and create sensitizing concepts (label and definition).
3. Choose three of your favourite songs and look up the lyrics on the Internet. Conduct a small analysis of the data by going through first and second cycle coding. Using a word-processing software program, complete the following:
   a. Create four to five codes deductively or inductively.
   b. Assign text segments to codes.
   c. Identify any patterns that exist in the data within or across codes.
   d. Identify any themes in the data.
4. Choose a journal article that has analyzed data using qualitative methods. Do you think the results have authenticity? Why or why not?

Online Exercises and Websites of Interest

Coding and Memos

www.google.com
Select one of the topics below and conduct a Google search. Using two website pages, code the data and determine if there are any themes within them. In a memo, note any disconfirming evidence or taken-for-granted knowledge.

- Burnout
- Course work
- Performance anxiety

- Emotional tsunami
- Writer's block
- Light bulb going off

Analyse This!! Learning to Analyse Qualitative Data

http://archive.learnhigher.ac.uk/analysethis/main/qualitative.html

This website provides an overview of analyzing survey, interview, focus group, and observational data. There is also information on discourse analysis.

The Listening Resource: Using Excel for Qualitative Data Analysis

www.qualitative-researcher.com/qualitative-analysis/using-excel-for-qualitative-data-analysis/

You can also use Excel to analyze qualitative data. Click on the hyperlink at the bottom of the post for step-by-step instructions.

Nvivo 10 for Windows: Getting Started

http://download.qsrinternational.com/Document/NVivo10/NVivo10-Getting-Started-Guide.pdf

This PDF is a step-by-step guide, which includes screen shots, on how to use the CAQDAS program NVivo.

Additional Resources

Corbin, J., & Strauss, A. (2015). *Basics of Qualitative Research: Techniques and Procedures for Developing Grounded Theory* (4th ed.). Thousand Oaks, CA: Sage.

This text is one of the most cited sources on how to conduct a grounded theory analysis. The authors provide detailed information on the rationale and steps on developing theory inductively from the data.

Miles, M.B., Huberman, A.M., & Saldaña, J. (2014). *Qualitative Data Analysis: A Methods Sourcebook* (3rd ed.). Thousand Oaks, CA: Sage.

This book provides a comprehensive, graphical, and easy-to-understand explanation of five approaches to qualitative data analysis: exploring, describing, ordering, explaining, and predicting.

Part V
Taking Methods a Step Further

Chapter 11

Evaluation Research

"One of the greatest mistakes is to judge policies and programs by their intentions rather than their results." M. Friedman, "Living within Our Means" (1975)

Learning Objectives

- To appreciate the role, goals, purpose, and types of evaluation research.
- To distinguish the differences between basic, applied, and evaluation research.
- To differentiate among program and evaluation theories, prospective and retrospective evaluations, and the system model for evaluation research.

- To formulate the research problem, accounting for utility, feasibility, propriety, and accuracy.
- To describe the formative evaluations of needs assessment, evaluability assessment, and process evaluations.
- To describe the summative evaluations of outcome, impact, cost-effectiveness, and cost–benefit evaluations.

Introduction

In one way or another, **evaluation research** is best seen as a research design that investigates whether or not a social intervention has produced the desired results. Evaluation design is not a type of data collection, as this form of research can be quantitative, qualitative, or mixed methods. Evaluations of criminal justice programs and policies can use evidence from documents (e.g. meeting minutes, websites, promotional material, or financial records), interviews, observations, secondary data, and surveys. Evaluations resemble more of a reason for conducting a study than a research method per se. In many cases, it is a type of explanatory research because it looks at cause and effect. That is, it asks, "Does

evaluation research
research that assesses the consequences (intentional and unintentional) of a policy, practice, or program and the extent to which its particular goals and objectives are met.

participating in the program result in the expected outcome?"

Evaluation studies are commonly referred to as applied research because the goal isn't necessarily to test theoretical explanations but to produce findings that are applicable and can be used immediately. For this reason, appropriate topics are diverse, but all share one characteristic: practical significance. This type of research is conducted in the real world and the findings have implications for proposed or current programs and initiatives. Evaluation studies scientifically determine program and policy merit and seek to identify "relevant values or standards that apply to what is being evaluated" (Coffman, 2003, p. 7). In contrast, social science research typically seeks to develop empirical rather than evaluative conclusions.

Evaluation studies are not just a small enclave in criminology and criminal justice research. The importance of this academic pursuit is seen in the creation of the peer-reviewed journal *Criminology & Public Policy* in 2001. Overall, journal articles follow the form of a comprehensive literature review, a detailed description of the methodology, a thorough presentation of the findings, and implications for future research. Evaluation research does not fit well into this model. *Criminology & Public Policy* is policy oriented and focuses on criminal justice policies, programs, and practice. Thus, its journal articles discuss the policy or practice under investigation, the significance or implications of studying this problem, and policy implications; review pertinent literature on the subject; give a brief description of the methodology; present results in a clear and succinct manner; and examine whether the findings provide empirical support for current, new, or modified policies and practices.

A good example of research published in this journal is Berk and MacDonald's (2010) evaluation of a targeted police intervention strategy used to implement a new crime prevention policy. The researchers examined the effectiveness of the Main Street Pilot Project and the larger Safer Cities Initiative in Los Angeles. The project's positive results on place-based targeted policing led to the full implementation of the Safer Cities Initiative, which addresses crime and disorder associated with homeless encampments on Skid Row. The policy objective of crime prevention led to a two-prong approach by the Los Angeles Police Department: it issued tickets and fines to reduce the density of homelessness in these areas and implemented strong enforcement practices, with arrests for public intoxication, drug use, and prostitution. After analyzing eight years of data from before and after the strategies were initiated, the researchers found reductions in violent, property, and nuisance (disorder) crimes. On the surface, the major policy implication is that the evidence supports the use of geographically targeted police interventions as an effective strategy to achieve crime prevention benefits. At the same time, Berk and MacDonald (2010) point out that the police cannot address the roots or consequences of homelessness; other programs, policies, and strategies are needed to tackle these issues.

Defining Evaluation Research

In everyday use, *to evaluate* means "to assess, appraise, or state the number or extent of a phenomenon." To evaluate is to make a judgment on the value of what something does and how well it does it. Evaluation research builds on our common-sense understanding; however, it is a systematic scientific investigation generating knowledge for evidence-based practice. Evaluation research scientifically investigates what works, to what extent, how best to proceed in specific contexts, and what process and effects exist in a social intervention. It allows us to see if what we want a program to accomplish is actually being achieved, thereby providing a type of accountability measure in our efforts to prevent and control crime.

Suchman (1967, p. 7) is credited with formalizing and defining evaluation research as a "social process of making judgments of worth" through the application of social research techniques. He adopted a pragmatist worldview with his assertion that evaluations should use whatever research methods are appropriate to the needs and context of a particular evaluative research question. Evaluation should be approached as a scientific process, and "the same procedures that we use to discover knowledge [can] be used to evaluate the degree of success in the application of this knowledge" (Stufflebeam & Shinkfield, 2007, p. 278).

Contemporary program evaluation is defined as "the systematic collection of information about the activities, characteristics, and outcomes of programs to make judgments about the program, improve program effectiveness, and/or inform decisions about future programming" (Patton, 2002, p. 10). In practice, evaluation research in criminology and criminal justice is conducted for several reasons: to use for

Vignette: Breaking It Down

Police Work: Is D.A.R.E. Successful?

The Drug Abuse Resistance Education (D.A.R.E.) program began in 1983 in Los Angeles. By the 1990s, it had spread across the United States and Canada. It is embraced by politicians and the public as a "feel good" program that fits well with the "War on Drugs" political mandate. The program gives police officers 80 hours of training to teach fifth-grade students how to resist drugs. The curriculum is delivered in 50-minute segments over a period of 17 consecutive weeks. The underlying premise is that police officers can teach children about drugs and the criminal problems drugs can cause for them, those around them, and society as a whole. The primary objective is to reduce the chances that youth will use drugs during their high-school years.

Does the program accomplish its goal? One evaluation, which compared fifth graders who participated in D.A.R.E. against a group that did not, found that the D.A.R.E. students had increased knowledge on the effects of drugs but there was little difference in awareness of why people shouldn't use drugs or in reduction of current or future drug use (Becker, Agopian, & Yeh, 1992). Rosenbaum and Hanson (1998) tracked youth from grades 6 to 12 and found that D.A.R.E. doesn't prevent drug use during these high-risk years when compared to youth who did not participate in the program. Many additional evaluations found small effects on drug use, with the effect decreasing over time. In fact, up to ten years after participating in the D.A.R.E. program, no differences were found in the likelihood of drug use, attitudes, or self-esteem (Lynam et al., 1999).

Despite extensive media coverage on such research findings, the program enjoyed a rapid growth in popularity and strong vested interests in its continuation developed. It's quite common for D.A.R.E. officers to be strong proponents of the program, as they see its success defined quite differently from the program's primary objective. For instance, D.A.R.E. can do "a great job of providing children with tools to handle problems more effectively and positive ways of seeking help" (Lundman, 2001, p. 79). Similarly, another officer states: "If good role models are used, in uniform, in the classroom, the positive influence cannot be denied, researchers' evaluations or not, because of the empirical evidence so prevalent during the interaction with students" (Lundman, 2001, p. 79). The evaluation results finding the program ineffective actually led to public and political cries for more D.A.R.E. and to a modified curriculum due to these perceived positive outcomes associated with deterring drug use.

management or administrative purposes; to test theoretical propositions; to identify ways to improve program delivery; or to decide whether a program should continue as is or be modified in some way or if funding should be discontinued. Naturally, this last reason makes program administrators the most nervous about giving criminologists access to their programs. A poignant example in police work is evaluations of the D.A.R.E. program.

Conducting an evaluation study on whether a program is achieving its stated goals and objectives is rarely a straightforward path devoid of ethical and political obstacles. Thus, it is increasingly important to structure the evaluation research design in a way that reduces these conflicts as much as possible, maintains scientific standards of evidence, and involves **stakeholders** in the research process. Evaluations can have more impact when accounting for stakeholder concerns, perspectives, and expectations based on quantitative and qualitative data (Birkeland, Murphy-Graham, & Weiss, 2005).

It is difficult to ignore the fiscal cutbacks, the need for efficiency, and the increased emphasis on accountability for a program's effectiveness to ensure continued funding. Thus, evaluation research is increasingly a venue for knowledge that is applicable to that program or to others targeting similar types of crime, offenders, or social problems. Historically, and to a large extent currently, prevention programs and intervention strategies are not necessarily rewarded for achieving their intended outcomes. Bureaucracy and red tape have created a situation whereby the successful completion and submission of required paperwork is sufficient to warrant continued funding. We shouldn't be surprised, then, that some criminal justice programs are not overly thrilled at the prospect of being scientifically taken to task for achieving their stated objectives.

Let's look at it in a different way, with you as a stakeholder. You have a vested interest in the content and delivery of your courses. Arguably, you also play a role in their delivery because teaching is an interactive process between the professor and student (e.g. class discussions, office hours). If you look at course assessments as a type of evaluation, you may feel as if your input has been included in evaluating your degree program's merit. However, you may define success or quality differently than your professors or other stakeholders define them. For instance, professors may define success as research productivity and satisfactory course evaluations. You may not be very concerned about the number of publications your professor had last year. Excluding different stakeholder definitions can reduce the validity of the findings.

In the case of the D.A.R.E. program, Birkeland, and colleagues (2005) conducted 128 interviews with school district officials and police officers to better understand why evaluation research findings can be dismissed by practitioners. Practitioners were not under the illusion that D.A.R.E. by itself can prevent drug use. For this reason, they were absolutely not surprised that the evaluation results found the program ineffective. Practitioners made a strong argument that researchers "missed the boat" because they measured the wrong outcomes when determining success or failure. Research measured the program goals, but the practitioners argued that the true measure of success was the relationship fostered between youth and authority figures. Finally, these stakeholders saw their personal experiences with the program as more compelling than scientific evidence gathered in an evaluation. If practitioners do not feel that the results are generalizable to their situation, the likelihood of their accepting and implementing the findings from evaluation research are slim.

An additional factor complicates matters for crime researchers: how we define effectiveness or success is still elusive. Is success avoiding further conflict with the law? If a person has completed an anger management program, is it effective when he or she doesn't commit another violent offence? For an employment program, is success getting a job, keeping a job, securing a job in the targeted occupation, or not reoffending? How do we hold a prevention

> **stakeholder** a person or organization invested in the program being evaluated or interested in what will be done with the results.

program or intervention strategy accountable for its funding if evaluation results differ depending on how success or effectiveness is defined?

This question is far from easy to address; however, a careful evaluation research design plays close attention to the purpose, procedural steps, stakeholders, measurement of success, and the ethical and political context. Equally important is developing methodological know-how that allows you to assess the quality and rigour of an evaluation study. As results are used for evidence-based practice, informed decision-making includes an assessment of the evidence presented in support of a recommendation or conclusion.

Goals and Purpose of Evaluation Research

At a basic level, evaluations focus on decisions about cost-effectiveness, improvements to program delivery, funding, or changes to improve success and achieve program goals. As a result, the primary difference between evaluations and other types of research is the orientation or focus, not the research methods employed. Given the possible resistance from stakeholders, it's important to appreciate the goals and purpose of evaluation research.

The overall goal is to provide program administrators and other stakeholders with information that helps them decide what programs to offer, how best to structure them, what clients are the most appropriate, and how to improve program delivery. The purpose of an evaluation study determines the type of program evaluation. Table 11.1 provides some of the common questions addressed in each of the primary types of evaluation research designs. Although we discuss them later in the chapter, introducing them here will help you to understand the purpose of evaluation research and its role in shaping the overall research design.

If the purpose of an evaluation is to assess why a program is needed or what the program is targeting, you would conduct a needs analysis. On the other hand, if your purpose is to determine whether a program is successful at achieving its objective of preventing reoffending, you would conduct an

Table 11.1 Purpose of program evaluations

Purpose	Type of evaluation	Possible research questions
Why and What	Needs analysis	Does the problem this program targets actually exist? How many people are affected by this problem? Can or will they use this program as a solution? What types of services can help reduce this problem?
How	Process analysis	Are individuals in the target population aware of the program's services? Does the intended target population use the program? How is the program structured and delivered? How do program elements work to achieve program objectives? Are any modifications to program delivery feasible or needed?
Success	Outcome	What is the impact or results of the program? Do these outcomes reflect successful achievement of the program objectives? Are there any unanticipated program outcomes?
Fiscal performance	Efficiency analysis	What is the cost of achieving objectives? Do the benefits outweigh the costs of the program?

outcome analysis. Whether you are reading an evaluation study, conducting one, or interpreting findings in the context of your future employment, the "key consideration is the need to ensure that the evaluation approaches used are appropriate both for the type of research being evaluated, and for the aims of the specific evaluation" (Marjanovic, Hanney, & Wooding, 2009, p. 40).

Theory and Practice in Evaluation Research

Theory and practice co-exist in evaluation research designs. The question you are probably asking is, "How is this possible with research that investigates whether policies and programs are working?" Findings that lead to improvements and accountability may have utility but fall short if the objective remains to inform evidence-based practices. If someone tells you that you need to change three things about how you communicate, you may be initially defensive. Why? The rationale for these suggestions and an explanation for the impact on others are missing.

In much the same way, evaluation findings need to help us understand why behavioural changes occur or why program changes are needed (Schilder, 1997). The use of theory in evaluation research helps us address the "why" question and determine how to structure the evaluation. The more a researcher knows about the substantive topic, theory, research design, and methodological techniques, the more likely he or she will accurately answer a particular research question (Miller & Salkind, 2002).

Basic, Applied, and Evaluation Research Designs

So far in this chapter, evaluation research has been consistently referred to as a type of applied research. Although this description is true in comparison to basic research, evaluation research has unique characteristics. If the goal of basic research is to create new knowledge and applied research to use this knowledge, the different purpose of evaluation research is more apparent if it is to inform evidence-based practice and decision-making. Evaluation research makes judgments on the application of knowledge to a particular social problem. Table 11.2 summarizes the key defining characteristics of basic, applied, and evaluation research designs.

The research question drives the method, but strong research designs also incorporate theory. Depending on the research design, the role of theory will differ during the formulation of research questions, data collection, and data analysis. The use of theoretical concepts and perspectives is more intuitive in basic and applied research. However, this intuitiveness by no means suggests that theory is not a part of evaluation research or is necessarily more difficult to incorporate within a research design. Evaluation research operates within the pragmatist worldview. Thus, the theoretical perspective is appropriate for the social problem under investigation.

As we discussed in Chapter 1, middle-range theory starts with specific aspects of a social phenomenon instead of abstract concepts and institutions in society. For evaluation research, these aspects entail a specific target population and tailored response to social phenomena. To create theoretical explanations about human behaviour, they have to be sufficiently grounded in the real world so we can empirically verify the statements in a variety of contexts and situations (e.g. other types of programs, different locations). Pawson and Tilley (2003, p. 116) summarize middle-range theory well: "Theory is the bridgehead between the goals of generalization and specification in evaluation research . . . evaluation research is thus about producing middle-range theory of a kind abstract enough to underpin the development of a range of program types yet concrete enough to withstand testing in the details of program implementation." Middle-range theories are integral in evaluations as they constitute a set of techniques to create explanations that are connected to the real world, communicate knowledge to academics,

Table 11.2 Comparing basic, applied, and evaluation research designs

Defining characteristic	Basic	Applied	Evaluation
Nature of the problem	Seeks new knowledge about social phenomena; hopes to establish general principles and theories	Seeks to understand how basic research can help alleviate a demanding social problem and provide policy-makers with evidence-based practices	Assesses outcomes of treatments applied to social problems
Research goal	Produce new knowledge, including the nature of the relationships between concepts	Explore the value of basic knowledge in an applied setting that can be useful to a policy-maker who seeks to eliminate or alleviate a social problem	Provide an accurate accounting of a program targeting a social problem
Theory	Selection of a theory to guide hypothesis testing	Selection of a theory, guidelines, or intuitive hunches to explore the dynamics of a social system	Selection of a theory to fit the problem under assessment
Appropriate techniques	Theory formulation, hypothesis testing, sampling, data collection techniques, statistical and textual analysis, inferences	Similar to basic research only in a setting where the implications of the research are immediately obvious	Use of conventional techniques appropriate to the evaluative research question

Source: Adapted from Miller & Salkind (2002, p. 3).

inform policy-makers, and stimulate new ideas and future research on the causes and responses to crime.

Use of Theory in Evaluation Research

Evaluation studies on the same topic, policy, or program can take different approaches. Let's look at the following question: How effective are intensive probation supervision programs at reducing recidivism? The study could examine one program in one location or two or more programs at more than one location. Alternatively, the research could investigate similar or different programs targeting the same issue or population, such as intensive supervision by specialized police youth squads, or the type of program could be the focus of a cross-national evaluation. Differences also exist in the complexity of the research design. Is there a single measure of success,

such as no new offences? Does the evaluation study incorporate multiple data sources and analytical techniques? Is it cross-sectional or longitudinal? As you can see, you can conduct an evaluation in a variety of ways and, consistent with a pragmatist worldview, you can use any theoretical perspective based on the research purpose and the program or policy under investigation.

If theory is so important, why are published evaluation studies typically atheoretical? Consider the concept of atheoretical from a different perspective. If we operate under the assumption that theory informs the research questions and the findings may or may not support the theoretical explanation, this criticism of evaluation research is largely accurate. On the other hand, theoretically based evaluation research designs create theory to improve policies and programs. From

Key Thinker

Frank R. Scarpitti

Frank Scarpitti's (2002) parents were working-class, first-generation Italian Americans who raised five children during the Great Depression and World War II. Scarpitti describes himself as a "college boy" (from Albert Cohen's middle-class measuring rod theory) because, as a young adult, he was determined to achieve middle-class status and respectability despite growing up in a high-delinquency, lower-class area. Based on his experiences growing up, a portion of his research focuses on ecological explanations for crime and juvenile delinquency. His research interests expanded as a graduate student working under the direction of Walter Reckless (containment theory) at Ohio State University; Scarpitti has published extensively ever since.

Doing research didn't always come easy. His first attempt was a job conducting a door-to-door marketing survey, for which he earned $1.00 per hour. On one cold night in January, Scarpitti called on an elderly woman. Instead of waiting for her to agree to participate in the study, he asked her if she knew what product was associated with Elsie the Cow. She asked him if he was crazy and slammed the door shut.

Scarpitti contextualizes the research process in the form of an analogy. Research is detective work and much like building a pyramid one pebble at a time. The findings from each research project are pebbles that accumulate, support, and inform one another. He argues that research doesn't have to be grand to have meaning, to be relevant, or to improve society. Research that allows us "to speak with greater certainty about social, political, or economic arrangements that have an impact on our daily lives empowers us with knowledge . . . that gives us the equipment we need to control our environment and to effect social change" (Scarpitti, 2002, p. 87). This crime and justice researcher conducts evaluations because the findings have the potential to make positive contributions toward solving social problems.

Conducting evaluation research is not an easy path to follow ideologically, logistically, or methodologically. Scarpitti (2002, p. 75) encourages us when he states that "believing that one's research may also have significant public policy implications and actually make a difference in the lives of thousands of people is a stimulant that becomes intoxicating." Despite scientific research's aim to maintain objectivity, absolute value neutrality is difficult to impossible to achieve. After forty years conducting basic, applied, and evaluation research, Scarpitti 2002, (p. 89) notes that "value judgments are exercised every time we choose to investigate one problem rather than another, or use one methodology rather than another."

Evaluation research is often the first type to come under attack for potential bias or funding agencies or other stakeholders' influence on the research design. Nonetheless, quality evaluation research is needed now more than ever. Scarpitti argues that research should continue to be socially significant. New and existing policies and programs will always require empirical testing, and theories on human behaviour that can better explain the causes of crime and effective responses by the criminal justice system are yet to be articulated.

this vantage point, theory-based evaluations not only make judgments about a program's success at achieving its objectives but also try to specify why it is successful (Neuman, 2003).

Suppose a researcher studies Mothers Against Drunk Driving (MADD)'s effectiveness in reducing alcohol-related car accidents and fatalities. The findings suggest that magazine, radio, billboard, and television advertising have only short-term effects. There is evidence that this result may partially be explained by perceptions surrounding the situation in which the alcohol is consumed. Individuals believe that consuming alcohol under certain circumstances is not necessarily bad (although it is depicted as such by MADD's media campaign), and they do not connect to the problem of drinking alcohol and then driving a car. These results could inform a theoretical explanation for the relationship among motivations for behaviour, depictions of that behaviour, and means of changing future behaviour.

Theory-Based Evaluation

Researchers who are more oriented toward basic research develop theory based on testing empirical data. For those oriented toward applied research, theory is a logical series of steps that are required for a program to get from point A to point B. Yet others amend the definition of theory further to suggest that it's a road map for a program's activities, from the beginning right up to completing program objectives. Thus, one variant of using theory in evaluation research studies is to base the investigation solely on the theory underlying the program. Any evaluation study that talks about program assumptions often uses them as a theoretical framework.

Program theories provide researchers with a programmatic road map and rationale for addressing a social problem in a particular way. Every program theory has three components. First, the problem is defined. The definition guides which services are offered and how the program is delivered. Researchers develop a problem definition based on data from within and across programs that respond to a given social problem. Second, program components are identified and logically linked to one another. The program theory explains how these program elements combine to produce the program objectives or outcomes. Think of this part much like a series of if/then statements. For example, *if* classes discuss the personal

> **program theory** a theory that specifies what needs to be done to accomplish program goals, what (if any) additional anticipated outcomes exist, and how these goals and outcomes are achieved.

and societal harms of drug use, *then* program participants stop consuming illicit drugs. Third, program theories outline program activities. This portion of the theory links the logical sequence of program components (step 2) to program activities by using performance indicators. Performance indicators are ways to measure if the program has successfully met its objectives, such as no subsequent drug-related arrests.

Studies adopting program theory have three clear methodological advantages. Program theory provides a framework for establishing research questions and determining the most appropriate data collection methods. Next, evaluators often cannot randomly assign participants to a group that enters the program (experimental group) or to a group of individuals who do not participate (control group). Yet the research goal of causality (i.e. whether program participation causes the expected outcome) remains. When you are unable to ensure that there are no significant differences between those who participate in the program and similar individuals who do not, any differences in the outcome of program participation may actually be due to other differences between participants and non-participants. Thus, any causal statement about program effectiveness is suspect. However, "if evaluators can show that the program moved along its expected sequence of steps, and that participants responded in expected ways at each step of the process, then they can claim a reasonable approximate of casual explanation" (Weiss, 2003, p. 3). Finally, a program theory is grounded in real-world practice and application. This quality helps the researcher explain why and how the program works.

Evaluation Theory

To conduct a methodologically sound evaluation of any policy or program, researchers need theories that help them choose and use data collection methods (Shadish, Cook, & Leviton, 1991). If theories are strategies and methods are the logistics, you will need both to assess different types of situations and social problems. **Evaluation theories** can provide guidance on what data collection methods to use, under which circumstances, and with what types of evaluations.

Evaluation theory is "a coherent set of conceptual, hypothetical, pragmatic, and ethical principles forming a general framework to guide the study and practice of program evaluation" (Stufflebeam & Shinkfield, 2007, p. 63). An evaluation theory stipulates five aspects of evaluation research in a coherent manner:

- core concepts such as process, outcome, and inputs
- hypotheses on how evaluation procedures and their order of implementation produce desired empirical outcomes
- feasible procedures for conducting the evaluation
- ethical considerations
- an overall framework or research design to guide the program evaluation

Given what constitutes an evaluation theory, it's not hard to see how useful this type of theory can be to structure the evaluation. Evaluation theories extend our knowledge on conducting program evaluations by illustrating best practices when investigating crime and justice policies and programs as well as why these methodological frameworks are effective.

According to Mark (2005), another reason to consider evaluation theory is that it consolidates lessons learned by prior researchers. As the saying goes, you don't want to make the same mistake twice. Evaluations in crime and justice often involve many methodological decisions that may not be encountered in the evaluation of responses to other social problems. Ethical constraints caused by judicial discretion or logistical problems of accessing data can limit how a researcher structures the study and assesses program success. In other words, in crime and justice research, evaluation theory helps

us figure out how to conduct the evaluation and why.

evaluation theory a theory about how evaluation research should be conducted in order to be valid.

Revisiting the Wallace Wheel

Chapter 2 introduced the Wallace Wheel (see Figure 2.2) as a depiction of the scientific method. Despite this structure for scientific inquiry, conducting research in criminology and criminal justice requires methodological flexibility. This couldn't be truer when it comes to evaluation research. Figure 11.1 is an adaptation of the Wallace Wheel, which better illustrates the role of theory and method in a scientific investigation of a criminal justice policy or program.

As with the original Wallace Wheel, you do not need to start the research process with theory. However, an evaluation theory guides research design—you would begin here when you develop a program theory. In the case of evaluation research, theory encompasses mechanisms (how), contexts (under what conditions), and outcomes. Hypotheses test propositions about what might work for whom and under what circumstances. Observations involve multimethod data collection and analysis to address

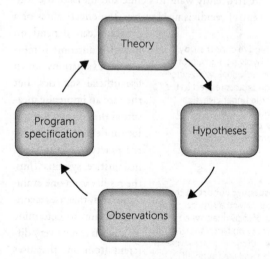

Figure 11.1 Phases of program evaluation

Sources: p. 85, Pawson, R., & Tilley, N. (2003). *Realistic evaluation*. Thousand Oaks, CA: Sage Publications.

the theoretically derived research question about the program mechanisms, contexts, and outcomes. Finally, program specification is the stage where the researcher determines what works for whom and in what context. Based on the findings from the program specification stage, this step can lead to modifications to substantive or program theory.

The Wallace Wheel is broken into informational components (theories, hypotheses, observations, and empirical generalizations) and methodological controls (logical deduction, research design, data analysis, and logical induction). In essence, none of these has changed. Instead of solely making inferences and empirical generalizations, the type of theory (substantive, program, or evaluation) and program specifications can change in evaluation research.

Evaluation Research Design

Contradictory findings in previous research can often be traced back to differences in the research design. In criminology and criminal justice research, we frequently want to define and measure the concept of recidivism. However, the effectiveness of a program can depend on how this outcome is measured. Evaluations often use official statistics, but they are an imprecise measure as they do not account for undetected crime or the practices of the criminal justice system. Thus, the results from one evaluation study that uses reconviction rates to determine recidivism can be very different from one that uses multiple measures, such as arrests, reconvictions, self-reported activity, and

prospective cohort study a study involving a group of similar individuals who differ only on factors related to the outcome under investigation and who are followed as the program or policy is implemented.

retrospective cohort study a study involving a similar group of individuals who differ only on factors related to the outcome under investigation and are followed using data from past records after the policy or program was implemented.

controls for the severity of the offence (Latessa & Holsinger, 1998; White, 2001).

Where Do I Start?

All research grapples with setting boundaries or specifying the parameters for data collection and analysis. Parameters fall into three general categories: time frame and selection of cases, type of data, and data collection methods. Time frame refers to the decision to evaluate a program or policy over a longer period of time or after the key events/interventions have occurred. Selecting your cases is critical, and the decision to conduct a quantitative, qualitative, or mixed methods evaluation study is directly influenced by the research question and program theory.

Specifying Parameters

A **prospective cohort study** follows a group of individuals for a period of time to make and test predictions. Farrington (1997) conducted a prospective evaluation of a community crime prevention program. The research goal was to carefully assess risk factors for youth crime and then test various prevention programs that were expected to reduce their impact. Program effectiveness is measured in multiple ways (e.g. reoffending, substance abuse, and other problem behaviours) before and after implementing the intervention strategy. Although prospective studies can represent a more robust approach to evaluating a criminal justice program, they are time-consuming, expensive, and less than ideal for evaluating a policy or program when results are needed sooner rather than later.

A **retrospective cohort study** analyzes data once the intervention is administered and all relevant events have occurred. Typically, this approach takes the form of analyzing large datasets where outcomes such as recidivism are already available. For example, Jones and Ross (1997) conducted a retrospective cohort study on the effectiveness of boot camps for repeat young offenders in North Carolina. They analyzed the differences between two groups: the experimental group that participated in the boot camp alternative and a group of offenders who were not sent to boot camp but were sentenced to probation. This second group was selected after program delivery by matching youth to a series of characteristics in an attempt to minimize any possible differences between the two groups. The effectiveness of this boot camp versus routine probation conditions was assessed by the number of new arrests for any crime, be it property, violent, drug-related, or public order offences, within 36 months. As the data were collected and analyzed after the records were created, there were limitations to the variables available and to the time frame for following the individuals when measuring the outcome, which in this case was recidivism. It's important to remember that retrospective studies are common and ideal in situations with funding limitations or ethical constraints in choosing cases.

Another way to look at the decision to conduct a prospective evaluation over a retrospective one is to return to the research question. Is the goal to evaluate the program or policy in terms of short-term or long-term objectives? Evaluating short-term objectives, such as the effect of not reoffending within 6 to 36 months, is well-suited to a retrospective study. Evaluating long-term objectives presents a larger challenge. A mechanism of change isn't necessarily the program characteristics or activities "but the response that the activities generate" (Sampson, 2007, p. 489). How long do you follow a cohort of individuals to assess behavioural changes accurately?

The manner of selecting cases creates additional difficulties in reconciling contradictory conclusions about program effectiveness. In prospective evaluations, you have more control over selection criteria that is informed by the program theory. Hayashi and colleagues (2010) conducted a prospective cohort evaluation on the effectiveness of a peer-run outreach-based syringe exchange program in Vancouver. This type of program is geared to intravenous drug users (IDU) who are not traditionally serviced by the conventional syringe exchange

programs available. Effectiveness was measured in two ways: reaching a group of IDU who are at a high risk for poor health outcomes and reducing the reuse of syringes. Participants were selected if they had injected drugs at least once in the past month, resided in the greater Vancouver area, and provided written consent to participate in the study. The results indicate that the program is successful at reaching its target clients, as participants self-reported unstable housing, frequent heroin and cocaine injection, injecting in public, and needle reuse. The study also concluded that this program is associated with lower levels of needle reuse.

In contrast, Salazar and Cook (2006) evaluated an intimate partner violence prevention program for youth to see whether changes occurred in attitudes and behaviour. Although this research may seem appropriate for a prospective research design, this type may not always be an option. Here the participants were selected by the criminal justice system and not the researchers. Adjudicated adolescent males who committed minor violent and abusive behaviours toward a female, experienced violence in the home, or (according to the court) were influenced by violence were referred by their probation officer to participate in the program as a condition of their probation order. Thus, in this retrospective study, the researchers selected cases that were predetermined.

Quantitative, Qualitative, or Mixed Methods?

Quantitative data tells us how much or how many, whereas qualitative data tells us how individuals feel and behave or why things are done in a certain way. Some may see quantitative as more objective and reliable than qualitative data. We need to remember that quantitative data requires just as much interpretation to make it meaningful and useful. Qualitative methods are empirical and systematic, and the analysis is grounded in the data. At all times, evaluation research must be empirically driven and adhere to scientific standards. No data type is appropriate for all evaluation studies. The choice should be driven by the research question, goals, and objectives.

Quantitative

Quantitative data is most commonly used in evaluation research, but researchers don't always use official statistics from the police, courts, or corrections. Serin, Gobeil, and Preston (2009) evaluated the Persistently Violent Offender Program, using data from 256 Canadian male violent offenders. The impact of participating in the program was assessed in three different ways: knowledge about program elements such as anger, empathy, and impulsivity; the number of institutional misconducts; and recidivism. Quantitative data were collected from self-report surveys to assess program element knowledge. This multimethod quantitative study also had to address the remaining two research questions, which required employing more traditional official statistics. Data for five years after program completion were examined, using institutional records for the number of misconduct offences while incarcerated and readmission to custody and police records for any subsequent arrests. Unfortunately, the results indicate that the program had little impact on knowledge, the number of misconduct offences, or recidivism upon release.

Qualitative

It is increasingly popular to use qualitative data in evaluation research because it allows the researcher to collect detailed, in-depth information. Certain elements of a program, such as decision-making or client perceptions, are difficult to quantify. Gideon (2009) evaluated a prison-based drug treatment program and, upon their release, interviewed 39 participants about their rehabilitation and reintegration experiences. Effectiveness was defined as the participants' perceptions on how essential continued treatment and supervision is for recovering addicts who received program support while incarcerated. The results indicate that continued treatment and supervision upon release are considered vital to

these recovering addicts, particularly in the first year. Qualitative data provides greater depth but sacrifices breadth. However, certain evaluation research questions are better addressed with qualitative data. This type of data is appropriate to understand perceptions on difficulties faced and the type of support needed.

Mixed Methods

Evaluation studies ideally need both types of data to be truly comprehensive. In practice, evaluation research is multi-faceted in terms of perspectives, methods, data, inferences, and conclusions. The decision to use mixed methods is driven by the purpose and role of the evaluation. Mixed methods evaluation research designs

> strive for knowledge claims that are grounded in the lives of the participants studied and that also have some generality to other participants and other contexts; that enhance understanding of both the unusual and the typical case; that isolate factors of particular significance while also integrating the whole; and that are full of emic meaning at the same time that they offer causal connections of broader significance. (Greene, 1997, p. 2)

Thus, assessments of program or policy impact on human behaviour can involve evaluating objectives that require different types of data.

Pauls (2005) examined the effectiveness of the Edmonton Police Service's Neighbourhood Empowerment Team Program. This study is a good example of using multiple methods to enhance reliability of the findings and to provide a more comprehensive understanding of the program. The evaluation involved reviewing program documentation, conducting interviews with community partners and key informants, running focus groups, analyzing crime statistics, and conducting a statistical comparison of crime rates and calls for service in similar non-participating communities. Each type of data addressed a particular program objective. The strengths and weaknesses of the program were identified from a number of different perspectives (e.g. official statistics, documents, and interviews) throughout data collection. The evaluation wasn't limited to changes in the crime rate, but it also gathered qualitative data from individuals with varying degrees of involvement and roles. In this way, a more comprehensive understanding of a program or policy's impact can be achieved.

Major Data Collection Methods

What type of information do you need to address your research questions? What do you need to measure the impact of a policy or program? How accurate is the information? Do you need to use more than one method? Will key decision-makers see the conclusions as credible? To answer these valid questions, we need to explore the purpose, advantages, and disadvantages of data collection methods commonly used in evaluation research to contextualize why more than one data collection method provides the researcher with a more comprehensive evaluation.

Table 11.3 describes six common data collection methods used in evaluation research. Surveys are predominantly quantitative. They allow for greater breadth, as you can collect data on considerably more topics from more people than with other methods. Surveys provide the most anonymity, which translates into the least bias because participants are less likely to provide socially acceptable responses to questions.

Interviews, observations, and focus groups are predominantly qualitative. Interviews are the least anonymous, which increases the risk of socially acceptable responses. However, if an interviewer establishes rapport with the participant, this bias can be minimized. The less structured the interview, the more flexible and responsive the researcher can be to unanticipated issues raised by the participant. The aim of this data collection method is to gain direct access to the interviewee's experiences and

authentic perceptions of social life. Observation of program delivery can provide the researcher with data that contextualizes information collected through other methods. For instance, there can be a difference between what people say they do and what actually occurs in real life. Additionally, participants may not realize various obstacles or factors when asked directly, but they can become evident to the researcher during observation sessions. Focus groups allow the researcher to gather information from an intensive discussion on a particular topic. The data can shed light on how opinions are formed or changed in the context of group interaction. Focus groups require a good facilitator who guides the discussion on various talking points. Moreover, it's important to note that the results from focus groups are often used to help design a survey.

Conducting a case study and analyzing documentation are accomplished with both quantitative and qualitative data. A case study focuses on one program and involves an intensive analysis of program specifics. An evaluation on one typical or atypical exemplar is an opportunity to achieve greater depth. However, it is more difficult to generalize the results to other similar programs elsewhere. Documentation from a program or policy is an integral source of data for an evaluator. It provides a picture of the program objectives, components, and outcomes, along with pertinent information such as the number of participants. Of course, this data collection method is limited, like all other methods, in terms of accessing the data. However, researchers can analyze documents not only for the content (what it says) but also for the form (how it is said) and compare this analysis to data collected through other methods.

Research Steps

An evaluator's primary role is to use his or her research expertise to assess the program's impact or efficiency and the initiative with judgments based on empirical data. The next step is to focus on how to perform this role. With the scientific method,

Table 11.3 Data collection methods in evaluation research designs

Method	Purpose	Advantages	Disadvantages
Survey	To gather a lot of information from people in a non-threatening manner	• Most anonymity • Inexpensive • Easier to compare and analyze • Sample surveys already exist	• Wording can bias responses • Impersonal • Difficult to get the full story
Interview	To understand impressions, experiences, or to gain in-depth information	• More range and depth • Develop rapport • Increased flexibility to gather unexpected information	• Least anonymity • Expensive and time-consuming • Can be difficult to compare responses • Interviewer could inadvertently bias responses
Documentation	To gain an appreciation of program operation, objectives, and other characteristics	• Comprehensive and historical • No disruption to program operations • Already exists • Can focus on content and form	• Need to know clearly what you are seeking • Less flexible as it's restricted to what is accessible
Observation	To gather information about how a program actually operates, particularly program activities	• View program operation as it actually occurs • Can adapt to events as they occur	• Difficult to interpret behaviours • Difficult to record observations • Can influence the behaviour of the participants by your presence
Focus group	To explore a topic in-depth through group discussion (e.g. reactions to an experience)	• Ideal to get common impressions • Efficient way to get a greater range and depth of information in less time • Can convey key program information	• Can be hard to analyze the responses • Requires a good facilitator • Hard to schedule six to eight people at the same time
Case study	To better understand experiences in a program and to conduct a comprehensive examination	• Detailed description of a particular program (process, impact)	• Represents depth of information, not breadth • Difficult to compare one case to another similar program elsewhere

Source: Adapted from McNamara (2010) and US Department of Health and Human Services (2005).

we state the hypothesis, collect data, analyze them, and then draw conclusions. The research steps for an evaluation are somewhat different:

- engage stakeholders
- describe the program

- develop an appropriate research design
- gather valid evidence
- draw inferences from the data
- support and justify conclusions
- play an active role in the use of the findings and share any lessons learned

In practice, this process entails identifying and measuring the program objectives, selecting an appropriate research design, collecting the data, and analyzing and interpreting the findings in relation to the research purpose and questions.

Prior to starting an evaluation study, you need to ask yourself a series of questions to help determine the type of evaluation needed for the specific program or policy. Table 11.4 organizes these questions into the categories of utility (purpose and use), feasibility (possibility to evaluate), propriety (suitability of methods), and accuracy (valid inferences to support conclusions).

In terms of utility, we ask ourselves, "Why conduct the evaluation in the first place?" Findings from an evaluation often serve more than one purpose. For instance, the results can assess whether the program yields the intended outcomes and can provide feedback to improve program implementation or judgments about social and economic value. Other utility questions include the following: Whom is the evaluation for? Who are the major stakeholders? What information will the stakeholders find useful? What will the final product of the evaluation be (e.g. report, executive summary, journal article)?

Feasibility ultimately involves addressing what exactly is being evaluated and if it can realistically be evaluated. Sometimes, researchers find it helpful to determine what is not being evaluated and proceed from there.

Propriety takes a closer look at the intervention strategy's intended outcomes. In other words, what is the program supposed to achieve and with whom? Equally important are being mindful of the unintended consequences produced by program activities and ensuring the research design allows for their discovery. Problem formulation occurs in this category, as the next step involves identifying the key questions that the study needs to address. These questions are often drafted in collaboration with the stakeholders, as is the identification of potential data sources.

Finally, accuracy requires careful consideration of which research design is most appropriate for achieving the evaluation objectives and addressing the research questions by collecting valid data. Specific questions to consider go beyond whether the program is achieving its goals and intended outcomes. How is the program accomplishing its intended and unintended outcomes? What mechanisms or processes make the program successful?

The fundamental step in all research, including evaluations, is to stipulate explicitly the problem to

Table 11.4 Research design questions

Criteria	Relevant questions
Utility	What is the purpose of the evaluation?
	Are stakeholder needs being met?
	What is the expected product of the evaluation?
	Who and how will the results be used?
Feasibility	What is the program's stage of development?
	How complex is the program?
	Can the components and outcomes be measured?
Propriety	Will the research design adequately detect any unintended consequences?
	Will the research design capture the experiences of those who are affected by the program?
Accuracy	Can program success or failure be detected?
	Will valid data be collected on program objectives or stakeholder concerns?

Source: Adapted from US Department of Health and Human Services (2005, p. 46).

be investigated and determine if program goals and objectives can be adequately measured. As we talked about earlier, identifying the expected outcomes and, in doing so, how success will be defined is equally thorny. If you were evaluating student learning, a student may have the objective of having fun with an outcome of a good grade. A professor might have an objective of teaching all the course material and an outcome of a good class average. A department chair may have the objective of ensuring all procedures for the classroom and grade submission are adhered to with an outcome of no grade disputes. The three stakeholders in this example differ, as is often the case in actual evaluations. The student and teacher have similar expected outcomes but differing objectives, and the administrator has a different agenda altogether. Thus, it is important to contact as many stakeholders as possible at the research problem formulation stage, to learn possible criteria for evaluation and program objectives from each of their points of view. Do not censor certain view points by disregarding any conflicting objectives. Allow the evidence to marshal whether there is support for these differing objectives or outcomes. As Neuman (2003, p. 526) aptly points out: "A researcher should be aware that measuring beliefs about program objectives can differ from measuring objectives directly."

Always remember that programs are evolving and policies are amended based on changing circumstances (Sampson, 2007). Identifying as many of these possible changes, measuring them, and collecting data that helps us figure out if the program or other external factors cause these changes are problems we face when conducting an evaluation. If we can't isolate what is supposed to change when someone participates in a program, it's extremely hard to evaluate program effectiveness.

inputs various financial, organizational, and human resources invested in a program.

outputs countable events or products derived from program activities.

program process the treatment or service provided by the program.

A large number of evaluations are case studies that investigate the effectiveness or efficiency of one particular program. During this stage in the research process, it is a good rule of thumb to remember that successful programs may not be successful in the future or that a program theory developed from the research is not necessarily applicable to similar programs elsewhere. Paying attention to the scope and nature of the social problem that the program addresses and linking the social problem to the program's objectives and outcomes increases the likelihood that certain aspects of successful programs will be transferable to other locations.

Basic Model: A One-System Approach

Adopting a system model means seeing all facets of the program as interrelated and affecting each other. Figure 11.2 represents the basic model for evaluation research. Think of it as a logic model you can follow to understand, track, and interpret program operation and delivery. A logic model "provides a graphic overview of a program, outlining the outcomes to be accomplished along with how they are to be achieved and for what groups" (Penna & Phillips, 2005, p. 4). The systems approach highlights the order in which things occur and the recursive feedback loop between stakeholders, clients, activities, and outcomes.

We have various **inputs** that enter the program, be they operating resources, staff, funding agencies, or clients. The clients are also referred to as the target population, or those for whom the program is intended to serve. Inputs lead to **outputs**, or direct products of the program's service delivery process. Outputs are immediate measures of what the program activities produce. It would seem that all we need to do is measure the inputs and then compare them to the outputs to see if the program's expected benefits are actually delivered. Unfortunately, it's not that easy. Between the inputs and the outputs is the **program process**, which constitutes the service or treatment that is administered in the intervention program being evaluated. Why is it important

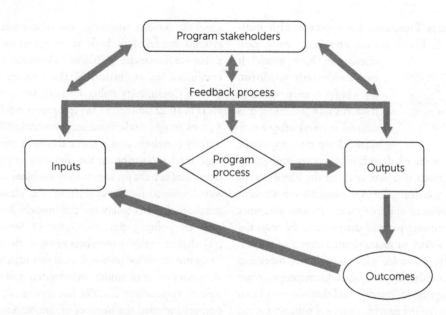

Figure 11.2 Basic model of an evaluation study

Source: Adapted from p. 365 of Bachman, R., & Schutt, R.K. (2007). *The practice of research in criminology and criminal justice* (3rd Ed.). Los Angeles, CA: Sage Publications.

to account for the program process when conducting an evaluation study? The incorrect or different administration of the service or treatment could be a possible explanation for any discrepancies found in the outputs and for any unexpected outcomes.

The outputs are the actual products of the program, such as the number of clients or the number of arrests. The **outcomes** are the impact of the program and are what we measure when assessing effectiveness. Stated differently, outcomes are the effects triggered by the program, such as increased knowledge, attitudinal changes, remaining drug-free, or not reoffending. Let's say the program is geared toward helping women released from a secure custodial facility to reintegrate into the community. The program activities work to develop their marketability and job skills. The output would be the number of women who went through the program process. The outcome would be a higher rate of employment or job retention for those who complete the program.

Program goals are statements on what the program intends to accomplish. Each goal will have at least one objective, which will have program activities associated with it. Objectives are more specific than goals, as they show how to accomplish the goal. Successful programs establish short- and long-term expected objectives. The long-term outcomes are usually the reason that the program was created in the first place. The short-term outcomes help us to understand progress toward achieving the long-term outcomes. Solid program objectives state the direction (expected change), time frame (when the objective is achieved), and the target (who is affected by the objective) (Poulin & Orchowsky, 2003, p. 5). Thus, each expected outcome must be considered in terms of activities, associated goals, and the sequence in which they are achieved by participants.

Once again, how we measure success arises when we come to outcomes. We have to decide whether we want one or more outcome measures of program

> **outcomes** the changes, effects, or accomplishments achieved by clients from participating in program activities.

effectiveness. Outcomes are measured with **indicators**, which can answer who, how many, how often, and how much. If we measure only recidivism for those women released from custody (assuming it is defined as committing a new offence), we miss important elements in the reintegration of women and ignore other elements that may relate to the likelihood of recidivism, such as substance abuse. Most evaluation studies measure multiple indicators and outcomes to avoid missing parts of the process, the ways the program works, or unanticipated effects of participation. The downside with multiple outcomes and indicators is that the analysis and interpretation are more complicated. You may find that one out of two indicators doesn't provide empirical support for the expected outcome. However, this contradiction is far outweighed by the need to measure program outcomes accurately. The results from an evaluation can have a profound impact on the program, and many researchers emphasize that measuring only involvement in the criminal justice system as an outcome indicator underrepresents the effectiveness of treatments geared to reducing criminal and analogous behaviour (Scott et al., 2003).

A feedback process occurs, as variation in both the outputs and outcomes can in turn influence the inputs. Let's go back to our example. If not enough women are served by the reintegration program that builds job skills, recruiting more women (inputs) could be a result. In the same way, conclusions will speak to how well program objectives are achieved and can lead to modifying goals, objectives, and activities.

To help clarify the relationship between inputs,

> **indicator** a characteristic or change observed to assess a program's progress toward achieving a particular outcome.

> **formative evaluation** a type of evaluation research that investigates what is and is not working so that actions can be taken to improve how the program or intervention functions.

> **summative evaluation** a type of evaluation research that investigates the effectiveness of or the extent to which a program achieves its objectives and the value of a program or process.

program process, outputs, and outcomes in a systems model, let's look at one evaluation of a law enforcement initiative. Dumaine (2005) conducted an evaluation of the Ottawa Police Service Community Police Centres, involving site visits to all 22 centres, 57 key informant interviews, 8 focus groups, a telephone survey with 1,006 community members, and a client feedback survey. A logic model, centring on the objective of the centres acting as hubs for community problem-solving, was developed for the evaluation. For illustration purposes, I focus solely on the model's problem-oriented policing portion. Some of the inputs included community members going to the centre. Program activities involved establishing contacts with relevant community stakeholders and centre officers responding to calls for service. Program outputs included the number of community organizations contacted by the police and the number of projects using problem-solving strategies. Intermediate outcomes were partnerships established with key community organizations and the implementation of problem-oriented policing strategies. The long-term objective for the problem-solving and crime prevention and management components was the Community Police Centres actively contributing to service delivery that reflects the Ottawa Police Service's commitment to community and problem-oriented policing, as stated in its organizational mission statement.

Types of Evaluation Research

A **formative evaluation** is meant to improve the program or intervention by looking at the program process (activities) and how well the services or treatment are delivered and to assess the organizational context, including logic model components of inputs, outputs, and outcomes. Common formative evaluations in criminal justice are needs assessments, evaluability assessments, and process evaluations. A **summative evaluation** examines the program's effect or impact. At this juncture, it is important to clarify effectiveness versus impact. Evaluating the effectiveness entails measuring the extent to which a program is meeting its objectives. To evaluate the impact is to measure whether the program or intervention creates the change anticipated for the social problem it is structured to address. Thus, we will look at outcome (effectiveness), impact, cost-effectiveness, and cost–benefit evaluations.

Formative Evaluations

These types of evaluations are change oriented, identifying any discrepancies between objectives and what is occurring in reality. Strengths, weaknesses, obstacles, and unexpected issues are identified to increase our understanding of how we can better implement the program. Formative evaluations are conducted at any point in the life cycle of a program, be it at the planning stages (needs assessment) or once the program is in operation (process evaluation). Organizations struggling to clarify objectives or likely to change program elements over time are ideal for these types of evaluations. The research design is predominantly qualitative in nature and asks exploratory and open-ended questions in order to ascertain program process, any changes since the program was initially conceived and launched, the relationship between components in the logic model, and the perceptions of staff. For this reason, formative evaluations are best approached using a case study design.

Several generic steps are involved in formative evaluations. First, a researcher needs to gain the co-operation of key stakeholders and their roles in the program and evaluation need to be clarified. For example, a program director may be concerned about identifying problematic areas in the program delivery process while staff is concerned about findings that address the impact of policies and procedures' ability to achieve program objectives. Thus, it is important in the first stage of a formative evaluation to identify, create relationships, and agree on what information is relevant with the various stakeholders. Second, the evaluation needs to be seen as an important contribution to program design and operation. Programs and policies in criminal justice do not operate in a vacuum but in an increasingly dynamic environment. Third, the evaluation research design should be structured to engage participants in a change-oriented activity that is meaningful to their work environment. Fourth, a researcher must identify who makes what decisions in the organization. Each stakeholder, including clients, will want to see answers to different questions. Finally, formative evaluations require the use of more than one data collection technique to address the research questions.

What makes formative evaluations unique is that they are prospective in nature. The results have the potential to create change and inform decision-making prior to program creation or modification during operations. In addition, the groundwork is laid for a summative evaluation to identify causal mechanisms. Unfortunately, we don't see the results of formative evaluations published very often for this very reason. The results are amalgamated with the findings from a summative evaluation to show whether improvements to a program produced the expected behavioural changes. In fact, the changes made in the program content and delivery examined in the summative evaluation almost always reflect the findings from a previous formative evaluation. Thus, I want you to view formative and summative evaluations as two integral components of evaluation research. Formative evaluations are often relegated to a lesser status than summative, as the policy implications are not the priority. Formative evaluations are the starting point for evaluating impact and effectiveness. Although practitioners have a preference for quantitative summative outcome studies, they could rarely be undertaken without having the results from at least a partial formative analysis (Bouffard et al., 2003).

Needs Assessment

Needs assessments answer the simple question of whether a program is needed and whether this particular program addresses the need. It can be difficult to know what social problems are the most important, and this type of assessment can be an excellent vehicle to allocate scare resources or to prioritize goals and objectives. For instance, a program for victims of domestic violence may service urban and rural areas. A needs assessment is ideal if, for example, stakeholders want to identify whether special services are needed for rural victims of domestic violence. Thus, this type of formative evaluation is an important step in the program development process, identifying any unmet needs, gaps in services provided, or emerging problems for victims, offenders, and service providers.

> **needs assessment** a process that investigates the nature of the problem to be addressed by the program, the clients who need the program, the level of need for the program, and the requirements for meeting this need.

As difficult as it can be to define success, it is equally difficult to settle on a definition of need. Evaluators must be sensitive to different perceptions of need held by the various stakeholders. By definition, a vested interest also influences an understanding of the problem and what a potential solution looks like. For this reason, needs assessments include interviews with key informants who are familiar with the social problem and involved in providing a service to this population. The data from these interviews can contextualize different definitions of need.

Royse, Thyer, and Padgett (2010) find six common reasons for conducting a needs assessment:

1. To explore the extent of a problem for a certain segment of the population in order to find evidence that justifies creating a new program.
2. To prioritize the need for a service and to provide guidance on resource allocation.
3. To determine if any other interventions or resources address this problem.
4. To determine if the target population is aware of existing services and see them as acceptable.
5. To determine if any barriers that keep the target population from accessing available services exist.
6. To inform the development of a program for a specific target population.

A needs assessment documents the magnitude of the problem, which is usually assessed with quantitative data and qualitative data so that unanticipated needs can be identified. In combination, quantitative and qualitative data provide a better understanding of the nature and extent of the targeted problem in the population.

A needs assessment's research steps are consistent with the overall approach to evaluation research. First, articulate the parameters or logistics for the assessment—amount of time required, budget, stakeholders, and purpose. Second, determine the type of information required by decision-makers. Stakeholders and members of planning committees can offer a unique perspective that you may not think about and that can be incorporated into the assessment to increase the utility of the findings. It goes without saying that the third step involves figuring out your access to the data. If existing secondary data exists, it doesn't make sense to reinvent the wheel and collect it yourself. For instance, if you need data on the socio-economic status in rural and urban areas, you can find them in the census. The next step is to develop a solid research design and get your hands dirty collecting data. You work closely with stakeholders at this stage, as they often serve as gatekeepers to information on the social problem and existing services. Finally, you write a preliminary report, shared with stakeholders for their input and interpretation. The final results can influence whether a program is launched. Further, how need is defined is often political, which means the results are likely to be used in the political arena.

Evaluability Assessment

Despite their importance, these types of evaluations are seldom conducted or published. An **evaluability assessment** is a tool that determines whether a program meets the criteria required to conduct an evaluation by engaging in "a systematic process that helps identify whether program evaluation is justified, feasible, and likely to provide useful information" (Kaufman-Levy & Poulin, 2003, p. 5). While needs assessments are conducted in the program planning stage, evaluability assessments occur once a program is operational.

Evaluability assessments clarify program goals, formalize relationships between the researcher and stakeholders, and provide information to anticipate possible problems when conducting an evaluation. Thus, there are only two conclusions that are derived from the assessment: an evaluation can be conducted or the program is not at the stage it needs to be for an evaluation. The important thing is the type of evidence leading to a conclusion that a process or summative evaluation should not be done.

All problems with program design centre on program theory and the logic model. A program needs to have a model that stipulates the goals, objectives, and outcomes with clear linkages to program activities. Without this information, it is virtually impossible to determine the activities' impact on participants. Even if there is a theory or model present, it could be flawed or unrealistic given the social problem. If you are looking to change the behaviour of all youth who break the law in a given community but the program activities are geared solely toward violent offenders, the goal is unreasonable. Problems with program implementation can also negate the viability of conducting an evaluation. If the actual program activities are not executed as intended, it is impossible to ascertain if the expected outcomes are the result of the program or other factors and experiences. We must also consider the question of data availability. An evaluation cannot be conducted if the program doesn't collect the data needed for an evaluation or doesn't have the ability to start gathering the appropriate data.

Kaufman-Levy and Poulin (2003) break down the steps to performing an evaluability assessment in the context of juvenile justice programs. First, the evaluator examines the program's history, design, and operation. It's important to understand what is on paper, what happens in real life, and why stakeholders believe the program activities will achieve the goals and objectives. Second, the evaluator watches the program delivered in real life to see if the implementation differs in any significant way from what is stated in the documentation examined in step one. Third, if an evaluation is to determine effectiveness or impact, the evaluator needs to know whether the program has the capacity to facilitate data collection and analysis. Fourth, the evaluator ascertains the likelihood that the program will reach its goals and objectives. This step goes back to program design issues of setting realistic goals and objectives. If they are unreasonable, they are unlikely to achieve their goals and objectives, no matter how well the program functions and implements the activities. The final step is arguably one of the hardest to accomplish. The evaluator documents why an evaluation will or will not assist the program. The results should indicate what needs to be developed further to allow for an evaluation. There is little point in evaluating a program that is not ready, as the findings will very likely be inconclusive or misleading.

> **evaluability assessment** a process that investigates the feasibility of conducting an evaluation and how findings have utility for the stakeholders.

> **process evaluation** a process that evaluates the systematic collection of information to document and assesses program operation and whether it functions as intended.

Process Evaluation

A **process evaluation** investigates the process of delivering the program and the ways in which it can be improved and documents any inconsistencies in delivering program activities and whether the program is functioning as intended. In other words, it examines how the program works and how it produces results. Is the target population receiving the services? How many clients are served and what types of services are offered? The answers to these questions and many others related to program process are vital if we are to truly assess whether program activities create the expected behavioural changes. The need for process evaluations prior to assessing effectiveness is highlighted by Christie and colleagues (2005), who argue that a program's structure largely depends on how the participants and stakeholders view the process and their respective roles. Unfortunately, process evaluations are often seen as a low priority by criminal justice agencies, as determining effectiveness and cost efficiency are a higher priority given fiscal downsizing and the need for ongoing program funding (Bouffard et al., 2003). Thus, process evaluations ask six fundamental questions:

1. To what extent is the program implemented as designed?
2. Is the program functioning and operating as intended?
3. To what extent are the target individuals reached by the program?
4. What resources are expended and required to operate the program?
5. Which parts of the program process are associated with intended outcomes?
6. Under what conditions is the program achieving its intended outcomes? If the program fails to meet its objectives due to problems with program implementation, a process evaluation seeks to stipulate why.

As with other formative evaluations, process evaluations include common research steps. First is the ever-important need to clarify who exactly the stakeholders are and what they are looking for from this evaluation. A process evaluation cannot tell stakeholders how well they are achieving their objectives. Instead, it provides information on program operation in relation to goals, objectives, activities, and outcomes. Second, develop a flexible research design. Programs are constantly changing,

and an emergent design is best suited to a process evaluation that is actively working in collaboration with stakeholders. In this way, the research design allows the researcher to be sensitive to evaluative program needs that arise during data collection, which increases the likelihood that the findings are utilized. Third, identify the stakeholders to be interviewed, especially the clients who provide integral information on program activities. Due to possible stakeholder bias during interviews, it is important to collect data from multiple sources to avoid inaccurate conclusions about the nature and functioning of the program (Bouffard et al., 2003). Fourth, develop the instruments, such as survey or interview questions, and collect the data. Fifth, examine any program documentation. Unlike evaluability assessments that begin with analyzing the documentation, the process evaluation gathers this information later in the research process so as not to influence data collection on how the program operates in real life. Finally, analyze the data and write the report; include feedback from administrators and stakeholders.

Summative Evaluations

Summative evaluations help practitioners determine whether to repeat, modify, or terminate a program or program component. The focus isn't on the implementation stage as in formative evaluations; instead, the goal is to inform decision-making after the intervention is complete. In other words, did it make a difference? Three major types of summative evaluations are conducted on criminal justice policies and programs. Outcome evaluations investigate whether the program causes the intended effects on the targeted individuals. Impact evaluations assess whether the outcomes (effects) are due to the program activities or other, external factors. Cost-effectiveness and cost–benefit evaluations assess fiscal efficiency by assigning monetary value to costs and benefits.

Outcome and Impact Evaluations

When conducting evaluations, you need to have implementation versus program failure on your radar screen (Harachi et al., 1999). A process evaluation can explain why a program has no effect due to a failure to implement the program in the intended manner. An outcome or impact evaluation provides information on the shortcomings in the program or intervention itself. The distinguishing characteristic is that the former investigates effectiveness in terms of achieving outcomes and the latter in terms of achieving goals.

An **outcome evaluation** is the systematic collection of information to assess program effectiveness, present conclusions about a program's merit or worth, and make recommendations about future program direction or improvements to achieve stated objectives. In short, this type of evaluation is an assessment of the intervention's immediate effects and its short-term and intermediate objectives. Criminal justice outcome evaluations often differentiate by demographics, level of risk for reoffending, and other pertinent characteristics of the target population to understand what works for whom under what circumstances to achieve the intervention objectives.

An **impact evaluation** measures the long-term effects of the intervention and determines whether program activities actually cause the changes in behaviour. Put differently, an outcome evaluation tells you about program performance, but impact evaluations also shed light on whether these outcomes occur because of program participation or factors external to the program. This means that the key difference is the timing of measurement or how long data are collected to see the impact of the program in their lives. Impact evaluations play an important role. If we restrict evaluating a program to the immediate effects, the success of an intervention becomes narrowly and prematurely defined.

In terms of outcome and impact evaluations, we need to clarify the different definitions of effects. Hughes, Black, and Kennedy (2008, p. 6) outline effects over time that an impact evaluation should consider. An ideal effect is an immediate and continuous improvement seen from program participation. A sleeper effect is one that you can't detect right after program participation. Thus, an outcome evaluation

may not capture this intended or unintended effect. A backsliding effect is immediate but doesn't last long. This situation is reminiscent of the best-case scenario found in evaluations of the D.A.R.E. program. A trigger effect occurs when the intervention elicits a behaviour that would have happened regardless of participating in the program. For example, the concept of aging out of crime could apply, as research finds that people are at less risk for recidivism as they age. Finally, the historical effect refers to a behaviour that gradually improves over time regardless of program participation. Thus, an evaluation may capture this effect and mistakenly attribute it to the program, as you see an improvement in the behaviour when compared to pre-intervention levels.

Establishing causality is at the heart of outcome and impact evaluations, and many researchers see experimental designs as the gold-standard approach for evaluation research. Two major types of experimental research are used in outcome and impact evaluations. In an **experimental evaluation design**, clients are randomly assigned to a group that receives the treatment under evaluation or to another group that doesn't receive the intervention. Both groups are measured before and after the intervention. In this way, the results can be compared to assess whether the program actually causes the anticipated outcomes and is thus effective at achieving its goals. For instance, you could randomly select schools to participate in the D.A.R.E. program and compare changes in attitudes and behaviour toward drugs before and after to results from a non-participating school.

outcome evaluation a process that assesses the progress toward achieving the short-term and intermediate outcomes that a program is designed to address.

impact evaluation a process that investigates the long-term effects of participating in a program to make a judgment on whether the intervention goal is achieved.

experimental evaluation design a research design that measures program effectiveness by randomly assigning individuals to a group that receives the intervention or to one or more groups that do not.

quasi-experimental evaluation design a research design that measures program effectiveness by using comparison groups that are as similar to each other as possible; individuals are not randomly assigned to a group.

A **quasi-experimental evaluation design** is used more often than the experimental approach, as it is often unethical or logistically difficult to randomly assign people who will or will not receive the intervention. In these studies, comparison groups are chosen so that, with the exception of participating in the program, they are as similar as possible. The evaluation's success depends on how similar the two groups are at the beginning of the evaluation. If there are significant differences between them, the impact of the program could just as easily be caused by these group differences. If you are evaluating a drug treatment program, it is unethical to tell the judge that individuals should be sentenced to participate at random because doing so removes judicial discretion. For this reason, a quasi-experimental evaluation design is the better choice; the researcher carefully matches the participants' characteristics to create a comparison group from those who were not referred by the judge.

Cost-Effectiveness and Cost–Benefit Evaluations

Efficiency evaluations seek to compare costs of competing interventions, with an underlying assumption that the program that produces the best results at the lowest cost is the most efficient and effective. Not surprisingly, increasing emphasis is placed on how money is spent in the criminal justice system, and cost-effectiveness and cost–benefit evaluations can assist stakeholders in allocating scarce resources.

cost-effectiveness evaluation a process that systematically examines the relationship between program costs and outcomes for two or more different interventions with similar desired outcomes.

cost–benefit evaluation a process that systematically compares the expected monetary benefits or savings from an intervention with its expected costs.

Cost-Effectiveness
A **cost-effectiveness evaluation** looks at the relationship between monetary inputs and the desired program outcomes. That is, two or more different interventions with similar outcomes are compared on the basis of the cost per unit or person. Let's take the example of a boot camp program for adolescents. We determine the effectiveness of each intervention strategy, such as militaristic discipline, by dividing the cost for each strategy by its effectiveness (i.e. the percentage increase in the number of boot camp graduates who do not break the law again). We get the cost for each per cent increase in the number of students who achieve this objective. This figure is then compared to the same analysis conducted on an alternative approach with the same expected outcome. For instance, the cost effectiveness can be calculated for similar youth's treatment in secure custody. Suppose the cost per each youth in secure custody who does not reoffend is $15,000, but boot camp achieves the same result for $10,000 per participant. This difference leads us to conclude that boot camps are more cost-effective than secure custody alternatives.

To conduct a cost-effectiveness evaluation, the first step is to compare the program characteristics, the indicators already used to measure success, and the comparable outcome indicators used in this evaluation and to create research questions and hypotheses. Second, the costs for personnel, facilities, equipment, and so forth must be assigned a monetary value and costs for each outcome calculated. Third, researchers calculate the cost-effectiveness ratio by dividing the total cost of the program by the effectiveness outcome indicator, such as the number of youth who do not come in conflict with the law again upon program completion. Lastly, the evaluator conducts a sensitivity analysis, which simply means testing how much the cost-effectiveness ratio varies when circumstances in a program change (e.g. increased operating costs due to personnel requirements as the number of clients increase).

Cost–Benefit
A **cost–benefit evaluation** quantifies the benefits of reducing crime with an intervention by identifying the benefits, placing a dollar value to them, calculating the total costs of the program, and then

comparing monetary benefits and costs. A cost-effectiveness evaluation compares the costs and outcomes of two or more alternative interventions, whereas a cost–benefit evaluation attributes a monetary value to the benefits. Think of this analysis as taking the benefits (avoided costs) associated with each program outcome (behavioural change) and dividing it by the total program costs. In a case where the monetary benefits to society exceed the costs, the program is justified in a cost–benefit analysis.

The most difficult aspect of this type of evaluation is how to quantify benefits in dollars and cents. What is the value of reducing crime by an average of 0.5 offences for each youth participating in boot camp? How much money is it worth to society and that individual to avoid committing an average of 0.5 crimes? What about non-crime related benefits such as substance abuse? Further, consider the challenges associated with the length of follow-up time once individuals complete a program. Due to logistical constraints, many program evaluations follow individuals for 6 to 12 months. Yet, most cost–benefit analyses are interested in the long-term costs and benefits as the focus is on achieving program goals, not specific objectives. Unfortunately, there is little agreement in the literature on how best to assign monetary value to indirect benefits such as reduced family conflict or victim fear and stress. When quantifying benefits is difficult, the cost-effectiveness approach is adopted so that you calculate the program's cost for each outcome but don't make a judgment on the monetary value of one less victim.

Which Efficiency Evaluation Should I Use?

Kee (1999) suggests considering two factors when deciding whether a cost-effectiveness or cost–benefit analysis is the most appropriate for evaluating a program. First, how will the results be used? Cost-effectiveness evaluations compare different strategies for addressing the same objective. Cost–benefit can analyze strategies that do not have the same expected outcome but a common goal. Second, how challenging will it be to assign a monetary value to costs and benefits? Each of these approaches can lead to different conclusions about the same program because of differences in assigning monetary value to costs and benefits. If the results are to be considered by stakeholders, it is important to remember the adage to "measure what you value, and others will value what you measure" (Bare, 2005, p. 6). Particularly in the case of estimating benefits, state the nature of it completely, as well as how it is being measured and any assumptions you made in assigning a monetary value. Remember, the key difference with cost-effectiveness is measuring the program outcomes (benefits) in non-monetary terms. However, the above still applies in relation to assigning value to program costs.

Methods in Action

Drugs and Crime

Criminologists conduct research to better understand the nature, causes, and conditions of drug use being associated with criminal and other analogous behaviour. Others conduct evaluations to ascertain the effectiveness and efficiency of approaches to address substance abuse with different target populations.

Program theory has two major components. Normative theory documents the relationship between inputs, process, outputs, and outcomes when conducting a process evaluation. Causative theory outlines the relationship between goals, objectives, activities, and outcomes and is properly addressed with outcome and impact evaluations. Chen (1997) conducted a process evaluation on a program that provides drug-using students with in-school counselling

Continued

services. This evaluation was conducted after an outcome evaluation found that the objectives were achieved but discrepancies existed between the program plan and its actual delivery, which affected how often the program was successful. Thus, this process evaluation was able to provide guidance on modification of program goals and objectives, required treatments, effective delivery strategies, and the conditions under which program implementation varied.

Magura and colleagues (1993) conducted a process and outcome evaluation on the effectiveness of an in-jail methadone maintenance program for heroin addicts. The outcome evaluation was conducted first, comparing methadone program participants' outcomes upon release to similar addicts who received only a seven-day heroin detoxification in jail. They found that program participants were more likely to continue treatment upon release and less likely to commit new offences. The process evaluation contextualized these findings. The in-jail program was most effective in maintaining post-release methadone treatment for those addicts who were already receiving methadone at the time of their arrest. Additionally, the researchers were able to make recommendations to help overcome client and administrative hurdles and improve outcomes for this target population of criminally involved addicts.

Logan and colleagues (2004) conducted a cost–benefit analysis of three drug court programs to assess the economic benefits of participation compared to eligible but non-participating offenders. They found that participation results in decreased incarceration rates, less use of mental health services, decreased legal costs, and increased earnings and child support payments. The highest return was for criminal justice outcomes. For every dollar invested in the drug court program, there was a return of $1.76 in reduced criminal justice costs for graduates. Even for those who did not finish the program, the return was $1.13 for every dollar spent on the program. These findings support a positive evaluation for the efficiency of drug courts.

Finally, Ogborne and colleagues (2008) conducted a process, impact, and efficiency evaluations on the INSITE supervised injection site located in Vancouver's Downtown Eastside. The process evaluation examined site usage, user characteristics, services provided, and the increased access to health and addiction care. The impact evaluation examined program participation's impact on overdose facilities, the transmission of blood-borne viral infections such as HIV, public order (e.g. people injecting in public), littering and loitering, drug-related crime, and drug use in the community. Interestingly, the cost-effectiveness estimates to prevent a new case of HIV transmission ranged from $52,000 to $155,000 and the benefits-to-costs ratios range from 0.97 to 2.90, which suggest that safe injection sites are efficient. The results from the process and impact evaluations also indicate positive benefits, albeit less in some areas than are seen with needle exchange programs.

Negotiating the Politics and Ethics of Evaluation Research

Conducting evaluation research has a high potential to be an ethical and political minefield. An evaluator has to be sensitive to the ways a social problem is defined and current efforts to resolve it. If the evaluation is not, to some extent, a collaborative endeavour with stakeholders, the risk of creating suspicion and compromising the validity of the data increases. Morris and Cohn's (1993) survey of researchers found that 65 per cent encountered ethical problems when conducting evaluation research. The most common ethical dilemma faced is pressure from stakeholders to distort the facts. Yet 35 per cent suggested no ethical or political difficulties. One respondent in this study states: "Any self-respecting evaluator who says 'no' to the question 'Have you ever encountered an ethical problem?' is lying" (p. 634).

In one way or another, every evaluation is seen as a political activity by those being evaluated. Funding agencies can pressure researchers in terms of defining the research problem and structuring access to data. The criminal justice agency may be at risk of losing its funding if negative information is disclosed. Pressure may also develop to limit the time frame of the evaluation so that the results are produced according to the stakeholder needs and not those of rigorous scientific inquiry (Emshoff, 2003).

The manner of reporting findings is equally political as it includes judgments on what should be occurring and on different interpretations of program theory. Findings can be used by some stakeholders who have a **conflict of interest** to further their own interests or agendas with particular interventions. The reality, particularly for efficiency studies, is that the results may be considered by stakeholders and published in peer-reviewed journals if the findings support preconceived beliefs about program efficiency and benefit those under evaluation (Moskowitz, 1993; Pinkerton et al., 2002). Morris and Cohn's survey results echo this sentiment as the greatest challenges faced when negotiating with stakeholders is that they have already decided what the findings should be or declare certain research questions off-limits despite substantive relevance. Unfortunately, this situation can lead to the black box syndrome—data is collected on hundreds of variables, but the results represent merely a "summative evaluation of an intervention's effects on a few measures" (Moskowitz, 1993, p. 3).

Differences in program delivery (theory versus practice) could be only one source for variations in the outcomes. The types of offenders, the context, and the research methods adopted can account for a larger share of any variation in achieving outcomes (Lösel, 2008). For example, the longer you collect data in a process evaluation, the higher the likelihood you may find something that can cause problems for someone if you report it (Morris & Cohn, 1993). Stakeholders may not all agree on which goals and objectives to measure or how to go about the measurement. Meet with stakeholders early in the planning stages to reach a consensus on the research objectives, methods, and the kinds of information and conclusions that will be made in the final report. Carefully define the research problem in a needs assessment, program success in an outcome or impact evaluation, and costs-and-benefits calculations in efficiency evaluations.

As Chelimsky (1987) points out, evaluation design and the dissemination of findings must be understood as enmeshed in a political context. Stakeholders are prospective in orientation and seek findings that look forward, whereas researchers often evaluate retrospectively and report what happened in the past and the implications for the present. Political and ethical challenges focus "on *what* the stakeholders expect the evaluator to find, on *what* the evaluator actually reports, and on *what* happens to that report once it is produced" (Morris & Cohn, 1993, pp. 639–640). Ethical and political challenges are unavoidable in evaluation research.

> **conflict of interest** a situation in which the influence of a secondary interest (e.g. continued funding) affects a person's professional judgment and decision-making about a primary interest (e.g. program success).

Stakeholders are not only information providers but also active partners, as evidenced by the fact that the majority of published evaluation research includes the program developer or director as an author (Gorman & Conde, 2007). They are more likely to challenge findings if they feel that their perspective, knowledge, and experience are not considered. The goal of any evaluation should not strictly be to explain the success or failure of a program but "to achieve consensus about the actions that should be taken to improve the program" (Abma, 2000, p. 200). Evaluation research must be an exercise in compromise if it is to achieve the objective of informing evidence-based practice.

When conducting evaluation research, maintain your independence and insist on editorial autonomy. The balance among autonomy, research integrity, and stakeholder negotiations is a difficult one. Focus on collecting data from multiple sources to contextualize findings and ensure as many perspectives as possible are captured in the analysis. Finally, explain the purpose and methods of the evaluation and then use meaningful and understandable language in the report. It helps to remember that the results are but one source of information influencing decision-makers and their impact increases if there is direct relevance and practical utility for stakeholders. A good approach is to present findings in a way that encourages practitioners to be reflective and critical of current practices so they find their own solutions to identified problems (Sampson, 2007).

Summary of Important Points

Introduction

- Evaluation research investigates what works, to what extent, how it works, whether program objectives are achieved, and fiscal efficiency.
- How success is defined is a challenge.
- The purpose for an evaluation determines the type of evaluation.

Theory and Practice in Evaluation Research

- The goal of basic research is to create new knowledge. The goal of applied research is to use this knowledge; for evaluation research, it is to inform evidence-based practice.
- Evaluations are based on program theory, which uses program assumptions and processes as the theoretical framework.
- Evaluation theory provides guidance on what data collection methods to use, under which circumstances, and with what types of evaluations.

Evaluation Research Design

- A prospective cohort study follows a group of individuals to test predictions as the program or policy is implemented.
- A retrospective cohort study follows a group of individuals, using data from past records after the policy or program is implemented.
- Comprehensive evaluations employ more than one data collection method.
- Questions about utility, feasibility, propriety, and accuracy help determine the type of evaluation.

- A systems approach adopts a logic model that outlines the relationship between inputs, program process, outputs, outcomes, feedback, and stakeholders.

Types of Evaluation Research

- Formative evaluations seek to improve a program by examining the program process.
- Summative evaluations examine the effect or impact of program participation.
- Needs assessments determine the demand for a program and if a particular program can address this need.
- An evaluability assessment examines the feasibility of conducting an evaluation.
- A process evaluation investigates whether the program is functioning as intended.
- An outcome evaluation assesses program effectiveness at achieving its objectives.
- An impact evaluation assesses the long-term effects of program participation and if these effects are due to the program or other, external factors.
- A cost-effectiveness evaluation determines the costs associated with successfully achieving program objectives.
- A cost–benefit analysis quantifies both costs and benefits to determine the efficiency of a program.

Negotiating the Politics and Ethics of Evaluation Research

- Evaluation research presents ethical and political challenges due to its collaboration with stakeholders and the potential impact of findings for evidence-based practice.

Key Terms

conflict of interest 363
cost–benefit evaluation 360
cost-effectiveness
evaluation 360
evaluability assessment 357
evaluation research 336
evaluation theory 345
experimental evaluation
design 359

formative evaluation 354
impact evaluation 359
indicator 354
inputs 352
needs assessment 356
outcome evaluation 359
outcomes 353
outputs 352
process evaluation 357

program process 352
program theory 344
prospective cohort study 346
quasi-experimental evaluation
design 360
retrospective cohort study 346
stakeholder 339
summative evaluation 354

Review Questions and Exercises

1. A program's inability to achieve its objectives is likely due to implementation or program failure. Discuss the merits of conducting a process and outcome evaluation on the same program.

2. The research plan for Correctional Service Canada is heavily based on evaluation research (http://www.csc-scc.gc.ca/research/005008-2000-eng.shtml). Choose any study from the identified strategic areas and determine the following:
   a. What type of evaluation research is it?
   b. What is the goal and purpose of the evaluation?
   c. What is the research problem?
   d. Why is this type of evaluation research design appropriate?
   e. Is there another type of evaluation study warranted? Why or why not?

3. What is the difference between a prospective and retrospective evaluation? How would you design a study in both ways if you were interested in evaluating zero tolerance arrest policies for incidents of domestic violence?

4. Do you think it is ethical to conduct cost-effectiveness and cost–benefit analyses? Does it matter if they are conducted in isolation or in conjunction with process and outcome evaluations? Give reasons to support your answers.

5. You are part of a team of highly skilled researchers who have been hired to evaluate the effectiveness of a pet-assisted therapy program for youth in secure custodial facilities. You ask yourself the following initial questions: Why use pets? What are the goals and objectives? How does the program work? How are youth selected? Who funds the program? Does it work?
   a. What is the research question for a process evaluation? What about an outcome evaluation?
   b. Describe the system components. For instance, the process could include pets from the local animal shelter visiting the correctional facility twice per week for three hours each time.
   c. What indicators could you use for the outcomes of pet-assisted therapy?
   d. What other types of data are important? For instance, which types of youth respond best?
   e. Who are the possible stakeholders?

Online Exercises and Websites of Interest

Evaluation Research Checklists

www.wmich.edu/evalctr/checklists

Produced and maintained by the Evaluation Center at Western Michigan University, this site has over thirty checklists that researchers can use to ensure the relevant questions are asked and methods used when conducting evaluation research.

Logic Models

www.epa.gov/evaluate/pdf/eval-guides/logic-model-development-guide.pdf

A PDF version of the widely cited W.K. Kellogg Foundation Logic Model Development Guide provides practical assistance on constructing logic models, particularly for outcome evaluations.

Non-Profit Evaluations

www.imaginecanada.ca/sites/default/files/www/en/library/csc/projectguide_final.pdf

The *Project Evaluation Guide for Nonprofit Organizations*, available in PDF form at this site, provides information on the different approaches to planning and implementing program evaluations on non-profit programs.

Additional Resources

Davidson, J.E. (2005). *Evaluation Methodology Basics: The Nuts and Bolts of Sound Evaluation*. Thousand Oaks, CA: Sage.

This text provides a detailed step-by-step guide for conducting all the types of evaluations discussed in this chapter.

Roman, J.K., Dunworth, T., & Marsh, K. (Eds.). (2010). *Cost–Benefit Analysis and Crime Control*. Washington, DC: The Urban Institute.

This edited compilation provides a perspective on policy-makers' increasing reliance on efficiency evaluations on crime control initiatives while also giving guidance on how to address thorny issues such as accurately measuring the pain and suffering caused by crime in monetary terms.

Royse, D., Staton-Tindell, M., Badger, K., and Webster, J.M. (2009). *Needs Assessment: A Basic Guide*. New York: Oxford University Press.

This text is an excellent resource on conducting the underutilized needs assessments on criminal justice policies and programs.

Chapter 12

Mixed Methods: An Integrated Approach

"The bias inherent in any particular data source, investigators, and particularly method will be cancelled out when used in conjunction with other data sources, investigators and methods ... the result will be a convergence upon the truth about some social phenomena." N.K. Denzin, *The Research Act: A Theoretical Introduction to Sociological Methods* (1978, p. 14)

"Under normal conditions the research scientist is not an innovator but a solver of puzzles and the puzzles upon [which] he concentrates are just those which he believes can be both stated and solved within the existing scientific tradition." T.S. Kuhn, *The Essential Tension: Selected Studies in Scientific Tradition and Change* (1977, p. 234)

Learning Objectives

- To articulate the definition, appropriateness, advantages, and disadvantages of mixed methods research.

- To appreciate the philosophical and substantive arguments for and against the use of mixed methods.

- To identify the different forms of triangulation and reasons for conducting mixed methods research.

- To specify a mixed methods research design by its characteristics and notation.

- To differentiate between common types of mixed methods research designs in criminology and criminal justice.

- To understand the unique considerations affecting the selection of a mixed methods research design.

Introduction

Every day we encounter all kinds of problems where we need different types of information to make informed decisions. In many cases, we gather this information from a variety of sources in more than one way. Perhaps we don't want to decide on the basis of a particular information source or we realize that more than one source is required to actually answer the question. Both are rationales for using mixed methods.

Consider the process of smoking cessation. If you were deciding whether to quit smoking or how to do so, you could start by visiting your doctor, who could provide you with medical information on quit aids, such as prescriptions and nicotine-based products. You would likely adopt an unstructured interview style with talking points to guide the discussion and follow-up questions to seek clarification. You might also use the same method with a different population, such as people you know who have successfully quit smoking. Another source could be official records from organizations such as the Canadian Lung Association, which would educate you on the dangers of smoking and the benefits of quitting. Next, you go to the Internet and look at other unobtrusive data sources, such as YouTube videos and articles. Lastly, you may join a smoking cessation forum, write a post, and (much like a focus group) interact with a larger group to gain information and support. This is an everyday example of a mixed methods approach to gathering and analyzing information.

Mixed methods offer researchers a mechanism to conduct more holistic, comprehensive, and balanced research consistent with the complexity of many research problems investigated in criminology and criminal justice. Mixed methods is referred to as a third movement, in addition to the quantitative and qualitative paradigms (Creswell, 2014; Teddlie & Tashakkori, 2012). Although these research designs are not as common in crime and justice research as in other disciplines, they are a viable approach because "mixed methods research has evolved to the point where it is a separate methodological orientation with its own worldview, vocabulary, and techniques" (Tashakkori & Teddlie, 2003a, p. x).

Defining Mixed Methods

In previous chapters, a mixed methods research design was defined as one that answers questions using quantitative and qualitative data collection and analytical techniques. In this chapter, you will gain an appreciation of the complexity of this type of research design and the simplicity of this definition. Consensus on a definition of mixed methods is lacking, partially because of the diversity of types coupled with the use of different terminology and typologies.

Nineteen definitions of mixed methods were compiled from leaders in this methodological field (Johnson, Onwuegbuzie, & Turner, 2007). The definitions vary in specificity and reflect five themes. Many address the question of what is meant by the "mixed" in mixed methods. A portion of the definition specifies when or where the mixing occurs during the research process. The definition mentions the breadth of the mixing along a continuum, from treating the collection and analysis of quantitative and qualitative data separately to fully integrating data types at all stages in the research process. Quite often, a rationale for why mixing occurs in research is provided. (The purpose and appropriateness of using mixed methods figures predominantly in definitions.) Finally, definitions include the orientation of the mixed methods design. The overwhelming majority of research is bottom-up, with the research question driving the process; however, it can be top-down, as is the case in a type of participatory action research.

An intuitive way of defining mixed methods is to take a closer look at some of its characteristics. The research process continues to be driven by the research question in terms of guiding the collection and analysis of quantitative and qualitative data. In doing so, researchers must ensure that all elements and standards expected in a monomethod research design are adhered to for each data type (Creswell, 2014). Then a type of research design is chosen to structure the research process into stages. At some point and to varying degrees, the findings from each data type are incorporated into the conclusions.

Integration means combining the findings from each type of data to form an overall conclusion or meta-inference. More specifically, integration is "a specific relationship between two or more methods where the different methods retain their paradigmatic nature but are intermeshed with each other in pursuit of the goal of knowing more" (Moran-Ellis et al., 2006, p. 51). Imagine integration as being like a seamless transportation system. Passengers buy one ticket for their entire journey, even when they need more than one mode of travel (e.g. plane, train) to achieve their goal of successfully reaching their destination.

Given this definitional ambiguity, we need to clarify what the concept of mixed methods means in this chapter. Mixed methods is considered a type of research that combines quantitative and qualitative methods, techniques, concepts, criteria, and language in one study. Thus, I adopt the definition developed by Johnson and colleagues (2007, p. 123):

> Mixed methods research is a type of research in which a researcher or team of researchers combines elements of qualitative and quantitative research approaches (e.g. use of qualitative and quantitative viewpoints, data collection, analysis, inference techniques) for the purposes of breadth and depth of understanding and corroboration.

Why Go to the Trouble?

To conduct mixed methods research, you do everything involved in a quantitative or qualitative project as well as the design issues specific to mixed methods. For example, the proposals, theses, and journal articles are longer and the logistics of mixed methods pose additional challenges that researchers must overcome. On average, quantitative articles are 22.0 pages long; qualitative, 23.9; and mixed methods the longest at 28.3 pages (Tewksbury et al., 2005, p. 275). The best way to address the question, "Why conduct mixed methods research?" is to look at the types of research most appropriate for mixed methods, the advantages, the disadvantages, and the methodological connoisseurs who conduct this type of research.

Appropriate Topics

Anytime you have a research problem that requires information in stages, a mixed methods research design is a good option to consider. On the other hand, the research topic and potential stages are less important than asking whether the research objectives can best be achieved using a monomethod approach. Recall the mantra referred to throughout this textbook: the research question drives the method. Mixed methods is no exception. Although combining quantitative and qualitative methods can provide more comprehensive knowledge on the issue or problem, this approach doesn't always apply when research questions do not require more than one type of data.

In general, mixed methods are appropriate under three conditions. The topic can be addressed within a post-positivistic and a constructivist paradigm. The existing literature and theory are investigated using both quantitative and qualitative data, whether monomethod or in mixed methods research designs. Either qualitative or quantitative data alone are inadequate for addressing the issues articulated in the research problem and questions.

Advantages and Disadvantages

As with all the research designs, data collection methods, and analytical techniques we have discussed in this textbook, there are also advantages and disadvantages to using a mixed methods research design. Lest I sound like a broken record, the framework for deciding on the research design continues to be what is needed to achieve the research objective and address the research questions. Each advantage and disadvantage should be considered in the context of each project in terms of the topic, research questions, and logistical constraints. Table 12.1 summarizes the main advantages and disadvantages associated with mixed methods research designs.

Advantages

There are three overall advantages to adopting a mixed methods research design. First, you can be more confident in your conclusions when inferences from different perspectives suggest the same or a similar interpretation and theoretical explanation. Thus, there is the potential to increase the validity of the findings and one's confidence in the conclusions.

A more holistic understanding of the research problem is possible, as the results synthesize findings, offer different perspectives, and better reflect the complexity of what we know as everyday life.

Second, when analyzing the data, you can use one type of data to provide insight on another one. In this way, mixed methods designs can develop inferences that represent multiple perspectives. For example, micro individual-level data and inferences can be situated in a larger context that is in the background of the social issue. In other words, you have the opportunity to uncover the larger significance of the findings in the overall conclusions. Incongruent results from each data type are just as welcome as similar findings. Incorporating divergent findings leads to modifying the conceptual framework and

Table 12.1   Strengths and weaknesses of mixed methods research designs

Strengths	Weaknesses
• Words, pictures, and narratives can be used to add meaning to numbers.	• Difficult for a single researcher, especially if both approaches are collected and analyzed simultaneously.
• Numbers can be used to add precision to words, pictures, and narratives.	• Researchers must be knowledgeable in quantitative and qualitative methods as well as how to mix them appropriately.
• Can generate and test a theory.	• More expensive and time-consuming.
• Ability to answer broader and a more complete range of research questions by adopting more than one approach.	• Controversial with purists who argue that mixing paradigms/worldviews is philosophically inconsistent.
• The strengths of one method can overcome the weaknesses and biases in another method.	• Potential to decrease validity and reliability if quantitative and qualitative portions are not executed up to their respective standards.
• Multiple types of data can provide stronger evidence to support a conclusion through convergence and corroboration of findings.	• Challenging to coordinate and manage data collection and analysis with complex mixed methods research designs (e.g. fully integrated model).
• Provide additional insight and understanding not possible with a single method.	
• Potential to increase the generalizability of the findings.	
• Produces more comprehensive knowledge to inform theory and practice.	

Source: Adapted from Brent & Kraska (2010, pp. 419–420); Johnson & Onwuegbuzie (2004, p. 21).

theoretical model that informed the research questions. Further, paradoxes or contradictions in the findings can offer clarification and initiate new ways of thinking about the social phenomenon (Johnson et al., 2007).

Third, mixed methods research designs provide the ability to answer multiple questions that are informed by different theories, thereby covering more substantive ground in the explanation. You can investigate both exploratory and confirmatory research questions in one study, which allows you to generate and test theories in the same research project.

Disadvantages

After everything is said and done, if the research is not conducted according to the standards associated with quantitative and qualitative research, the data collected and inferences made during data analysis have even less reliability and validity in comparison to a monomethod research project. An indicator of this problem is methods being used neither as systematically nor as thoroughly as they would be in a monomethod project. It's much like the bull's eye analogy used for measurement. Just because you throw a bucketful of darts at the dartboard doesn't mean you will hit the bull's eye (which here represents valid conclusions). Similarly, darts may land on the target randomly, yielding unreliable findings.

We must also consider logistics. One disadvantage is that mixed methods research projects take longer than monomethod investigations. They require more financial and time resources. Researchers must have the requisite skill in both qualitative and quantitative methods and an acute awareness of each method's strengths and weaknesses. Finally, the research process can be very complicated. It can have more integrated designs, be difficult to manage, be challenging in terms of coordinating data collection and analysis, and become an analytical minefield when sorting the inferences to formulate overall conclusions.

Methodological Connoisseur

As mixed methods researchers gain expertise in both qualitative and quantitative research methods, they become methodological connoisseurs. Why is this process critical? The basic principle underlying mixed methods designs is to choose methods that have complementary strengths but do not share the same weaknesses (Tashakkori & Teddlie, 1998). The validity of the findings is enhanced because the limitations of one method are overcome by using an additional method. For example, surveys are not the most appropriate way for understanding processes, but this weakness can be overcome by combining this data collection method with participant observation. I hope you can see that the only way a researcher can do so effectively is to be knowledgeable and have expertise in the full spectrum of qualitative and quantitative methods and techniques.

Methodological connoisseurs are not purists adhering to one worldview but are knowledgeable in both post-positivism and constructionist philosophies, conduct research consistent with pragmatism, and adopt the philosophy of **methodological pluralism** (Teddlie & Tashakkori, 2011). This philosophy can apply to using multiple methods within the same approach or combining qualitative and quantitative methods. As Sechrest and Sidani (1995, p. 77) say, "Good science is characterized by methodological pluralism." The connoisseurs consider the research question and let it dictate the design and the methods that are combined in the study. They are eclectic in their approach to the pursuit of knowledge, with methodological flexibility in how research is structured and carried out. As summarized well by two leading authorities, "a researcher employing methodological eclecticism is a *connoisseur of methods* who knowledgably, and often intuitively, selects the best techniques available to answer research questions

> **methodological pluralism** the view that no method is superior over another, as multiple approaches are legitimate scientific methods of acquiring knowledge.

that may evolve as the study unfolds" (Teddlie & Tashakkori, 2012, p. 777; emphasis original).

Methodological Controversies

From the late 1950s to the 1960s, the idea of methodological pluralism developed with work in unobtrusive methods (Campbell & Fiske, 1959; Webb et al., 1966). Initially based on improving measurement validity, the argument stated that using more than one method could measure multiple dimensions and ultimately increase the validity of conclusions. Pluralism was extended to researchers themselves. Unlike much research produced in the natural sciences, social scientists were more likely to conduct research unilaterally. Thus, these scholars advocated for the benefits of collaboration in bringing a variety of knowledge and experience to bear in a research project. This type of mixing continues to occur today.

Overall, **methodological exclusivism** could characterize much of the research published in criminology and criminal justice (Brent & Kraska, 2010; Tewksbury et al., 2005). As exemplified by the quote from Thomas Kuhn at the beginning of this chapter, this ideological position assumes that only a single paradigm is credible to create valid scientific research. It constitutes erecting rigid methodological boundaries between the quantitative and qualitative approaches to research. This unnecessary great divide inhibits the building of our knowledge base (Brent & Kraska, 2010). It not only minimizes the contribution made by research adhering to each approach, but it also diminishes the potential contribution of mixed methods research. Some researchers are dedicated to using only one approach and see it as the only way to approach all research problems. Researchers are in one camp or another (a situation

methodological exclusivism in contrast to methodological pluralism, the position that there is only one credible method of inquiry to acquire knowledge.

often referred to as the paradigm wars), and the mixed methodologists are vilified by both parties on the grounds of violating philosophical assumptions.

Philosophical Assumptions

In Chapter 1, we discussed that quantitative research is consistent with the worldview of post-positivism, qualitative research with constructionism, and mixed methods with pragmatism (see Table 1.2 for a summary). To briefly review, those who believe that there is one truth that we need to discover by deductively gathering empirical evidence to test theories are at one end of the continuum. At the other end are those who adhere to a philosophy that reality is a social construction. There are multiple truths, which are all located within a social and historical context. We can't profess to predict but, at best, can only understand and generate theories that better reflect social reality and the ways we make sense of the world around us. This methodological exclusivism fostered the view of an incompatibility between quantitative and qualitative methods' oppositional philosophical assumptions.

Incompatibility Thesis and Pragmatism

Methodological purists adhere to the incompatibility thesis, which argues that mixed methods can't work because methods are definitively linked to worldviews and, by mixing them, we violate the philosophical assumptions of both. The counterargument is within the pragmatist worldview: methods are compatible, providing that the research question plays the central role. Some research questions are quantitative and others are qualitative. Adopting this problem-centred point of view, the quantitative phase is associated with post-positivism, whereas qualitative data collection and analysis has the researcher switch to a constructionist paradigm. This approach, where integration occurs at the interpretation stage, is the most common in mixed methods research.

Not surprisingly, mixed methodologists reject the incompatibility thesis. Instead, they argue that mixed methods is a better approach if we really want to understand this social phenomenon. Recall that pragmatism rejects the methodological duality creating this divide in favour of adopting the most appropriate method to investigate the research problem. Pragmatists are pluralists in terms of methods; they focus on evidence-based practice, where theory informs decisions and problems in everyday life. They also place priority on discovering knowledge in the best way possible instead of on justifications for the approach adopted. Thus, the principles of mixed methods are consistent with the breadbasket of the pragmatist worldview. Unfortunately, things aren't that simple. If they were, the methodological divide and debate would be ancient history.

State of the Discipline

A mixed methods research design gives researchers a road map to develop an understanding that has both depth and breadth. Working in this third paradigm means you adopt the mindset that all methods occupy similar territory in the research process and there is no great methodological divide, provided that the design balances the strengths and weaknesses of each method. More holistic conclusions are possible if we think outside the box and incorporate multiple theoretical perspectives and research questions that are investigated with the most appropriate methods, be they quantitative or qualitative.

As illustrated in the Research Highlights box below, mixed methods is underutilized and the controversy is not over. The table shows that one of the disadvantages is facing purists' arguments. Right or wrong, the incompatibility thesis is still alive and well in criminology and criminal justice. Here is one example from a crime and justice researcher (Worrall, 2000, p. 360):

> Quantoids can sleep better at night knowing that their methods provide the tools to make probabilistic claims about what lies in store for trends in crime, causes of crime, and solutions to crime. Prediction is a powerful tool. Where prediction errs—and where the connection between quantitative research and policy is tenuous—it is because of flawed theory, not method.

Other evidence suggests that, because of personal, political, and social orientations, some researchers pit themselves against one another, become defensive, and may neglect the contribution of the others on the basis of methodological choices (Tewksbury et al., 2005).

Research Highlights

The Methodological Road Map to Published Crime and Justice Research

Mixed methods studies have become more popular than they were in the past, but this change by no means suggests that the approach is a common occurrence. Methodological exclusivism "may be showing signs of cracks" (Crow & Ortiz Smykla, 2013, p. 553). However, evidence continues to indicate a quantitative dominance in the discipline.

Several content analyses of articles published in top-tier (e.g. *Criminology, Justice Quarterly*) and lower-tier journals (e.g. *Southwest Journal of Criminal Justice*) find that an overwhelming majority of published research uses exclusively quantitative data (Buckler, 2008; Crow & Ortis Smykla, 2013; Kleck et al., 2006; Tewksbury et al., 2005). To put this in perspective, consider the results presented in the following table.

Continued

State of the discipline

Primary method of analysis	Tewksbury et al. (2005)[1] (%)	Crow & Ortis Smykla (2013)[2] (%)
Quantitative	73.1	85.4
Theoretical	7.0	–
Qualitative	6.3	5.1
Evaluation	5.2	–
Methodological	5.1	–
Mixed methods	1.4	9.6
Legal	1.0	–
Meta-analysis	0.6	–
Historical	0.3	–
Year range	1998–2002	2008–2010
Total (N)	725	314

Notes
1. p. 273
2. p. 542

These studies use slightly different combinations of journals, but they give us an idea of methodological orientation. The number of qualitative studies remains relatively stable over the ten-year span. On the other hand, the dominance of quantitative research increases by 12 per cent, even once lower tier journals (which are more inclined to publish qualitative research) are taken into account. Not surprisingly, four out of five authors surveyed associated the top-tier journals with quantitative research (Crow & Ortiz Smykla, 2013).

As you can also see, mixed methods studies are becoming more common. However, they require methodological connoisseurs, along with investigator collaboration, to ensure sufficient substantive and methodological knowledge. When looking at single versus multiple authorship, 90 per cent of mixed methods research is co-authored, compared to 65.2 per cent of qualitative and 75.3 per cent of quantitative studies (Tewksbury et al., 2005, p. 276). Surveys are the dominant data collection method (45 per cent), followed by archival data (32 per cent) and official statistics (26 per cent) (Kleck et al., 2006, p. 149). Further, only 5.5 per cent of graduate courses focus on qualitative methods, whereas 48.8 per cent are dedicated to quantitative methods and analysis (Buckler, 2008, p. 390).

There is little consensus on why quantitative methods are more commonly used in crime and justice research. One-third of researchers surveyed feel significant pressure to conduct quantitative research because it's seen as easier to publish and superior to both qualitative and mixed (Buckler, 2008). Perceptions on why qualitative research is underutilized are similar to those for mixed methods, including pragmatic concerns (e.g. page length, likelihood of publication), little training, less legitimacy than quantitative research, and less precise evaluative standards available (Buckler, 2008). Journal editors would like to see more non-quantitative research, but they feel reviewers are ill-prepared to assess the manuscripts with an inclination toward using a "quantitative ruler" (p. 392).

Is the fact that the overwhelming majority of published articles are quantitative attributable to a cultural trend, few courses, funding priorities, devaluing of qualitative and mixed methods research, or biased reviewers? The jury is still out. As concluded by Tewksbury and colleagues (2005, p. 278), "the social sciences have been hampered by efforts to emulate the physical sciences, instead of evolving into a field that incorporates, not ranks, methodological approaches."

Can We? Should We?

By definition, mixed methods research is more complex in terms of structure, analysis, and interpretation than a monomethod quantitative or qualitative research design. There is a developing appreciation for the types of inferences each approach can produce and the commonalities that exist when you move beyond a methodological divide perspective. As Maruna (2010, p. 137) argues, "such work, then, draws on the entire body of criminological research and theory far better than monomethodological approaches can."

The theoretical perspective provides the framework for methodological decisions on the design, data source, analysis, interpretation, and the reporting of results (Creswell et al., 2003; Schulenberg, 2007a). Quantitative research questions focus on variation and the qualitative on process. While the research questions inform the appropriate methods to be included, the research design tells us how the methods will work in combination with one another. The next step is to explore this relationship further by unpacking the underlying rationale, components of mixed methods designs, the objectives, and common characteristics.

What Are We Trying to Do with Mixed Methods?

There are several ways to answer this question. In all cases, there is one or more types of triangulation. There are four reasons to use mixed methods: complementarity, initiation, development, and expansion (Greene, Caracelli, & Graham, 1989). One also considers the research objective: What is the project trying to accomplish?

The answers to these foundational questions provide the framework for considering the mixed methods design characteristics used to distinguish one model from another. Model characteristics to be determined include identifying the order of the different types of data in the research process, the priority or weight given to each one, and whether it occurs in stages or is transformative. Finally, prior to

looking closer at the different types of mixed methods research designs, we review the design notation. Just as experimental designs have specific symbols and acronyms to differentiate between types, so do mixed methods research designs.

Triangulation

The concept of **triangulation** is based on a trigonometry formula used for naval navigation, land surveying, and military practices. Don't panic: you are not expected to calculate angles for this course! That said, it is important to appreciate the conceptual origins as they provide the framework for how this strategy manifests itself in mixed methods research.

> **triangulation** a research strategy that uses more than one theory, method, or investigator in order to increase the validity of the findings.

Figure 12.1 presents a visual for this trigonometric formula. Angle A is known as alpha (α), angle B as beta (β), and our unknown, angle C, as gamma (γ). Regardless of the triangle's shape, the three angles will equal 180 degrees. Thus, if we know the value of two angles, we can calculate the third one.

In general terms, triangulation in research often refers to the combination of quantitative and qualitative data to see if different methods yield similar results. Different types of data are collected to measure and assess the same social problem and to increase our confidence in the inferences. Think of alpha and beta as types of data collected using different methods. In combination, each helps us to better

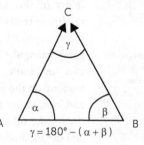

$$\gamma = 180° - (\alpha + \beta)$$

Figure 12.1 Origins of triangulation

identify the truth represented by angle C. Methods A and B provide multiple lines of sight for the larger picture we refer to as gamma.

Denzin (1978) built on the ideas of Webb and colleagues (1966) by appropriating the term *multiple operationalism* for triangulation and applying it to the social sciences. Denzin made distinctions and identified four possible variations of triangulation. Remember, with mixed methods the results may converge, be partially consistent, or entirely contradictory. Pragmatists consider all these possibilities welcome outcomes from the analysis. They are not concerned about contradictions because claims to knowledge are stronger when the findings do or do not converge with one another, constituting a finding in and of itself (Creswell et al., 2003).

Investigator Triangulation

The reality is that one person cannot be an expert in everything. Admitting weakness is not easy; however, it is important to be realistic about our competency in different types of data collection and analysis techniques, and this factor becomes even more significant when using more than one technique in the same study. To improve the credibility of the data and the validity or trustworthiness of the interpretations, **investigator triangulation** involves two or more researchers working on the same project and combining their expertise on the substantive topic and the methods used in the study. Each researcher is involved in all stages of the research process, from choosing the design to writing up the results. Investigator triangulation has become more common in criminology and criminal justice as research brings together ideas from different disciplines, further necessitating methodological pluralism.

Theoretical Triangulation

Another variation common in mixed methods research is **theoretical triangulation**, in which researchers use two or more theories to inform the research process. Social phenomenon have more than one explanation, and different theories require different research approaches to see if the explanation works in a particular context. Thus, when conducting a study with theoretical triangulation, research questions are created from each theory to incorporate more than one perspective on the research problem. With the research question driving the method, each question clarifies the type of data, the mixed methods research design, data collection methods, analytical techniques, and the interpretation of the findings.

Methodological Triangulation

This next form of triangulation is what we usually think about when we hear the term *mixed methods*. **Methodological triangulation** is adopted when two or more methods are incorporated in the same research study. As we have learned throughout this textbook, each method has strengths and weaknesses. Triangulation is a way to overcome these inherent biases. The methods are chosen based on the research questions but are combined systematically. The foundational principle of all mixed methods research designs is to combine methods with complementary strengths and non-overlapping weaknesses.

Denzin (1978) points out two different types of methodological triangulation. Also referred to as a within-method strategy, **multimethod research** uses more than one type of quantitative method or qualitative method in the same research study. With

---

investigator triangulation a research strategy in which more than one researcher is involved in data collection, analysis, and interpretation to improve the credibility of the findings.

theoretical triangulation a research strategy that uses more than one theory to inform research questions, data collection, analysis, and interpretation.

methodological triangulation a research strategy that uses more than one method to study a research problem, with the objective of overcoming the weaknesses associated with one method by using an additional method.

multimethod research a form of methodological triangulation that uses more than one type of quantitative method or multiple qualitative methods in one research study.

this strategy, you remain within one paradigm and worldview, which Denzin argues limits value due to the inherent methodological limitations shared by all methods in one approach. For instance, quantitative methods are excellent ways to understand factors affecting a particular outcome but are less than ideal for understanding a generic social process or the reasons a relationship exists. An example of a study that uses multiple quantitative data is Eitle, D'Alessio, and Stolzenberg's (2014) investigation of the association between organizational characteristics and environmental factors with police misconduct. Adopting theoretical triangulation, the theories of discretion control, minority group threat, and the ecological theory of patrol informed the development of research questions, which required three different types of quantitative data.

The second type is between-method, a combination of quantitative and qualitative methods in the same study. We typically associate mixed methods research with this type. This chapter largely devotes its attention to these between-method designs.

Analytical Triangulation

Researchers use **analytical triangulation** when they analyze the data in more than one way. For example, they might analyze interview data qualitatively with grounded theory and quantitatively with a content analysis. Similarly, they could analyze the data from survey answers qualitatively with thematic analysis and create variables to be analyzed statistically. Both of these examples are types of analytical triangulation. Although this strategy can improve the validity of the findings, converting data is also the most controversial approach. Purists argue that it violates the epistemological and ontological assumptions that underlie quantitative and qualitative data. Transforming one type of data into the other is philosophically inconsistent and a "no-no."

One example of the most common form of converted data—percentages demonstrating the prevalence of a qualitative theme in the data—was introduced in Chapter 10. Bowen (2009) used a qualitative database to investigate plea bargaining strategies and discourse. In this sequential multi-method qualitative dominant study, Bowen collected direct observation data on 42 cases and conducted one or more interviews with 25 attorneys. Finally, she coded characteristics and dispositional data qualitatively to understand contextual factors and converted them into quantitative data to analyze dispositional prevalence and the dominance of various factors affecting bargaining strategies.

Complementarity

Consistent with methodological triangulation, **complementarity** uses quantitative and qualitative methods to look at different aspects of the same social phenomenon to produce a more grounded, holistic, and meaningful understanding. When a single approach is insufficient for investigating the research problem, complementarity involves combining methods that do not share the same weaknesses. The ability of one method to compensate for the weaknesses inherent in another one is predicated on the belief that a type of data can produce only a certain type of knowledge.

What impact do life circumstances have on the development of criminal behaviour? Does it differ by the type or age of the offender? Blockland and Nieuwbeerta (2005) asked these questions and required a robust measure of crime and reoffending to answer them. As we learned in Chapter 8, official and self-report crime data have strengths and particular disadvantages unique to each. Official data are not affected by memory (e.g. under-reporting, sequence of events), while self-report data have the advantage of providing data on crimes not known to the police. Arguably, they are both good measures of

analytical triangulation a research strategy that analyzes data in more than one way, using quantitative and qualitative techniques.

complementarity the use of quantitative and qualitative methods with non-overlapping weaknesses in the same study to provide a more meaningful and holistic understanding of a social phenomenon through the different types of knowledge created by each data type.

criminal behaviour; however, with non-overlapping weaknesses, this combination of methods can provide a better understanding of criminal behaviour.

Using two or more approaches to investigate a research problem allows for investigating static and dynamic features of the aspect of reality under investigation. In other words, research can investigate static characteristics that are fixed (e.g. sex, prior record) and dynamic features (motivation to offend). Quantitative methods identify the "what" and qualitative provide insight on the "why"; therefore, findings from different methods elaborate, clarify, unpack, or extend the overall conclusions. For example, when using mixed methods for the purpose of complementarity, the generalizability of findings generated from qualitative methods can be explored by collecting quantitative data from the same or similar populations.

Initiation

Similar to complementarity, different methods are used to investigate dimensions of the same social phenomenon; however, the purpose here is to generate dissimilar findings. This is an iterative approach that encourages paradigm mixing because it increases the odds of discovering inconsistent patterns and explanations. The intent is to explore the unexpected—the contradiction—to develop new perspectives, questions, and avenues for future research. If the reason for mixing methods is complementarity, **initiation** is also absolutely "consistent with a mixed methods way of thinking to actively pursue this puzzle rather than interpret it as a failure to attain convergence" (Greene, 2007, p. 103). Initiation can

initiation the use of quantitative and qualitative methods to uncover contradictions, understand why they occur, and develop new perspectives on the social phenomenon.

development a strategy of using one method to inform decisions about research questions, sampling, data collection, and analysis of a second method.

expansion the use of quantitative and qualitative methods in the same study to assess different phenomena.

be the rationale for adding a second data strand and method to expand or clarify unexpected findings from the first method. A good way to understand initiation is to compare it to development.

Development

Another reason to use mixed methods is **development**, whereby one method is used to inform methodological decisions about another one. With complementarity and initiation, the research process for each data strand can occur concurrently or consecutively. With development, one method will always occur before another one. The first method may assess one aspect of the social phenomenon; the second method uses all or some of the findings to explore it in a different way. For instance, surveys can investigate the attitudes on the causes of crime. These causes become the concepts investigated when using the second method of interviews, which are better at understanding how these ideas are defined by respondents. The results from method 1 identify and shape the use of method 2. With initiation, method 1 and method 2 are combined with the expectation that the results will differ so that we will have a better picture of what we do and do not know about the social phenomenon.

According to Greene (2007), the rationale of development isn't new to mixed methods research. You will frequently see it in crime and justice research. You may have a situation where you don't know a lot about a social phenomenon. In such a case, you could use qualitative methods to learn more about it in this research context and develop survey questions based on the knowledge. The development can become iterative: the results from this quantitative survey can identify deviant cases, and interviews can then provide additional insight into these unique perspectives.

Expansion

The final purpose for mixed methods can be **expansion**—to expand the scope and breadth of the findings. Multiple methods are used to investigate different phenomena associated with the research problem. Methodological choices extend beyond one tradition or worldview because the different phenomena require different approaches.

A good example of expansion is evaluation research, the most common reason to use mixed methods when evaluating a policy or program. Quantitative methods are ideal for targeting whether the program outcomes are achieved. Qualitative methods investigate a completely different phenomenon of how the program was implemented. As seen in Chapter 11, implementation and outcome are different conceptually and practically in the real world, although both constitute a component of evaluating a program (i.e. a process and outcome evaluation).

Lewis (2004) used a longitudinal quasi-experimental design to evaluate criminal justice sanctions for domestic violence offenders and a mixed methods design adopted for expansion reasons. The men either received a traditional criminal justice sanction or had a probation condition to attend the intervention program. The population sample consisted of all cases heard in two courts during the study period and was used for both data strands. Lewis collected qualitative interview data shortly after the intervention and used surveys as a follow-up measurement of the dependent variable. Qualitative data were prioritized when drawing conclusions, as the focus was on the lived experience of the offenders. The quantitative data expanded on these results by focusing on the legal intervention itself and on outcomes. Incidentally, the program was found to increase women's feelings of safety, reduce recidivism, and improve offender attitudes.

Common Characteristics in Mixed Methods Designs

Four characteristics describe all mixed methods research designs. First, the data strands have a particular order or sequence. Second, each data strand is given the same or different priority in terms of the inclusion purpose and weight when drawing

inferences from the data. Third, the research project is either independent or part of a series of studies. Finally, data collection and analysis can be participatory and classified as a transformative mixed methods research design. Each of these characteristics help us to distinguish one mixed methods research design from another and to form part of the decision-making process when selecting the most appropriate one for the project.

Sequence

Morse (1991, 2003) was the first to articulate the two types of order in methodological triangulation—concurrent and sequential—and emphasize that the decision on how to sequence data collection and analysis depends on the research question. The first step is to identify the rationale for using mixed methods (i.e. complementarity, initiation, development, expansion). Obviously, if the purpose is development, sequential is the only logical order. However, the decision on the order of each data strand is not always this clear cut.

Concurrent

Concurrent designs, also known as parallel, have quantitative and qualitative data collected simultaneously. One type of data can provide insight into what is going on and the other why it is happening, but the key distinction is that they are collected at the same time. This sequencing is more common with deductive research, which tests theoretical propositions. It is also ideal if you have concerns about potential reactivity. For instance, you can conduct systematic social observation and simultaneously collect and analyze official records if you are worried that the geographic areas or shifts are not indicative of general police work for that police service.

Sequential

In this case, data collection occurs in stages; the research process associated with one type of data is completed before the next phase begins. Often, the first type of data are not only collected but also inform the research question for the next method. You often see this practice when supplementary data are collected to clarify relationships and findings from the first method.

The best order for data collection and analysis is determined in one of three ways. First, the sequence can be informed by the approaches used in prior research on the topic. If interviews were conducted first and then other researchers were able to secure ethics clearance to obtain a criminal record check verifying the self-reported criminality, this sequence might be one to adopt. Second, consider the primary research strategy adopted. Is the research best characterized as inductive? If so, it makes sense to collect qualitative data first. If it is deductive, the quantitative method should be first in the sequence. Finally, the characteristics of the social setting or research problem are important considerations. The only way to conduct a survey with the target population might depend on achieving rapport and trust. Thus, in this social setting, qualitative methods would precede quantitative. If the research problem involves understanding trends and the process leading up to these patterns, starting with quantitative methods makes sense.

embedded (or nested) mixed methods design a mixed methods research design that has a primary data strand but contains a smaller secondary method for convergence, exploratory, or explanatory reasons.

Integrated

We can think of an integrated sequence in two ways. First, studies can be concurrent and sequential in their design. Now, you're probably thinking these two are mutually exclusive. That isn't always the case; for example, several studies can be combined within a larger research project. Multiple researchers can collect data simultaneously (concurrent) and the actual data collection by each researcher can be completed in a certain order (sequential).

Second is the fully integrated model, which we will discuss further later in the chapter. This type of integrated mixed methods research is iterative because of the constant interplay between the different methods at all stages of the research process. Thus, the data collection from one method informs the research question, collection, and even analysis of another method and vice versa.

Priority

Whether the design is concurrent, sequential, or integrated, the priority given to each data strand varies. There are several different ways to go about this question of emphasis and dominance of one method over another. The best way to determine the priority within a research design is to see whether inferences from that data strand are combined with the other method, if they are used sequentially to inform the second method, or if the research problem has a primary emphasis on either qualitative or quantitative research questions. The priority is most evident when looking at the conclusions and the type of data that form the bulk of the interpretation. A special type of priority is an embedded research design, which combines the characteristics of sequence and priority.

An **embedded**, or **nested**, **mixed methods design** is one type of an integrated model. Data collection and analysis can occur before, during, or after that of the primary method (concurrently or sequentially). A good way to think about embedded mixed methods is to picture the dominant method as a large box and the secondary method as a smaller box inside it.

Imagine collecting more than one type of data from the same people or organization. The most common nested design features a sample of individuals completing a survey and then a researcher choosing a subset for in-depth interviewing. With surveys as the primary method and interviews as the secondary, this example is a within-subject design. Multiple data points are created for each person, using different data. A between-subject design involves using the primary and secondary methods to collect data from different samples.

In nested designs, the secondary type of data wouldn't be meaningful if it were not a small portion of the other method. With that said, this design may be an option when resources dictate that prioritizing both types of data in the research process is unfeasible. Thus, quantitative and qualitative data are collected *within* a quantitative or qualitative research design.

For instance, in a nested quantitative design, the qualitative data can examine the intervention process experiences in evaluation research or explain reactions to participation after the experiment is complete. The secondary method is incorporated into the research design to enhance the overall findings. The general rule of thumb is that correlational research will have quantitative data as primary and observation data as nested. In case-study research, qualitative data are primary and quantitative survey data are embedded in the design.

Let's look at Ratcliffe and colleagues' (2011) study as an example. Previous research finds that foot patrol improves citizen perceptions of the police and lessens fear of crime but is largely ineffective in reducing crime. However, these researchers recognized that there are concerns about statistical and measurement techniques (validity) in prior research and developed this study partially in response to these issues. They conducted a randomized experiment in sixty violent crime hot spots. The dominant quantitative data came from violent crime reports in the police department's computer records. The embedded observational data were not meaningful outside the quantitative data strand. The qualitative data were collected to improve reliability in the experimental versus control groups' hot spots and to document the types of strategies used by officers on foot patrol. In all areas, observers documented police behaviour so that researchers could assess the consistency of officers using strategies assigned to the control and experimental hot spot. With this methodological safeguard embedded within the design, they found that, unlike previous research results, violent crime did in fact decrease in the foot patrol zones after three months.

Multiphase

In **multiphase mixed methods** research, more than one study is conducted under the umbrella of an overarching, larger study. The smaller projects can be monomethod or mixed methods. The key distinction here is that the mixing is at the level of a research project and conclusions are based on findings for the combination of studies. Thus, two or more individual studies are conducted and then mixed in this larger research endeavour.

> **multiphase mixed methods design** a mixed methods research design that conducts more than one study within a larger project; the studies share a common research objective.

It is not surprising to see the studies occur sequentially. Data for study 1 are collected and analyzed. The results are used to inform study 2, from the research question onwards. The results from study 2 inform study 3 and so forth. Each monomethod or mixed methods study informs the design and execution of the next one.

Transformative

A **transformative mixed methods design** can be sequential, concurrent, or integrated. The distinguishing feature of the research objective is to collect data from a vulnerable population. Social justice theory is used as the framework to combine methods, with the goal of improving an at-risk, marginalized, or vulnerable population's condition. Thus, this characteristic is more common when conducting research using feminist or race theories.

> **transformative mixed methods design** a type of participatory action research that combines methods for the purpose of improving the condition of marginalized populations.

A transformative mixed methods research design allows for multiple perspectives on the lives of society's disenfranchised populations. Think of this characteristic as a participatory action mixed methods research design. The point is to create change by working collaboratively with research subjects (see Chapter 7 for participatory action research). The ultimate outcome and the conclusions' aim is to empower the population under study.

Ronel and colleagues (2009) sought to understand the influence of at-risk youths' perceptions of altruism on the part of volunteers at drop-in centres. They used four types of data from seven centres: interviews with volunteers, complete observer participant observation, case studies, and surveys with youth. As the youth couldn't be interviewed, the quantitative surveys "enabled [the researchers] to validate the qualitative results and to study the quantitative correlations between various qualitative variables" (p. 194). Thus, this research was iterative, with the findings from each strand influencing others'. The research design allowed the researchers to explore volunteers' and youths' perspectives by involving volunteers in the design and data collection process. This approach created an "extended community of researchers and provided a point of view from within, not just from without" that was considered critical because the youth benefited from volunteers gaining context-specific knowledge and experience (p. 194).

Design Notation

The next section provides an overview of the more common mixed methods designs in crime and justice research. Before we look at these types, however, we need to understand the scientific notation used to identify the study characteristics. The notation will also tell us how the design types compare with one another.

Symbols and upper- and lower-case letters are used to indicate sequence, priority, and process. A plus sign (+) indicates a concurrent sequence; both data types of data are collected, analyzed, and interpreted simultaneously. In contrast, an arrow (→) symbolizes sequential data collection and analysis, with one method informing the design and execution of a second method. A double-headed arrow (↔) indicates a back-and-forth pattern, which is iterative and consistent with an integrated sequence.

Capitalizing quantitative (QUAN) or qualitative (QUAL) represents that data type being considered primary in terms of data collection, analysis, and interpretation. The data that are given less emphasis, and classified as secondary, are in lower-case letters (quan, qual). If the research design is embedded, the secondary data method is in parentheses ( ). Last but not least, a dashed arrow (-–→) reflects an iterative interpretation process (e.g. going from inference back to data collection, as one would see with grounded theory).

Methods in Action

New Directions: The Who, What, Where, and Why of Social Media

What do Facebook, Twitter, Google+, LinkedIn, YouTube, Flickr, Instagram, Pinterest, Reddit, and Tumblr all have in common? They are social media and networking sites, difficult to research, yet increasingly becoming a police communication strategy. According to the International Association of Chiefs of Police's (2014) Social Media Survey, 95.9 per cent use social media in some capacity; the sites most frequently used are Facebook (92.1 per cent), Twitter (64.8 per cent), and YouTube (42.9 per cent). But these numbers tell us only part of the story.

Consider these statistics: the fastest growing demographic on Twitter is between 55 and 64 years of age; YouTube reaches more 18- to 34-year-olds than cable networks do; someone joins LinkedIn every two seconds; and social media has replaced pornography as the number one online activity (Cooper, 2013). Seventy-three per cent of online adults use social networking sites, of which 71 per cent use Facebook, 22 per cent LinkedIn, and 18 per cent Twitter (Pew Research Center, 2014). As important as it is to identify trends with quantitative data, using qualitative data to see how ideas are expressed is also necessary (Zaltzman & Leichliter, 2014). For precisely the same reason, there is concern that statistics quantifying the extent of contact (e.g. retweets, followers) between the police and community is only a crude measure of process when outcomes, such as improved relations, are of greater importance (Davis III, Alves, & Sklansky, 2014). All these trends point to the appropriateness of investigating the use of social media with mixed methods.

Kietzmann and colleagues (2012) offer a framework for unpacking the social media phenomenon by breaking the concept into several functions that require using quantitative and qualitative data. The concept of identity captures the ways and the extent that users reveal personal information about themselves. The challenge is incorporating triangulation because people can reinvent themselves online. Groups are communities that develop within the social networking sites. New relationships develop or long-lost ones are rekindled. Qualitative analyses of message content can unpack this idea further. There is also the question of how reputation is based on past actions and how trust is maintained. An online presence and the extent that users communicate with one another are important dimensions; it's not simply the frequency but the direction and content of the interactions. Finally, sharing involves examining what content is distributed to others (QUAN) and the motivations for doing so (QUAL). Thinking in terms of these social media characteristics and their relevance to a research problem, such as police–community relations, can inform the researcher on the most appropriate mixed methods design.

Analytic induction is at work in a study that investigated police departments' use of Facebook (Lieberman, Koetzle, & Sakiyama, 2013). The researchers used a sequential multi-strand mixed methods design, reviewing official statistics to identify the twenty largest police departments, department websites to identify Facebook users, and a web crawler to capture posted messages and URL links. A content analysis used quantitative and qualitative data from these posts. The data revealed that departments that frequently post or send crime-related messages are more likely to distribute public relations messages than are less frequent posters.

Crump (2011) investigated the effectiveness of using social media to reach out to those typically not in a dialogue with police services. He analyzed the content of Twitter messages from 140 police accounts to ascertain motivation and online behaviour. In this sequential design, findings were contextualized with interview data from three police services. Crump concluded that the police culture results in cautious use of Twitter, largely in order to reinforce existing communication messages.

Types of Mixed Methods Research Designs

We have discussed the common characteristics and design notation of mixed methods research. The next step is to review the most common designs used in criminology and criminal justice research. Equivalent status and dominant-less-dominant designs focus specifically on the priority of each quantitative and qualitative data strand. Both types become part of concurrent and sequential mixed methods research designs. The final design, fully integrated, is the most complex. Although not suitable for many research problems, it is a powerful tool—when appropriate—to harness multiple perspectives on the topic.

Equivalent Status Designs

In **equivalent status designs,** each data strand is given the same emphasis when developing an overall conclusion. The design can be concurrent (QUAN + QUAL; QUAL + QUAN) or sequential (QUAN → QUAL; QUAL → QUAN). Notice that both strands are in capital letters, indicating the same priority for each. Inferences are made from each strand and then given equal weight when drawing conclusions.

> **equivalent status design** a mixed methods research design in which each data strand is given equal priority and findings from each create one overall conclusion.

In Figure 12.2, designs A and B are sequential; data for either the quantitative or qualitative strand

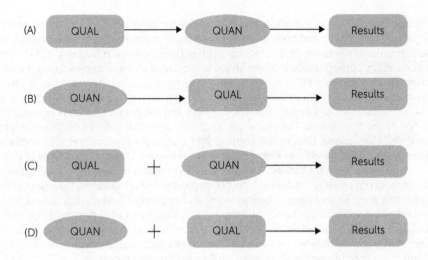

Figure 12.2 Equivalent status designs

is collected first, followed by the other type of data. Designs C and D are concurrent, or parallel, equivalent status designs. Both quantitative and qualitative data are collected simultaneously and given equal priority.

Let's put this figure in more concrete terms. Design A uses qualitative measures to develop quantitative tools. In contrast, design B employs quantitative data to examine breadth, which is followed by using qualitative data to understand specific aspects of the quantitative results in more depth. In designs C and D, both strands measure different perspectives on the same social phenomenon, which, in combination, provides a more holistic understanding. The findings from each equally contribute to the conclusions.

With equivalent status designs, the mixing occurs at the point of interpretation when a meta-inference is created. The findings from different methods are integrated at the theoretical level. Each strand is analyzed, consistent with the assumptions of its respective paradigms. The findings from each are then brought together to create the overall conclusion.

All mixed methods research can have two or more data strands. For example, one study used two quantitative and one qualitative strand when evaluating a directed police patrol project (McGarrell et al., 2001). The study used a pre–post quasi-experimental design with a nonequivalent control group (see Chapter 5). The mixed methods component was sequential equivalent status design (QUAN→QUAN→QUAL). The researchers used Uniform Crime Report official statistics to discern patterns in violent crime. On the basis of these results, they created models for the experimental and control group patrol zones that informed the police incident reports officers completed after each call. Finally, they conducted police ride alongs to collect qualitative findings to better understand the process of the patterns identified in the police reports. The results suggest that directed patrol focused on suspicious activities and geographical areas is more effective at reducing violent gun crime than the general deterrence approach of increasing the number of random vehicle stops.

Dominant-Less-Dominant Designs

In contrast to equivalent status, **dominant-less-dominant designs** have one paradigm, its methods have priority, and a smaller component of the overall study is drawn from another type of data. Figure 12.3 splits these designs into qualitative or quantitative dominant. Under each of these larger categories are four variations that are appropriate with certain types

dominant-less-dominant design a mixed methods research design in which one data strand is dominant and the findings play a larger role when creating an overall conclusion.

of research objectives. The first two involve two different methods from the same paradigm and the last two mix quantitative and qualitative data.

QUAL Dominant

In the first two designs in Figure 12.3, the two methods come from the same paradigm. In design 1, two qualitative methods are used simultaneously, with one dominant method forming the basis for conclusions. This design is ideal when you want more than one perspective to inform conclusions suggesting the existence of a generic social process. Design 2 also uses two qualitative methods, but they are executed sequentially, with the first being dominant. Both studies are independent, but data from the first is used to inform the second. Despite the logical progression in design 2, researchers typically publish the results in separate articles.

The next two designs mix different types of data. With design 3, a qualitative method is used concurrently with a less dominant quantitative method. In this case, the quantitative measurement enhances the qualitative description or interpretation. Thus, quantitative data are used as further information for the qualitative findings. Qualitative and quantitative methods are used sequentially with an inductive theoretical focus in design 4. This approach is common when developing a typology or theoretical model. However, it's difficult to find research examples, as findings resulting in only minor theoretical modifications are rarely published.

Although Figure 12.3 depicts the qualitative method occurring first in the sequence, the dominant method can just as easily come second (quan→QUAL). Brunson and Miller (2009) wanted to understand how conflicts are shaped in schools and how and when they occur in the community. The researchers used purposive sampling to select at-risk and delinquent youth between the ages of 13 and 19. They conducted quantitative surveys first to provide a guide for the qualitative interviews conducted later in the day. Here, the less dominant survey provided baseline information on the youth's exposure to violence, whereas the dominant qualitative method provided in-depth information on baseline themes organized into the context and on attitudes toward violence.

QUAN Dominant

Designs 5 through 8 in Figure 12.3 give priority to a quantitative method. In design 5, both types of quantitative data are collected concurrently. This is the most common type of triangulation, largely because you can remain within the post-positivistic paradigm. Other quantitative instruments are used as a validity check. The results are triangulated by determining statistical correlations between measures. However, the key is that the first method is dominant, with the second used as a tool for verification. Design 6 is sequential; researchers use the second study to elicit further information about particular dimensions in the first study. This design is used when there is considerable past research providing enough information for method 1 to know the relevant variables to create hypotheses for testing a theoretical explanation. Theoretical developments are then tested further with quantitative method 2.

Design 7 is concurrent in order to create a theoretical model based on findings from prior research. The model is tested quantitatively, while a less dominant qualitative method is conducted at the same time to address components of the theory that cannot be quantified. Finally, in design 8,

Qualitative dominant	Quantitative dominant
1. QUAL + qual	5. QUAN + quan
• More perspectives	• Most common
2. QUAL→qual	6. QUAN→quan
• Independent studies	• Elicit further information
3. QUAL + quan	7. QUAN + qual
• Enhance interpretation	• Create and test model
4. QUAL→quan	8. QUAN→qual
• Develop theory	• Unexpected QUAN results

Figure 12.3 Dominant-less-dominant designs

Source: Morse (2003, pp. 189–208). Copyright © 2002, CCC Republication.

convergent parallel design a mixed methods research design in which both data strands are collected and analyzed concurrently and the overall conclusion is based on a comparison of each data strand's findings.

quantitative and qualitative data are collected sequentially with a deductive theoretical focus. This process is typically used when the quantitative results are unexpected and the qualitative study is conducted to ascertain potential reasons for the anomalous findings. In other words, the qualitative study provides explanations for a particular part of the quantitative study.

To bring all this information together, the next step is to look at the three common design frameworks used to conduct mixed methods research. The first is convergent parallel designs, which involve comparing findings. The second is a sequential mixed methods design that can be exploratory, with the qualitative data strand first, or explanatory, with quantitative methods first. Finally, a fully integrated model, which is equivalent status, combines all variations in one design

and data collection and analysis occur simultaneously for both strands.

Convergent Parallel Design

In a **convergent parallel design**, the different types of data are collected and analyzed concurrently, the findings from each are interpreted at the same time, and conclusions integrate the findings from each by asking whether they support the same conclusion. Each type of data provides a different perspective on the research problem.

Figure 12.4 depicts any parallel mixed methods research design. In this design, the comparisons occur at the interpretation level. The comparisons of findings from each strand can be direct or merged. Consistent with the initiation rationale for conducting mixed methods research, direct comparisons take the findings from each and directly compare whether they support or contradict one another. For example, the statistical analyses from survey data on citizen opinions and the results from a thematic analysis of interview data on the Scared Straight

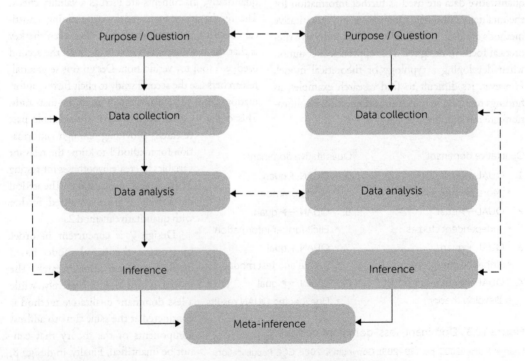

Figure 12.4 Convergent parallel mixed methods research design

program are compared to see if the same conclusions can be drawn. Merged comparisons involve transforming the data, such as you find when qualitative codes are counted. In either of these cases, this design is appropriate for gaining a more comprehensive understanding or corroboration between two different perspectives or for comparing across levels (e.g. within an organization—management versus front-line workers). This is an equivalent status design, as both types of data make an equal contribution to our understanding of the issue or problem.

Exploratory and Explanatory Sequential Designs

Sequential mixed methods research executes one data strand first, with the results informing the second strand, often at the research question development stage (see Figure 12.5). The two different types of sequential designs are exploratory and explanatory. The sequence of data strands depends on the research purpose. In both situations, the design is often equivalent status but can just as easily be dominant-less-dominant (designs 3, 4, 7, or 8).

Exploratory Sequential Design

The distinguishing feature of an **exploratory sequential design** is that the research purpose determines that the sequence starts with the qualitative data strand. The qualitative findings are then used to create the research question and process for the quantitative strand. Researchers use this design to develop a data collection instrument or test an inductive theoretical model. This sequential mixed methods design explores new theories, develops instruments, creates typologies, and investigates whether qualitative themes are generalizable to a larger population.

> **exploratory sequential design** a sequential mixed methods research design that conducts the study in two stages, with the qualitative data strand first in sequence and the findings used to inform the collection and analysis of quantitative data.

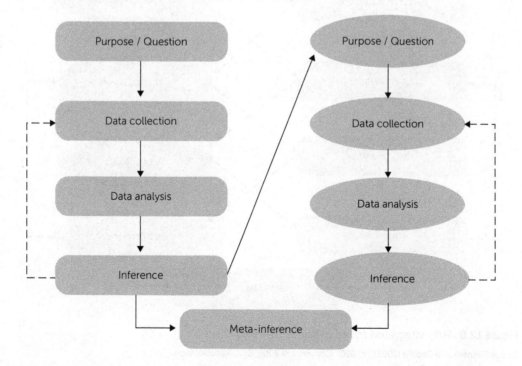

Figure 12.5 Sequential mixed methods research design

Explanatory Sequential Design

An **explanatory sequential design** is identical to an exploratory design with one exception: the quantitative data are collected and analyzed first and then the findings are used to inform the collection and analysis of the qualitative data strand. The qualitative research question is developed on the basis of the quantitative findings and the results from both strands are linked together in the conclusion. In this design, the qualitative findings help to *explain* the quantitative results to come to a more comprehensive conclusion.

> **explanatory sequential design** a sequential mixed methods research design that conducts the study in two stages, with the quantitative data strand first in sequence and the findings used to inform the collection and analysis of qualitative data.

> **fully integrated design** a research design in which both data strands mix interactively at all stages in the research process.

The results from the qualitative data add more depth to the results that have breadth using quantitative methods. Alternatively, the qualitative data are used to expand on aspects of the quantitative results that cannot be fully explained. This process develops new questions as a result of phase one. Thus, this design can be used when the purpose for conducting mixed methods research is complementarity, development, or expansion.

Fully Integrated Mixed Methods Design

A **fully integrated design** is the most dynamic and interactive form of mixed methods. Each stage in the research process is iteratively mixed for both data strands. In this way, the approach and findings from one strand directly affect various stages in the other strand. By definition, this design is equivalent status. Quantitative and qualitative methods are collaboratively used to answer multiple questions

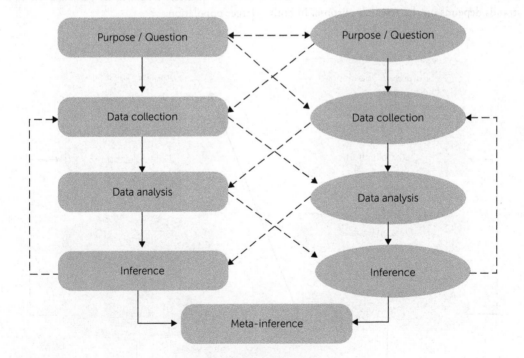

Figure 12.6 Fully integrated mixed methods research design

that are both exploratory and confirmatory. Instead of the findings from each strand mixing only at the interpretation level, results from each stage in the research process inform methodological decision-making in the other strand and vice versa.

In Figure 12.6, the dashed arrows indicate the iterative process at every stage in the research process for each strand, informing each other in a recursive pattern. As seen by the double-headed dashed arrow between the two research questions boxes, the conceptualization of the quantitative research question informs the formulation of the qualitative question and vice versa. The same interactive activities occur at data collection, analysis, and interpretation stages. However, please note that the arrows point downwards.

If the first data strand is quantitative, QUAN data collection informs QUAL data analysis and the same applies for QUAL data collection to QUAN analysis. At the end of this complex process, a meta-inference is created from the findings from both strands. As I am sure you can imagine, this type of design is an excellent example of investigator triangulation becoming an important consideration. A research team will have a wide array of methodological and substantive knowledge and experience. The greater the amount of human and financial resources required, the greater the need for this type of triangulation. It is also needed when three or more data strands are incorporated in the design.

Vignette: Breaking It Down

Predicting and Understanding Police Work

"In our goal to pursue the more 'scientific' aspects of research on the police we have often settled for statistical results—absent contextual meaning ... without the associated social interpretation."

J.R. Green, "New Directions in Policing: Balancing Prediction and Meaning in Police Research" (2014, p. 202)

Policing researchers are increasingly moving outside the comfort zone of monomethods and conducting research that is inductive and deductive, tests theoretical predictions, develops theories, and seeks to provide more holistic understandings of police work. The research problems span policing policy and practice, investigation patterns, perceptions, decision-making processes, and the effectiveness of patrol strategies. Let's take a look at some examples of approaching these topics with mixed methods so you can see how a single study captures prediction and contextual meaning.

Design by Research Purpose

The circumstances of citizens being stopped and searched by police is controversial. Is the use of discretion racially biased? What is the impact of visibility, time, place, and type of car on this decision? For the purpose of complementarity, one mixed methods study had four concurrent data strands executed in pairs sequentially to address these questions (Waddington, Stenson, & Don, 2004).

Continued

The first stage involved direct observation by driving through areas of high rates of stop-and-search to record the race, age, and sex of pedestrians. The weaknesses of this method were misidentification and insufficient time to record observations. Thus, CCTV footage was subsequently reviewed to compensate for these problems and to capture data in the foot-only zones in the downtown core.

The second stage collected quantitative data from police computer records to determine who was stopped, when, and for what purpose. Official police reports do not record perceptions well, so this step was followed up by interviewing sixty front-line officers and asking them to recount three recent stop-and-search incidents. Although official records indicate disproportionate contact, little evidence suggests that officers selectively target racial minorities, as other reasons explain the decision to stop citizens.

Vargas (2014) wanted to understand the impact on violent crime in an area once a gang leader was arrested. The purpose for using mixed methods was expansion. Qualitative data from field work, police reports, court cases, and interviews (dominant) were used to assess changes in gang behaviour post-arrest. Official statistics were used to determine whether the arrests resulted in short- or long-term changes in the violent crime within these gang territories. Thus, qualitative is dominant with an embedded less dominant quantitative outcome measure (QUAL + [quan]). It turns out that, within the first month after arrest, violent crime spikes in these areas.

Design by Research Question

A study investigating police strategies with migrants combined data from two different studies (Leerkes, Varsayi, & Engbersen, 2012). Using a national database of registered person stops, the quantitative analysis was integrated with the qualitative observation data from an ethnographic study conducted in two large cities. Thus, the integration occurred iteratively at the analysis and interpretation stages using two sources of secondary data. The context in which apprehension patterns occur was followed by evidence of highly selective apprehension practices, leading to conclusions about the interests of the police and community.

Whether it's the research purpose connecting the data strands or it's the research questions, these studies are examples of a monomethod approach being inappropriate. The inferences from each strand suggest areas for future research. The meta-inferences then combine multiple perspectives on the research problem to guide research and policy development.

Methodological Gymnastics

Mixed methods research requires methodological gymnastics on the part of the researcher and reader. Most academics and practitioners are more comfortable with one approach and identify as quantitative or qualitative researchers. One view of reality and method of research is more consistent with the types of questions that are of interest to them. Further, with the quantitative dominance evident in criminology and criminal justice scholarship, adopting a mixed methods research design makes one "to some extent a scholarly deviant [who] can expect to experience the disapprobation arising from the natural discomfort which this scholarly deviance arouses in its audience" (Schulenberg, 2007a, p. 117).

Unique Considerations for Mixed Methods Designs

In previous chapters, we talked about all stages in the quantitative and qualitative research processes. However, mixed methods research requires additional steps and three areas that need greater attention to design and implementation. These issues include the purpose statement and number of research questions; sampling; and data analysis and meta-inferences.

Purpose and Questions

In Chapter 3, the purpose statement was defined as a statement outlining the research intent and objectives. In mixed methods research, this statement needs additional information. Similar to a monomethod study, the statement articulates the research objective. The statement specifies the role played by each data strand (quantitative, qualitative) in the research design. For instance, questions to be considered are whether a strand is dominant and what aspect of the research problem this data will address. The statement clarifies why both types of data are needed to achieve the research objective. Thus, in several sentences, the purpose statement outlines why the research is being conducted and provides information on the type of design, the different data strands, and why the study requires more than one type of data to address the research problem (Creswell, 2014).

Similarly, research questions are expanded in mixed methods research designs. There are three different types of research questions all linked to data strands. Just as monomethod research has questions that drive the method, so do mixed methods, with separate quantitative and qualitative questions. In addition to the specific data-type questions, each study has an overarching research question bridging the qualitative and quantitative questions. When we think of a central research question, it's often in association with qualitative research. Here, the central mixed methods research question guides the creation of a meta-inference. It plays a pivotal role in mixed methods research because it provides the framework for how the data are combined to address the research problem.

Consider Marshall's (2012) research that explored why African-American youth are disproportionately represented in those who start in the child welfare system and then enter the juvenile

justice system. In this concurrent qualitative dominant design (QUAL + quan), the rationale for adopting mixed methods was complementarity, as the quantitative survey data were used to enrich the qualitative interview data. Three research questions informed the research design and data strands:

- Interviews addressed qualitative research question 1: How do professionals understand and explain the disproportionate crossing over (Marshall, 2012, p. 52)? Practitioners described several interrelated reasons for crossing over, including poverty, education, emotional and behavioural problems, parents, family, and larger social systems.
- Surveys were the most appropriate method for answering the quantitative research question 2: How racially sensitive and aware are these professionals (p. 53)? The results suggest that black practitioners who are less colour blind also identify more as racialized Americans.
- The central mixed methods research question 3 brings the quantitative and qualitative findings together: Is there a relation between professionals' interpretations of disproportionate crossing over and their racial sensitivity and awareness (p. 53)? Thus, the point of interaction between the two data strands was at the level of data analysis and inferences. The meta-inference is that practitioners who are less colour blind and identify as racialized Americans put more weight on larger social system factors than on individual- and family-level contributors to explain why more African-American youth in the juvenile justice system have a history in the child welfare system (p. iii).

Sampling

As is the case with monomethod research, the sampling strategy is dictated by the research question. The most appropriate technique collects the information required to address the research questions and is consistent with that type of data. The same principles apply in mixed methods research, with the exception that you will likely use more than one sampling technique in the same study.

The goal of using methods with complementary strengths and non-overlapping weaknesses applies to sampling decisions as well. Be careful when combining probability and nonprobability techniques. You are striving for a balance between saturation or theoretical sampling (qualitative) and representativeness (quantitative). Go back to that particular research question. If you want to generalize to a larger population, probability sampling is needed. If the research question requires gathering in-depth information on a few cases, nonprobability techniques are appropriate.

The research subjects in the sample may or may not be different for each data strand. In a sequential study, the sample obtained for the first quantitative phase of the research is created using random sampling. For the second strand, the quantitative findings serve as a catalyst for finding additional research subjects with the same or different sampling technique. Alternatively, the second phase could use the same research subjects. The first stage is quantitative, but the second qualitative method adopts purposive sampling to select deviant cases from the larger random sample.

Data Analysis and Inferences

Despite the ability to collect data concurrently and sequentially, there is no way to develop a meta-inference analyzing quantitative and qualitative data simultaneously using the same analytical tool. For instance, an analytical software program that combines the full functionality of SPSS and NVivo does not exist. However, each program has some basic tools to analyze converted data. SPSS allows for descriptive statistics on text data by counting words instead of numerical data. NVivo and other CAQDAS programs can also create descriptive statistics and run procedures such as cluster analysis, as you saw in Figure 10.7. NVivo allows datasets to be exported to statistical software programs. That said, they remain separate programs.

An analytical challenge in many mixed methods research designs is creating a meta-inference from each data strand's inferences. Specifically, how do you combine inferences that are based on different questions, philosophical assumptions, and often different aspects of the research problem? The first step is to recall which quantitative or qualitative research question is being addressed by this quantitative or qualitative finding. Next, go back to the central overarching research question that bridges the qualitative and quantitative data strands. How do the combination of inferences from each data type address this larger question? Finally, keep in mind the priority assigned to each strand in the design. If qualitative is dominant, those findings play a larger role in creating the meta-inference by virtue of the fact that the research problem predominantly requires a qualitative approach. If it is an equivalent-status design, inferences from both strands are equally important in developing a meaningful understanding of the issue or problem investigated.

Ethics and Politics

Every aspect of conducting research involves a consideration of ethics. The only difference in a mixed methods research study is that ensuring the research participants' rights are protected is more complex. Ethical considerations associated with quantitative and qualitative data collection methods and analysis are all applicable in a mixed methods study. There may also be additional ethical considerations. For example, collecting data from the same respondents with different methods and then linking the data increases concerns about their anonymity, particularly when publishing the results.

The politics surrounding mixed methods are more of a minefield. It goes beyond the methodological divide and paradigm wars. Not only does the controversy continue to varying degrees in the discipline, but there is also the occasional political mudslinging. While engaging in the controversy, when "each faction—the *quants* and *quals*—[is] adopting a type of binary or exclusionary logic, our methodological choices are limited to either one or the other approach, with both camps viewing each other's as inferior" (Brent & Kraska, 2010, pp. 416–417).

The other political aspect is the influence of crime and justice research on policy-makers and vice versa. Over the years, mixed methods research has become more valued. Evidence-based policy requires a research environment of methodological pluralism because multiple methods give policy-makers a comprehensive understanding of complex questions on how to prevent and respond to crime (Fielding, 2010). However, it appears that policy-makers contribute to the quantitative dominance by paying more attention to quantitative dominant mixed methods designs.

Making the qualitative monomethod or portion of mixed methods designs fit neatly into the checklist mentality associated with post-positivistic standards is challenging. With that said, use caution before generalizing to all policy-makers and research on criminology and criminal justice topics. The political environment is likely less concerned with the type of method as with why the research is commissioned in the first place, how the results are to be used, and what role the findings play in evidence-based practice and policy-making (Fielding, 2010). Yet, when professional associations and government entities call for additional research, there can be a methodological preference. This situation has led some to argue quite persuasively that "in this politically driven process legitimacy has been given to ... a renewed form of positivism, ironically masquerading under the guise of 'evidence-based practice'" (Scraton, 2002, p. 33, cited in Fielding, 2010, p. 136).

There is no clear-cut answer or solution to the politics surrounding mixed methods research. But knowledge is power, and developing an awareness of potential problems allows you to take appropriate steps to minimize the issue. The other undeniable truth is that the research question drives the method and, when a mixed methods design is called for, it makes no sense to design the research in any other way. Perhaps the day will come when "the crime and justice research community won't question why someone mixed quantitative and qualitative methods but, rather, why they did not" (Brent & Kraska, 2010, p. 428).

Conclusion

The type of mixed methods research design is influenced by logistical concerns such as the research objective (e.g. evaluation), research questions, sequence, priority, and the context or field setting. You may run into a perplexing problem. Therefore, when designing a mixed methods study, critically examine the research questions and determine the extent of interaction between strands, the sequence that makes the most sense, the priority and emphasis of each data strand, and at what point the strands interface or mix (i.e. the stage in the research process when the strands directly interact).

What happens if existing designs don't make sense but the project requires quantitative and qualitative data to address the research problem? The answer is daunting but simple. You may have to develop a new mixed methods design because the current options are not the most appropriate for this research study (Teddlie & Tashakkori, 2006). This situation happens more frequently than you may think. You need only open several books on mixed methods to see that the same concepts are discussed, but there are small or large variations in the terminology and structure of the design.

In a more general sense, three factors should be kept at the forefront when developing mixed methods research. The first cannot be emphasized enough. At the substantive level, give priority to the purpose statement and research questions. Second, at the paradigm level, bear in mind the assumptions about the social world contained in each worldview. Whether you align with pragmatism or not, you do have to have a central mixed methods research question and specific qualitative and quantitative questions in order to be epistemologically and ontologically consistent. Finally, at the technical level, the skills required to collect and analyze both types of data are needed to create valid inferences and meta-inferences. If you feel uncertain, investigator triangulation is a good solution.

What does a well-designed and executed mixed methods research study look like? Depending on the type of design, there are a multitude of answers. However, it is possible to talk about six overall features of good mixed methods research projects (Ponterotto, Mathew, & Raughley, 2013, p. 47):

1. Inclusion of a convincing rationale for why a mixed methods design is appropriate;
2. Awareness of the research paradigm and philosophy of science parameters for each of the methods, including a discussion of how the variant paradigms combine to enhance the study;
3. Demonstrated expertise in both methodological components of the mixed design;
4. High multicultural awareness of the research team;
5. Ethical vigilance that transcends both the quantitative and qualitative components;
6. Strong writing skills that incorporate "thick description" for the qualitative component and objective precision in the quantitative component with a fluid integration of the findings across the methods.

By discussing mixed methods research, this chapter has amalgamated the material covered throughout the textbook. Congratulations on making it to the end! Hopefully, you can see how all the pieces come together and the methodological gymnastics and creativity possible, when appropriate, for the research objective and questions. Perhaps the best way to summarize mixed methods research and exemplars is to conclude with the following words from Greene (1997, p. 2):

A mixed-method design combining these two traditions would strive for knowledge claims that are grounded in the lives of the participants studied and that also have some generality to other participants and other contexts; that enhance understanding of both the unusual and the typical case; that isolate factors of particular significance while also integrating the whole; and that are full of emic meaning at the same time that they offer causal connections of broader significance.

Mixed methods research is not for the faint of heart. It requires more resources and skills, but it certainly has the potential to push our knowledge into new areas, with comprehensive findings that contribute to a greater understanding of our social world.

Summary of Important Points

Introduction

- Mixed methods research combines quantitative and qualitative approaches at various stages in the research process to corroborate findings and increase the breadth and depth of our knowledge.
- Advantages of adopting a mixed methods research design include increased confidence in the conclusions and the ability to present multiple perspectives and to address different types of research questions.
- Disadvantages include the requirement of becoming a methodological connoisseur, increased time and human resources, difficulty coordinating the research process, and challenges creating overall conclusions.

Methodological Controversies

- Mixed methodologists adhere to methodological pluralism, whereas purists are advocates of methodological exclusivism.
- The incompatibility thesis argues that one cannot mix methods as the philosophical assumptions associated with post-positivism and interpretivism are both violated.
- Mixed methods is becoming more common in criminology and criminal justice research, but evidence continues to indicate a quantitative dominance.

What Are We Trying to Do with Mixed Methods Research?

- Originating from a trigonometry formula used for naval navigation, triangulation increases the validity of the findings by incorporating multiple investigations, theoretical perspectives, methods, and analytical techniques in the same study.
- Within-method multimethod research uses more than one type of method in the quantitative or qualitative paradigm to generate the same type of data and findings.
- Between-method mixed methods research combines a quantitative and at least one more qualitative method in the same study.
- There are four reasons for conducting mixed methods research: complementarity (comprehensive understanding); initiation (generate dissimilar findings, illuminating new directions); development (findings from one method inform another method); and expansion (clarify the findings from the first method by using an additional method).
- Strong mixed methods research combines methods with complementary strengths and non-overlapping weaknesses.

Common Characteristics in Mixed Methods Designs

- The research process associated with each data strand can be concurrent, sequential, or integrated.

- Mixed methods designs differ based on how much priority is given to each data strand: equivalent, primary/secondary, or embedded.
- Multiphase research combines multiple studies with the same research objective into one larger research project.
- Consistent with participatory action research, a transformative research design involves research subjects in the research process for one or more data strands.

Types of Mixed Methods Designs

- In equivalent status designs, the findings from each data strand make equal contributions to overall conclusions.
- In dominant-less-dominant designs, the findings from one data strand make a larger contribution to the overall conclusions.
- In a convergent parallel design, quantitative and qualitative data are collected concurrently with the findings from each data strand compared when drawing conclusions.
- In an exploratory sequential design, the qualitative data strand is first followed by the quantitative method.
- In an explanatory sequential design, the quantitative method is first followed by collecting and analyzing a qualitative data strand.
- In a fully integrated design, data strands interact iteratively at all stages in the research process.

Methodological Gymnastics

- The purpose statement outlines the rationale for the study, type of design, data strands, and appropriateness of mixed methods.
- A central mixed methods research question provides the framework for drawing conclusions that combine findings from each data strand.
- Mixed methods research may use the same or different samples for each data strand.

- To create a meta-inference, refer to the research questions and priority assigned to types of data in the research design.
- All ethical and political concerns associated with quantitative and qualitative research must be considered in mixed methods research.

Conclusion

- Strong mixed methods research provides a clear rationale for its use, demonstrates awareness of the methodological divide, is conducted by methodological connoisseurs, is ethically vigilant, and integrates the findings well.

Key Terms

analytical triangulation 377
complementarity 377
convergent parallel design 386
development 378
dominant-less-dominant design 384
embedded (or nested) mixed methods design 380
equivalent status design 383

expansion 378
explanatory sequential design 388
exploratory sequential design 387
fully integrated design 388
initiation 378
investigator triangulation 376
methodological exclusivism 372
methodological pluralism 371

methodological triangulation 376
multimethod research 376
multiphase mixed methods design 381
theoretical triangulation 376
transformative mixed methods design 381
triangulation 375

Review Questions and Exercises

1. Why is using mixed methods research designs seen as controversial?
2. What characteristics do mixed methods research designs have in common?
3. On a topic of your choice, find one qualitative and one quantitative article that investigates a similar type of research problem. For each article, identify the research objective, purpose statement, and research questions. Next, design a mixed methods study that could have combined the research in these articles into one study. Specify the following in your answer:
   a. central mixed methods research question
   b. one quantitative and one qualitative research question
   c. quantitative and qualitative methods
   d. sequence, priority, or integrated
   e. type of mixed methods design
4. Review one of the mixed methods research studies described in this chapter and state what logistical, ethical, and political factors need to be addressed.

Online Exercises and websites of Interest

Pulling It Apart

www.scholar.google.com
Using Google Scholar, select a journal article that uses a mixed methods research design. Alternatively, you can use one of the articles cited in this chapter. Review the methods and identify the following:

   a. research objective
   b. purpose statement

    c. central mixed methods research question
    d. quantitative and qualitative research methods used
    e. manner of structuring findings
    f. overall conclusion that integrates both types of data

"Social Media Hell"

http://ca.adforum.com/agency/5612/creative-work/34467713

Design a mixed methods study that investigates the notion of "social media hell." This idea can be the phone application itself, the organization, or the concept.

International Journal of Social Research Methodology

www.tandfonline.com/toc/tsrm20/current#.U4zrwLGZggo

This interdisciplinary journal publishes articles on methodological debates and practices across the spectrum of approaches: qualitative, quantitative, and mixed methods. Issues covered include philosophical, theoretical, ethical, political, and practice.

Journal of Mixed Methods Research

http://mmr.sagepub.com

This journal publishes articles on when mixed methods is the most effective alternative, as well as design and procedure issues and the logistics of using these types of research designs.

Additional Resources

Creswell, J.W. (2014). *Research Design: Qualitative, Quantitative, and Mixed Methods Approaches* (4th ed.). Thousand Oaks, CA: Sage.

This text is a hands-on guide to conducting quantitative, qualitative, and mixed methods research that takes you from the research objective, purpose statement, and research questions to writing up the results.

Tashakkori, A., & Creswell, J.W. (2007). "Exploring the Nature of Research Questions in Mixed Methods Research." *Journal of Mixed Methods Research, 1,* 207–211.

This article highlights how research questions are used in mixed methods research and provides an overview of central mixed methods, quantitative, and qualitative research questions.

Tashakkori, A., & Teddlie, C. (1998). *Mixed Methodology: Combining Qualitative and Quantitative Approaches.* Thousand Oaks, CA: Sage.

This ground-breaking publication reviews the methodological controversies and outlines a comprehensive list of mixed methods research designs.

The Research Proposal and "Writing It Up"

Advice on combatting the blank computer screen disease: "You cannot overcome the fear without doing the thing you are afraid of and finding out that it is not as dangerous as you imagined. So the solution for writing something that will not fully, logically, and completely master the chaos is to write it anyway and discover that the world will not end when you do. . . . So here is where the advice stops. You can't start swimming until you get in the water." H.S. Becker, *Writing for Social Scientists: How to Start and Finish Your Thesis, Book, or Article* (2007, p. 135)

Introduction

I'm sure you can relate to facing a blank page, typing a paragraph and deleting the whole thing shortly thereafter, or not even making it to the computer because you are perfecting the art of procrastination. You are not alone. Part of the solution to these problems is gaining a better understanding of what constitutes a research proposal, a typical report, and ways to reframe the writing process. Taking some of the mystery out of the process can help you sort the noodles from the soup.

A research proposal is a document that presents information to support why a potential research project should be completed. It can be a course assignment, thesis or dissertation requirement, part of the ethics approval process, an application for a research grant, or a response to a request for proposals (RFP) to secure a contract for practitioner- or government-sponsored research. It is written before the research is conducted and provides a road map for the entire research process. The goal is to convince the audience that the research should be conducted and that what you propose is feasible. The proposal presents the research purpose, objective, and questions; identifies the gaps in knowledge (how this study builds on prior research); explains why the methods chosen are the most appropriate; and outlines steps to ensure ethical treatment of research subjects, a timeline for completion, and perhaps a budget.

The written report will have an abstract or an executive summary, depending on whether you are writing for an academic or practitioner audience.

The structure is what you would expect: sections for the introduction, literature review, theoretical framework, research questions, methods, findings, discussion, and conclusion. Taking a look at each of these sections in greater detail will help you read published research (see Appendix B).

Finally, there is the issue of writing advice, raised with the opening quotation. How do you get the quantitative and qualitative findings to tell a story? What are some of the ways you can get words onto the page? These and other questions can be answered by keeping a few pieces of advice in mind.

Research Proposal

As one of your course requirements, you may have to write a research proposal. Before you go tearing out of the room screaming and pulling your hair, be assured that even seasoned researchers are unable to develop a perfect research proposal. Remember, there is no such thing as a perfect research design because conducting research is a messy process. The research proposal is one tool used to make the process smoother and to clarify your thinking on what you are doing and why.

If you have to submit a proposal for this course, think of it as a way to demonstrate your understanding of methodological principles by applying them in a research context. You will likely be assessed on your ability to provide the rationale for your methodological decisions and the application of research methods, not your understanding of the substantive topic. To help make this process less intimidating, let's take a closer look at some of the key items that should be included in your proposal.

Research Purpose

In this section, describe why your topic constitutes a problem in society, what the proposed research is trying to understand, and why the study should be conducted. Include the purpose statement and the research objective and address the "so what" question. In describing the research purpose, the proposal must communicate to the reader why it's important to find the answers to the research problem or to better understand why things occur in the way that they do.

Literature Review and Theoretical Framework

A literature review highlights what we know and what remains unanswered in relation to this social phenomenon. In this context, a social phenomenon is what the research study focuses on and what you are trying to explain. For instance, if your topic is love, the social phenomenon could be falling in love. The research purpose is to understand how people fall in love.

The length of the literature review depends on the audience. If it is for a course, take your direction from your professor. The focus is likely on the methods, which means that the literature review doesn't need to be long or cover everything but provide sufficient information to show how the literature informed the development of your research questions. For a thesis proposal, the literature review is longer and must cover all facets associated with the research problem. For funding proposals, the agency often stipulates the overall number of pages for the proposal and all the information has to be within that page limit.

Where do you start? Look up previous research on your topic to provide a context for the proposed research. In other words, provide enough background information so that it is clear to the reader what your study will address. For instance, even falling in love is a very large topic. What are some examples of research problems that have been investigated in this area? Why have other researchers felt that this is an important social phenomenon to study? Are there any areas that previous researchers believe warrant further investigation?

The same principle applies to the theoretical framework. What existing theories can potentially provide an explanation for your research problem? Provide an overview of the theory and draw connections to the research topic and problem. The gaps in knowledge uncovered in the literature review and the theoretical propositions inform the development of the research questions.

Research Questions and Design

The backbone of the proposal is the research questions. In our example, the research question could be "What are the stages of falling in love?" or "What factors affect the likelihood of falling in love?" This stage is always challenging with qualitative research proposals because of the iterative and recursive research process. However, all qualitative projects have a central research question, such as "How do people know they are in love?"

A quantitative research design can involve testing whether a hypothesis is true or false. Remember, a hypothesis is a causal statement that posits a relationship between two variables and how that relationship works. Back to our example: our hypothesis could be that the longer two people date each other, the more likely they are to get married. The two concepts are time and falling in love. The variables are length of time in days and relationship status. Identify which is the independent variable (X), being the cause, and the dependent variable (Y), which is the effect. A change in X causes a specific change in Y.

Once you have stated the research questions and hypotheses, identify the research design. Is this a qualitative, quantitative, or mixed methods research study? If it is an experiment, evaluation research, or mixed methods, discuss the type or model being used. With all methodological decisions, explain why this approach is the most appropriate for addressing the research questions.

Measurement

Create a nominal definition for all the concepts under investigation (conceptualization) or sensitizing concepts in qualitative research. For example, a nominal definition of love could be a tender, passionate affection for another person. This description is not operationalized because the dictionary-style definition includes three additional concepts—tender, passionate, and affection.

Create an operational definition for each concept (operationalization). For example, an indicator of affection could be hugging. At this stage, you may find it helpful to use concrete examples, such as survey or interview questions that are included in their entirety in an appendix.

Sampling and Data Collection

Based on your research questions and approach adopted in the proposed study, how will you go about finding the right people to participate in the study? You will need to address the following questions:

- Which probability or nonprobability sampling technique will you adopt? Why is this one appropriate in comparison to the other alternatives?
- What constitutes the population for your study? As a result of defining the population in this way, state the generalizability of the findings.
- Given your research question, are you targeting certain types of people in the population? For instance, will your sampling elements be adults (individuals over the age of 18)? Those involved in certain types of relationships (e.g. married persons)? Why?
- What is your projected sample size?
- Do you anticipate any sampling problems that could affect the extent of sampling error?

Whether the proposed research is quantitative, qualitative, or mixed methods, discuss the data collection methods next. How will you collect each type of data? Why is this method the most appropriate way to collect the data needed to address the research questions?

Additional Methods Information

A research proposal also discusses any ethical considerations that may be of concern for the project, including how the risks will be minimized. There should be enough detail for you to use this section for an ethics application. Refer to the ethics appendix if you are required to provide an example of an informed consent form. Determine if there are any risks to the study participants. What steps are you going to take to minimize these potential risks? Is informed consent possible? If you propose covert research, you need a strong rationale to justify why the benefits outweigh the risks associated with non-disclosure. Don't forget to point out the benefits to participants, knowledge, and society.

Lastly, you are often expected to include a timeline that stipulates the expected time required to complete each stage in the research process. The timeline includes proposal acceptance, ethics clearance, data collection, analysis, and writing up the results. If you are requesting funding, provide a budget with the projected use of funds and a rationale for the expenses in an appendix.

Written Reports

Sometimes it is easier to figure out what goes into a proposal by taking a closer look at what appears in the final product once the research is complete. Naturally, this structure doesn't work for all the different ways that research findings are disseminated. For instance, you would include an abstract for an academic audience but an executive summary for practitioners. However, this general overview will help you whether you're writing or reading research results.

Front Matter

As tempting as it may be to come up with a clever, catchy title, it's probably not a good idea. The title needs to give the reader enough information to know the research topic and the issue being addressed. Abstracts are typically between 100 to 200 words and summarize the research project. They usually include the purpose, rationale, objective, research questions, design, data source, analytical technique(s), main findings, and implications. If the proposal is for a practitioner or government audience, the executive summary also includes a bulleted list of the major findings and the resulting recommendations.

I typically leave writing the introduction until I have completed the rest of the paper. It is difficult to introduce something that hasn't been written yet. The saying "You don't have a second chance to make a first impression" applies here. In the introduction, your job is to grab the reader's attention strategically. Interest is piqued when what we believe to be true is challenged, when information suggests a new way of thinking about the problem, or when we gain knowledge on something we know little about (Palys & Atchison, 2014, pp. 380–381). How do you create interest strategically? If findings challenge our thinking, the introduction makes this clear. In real life, we may avoid controversy, but we are attracted to it intellectually. You will see arguments such as "Some people think X is true and others do not. This study will investigate this contradiction." Overall, provide the reader with a statement on what we know, the pervasiveness of the issue, the attention it has received, and the reasons that knowing more about it is important. Within this larger context, present the problem and a road map to the rest of the paper.

Literature Review

An effective literature review goes beyond citing literature relevant to the study and research questions. It involves synthesizing information to identify our existing knowledge, unanswered questions, disagreements, and the ways this study contributes by addressing a particular gap in our knowledge. The common mistake is to write a shopping list summarizing one study after another instead of synthesizing and interpreting by theme. Approaching the literature review thematically will help you draw connections, determine our state of knowledge, and (later in the discussion section) demonstrate how your findings build on prior research. In essence, a systematic literature has six general characteristics (Boote & Beile, 2005):

1. The research problem is situated in the larger context.
2. It is clear why these prior research studies are included in the review and why others were excluded. There is either a statement of coverage in relation to the research questions or the scope is established in the introduction.
3. The state of knowledge on the research problem is examined so that a statement can be made about what we do and don't know about the problem or issue. This sets the stage for answering why the research is needed (the "so what" question).
4. A history of the topic is provided to contextualize the current research study.
5. The review identifies ambiguous definitions and contradictory findings.
6. The results from prior research are synthesized to offer new perspectives and demonstrate how the proposed research will address this gap in our knowledge.

Next, the methods section provides all the information that would be included in a proposal. The difference is that, instead of saying you *will* collect the data, you describe how the data *were* collected. The findings present the results from your data analysis in an order that is logical substantively in quantitative research and thematically in qualitative research.

Discussion and Conclusions

Think about an article as being structured in the shape of an hourglass. The introduction is broad, the literature review goes from general to specific, the methods and findings are specific, the discussion moves to more general with linkages between the findings to the research questions, and the conclusions draw connections to the larger context. In the discussion, the first order of business is to summarize the findings in relation to the research questions. Do the findings support or depart from past research? Why might this be the case? The discussion is followed by the conclusion, which makes broader statements on the implications of the findings, study strengths and limitations, and areas for future research.

You may see limitations as the skeleton in the closet, but don't fear putting them into the universe. Every study has limitations. They don't make your research any less of a contribution to our knowledge base. Limitations help us understand the context in which the findings should be interpreted. By critically thinking about the limitations, you can draw better conclusions and make more informed recommendations for future research. Ask yourself: If you could do this all over again, what would you do differently? Odds are that the changes you have in mind reflect limitations of the current study.

Words to Maintain Sanity

Some of the advice in this section may seem obvious, but it's worth repeating. When we are in the midst of a task, we can sometimes lose sight of where we are trying to go. Here are some ideas on how to get from point A to point B with as few hiccups as possible along the way.

If procrastination has become your constant companion, consider creating a writing ritual. Do you have favourite paper or a favourite pen? Do you work best in a particular room or time of day? Set yourself up for success. Also consider scheduling writing into your daily routine. Believe it or not, you are much more productive if you write every day than when you go on writing marathons or pull all-nighters.

Regardless of the type of report, your goal is to tell a story. What does the reader need to know in order to understand the research study and findings? Try stating your research problem in the form of a question or in a declarative statement (e.g. "The purpose of this research is . . . "). Know your story. If you were in an elevator and someone asked you what your research is about, could you convey the purpose and main findings in a minute or less? Being able to do so can go a long way to helping you organize how to write your story.

Start writing early. Begin with free-flow writing. In other words, don't worry about paragraphs, spelling, or grammar. Just aim to get your ideas onto paper. This process can help you get past that "white screen" staring at you. When you start to turn these early drafts into a paper, avoid jargon. Be succinct because long and wordy doesn't equal quality.

Consider your audience. Writing for an academic audience is much different than writing for practitioners. The former can use technical terms, whereas the latter should be written with clear and accessible language. Course papers are assigned for different reasons and journal articles are on topics investigated using a variety of methods. For course papers, include a thesis statement, be sure to answer the research question, demonstrate a grasp of the substantive material, define key terms, and use headings and subheadings. In addition to including an executive summary in practitioner and government reports, keep tables and graphs simple and present findings in the context of practical examples.

A great way to organize your thinking about the study and research findings is to use an outline. Sections in an outline will likely turn into headings and subheadings in your paper, which guide your writing and the reader's focus. Outlines can also help you present a cogent argument by grouping information into a logical order by related ideas. Different levels in the outline discern the central ideas from supporting information, thereby improving the flow of your argumentation. It's okay if you have gaps in the outline at first. As you become more immersed in the material and start writing, you will move things around and the outline will become more specific and complete.

When you have a draft, edit, edit, and—when you think you are done—edit again. Revisions involve inserting new information, moving blocks of text, and strengthening the links between ideas, arguments, and evidence. Editing involves making each sentence and paragraph as correct as possible by checking spelling, grammar, and sentence structure; changing sentences from passive to active voice; and having only one idea discussed in a paragraph. A paragraph should never be longer than one page. I revise and edit a journal article draft easily over 15 times before I submit it for publication consideration. I'm also a paper person and find that using a hard copy makes the process easier. It's much like a clean slate; I can see what changes I have made each time. This possibility can be important if you need to backtrack. You have a record of every change you've made. Writing is not an event but a process and a journey.

The final suggestion is to create a reverse outline during the editing process. Once the first draft is written, go through the paper and write out the headings, subheadings, and each idea as it's introduced. Then compare this outline with the original one. You draft might make more substantive sense than your original outline, but the opposite can also be true. The reverse outline can help you see when you are making leaps in logic and where you need to make changes to strengthen your argument.

Websites of Interest

"A Quick and Dirty Guideline to Academic Essay Writing Success"

http://elab.athabascau.ca/workshop/essay-writing-tips

Written by Kirsten C. Uszkalo, this humorous yet extremely informative review of writing an essay takes you from the thesis statement and literature review to general advice, such as "Write well in advance. Everything sounds brilliant at 2 am."

"Some General Advice on Academic Essay Writing"

www.writing.utoronto.ca/advice/general/general-advice

C.A. Silber's article provides information on thesis statements, organization, and the writing process for course-based essays.

"This Itch of Writing: Twenty Top Tips for Academic Writing"

http://emmadarwin.typepad.com/thisitchofwriting/2013/05/twenty-top-tips-for-academic-writing.html

Whether you are writing a research proposal or course essay, academic writing can be an alienating and bewildering experience. Emma Darwin has twenty tips to help with structure, content, style, and grammar.

Additional Resources

Jewell, C. *Academic Integrity and Plagiarism.* Retrieved from www.youtube.com/watch?v=sWrFrB9EsAo

Presented by Christine Jewell, this narrated PowerPoint presentation takes you through the different types of plagiarism and, most important, provides you with techniques to avoid committing this type of academic misconduct.

Academic Writing Help Centre. (2007). *Writing a Thesis Proposal: A Systems Approach.* Retrieved from http://sass.uottawa.ca/sites /sass.uottawa.ca/files/thesis.pdf

This article presents a framework for writing a thesis proposal, with advice on research questions, rationale, literature review, theoretical framework, and methodology sections.

Becker, H.S. (2007). *Writing for Social Scientists: How to Start and Finish Your Thesis, Book, or Article.* Chicago: University of Chicago Press.

This book is a highly recommended read that will tell you as much about yourself as a writer as it will the mechanics of putting words to paper.

Reading and Interpreting Published Research

"The measure of greatness in a scientific idea is the extent to which it stimulates thought and opens up new lines of research." Paul A.M. Dirac

Introduction

When you read published research, think of yourself as a detective on a case. Providing that the article is logical in its presentation of the material, your job is to extract the information that tells you how and what was found, along with the significance, implications, and areas of future research. This appendix provides three methods for reading and interpreting research articles and books. First are some suggestions on what order to read the sections of an article, what to record in your notes, and how to avoid plagiarism. Second are questions you can ask yourself while reading an article; these are organized by article sections. Finally, additional questions are listed by type of research design and method.

Where Do I Start Reading?

There is no right or wrong way to read a journal article. The more you read, the more you will discover what works best for you. It may be unnerving, but there are no hard and fast rules. With that said, what follows is one way to start digesting and evaluating published research. Included at the end of the appendix are several sources that provide greater detail or offer alternatives that may work better with your learning style.

Step one is a given. You start by reading the title and abstract. As you conduct your search of the literature, this is the best way to initially screen an article and decide whether it is relevant for your research purposes. A well-written abstract also gives you a framework for reading the rest of the article. Then read the introduction to get a better picture of the larger context, purpose, and research questions. The next stop is the methods section. You want to have a better understanding of how the research problem was investigated to provide a framework for interpreting the findings. Scan the article, taking note of headings and subheadings; if you see something interesting, stop and read that portion. Only after these initial steps are complete do you read the article in detail from beginning to end. As you read and take notes, you may see citations in the literature review and discussion sections as potential sources. You can pursue these leads in the same way a detective would explore alternative explanations or new evidence.

What you record in your notes largely depends on what works best for you. This part of the process may take some experimentation, as your note-taking will differ from the style you use when reading a course textbook or listening to a lecture. The goal is to take notes not only on the specific details but also in a way that you can discern the forest from the trees. What is the study's overall conclusion? What is the significance of the findings? And of equal importance, how does this article compare and fit into what you have learned from other sources? In respect to specifics, make note of the research questions, major points from the literature review, pertinent methodological details that affect how data are interpreted, concepts, key findings, overall conclusion, and any areas for future research. Once you've completed your notes, write a paragraph that summarizes the entire article in your own words.

Avoiding plagiarism is a paramount concern, and it starts with the note-taking process. Develop a system that clearly indicates what information is taken from the article and what is your original work. For example, you should include the page numbers with any material taken verbatim from the article so that there is no question that they are not your words. You could also put any ideas you paraphrase in italics and your thoughts and interpretations in square brackets. Sometimes it is helpful to have separate documents for themes that start to develop across articles. You would cut and paste relevant quotations and paraphrased material from the article summary into these thematic documents, being sure to document the source. If you are paper person, you could use index cards, but that is a labour-intensive approach.

Questions by Article Section

This section is by no means exhaustive, but it provides a guide to interpreting the results, evaluating the findings, and revealing potential problems. The questions may not apply to every single article. However, you can also ask yourself these questions when writing a research proposal or a study's results. The chapters that cover the material referred to in each subsection are indicated in parentheses.

Introduction (Chapters 1 and 2)

- Are the research purpose, objective, and problem clear?
- What is the larger context for this problem? Can you identify why answering the research questions is important?
- What is the potential significance of the findings? In other words, has the "so what" question been addressed?
- Are the research questions provided?

Literature Review (Chapter 2)

- Does the type of literature review (e.g. chronological, thematic) make sense for this study?
- Is the research problem clearly defined?
- Is the research included in the review related to the research questions?
- Does the researcher(s) critically evaluate the literature and synthesize the findings categorically? Are contradictory findings discussed?

- Are connections made between prior research and theoretical propositions?
- Are you able to identify the gaps in knowledge (what we do and do not know) about this research problem?
- Is it clear how the literature and theory informed the research questions?

Research Design (Chapter 2)

- What is the type of research (exploratory, descriptive, explanatory, or a combination)? Is it consistent with the research questions?
- Is the study cross-sectional or longitudinal?
- Is the research design (quantitative, qualitative, mixed, experimental, evaluation) appropriate for achieving the research objective?
- Are the data sources adequately described so that you can determine their appropriateness?
- Do the data collection methods chosen provide the data required to address the research questions?
- Are reasons provided for methodological decisions?

Measurement (Chapter 3), Sampling (Chapter 4), and Ethics (All Chapters)

- Are nominal and operational definitions or sensitizing concepts adequately defined?
- Are the measures reliable and valid? What is really being measured and will it provide the data needed to address the research question?
- Are the sampling techniques used appropriately for the research design (e.g. probability sampling in quantitative research)?
- What population does the researcher want to draw conclusions about? Will this be possible with the sample?
- Is the sample size discussed?
- Are the ethical considerations recognized? Were appropriate steps taken to minimize risks and maximize benefits to participants? (Note: Not all articles will provide this information.)

Data Analysis and Findings (Chapters 9 and 10)

- Are the article's analytical techniques capable of providing answers to the research questions?
- To the best of your knowledge, are the findings (e.g. contingency table, statistical significance) interpreted correctly?
- Is there evidence of substantive significance? Recall that even unreliable, invalid, and ambiguous numbers can be statistically significant with a large enough sample.
- Are exemplars and thick description used to establish trustworthiness?
- Does the researcher refer back to the research purpose, research question(s), or hypotheses?

Discussion and Conclusion

- Are the findings summarized by the research question? Unfortunately, the question answered in the discussion is not always the same as the research question posed in the introduction or literature review.
- Does the researcher go beyond the findings when making inferences, drawing conclusions, or stating implications? In other words, are the statements supported by the data presented in the findings section?
- Does the research add to, modify, replicate, or contradict prior research findings discussed in the literature review?
- How do the findings add to our knowledge of the research problem? What are the implications? Has that "so what" question been addressed?
- Are the limitations and areas for future research discussed in light of the research design and findings?

Questions by Method

The following questions can be used in conjunction with those in the previous section. Please note that they are general and do not go into specifics. For example, in an experimental design, you want to check for any problems with internal validity. You can then refer to your notes (e.g. for the different threats to validity, such as history or maturation).

Experiments (Chapter 5)

- Is the type of experimental design appropriate for addressing the research questions?
- What is the experimental stimulus (independent variable) and the outcome (dependent variable)?
- How are the research subjects assigned to the control and experimental groups (randomization, matching)? Are the groups comparable?
- Are the conditions the same for all groups?
- Are there any problems of internal and external validity?
- Are there any ethical concerns about the treatment or its administration? If deception is used to some degree, is it justifiable?

Survey and Interview Research (Chapter 6)

- Are there any problems with question wording, measurement of concepts, or question order?
- Are closed-ended questions free of errors (e.g. double-barrelled, exhaustive, mutually exclusive)?
- Are open-ended questions thematically organized?
- Did the researcher guard against his or her own bias creeping in during the coding of qualitative data?
- Is there a potential for a social desirability bias?
- Are steps taken to avoid pitfalls, such as a response set bias?
- Are risks to participants considered, especially for sensitive topics and vulnerable populations?

Field Research (Chapter 7)

- What are the main sensitizing concepts in the study?

- Is sufficient information on the study site and participants provided?
- How was access secured and maintained?
- Are the findings presented using thick description? Did the researcher allow the data to speak?
- Is there evidence of reflexivity?
- To what degree did the researcher participate in the social setting? Are there potential reactivity effects?
- How was access achieved and maintained?
- Were ethical considerations discussed and recognized when interpreting the findings?
- Are the criteria for dependability, credibility, and trustworthiness met?

Secondary Data (Chapter 8)

- What are the weaknesses in the original data collection methods?
- What was the research purpose of the original study? What is the substantive connection to the current study?
- Does the dataset have the key variables needed to address the research questions? If not, how valid is the proxy operationalization?

Evaluation Research (Chapter 11)

- Is the type of evaluation research used appropriate for achieving the research objective?
- To what extent are the stakeholders involved in the research process? Does this involvement impact the research process in a positive or negative way?
- What is the intervention and is it measured consistently with the type of evaluation research?
- How is success defined? Are the outcomes being assessed associated with immediate, short-term, intermediate, or long-term program objectives?
- Who paid for the research? Are there any ethical or political considerations that could have affected the findings or interpretations?

Websites of Interest

"Critically Reading Journal Articles"

http://faculty.ksu.edu.sa/77632/Documents/CriticallyReadingJournal%20Articles%201.pdf
This article offers tips for reading journal articles, such as selective reading techniques and the types of information to write notes on from each section.

"How to Read Academic Research"

www.youtube.com/watch?v=XvnUojPCftk
Presented by Russell James, this video uses everyday and research examples to give a framework for reading research articles. Although the PowerPoint is narrated quickly, there are excellent tips highlighted on the slides.

"How to Read and Understand a Scientific Paper: A Guide for Non-Scientists"

http://violentmetaphors.com/2013/08/25/how-to-read-and-understand-a-scientific-paper-2/
This blog posting provides information on what to do before you begin reading, what specific questions to ask yourself when reading each section, and how to process the information when you are finished reading and taking notes.

"How to Read a Paper"

http://blizzard.cs.uwaterloo.ca/keshav/home/Papers/data/07/paper-reading.pdf
In this article, Keshav provides an alternative framework—a three-pass approach—for reading published research: gain a general idea, grasp the content, and understand in-depth by focusing on the details.

Additional Resources

Ho Shon, P.C. (2012). *How to Read Journal Articles in the Social Sciences: A Very Practical Guide for Students*. Sage Study Skills. Thousand Oaks, CA: Sage.

In this easy-to-understand study guide, Chapters 4 ("Should I Even Read This?—Abstract, Introduction, Methods") and 5 ("So What?—Literature Review, Results, Conclusion") are particularly relevant and useful.

Plano Clark, V.L., & Creswell, J.W. (2014). *Understanding Research: A Consumer's Guide* (2nd ed.). Upper Saddle River, NJ: Pearson.

This step-by-step, user-friendly guide offers strategies to read, interpret, and evaluate the quality of published research.

Random Number Table

	A	B	C	D	E	F	G	H
1	98536	18350	75552	14193	22999	30504	54278	32442
2	22855	81245	21254	52843	98476	52451	21208	11500
3	30620	98460	30664	50020	53234	09310	86698	51382
4	29418	14648	60123	10638	54752	06715	48374	15231
5	34365	86960	68408	47418	63630	24684	74926	49597
6	87204	27767	66059	49906	96513	20356	02986	32620
7	64592	04630	50756	84948	03518	90054	29426	03065
8	42921	17490	02810	06512	16899	09275	62167	13398
9	61082	17500	30097	66561	91014	41018	38789	81438
10	15164	79845	23140	69026	34795	23853	86247	58609
11	71626	40148	16812	02196	92305	97819	62565	78249
12	90856	46411	56788	16860	69104	21628	64552	43812
13	11553	11366	20202	22552	44513	74243	21381	23697
14	66901	27433	62300	51456	41287	04791	82419	44043
15	86590	88282	35360	52335	14802	21015	78696	94879
16	65010	07986	55365	88159	02319	12383	84931	17740
17	37316	70776	24707	26677	74058	11086	46257	88137
18	95910	27319	89702	53268	02471	53829	22965	16170
19	93157	44767	07718	58613	32054	36396	74068	39268
20	97852	62430	28811	57142	95215	10370	86183	06513
21	15782	15513	21563	13552	13236	00145	40685	70189

	A	B	C	D	E	F	G	H
22	74729	69176	33960	25177	72645	25091	94565	68968
23	91774	39309	44038	28556	47728	07584	12471	76810
24	42986	45122	60959	13771	74915	53611	98778	57134
25	03874	58254	49827	36765	99171	44921	15455	92732
26	71390	47262	49342	70804	50023	26658	68698	03180
27	29591	23009	98260	73773	96945	65030	48708	65155
28	21436	98521	80197	73670	85307	59294	36371	39890
29	52183	07261	19421	94115	75708	87113	21986	51748
30	21390	34632	15480	86239	90564	92901	30440	97173
31	73221	35626	51600	74364	06364	83349	69522	18216
32	45760	70595	29784	46344	89274	93201	74990	80782
33	01405	09496	49854	06240	52406	73365	24256	09901
34	73667	17838	81906	89901	72169	38491	68082	19241
35	59595	39594	83990	49081	17175	26542	96330	40034
36	38757	23503	71959	20001	58900	40704	25093	48759
37	06039	38174	08676	33642	17591	35550	67146	76540
38	86723	65722	88017	50878	90691	66886	46774	40270
39	97603	55170	99433	57456	02672	69023	73605	41137
40	13342	06199	27095	41872	96133	05445	71445	74980
41	63032	27444	06403	26868	31918	43264	81410	44981
42	66662	59097	18599	77237	07208	20244	91995	63490
43	47148	23784	06727	66841	56563	33319	42485	89510
44	45957	58469	45063	50851	94320	21621	69549	15769
45	98668	26237	49290	82089	82697	33761	74811	34733
46	90436	06618	76544	00936	89582	32117	54014	82928
47	00386	23189	94099	35522	07851	32087	81144	62583
48	08391	61862	09223	75053	35874	42623	34527	13820
49	50115	41728	67440	74075	53435	32416	25032	46438
50	82435	97208	74920	65153	91664	97664	94007	02696
51	93273	55293	42046	18334	30453	67180	16749	23962
52	16668	16956	85115	83915	44361	63000	24007	27913
53	35718	93502	38283	03932	88771	84014	83899	40296
54	00988	39200	80764	11198	76210	33105	33821	45621
55	83262	04445	01224	59388	09298	65158	63353	27738
56	66990	00607	90415	32993	30408	80222	10255	51183
57	97113	60951	25617	40839	95832	08710	50643	17448
58	48101	98779	58737	32889	00007	07638	97463	58911

(Continued)

	A	B	C	D	E	F	G	H
59	43354	01373	51261	20109	52748	11237	26617	22703
60	27563	52866	98420	68788	82821	40056	47583	87797
61	63325	27792	46328	08871	42622	67804	71896	73512
62	59269	06918	49093	06006	96463	05052	02901	89537
63	46478	26649	61801	61665	22511	38559	81913	85981
64	73647	65434	16624	67357	50727	64009	57451	46835
65	45540	21804	80948	19689	31610	61972	22387	94417
66	34761	15649	20269	35663	64460	99524	07574	91790
67	94899	60543	30673	64680	70760	04724	99513	50106
68	20001	93516	11939	73489	71661	29614	02967	35020
69	50408	13046	63231	68286	96020	95294	74504	84997
70	38607	11376	60081	67759	06558	00845	95233	74654
71	83776	46077	44561	52981	25791	21049	79049	45695
72	37506	58412	09053	38462	36190	43694	73513	37689
73	73517	19782	15662	51229	79451	16899	35985	67674
74	12710	16610	26803	99998	25891	53779	94881	13778
75	97900	70672	24527	31459	59432	61799	66516	19786
76	60999	51394	35670	65393	88348	15667	97301	32511
77	73463	72204	15840	59619	00115	40202	44697	36856
78	21960	43109	03787	91329	18907	90653	20160	64114
79	91274	48586	24643	55194	94163	55027	31716	97697
80	17920	63895	50531	24999	82072	67274	01291	73295
81	03320	33370	38516	72900	95159	11456	63447	62304
82	91753	69676	54762	21844	71803	38692	27144	76781
83	66479	11388	34073	39680	55968	06115	99951	72133
84	50052	23218	78021	27700	73547	90086	18697	93052
85	59784	48630	10851	09592	82485	07563	50335	05786
86	68075	88159	72065	21273	78824	06086	90761	52823
87	64297	98454	12698	26294	25760	55207	67289	53481
88	50944	89169	98877	57784	82584	13642	11017	29269
89	83868	76446	02383	43957	61727	10316	40753	22859
90	30658	28626	74085	81841	91493	43916	62103	15899

Sources of Secondary Data in Social Science Research

Sources of secondary data are increasingly available online and are downloadable in file formats accepted by common statistical analysis programs. This appendix is not a comprehensive list for all sources of secondary data. However, it should give you a better idea of the possibilities and of where to start looking for a dataset online, in research data centres, or via university libraries. Finally, all these websites provide the information you need to determine if a particular secondary dataset is appropriate for addressing your research questions.

General International Sources of Data

Organisation for Economic Co-operation and Development (OECD): Data Lab

www.oecd.org/statistics/

This webpage is an excellent source of statistical data on a variety of social science topics, including child poverty, substance abuse, cost of living, and the experience and fear of crime.

United Nations

General: www.un.org/english/
Database Search Engine: http://data.un.org

This website contains links to United Nations data and other international publications.

United States Census Bureau: International Programs

www.census.gov/population/international/data/idb/informationGateway.php

This website provides links to demographic indicators and population trends for 229 countries around the world.

Secondary Data Depositories

Council of European Social Sciences Data Archives (CESSDA)

www.cessda.org

This European version of ICPSR contains over 25,000 secondary datasets.

Inter-University Consortium for Political and Social Research (ICPSR)

www.icpsr.umich.edu/index.html

The ICPSR is the largest depository for academic, government, and international datasets available for secondary analysis. All substantive topics are represented and the data are downloadable free of charge.

Statistics Canada

www.statcan.gc.ca/start-debut-eng.html

Statistics Canada is the federal government organization that uses national or global samples to collect data on social and economic issues. From this site, you can access *The Daily* and browse datasets by subject.

Historical Data Sources

CBC Digital Archives

http://archives.cbc.ca

This archive contains over 13,000 video, film, and radio clips in English and French.

Library and Archives Canada

www.collectionscanada.gc.ca/index-e.html

Featured in the Methods in Action box in Chapter 8, Library and Archives Canada has hundreds of thousands of documents, pictures, maps, and other historical cultural data available for viewing and analysis online or at the archives.

Online Newspaper Archives

http://en.wikipedia.org/wiki/Wikipedia:List_of_online_newspaper_archives

This webpage lists all newspapers published in 74 countries, including all provinces and territories in Canada. Once you select a newspaper, you can conduct an online search of historical articles scanned from microfilm and downloadable for free.

Crime- and Justice-Specific Depositories

National Archive of Criminal Justice Data (NACJD)

www.icpsr.umich.edu/NACJD/archive.html
A division of ICPSR, this archive contains only downloadable datasets on virtually every criminological and criminal justice topic.

Statistics Canada: Crime and Justice

www5.statcan.gc.ca/subject-sujet/theme-theme.action?pid=2693&lang=eng&more=0&HPA
This website contains links to datasets and publications on the nature and extent of crime as well as the administration of justice.

United Nations Survey on Crime Trends and the Operations of Criminal Justice Systems (UN-CTS)

www.unodc.org/unodc/en/data-and-analysis/United-Nations-Surveys-on-Crime-Trends-and-the-Operations-of-Criminal-Justice-Systems.html
This website provides access to surveys and other sources of international crime statistics on topics such as drug trafficking, organized crime, and responses to crime.

Individual Crime and Criminal Justice Surveys

General Social Survey (GSS)

www5.statcan.gc.ca/bsolc/olc-cel/olc-cel?catno=89F0115XWE&lang=eng
www.statcan.gc.ca/pub/89f0115x/89f0115x2009001-eng.htm
Until 2012, Statistics Canada collected GSS data annually. Each survey classifies topics by demographic characteristics of age, sex, education, and income, with the same questions repeated over time in the areas of personal risk, family and friends, substance use, and victimization.

International Crime Victimization Survey (ICVS)

www.statcan.gc.ca/pub/85-002-x/2008010/article/10745-eng.htm
www.icpsr.umich.edu/icpsrweb/ICPSR/series/175
The first wave of data for this survey was collected in 1989. The fourth wave collected data from 47 countries, including Canada.

International Youth Survey (IYS)

www23.statcan.gc.ca/imdb/p2SV.pl?Function=getSurvey&SDDS=5117&Item_Id=22726
This survey is Canada's contribution to the International Self-Report Delinquency Study (ISRD). Data from youth in grades 7 to 9 are collected in over 30 European countries, the United States, and Canada.

National Longitudinal Study of Adolescent Health (ADD Health)

www.cpc.unc.edu/projects/addhealth

This longitudinal survey collects data on social, economic, psychological, and physical well-being from youths in grades 7 to 12. It is commonly used in crime and justice research to investigate topics such as risk factors (e.g. genetic, family, peers), criminal careers, and the propensity to commit certain types of crime.

Glossary

acceptable incompetent a field role in which a researcher learns more about the setting by portraying himself or herself as being less knowledgeable than is truly the case; can be used in observer as participant and participant as observer roles.

accretion the addition of an object or substance to a setting once an individual leaves.

agency records records created by a criminal justice agency as part of normal operations.

alternative hypothesis an empirically testable statement that specifies the relationship expected between two variables.

analysis of variance (ANOVA) a statistical technique that uses a continuous dependent variable to investigate whether the means of two or more groups are different from one another.

analytic comparison the development of theoretical ideas, using the methods of agreement and difference, based on patterns in existing theories when compared to alternative explanations in a particular social context.

analytical notes a researcher's notes on ideas and themes that develop when reviewing data.

analytical triangulation a research strategy that analyzes data in more than one way, using quantitative and qualitative techniques.

analytic induction an iterative process in which hypotheses develop early in the data analysis process and subsequent evidence is compared to either support or refute themes and relationships between concepts.

annotation a type of memo associated with a particular text segment rather than a larger concept.

anonymity the guarantee that no one, not even the researcher, can link the study's data to the identity of a research subject.

applied research research that aims to address an identified concern or to solve a specific problem.

archival data existing records that contain information on the past; usually stored in libraries and depositories.

argot shared terminology, which signals group membership.

attribute a representation of a variable's categories or numerical values.

axial coding analytical processes that combine two or more codes to form thematic categories and relationships across codes; categories are identified and specified.

bar chart a visual depiction using bars to represent the categories of nominal or ordinal variable frequency distributions.

basic research research that attempts to advance knowledge and theoretical understanding of a particular social phenomenon; the intent of the research and the results are not explicitly meant to address a concern or to solve a problem.

before-and-after design a quasi-experiment design that measures the dependent variable several times before and after the intervention for intact groups.

bivariate analysis a statistical analysis of two variables that assesses the empirical relationship.

bivariate regression a statistical analysis used to assess the relationship between one independent (predictor) and one dependent (criterion) variable.

box-and-whisker plot (or boxplot) a graphical representation of a distribution's shape, central tendency, and dispersion; based on the interquartile range.

categorical variable (or discrete variable) a variable that can adopt a value of two or more fixed categories.

causal time order a threat to internal validity involving the violation of the temporal order.

Central Limit Theorem a theory stating that, with an infinite number of samples from a population, the sampling distribution will be normally distributed around the population average for that characteristic.

chi-square a test of statistical significance determining the degree of confidence that an association between two categorical variables did not occur by chance (i.e. the null hypothesis can be rejected).

chronological review a literature review that presents theory and prior research on a subject in order of chronological time.

close-ended question a survey question in which respondents select an answer from a pre-defined list of options.

clusters naturally occurring groups in a population, such as schools, neighbourhood blocks, or police agencies.

cluster sampling a sampling technique that selects groups from the target populations (clusters) and then randomly selects members within each group to create a sample.

codebook a document outlining the structure, layout, and content of a data file; used by researchers for data entry and analysis.

coding a systematic process of categorizing groups of text segments together and assigning a term or phrase to summarize that topic, event, or person.

coding system a classification system or set of rules to code words, phrases, symbols, sounds, or images.

coefficient of determination (r^2) a statistic summarizing the extent to which variation in the dependent variable can be explained by changes in one or more independent variables.

cohort study longitudinal research in which data are collected at different points in time from individuals who belong to a particular group or category. ·

compensation a threat to internal validity that occurs when researchers compensate control group members for being deprived of the treatment.

compensatory rivalry a threat to internal validity that involves control group members trying to perform as well as or better than the experimental group.

complementarity the use of quantitative and qualitative methods with non-overlapping weaknesses in the same study to provide a more meaningful and holistic understanding of a social phenomenon through the different types of knowledge created by each data type.

complete observer a field role in which the researcher is an unobtrusive observer (i.e. does not interact with group members in any way).

complete participant a field role that involves the researcher adopting an active role as a full-fledged group member and participants being unaware of his or her researcher status.

concept an abstract, general idea inferred or derived from particular instances or occurrences; describes the general characteristics or the essential features of something.

conceptual definition an explicit, working definition of a concept, resembling a dictionary definition.

concurrent validity a validity test that determines the extent to which the scores from one measure correspond to those of an existing measure.

confidence interval a range of values—including the value of the population parameter—with a specific probability.

confidence level an indication of how confident one is about the accuracy of a sample statistic's estimation of the true population parameter.

confidentiality the guarantee that the identities of a study's subjects are known to the researcher but will not be revealed.

confirmability an assessment of trustworthiness referring to the degree that research findings can be confirmed or corroborated by others.

conflict of interest a situation in which the influence of a secondary interest (e.g. continued funding) affects a person's professional judgment and decision-making about a primary interest (e.g. program success).

confounding variable a variable representing an unmeasured factor that, when it causes a change in the independent and dependent variables, creates a spurious relationship.

constant comparison method a comparison of empirical indicators that describe people, events, and situations to other data for similarities and differences.

constructivism a theoretical worldview that emphasizes how people interpret the social world around them.

construct validity a validity test that finds the extent to which scores on multiple indicators are related to one another as predicted by theory.

content analysis the systematic analysis of communication found in text, audio, video, or images.

content validity a validity test in which a knowledgeable person's judgment validates a measure by concluding that it covers the range of the concept.

contextual review a systematic summary, synthesis, and comparison of theory and research to provide the rationale for new research.

contingency question a question that respondents answer solely on the basis of their answers to a filter question.

continuous variable a variable that adopts any of a range of values, thereby allowing a researcher to find an intermediate value between any two given numerical scores.

control group in an experiment, the group that is not exposed to the stimulus or intervention (independent variable) and is therefore expected to remain unchanged.

control variable a variable that does not vary but can affect independent and dependent variables.

convenience sampling a sampling technique in which cases are selected because they are convenient, regardless of their characteristics.

convergent parallel design a mixed methods research design in which both data strands are collected and analyzed concurrently and the overall conclusion is based on a comparison of each data strand's findings.

convergent validity a validity test that assesses whether two measures associate in a manner consistent with theoretical predictions.

conversation analysis analysis that examines verbal interchanges to understand the structure of social interaction.

correlation coefficient (or Pearson's product-moment correlation coefficient) a statistic that describes the association between two variables in terms of strength and direction.

cost–benefit evaluation a process that systematically compares the expected monetary benefits or savings from an intervention with its expected costs.

cost-effectiveness evaluation a process that systematically examines the relationship between program costs and outcomes for two or more different interventions with similar desired outcomes.

counterfactual a conceptualization of alternate conditions, factors, or outcomes.

credibility the trustworthiness of interpretations based on the research subjects' perspective.

criterion validity a validity test that compares a measurement's scores to an external, established instrument or criterion.

cross-sectional research a research design in which data are collected at a single point in time.

cross-tabulation a contingency table that displays the frequencies and percentages for specific combinations of at least two categorical variables.

deductive coding an approach to the data in which coding occurs with certain concepts and themes in mind.

deductive reasoning an approach to research that moves from the general to specific by taking an existing idea or theory and applying it to a situation to test whether it is true.

demoralization a threat to internal validity that is a form of attrition caused by control group members feeling deprived.

dependability the consistency of qualitative findings, along with the ability to replicate them, trace their methods, and develop their findings.

dependent variable the effect or outcome of one or more causes whereby their values are altered by a change in an independent variable.

descriptive coding a type of first cycle coding that assigns text segments to a code because they describe the concept or idea.

descriptive research research that creates a picture or profile with words or numbers to answer who, when, where, or how.

descriptive statistics statistics that describe sample characteristics and relationships between variables.

determinism a view that sees all behaviours and events as determined, or caused by, prior events, conditions, and laws.

development a strategy of using one method to inform decisions about research questions, sampling, data collection, and analysis of a second method.

dichotomous variable a type of categorical variable that adopts one of only two possible values.

diffusion a threat to internal validity in which treatment information is passed from the experimental group to the control group.

discourse analysis analysis that examines language to understand communication patterns that occur during social interactions.

discriminant validity a validity test that determines whether two concepts differ from one another as predicted by theory.

disproportionate stratified sampling a sampling technique in which the proportion of each stratum is intentionally different from the proportion in the target population.

distorter variable a third variable that reverses the direction of the relationship between independent and dependent variables.

dominant-less-dominant design a mixed methods research design in which one data strand is dominant and the findings play a larger role when creating an overall conclusion.

double-barrelled question a question that includes two or more ideas, resulting in more than one possible answer.

double negative question a question that includes two negative words, making it difficult to understand.

ecological fallacy overgeneralization of group-level data to describe individual-level processes, behaviour, or attitudes.

elaboration model the model that examines the relationship in each category for two variables by controlling for the effects of one or more control variables (symbolized by Z).

embedded (or nested) mixed methods design a mixed methods research design that has a primary data strand but contains a smaller secondary method for convergence, exploratory, or explanatory reasons.

emic an insider perspective; events and behaviours under investigation are interpreted based on what they mean to the social actors involved.

emotion coding a type of first cycle coding that assigns text segments to a code because they describe the nature, scope, and circumstances of emotions.

empirical generalization a statement based on a pattern or regularity across different empirical observations that is not necessarily occurring in all circumstances.

empirical indicator an exact indication of how a concept is recognized and measured.

epistemology a philosophical concept regarding the nature and criteria of legitimate knowledge based on how we know what we know.

equal probability of selection method (EPSEM) the theory that each element in the sampling frame has a known, equal, and nonzero probability of sample selection.

equivalent status design a mixed methods research design in which each data strand is given equal priority and findings from each create one overall conclusion.

erosion the wearing away or removal of an object once an individual leaves the setting.

ethnocentrism an interpretation of the world based on one's own understanding and not from the participants' perspective.

ethnography a research method that uses the research subjects' perspective to describe a culture and alternate way of life.

ethnomethodology a field research method focusing on how social actors create meaning in everyday life.

etic an outsider perspective; the researcher interprets the events and behaviour under investigation.

evaluability assessment a process that investigates the feasibility of conducting an evaluation and how findings have utility for the stakeholders.

evaluation research research that assesses the consequences (intentional and unintentional) of a policy, practice, or program and the extent to which its particular goals and objectives are met.

evaluation theory a theory about how evaluation research should be conducted in order to be valid.

exhaustive response options that represent every view or experience.

expansion the use of quantitative and qualitative methods in the same study to assess different phenomena.

experiment a research design that isolates, controls, and manipulates an independent variable to measure its effect on the dependent variable.

experimental evaluation design a research design that measures program effectiveness by randomly assigning individuals to a group that receives the intervention or to one or more groups that do not.

experimental group in an experiment, the group exposed to the stimulus or intervention.

experimental mortality (or attrition) a threat to internal validity that occurs when groups differ because the subjects in one are more likely to drop out than those from the other.

explanatory research research conducted to explain why something occurs and to test and refine theory.

explanatory sequential design a sequential mixed methods research design that conducts the study in two stages, with the quantitative data strand first in sequence and the findings used to inform the collection and analysis of qualitative data.

exploratory research research that is directed at little-understood subjects or developing ideas and that refines research questions for future research.

exploratory sequential design a sequential mixed methods research design that conducts the study in two stages, with the qualitative data strand first in sequence and the findings used to inform the collection and analysis of quantitative data.

ex post facto control group a quasi-experimental design in which a researcher creates a comparison group and examines the impact of an intervention but conducts the study after the event has occurred.

face-to-face survey a survey administered by a researcher, who asks respondents questions in person.

face validity a validity test in which a person's judgment validates a measure based on its appearance and appropriateness.

factor analysis a statistical technique used to assess whether a number of indicators tend to group together and are interrelated to form a latent construct.

fence-sitters respondents who choose neutral response options because they do not have a definitive opinion on the topic.

field experiment an experiment conducted in a real-life setting where the researcher controls the administration of the treatment, program, or event.

field relations the logistics, procedures, ethics, and personal dimensions related to informants, gatekeepers, and social actors in the field setting.

field research a research approach that collects data to understand a natural setting in which the behaviour being investigated actually occurs.

field role a role that defines the degree to which a researcher participates in the research setting's activities.

filter question a question that identifies whether a respondent should answer the contingency questions or be directed to a question later in the survey.

first cycle coding the coding cycle stage during which text segments are assigned to descriptive, process, in vivo, and emotion codes.

floaters respondents who choose a response option to a close-ended question even though they are not sure how to answer or what their views are on the issue.

focus group a group of respondents who are interviewed together in order to facilitate discussion.

formative evaluation a type of evaluation research that investigates what is and is not working so that actions can be taken to improve how the program or intervention functions.

frequency distribution a distribution that summarizes nominal and ordinal variables in a table by presenting the total number and percentage for each score in the dataset.

frequency polygon a graph with a continuous line used to present the frequency distribution of interval/ratio variables visually; also known as a line graph.

F-test a test of statistical significance determining the probability that differences between samples for two or more means are the result of sampling error.

full field notes field notes documenting, in as much as detail as possible, what the researcher hears, sees, and does while in the field setting.

fully integrated design a research design in which both data strands mix interactively at all stages in the research process.

gatekeeper a person who has informal or formal authority that influences or controls whether a researcher has access to the research site.

generalizability the process of extending a study's findings and conclusions to the population; occurs after analyzing data from a sample.

going native the situation of a researcher becoming too immersed in the research setting and losing objectivity by adopting the participants' worldview.

grounded theory an emergent theory and method that uses constant comparison and coding procedures to develop a theoretical explanation grounded in the data.

halo effect a predisposition to admire all actions and words of a person, based on the perception of a distinguished quality demonstrated in the past.

Hawthorne effect a threat to external validity in which control group members are aware that they are participating in a study and modify their behaviour accordingly.

histogram a graph that uses vertical bars on the horizontal axis to represent a continuous variable's frequency distribution.

historical comparative research a research approach that compares two or more countries, time periods, or different social groups in one country.

historical review a systematic presentation of key developments in theory and research over time.

historical specificity an examination of past events that are specific in time and space.

history a threat to internal validity in which events external to the experiment affect the posttest scores.

hypothesis an untested statement or proposition that specifies the relationship between two theoretical concepts and their indicators.

hypothetico-deductive method a research method that formulates a testable hypothesis to explain a social phenomenon, deduces predictions from the hypothesis, and, when the prediction is falsified by observable data, rejects the theory and develops a new hypothesis.

ideal type an abstract description of the social phenomenon that is a model used to compare data.

idiographic research research that focuses on understanding behaviours and events within a socio-historic situated approach.

illustrative method a qualitative method that applies an existing theory to a situation, setting, group, or experience and uses the data as theoretical examples.

impact evaluation a process that investigates the long-term effects of participating in a program to make a judgment on whether the intervention goal is achieved.

impression management the act of controlling and manipulating the impression left on others.

independent variable the cause that changes, influences, or predicts the values of a dependent variable.

index the total score of two or more variables; used to create a numerical score measuring a single construct.

indicator a characteristic or change observed to assess a program's progress toward achieving a particular outcome.

inductive coding a type of coding that elaborates on meaning by creating larger conceptual categories.

inductive reasoning an approach to research that moves from the specific to the general by using observations to formulate an idea or theory.

inferential statistics techniques that use sample observations to make inferences about the population.

informant a person in the field setting who the researcher develops a relationship with and gains insider knowledge as a result.

informed consent agreement to participate in a research study after being made aware of the purpose, process, risks and benefits, and intended use of the data.

initiation the use of quantitative and qualitative methods to uncover contradictions, understand why they occur, and develop new perspectives on the social phenomenon.

inputs various financial, organizational, and human resources invested in a program.

instrumentation a threat to internal validity in which different outcomes are caused by variations in the experimental conditions or the measurement of the dependent variable.

intercept the point at which the regression line intercepts with the Y-axis; symbolized as a.

inter-coder reliability the extent of agreement between two or more coders to ensure that the code is assigned in the same way.

interpretivist a worldview that sees meaning as socially constructed, action as intentional, and the goal of research as understanding how people create and maintain meaning about the world around them.

interquartile range (IQR) in a frequency distribution, a measure of dispersion that is the distance between the twenty-fifth and seventy-fifth percentile.

intersubjectivity a term that describes a situation with a meaning or definition held by more than one person and that is constructed through interactions with others.

interval variable a variable that organizes data in order and includes a discernable numerical distance between data points.

intervening variable a variable that explains a causal relation between others by accounting for how an independent variable affects the dependent variable.

interview a conversation with structure and purpose eliciting a person's point of view and the meaning he or she gives to life experiences.

interview schedule a list of interview topics and questions; depending on the type of interview, the question order may change, questions may be skipped if they are no longer relevant or repetitive, and probes may be inserted.

intra-rater reliability the extent to which assigned codes for the same text are equivalent and stable when coded by the same person at two different periods of time.

investigator triangulation a research strategy in which more than one researcher is involved in data collection, analysis, and interpretation to improve the credibility of the findings.

in vivo coding a type of first cycle coding that assigns text segments to a code because they describe a meaningful word or phrase used by a respondent.

jotted notes field notes that are written while still in the field and use cue words to increase memory recall for writing the full field notes.

laboratory experiment an experiment conducted under highly controlled conditions in an artificial environment.

latent content a subjectively derived theme implied from underlying and implicit content in words, phrases, and images.

leading question a question that indirectly encourages respondents to answer in a certain way regardless of their true opinion.

life history an account of a person's life story, told using his or her own words and placed within a specific larger context.

literature review the systematic summary, synthesis, classification, and comparison of scientific knowledge published on a topic.

loaded question a question that assumes the respondent has experienced or done something.

longitudinal research a research design in which data are collected more than once over a period of time.

macro-level a theory and research focus on explaining phenomena that occur in large-scale settings, exist across significant periods of time, or involve the relations and impact of social institutions in society.

manifest content the words, phrases, and images in a communication that illustrate themes with a concrete, explicit meaning.

matching a selection method in which participants are assigned to the experimental and control groups based on similar individual or aggregate characteristics.

matrix question a series of questions with the same response options.

maturation a threat to internal validity that occurs when posttest scores are affected by biological or psychological changes within subjects.

mean a measure of central tendency that provides the average score in a frequency distribution; calculated by adding the scores and then dividing the total by the number of cases.

median a measure of central tendency that is the middle point found in the distribution when the values are listed from lowest to highest.

memo a document that explains coding, defines concepts, brainstorms theories, and records methodological issues that arise during data analysis.

meso-level a theory and research focus on explaining phenomena that link micro- and macro-level social processes at an intermediate level (e.g. organizations, time periods of several months or years).

meta-analysis a systematic analytical strategy used to statistically combine and summarize the results from more than one study.

method of agreement an analytical technique that involves comparing data characteristics that are similar to other cases and results in the same or similar outcome.

method of difference an analytical technique that involves comparing data characteristics that are different for cases that have the same or similar outcome.

methodological exclusivism in contrast to methodological pluralism, the position that there is only one credible method of inquiry to acquire knowledge.

methodological pluralism the view that no method is superior over another, as multiple approaches are legitimate scientific methods of acquiring knowledge.

methodological review a systematic summary of research methods adopted in prior research; used to assess the methods' effects on findings and conclusions.

methodological triangulation a research strategy that uses more than one method to study a research problem, with the objective of overcoming the weaknesses associated with one method by using an additional method.

micro-level a theory and research focus on explaining processes that occur over short periods of time, involve a small-scale setting, or include only a few people in a social interaction or encounter.

middle-range theory a theoretical approach (or set of theoretical statements) that create a bridge between empirical evidence and abstract theories.

mode a measure of central tendency that is the most frequent value found in a frequency distribution.

multimethod research a form of methodological triangulation that uses more than one type of quantitative method or multiple qualitative methods in one research study.

multiphase mixed methods design a mixed methods research design that conducts more than one study within a larger project; the studies share a common research objective.

multiple regression a statistical technique used to assess the ability of two or more independent variables to predict variation in one continuous dependent variable.

multivariate analysis a statistical analysis of three or more variables that assesses the empirical relationship between them.

mutually exclusive response options that do not overlap, allowing respondents to choose only one answer.

narrative analysis an interpretation of stories in terms of organization, development, and function within the context of life experiences as they are described in the social interaction.

natural experiment an experiment conducted in a real-life setting where the researcher does not control the administration of the treatment, program, or event.

needs assessment a process that investigates the nature of the problem to be addressed by the program, the clients who need the program, the level of need for the program, and the requirements for meeting this need.

negative (or left) skew distributions with a long tail on the left side, a large number of high scores, and— from lowest to highest—the mean, median, and mode.

netnography the use of field research methods to study online communities.

node a coding unit used as a label for a concept, category, or theme in computer-assisted qualitative data analysis.

nominal variable a variable that distinguishes categorical names by assigning numbers to them.

nomothetic research research that focuses on establishing universal principles or laws about social reality.

nonequivalent control group a quasi-experiment design that lacks randomization but includes pretests, posttests, and two groups.

nonprobability sampling sampling techniques in which individuals or observations are not randomly selected and do not have the same chance of selection.

null hypothesis an empirical and falsifiable statement that specifies no difference between two variables that are expected to vary in a predictable way.

observer as participant a field role in which the status of researcher is known to group members and the researcher participates minimally in group activities.

one-group pretest–posttest a pre-experimental design that measures one group before and after an independent variable is introduced.

one-shot case study a pre-experimental design that observes one group at one point in time after a treatment is introduced.

ontology a philosophical concept about establishing truth.

open coding the process of identifying and creating a label for ideas and assigning text segments to these codes to develop an initial framework for further analysis.

open-ended question a survey question in which respondents answer the question in their own words.

operational definition a definition that specifies the operations or criteria used to identify and empirically measure a concept.

ordinal variable a variable in which data are organized in rank order with no numerical difference between categories.

outcome evaluation a process that assesses the progress toward achieving the short-term and intermediate outcomes that a program is designed to address.

outcomes the changes, effects, or accomplishments achieved by clients from participating in program activities.

outputs countable events or products derived from program activities.

panel study longitudinal research in which data are collected from the same individuals at different points in time.

participant as observer a field role that involves the group's members knowing the status of researcher and the researcher actively participating in group activities.

participant observation a data collection technique in which researchers immerse themselves in the culture and collect observational data to produce descriptions of everyday life and how it is understood by participants.

participatory action research (PAR) a research design that empowers a community through collaboration at all stages in the research process in order to create change and understand social reality.

periodicity a phenomenon that creates sampling bias when elements in the sampling frame are listed cyclically and the pattern coincides with the sampling interval.

personal notes field notes on the researcher's feelings while in the field and his or her personal reactions to observations.

pie chart a circular graphic that visually represents a variable's frequency distribution, using percentages of the total.

population theoretically, all individuals, groups, or objects that share particular characteristics.

population parameter a characteristic of the population whose value is unknown and is estimated based on findings from the sample.

positive (or right) skew distributions with a long tail on the right side, a large number of low scores, and— from lowest to highest—the mode, median, and mean.

positivism a worldview that asserts that scientific knowledge, which describes and explains observable phenomena, is the only true knowledge.

posttest a test—the same as the pretest—administered after a subject is exposed to a treatment; used to assess any changes in the dependent variable.

pragmatism the position that knowledge is a tool for organizing experience and for merging theory and practice and that scientific inquiry cannot avoid the multiple theoretical foundations, perspectives, and philosophical assumptions if it is to fully understand social phenomena.

predictive validity a validity test that examines the degree to which a measurement instrument can predict a future behaviour or event.

pre-experimental design an exploratory research design that does not control for alternative explanations or use random assignment.

pretest a test administered before a subject is exposed to a treatment; used to collect baseline data on the dependent variable.

primary data original sources and data collected by the researcher.

probability proportionate to size (PPS) a type of cluster sampling in which clusters are chosen proportionately based on their size in the population.

probability sampling random sampling techniques in which each individual or observation has the same chance of being selected.

probe an interview technique used to get respondents to elaborate on their answer.

process coding a type of first cycle coding that assigns text segments to a code because they describe actions and sequences.

process evaluation a process that evaluates the systematic collection of information to document and assesses program operation and whether it functions as intended.

program process the treatment or service provided by the program.

program theory a theory that specifies what needs to be done to accomplish program goals, what (if any) additional anticipated outcomes exist, and how these goals and outcomes are achieved.

proportionate stratified sampling a sampling technique in which each stratum is proportional in size to what exists in the target population.

prospective cohort study a study involving a group of similar individuals who differ only on factors related to the outcome under investigation and who are followed as the program or policy is implemented.

purpose statement a statement outlining a research study's objectives.

purposive sampling a sampling technique in which elements are selected based on the researcher's judgment, knowledge, and substantive criteria.

quasi-experimental design an exploratory research design that does not use random assignment but measures the dependent variable before and after the intervention and gives the researcher some control over the independent variable.

quasi-experimental evaluation design a research design that measures program effectiveness by using comparison groups that are as similar to each other as possible; individuals are not randomly assigned to a group.

quota sampling a sampling technique in which elements are selected based on predetermined characteristics that are proportionately similar in the population.

random assignment (or randomization) a selection method that uses probability sampling techniques to assign participants to experimental and control groups.

random measurement error an error that is always present to some degree, is unpredictable, affects reliability, and varies from one measurement to the next.

random sampling error error that occurs by chance and affects the accuracy of the sample statistic.

random selection the process of creating a representative sample in which the elements are randomly selected and have a known and independent chance of selection.

range a measure of dispersion that is the difference between the highest and lowest value found in a frequency distribution.

rapport an open and trusting relationship between a researcher and subjects, which fosters mutual understanding.

rate a standardized value assigned to a frequency to allow comparisons between groups on the particular measure.

ratio variable a variable that includes ordered data, an equivalent numerical distance between points, and a true zero.

reciprocity a give-and-take relationship of sharing information and doing small favours for the privilege of gaining access to a social world.

reductionism overgeneralization of individual-level data to make statements about societal-level processes.

reflexivity a process in which a researcher considers his or her role and how it influences or is influenced by the data and research participants.

regression line the line running through points on a scattergram that shows the direction of the relationship; used to understand the relationship between an independent and dependent relationship.

reification the practice of treating a concept as though it has a material existence.

reliability the extent to which repeated testing of a concept produces the same result.

representativeness the quality that occurs when sample characteristics important to the study resemble what is found in the population.

research ethics ethical standards that are accepted by the scientific community and hold researchers responsible for their professional conduct.

response rate the percentage of the survey sample that completes the survey; the item response rate is the percentage of respondents who answer a particular question.

response set effect the tendency for respondents to answer multiple matrix questions in the same way.

retrospective cohort study a study involving a similar group of individuals who differ only on factors related to the outcome under investigation and are followed using data from past records after the policy or program was implemented.

sample a subset of individuals or objects selected from the population and used to draw conclusions about the larger group.

sample statistic a characteristic of the sample used to estimate an attribute of the population (the population parameter).

sampling the process of selecting a number of individuals, objects, or observations from a larger group.

sampling distribution a statistic based on multiple samples of a given population and the probability of it occurring.

sampling element a person, group, organization, document, or event sampled from the population.

sampling error the difference between the value of the sample statistic and the value of the population parameter.

sampling fraction the ratio of sample size to stratum size; used to determine the number of elements selected from the strata.

sampling frame a list of the elements from the target population that are used to create a sample.

sampling interval the standard distance between each sampling element selected.

sampling ratio the proportion of elements to be selected from the target population; this numerical value determines the range for a random start.

scale a logical arrangement of scores on the variable that represents patterns of responses and captures the intensity of emotions or attitudes.

scattergram (or scatterplot) a graphical representation of scores for two continuous variables distributed across the range of all possible values; used to indicate a relationship's strength and direction.

scientific method a model of inquiry used to systematically create knowledge based on a set of principles and procedures.

scientific misconduct intentional fabricating, falsifying, or plagiarizing of research data or other means of violating commonly accepted practices within the scientific community for proposing, conducting, and reporting research.

secondary data data collected by someone other than the researcher.

secondary data analysis analyzing, reclassifying, and interpreting data collected by other researchers.

second cycle coding the coding cycle stage that creates categories' grouping codes and identifies patterns in the data.

selection bias a threat to internal validity in which characteristics of experimental and control group members differ prior to independent variable manipulation.

selective coding the process of developing a theoretical explanation by creating a central concept that organizes all the other categories and codes developed in open and axial coding.

self-administered survey a survey completed without interaction between respondents and the researcher; respondents receive the surveys in the mail or via an e-mail or a hyperlink directing them to a website.

semiotics analysis that focuses on symbols, signs, and their meanings in social interactions.

semi-structured interview a type of interview that, when responses are substantively significant, gives the interviewer the flexibility to ask questions that are not on the interview schedule.

sensitizing concept a preliminary conceptual definition based on prior research and theory that is used to recognize this idea in the field and during the initial stages of data analysis.

simple random sampling (SRS) a probability sampling technique that uses a lottery or random number table to select sequentially numbered elements randomly from a sampling frame.

skip pattern a set of filter and contingency questions used to ensure that the appropriate respondents are answering the questions.

slope the angle of the regression line; symbolized as b.

snowball sampling a sampling technique in which researchers begin with one informant, who refers them to other participants who possess the required knowledge.

social desirability bias the tendency for respondents to answer questions in a manner that makes them look socially acceptable; particularly common with sensitive questions on deviant and criminal behaviour.

Solomon four group an experimental research design in which subjects are randomly assigned to two experimental and two control groups and one of each group does not receive a pretest.

spuriousness the situation of a possible causal relationship being caused by a third, alternative, and unmeasured variable.

stakeholder a person or organization invested in the program being evaluated or interested in what will be done with the results.

standard deviation an estimate of how widely the scores are spread around the mean in a frequency distribution.

standard error the measurement of the total sampling error and of the sample mean's ability to estimate the population mean.

static group comparison a pre-experimental design that does not randomly assign participants to the two groups and that measures the dependent variable with only a posttest after exposure to the independent variable.

statistical regression a threat to internal validity in which extreme scores on the pretest are less extreme on the posttest.

statistical significance a coefficient that indicates the chances of a relationship found in the sample occurring by chance and not existing in the population.

strata subgroups within the target population.

stratified random sampling a probabilistic technique that divides the target population into homogenous subgroups (strata) and randomly chooses elements within each subgroup (stratum).

structured interview an interview in which questions are read verbatim to all respondents and are asked in the same order.

successive approximation iterative movements between data and existing theoretical concepts that guide further data collection, refine theory, and develop empirical generalizations.

summative evaluation a type of evaluation research that investigates the effectiveness of or the extent to which a program achieves its objectives and the value of a program or process.

suppressor variable a variable that prevents a true relationship from appearing because the independent variable may not be associated with the dependent variable but correlated with one or more other independent variables.

survey a data collection method used to gather information from individuals on facts, opinions, or experiences.

systematic measurement error an error that affects the validity of the measure, represents an inaccuracy in the instrument, and impacts the results in a predictable way.

systematic random sampling a technique in which a sampling interval is calculated and, with a random start, every kth element is selected until the desired sample size is reached.

systematic sampling error (or sampling bias) errors—resulting from mistakes or deficiencies in how the sample is created or how the data are analyzed—that affect the accuracy of a sample statistic.

systematic social observation (SSO) a mixed methods structured observation that uses explicit rules for observing, categorizing, and recording behavioural data.

tacit knowledge a person's unconscious or unwritten knowledge.

target population the group of individuals or cases that provide data to best address the research questions and to whom the findings will apply.

tautology circular reasoning; employed when the causal statement is true by definition.

teleology a type of faulty causal reasoning that cannot be empirically tested or falsified.

telephone survey a survey in which an interviewer asks respondents questions over the telephone, reducing the costs in comparison to face-to-face surveys and enabling a representative sample.

telescoping a recall problem in which respondents have trouble accurately remembering when, for how long, or how often something occurred in the past.

testing effect a threat to internal validity in which the completion of a pretest affects posttest scores.

thematic review a literature review that presents theories, methods, or findings on a subject in groups related to future research endeavours.

theoretical review a systematic comparison and assessment of theoretical explanations of crime and criminality.

theoretical triangulation a research strategy that uses more than one theory to inform research questions, data collection, analysis, and interpretation.

theory a set of statements or model based on empirical evidence and reasoning that helps to explain and predict social phenomena.

thick description description that explains behaviour, the context in which it occurs, and understandings that make it meaningful to participants.

time-series research (or trend study) a research design in which given characteristics of a population are analyzed at regular intervals over time.

transcript a written version of an interview, documenting verbatim responses to the questions.

transferability an assessment of trustworthiness that determines the degree to which research findings can be generalized or transferred to other settings, situations, and people.

transformative mixed methods design a type of participatory action research that combines methods for the purpose of improving the condition of marginalized populations.

triangulation a research strategy that uses more than one theory, method, or investigator in order to increase the validity of the findings.

true experiment a design that randomly assigns participants to one of two groups and measures the dependent variable before and after the independent variable is administered.

t-test a test of statistical significance determining whether the means for two groups differ from one another beyond what would occur by random chance.

two-group posttest only an experimental research design that adopts all elements of a true experiment, with the exception of a pretest.

Type I error the rejection of the null hypothesis when it is true (i.e. the relationship found in the sample occurred by chance); also known as an alpha (α) error.

Type II error acceptance of the null hypothesis when it is false (i.e. the relationship found in the sample did not occur by chance); also known as a beta (β) error.

univariate analysis a statistical analysis that describes one variable.

unobtrusive methods research methods in which the researcher does not directly interact with research subjects, thereby removing the threat of reactivity possible with other data collection methods.

unstructured interview a type of interview in which the question content, wording, and order vary each time.

variable something that can be observed and measured at different levels, amounts, or strengths in the real world.

vignette question a question placed in the context of a hypothetical scenario.

voluntary participation a person's informed consent to participate in a research study; gained without coercion, manipulation, or other controlling influences.

References

Abbate, G. (2003, February 21). Paper's racial-profiling reports called quackery. *The Globe and Mail*, p. A16.

Abma, T. A. (2000). Stakeholder conflict: A case study. *Evaluation and Program Planning, 23*, 199–210.

Abram, K. M., Teplin, L. A., McClelland, G. M., & Dulcan, M. K. (2003). Comorbid psychiatric disorders in youth in juvenile detention. *Archives in General Psychiatry, 60*, 1097–1108.

Adler, P. (1984). The sociologist as celebrity: The role of the media in field research. *Qualitative Sociology, 7*, 310–326.

Adler, P. A. (1985). *Wheeling and dealing: An ethnography of an upper-level drug dealing and smuggling community.* New York: Columbia University Press.

Adler, P. A., & Adler, P. (1994). Observation techniques. In N. K. Denzin & Y. S. Lincoln (Eds.), *Handbook of Qualitative Research* (pp. 377–392). Thousand Oaks, CA: Sage.

Alcula (2013). *Statistics calculator: Scatter plots generator.* Retrieved from http://www.alcula.com/calculators/statistics/scatter-plot/

Alison, L. J., Snook, B., & Stein, K. L. (2001). Unobtrusive measurement: Using police information for forensic research. *Qualitative Research, 1*, 241–254.

Alwin, D. F. (1977). Making errors in surveys: An overview. *Sociological Methods & Research, 6*, 131–150.

Amatrudo, A. (2010). Adolphe Quetelet (1796–1874). In K. Hayward, S. Maruna, & J. Mooney (Eds.), *Fifty key thinkers in criminology* (pp. 12–18). New York: Routledge.

Amnesty International (2000). The death penalty in Canada: Twenty years of abolition. *Amnesty International Canada.* Retrieved from http://www.amnesty.ca/deathpenalty/canada.php

Anderson, E. (1999). *Code of the street: Decency, violence, and the moral life of the inner city.* New York: Norton.

Anderson, J., & Linden, R. (2014). Why steal cars? A study of young offenders involved in auto theft. *Canadian Journal of Criminology and Criminal Justice, 56*, 241–260.

Anderson, S. A., Sabatelli, R. M., & Trachtenberg, J. (2007). Community police and youth programs as a context for positive youth development. *Police Quarterly, 10*, 23–40.

Andreson, M. A., & Felson, C. (2012). An investigation into the fundamental regularities of co-offending for violent and property crime classifications. *Canadian Journal of Criminology and Criminal Justice, 54*, 101–115.

Applegate, B. K., & Davis, R. K. (2006). Public views on sentencing juvenile murderers: The impact of offender, offense, and perceived maturity. *Youth Violence and Juvenile Justice, 4*, 55–74.

Babbie, E. (2013). *The practice of social research* (13th ed.). Belmont, CA: Thomson Wadsworth.

Bachman, R., & Schutt, R. K. (2007). *The practice of research in criminology and criminal justice* (3rd ed.). Los Angeles: Sage.

Bala, N., Carrington, P. J., & Roberts, J. V. (2009). Evaluating the Youth Criminal Justice Act: A qualified success. *Canadian Journal of Criminology and Criminal Justice, 51*, 131–167.

Baluja, T. (2012, September 10). Majority wants bullying criminalized, poll finds. *The Globe and Mail.* Retrieved from http://www.theglobeandmail.com/news/politics/ottawa-notebook/most-canadians-want-bullying-criminalized-poll-finds/article549959/

Bank of Canada (2013). Inflation calculator. Retrieved from http://www.bankofcanada.ca/rates/related/inflation-calculator/

Bare, J. (2005). Evaluation and the sacred bundle. *The Evaluation Exchange: A Periodical on Emerging Strategies in Evaluating Child and Family Services, 11*(2), 6.

Baron, S. W., & Forde, D. R. (2007). Street youth crime: A test of control balance theory. *Justice Quarterly, 24*, 335–355.

Batton, C., & Kadleck, C. (2004). Theoretical and methodological issues in racial profiling research. *Police Quarterly, 7*, 30–64.

Beaumont Organization (1981). *The benefits of cigarettes: Exploratory research.* Retrieved from http://tobaccodocuments.org/landman/9955.html

Beauregard, E., & Mieczkowski, T. (2012). From police interrogation to prison: Which sex offender characteristics predict confession? *Police Quarterly, 15*, 197–214.

Becker, H. S. (1953). Becoming a marijuana user. *American Journal of Sociology, 59*, 235–242.

Becker, H. S. (1963). *Outsiders: Studies in the sociology of deviance.* Glencoe, IL: Free Press.

Becker, H. S. (1998). *Tricks of the trade: How to think about your research while you're doing it.* Chicago: University of Chicago Press.

Becker, H. S. (2007). *Writing for social scientists: How to start and finish your thesis, book, or article.* Chicago: University of Chicago Press.

Becker, H. K., Agopian, M. W., & Yeh, S. (1992). Impact evaluation of Drug Abuse Resistance Education (DARE). *Journal of Drug Education, 24*, 284–285.

Becker, H. S., & Geer, B. (1957). Participant observation and interviewing: A comparison. *Human Organization, 16*(3), 28–32.

Beirne, P. (1987). Adophe Quetelet and the origins of positivist criminology. *American Journal of Sociology, 92*, 1140–1169.

Berger, P. L., & Luckmann, T. (1967). *The social construction of reality: A treatise in the sociology of knowledge.* New York: Random House.

Berk, R. A., Ladd, H., Graziano, H., & Baek, J.-H. (2003). A randomized experiment testing inmate classification systems. *Criminology & Public Policy, 2*, 215–242.

Berk, R., & MacDonald, J. (2010). Policing the homeless: An evaluation of efforts to reduce homeless-related crime. *Criminology & Public Policy, 9*, 813–840.

Bernard, H. R. (2013). *Social research methods: Qualitative and quantitative approaches* (2nd ed.). Thousand Oaks, CA: Sage.

Birkeland, S., Murphy-Graham, E., & Weiss, C. (2005). Good reasons for ignoring good evaluation: The case of the drug abuse resistance education (D.A.R.E.) program. *Evaluation and Program Planning, 28*, 247–256.

Black, D. J. (1984). *Toward a general theory of social control.* Orlando: Academic Press.

Blair, J. P., Pollock, J., Montague, D., Nichols, T., Curnutt, J., & Burns, D. (2011). Reasonableness and reaction time. *Police Quarterly, 14*, 323–343.

Blatchford, C. (2003, February 21). Study finds race treated equally: Chief ends months of silence with a barrage of facts. *National Post*, A1.

Blockland, A., & Nieuwbeerta, P. (2005). The effects of life circumstances on longitudinal trajectories of offending. *Criminology, 43*, 1203–1240.

Bloomberg, S. A., & Wilkins, L. T. (1977). Ethics of research involving human subjects in criminal justice. *Crime & Delinquency, 23*, 435–444.

Blumer, H. (1969). *Symbolic interactionism: Perspective and method.* Berkeley: University of California Press.

Boas, F. (1911). *The mind of primitive man.* New York: Macmillan.

Boivin, R. (2013). On the use of crime rates. *Canadian Journal of Criminology and Criminal Justice, 55*, 263–277.

Boivin, R., & Cordeau, G. (2011). Measuring the impact of police discretion on official crime statistics: A research note. *Police Quarterly, 14*, 186–203.

Boote, D. N., & Beile, P. (2005). Scholars before researchers: On the centrality of the dissertation literature review in research preparation. *Educational Researcher, 34* (6), 3–15.

Boruch, R. F., Victor, T., & Cecil, J. S. (2000). Resolving ethical and legal problems in randomized experiments. *Crime & Delinquency, 46*, 330–353.

Bouffard, J. A., Taxman, F. S., & Silverman, R. (2003). Improving process evaluations of correctional programs by using a comprehensive evaluation methodology. *Evaluation and Program Planning, 26*, 149–161.

Bowen, D. M. (2009). Calling your bluff: How prosecutors and defense attorneys adapt plea bargaining strategies to increase formalization. *Justice Quarterly, 26*, 2–29.

Braga, A. A., & Bond, B. J. (2008). Policing crime and disorder hot spots: A randomized controlled trial. *Criminology, 46*, 577–607.

Braga, A. A., Weisburd, D. L., Waring, E. J., Mazerolle, L. G., Spelman, W., & Gajewski, F. (1999). Problem-oriented policing in violent crime places: A randomized controlled experiment. *Criminology, 37*, 541–580.

Braithwaite, J. (1989). *Crime, shame and reintegration.* New York: Cambridge University Press.

Brennan, S. (2012). *Police-reported crime statistics in Canada, 2011.* Ottawa: Statistics Canada.

Brent, J. J., & Kraska, P. B. (2010). Moving beyond our methodological default: A case for mixed methods. *Journal of Criminal Justice Education, 21*, 412–430.

Brinkmann, S. (2012). *Qualitative inquiry in everyday life.* Los Angeles: Sage.

Brodbeck, T. (2012, April 3). Youth Justice Act experiment failing us. *Winnipeg Sun*, A1.

Bruce, A. S., & Desmond, S. A. (1998). A classroom exercise for teaching the problems of offence classification and tabulation associated with the UCR. *Journal of Criminal Justice Education, 9*, 119–129.

Brunson, R. K., & Miller, J. (2009). Schools, neighborhoods, and adolescent conflicts: A situational examination of reciprocal dynamics. *Justice Quarterly, 26*, 183–210.

Buckler, K. (2008). The quantitative/qualitative divide revisited: A study of published research, doctoral program curricula, and journal editor perceptions. *Journal of Criminal Justice Education, 19*, 383–403.

Burns, K. E. A., Duffett, M., Kho, M. E., Meade, M. O., Adhikari, N. K. J., Sinuff, T., & Cook, D. J. (2008). A guide for the design and conduct of self-administered surveys of clinicians. *Canadian Medical Association Journal, 179*(3), 245–252.

Burton, C., & Tewksbury, R. (2013). How families of murder victims feel following the execution of their loved one's murderer: A content analysis of newspaper reports of executions from 2006–2011. *Journal of Qualitative Criminal Justice and Criminology, 1*, 53–77.

Calvey, D. (2008). The art and politics of covert research: Doing "situated ethics" in the field. *Sociology, 42*, 905–918.

Campbell, D. T., & Fiske, D. W. (1959). Convergent and discriminant validation by the multitrait-multimethod matrix. *Psychological Bulletin, 56*, 81–105.

Campbell, D. T., & Stanley, J. C. (1963). *Experimental and quasi-experimental designs.* Chicago: Rand McNally.

Campbell, E. (2004). Police narrativity in the risk society. *British Journal of Criminology, 44*, 695–714.

Campbell, M. A., French, S., & Gendreau, P. (2009). The prediction of violence in adult offenders: A meta-analytic comparison of instruments and methods of assessment. *Criminal Justice and Behavior, 36*, 567–590.

Canadian Association of University Teachers. (2003). *CAUT policy statement on fraud and other misconduct in academic research.* Retrieved from http://www.caut.ca/pages.asp?lang=1&page=275

Canadian Institutes of Health Research, Natural Sciences and Engineering Research Council of Canada, & Social Sciences and Humanities Research Council of Canada. (2014, December). *Tri-council policy statement: Ethical conduct for research involving humans.* Retrieved from http://www.pre.ethics.gc.ca/pdf/eng/tcps2-2014/TCPS_2_FINAL_Web.pdf

Carbone-Lopez, K., & Miller, J. (2012). Precocious entry as a mediating factor in women's methamphetamine use: Implications for life-course and pathways research. *Criminology, 50,* 187–220.

Carlan, P. E., & Lewis, J. A. (2009). Professionalism in policing: Assessing the professionalization movement. *Police Quarterly, 12,* 370–387.

Carrington, P. J. (2013). Trends in the seriousness of youth crime in Canada, 1984–2011. *Canadian Journal of Criminology and Criminal Justice, 55,* 293–314.

Carrington, P. J., & Schulenberg, J. L. (2008). Structuring police discretion: The effect on referrals to youth court. *Criminal Justice Policy Review, 19,* 349–367.

Castellano, T. C., & Schafer, J. A. (2005). Continuity and discontinuity in competing models of criminal justice education: Evidence from Illinois. *Journal of Criminal Justice Education, 16,* 60–78.

Castillo, M., Petrie, R., Torero, M., & Visceiza, A. (2012). Lost in the mail: A field experiment on crime. Retrieved from http://mason.gmu.edu/~rpetrie1/LostMailRevised12.pdf

CBC (2012, 29 October). Crime hot spots in Toronto revealed in online map. Retrieved from http://www.cbc.ca/news/canada/toronto/story/2012/10/26/toronto-crime-hotspots-map213.html

Chaiyavej, S., & Morash, M. (2009). Reasons for policewomen's assertive and passive reactions to sexual harassment. *Police Quarterly, 12,* 63–85.

Chambliss, W. (1973). The saints and the roughnecks. *Society, 11*(2), 4–31.

Charmaz, K. (2006). *Constructing grounded theory: A practical guide through qualitative analysis.* Thousand Oaks, CA: Sage.

Charron, M. (2009). *Neighbourhood characteristics and the distribution of police-reported crime in the City of Toronto.* Ottawa: Statistics Canada.

Chelimsky, E. (1987). What have we learned about the politics of program evaluation? *Evaluation Practice, 8,* 5–21.

Chen, H.-T. (1997). Normative evaluation of an anti-drug abuse program. *Evaluation and Program Planning, 20,* 195–204.

Christie, C. A., Montrosse, B. E., & Klein, B. M. (2005). Emergent design evaluation: A case study. *Evaluation and Program Planning, 28,* 271–277.

Cihan, A., & Wells, W. (2011). Citizens' opinions about police discretion in criminal investigations. *Policing: An International Journal of Police Strategies & Management, 34,* 347–362.

Clarke, M. (1975). Survival in the field: Implications of personal experience in the field. *Theory and Society, 2,* 95–123.

Cloward, R. A., & Ohlin, L. E. (1960). *Delinquency and opportunity: A theory of delinquent gangs.* Glencoe, IL: Free Press.

Cochran, W. G., Mosteller, F., & Tukey, J. W. (1954). *Statistical problems of the Kinsey report on sexual behavior in the human male.* Washington, DC: American Statistical Association.

Cockcroft, T. (2013). *Police culture: Themes and concepts.* New York: Routledge.

Coffman, J. (2003). Michael Scriven on the differences between evaluation and social science research. *The Evaluation Exchange, 9*(4), 7.

Cohen, S. (1973). *Folk devils and moral panics.* St. Albans: Paladin.

Cohn, E. G. (2011). Changes in scholarly influence in major international criminology journals, 1986–2005. *Canadian Journal of Criminology and Criminal Justice, 53,* 157–188.

Comack, E., & Brickey, S. (2007). Constituting the violence of criminalized women. *Canadian Journal of Criminology and Criminal Justice, 49,* 1–36.

Comack, E., & Seshia, M. (2010). Bad dates and street hassles: Violence in the Winnipeg street sex trade. *Canadian Journal of Criminology and Criminal Justice, 52,* 203–214.

Committee on Identifying the Needs of the Forensic Sciences Community, National Research Council. (2009, August). *Strengthening forensic science in the United States: A path forward.* Washington, DC: National Academies Press.

Connell, N. M., Miggans, K., & McGloin, J. M. (2008). Can a community policing initiative reduce serious crime? A local evaluation. *Police Quarterly, 11,* 127–150.

Cook, T. D., & Campbell, D. T. (1979). *Quasi-experimentation: Design and analysis issues for field settings.* Chicago: Rand McNally.

Cooper, B. B. (2013). 10 surprising social media statistics that will make you rethink your social strategy. *Work Smart.* Retrieved from http://fastcompany.com/3021749/worksmart/10-surprising-social-media-statistics-that-will-make-you-rethink-your-social-stra

Copes, H., Brown, A., & Tewksbury, R. (2011). A content analysis of ethnographic research published in top criminology and criminal justice journals from 2000 to 2009. *Journal of Criminal Justice Education, 22,* 341–359.

Copes, H., & Tewksbury, R. (2011). Criminal experience and perceptions of risk: What auto thieves fear when stealing cars. *Journal of Crime and Justice, 34,* 62–79.

Corbin, J., & Strauss, A. (2007). *Basics of qualitative research: Techniques and procedures for developing grounded theory* (3rd ed.). Thousand Oaks, CA: Sage.

Cortoni, F., & Hanson, R. K. (2005). *A review of recidivism rates of adult female sexual offenders.* Research Report No. R-169. Ottawa: Correctional Service of Canada.

Cosgrove, J. F., & Klassen, T. R. (Eds.) (2009). *Casino state: Legalized gambling in Canada.* Toronto: University of Toronto Press.

Coupe, T., & Blake, L. (2006). Daylight and darkness targeting strategies and the risks of being seen at residential burglaries. *Criminology, 44*, 431–464.

Creswell, J. W. (2014). *Research design: Qualitative, quantitative, and mixed methods approaches* (4th ed.). Thousand Oaks, CA: Sage.

Creswell, J. W., Plano Clark, V. L., Gutmann, M. L., & Hanson, W. E. (2003). Advanced mixed methods research designs. In A. Tashakkori and C. Teddlie (Eds.), *Handbook of mixed methods in social and behavioral research* (pp. 209–240). Thousand Oaks, CA: Sage.

Cronenberg, D. (2012). David Cronenberg quotes. Brainy Quotes. Retrieved from http://www.brainyquote.com/quotes/authors/d/david_cronenberg.html

Crow, M. S., & Ortiz Smykla, J. (2013). A mixed methods analysis of methodological orientation in national and regional criminology and criminal justice journals. *Journal of Criminal Justice Education, 24*, 536–555.

Crump, J. (2011). What are the police doing on Twitter? Social media, the police and the public. *Policy & Internet, 3*(4), Article 7. Retrieved from http://www.psocommons.org/policyandinternet/vol3/iss4/art7

Daintith, J., Egerton, H., Fergusson, R., Stibbs, A., & Wright, E. (Eds.). (2000). *The Macmillan dictionary of quotations: A unique reference combination.* Edison, NJ: Chartwell Books.

Davis III, E. F., Alves, A. A., & Sklansky, D. A. (2014, March). Social media and police leadership: Lessons from Boston. *New Perspectives in Policing*. Washington, DC: Harvard Kennedy School and the National Institute of Justice.

Dean, D., Hollinger, R. C., & Dugan, L. (2004). Who actually steals? A study of covertly observed shoplifters. *Justice Quarterly, 21*, 693–729.

DeLorenzi, D., Shane, J. M., & Amendola, K. L. (2006). The CompStat process: Managing performance on the pathway to leadership. *The Police Chief, 73*(9). Retrieved from http://www.policechiefmagazine.org/magazine/index.cfm?fuseaction=display&article_id=998&issue_id=92006

Demetriou, C., & Silke, A. (2003). A criminological Internet "sting": Experimental evidence of illegal and deviant visits to a website trap. *British Journal of Criminology, 43*, 213–222.

Denzin, N. K. (1978). *The research act: A theoretical introduction to sociological methods.* New York: McGraw-Hill.

DiCristina, B. (1995). *Method in criminology: A philosophical primer.* New York: Harrow and Heston.

Dillman, D. A. (1999). Mail and other self-administered surveys in the 21st century: The beginning of a new era. *The Gallup Research Journal, 2*, 121–140.

Dillman, D. A. (2004). *Mail and Internet surveys: The tailored design method.* New York: Wiley.

do Mar Pereira, M. (2013). Media coverage of ethnographic work: Opportunities, problems and dilemmas. Retrieved from http://ceas.iscte.pt/ethnografeast/papers/maria_pereira.pdf

Dobrzynski, J. H. (2010, May 6). Don't get stumped in the interview: The new, NEW interview questions. http://www.forbes.com/2010/05/06/job-interview-questions-personality-forbes-woman-leadership-career.html

Dodge, M. (2006). Juvenile police informants: Friendship, persuasion, and pretense. *Youth Violence and Juvenile Justice, 4*, 234–246.

Doyle, Sir A. C. (2009). *The Penguin Complete Sherlock Holmes.* London: Penguin.

Dugan, L., Lafree, G., & Piquero, A. R. (2005). Testing a rational choice model of airline hijackings. *Criminology, 43*, 1031–1065.

Dumaine, F. (2005). Future directions in community policing: Evaluation of the Ottawa Police Service Community Police Centres. *The Canadian Review of Policing Research, 1*. Retrieved from http://crpr.icaap.org/index.php/crpr/article/view/43/49

Dunham, R. G., & Alpert, G. P. (2009). Officer and suspect demeanor: A qualitative analysis of change. *Police Quarterly, 12*, 6–21.

Dupuis, T. (2009). *Legislative summary LS-658E. Bill C-34: Protecting victims from Sex Offenders Act.* Ottawa: Parliamentary Information and Research Service, Library of Parliament.

Eck, J. E., Chainey, S., Cameron, J. G., Leitner, M., & Wilson, R. E. (2005). *Mapping crime: Understanding hot spots.* Washington, DC: National Institute of Justice.

Edmonds, W. A., & Kennedy, T. D. (2013). *An applied reference guide to research designs: Quantitative, qualitative, and mixed methods.* Los Angeles: Sage.

Eitle, D., D'Alessio, S. J., & Stolzenberg, L. (2014). The effect of organizational and environmental factors on police misconduct. *Police Quarterly, 17*, 103–126.

Emshoff, J. (2003). Commentary: Practical realities and ethical choices. *American Journal of Evaluation, 24*, 419–422.

Exum, M. L. (2002). The application and robustness of the rational choice perspective in the study of intoxicated and angry intentions to aggress. *Criminology, 40*, 933–966.

Famega, C. N., Franck, J., & Mazerolle, L. (2005). Managing police patrol time: The role of supervisor directives. *Justice Quarterly, 22*, 540–559.

Farrington, D. P. (1997). Evaluating a community crime prevention program. *Evaluation, 3*, 157–173.

Farrington, D. P. (2010a). Crime and the family. *The Criminologist, 35*(2), 1, 3–6.

Farrington, D. P. (2010b). Joan McCord (1930–2004). In K. Hayward, S. Maruna, & J. Mooney (Eds.), *Fifty key thinkers in criminology* (pp. 179–185). New York: Routledge.

Farrington, D. P., & Welsh, B. C. (2007). Saving children from a life of crime: Early risk factors and effective interventions. Foreword by J. Q. Wilson. *Studies in Crime and Public Policy.* New York: Oxford University Press.

Faupel, C. E. (1987). Heroin use and criminal careers. *Qualitative Sociology, 10*, 115–131.

Felch, J., & Dolan, M. (2009, February 19). Report questions science, reliability of crime lab evidence. *Los Angeles Times*. Retrieved from http://articles.latimes.com/2009/feb/19/nation/na-crime-science19

Ferrell, J. (1997). Criminological verstehen: Inside the immediacy of crime. *Justice Quarterly, 14*, 3–23.

Fielding, N. (2010). Mixed methods research in the real world. *International Journal of Social Research Methodology, 13*, 127–138.

Fitzgerald, A., & Baralt, L. B. (2010). Media constructions of responsibility for the mitigation and mitigation of environmental harms: The case of mercury-contaminated fish. *Canadian Journal of Criminology and Criminal Justice, 52*, 341–368.

Frank, J. (2009). Conceptual, methodological, and policy considerations in the study of police misconduct. *Criminology & Public Policy, 8*, 733–736.

Frankel, M. S. (1998). Scientific community must set standards. *Forum for Applied Research and Public Policy, 13*, 57–60.

Friedman, M. (1975, December 7). Living within our means. Interview with Richard Heffner on *The Open Mind*. Retrieved from http://www.theopenmind.tv/searcharchive_episode_transcript.asp?id=494

Gabor, T. (2004). Inflammatory rhetoric on racial profiling can undermine police services. *Canadian Journal of Criminology and Criminal Justice, 46*, 457–466.

Galliher, J. F., Brekhus, W. H., & Keys, D. P. (2004). *Laud Humphreys: Prophet of homosexuality and sociology*. Madison: University of Wisconsin Press.

Gans, H. J. (2010). Public ethnography: Ethnography as public sociology. *Qualitative Sociology, 33*, 97–104.

Garaway, G. B. (1997). Evaluation, validity, and values. *Evaluation and Program Planning, 20*, 1–5.

Garwood, J., Rogerson, M., & Pease, K. (2000). Sneaky measurement of crime and disorder. In V. Jupp, P. Davies, & P. Francis (Eds.), *Doing criminological research* (pp. 157–167). Thousand Oaks, CA: Sage.

Geertz, C. (1973). *The interpretation of cultures: Selected essays*. New York: Basic Books.

Gibbons, D. C. (1994). *Talking about crime and criminals: Problems and issues in theory development in criminology*. Englewood Cliffs, NJ: Prentice Hall.

Gideon, L. (2009). What shall I do now? Released offenders' expectations for supervision upon release. *International Journal of Offender Therapy and Comparative Criminology, 53*, 43–56.

Gill, M., & Taylor, G. (2004). Preventing money laundering or obstructing business? Financial companies' perspectives on "know your customer" procedures. *British Journal of Criminology, 44*, 582–594.

Gillis, W. (2010a, June 30). Most think G20 police actions justified, poll finds. *Toronto Star*. Retrieved from http://www.thestar.com/news/gta/g20/2010/06/30/most_think_g20_police_actions_justified_poll_finds.html

Gillis, W. (2010b, August 4). Toronto residents fail to report crime due to perceived hassle, insignificance. *Toronto Star*. Retrieved from http://www.thestar.com/news/gta/2010/08/04/toronto_residents_fail_to_report_crime_due_to_perceived_hassle_insignificance.html

Gladwell, M. (2007, November 12). Dangerous minds: Criminal profiling made easy. *The New Yorker*, pp. 36–45.

Glaser, B., & Strauss, A. (1967). *The discovery of grounded theory*. Hawthorne, NY: Aldine.

Godfredson, J. W., Ogloff, J. R. P., Thomas, S. D. M., & Luebbers, S. (2010). Police discretion and encounters with people experiencing mental illness. *Criminal Justice and Behavior, 37*, 1392–1405.

Goering, P., Veldhuizen, S., Watson, A., Adair, C., Kopp, B., Latimer, E., & Ly, A. (2012). *At Home/Chez Soi interim report: September 2012*. Ottawa: Mental Health Commission of Canada.

Goffman, E. (1959). *The presentation of self in everyday life*. New York: Anchor Books.

Golafshani, N. (2003). Understanding reliability and validity in qualitative research. *The Qualitative Report, 8*, 597–607.

Goode, W. J., & Hatt, P. K. (2002). Methods in social research. In D. C. Miller & N. J. Salkind, (Eds.), *Handbook of research design and social measurement* (6th ed.) (pp. 33–36). Thousand Oaks, CA: Sage.

Gorman, D. M., & Conde, E. (2007). Conflict of interest in the evaluation and dissemination of "model" school-based drug and violence prevention programs. *Evaluation and Program Planning, 30*, 422–429.

Gottfredson, D. C., Najaka, S. S., & Kearley, B. (2003). Effectiveness of drug treatment courts: Evidence from a randomized trial. *Criminology & Public Policy, 2*, 171–196.

Green, J. R. (2014). New directions in policing: Balancing prediction and meaning in police research. *Justice Quarterly, 31*, 193–228.

Greene, C., Sprott, J. B., Madon, N. S., & Jung, M. (2010). Punishing processes in youth court: Procedural justice, court atmosphere and youths' view of the legitimacy of the justice system. *Canadian Journal of Criminology and Criminal Justice, 52*, 527–544.

Greene, J. C. (1997). Advancing mixed-method evaluation. *The Evaluation Exchange: Emerging Strategies in Evaluating Child and Family Services, 3*(1), 2–3.

Greene, J. C. (2007). *Mixed methods in social inquiry*. San Francisco: Wiley.

Greene, J. C., Caracelli, V. J., & Graham, W. F. (1989). Toward a conceptual framework for mixed-method evaluation designs. *Educational Evaluation and Policy Analysis, 11*, 255–274.

Guay, J.-P. (2012). *Predicting recidivism with street gang members*. Ottawa: Public Safety Canada.

Gubrium, J. F., & Holstein, J. A. (2000). Analyzing interpretive practice. In N. Denzin & Y. S. Lincoln (Eds.), *The handbook of qualitative research* (2nd ed.) (pp. 487–508). Thousand Oaks, CA: Sage.

Guevara, L., Herz, D., & Spohn, C. (2008). Race, gender, and legal counsel. *Youth Violence and Juvenile Justice, 6,* 83–104.

Ha, T. T. (2012, April 12). Police-reported hate crimes down sharply in 2010: StatsCan. *The Globe and Mail.* Retrieved from http://www.theglobeandmail.com/news/national/police-reported-hate-crimes-down-sharply-in-2010-statscan/article4101763/

Haar, R. N., & Morash, M. (2013). The effect of rank on police women coping with discrimination and harassment. *Police Quarterly, 16,* 395–419.

Habermeyer, E., Passow, D., Puhlmann, P., Vohs, K., & Herpetrtz, S. (2009). Sexual offenders in preventive detention: Data concerning the inmates and expert witness practice. *International Journal of Offender Therapy and Comparative Criminology, 53,* 373–384.

Hadfield, P. (2007). A hard act to follow: Assessing the consequences of licensing reform in England and Wales. *Addiction, 102,* 177–180.

Haggerty, K. D. (2001). *Making crime count.* Toronto: University of Toronto Press.

Harachi, T. W., Abbott, R. D., Catalano, R. F., Haggerty, K. P., & Fleming, C. B. (1999). Opening the black box: Using process evaluation measures to assess implementation and theory building. *American Journal of Community Psychology, 27,* 711–731.

Hayashi, K., Wood, E., Wiebe, L., Qi, J., & Kerr, T. (2010). An external evaluation of a peer-run outreach-based syringe exchange in Vancouver, Canada. *International Journal of Drug Policy, 21,* 418–421.

Hays, K. L., Regoli, R. M., & Hewitt, J. D. (2007). Police chiefs, anomia, and leadership. *Police Quarterly, 10,* 3–22.

Herman, E. S., & Chomsky, N. (1988). *Manufacturing consent: The political economy of the mass media.* New York: Pantheon Books.

Herzog, S. (2004). The effect of motive on public perceptions of the seriousness of murder in Israel. *British Journal of Criminology, 44,* 771–782.

Hine, C. (2011). Internet research and unobtrusive methods. *Social Research Update, 61,* 1–4.

Hirschi, T. (1969/2009). *Causes of delinquency.* Piscataway, NJ: Transaction.

Hirschi, T. (1980). Causes of delinquency. *This Week's Citation Classic, 200*(38), 302.

Hollin, C. (2001). Prediction Studies. In E. McLaughlin & J. Muncie (Eds.), *The Sage dictionary of criminology* (pp. 221–222). Thousand Oaks, CA: Sage.

Holt, T. J. (2010). Exploring strategies for qualitative criminological and criminal justice inquiry using on-line data. *Journal of Criminal Justice Education, 21,* 466–487.

Holt, T. J., Zeoli, A. M., & Bohrer, K. (2013). Examining the decision-making processes of sex tourists using on-line data. *Journal of Qualitative Criminal Justice and Criminology, 1,* 122–151.

Homan, R. (1992). The ethics of open methods. *British Journal of Sociology, 43,* 321–332.

Honkatukia, P., Nyqvist, L., & Pösö, T. (2006). Violence from within the reform school. *Youth Violence and Juvenile Justice, 4,* 328–344.

Hopper, C. B., & Moore, J. (1990). Women in outlaw motorcycle gangs. *Journal of Contemporary Ethnography, 18,* 363–387.

Howard, C. (2010, August 27). Best questions to ask in your job interview. Forbes.com. Retrieved from http://www.forbes.com/sites/carolinehoward/2010/08/27/best-questions-to-ask-in-your-job-interview/

Hubbard, D. W. (2010). *How to measure anything: Finding the value of intangibles in business* (2nd ed.). Hoboken, NJ: Wiley.

Huff, D. (1954). *How to lie with statistics.* New York: Norton.

Hughes, R., Black, C., & Kennedy, N. P. (2008). *Public health nutrition intervention management: Impact and outcome evaluation.* Dublin: JobNut Project, Trinity College. Retrieved from http://www.medicine.tcd.ie/nutrition-dietetics/assets/pdf/3-Evaluation-module/Unit-14-Impact-and-Outcome-Evaluation-090128.pdf

Humphreys, L. (1975). *Tearoom trade: Impersonal sex in public places.* New York: Aldine de Gruyter.

Hurston, Z. N. (1942). *Dust tracks on a road: An autobiography.* New York: Harper Perennial.

Hyshka, E. (2009). The saga continues: Canadian legislative attempts to reform cannabis law in the twenty-first century. *Canadian Journal of Criminology and Criminal Justice, 51,* 73–91.

Institute for Social Research. (2013). Telephone surveys. *York University.* Retrieved from http://isr.yorku.ca/services/telephone.html

International Association of Chiefs of Police. (2014). *2013 social media survey results.* Retrieved from http://www.iacpsocialmedia.org/Resources/Publications/2013SurveyResults.aspx

Ioannidis, J. P. A. (2005). Why most published research findings are false. *Public Library of Science Medicine, 2,* 696–701.

Israel, M. (2004). Strictly confidential? Integrity and disclosure in criminological and socio-legal research. *British Journal of Criminology, 44,* 715–740.

Jackson, J. (2004). Experience and expression: Social and cultural significance in the fear of crime. *British Journal of Criminology, 44,* 946–966.

Jacobs, B. A. (1998). Researching crack dealers: Dilemmas and contradictions. In J. Ferrell & M. S. Hamm (Eds.), *Ethnography at the edge: Crime, deviance, and field research* (pp. 160–177). Boston: Northeastern University Press.

Jacobs, B. A., Topalli, V., & Wright, R. (2003). Carjacking, streetlife, and offender motivation. *British Journal of Criminology, 43,* 673–688.

Jacques, S., & Wright, R. (2011). Informal control and illicit drug trade. *Criminology, 49,* 729–765.

Jeffords, C. R. (2007). Gaining approval from a juvenile correctional agency to conduct external research: The perspective of a gatekeeper. *Youth Violence and Juvenile Justice, 5,* 88–99.

Jen Der Pan, P., Deng, L.-Y. F., Chang, S. S. H., & Jiang, K. J.-R. (2011). Correctional officers' perceptions of a solution-focused training program: Potential implications for working with offenders. *International Journal of Offender Therapy and Comparative Criminology, 55,* 863–879.

Johnson, R. B., & Onwuegbuzie, A. J. (2004). Mixed methods research: A research paradigm whose time has come. *Educational Researcher, 33*(7), 14–26.

Johnson, R. B., Onwuegbuzie, A. J., & Turner, L. A. (2007). Toward a definition of mixed methods research. *Journal of Mixed Methods Research, 1,* 112–133.

Jones, M. (2003). *Criminal justice pioneers in US history.* Boston: Pearson.

Jones, M., & Ross, D. L. (1997). IS LESS BETTER? Boot camp, regular probation and rearrest in North Carolina. *American Journal of Criminal Justice, 21,* 147–161.

Kahane, H. (1988). *Logic and contemporary rhetoric.* Belmont, CA: Wadsworth.

Kaufman-Levy, D., & Poulin, M. (2003). *Evaluability assessment: Examining the readiness of a program for evaluation.* Program Evaluation Briefing Series #6. Washington, DC: Juvenile Justice Evaluation Center, Justice Research and Statistics Association, Office of Juvenile Justice and Delinquency Prevention, and the United States Department of Justice.

Kee, J. E. (1999). At what price? Benefit-cost analysis and cost-effectiveness analysis in program evaluation. *The Evaluation Exchange: Emerging Strategies in Evaluating Child and Family Services, 5*(2/3), 4–5.

Kelling, G. (1999). Measuring what matters: A new way of thinking about crime and public order. In R. H. Langworthy (Ed.), *Measuring what matters: Proceedings from the Policing Research Institute meetings* (pp. 27–36). Washington, DC: National Institute of Justice.

Kelling, G. L., Pate, T., Dieckman, D., & Brown, C. E. (1974). *The Kansas City preventative patrol experiment: A summary report.* Washington, DC: Police Foundation.

Kelling, G. L., & Wilson, J. Q. (1982, March). Broken windows: The police and neighborhood safety. *Atlantic Monthly.* Retrieved from http://www.theatlantic.com/magazine/archive/1982/03/broken-windows/304465/?single_page=true

Kent, D. R., Donaldson, S. J., Wyrick, P. A., & Smith, P. J. (2000). Evaluating criminal justice programs designed to reduce crime by targeting repeat gang offenders. *Evaluation and Program Planning, 23,* 115–124.

Kietzmann, J. H., Silvestre, B. S., McCarthy, I. P., & Pitt, L. (2012). Unpacking the social media phenomenon: Towards a research agenda. *Journal of Public Affairs, 12,* 109–119.

Killey, J.-C. (2003, April 19). Profiling racial profiling. Letter to the Editor. *The Globe and Mail,* A20.

King, A., & Thomas, J. (2009). You can't cheat an honest man: Making ($$$ and) sense of the Nigerian e-mail scams. In F. Schmalleger and M. Pittaro (Eds.), *Crimes of the Internet* (pp. 206–224). Upper Saddle River, NJ: Pearson Prentice Hall.

King, I. T. (1994). *Explorations beyond the machine: A philosophy of social science for the post-Newtonian age.* Commack, NY: Nova Science Publishers.

Kirk, D. S., & Matsuda, M. (2011). Legal cynicism, collective efficacy, and the ecology of arrest. *Criminology, 49,* 443–472.

Kitchenham, B., & Pfleeger, S. L. (2002). Principles of survey research: Populations and samples. *Software Engineering Notes, 27*(5), 17–20.

Kleck, G., Tark, J., & Bellows, J. J. (2006). What methods are most frequently used in research in criminology and criminal justice? *Journal of Criminal Justice, 34,* 147–152.

Klein, M. W. (2002). Surrounded by crime: Lessons from one academic career. In G. Geis & M. Dodge (Eds.), *Lessons of criminology* (pp. 47–63). Cincinnati: Anderson Publishing.

Klinesmith, J., Kasser, T., & McAndrew, F. T. (2006). Guns, testosterone, and aggression: An experimental test of a mediational hypothesis. *Psychological Science, 17,* 568–571.

Klinger, D. A. (1996). Quantifying law in police–citizen encounters. *Journal of Quantitative Criminology, 12,* 391–415.

Klinkenberg, W. D., Calsyn, R. J., Morse, G. A., McCudden, S., Richmond, T., Burger, G. K., & Petri, P. (2003). Effect of data collection mode on self-reported sexual and drug using behaviors for persons with severe mental illness. *Evaluation and Program Planning, 26,* 275–282.

Klockars, C. B. (1999). Some really cheap ways of measuring what really matters. In R. H. Langworthy (Ed.), *Measuring what matters: Proceedings from the Policing Research Institute meetings* (pp. 195–214). Washington, DC: National Institute of Justice.

Klofas, J. M., & Cutshall, C. R. (1985). The social archaelology of a juvenile facility: Unobtrusive methods in the study of institutional cultures. *Qualitative Sociology, 8,* 368–387.

Kochel, T. R., Wilson, D. B., & Mastrofksi, S. D. (2011). Effect of suspect race on officers' arrest decisions. *Criminology, 2011,* 473–512.

Kohm, S. A., Waid-Lindberg, C. A., Weinrath, M., O'Connor Shelley, T., & Dobbs, R. R. (2012). The impact of media on fear of crime among university students: A cross-national comparison. *Canadian Journal of Criminology and Criminal Justice, 54,* 67–100.

Korf, D. J., van Ginkel, P., & Benschop, A. (2009). How to find non-dependent opiate users: A comparison of sampling methods in a field study of opium and heroin users. *International Journal of Drug Policy, 21,* 215–221.

Kraska, P. B., & Neuman, W. L. (2012). *Criminal justice and criminology research methods* (2nd ed.). Upper Saddle River, NJ: Pearson.

Kruttschnitt, C., & Carbone-Lopez, K. (2006). Moving beyond the stereotypes of women's subjective accounts of their violent crime. *Criminology, 44,* 321–351.

Kuhn, T. (1970/1996). *The structure of scientific revolutions* (3rd ed.). Chicago: University of Chicago Press.

Kuhn, T. S. (1977). *The essential tension: Selected studies in scientific tradition and change.* Chicago: University of Chicago Press.

Kupchik, A. (2007). The correctional experiences of youth in adult and juvenile prisons. *Justice Quarterly, 24,* 247–270.

Labriola, M., Rempel, M., & Davis, R. C. (2008). Do batterer programs reduce recidivism? Results from a randomized trial in the Bronx. *Justice Quarterly, 25,* 252–282.

Lam, A., Mitchell, J., & Seto, M. C. (2010). Lay perceptions of child pornography offenders. *Canadian Journal of Criminology and Criminal Justice, 52,* 173–201.

Lamiell, J. T. (1998). Nomothetic and idiographic: Contrasting Windelband's understanding with contemporary usage. *Theory and Psychology, 8,* 23–38.

Land, K. C., Teske, Jr., R. H. C., & Zheng, H. (2009). The short-term effects of executions on homicides: Deterrence, displacement, or both? *Criminology, 47,* 1009–1043.

Landau, T. (1996). Policing and security in four remote Aboriginal communities: A challenge to coercive models of police work. *Canadian Journal of Criminology, 38,* 1–32.

Lane, J. (2006). Exploring fear of general and gang crimes among juveniles on probation: The impacts of delinquent behaviors. *Youth Violence and Juvenile Justice, 4,* 34–54.

La Pelle, N. (2004). Simplifying qualitative data analysis using general purpose software tools. *Field Methods, 16,* 85–108.

Lappi-Seppälä, T. (2011). Explaining imprisonment in Europe. *European Journal of Criminology, 8,* 303–328.

Latessa, E. J., & Holsinger, A. (1998). The importance of evaluating correctional programmes: Assessing outcome and quality. *Corrections Management Quarterly, 2,* 22–29.

Lawton, B. A., & Schulenberg, J. L. (2007). Assessing the impact of Hurricane Katrina on space-time clusters of crime patterns in Houston, TX. National Institute of Justice MAPS Conference, Pittsburgh.

Lawton, B. A., Taylor, R. B., & Luongo, A. J. (2005). Police officers on drug corners in Philadelphia, drug crime, and violent crime: Intended, diffusion, and displacement effects. *Justice Quarterly, 22*(4), 427–451.

Lee, R. M. (2000). *Unobtrusive methods in social research.* Philadelphia: Open University Press.

Lee, Y.-F., Altschuld, J. W., & White, J. L. (2007). Problems in needs assessment data: Discrepancy analysis. *Evaluation and Program Planning, 30,* 258–266.

Leedy, P. D. (1997). *Practical research: Planning and design* (6th ed.). Upper Saddle River, NJ: Prentice Hall.

Leerkes, A., Varsayi, M., & Engbersen, G. (2012). Local limits to migration control: Practices of selective migration policing in a restrictive national policy context. *Police Quarterly, 15,* 446–475.

Leiber, M. J., & Mawhorr, T. L. (1995). Evaluating the use of social skills training and employment with delinquent youth. *Journal of Criminal Justice, 23,* 127–141.

Leschied, A., Chiodo, D., Nowicki, E., & Rodger, S. (2008). Childhood predictors of adult criminality: A meta-analysis drawn from the prospective longitudinal literature. *Canadian Journal of Criminology and Criminal Justice, 50,* 435–467.

Levitt, S. D. (1998). The relationship between crime reporting and police: Implications for the use of Uniform Crime Reports. *Journal of Quantitative Criminology, 14,* 61–81.

Levitt, S. D., & List, J. A. (2006). What do laboratory experiments tell us about the real world? Retrieved from http://pricetheory.uchicago.edu/levitt/Papers/jep%20revision%20Levitt%20&%20List.pdf

Lewis, J., & Maticka-Tyndale, E. (2000). Licensing sex work: Public policy and women's lives. *Canadian Public Policy—Analyse de Politiques, 26,* 437–449.

Lewis, R. (2004). Making justice work: Effective legal interventions for domestic violence. *British Journal of Criminology, 44,* 204–224.

Library and Archives Canada (2008). *Using archives: A practical guide for researchers.* Retrieved from http://www.collectionscanada.gc.ca/04/0416_3.html

Lieberman, J. D., Koetzle, D., & Sakiyama, M. (2013). Police departments' use of Facebook: Patterns and policy issues. *Police Quarterly, 16,* 438–462.

Liederbach, J., & Travis III, L. F. (2008). Wilson redux: Another look at varieties of police behaviour. *Police Quarterly, 11,* 447–467.

Lincoln, Y. S., & Guba, E. G. (1985). *Naturalistic inquiry.* Beverly Hills: Sage.

Locke, L. F., Spirduso, W. W., & Silverman, S. J. (2007). *Proposals that work: A guide for planning dissertations and grant proposals* (5th ed.). Thousand Oaks, CA: Sage.

Lofland, J., Snow, D. A., Anderson, L., & Lofland, L. H. (2006). *Analyzing social settings: A guide to qualitative observation and analysis* (4th ed.). Belmont, CA: Wadsworth.

Logan, T. K., Hoyt, W. H., McCollister, K. E., French, M. T., Leukefeld, C., & Minton, L. (2004). Economic evaluation of drug court: Methodology, results, and policy implications. *Evaluation and Program Planning, 27,* 381–396.

Lombard, M., Snyder-Duch, J., & Campanella-Bracken, C. (2004). *Practical resources for assessing and reporting intercoder reliability in content analysis research projects.* Retrieved from http://ils.indiana.edu/faculty/hrosenba/www/Research/methods/lombard_reliability.pdf

Lösel, F. (2008). Doing evaluation research in criminology. In R. D. King & E. Wincup (Eds.), *Doing research on crime and justice* (2nd ed.) (pp. 141–170). New York: Oxford University Press.

Lowman, J., & Palys, T. (2001). The ethics and law of confidentiality in criminal justice research: A comparison of Canada and the United States. *International Criminal Justice Review, 11,* 1–33.

Lundman, R. J. (2001). *Prevention and control of juvenile delinquency* (3rd ed.). New York: Oxford University Press.

Lynam, D. R., Milich, R., Zimmerman, R., Novak, S. P., Logan, T. K., Martin, C., Leukefeld, C., & Clayton, R. (1999). Project DARE: No effects at 10-year follow-up. *Journal of Consulting and Clinical Psychology, 67,* 590–593.

Magura, S., Rosenblum, A., Lewis, C., & Joseph, H. (1993). Effectiveness of in-jail methadone maintenance. *Journal of Drug Issues, 23,* 75–99.

Maher, T. M. (2003). Police sexual misconduct: Officers' perceptions of its extent and causality. *Criminal Justice Review, 28,* 355–381.

Mahoney, T., & Turner, J. (2012). *Police-reported clearance rates, 2010.* Ottawa: Statistics Canada.

Maier, S. L., & Monahan, B. A. (2010). How close is too close? Balancing closeness and detachment in qualitative research. *Deviant Behavior, 31,* 1–32.

Maimon, D., Antonaccio, O., & French, M. T. (2012). Severe sanctions, easy choice? Investigating the role of school sanctions in preventing adolescent violent offending. *Criminology, 50,* 495–524.

Malinowski, B. (1961). *Argonauts of the Western Pacific.* New York: E. P. Dutton.

Maltz, M. D. (2001). *Recidivism.* Orlando: Academic Press.

Manning, P. K. (1999). High risk narratives: Textual adventures. *Qualitative Sociology, 22,* 285–299.

Marinos, V., & Innocente, N. (2008). Factors influencing police attitudes towards extrajudicial measures under the Youth Criminal Justice Act. *Canadian Journal of Criminology and Criminal Justice, 50,* 469–489.

Marjanovic, S., Hanney, S., & Wooding, S. (2009). *A historical reflection on research evaluation studies, their recurrent themes and challenges.* Santa Monica: RAND Corporation.

Mark, M. (2005). Evaluation theory or what are evaluation methods for! *The Evaluation Exchange, 11*(2), 2–3.

Marks, M. (2004). Research police transformation: The ethnographic imperative. *British Journal of Criminology, 44,* 866–888.

Marshall, C., & Rossman, G. B. (1990). *Designing qualitative research.* Newbury Park, CA: Sage.

Marshall, J. M. (2012). *A mixed method examination of racial disproportionalities among youth who cross over from the child welfare to the juvenile justice system: Child welfare and juvenile justice professionals' perspectives and racial attitudes* (Unpublished doctoral dissertation). University of Illinois at Urbana-Champaign, Urbana, IL.

Martinson, R. (1974). What works? Questions and answers about prison reform. *The Public Interest, 35,* 22–54.

Martinson, R. (1979). New findings, new views: A note of caution regarding sentencing reform. *Hofstra Law Review, 7,* 243–258.

Maruna, S. (2010). Mixed method research in criminology: Why not go both ways? In A. R. Piquero and D. Weisburd (Eds.), *Handbook of quantitative criminology* (pp. 123–140). New York: Springer.

Mastrofski, S. D., & Parks, R. B. (1990). Improving observational studies of the police. *Criminology, 28,* 475–496.

Mastrofski, S. D., Parks, R. B., & McClusky, J. D. (2010). Systematic social observation in criminology. In A. R. Piquero & D. Weisburd (Eds.), *Handbook of quantitative criminology* (pp. 225–247). New York: Springer.

Matas, R. (2012, September 6). Tackling chronic offenders key to reducing Vancouver's high crime rates. *The Globe and Mail.* Retrieved from http://www.theglobeandmail.com/news/british-columbia/tackling-chronic-offenders-key-to-reducing-vancouvers-high-crime-rates/article2310419/

Maxwell, J. A. (2004a). Causal explanation, qualitative research, and scientific inquiry in education. *Educational Researcher, 33,* 3–11.

Maxwell, J. A. (2004b). Using qualitative methods for causal explanation. *Field Methods, 16,* 243–264.

McCord, J. (2002). Joan McCord. In G. Geis & M. Dodge (Eds.), *Lessons of criminology* (pp. 95–108). Cincinnati: Anderson Publishing.

McCue, C., & Beck, C. (2009). Predictive policing: What can we learn from Walmart and Amazon about fighting crime in a recession? *The Police Chief, 76*(11), 18–20, 22–24.

McGarrell, E. F., Chermak, S., Weiss, A., & Wilson, J. (2001). Reducing firearms violence through directed police patrol. *Criminology & Public Policy, 1,* 119–148.

McKillop, D., & Pfeiffer, J. (2004). Decision-making and young offenders: Examining the role of discretion in police judgments. *Canadian Journal of Police and Security Services, 2,* 209–214.

McNamara, C. (2010). Basic guide to program evaluation. Retrieved from http://managementhelp.org/evaluatn/fnl_eval.htm

McSkimming, M. J., Sever, B., & King, R. S. (2000). The coverage of ethics in research methods textbooks. *Journal of Criminal Justice Education, 11,* 51–63.

Media Matters for America (2010). Boortz again referred to victims of Hurricane Katrina as "parasite[s]." Retrieved from http://mediamatters.org/mmtv/200806190009

Melchers, R. (2003). Do Toronto Police engage in racial profiling? *Canadian Journal of Criminology and Criminal Justice, 45,* 347–366.

Mellor, N. (2001). Messy method: The unfolding story. *Education Action Research, 9,* 465–484.

Merriam-Webster (1996). Ethics. *Miriam-Webster's dictionary of law*. Retrieved from http://dictionary.lp.findlaw.com/scripts/results.pl?co=dictionary.lp.findlaw.com&topic=e8/e8ea9f107b9ada6959b32ff1a9b395da

Merton, R. K. (1968). *Social theory and social structure*. New York: The Free Press.

Miles, M. B., & Huberman, A. M. (1984). Drawing valid meaning from qualitative data: Toward a shared craft. *Educational Researcher, 13*(5), 20–30.

Miles, M. B., & Huberman, A. M. (1994). *Qualitative data analysis: An expanded sourcebook*. Thousand Oaks, CA: Sage.

Miles, M. B., Huberman, A. M., & Saldaña, J. (2014). *Qualitative data analysis: A methods sourcebook* (3rd ed.). Thousand Oaks, CA: Sage.

Milgram, S. (1963). Behavioral study of obedience. *Journal of Abnormal and Social Psychology, 67*: 371–378.

Miller, D. C., & Salkind, N. J. (2002). *Handbook of research design & social measurement* (6th ed.). Thousand Oaks, CA: Sage.

Miller, H. V., & Miller, J. M. (2010). Community in-reach through jail re-entry: Findings from a quasi-experimental design. *Justice Quarterly, 27*, 893–910.

Miller, P. R. (n.d.). Tipsheet—Survey modality. *Duke initiative on survey methodology*. Retrieved from http://www.dism.ssri.duke.edu/pdfs/Tipsheet - SurveyModality.pdf

Molotch, H. (2012). Interview: Howard S. Becker. *Public Culture, 24*, 421–443.

Moran-Ellis, J., Alexander, V. D., Cronin, A., Dickinson, M., Fielding, J., Sleney, J., & Thomas, H. (2006). Triangulation and integration: Processes, claims and implications. *Qualitative Research, 6*, 45–59.

Morgan, G. A., Harmon, R. J., & Gliner, J. A. (2001). Ethical issues related to publishing and reviewing. *Journal of the American Academy of Child Adolescent Psychiatry, 40*, 1476–1478.

Morris, M., & Cohn, R. (1993). Program evaluators and ethical challenges: A national survey. *Evaluation Review, 17*, 621–642.

Morrison, W. (2010). Travis Hirschi (1935–). In K. Hawyard, S. Maruna, & J. Mooney (Eds.), *Fifty key thinkers in criminology* (pp. 220–226). New York: Routledge.

Morse, J. M. (1991). Approaches to qualitative–quantitative methodological triangulation. *Nursing Research, 40*, 120–123.

Morse, J. M. (2003). Principles of mixed methods and multimethod research design. In A. Tashakkori & C. Teddlie (Eds.), *Handbook of mixed methods research in social and behavioral research* (pp. 189–208). Thousand Oaks, CA: Sage.

Morse, J. M., Barrett, M., Mayan, M., Olson, K., & Spiers, J. (2002). Verification strategies for establishing reliability and validity in qualitative research. *International Journal of Qualitative Methods, 1*, 1–19.

Moskowitz, J. M. (1993). Why reports of outcome evaluations are often biased or uninterpretable: Examples from evaluations of drug abuse prevention programs. *Evaluation and Program Planning, 16*, 1–9.

Mullins, C. W., & Wright, R. (2003). Gender, social networks, and residential burglary. *Criminology, 41*, 813–839.

Mullis, K. B. (2009). The benefits of science. Retrieved from http://www.karymullis.com/science.html

Murray, C. A., & Cox, Jr., L. A. (1979). *Beyond probation: Juvenile corrections and the chronic delinquent*. Beverly Hills: Sage.

Muschert, G. W. (2007). The Columbine victims and the myth of the juvenile superpredator. *Youth Violence and Juvenile Justice, 5*, 351–366.

Myers, N. M., & Dhillon, S. (2013). The criminal offence of entering any Shoppers Drug Mart in Ontario: Criminalizing ordinary behaviour with youth bail conditions. *Canadian Journal of Criminology and Criminal Justice, 55*, 187–214.

National Institute of Justice. (2013). *NIJ's drugs and crime research: Arrestee Drug Abuse Monitoring Programs*. Retrieved from http://www.nij.gov/topics/drugs/markets/adam

Neuman, L. W. (2003). *Social research methods: Qualitative and quantitative approaches* (5th ed.). Boston: Allyn and Bacon.

Neuman, L. W. (2011). *Social research methods: Qualitative and quantitative approaches* (7th ed.). Boston: Allyn and Bacon.

Neuman, L. W., & Robson, K. (2012). *Basics of social research: Qualitative and quantitative approaches* (2nd ed.). Toronto: Pearson.

Newton, R. R., & Rudenstam, K. E. (1999). *Your statistical consultant: Answers to your data analysis questions*. Thousand Oaks, CA: Sage.

Nobles, M. R., Fox, K. A., Piquero, N., & Piquero, A. (2009). Career dimensions of stalking victimization and perpetration. *Justice Quarterly, 26*, 476–503.

Nolasco, C. A. R. I., Vaughn, M. S., & del Carmen, R. V. (2010). Toward a new methodology for legal research in criminal justice. *Journal of Criminal Justice Education, 21*, 1–23.

O'Beirne, M., Denney, D., & Gabe, J. (2004). Fear of violence as an indicator of risk in probation work. *British Journal of Criminology, 44*, 113–126.

Ogborne, A., Larke, B., Plecas, D., Waller, I., & Rehm, J. (2008). *Vancouver's INSITE service and other supervised injection sites: What has been learned from research?* Final Report of the Expert Advisory Committee prepared for the Honourable Tony Clement Minister of Health. Ottawa: Health Canada.

Palys, T., & Atchison, C. (2014). *Research decisions: Quantitative, qualitative, and mixed methods approaches* (5th ed.). Toronto: Nelson Education.

Palys, T., & Lowman, J. (2000). Ethical and legal strategies for protecting confidential research information. *Canadian Journal of Law & Society, 15,* 39–80.

Paoline, III, E. A., & Terrill, W. (2011). Listen to me! Police officers' views of appropriate use of force. *Journal of Crime and Justice, 34,* 178–189.

Park, R. L. (2003, January 31). Seven warning signs of bogus science. *The Chronicle of Higher Education.* Retrieved from http://chronicle.com/article/The-Seven-Warning-Signs-of-/13674

Patchin, J. W., & Hinduja, S. (2006). Bullies move beyond the schoolyard: A preliminary look at cyberbullying. *Youth Violence and Juvenile Justice, 4,* 148–169.

Patton, M. Q. (2002). *Qualitative research & evaluation methods* (3rd ed.). Thousand Oaks, CA: Sage.

Pauls, M. (2005). An evaluation of the Neighbourhood Empowerment Team (NET): Edmonton Police Service. *The Canadian Review of Policing Research, 1.* Retrieved from http://crpr.icaap.org/index.php/crpr/article/view/42/38

Payne, B. K., & Button, D. M. (2009). Developing a citywide youth violence prevention plan: Perceptions of various stakeholders. *International Journal of Offender Therapy and Comparative Criminology, 53,* 517–534.

Payne, B. K., & Chappell, A. (2008). Using student samples in criminological research. *Journal of Criminal Justice Education, 19,* 175–192.

Pawson, R., & Tilley, N. (2003). *Realistic evaluation.* Thousand Oaks, CA: Sage.

Peak, K. J., Barthe, E. P., & Garcia, A. (2008). Campus policing in America: A twenty-year perspective. *Police Quarterly, 11,* 239–260.

Peelo, M., Francis, B., Soothill, K., Pearson, J., & Ackerley, E. (2004). Newspaper reporting and the public construction of homicide. *British Journal of Criminology, 44,* 256–275.

Penna, R., & Phillips, W. (2005). Eight outcome models. *The Evaluation Exchange: A Periodical on Emerging Strategies in Evaluating Child and Family Services, 11*(2), 4–5.

Peterson, S. L. (1999). Building scholars: A qualitative look at mentoring in a criminology and criminal justice doctoral program. *Journal of Criminal Justice Education, 10,* 247–261.

Peterson-Badali, M., & Broeking, J. (2010). Parents' involvement in the youth justice system: Rhetoric and reality. *Canadian Journal of Criminology and Criminal Justice, 52,* 1–27.

Pew Research Center. (2014). Social networking fact sheet. *Pew Research Internet Project.* Retrieved from http://pewinternet.org/fact-sheets/social-networking-fact-sheet/

Piff, P. K., Stancato, D. M., Côté, S., Mendoza-Denton, R., & Keltner, D. (2012). Higher social class predicts increased unethical behavior. *Proceedings of the National Academy of Sciences (PNAS),* PNAS Early Edition, 1–6.

Pinkerton, S. D., Johnson-Masotti, A. P., Derse, A., & Layde, P. M. (2002). Ethical issues in cost-effectiveness analysis. *Evaluation and Program Planning, 25,* 71–83.

Piquero, A. R. (2009). Methodological issues in the study of persistence in offending. In J. Savage (Ed.), *The development of persistent criminality* (pp. 271–287). New York: Oxford University Press.

Piquero, N. L., & Piquero, A. R. (2006). Control balance and exploitative corporate crime. *Criminology, 44,* 397–429.

Piza, E. L., & O'Hara, B. A. (2014). Saturation foot-patrol in a high-violence area: A quasi-experimental evaluation. *Justice Quarterly, 31,* 693–718.

Pogrebin, M. (2002). *Qualitative approaches to criminal justice: Perspectives from the field.* Thousand Oaks, CA: Sage.

Pogrebin, M. (2010). On the way to the field: Reflections of one qualitative criminal justice professor's experiences. *Journal of Criminal Justice Education, 21,* 540–561.

Pogrebin, M., & Poole, E. (1988). Humor in the briefing room: A study of the strategic uses of humor among police. *Journal of Contemporary Ethnography, 17,* 183–210.

Pogrebin, M., & Poole, E. (1997). The sexualized work environment: A look at women jail officers. *The Prison Journal, 77,* 41–57.

Polit, P. F., & Beck, C. T. (2010). Generalization in quantitative and qualitative research: Myths and strategies. *International Journal of Nursing Studies, 47,* 1451–1458.

Ponterotto, J. G., Mathew, J. T., & Raughley, B. (2013). The value of mixed methods designs to social justice research in counselling and psychology. *Journal for Social Action in Counselling and Psychology, 5,* 42–68.

Popper, K. R. (1959). *The logic of scientific discovery.* New York: Basic Books.

Popper, K. R. (1963). *Conjectures and refutations.* London: Routledge and Keagan Paul.

Porter, C. (2005, June 9). Kingston race study attacked: Report tracked police arrests, critics dispute claim of racial bias. *The Toronto Star,* A4.

Pottie-Bunge, V., Johnson, H., & Baldé, T. (2005). *Exploring crime patterns in Canada.* Ottawa: Statistics Canada.

Poulin, M., & Orchowsky, S. (2003). *Juvenile justice program evaluation: An overview* (2nd ed.). Program Evaluation Briefing Series #1. Washington, DC: Juvenile Justice Evaluation Center, Justice Research and Statistics Association, the Office of Juvenile Justice and Delinquency Prevention, and the United States Department of Justice.

Poulin, M., Orchowsky, S., & Trask, J. (2011). *Is this a good quality outcome evaluation report? A guide for practitioners.* Washington, DC: Justice Research and Statistics Association and the Bureau of Justice Statistics.

Prairie Research Associates (2004). *Multi-site survey of victims of crime and criminal justice professionals across Canada.* Ottawa: Department of Justice Canada.

Pratt, A., & Thompson, S. K. (2008). Chivalry, "race" and discretion at the Canadian border. *British Journal of Criminology, 48*, 620–640.

Pratt, T. C. (2010). Meta-analysis in criminal justice and criminology: What it is, when it's useful, and what to watch out for. *Journal of Criminal Justice Education, 21*, 152–168.

PredPol (2012). PredPol: Predict crime in real time. Retrieved from http://predpol.com.

Presser, L. (2010). Collecting and analyzing the stories of offenders. *Journal of Criminal Justice Education, 21*, 431–466.

Prus, R. C. (1996). *Symbolic interaction and ethnographic research: Intersubjectivity and the study of human lived experience.* Albany: State University of New York Press.

Quan, D. (2012, April 23). Canadian police officers overworked, understaffed, stressed-out: survey. *Edmonton Journal.* Retrieved from http://www.edmontonjournal.com/health/Canadian+police+officers+overworked+understaffed+stressed+survey/6506477/story.html

Rabe-Hemp, C. E., & Schuck, A. M. (2007). Violence against police officers: Are female officers at greater risk? *Police Quarterly, 10*, 411–428.

Rainone, G. A., Schmeidler, J. W., Frank, B., & Smith, R. B. (2006). Violent behaviour, substance use, and other delinquent behaviors among middle and high school students. *Youth Violence and Juvenile Justice, 4*, 247–265.

Ratcliffe, J. H., Taniguchi, T., Groff, E. R., & Wood, J. D. (2011). The Philadelphia foot patrol experiment: A randomized controlled trial of police patrol effectiveness in violent crime hot spots. *Criminology, 49*, 795–831.

Read, T., & Tilley, N. (2000). *Not rocket science? Problem-solving and crime reduction.* Crime Reduction Research Series Paper 6. London: Research, Development, and Statistics Directorate of the Home Office.

Renauer, B. C. (2007). Reducing fear of crime: Citizen, police, or government responsibility? *Police Quarterly, 10*, 41–62.

Richardson, C., & Kennedy, L. (2012). "Gang" as empty signifier in contemporary Canadian newspapers. *Canadian Journal of Criminology and Criminal Justice, 54*, 443–479.

Roberts, J. V., & Gabor, T. (2004). Living in the shadow of prison: Lessons from the Canadian experience in decarceration. *British Journal of Criminology, 44*, 92–112.

Rojek, J., & Decker, S. H. (2009). Explaining racial disparity: Police discipline process. *Police Quarterly, 12*, 388–407.

Ronel, N., Haski-Leventhal, D., Ben-David, B. M., & York, A. S. (2009). Perceived altruism: A neglected factor in initial intervention. *International Journal of Offender Therapy and Comparative Criminology, 53*, 191–210.

Root-Berstein, R. S., Berstein, M., & Garnier, H. (1993). Identification of scientists making long term, high impact contributions, with notes on their methods of working. *Creativity Research Journal, 6*, 329–343.

Rose, C., Reschenberg, K., & Richards, S. (2010). The inviting convicts to college program. *Journal of Offender Rehabilitation and Comparative Criminology, 49*, 293–308.

Rosenbaum, D. P., Graziano, L. M., Stephens, C. D., & Schuck, A. M. (2011). Understanding community policing and legitimacy—Seeking behaviour in virtual reality: A national study of municipal police websites. *Police Quarterly, 14*, 25–47.

Rosenbaum, D. P., & Hanson, G. S. (1998). Assessing the effects of school-based drug education: A six-year multilevel analysis of project D.A.R.E. *Journal of Research in Crime and Delinquency, 35*, 381–412.

Rosenfeld, R. (2011). The big picture: 2010 presidential address to the American Society Of Criminology. *Criminology, 49*, 1–26.

Rossler, M. T., & Terrill, W. (2012). Police responsiveness to service-related requests. *Police Quarterly, 15*, 3–24.

Rowe, S. C., Wiggers, J., Wolfenden, L., Francis, J. L., & Freund, M. (2012). Evaluation of an educational policing strategy to reduce alcohol-related crime associated with licensed premises. *Canadian Journal of Public Health, 103*(Supplement 1), S8–S14.

Royse, D., Thyer, B. A., & Padgett, D. K. (2010). *Program evaluation: An introduction* (5th ed.). Belmont, CA: Wadsworth Cengage Learning.

Rubin, H. J., & Rubin, I. S. (1995). *Qualitative interviewing: The art of hearing data.* Thousand Oaks, CA: Sage.

Ruelle, D. (2007). *The mathematician's brain.* Princeton, NJ: Princeton University Press.

Russell, B. (1946/2004). *A history of western philosophy* (2nd ed.). London: Routledge.

Sabbagh, C., & Golden, D. (2007). Reflecting upon etic and emic perspectives on distributive justice. *Social Justice Research, 20*, 372–387.

Salazar, L. F., & Cook, S. L. (2006). Preliminary findings from an outcome evaluation of an intimate partner violence prevention program for adjudicated, African American, adolescent males. *Youth Violence and Juvenile Justice, 4*, 368–385.

Saldaña, J. (2013). *The coding manual for qualitative researchers* (2nd ed.). Thousand Oaks, CA: Sage.

Sampson, A. (2007). Developing robust approaches to evaluating social programmes. *Evaluation, 13*, 477–493.

Sampson, R. J., & Laub, J. H. (2003). Life-course desisters? Trajectories of crime among delinquent boys followed to age 70. *Criminology, 41*, 555–592.

Sandberg, S. (2010). What can "lies" tell us about life? Notes towards a framework of narrative criminology. *Journal of Criminal Justice Education, 21*, 47–465.

Sardar, Z. (1998). Practicing to deceive. *New Statesman, 127*(4409), 41–42.

Satzewich, V., & Shaffir, W. (2009). Racism versus professionalism: Claims and counter-claims about racial profiling. *Canadian Journal of Criminology and Criminal Justice, 51*, 199–226.

Sauvé, J., & Hung, K. (2008). *An international perspective on criminal victimisation.* Retrieved from http://www.statcan.gc.ca/pub/85-002-x/2008010/article/10745-eng.htm

Savelsberg, J. J., & Flood, S. M. (2004). Criminological knowledge: Period and cohort effects in scholarship. *Criminology, 42,* 1009–1041.

Scarpitti, F. R. (2002). The good-boy in a high-delinquency area—40 years later. In G. Geis & M. Dodge (Eds.), *Lessons of criminology* (pp. 65–94). Cincinnati: Anderson Publishing.

Schachter, H. (2011, January 3). Ten must-ask job interview questions. *The Globe and Mail.* Retrieved from http://www.theglobeandmail.com/report-on-business/careers/management/ten-must-ask-job-interview-questions/article610545/

Schaefer, D. R., & Dillman, D. A. (1998). Development of a standard e-mail methodology: Results of an experiment. *Public Opinion Quarterly, 62,* 378–397.

Schafersman, S. D. (1991). *An introduction to critical thinking.* Retrieved from http://www.freeinquiry.com/critical-thinking.html

Schilder, D. (1997). Canadian Social Services Senior Manager Forum. *The Evaluation Exchange, 3*(1), 6.

Schneider, A. L. (1990). *Deterrence and juvenile crime: Results from a national policy experiment.* New York: Springer-Verlag.

Schulenberg, J. L. (2007a). Analysing police decision-making: Assessing the application of a mixed-method/mixed-model research design. *International Journal of Social Research Methodology, 10,* 99–119.

Schulenberg, J. L. (2007b). Predicting noncompliant behavior: Disparities in the social locations of male and female probationers. *Justice Research and Policy, 9,* 25–57.

Schulenberg, J. L. (2008). *The language of leadership: Effective communication for law enforcement command personnel.* Huntsville: Law Enforcement Management Institute of Texas.

Schulenberg, J. L. (2013a). *The Ontario Police Complaints System Forum: Perspectives from the community, police and policy-makers.* Final Report. Toronto: Scadding Court Community Centre.

Schulenberg, J. L. (2013b). *A view from the streets: Preliminary findings.* Report to Waterloo Regional Police Service. Waterloo, ON: University of Waterloo.

Schulenberg, J. L. (2014). Systematic Social Observation of police behaviour: The process, logistics, and challenges in a Canadian context. *Quality & Quantity: International Journal of Methodology, 48,* 297–315.

Schulenberg, J. L., & Chenier, A. (2014). International protest events and the hierarchy of credibility: Media frames defining the police and protestors as social problems. *Canadian Journal of Criminology and Criminal Justice, 56,* 261–294.

Schulenberg, J. L., & Warren, D. (2009). Police discretion with apprehended youth: Assessing the impact of juvenile specialization. *Police Practice and Research: An International Journal, 10,* 3–16.

Schuman, H., & Presser, S. (1981). *Questions and answers in attitude surveys: Experiments on question form, wording, and context.* New York: Academic Press.

Schwandt, T. (2001). *Dictionary of qualitative inquiry* (2nd ed.). Thousand Oaks, CA: Sage.

Scott, C. K., Foss, M. A., Lurigio, A. J., & Dennis, M. L. (2003). Pathways to recovery after substance abuse treatment: Leaving a life of crime behind. *Evaluation and Program Planning, 26,* 403–412.

Scott, J. (1990). *A matter of record.* Cambridge: Polity.

Scott, M. S. (2003). *The benefits and consequences of police crackdowns.* Problem-Oriented Guides for Police Response Guide Series, No. 1. Washington, DC: Office of Community Oriented Policing Services, US Department of Justice.

Scraton, P. (2002). Defining "power" and challenging knowledge: Critical analysis as resistance in the UK. In K. Carrington & R. Hogg (Eds.), *Critical criminology: Issues, debates, challenges* (pp. 15–40). Devon, UK: Willan Publishing.

Seale, C., Charteris-Black, J., MacFarlane, A., & McPherson, A. (2010). Interviews and internet forums: A comparison of two sources of qualitative data. *Qualitative Health Research, 20,* 595–606.

Seawright, J. (2002). Testing for necessary and/or sufficient causation: Which cases are relevant? *Political Analysis, 10,* 178–193.

Seawright, J., & Gerring, J. (2008). Case selection techniques in case study research: A menu of qualitative and quantitative options. *Political Research Quarterly, 61,* 294–308.

Sechrest, L., & Sidani, S. (1995). Quantitative and qualitative methods: Is there an alternative? *Evaluation and Program Planning, 18,* 77–87.

Sengo, S. R., & Dhungana, K. (2009). A field data examination of policy constructs related to fatigue conditions in law enforcement personnel. *Police Quarterly, 12,* 123–136.

Serin, R. C., Gobeil, R., & Preston, D. L. (2009). Evaluation of the Persistently Violent Offender Treatment Program. *International Journal of Offender Therapy and Comparative Criminology, 53,* 57–73.

Seron, C., Pereira, J., & Kovath, J. (2006). How citizens assess just punishment for police misconduct. *Criminology, 44,* 925–960.

Sever, B. (2005). Ranking multiple authors in criminal justice scholarship: An examination of underlying issues. *Journal of Criminal Justice Education, 16,* 79–100.

Shadish, W. R., Cook, T. D., & Leviton, L. C. (1991). *Foundations of program evaluation: Theories of practice.* Newbury Park, CA: Sage.

Shapiro, F. R. (2006). *The Yale book of quotations.* New Haven, CT: Yale University Press.

Shaw, C. R. (1930). *The jack-roller: A delinquent boy's own story*. Chicago: University of Chicago Press.

Shaw, C. R., & McKay, H. D. (1942). *Juvenile delinquency in urban areas*. Chicago: University of Chicago Press.

Shenton, A. K. (2004). Strategies for ensuring trustworthiness in qualitative research projects. *Education for Information, 22*, 63–75.

Sherman, L. W., Gartin, P. R., & Buerger, M. E. (1989). Hot spots of predatory crime: Routine activities and the criminology of place. *Criminology, 27*, 27–55.

Sherman, L., & Weisburd, D. (1995). General deterrent effects of police patrol in crime "hot spots": A randomized, controlled trial. *Justice Quarterly, 12*, 625–648.

Shermer, M. (2003). Psychic for a day: How I learned tarot cards, palm reading, astrology, and mediumship in 24 hours. *Skeptic Magazine, 10*(1), 48–55.

Silverman, D. (2013). *Doing qualitative research: A practical handbook* (4th ed.). Thousand Oaks, CA: Sage.

Singer, E. (1978). Informed consent: Consequences for response rate and response quality in social surveys. *American Sociological Review, 43*, 144–162.

Skogan, W. G. (1999). Measuring what matters: Crime, disorder, and fear. In R. H. Langworthy (Ed.), *Measuring what matters: Proceedings from the Policing Research Institute meetings* (pp. 37–54). Washington, DC: National Institute of Justice.

Skogan, W. G. (2009). Concern about crime and confidence in the police: Reassurance or accountability? *Police Quarterly, 12*, 301–318.

Smith, J., & Godlee, F. (2005). Investigating allegations of scientific misconduct. *British Medical Journal, 331*, 245–246.

Smith, M., Sviridoff, S., Sadd, S., Curtis, R., & Grinc, R. (1992). *The neighbourhood effects of street-level drug enforcement: Tactical narcotics teams in New York: An evaluation of TNT*. New York: Vera Institute of Justice.

Smith, R. (2001). Police-led crackdowns and cleanups: An evaluation of a crime control initiative in Richmond, VA. *Crime and Delinquency, 47*, 60–83.

Snook, B., Eastwood, J., & MacDonald, S. (2010). A descriptive analysis of how Canadian police officers administer the right-to-silence and right-to-legal-counsel cautions. *Canadian Journal of Criminology and Criminal Justice, 52*, 545–560.

Snyder, G. J. (2010). Howard S. Becker. In K. Haward, S. Maruna, & J. Mooney (Eds.), *Fifty Key Thinkers in Criminology* (pp. 163–168). New York: Routledge.

Social Sciences and Humanities Research Council (2014). Insight program. Retrieved from http://www.sshrc-crsh.gc.ca/funding-financement/umbrella_programs-programme_cadre/insight-savoir-eng.aspx

Son, I. S., & Rome, D. M. (2004). The prevalence and visibility of police misconduct: A survey of citizens and police officers. *Police Quarterly, 7*, 179–204.

Sorg, E. T., Haberman, C. P., Ratcliffe, J. H., & Groff, E. R. (2013). Foot patrol in violent crime hot spots: The longitudinal impact of deterrence and posttreatment effects of displacement. *Criminology, 51*, 65–101.

Spano, R. (2003). Concerns about safety, observer sex, and the decision to arrest: Evidence of reactivity in a large-scale observational study of police. *Criminology, 41*, 909–932.

Spano, R., Freilich, J. D., & Bolland, J. (2008). Gang membership, gun carrying, and employment: Applying routine activities theory to explain violent victimization among inner city, minority youth living in extreme poverty. *Justice Quarterly, 25*, 381–410.

Spradley, J. P. (1979). *The ethnographic interview*. Toronto: Harcourt Brace Jovanovich.

Sprinkle, J. E. (2008). Animals, empathy, and violence: Can animals be used to convey principles of prosocial behaviour to children? *Youth Violence and Juvenile Justice, 6*, 47–58.

Sprott, J. B., & Doob, A. N. (2008). Youth crime rates and the youth justice system. *Canadian Journal of Criminology and Criminal Justice, 50*, 621–639.

Sprott, J. B., & Doob, A. N. (2009). *Justice for girls? Stability and change in the youth justice systems of the United States and Canada*. Foreword by F. E. Zimring. Adolescent Development and Legal Policy Series. Chicago: University of Chicago Press.

Sprott, J. B., Webster, C. M., & Doob, A. N. (2013). Punishment severity and confidence in the criminal justice system. *Canadian Journal of Criminology and Criminal Justice, 55*, 279–292.

Stack, S., Cao, L., & Adamzyck, A. (2007). Crime volume and law and order culture. *Justice Quarterly, 24*, 291–308.

Statistics Canada (2012). Uniform Crime Reporting Survey (UCR). Retrieved from http://www23.statcan.gc.ca/imdb/p2SV.pl?Function=getSurvey&SDDS=3302&Item_Id=1044&lang=en

Statistics Canada (2013a). *Misinterpretation of statistics*. Retrieved from http://www.statcan.gc.ca/edu/power-pouvoir/ch6/misinterpretation-mauvaiseinterpretation/5214805-eng.htm

Statistics Canada. (2014). Data analysis and presentation. Retrieved from http://www.statcan.gc.ca/pub/12-539-x/2009001/analysis-analyse-eng.htm

Steiner, B., Travis, III, L. F., & Makarios, M. D. (2011). Understanding parole officers' responses to sanctioning reform. *Crime & Delinquency, 57*, 222–246.

Stephens, D. W. (1999). Measuring what matters. In R. H. Langworthy (Ed.), *Measuring what matters: Proceedings from the Policing Research Institute meetings* (pp. 55–64). Washington, DC: National Institute of Justice.

Stitt, B. G., Leone, M. C., & Jennings-Clawson, H. (1998). Focus groups and evaluation of criminal justice programs. *Journal of Criminal Justice Education, 9*, 71–80.

Stoddard-Dare, P., Mallett, C. A., & Boitel, C. (2011). Association between mental health disorders and juveniles' detention for a personal crime. *Child and Adolescent Mental Health, 16,* 208–213.

Stoeffer, S. A. (1950). Some observations on study design. *American Journal of Sociology, 55,* 355–361.

Strauss, A., & Corbin, J. (1998). *Basics of qualitative research: Grounded theory procedures and techniques* (2nd ed.). Newbury Park, CA: Sage.

Stroshine, M., Alpert, G., & Dunham, R. (2008). The influence of "working rules" on police suspicion and discretionary decision making. *Police Quarterly, 11,* 315–337.

Stufflebeam, D. L., & Shinkfield, A. J. (2007). *Evaluation theory, models, and applications.* San Francisco: Jossey-Bass.

Suchman, E. A. (1967). *Evaluative research: Principles and practices in public service and social action programs.* New York: Russell Sage Foundation.

Surette, R. (2009, 17 August). Youth crime and flawed statistics. *Rabble.ca: News for the rest of us.* Retrieved from http://rabble.ca/columnists/2009/08/youth-crime-and-flawed-statistics

Swazey, J. P. (1998). Research integrity: Why it matters. *Forum for Applied Research and Public Policy, 13,* 61–64.

Sword, W. (1999). Accounting for the presence of self: Reflections on doing qualitative research. *Qualitative Health Research, 9,* 270–278.

Tallichet, S. E., & Hensley, C. (2009). The social and emotional context of childhood and adolescent animal cruelty: Is there a link to adult interpersonal violence? *International Journal of Offender Treatment and Comparative Criminology, 53,* 596–606.

Tansey, O. (2007). Process tracing and elite interviewing: A case for non-probability sampling. *PSOnline, October,* 765–772.

Tashakkori, A., & Teddlie, C. (1998). *Mixed methodology: Combining qualitative and quantitative approaches.* Thousand Oaks, CA: Sage.

Tashakkori, A. & Teddlie, C. (2003a). *Handbook of mixed methods in social and behavioral research.* Thousand Oaks, CA: Sage.

Tashakkori, A., & Teddlie, C. (2003b). The past and future of mixed methods: From data triangulation to mixed model designs. In A. Tashakkori & C. Teddlie (Eds.), *Handbook of mixed methods in social and behavioral research* (pp. 671–701). Thousand Oaks, CA: Sage.

Taylor, B., Koper, C. S., & Woods, D. J. (2011). A randomized control trial of different policing strategies at hot spots of violent crime. *Journal of Experimental Criminology, 7,* 149–181.

Taylor, B., Kowalyk, A., & Boba, R. (2007). The integration of crime analysis into law enforcement agencies: An exploratory study into perceptions of crime analysis. *Police Quarterly, 10,* 154–169.

Taylor, H. (1998, May 4). Myth and reality in reporting sampling error: How the media confuse and mislead readers and viewers. *The Polling Report.* Retrieved from http://pollingreport.com/sampling.htm

Taylor, S. C., & Norma, C. (2011). The "symbolic protest" behind women's reporting of sexual assault crime to police. *Feminist Criminology, 7,* 24–47.

Teddlie, C., & Tashakkori, A. (2006). A general typology of research designs featuring mixed methods. *Research in the Schools, 13,* 12–28.

Teddlie, C., & Taashakkori, A. (2011). Mixed methods research: Contemporary issues in an emerging field. In N. K. Denzin & Y. S. Lincoln (Eds.), *The Sage handbook of qualitative research* (pp. 1–41). Thousand Oaks, CA: Sage.

Teddlie, C., & Tashakkori, A. (2012). Common "core" characteristics of mixed methods research: A review of critical issues and call for greater convergence. *American Behavioral Scientist, 56,* 774–788.

Tewksbury, R., DeMichele, M. T., & Miller, J. M. (2005). Methodological orientations of articles appearing in criminal justice's top journals: Who publishes what and where. *Journal of Criminal Justice Education, 16,* 265–279.

Thomas, W. I., & Thomas, D. S. (1928). *The child in America: Behavior problems and programs.* New York: Knopf.

Thompson, K. (2011, November 1). The Santa Cruz experiment: Can a city's crime be predicted and prevented? *Popular Science.* Retrieved from http://www.popsci.com/science/article/2011-10/santa-cruz-experiment

Thrasher, F. (1927). *The gang: A study of 1,313 gangs in Chicago.* Chicago: University of Chicago Press.

Tille, J. E., & Rose, J. C. (2007). Emotional and behavioral problems of 13- to 18-year-old incarcerated female first-time offenders and recidivists. *Youth Violence and Juvenile Justice, 5,* 426–435.

Tillyer, R., & Klahm IV, C. (2011). Searching for contraband: Assessing the use of discretion by police officers. *Police Quarterly, 14,* 166–185.

Tittle, C. R. (2002). Reflections of a reluctant but committed criminologist. In G. Geis & M. Dodge (Eds.), *Lessons of criminology* (pp. 23–45). Cincinnati: Anderson Publishing.

Tong, L. S. J., & Farrington, D. P. (2006). How effective is the "Reasoning and Rehabilitation" programme in reducing reoffending? A meta-analysis of evaluations in four countries. *Psychology, Crime & Law, 12,* 3–24.

Tourangeau, R., & Smith, T. W. (1996). Asking sensitive questions: The impact of data collection mode, question format, and question context. *Public Opinion Quarterly, 60,* 275–304.

Trulson, C., Marquart, J., & Mullings, J. (2004). Breaking in: Gaining entry to prisons and other hard-to-access criminal justice organizations. *Journal of Criminal Justice Education, 15,* 451–479.

Turvey, B. (1999). *Criminal profiling*. London: Academic Press.

United Nations (1948). *The universal declaration of human rights*. Retrieved from http://www.un.org/en/documents/udhr

US Department of Health and Human Services. (2005). *Introduction to program evaluation for public health programs: A self-study guide*. Atlanta: Office of the Director, Office of Strategy and Innovation, Centers for Disease Control and Prevention.

Valla, J. M., Ceci, S. J, & Williams, W. M. (2011). The accuracy of inferences about criminality based on facial appearance. *Journal of Social, Evolutionary, and Cultural Psychology, 5*, 66–91.

Van Maanen, J. (1973). Observations on the making of a policeman. *Human Organization, 32*, 407–418.

Van Maanen, J. (1998). *Tales of the field on writing ethnography*. Chicago: University of Chicago Press.

Van Maanen, J. (2003). The moral fix: On the ethics of fieldwork. In M. R. Pogrebin (Ed.), *Qualitative approaches to criminal justice: Perspectives from the field* (pp. 363–376). Thousand Oaks, CA: Sage.

Vannini, P. (2013). Early reflections on public ethnography. Retrieved from http://www.publicethnography.net/projects/early-reflections-public-ethnography

Vargas, R. (2014). Criminal group embeddedness and the adverse effects of arresting a gang's leader: A comparative case study. *Criminology, 52*, 143–168.

Viren, S. (2008, May 9). Survey of youths in custody finds half have mental health problems. *Houston Chronicle*, B1, B6.

Waddington, P. A. J. (1999). Police (canteen) sub-culture: An appreciation. *British Journal of Criminology, 39*, 287–309.

Waddington, P. A. J., Stenson, K., & Don, D. (2004). In proportion: Race, police stop and search. *British Journal of Criminology, 44*, 889–914.

Wallace, M., Turner, J., Matarazzo, A., & Babyak, C. (2009). *Measuring crime in Canada: Introducing the Crime Severity Index and improvements to the Uniform Crime Reporting Survey*. Catalogue no. 85-004-X. Ottawa: Canadian Centre for Justice Statistics, Statistics Canada.

Wallace, W. L. (1971). *The logic of science in sociology*. Hawthorne, NY: Aldine de Gruyter.

Wallis, A., & Roberts, H. V. (1956). *Statistics: A new approach*. Glencoe, IL: The Free Press.

Wansink, B., Kniffin, K. M., & Shimizu, M. (2012). Death row nutrition: Curious conclusions of last meals. *Appetite, 59*, 837–843.

Warren, D. (2009). *The social construction of the Katrina evacuee: Formal and informal responses in Houston, Texas post-Hurricane Katrina* (Unpublished doctoral dissertation). Sam Houston State University, Huntsville, TX.

Warwick, D. P., & Lininger, C. A. (1975). *The sample survey: Theory and practice*. New York: McGraw-Hill.

Waters, I., & Brown, K. (2000). Police complaints and the complainants' experience. *British Journal of Criminology, 40*, 617–638.

Webb, E. J., Campbell, D. T., Schwartz, R. D., & Sechrest, L. (1966). *Unobtrusive measures: Nonreactive research in the social sciences*. Chicago: Rand McNally.

Weber, M. (1904/1949). *The methodology of the social sciences* (E. A. Shils & H. A. Finch, Trans. and Eds.). New York: The Free Press.

Weber, M. (1921/1978). *Economy and society, Volume 1* (G. Roth & C. Wittich, Eds.). Berkeley, CA: University of California Press.

Weber, R. P. (1990). *Basic content analysis* (2nd ed.). Newbury Park, CA: Sage.

Webster, C. M., Doob, A. N., & Myers, N. M. (2009). The parable of Ms. Baker: Understanding pretrial detention in Canada. *Current Issues in Criminal Justice, 21*, 79–102.

Weed, D. L. (1998). Health law and ethics: Preventing scientific misconduct. *American Journal of Public Health, 88*, 125–129.

Wehrman, M. M., & de Angelis, J. (2011). Citizen willingness to participate in police–community partnerships: Exploring the influence of race and neighborhood context. *Police Quarterly, 14*, 48–69.

Weinrath, M. (2009). Inmate perspectives on the remand crisis in Canada. *Canadian Journal of Criminology and Criminal Justice, 51*, 355–379.

Weisburd, D. (2000). Randomized experiments in criminal justice policy: Prospects and problems. *Crime & Delinquency, 46*, 181–193.

Weisburd, D., & Braga, A. A. (2006). Hot spots policing as a model for police innovation. In D. Weisburd & A. A. Braga (Eds.), *Police innovation: Contrasting perspectives* (pp. 225–244). Cambridge Studies in Criminology Series. New York: Cambridge University Press.

Weisburd, D., & Green, L. (1995). Policing drug hot spots: The Jersey City drug market analysis experiment. *Justice Quarterly, 12*, 711–736.

Weisburd, D., Lum, C. M., & Petrosino, A. (2001). Does research design affect study outcomes in criminal justice research? *The Annals, 578*, 50–70.

Weisner, M., Capaldi, D. M., & Kim, H. K. (2007). Arrest trajectories across a 17-year span for young men: Relation to dual taxonomies and self-reported offence trajectories. *Criminology, 45*, 835–863.

Weiss, C. H. (2003). On theory-based evaluation: Winning friends and influencing people. *The Evaluation Exchange, 9*(4), 2–3.

Weitzer, R. (1999). Citizens' perceptions of police misconduct: Race and neighborhood context. *Justice Quarterly, 16*, 819–846.

Wells, E. (2009). Uses of meta-analysis in criminal justice research: A quantitative review. *Justice Quarterly, 26*, 268–294.

Wells, J. B., Minor, K. I., Angel, E., & Stearman, K. D. (2006). A quasi-experimental evaluation of a shock incarceration and aftercare program for juvenile offenders. *Youth Violence and Juvenile Justice, 4*, 219–233.

Welsh, B. C. (2007). *Evidence-based crime prevention: Scientific basis, trends, results, and implications for Canada.* Ottawa: National Crime Prevention Centre, Public Safety Canada.

Welsh, B. C., & Farrington, D. P. (2009). Public area CCTV and crime prevention: An updated systematic review and meta-analysis. *Justice Quarterly, 26*, 716–745.

Westheimer, J., & Kahne, J. (2004). What kind of citizen? The politics of education for democracy. *American Educational Research Journal, 41*, 237–269.

White, C. (2004). Three journals raise doubts on validity of Canadian studies. *British Medical Journal, 328*, 67–69.

White, D. G. (2001). Evaluating evidence and making judgments of study quality: Loss of evidence and risks to policy and practice decisions. *Critical Public Health, 11*, 3–17.

White, M. D., & Ready, J. (2007). The TASER as a less lethal force alternative: Findings on use and effectiveness in a large metropolitan police agency. *Police Quarterly, 19*, 251–274.

Whitton, B. (1999, 25 February). UW prof finds little change in youth crime rates. Retrieved from http://www.adm.uwaterloo.ca/infonews/release/1999/037%20Little%20change%20in%20youth%20crime,%20prof%20finds,%20February%2024,%201999.html

Whyte, W. F. (1955). *Street corner society.* Chicago: University of Chicago Press.

Whyte, W. F. (1993). Revisiting "Street corner society." *Sociological Forum, 8*, 285–298.

Wilkinson, D. L. (2007). Local social ties and willingness to intervene: Textured views among violent urban youth of neighborhood social control dynamics and situations. *Justice Quarterly, 24*, 185–220.

Williams, T., Dunlap, E., Johnson, B. D., & Hamid, A. (1992). Personal safety in dangerous places. *Journal of Contemporary Ethnography, 21*, 343–374.

Willmott, P. (1998). Integrity in social science—The upshot of a scandal. *International Social Science Journal, 50*, 370–374.

Wilson, S. J., & Lipsey, M. W. (2000). Wilderness challenge programs for delinquent youth: A meta-analysis of outcome evaluations. *Evaluation and Program Planning, 23*, 1–12.

Winterdyk, J., & Thompson, N. (2008). Student and non-student perceptions and awareness of identity theft. *Canadian Journal of Criminology and Criminal Justice, 50*, 153–186.

Wolcott, H. F. (2005). *The art of fieldwork* (2nd ed.). Walnut Creek, CA: AltaMira Press, Rowman & Littlefield.

Wolfer, K. M., & Friedrichs, D. O. (2001). Commitment to justice at a Jesuit university: A comparison of criminal justice majors to non-majors. *Journal of Criminal Justice Education, 12*, 319–336.

Wolfgang, M. E. (1980). On an evaluation of criminology. In M. W. Klein & K. S. Teilmann (Eds.), *Handbook of criminal justice evaluation* (pp. 19–52). Beverly Hills, CA: Sage.

Worden, R. E. (1989). Situational and attitudinal explanations of police behavior: A theoretical reappraisal and empirical assessment. *Law & Society Review, 23*, 667–711.

Worden, R. E., & Brandl, S. (1990). Protocol analysis of police decision-making: Toward a theory of police behavior. *American Journal of Criminal Justice, 14*, 297–318.

Worrall, J. L. (2000). In defense of the "quantoids": More on reasons for the quantitative emphasis in criminal justice education and research. *Journal of Criminal Justice Education, 11*, 353–361.

Wortley, S. (2005). *Racial profiling in Canada: Evidence, impacts and policy debates.* Retrieved from http://www.toronto.ca/metropolist/metropolistoronto2005/pdf/wortley_metro_profile.pdf

Wortley, S., & Marshall, L. (2005). *Race and police stops in Kingston, Ontario: Results of a pilot project.* Kingston, ON: Kingston Police Services Board.

Wright, R., Decker, S. H., Redfern, A. K., & Smith, D. L. (1992). A snowball's chance in hell: Doing fieldwork with active residential burglars. *Journal of Research in Crime and Delinquency, 29*, 148–161.

Yeager, M. G. (2006). The Freedom of Information Act as a methodological tool: Suing the government for data. *Canadian Journal of Criminology and Criminal Justice, 48*, 499–521.

Young, J. [Jerome]. (2010, September 4). How to answer the hard interview questions. Forbes.com. Retrieved from http://www.forbes.com/2010/04/09/hard-interview-questions-leadership-careers-employment.html

Young, J. [Jock]. (2010). Robert Merton (1910–2003). In K. Hayward, S. Maruna, & J. Mooney (Eds.), *Fifty key thinkers in criminology* (pp. 220–226). New York: Routledge.

Youth Canada (2012). Preparing for a job interview. Retrieved from http://www.youth.gc.ca/eng/topics/jobs/interview.shtml

Zaltzman, J., & Leichliter, B. (2014). Social media–related qualitative research. *New Qualitative Research.* Retrieved from http://www.newqualitative.org/qualitative-research/social-media-qualitative/

Zhang, S., & Chin, K.-L. (2002). Enter the dragon: Inside Chinese human smuggling organizations. *Criminology, 40*, 737–768.

Ziman, J. (2002). The continuing need for disinterested research. *Science and Engineering Ethics, 8*, 397–399.

Zimbardo, P. G., Maslach, C., & Haney, C. (1999). *Reflections on the Stanford Prison Experiment: Genesis, transformations, consequences.* Retrieved from http://www.prison-exp.org/pdf/blass.pdf

Zimbardo, P., & Wang, C. X. (2010). Resisting influence: Dr. Z's 20 hints about resisting unwanted influences on you. *The Lucifer Effect by Philip Zimbardo.* Retrieved from http://www.lucifereffect.com/guide_hints.htm

Court Cases Cited

Daubert v. Merrell Dow Pharmaceuticals, Inc., 509 U.S. 579, 589 (1993).

R. v. Mohan, [1994] 2 S.C.R. 9

Index

Credits

Photo and Figure Credits